Intercultural Communication: A Reader

Second Edition

Larry A. Samovar
San Diego State University

Richard E. Porter
California State University,
Long Beach

Wadsworth Publishing Company, Inc.
Belmont, California

ISBN 0-534-00448-2

L.C. Cat. Card No. 75-40644

Printed in the United States of America

3 4 5 6 7 8 9 10—80 79 78

Preface

To present a second edition of our intercultural communication reader is pleasing to us in a variety of ways. Pleasure obviously comes from knowing that the first edition was successful, warranting a second edition. It also comes from receiving and utilizing the helpful suggestions of many who used the original edition and from the knowledge that the intercultural communication field is viable and growing. In this edition, as in the first, the articles and essays are intended for the general reader. Consequently, we again have selected materials that are broadly based and comprehensive in nature and that are suitable for both undergraduate and graduate students. Although the level of difficulty does vary from article to article, we believe that, with only one or two exceptions, we have not gone beyond the difficulty level found in most texts for advanced undergraduate students. Twenty-two essays are new to this volume and six are original, written especially for this edition.

Intercultural Communication: A Reader is designed to meet three specific needs. The first comes from our belief that successful intercultural communication is a matter of highest importance if humanity and society are to survive. This book, then, is designed to serve as a basic anthology for courses providing theoretical and practical knowledge about intercultural communication processes. Our intention is to make this book useful not only to students of communication theory but also to readers seeking practical and immediately usable knowledge. Second, the book should be useful as a *supplementary text* in existing basic communication skills and service courses and in interpersonal communication courses. Third, we have found the book to be useful as *resource material* for advanced courses in public speaking, communication theory, group communication, organizational and business communication, and mass communication as well as courses in anthropology, sociology, social psychology, social welfare, business, and political science or international relations. It may also serve as a resource manual for persons who find themselves in programs and situations necessarily involving intercultural communication.

The book is organized around four closely related parts. In Part One, Approaches to Intercultural Communication, the first chapter contains essays that discuss what intercultural communication is, what it tries to accomplish, and the nature of intercultural communicators. Parts Two, Three, and Four trace the intercultural communication experience by means of a topical sequence. Part Two, Socio-Cultural Influences: What We Bring to Intercultural Communication, examines the influences socio-cultural factors have on intercultural interaction. In this section, Chapter 2 details experiential backgrounds—*what we bring* to an intercultural encounter. Chapter 3 explores the influence of culture on our perceptual processes. We believe that by examining the cultural differences in what we bring to our intercultural communication acts, we are better able to understand and appreciate what goes on during the communication event itself. In Part Three, Intercultural Interaction: Taking Part in Intercultural Communication, our analysis focuses on the problems of intercultural interaction. Chapter 4 in this section examines cultural differences in verbal interaction while Chapter 5 focuses on differences in nonverbal interaction. Part Four, Intercultural Communication: Becoming More Effective, is concerned with improving intercultural communication. In Chapter 6 are readings that bring us the knowledge and experiences of successful intercultural communicators and practical suggestions for improving our intercultural communication. Chapter 7, the final chapter in the book, examines the future of intercultural communication and charts directions for research, change, and improvement.

This book continues to be the outcome of a joint venture. The ideas reflected in it and the decisions necessary for its development and preparation grew out of an association and dialog that has persisted since 1967. Both of us share a mutual concern that if the human race is to endure during the decades ahead, decades that will in both time and space bring us closer together, we must be able to communicate with individuals from cultures far removed from our own.

We wish to express our appreciation to the many authors, professional associations, and publishers whose cooperation has helped make this book possible. In addition, various individuals have played a significant role in the development and completion of this project. Especially, we should like to acknowledge the thoughtful reviews of the manuscript by LaRay M. Barna of Portland State University, H. Peter Kuiper of Fresno City College, and Michael H. Prosser of the University of Virginia; and we are grateful to those instructors who have used the previous edition and who offered suggestions for the new edition: Nobleza Asuncion-Landé, University of Kansas; Kenneth D. Bryson, Montana State University; Jean M. Civikly, University of New Mexico; F. H. Goodyear, Madison College; Jack Gregory, University of West Florida; D. Ray Heisey, Kent State University; Howard P. Holladay, California State University, Los Angeles; Fred E. Jandt, State University College at Brockport; Raghu Raj Kumar, Weber State College; Rebecca Leonard and Bailey B. Baker, Purdue University; the late Jean E. Liedman, Monmouth College; Frain G. Pearson, Southern Utah State College; Robley Rhine, University of Colorado, Denver; Rose Marie Smith, Arizona State University; Gordon I. Zimmerman, University of Nevada, Reno. We also wish to thank Rebecca Hayden of Wadsworth Publishing Company for her advice and editorial direction. The work of Cora Cochran, who served as secretary, typist, and proofreader is also appreciated. And we wish to thank our research assistants Diana Meehan and Audrey A. Guenther.

Larry A. Samovar
Richard E. Porter

Contents

Contents

Part One   Intercultural Communication: An Introduction

Interest in the communication phenomenon that occurs when message producer and message receiver come from different cultures has mushroomed in the past five years. What we once termed intercultural communication has increasingly become known also as cross-cultural communication, trans-cultural communication, trans-racial communication, interracial communication, intercommunication, interethnic communication, and international communication. Simultaneously, a variety of books have been published, and new organizations professing interest in the study of intercultural communication have come into being. Unfortunately, all of this activity has done little to reduce the confusion of multiple labels and varying conditions requisite to intercultural communication. We still hold to the view expressed in our first edition that the best label for the form of communication represented in this volume is *intercultural communication.* And, we still believe that whenever the parties to an act of communication bring with them different experiential backgrounds that reflect a long-standing deposit of group experience, knowledge, and values, we have *intercultural communication.* Although it may often involve racial or ethnic differences, or both, we still argue that intercultural communication also occurs when there are gross socio-cultural differences without accompanying racial or ethnic differences.

Intercultural communication is not new. It is as old as humanity. Yet only during the last two decades have we really begun to concern ourselves about it; perhaps knowing our technology has produced the means of our own self-destruction has prompted this concern. Historically, intercultural communication, more often than not, has employed a rhetoric of force rather than reason. Maybe we are now seeking something other than traditional force. Or perhaps the reason is more pragmatic, being brought about by our mobility, increased contact between cultures, and a widening world marketplace. Traditionally, intercultural communication took place only within an extremely small minority. Ministers of government and certain merchants were the travelers and visitors of foreign lands. Until rather recently, we had little contact even with other cultures within our own country. The ghetto or barrio dwellers remained in the barrio or ghetto. If they did emerge, it was to serve the upper class, not to interact as equals. And those who made up the vast white middle America remained at home, rarely leaving their own county. But this has changed markedly; we are now a mobile society among ever-increasing mobile societies. And, whatever the reason, more thought has been given to intercultural communication in the last decade than in any other period of our history.

Inquiry into the nature of intercultural communication has raised many questions, but it has produced only a few answers and far fewer theories. Most of the inquiry has been associated with fields other than communication: anthropology, international relations, social psychology, and socio- and psycholinguistics primarily. Although the direction of research has been diverse, the knowledge has not been coordinated. Much that has emerged has been more of a reaction to current socio-racial-ethnic concerns than an attempt to define and to explain intercultural communication. In recent years, for instance, there have been numerous books and articles dealing with the rhetoric of agitation, the communication of protest, and the language of the urban poor.

The arena of intercultural communication has not been completely established although there appears to be increasingly greater agreement about what it is. However, there is still a great need to specify the nature of intercultural communication and to recognize various viewpoints that see the phenomenon somewhat differently.

1

Approaches to Intercultural Communication

In Chapter 1 we present three views of intercultural communication, each of which sets forth concepts, suggests parameters, and attempts to explain the nature of intercultural communication.

We begin with a general orientation and overview of intercultural communication. The first essay introduces some of the topics and issues associated with the study of intercultural communication and presents in rather broad terms what it involves. We start by defining and explaining the role of human communication. We then turn our attention to the specific areas of culture and communication and show how these relate one with the other to form the field of intercultural communication. By examining the major variables that affect intercultural communication, we better understand how it operates. We believe that the reader, by knowing at the outset of the book what the study of intercultural communication entails, will have a greater appreciation for the selections that follow.

Turning to a viewpoint primarily concerned with understanding the dynamics of domestic intercultural communication, Rich and Ogawa in "A Model of Intercultural and Interracial Communication" offer us a structure within which concepts and hypotheses concerning intercultural and cross-racial communication can be examined. To facilitate understanding, they view these issues through the methodology of models that effectively show necessary definitions and theoretical structures. By these means, Rich and Ogawa look at intercultural communication from a variety of orientations. They examine intercultural, contracultural, interracial, and interethnic communication and help draw boundaries for these areas.

The last selection, by D. Price-Williams, examines the relationship between culture and a host of psychological factors. He maintains that studies of individual differences show to what degree a particular person is similar to or different from others; so cross-cultural studies focus on the similarities and differences of whole societies and cultures. The author discusses how the factors of perception, thought, socialization, and personality differ from culture to culture. When analyzed and understood, these concepts tell us a great deal about many of the essential components of intercultural communication.

Communicating Interculturally

Richard E. Porter and Larry A. Samovar

Two seemingly unrelated occurrences took place during the late 1960s and early 1970s. Events transpired that had profound effects on the field of communication. On one front the world, in a figurative sense, had begun to shrink; the global village prophecy was upon us. For a variety of reasons, we had improved our mobility until distances no longer mattered. A jet airplane could place us anywhere within hours. This new-found mobility was not exclusively ours; people around the world were on the move. International tradesmen, foreign students, diplomats, and especially tourists were moving in and out of an assortment of cultures—cultures that often appeared unfamiliar, alien, and at times mysterious. Close cultural contact was further underscored as the United States inaugurated communication satellites that could provide education as well as entertainment. As many as 400 million people could be taught to read at the same time. People in remote areas of countries like India could now be reached by television.

While this global phenomenon was taking place, there also was a kind of cultural revolution within our own boundaries. Domestic events forced all of us to focus our attention upon new, and often demanding, cultures and subcultures. Blacks, Chicanos, women, homosexuals, the poor, "hippies," and countless other groups became highly visible and vocal—and they disturbed many of us. Frequently, their communicative behaviors seemed strange or even bizarre and failed to meet our normal expectations.

The focus of attention on minority cultures just described made us realize not only that intercultural contact was inevitable but that it was often unsuccessful. We found, in short, that intercultural communication was difficult. Even when we overcame natural barriers of language, we could still fail to understand and be understood. These failures in both the international arena and the domestic scene gave rise to the marriage of culture and communication and to the recognition of intercultural communication as a field of study. Inherent in this fusion of academic disciplines was the idea that the study of intercultural communication entails the investigation of culture and the difficulties of communicating across cultural boundaries.

Intercultural communication occurs whenever a message producer is a member of one culture and a message receiver is a member of another. Therefore, in this essay we shall discuss intercultural communication and point out the relationships among communication, culture, and intercultural communication.

This original essay appears here in print for the first time. All rights reserved. Permission to reprint must be obtained from the publisher and the author. Professor Porter teaches in the Department of Speech Communication, California State University, Long Beach, and Professor Samovar teaches in the Speech Communication Department at San Diego State University.

Communication

As we have already indicated, intercultural interaction occurs through the process of communication. By definition, and in practice, communication and intercultural communication are inseparable. It is impossible to talk about one without the other. It is even more obvious that we cannot share ideas and feelings cross-culturally if we do not communicate. Culture A can contact Culture B only by sending messages. In short, intercultural interaction means communication between individuals of different cultures.

Because human communication is such a vital part of intercultural interaction, we believe that an understanding of the workings of communication is paramount if one is to understand intercultural interaction. Therefore, let us define what communication is and explain how it operates.

Definitions and descriptions of communication are legendary and numerous. They run from the very general "Communication is the discriminatory response of an organism to a stimulus" (Stevens, 1950, p. 698) to the specific "Communication has as its central interest those behavioral situations in which a source transmits a message to a receiver(s) with conscious intent to affect the latter's behavior" (Miller, 1966, p. 92). There are even definitions that speak only of the verbal elements—"Communication is the verbal interchange of thought or idea" (Hoben, 1954, p. 77). It is easy to see that the term communication is indeed an enigma. Communication is an activity in which we all engage, yet it is very difficult to specify its parameters. However, for our purposes we would suggest that *communication is a dynamic process whereby human behavior, both verbal and nonverbal, is perceived and responded to.* A closer examination of this definition will enable us to see most of the specific components and ingredients of communication.

1. *Communication is a dynamic process.* It is ongoing and active, rather than static and passive. In this sense, communication has no beginning or end. There are, instead, a series of behaviors—actions, activities, and responses—taking place during an encounter. Most of these patterns are in operation before people make contact. So communication seems to be a flowing together of many interdependent functions. We are capable of seeing, hearing, thinking, talking, moving, and countless other activities all at the same time. In short, it is foolish to try to visualize communication as a "still-life" picture.

2. *Communication is symbolic behavior.* All communication entails the use of symbols of some kind. They are used to express our ideas and feelings. We cannot transfer internal notions or states directly; they must be symbolized in a code that stands for and represents our internal states. The process of producing a symbolic code is called *encoding* and is a form of human behavior. Any behavior, consciously or unconsciously produced, has the potential to function as a symbol. In fact, a symbol may be thought of as any human behavior, verbal or nonverbal, to which meaning may be attached. Simply, "one cannot not communicate" (Watzlawick, 1967, p. 48) as long as he or she is capable of behavior and there is someone to attribute meaning to the behavior. Linguistic

or verbal symbols are, of course, the most manifest coding system we employ. However, we also use nonverbal symbols to share experiences and feelings. Our clothes, actions, facial expressions, and use of time and space are just a few of the nonverbal symbolic codes we use. Whether we call on word symbols or nonverbal symbols, we are creating and using behaviors as a code to represent thought.

3. *Communication elicits a response.* Whenever we become aware of another person's verbal or nonverbal behaviors we must transform them into meaningful experience. By this we mean that the behaviors only have meaning for us in the context of our past experiences, and it is from these experiences that we derive the meaning we attach to the observed behaviors. This process of deriving meaning for symbols is called *decoding,* and it is an internal activity. Attaching meaning to someone else's symbolic behavior carries with it a corresponding effect on the behavior of the perceiver. If you see a Japanese woman and she smiles at you, you interpret her symbolic behavior (smile) as communicating something to you. Obviously, communication is taking place. But there is also communication when this same woman puts on her ceremonial tea-serving costume and you attach meaning to her attire. In both cases you perceived her behavior and responded to it by attributing meaning to her smile and to her dress. In addition, your behavior of attributing meaning may have led to additional behavior on your part—you may have returned her smile or commented on the beauty of her costume.

4. *Communication is a receiver phenomenon.* Weaving its way throughout our discussion is the idea that Person A produces a message that travels via a channel to Person B. Person B then attaches meaning to the message. No communication occurs unless we have Person B—the receiver—someone to interpret and give meaning to symbolic behavior. If someone waves a hand as if to symbolize the concept "good-bye," but you fail to see it, communication has not taken place. If, however, you see the arm movement and decide someone is leaving, communication has occurred. It matters little if the arm action was produced to swat at a bee, for it is the *receiver* who must eventually determine what the behavior symbolizes.

5. *Communication is complex.* One fact is evident from our brief analysis—human communication is not a simple matter. It is a process that calls for the simultaneous production of a number of highly intricate and interdependent activities. If communication were a linear phenomenon, with one action producing one response, the issue of complexity would not be so prevalent. Furthermore, communication is complex because it contains so many variables. Among these variables are the many aspects of the human personality that each person brings to the encounter, the diverse forms that messages can take, the various channels the message can use, and the influence of the context and environment on communication.

Having briefly sketched the essential characteristics of communication, we are now ready to talk about culture and its relationship to communication. Culture is a communication problem because it is not constant; it is a variable. And, as cultural variance increases, so do the problems of communication.

Culture, Communication, and Social Perception

The concept of culture presents some difficulties in the discussion of intercultural communication. In the classic anthropological sense, culture refers to the cumulative deposit of knowledge, experience, meanings, beliefs, values, attitudes, religions, concepts of self, the universe, and self-universe relationships, hierarchies of status, role expectations, spatial relations, and time concepts acquired by a large group of people in the course of generations through individual and group striving. Culture manifests itself both in patterns of language and thought and in forms of activity and behavior. These patterns become models for common adaptive acts and styles of expressive behavior, which enable people to live in a society within a given geographical environment at a given state of technical development.

This definition is extremely useful when considering intercultural communication as an international event, where people come from widely diverse geographic areas separated and isolated from one another. But what about our domestic events? We earlier pointed out that domestic events during the 1960s and 1970s were partly responsible for the development of intercultural communication as a field of study. Obviously if there are ethnic or racial groupings our definition is still applicable. But how does an emerging minority such as the drug culture or the gay liberation movement meet our definition, which calls for the acquisition of a cumulative deposit of knowledge and other aspects of culture over generations? Obviously it doesn't. However, there are significant minority groups within our society—within any society—whose memberships transcend racial and ethnic lines that nevertheless are unique enough to be viewed as cultures, at least for the purposes of intercultural communication. This may be stretching the traditional concept of culture a bit, but we believe that the communication problems we must deal with can best be considered as deriving at least in part from cultural differences, even if these differences developed during a single generation.

Culture is extremely complex, varying along many dimensions. Any attempt to factor out the dimensions and to provide a scale for their measurement is far beyond our purposes in this article. But, if we think of cultural differences varying along a minimal-maximal dimension (see Figure 1), the amount of difference between two cultural groups depends on the social uniqueness of the two groups. Although this is a crude scale, it does permit us to examine an intercultural communication act and to understand the effect of cultural difference. To illustrate how the dimension helps us, let us look at the examples of cultural difference positioned along the scale.

The first example is maximal—differences between Asian and Western cultures. Here we find the greatest number of cultural factors subject to variation; we also find the least commonality. Physical appearance, religion, philosophy, social attitudes, language, heritage, and basic conceptualizations of self and the universe are among the cultural factors that differ sharply.

An example nearer the center of the scale is the difference between American culture and French culture. Less variation is found; physical characteristics are

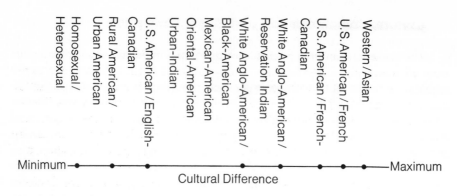

Figure 1. Arrangement of compared cultures along a scale of minimum to maximum cultural difference.

similar, and the English language is in part derived from French and its ancestor languages. The roots of both French and American philosophy lie in ancient Greece, and most Americans and French share the Christian religion.

Examples near the minimal end of the scale are characterized in two ways. First are the variations found between members of separate but similar cultures —for instance, between U.S. Americans and Canadians. The difference is less than that found between American and French cultures but greater than that generally found within a single culture. Even in this case we are not totally accurate, because we must distinguish between English-Canadian and French-Canadian cultures (note the differences on the scale). Second, minimal differences may be seen in the variance between subgroups of the same general culture—for instance, Anglo-Americans, and Mexican-Americans residing in separate parts of the same city. Similarly, socio-cultural differences can be found between members of the John Birch Society and the Americans for Democratic Action, between mainstream middle class Americans and the urban poor or the "drug culture," and between heterosexuals and homosexuals.

In both categorizations, members of each cultural group share much more in common than in the prior examples. They probably speak the same language, share the same general religion, attend the same schools, and inhabit the same geographical area. Yet, these groups of people are culturally different; they do not share the same experiences nor do they share the same perceptions. They see the world differently. Their life styles are vastly different, and their beliefs, values, and attitudes are far from being the same.

Social perception, which is the process by which we attach meaning to the social objects and events we encounter in our environment, is an extremely important aspect of any communication act. It is the means by which we assign meanings to the messages we receive. Social perception becomes even more important when we consider intercultural communication, because culture conditions and structures our perceptual processes in such a way that we develop culturally determined perceptual sets. These sets not only influence which stimuli reach our awareness, but more importantly they have a great influence on the judgmental aspect of perception—the attachment of meaning to these stimuli. It is our contention that *intercultural communication can best be understood as cultural variance in the perception of social objects and events. The barriers to communication caused by this perceptual variance can best be lowered by a knowledge and understanding of cultural factors that are subject to variance, coupled with an honest and sincere desire to communicate successfully across cultural boundaries.*

The ultimate aim of social perception is to give us an accurate account of the social aspects of our environment. Unfortunately, this often is *not* the result, because various cultural elements prejudice the meanings we attach to social stimuli. A social object or event perceived simultaneously by members of different cultures may be and often is interpreted quite differently by each member. For example, Bagby (1957), in a study of cross-cultural perceptual predominance in binocular rivalry, found that culture influenced the outcome of the perceptual process. Matching twelve Mexican children with twelve U.S. American children, Bagby flashed a series of stereograms in which one eye was exposed to a scene of a bullfight and the other eye exposed to a scene of a baseball game. Under these conditions, Bagby found the viewers predominantly reported the scene appropriate to their culture: Mexican children tended to see the bullfight and American children tended to see the baseball game, although they were simultaneously exposed to both scenes. Even physical objects are subject to different interpretations in different cultures. For instance, the star constellation we refer to as the "Big Dipper" is often called the "Big Bear" or the "Big Plow" in parts of Northern Europe.

There are many variables in the communication process whose values are determined, at least in part, by culture. These variables have the ability to influence our perceptions and to affect the meaning we assign to communicative acts. In the following sections, we will discuss eight such variables: (1) attitudes, (2) social organization, (3) patterns of thought, (4) roles and the role prescriptions, (5) language, (6) use and organization of space, (7) time conceptualization, and (8) nonverbal expression. The isolation of these variables is somewhat arbitrary and artificial because they overlap and interact with one another. For instance, a person's concept of the universe is in part derived from his culturally influenced thinking and reasoning habits and patterns; it is also a function of his attitudes. Yet, because of the interactive effect, attitudes are a function of a person's views of the universe as well as his beliefs, values, perceptions, stereotypes, and thought patterns. Thus, although we will use the eight categories as a convenient means of division, do not assume these factors exist or exert influence in isolation. In reality, they all work with and against one another in affecting our intercultural communicative behaviors.

Attitudes

Attitudes are psychological states that predispose us to act in certain ways when we encounter various social events or objects in our environment. Not only do attitudes influence our overt behaviors, they also cause us to distort our perceptions— that is, to interpret events so they are in accord with our predispositions. We often tend, therefore, to see things as we *want* them to be rather than as they *are*. Attitudes that affect intercultural communication the most can be categorized as ethnocentrism, world view, absolute values, stereotypes, and prejudices.

ETHNOCENTRISM   A major source of cultural variance in attitudes is *ethnocentrism,* which is a tendency to view people unconsciously by using our own group and our own customs as the standard for all judgments. We place ourselves, our racial, ethnic, or social group, at the center of the universe and rate all others accordingly. The greater their similarity to us, the nearer to us we place them; the greater the dissimilarity, the farther away they are. We place one group above another, one segment of society above another, one nation-state above another. We tend to see our own groups, our own country, our own culture as the best, as the most moral. This view also demands our first loyalty and produces a frame of reference that denies the existence of any other frame of reference. It is an absolute position that prohibits any other position from being appropriate for another culture.

Political and nationalistic ethnocentric attitudes are a chief barrier to intercultural communication. When we identify with specific political units—cities, counties, states, nations—we restrict our area of moral obligation. Our ability to accept cultural differences is affected by this restriction. When a boundary, even a state or local line, is present, our allegiance to one group restricts our ability to accept another or to view them favorably. This boundary may be something as definite as a political division or as arbitrary as a railroad track or river.

Another and sometimes more potent source of ethnocentristic attitudes is religion. Many religious denominations emphasize the rightness of their way as distinguished from that of others. Some of us even become dogmatic in our views and see anyone else as an "infidel." This type of religious fervor has led sociologist Talcott Parsons to observe:

> Ethnocentrism is accentuated by this religious dogmatism because it interferes with the understanding of other cultural groups. . . . So far as one cultural group differs from another, it tends to be held as suspect. This dogmatism often extends beyond matters of religion to include extreme hostility to other aspects of culture (1964, p. 500).

Our problem lies in the fact that we have a carryover from religion to other aspects of culture. Not only do we sometimes feel hostility toward another culture's religion, but that hostility also affects our perception of customs, modes of dress, food, art, traditions, and racial characteristics. To give an extreme case, how can two people interact successfully if one believes the other to be guilty of deicide? Or, in a less extreme case, how can we successfully communicate interculturally if we perceive another's cultural customs as foolish if not utterly ridiculous?

Ethnocentrism has also manifested itself as a colonial attitude toward racial minorities in the United States. We have generally viewed racial minorities as less than equal; they have been viewed as second class members of society—not quite as good as the white majority—and treated as such. Historically the development of this attitude is easy to see. Blacks came to America as slaves; the Indians and the Mexicans were defeated by the white man's guns; and the Orientals, although not technically slaves, were brought here to live in wretched conditions and perform menial labor. This attitude has prevailed throughout our history and has been epitomized in such slogans as "The only good Indian is a dead Indian." Today the laws have changed to some degree, but the attitudes remain. Blacks, Mexican-Americans, Indians, and Orientals are still subject to prejudice and discrimination and treated in many respects as colonized subjects.

This treatment of racial minorities is different from that accorded to emigrant ethnic minorities who were white. True, many ethnic minorities were the object of prejudice and discrimination upon their arrival. But they were able to assimilate into the general population and lose their visibility as someone different. The melting pot concept we idealize in the United States has worked for many who came to this country—as long as they were white enough and Anglo enough to be assimilated. Today many of these ethnic minorities are idealized in our folklore and, instead of being the butt of ridicule, they are looked upon with pride. How many Americans without a trace of Irish ancestry wear green on St. Patrick's day?

Yet, all ethnic minorities are not fully assimilated—especially those who attempt to maintain their ethnic identity. Especially for Jews, prejudice and discrimination still result from our ethnocentristic views. We welcome those who will become like us, but we reject those who wish to retain their own cultural heritage.

When we allow ethnocentrism to interfere with our social perception, the effectiveness of intercultural communication is reduced because we are unable to view aspects of another culture that differ from our own in an objective manner. The degree to which these attitudes reduce our communication effectiveness cannot be predicted because of the variety of circumstances under which they can be present. However, we do know that ethnocentrism is strongest in moral and religious contexts, where emotionalism may overshadow rationality and cause so much hostility that communication ceases. And, finally, at the extreme, ethnocentrism robs us of the willingness and desire to communicate interculturally.

WORLD VIEW   The way we view our world is a function of our culture, and it affects our social perception. As Americans, we tend to have a human-centered view. The world is a vast space in which we may carry out our desires. We build what we wish, we control nature as we can, and when we are displeased we tear it all down and start again.

In other cultures the relationship between the person and the cosmos is viewed differently. An Oriental world view is apt to be one of balanced relationships in which humans share a place with heaven and earth. Each thing that a person does has some effect on the balance of that relationship. Consequently, he must act carefully so as not to upset the balance because it is the nature of the cosmos to tend toward harmony.

Our world view gives us a perspective from which we shape and form our attitudes. As we encounter people with differing world views, our communicative behavior is hampered because we view events differently; we use frames of reference that may seem vague or obscure to others, just as theirs may seem to us. Our perceptions become clouded and our attitudes interfere with our ability to share perceptions with others.

ABSOLUTE VALUES   Closely related to and often derived from ethnocentrism and world view are absolute values. Or perhaps systems of absolute values lead to ethnocentrism and world view. The antecedent-consequent relationship is not really clear. Anyway, absolute values are culturally derived notions we have of right and wrong, good and bad, beautiful and ugly, true and false, positive and negative, and so on. They influence our social perception by providing us with a set of basic precepts from which we judge the behavior and beliefs of others. We take these notions to be absolute—to be "truth"—and do not or cannot realize that these "absolutes" are subject to cultural variation. An absolute value or a concept of right and wrong that is "truth" should be meaningful to us only in the relative sense of what is accepted or believed within a given culture.

In our social perception, we find that absolute value systems lead us to inaccurate judgments about social reality. What we regard as "truth," as an absolute, may be seen as sheer folly by someone from another culture. For example, in the American culture it is generally held that one can attain salvation only through the acceptance of Christ. But to a Jew, Moslem, Shintoist, Hindu, Taoist, or Buddhist, this notion may seem foolish. Because of absolute values, we can find ourselves in situations where we oppose someone else because of our conviction that he sees reality in a completely mistaken way. If we hold to the absoluteness of our position, we find ourselves where compromise is impossible; we *know* the "truth" and to yield would be a confession that we really do not. Admitting that we do not know is probably the most difficult confession for us to make. Because of the religious and moral context found in most absolute values, we can be emotionally involved to such a degree that our behavior becomes totally irrational, reducing our communicative capacities.

STEREOTYPES AND PREJUDICES   Stereotypes are attitudinal sets in which we assign attributes to another person solely on the basis of the class or category to which that person belongs. Stereotyping might lead us to believe, for example, that all Irish are quick-tempered and red-headed; that all Japanese are short, buck-toothed, and sly; that all Jews are shrewd and grasping; or that all Blacks are superstitious and lazy. Although these generalizations are commonly held stereotypes, they are untrue! Prejudices, on the other hand, are attitudinal sets that predispose us to behave in certain ways toward people solely on the basis of their membership in some group. For example, because a person is an Oriental, a Jew, or a Black, he may be denied membership in a country club, be forced to live in a ghetto or barrio, or be restricted to low-paying jobs and the performance of menial tasks. Stereotypes and prejudices are closely related.

An example of the effect stereotypes and prejudices can have on perceptual judgments was reported by Lambert (1960). Lambert and his associates had five bilinguals speak to English-Canadian test subjects in both French and English. When asked to judge personality traits of ten speakers (the five bilinguals) heard over a telephone, test subjects judged the English speakers more favorably than the French. In a parallel study, Lambert and his associates (1966) found, on the basis of speech patterns, language, and dialect, that English-Canadians rated French-Canadians unfavorably in a number of personality traits including ambition, self-confidence, religiousness, intelligence, dependability, likeability, and character. In these examples, English-Canadians held stereotypes of French-Canadians that led them to behave in a prejudicial manner toward stimuli identified as being French-Canadian. What this tells us is that we are likely to make social judgments about others based not on their true attributes but on stereotype attributes we assign to them on the basis of such insufficient evidence as the sound of their voice.

Prejudice and stereotype effects on social perception are further illustrated by Secord and Backman:

> A prejudiced person perceives selectively certain aspects of the behavior of the Negro: those that fit in with his preconceived ideas concerning the Negro. Thus he observes and notes behavior incidents that demonstrate stupidity, laziness, irresponsibility, or superstition; he overlooks other incidents that might contradict his prevailing ideas. The behavior of the Negro as he observes it thus supports his prejudicial beliefs (1964, p. 15).

Stereotypes and prejudices work in various ways to affect our communication. By predisposing us to behave in specific ways when confronted by a particular stimulus and by causing us to attach generalized attributes to people whom we encounter, we allow stereotypes and prejudices to interfere with our communicative experiences and to limit their effectiveness. We spend our time looking for whatever reinforces our prejudices and stereotypes and ignore what is contradictory.

Social Organization

The societal composition of cultures can also affect our perception. Flack (1966) has described two societal compositions related to the perception and communication processes. The first is based on *geographic* societies and is composed of members of a nation, nationality, tribe, cast, or religious sect. The second, based on *role* societies, acts within or transcends geographic cultures; it is composed of members of a profession, elite, or ideological, racial, or religious confraternity.

This concept is especially useful in relating to such diverse cultural groups as Russian wheat farmers or gay liberationists. In the first instance, the Russian farmer is a member of a geographic society. The gay liberationist, however, belongs to a role society and may be found in many geographic locales—even perhaps among Russian wheat farmers. Most international intercultural communication is based upon cultural differences in geographic societies while domestic intercultural communication is usually more a matter of cultural differences in role societies. This is especially true when we consider such culturally diverse groups as the gay community, the drug culture, youth, the urban poor, women's rights advocates, and pimps. Domestically, there also exists what we might call a hybrid form that relies on both geographic and role differences. Racial and ethnic minorities who are limited in geographic location by ghetto, barrio, or reservation may in part reflect a cultural difference resulting from geographic separation. They also are partly influenced by role differences.

These cultures have different effects on their members. In the geographic culture, people tend to live and feel a "common way of life" and to perceive relatively similar contexts, meanings, and motives. In the role culture, people share common definitions of situations and perceive intra- and intersocietal functions, codes of procedure, and specialized contexts, meanings, and motives in relatively similar terms.

Based on these two types of cultures, Flack (1966) has divided communication into two types: *cognitive* and *experiential.* Cognitive communication deals with things we know about; and it is possible between members of both geographic and role cultures. In contrast, experiential communication, which occurs when knowledge inheres in feeling, occurs only between members of geographic cultures. Basically, intercultural communication is dependent upon the ability to share social perceptions. As perceptions vary culturally, the experiential level of communication diminishes. For example, what are the circumstances when both a Mexican and a North American view the film *Viva Zapata?* If both are members of the same role culture, such as professional motion picture producer, they could communicate intraculturally about the technical and artistic aspects of producing the film. But, were the subject to leave the cognitive level and focus on the character of Zapata the man, the differences in experience could make communication difficult. To many North Americans, Zapata is remembered as a ruthless bandit, but to many Mexicans he is a national hero. These experiential differences place our communicators in different experiential cultures, and now we have a form of intercultural communication.

Hayakawa (1958) has divided the development of human cooperation and communication into three organizational stages: societies organized around physical symbols, around "master" verbal symbols, or around shared perceptions. The first is typified by the pyramids of Egypt and Mexico, Indian burial mounds, and various shrines, churches, and temples. The second is represented by master symbols held in respect by groups—for example, the secret world of a fraternity or a greeting such as "Allah is Great." In societies built around master symbols, agreement reached at the highest levels of abstraction—"God," "Divine Right of Monarchs," and so on—provides the basis for agreement at lower levels of abstraction. The third level of organization transcends local or regional loyalties. In these societies, the agreement process is opposite to that of the second stage; here agreement is first reached at the lowest levels of abstraction and then the sharing of perceptions proceeds step-by-step to higher levels. Unfortunately, religious notions do not lend themselves to being shared perceptions at low levels of abstraction. "Allah is Great" or "Christ is my Savior" are perceptions shared by millions, but they are such high level abstractions that they function as master symbols. Hayakawa's (1958) notion of shared perceptions at low levels of abstraction proceeding step-by-step to higher levels of abstraction is best illustrated mathematically: $1 + 1 = 2$, $2(a + b) = 2a + 2b$, $ax^2 + bx + c = 0$,

$$x = \frac{-b \pm \sqrt{b^2 + 4ac}}{2a}$$

and so on. Each mathematical step is agreed upon and serves as the basis for the next, which is more complex and abstract.

Hayakawa (1958) suggests that when there is too much social organization around master symbols, the sharing of perceptions cross-culturally is difficult if not impossible. For instance, the history and current events of the Near East reflect what happens when the master symbol "Allah is Great" is answered by the master symbol "Christ is my Savior."

Another effect of cultural variance in social organization is seen in the ways by which legal systems are administered. Hall (1959, pp. 81–82) has cited an example of this cultural difference as it existed in a small Western U.S. town. The town was predominantly Mexican-American in population and government with the Latin culture prevailing. A 15-mph speed limit was rigidly enforced by a Mexican-American motorcycle policeman. Acting on the letter of the law he would arrest people for driving 16 mph. Mexican-Americans brought before the court usually had a cousin or an uncle sitting on the bench and were quickly acquitted. Anglos were rarely that lucky and usually had to pay a fine. Unhappy with their treatment, the Anglos led the policeman out of town at a high rate of speed and ran him off the road. His legs were severely broken, and he could no longer ride a motorcycle as a result of his injuries.

At the heart of the matter was the different view each culture took of law, government, and family. Law in Mexico and Latin America tends to be enforced technically, or by the book, but it is mediated by the family. U.S. law tends to be enforced in accordance with the formal systems of the culture. North American law is not expected to be stricter than the rest of the culture. When the North American considers a law unjust, he is more likely to violate it than when he considers it to be realistic and sensible.

These approaches to law enforcement are differences in the way both cultures organize themselves for the enforcement and administration of their legal systems. Although it might be argued that the foregoing incident was merely one group of people disliking their treatment at the hands of another and seeking revenge, it also seems obvious that no successful intercultural communication was achieved. Both groups looked at the situation and perceived it in accordance with their culturally derived perceptual sets. The Anglos could see it as strange and unfair. The Latins perceived it as normal and quite possibly could not understand the Anglos' dislike of the procedure. Because there was an almost total lack of shared perceptions, however, these groups had little or no understanding of one another.

Patterns of Thought

The form of reasoning prevalent in a society is another aspect of culture that influences social perception. Pribram has suggested:

> Mutual understanding and peaceful relations among the peoples of the earth have been impeded not only by the multiplicity of languages but to an even greater degree by differences in patterns of thought—that is, by differences in the methods adopted for defining the sources of knowledge, and for organizing coherent thinking. . . . the most striking differences among philosophical doctrines are attributable to deepseated divergencies in the methods of forming fundamental concepts and of defining the functions of Reason—that is, the cognitive power of the human mind and the extent and validity of that power (1949, p. 1).

In analyzing Western thought, Pribram found the Western mind to be capable of arriving directly at insight into the order of the universe. But, as he points out, societies have arrived at vastly different concepts of the order of the universe and of the methods to be employed in comprehending the laws underlying that order.

Oliver (1962, pp. 77–78) has suggested that a major difficulty in intercultural communication is the differences between Aristotelian modes of reasoning prevalent in Western cultures and the non-Aristotelian systems of the Orient. The Aristotelian system was developed by men presumed to be free and having the right to cast ballots; it views man as a rational being available to factual and sound reasoning.

But Western assumptions are not universal. There are many modes of thinking, many standards of value, many ways in which people conceive of their relationship to the universe. In the Taoist view, humans are not rational beings, nor is truth to be conceived in terms of reason and logic. Taoist philosophy states that human life is conditioned and unfree and only when a person recognizes this limitation and makes himself dependent upon the harmonious and beneficent forces of the cosmos does he achieve success. Tao holds that truth is most likely to emerge when we waits for it, when we accept it as it comes rather than setting forth along a preconceived path in a predetermined manner to define a preconceived truth.

The extent of variance that may be found among cultural patterns of reasoning may be found by contrasting Western Aristotelian and Oriental Taoist modes of reasoning. Tao teaches the wisdom of being foolish, the success of failure, the strength of weakness, and the futility of contending for power—all of which might be seen as irrational by the traditional Western mind. The Taoist, whose basic philosophy is based upon the need to achieve harmony with the cosmos, observes nature in order to achieve this relationship. Instead of perceiving the concept of

strength-in-weakness as an irrational attempt to be both A and not-A simultaneously, the Taoist sees a rational relationship because he has observed such in
nature. A tree limb that is strong and does not bend eventually breaks under the
increasing weight of winter snow, but the weak limb—the one that is limber and
bends—gives way to the weight of the snow and lets it fall to the ground before
enough can accumulate to break the limb. Weakness is perceived as strength;
strength is seen as weakness. In Tao, this is rational.

To improve our intercultural communication abilities, we must determine
what effect differences in reasoning patterns have on communicative behavior. If,
for example, a Taoist does not actively search for truth but is content to wait for
it to appear, his passiveness could present a difficult problem to those of us who
have been influenced by Western tradition to seek the truth. To search for truth
when it must be waited for most certainly could be perceived as foolish or
improper behavior by a Taoist, and to quietly wait for truth when it must actively
be sought would quite probably exasperate the Western mind.

Roles and Role Prescriptions

Roles are important in intercultural communication because role expectations or prescriptions vary culturally. If we encounter members of other cultures
and their behavior seems strange to us, it could very well be a matter of different
role prescriptions. And, although we might want to argue the value of such
prescriptions, we must realize—if we are to succeed in our task of communication
—that, for members of the culture with which we are in contact, their behaviors
are completely natural, normal, and *moral.*

A good example of cultural differences in role prescriptions and the effect it
had on intercultural communication comes from England during World War II.
British women saw American servicemen stationed in England as immoral and
lustful. Simultaneously, American servicemen found English girls to be wanton
and without morals. Yet neither of these was the general case. Cultural differences
in the role of moderating sex behavior caused social misperceptions. In America,
this responsibility is prescribed for the female role; in England, the responsibility
was a male role behavior. Thus, American servicemen, used to being told "no"
by American women, suddenly found themselves dating English women who had
not learned to say "no." And English women, used to men not making advances
unless they were seriously intended, found themselves dating Americans who
were used to making sexual advances until told to stop.

Another example of how the values associated with roles vary and lead to
conflict and lack of successful communication may be seen domestically in the
case of so-called victimless crime. One segment of society fulfills the role of society
protector and has a value system that holds such things as nude sunbathing,
homosexual acts, getting stoned, buying sex, or viewing "pornographic" matter
as absolutely evil and not to be permitted under any circumstance. On the other
hand, those who fulfill the roles of nude sunbather, homosexual, pot smoker, pimp
or prostitute, and explicit sex film producer or viewer hold a vastly different set

of values. Their values allow these acts and hold that they are not evil but are the exercise of free choice by mature people in a free society. The values held by these various role groups often conflict and may lead to ineffective communication or even violent interaction. At the very least, one value system will be attempting to prevent the other from existing or at least being visible.

These examples have shown how cultural variance in role prescriptions can cause confusion and misunderstanding. When we assume that the rest of the world should and does share the same role behaviors as we, our ability to communicate will be reduced sharply. Again, although we might want to argue the value of a particular role prescription, we must remember that what seems strange and perhaps wrong to us is completely natural and normal for others. And, our customs and behaviors probably seem just as strange to others.

Language

We obviously are aware that there are language differences between cultural groups. But many of us naively believe that a competent interpreter is all that is necessary for people of different cultures to communicate. This notion fails to acknowledge the relationship between culture and language. To a very great extent our language is a product of our culture. At the same time, our culture is very much a product of our language. Culture and language are inseparably intertwined. What we think about and how we think about it are direct functions of our language; and what we think about and how we think about it in part determine the nature of our culture.

A major problem found in language differences is the part words play in the perception process. Since judgment and attachment of meaning are a part of perception, the ultimate meaning associated with a word is culturally determined. Even within our "American culture," there are groups that share perceptions not shared by others. For instance, if we ask a Christian Scientist, a pharmacist, and an addict what the word "drug" means, we would expect and most likely receive quite different responses. These different responses result from the dissimilar perceptions each person has of drugs. A Christian Scientist, a pharmacist, and an addict each have a unique set of experiences with drugs. These experiences influence their perception and thus affect the meaning they attach to the word "drug." The background of experience provides the connotative meanings for the symbol "drug."

When we communicate interculturally, we are likely to encounter problems where cultural differences in word *connotations* affect our ability to communicate. And many times these difficulties are likely to turn up when least expected. Let's take, for instance, the word "ancestor," a word that seems neutral enough not to cause meaning problems. Yet, look at these cultural differences: North Americans tend to perceive ancestors as distant relatives of foreign origin; Colombians tend to see them in terms of national and family history; and Koreans look upon ancestors as mythical persons of supernatural character with nearly divine status.

Another language problem is cultural differences in *denotative meanings*. In America, we think of all cars as automobiles, whereas in certain parts of the Arab world only the Cadillac is considered an automobile. This fact might not seem too important, but consider the ramifications of offering someone from that culture the use of your automobile. If you owned a Cadillac, there would be no problem; if your "automobile" turned out to be a psychedelically painted van, some obvious problems might arise.

Language also provides us with another important problem. Because the meanings we assign to words are in part the result of our cultural experiences, we often lack applicable experiences in encountering foreign words. This is why some words and phrases do not lend themselves to direct translation; or if directly translated, we fail to experience them as we do the same words in our own language. The term "My God" evokes much more of an emotional response from us than the comparable Spanish *¡Dios Mios!*

Use and Organization of Space

The way people use and organize space is another cultural variable we must consider. Cultures often attach different meanings to the same or similar interpersonal distances. We unconsciously structure space as a function of our culture, and it often serves as a nonverbal means of communication. Hall has observed:

> Space communicates in very much the same ways as the tone of voice. It can be, like language, formal or informal, warm or cold, public or private, masculine or feminine, and indicative of high or low stature (1960, pp. 41–42).

The manner in which a culture views space is manifest throughout its society. For instance, in the United States we live in close relationships with one another; we borrow things, share rides to work, provide social activities, and serve as sources of help in emergencies. Other cultures are often different. The Latin American culture tends to build houses around patios, which are hidden from outsiders behind walls. About this Hall has commented:

> It is not easy to describe the degree to which small architectural differences such as this affect the outsiders. American Point Four technicians living in Latin America used to complain that they felt "left out" of things, that they were "shut off." Others kept wondering what was going on "behind those walls" (1959, p. 99).

The effect of space on communication, both intra- and interculturally is only beginning to become known. Sommer (1962) has found that North Americans seated in a large room find the most comfortable conversation distance to be about five and one-half feet and that they show a preference to be seated face-to-face rather than side-by-side. He has also hypothesized that the distance for comfortable conversation varies as an inverse function of the size of the room. As the room becomes larger, the distance for comfortable conversation becomes smaller.

Hall (1966, pp. 144–153) has described how interpersonal distances vary cultur-ally, with vast differences existing for the Arab and Latin American compared to the North American. In the United States, we tend to keep a greater distance between ourselves when engaged in face-to-face interpersonal communication; Arabs and Latins tend to stand closer. In our culture physical contact tends to be reserved for intimate events, whereas other cultures do not make this reserva-tion.

Cultures develop appropriate distances for people engaged in conversation, depending on the purpose and nature of the message. A culturally influenced zone of personal space surrounds each individual. People are allowed to enter this space only for the most intimate forms of interaction. When personal space is violated, we usually experience feelings of intrusion, overbearing, and dominance, often with negative sexual connotations. Depending on the social relationships involved, the intruder may be perceived as pushy, overbearing, disrespectful, sexually aggressive, homosexual, or even a boor. Though the result of ignorance, such intrusions can disrupt interaction.

Time Conceptualization

An American agriculturalist, recently arrived on assignment in a Latin American country, had this experience:

> After what seemed to him a suitable period he let it be known that he would like to call on the minister who was his counterpart. For various reasons, the suggested time was not suitable; all sorts of cues came back to the effect that the time was not yet ripe to visit the minister. Our friend, however, persisted and forced an appointment which was reluctantly granted. Arriving a little before the hour (the American respect pattern), he waited ... five minutes—ten minutes—fifteen minutes ... forty-five minutes (the insult period)! He jumped up and told the secretary that he had been "cooling his heels" in an outer office for forty-five minutes and he was "damned sick and tired" of this type of treatment. The message was relayed to the minister, who said, in effect, "Let him cool his heels." The attache's stay in the country was not a happy one (Hall, 1959, p. 18).

The difficulty between the attache and the minister resulted from differences in the way the North American and the Latin cultures conceive of time. Not only were there misperceptions about the appropriate "time" to call on the minister, but there were gross misperceptions about waiting patterns. The North Ameri-can's concept caused him to perceive the 45-minute delay as an insult; in the Latin concept, 45 minutes, instead of being at the end of the waiting scale, was just barely at the beginning. The minister's manner of handling time caused him to perceive the visitor's protestations to be as absurd as if the visitor had raised a storm about cooling his heels after five minutes of North American time.

The manner in which time is conceptualized is another cultural variable. Western cultures tend to conceptualize time in *lineal-spatial* terms, meaning that we are aware of a past, a present, and a future. Time is something we can manipulate, something we can save, waste, make up, or spend. We place a strong emphasis on time as an aspect of history rather than as an aspect of immediate experience. We treat the present as a way-station, an intermediate point between past and future, and an immersion in the present is considered by some of us to be paganistic.

Unlike us, others are more concerned with immediacy or what is called *felt time.* Japanese Zen treats time like a limitless pool in which events occur, cause ripples, and then subside. There is no past, no present, no future—only the event in the absolute present. The Navajo concept of time assigns reality only to the immediate; thoughts of the future are not worth much consideration. The Sioux Indian presents an even greater problem; that language does not contain words for time, late, or waiting.

As time conceptualizations vary culturally, so will the norms concerning time sequences in communication. Moore states:

> Communication effectiveness may be influenced or affected by the speed of response. The fast talker may be regarded as foolish or with suspicion. The response that comes "too fast" may cause doubt about the consideration given to the stimulus, and the response that is "too slow" may raise doubt about the quality of the reception or the receiver's interest in the message (1963, pp. 49–50).

The problem for us is to know what the appropriate speed of response is in intercultural communication situations. Culture determines when a response is too fast or too slow, when a person talks too fast or too slowly. As the complexity of these cultural norms increases, our perceptual problems increase, and errors or failures may occur in the interpretation we make of messages we receive from persons in other cultures.

Nonverbal Expression

> It is a common experience among people who travel to find that it is difficult to interpret the facial expressions of peoples of cultures other than their own. This difficulty has frequently been voiced with reference to Oriental people whose modes of expression are found to differ from those of Caucasians (Vinacke, 1949, p. 407).

Another cultural variable that affects the social perception process is nonverbal expression. Culture determines the form nonverbal messages take as well as the circumstances calling for their expression and the amount of expression permitted. Klineberg has pointed out:

> We find that cultures differ widely from one another in the amount of emotional expression which is permitted. We speak, for example, of the imperturbability of the American Indian, the inscrutability of the Oriental, the reserve of the Englishman, and at the other extreme of the expressiveness of the Negro or the Sicilian. Although there is always some exaggeration in such cliches, it is probable that they do correspond to an accepted cultural pattern, at least to some degree (1954, p. 174).

The Japanese smile is a law of etiquette that has been elaborated and culturated from early times; and it is not necessarily a spontaneous expression of amusement. This smile is a silent language that is often inexplicable to Westerners. The Japanese child is taught to smile as a social duty so that he will always show an appearance of happineśs and avoid inflicting sorrow upon his friends.

The problem as it affects social perception can be seen in the following anecdote. A Japanese woman servant smilingly asked her Western mistress if she might go to her husband's funeral. Later she returned with his ashes in a vase, and actually laughing, said, "Here is my husband." Her mistress regarded her as a cynical creature, although her smile and laughter may have been reflecting pure heroism.

The amount of emotional expression permitted by a culture also varies according to the emotion involved.

> The Chinese, who feel that a display of anger is never warranted and that affection should be shown only in privacy, insist upon a public manifestation of grief or sorrow. . . . Not only is grief expressed, but there is an elaborate set of rules and regulations which ensure that it will be properly expressed. One of the Chinese classics is the *Book of Rites,* a considerable portion of which is devoted to the technique of the mourning ceremonial, with elaborate instructions as to just what procedure should be followed in order that the expression of the grief may be socially acceptable. The Plains Indians, in spite of their deserved reputation for imperturbability, expected a man literally to wail and howl for hours at a stretch at the death of his wife or child. . . . It is clear that the repressive influence of a culture with regard to emotional behavior is not applied equally in all directions. It is perhaps unnecessary to add that the absence of the manifestation of an emotion does not prove that it is not experienced. It merely prevents our direct knowledge of its existence (Klineberg, 1954, pp. 177–178).

Even in what may be considered a more basic form of expression—the nonverbal expression of what we call verbal expressions, there are cultural variations. In our culture, the verbal statement "no" is often expressed nonverbally by moving the head from side to side. Yet an Abyssinian is apt to express "no" by jerking the head to the right shoulder; a Dyand of Borneo may express it by contracting the eyebrows slightly; and Sicilians express "no" by raising the head and chin. Among the Ainu of northern Japan our particular head noddings are unknown; "no" is expressed by a movement of the right hand and affirmation by a simultaneous movement of both hands.

The importance of the nonverbal aspect of communication cannot be overlooked. We rely on nonverbal cues to help interpret verbal cues. When we detect incongruencies between the verbal and nonverbal, we tend to assign greater credibility to the nonverbal. This may be all right within a culture where perhaps we know what the cues mean. But when we encounter new or different cues, we are unable to interpret them correctly. In fact, we may assign totally wrong meanings to nonverbal cues and react to them as if they implied what we take them to mean. Remember the Japanese woman who "laughingly" displayed her dead husband's ashes. The *judgment* of "laughingly" is purely from our culture. To another Japanese, the smile and appearance of "joy" might have been perceived as a sign of bravery under trying emotional circumstances and probably would have evoked an interpretation of respect and admiration as well as sympathy.

There is much for us to learn about how people from other cultures use nonverbal cues to express themselves. Until we gain this knowledge we are going to encounter trouble whenever we interact with people from other cultures. Nonverbal aspects of intercultural communication are probably among the most difficult because of the reliance we place on the interpretation of nonverbal cues in decoding verbal cues.

Summary

Here we have suggested that the chief problem associated with intercultural communication is error in social perception brought about by cultural variations that affect the perceptual process. The attribution of meaning to messages is in many respects influenced by the culture of the message decoder. When the message being interpreted was encoded in another culture, the cultural influences and experiences that produced that message may be entirely different from the cultural influences and experiences that are being drawn upon to decode the message. Consequently, grave errors in meaning may arise that are not intended nor really the fault of the communicators. They are the result of entirely different backgrounds being unable to accurately understand one another.

The approach we have taken is also based upon a fundamental assumption: The parties to intercultural communication must have an honest and sincere desire to communicate and seek mutual understanding. This assumption, therefore, requires favorable attitudes on the part of intercultural communicators and an elimination of superior-inferior relationships based upon membership in particular cultures. Unless this basic assumption has been satisfied, our theory of cultural variance in social perception will not produce improvement in intercultural communication.

We have discussed eight cultural variables that are major sources of communication difficulty: attitudes, social organization, patterns of thought, roles and role expectations, language, space, time, and nonverbal expression. Although they were discussed in isolation, we cannot allow ourselves to conclude they are unrelated. They are all related in a matrix of cultural complexities.

For there to be successful intercultural communication, we must be aware of the cultural factors affecting communication in both our own culture and the culture of the other party. We need to understand not only cultural differences but also cultural similarities. While understanding differences will help us know where problems lie, understanding similarities may help us be closer.

This discussion is only an introduction to the arena of intercultural communication. The variables discussed here have merely been highlighted, and not all of the relevant variables have been mentioned. One reason is the obvious lack of space. Another is that our knowledge of the effect of culture on communication is woefully inadequate.

References

Bagby, J. W., "A Cross-Cultural Study of Perceptual Predominance in Binocular Rivalry," *Journal of Abnormal and Social Psychology,* 54 (1957), 331–334.

Flack, M. J., "Communicable and Uncommunicable Aspects in Personal International Relations," *Journal of Communication,* 16 (1966), 283–290.

Hall, E. T., *The Silent Language,* Greenwich, Conn., 1959.

Hall, E. T., "Language of Space," *Landscape,* 10 (1960), 41–42.

Hall, E. T., *The Hidden Dimension,* Garden City, N.Y., 1966.

Hayakawa, S. I., "Communication and the Human Community," *ETC.,* 60 (1958), 5–11.

Hoben, J. B., "English Communication at Colgate Re-Examined," *Journal of Communication,* 4 (1954), 77.

Klineberg, O., *Social Psychology,* rev. ed., New York, 1954.

Lambert, W. E., et al., "Evaluation Reactions to Spoken Languages," *Journal of Abnormal and Social Psychology,* 60 (1960), 44–51.

Lambert, W. E., et al., "Judging Personality Traits through Speech: A French-Canadian Example," *Journal of Communication,* 16 (1966), 305–321.

Miller, G. A., "On Defining Communication: Another Stab," *Journal of Communication,* 16 (1966), 92.

Moore, W. E., *Man, Time, and Society,* New York, 1963.

Oliver, R. T., *Culture and Communication,* Springfield, Ill., 1962.

Parsons, T., "Intercultural Understanding and Academic Social Science," in *Approaches to Group Understanding,* ed. L. Bryson, L. Finkelstein, and R. M. MacIver, New York, 1964.

Pribram, K., *Conflicting Patterns of Thought,* Washington, D.C., 1949.

Secord, P. F., and C. W. Backman, *Social Psychology,* New York, 1964.

Sommer, R., "The Distance for Comfortable Conversation," *Sociometry,* 25 (1962), 111–116.

Stevens, S. S., "A Definition of Communication," *Journal of the Acoustical Society of America,* 22 (1950), 698.

Vinacke, E. W., "The Judgment of Facial Expressions by Three National-Racial Groups in Hawaii: I, Caucasian Faces," *Journal of Personality,* 17 (1949), 407–429.

Watzlawick, P., J. Beavin, and D. Jackson, *The Pragmatics of Human Communication,* New York, 1967.

Intercultural and Interracial Communication: An Analytical Approach

Andrea L. Rich and Dennis M. Ogawa

In our internationally troubled world and racially tense society, the study of intercultural and interracial communication has become critically important to

This paper was first presented to the Intercultural Division of the International Communication Association in the annual convention at Phoenix, Arizona, April 1971. Reproduced by permission of the authors. Professor Rich is with the Speech/Communications Department at the University of California at Los Angeles, and Professor Ogawa is Director of Ethnic Studies at the University of Hawaii.

researchers concerned with the processes and effects of human interaction. This paper is designed to provide a hitherto absent structure within which concepts and hypotheses concerning cross-cultural and cross-racial communication can be tested and analyzed.

To provide some framework for the analysis of intercultural and interracial communication, we must explore factors in the macrocosm or larger environment in which this communication occurs. Specifically, our paper will attempt to answer the following questions:

> 1. What are the defining societal and interpersonal patterns and relationships which distinguish the terms "intercultural," "contracultural," "interracial," and "interethnic" communication?
>
> 2. What are some of the major factors which may influence patterns of interracial communication?

By suggesting the defining patterns and relationships of these terms and by delineating some of the factors influencing interracial communication, we hope to clear up the confusion and looseness with which the terms have been employed.

Distinguishing Societal and Interpersonal Patterns and Relationships

INTERCULTURAL COMMUNICATION   "Culture is the sum total of the learned behaviors of a group of people which are generally considered to be the tradition of that people and are transmitted from generation to generation (1)." By "intercultural communication" we mean comunication (2) between *peoples* of different cultures (as opposed to communication between official representatives of nations, i.e., international communication). Figure 1 represents our concept of intercultural communication.

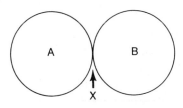

Figure 1

A and *B* represent the two communicating cultures. (A_1 and B_1 would represent the individuals within those cultures who are actually interacting.) The important assumption here is that these cultures do not and have not historically existed in a colonial relationship where one of the cultures has taken over or dominated the other for any long period of time. (Hence, the circles do not overlap.)

The communicators may or may not share a symbolic system in intercultural communication. When the system is shared (e.g., an American speaking with an Australian), the *X* of our diagram would refer to that shared system (the English language). When communication is conducted between people of different cultures who do not share a symbolic system (a Frenchman and a German, for example), the X portion of the diagram represents whatever improvised system they invent to make contact.

As we shall see in sections on interracial and contracultural communication, the important distinction between intercultural, contracultural, and interracial communication is the interpersonal relationship of the communicating individuals. In intercultural communication situations, individuals are strange to each other; they have had a relatively separate historical development. As such, they tend to communicate more or less as equals.

INTERRACIAL COMMUNICATION   Figure 2 applies to interracial communication as it occurs in the United States. Circle A represents the dominant power structure, or, specifically, "white America." A includes the physical, social, and psychological space occupied by white America. The individuals who occupy that space we shall refer to as A_1.

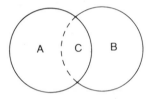

Figure 2

Circle B represents the non-white racial group as it exists in its purest form, uninfluenced by the structure of white America. For example, B_1 (the individual who occupies the physical, social, and psychological space of B) could be the immigrant Japanese *before* he reaches the shores of America or the Mexican *abuela* (grandmother) who was brought to the United States by her family to dwell in the ethnic shelter of an East Los Angeles barrio. She speaks no English and may have created her own pure and unaffected racial subculture. There is some doubt, however, as to whether one may dwell in the United States and still be unaffected by the white structure. It is possible that B may exist only on its native soil or as an idealized concept in the mind of C_1 (to be defined shortly).

Circle C represents the experience of being a racial minority in a white-dominated structure. It is the geographical, social, and psychological space allotted to the non-white American. C_1 (and C_2, C_3, etc.) are the individuals confined to that space, the ethnic-American (Mexican-American, Black-American, Japanese-American, etc.). The line of C transversing A is broken, not to suggest the possibility of C_1 ever entering into A, but to demonstrate that the size of C is elastic; it may vary depending upon the whim of A and, to a certain extent, upon the tenacity of C to remain close to B. For example, when Congress passes certain Civil Rights legislation, it enlarges the size of C. Such expansion of C into the domain of A, however, is under the control of A; the outside limit to which C can intrude upon A is dictated by A.

On the other hand, C could, by its own choice, choose to remain small and closer to B. Members of certain Mexican-American barrios, for example, have attempted to keep Mexican culture intact by speaking the Spanish language and generally preserving Mexican custom rather than white Anglo-Saxon custom. The size of C will also vary depending upon which group we consider as occupying C at any given time. Let us say, for example, that C_1 represents Black America and C_2 represents Mexican America (Figure 3). C_1 may be larger than C_2 because, at least until recently, Black America has depended more upon white America for its culture (language, customs, etc.) than has Mexican America.

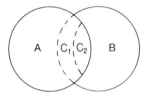

Figure 3

There are certain assumptions which can be drawn from Figure 3. First, a member of C can never totally move within the realm of A. This is, at present, a fact of life in white-dominated America. Despite the thrust toward integration, white America has tenaciously maintained a portion of A into which, on the basis of color, non-white Americans may not enter. As long as a member of C can be identified as non-white, he cannot pass completely into the realm of A.

On the other hand, a member of C can move within his allotted space of C, and also within B, unless he has rejected B or has been rejected by B. That is to say, a Japanese-American is relatively free to return to Japan and drop the hyphenate of being a Japanese-American, if he so desires. Though his ethnic minority experience in the United States may cause him certain problems in acculturation within his new environment, in most cases there are few or no legal or social barriers preventing a member of C from entering into B, such as there are racial barriers preventing a member of C from entering into A in the United States.

A third and significant assumption for interracial communication is that a member of A can never become a member of C. A white American, despite his good intentions, can never fully contemplate the experience of being a racial minority in a white-dominated America. Communication between members of A and members of C, or between white and any non-white groups, is therefore highly difficult because of this lack of shared experience. The outstanding characteristic of communication between members of A and C (interracial communication, as opposed to international or intercultural communication) is that the very existence of C (a segregated physical and psychological space dictated by A) has to cause hostility and resentment on the part of C members; therefore, tension and great strain arise in any attempts at communication between individuals in A and C.

On the other hand, communication between C_1, C_2, C_3, C_4, etc. (Black Americans, Mexican Americans, Japanese Americans) stands a better chance of positive response because all these non-white groups, to some degree, share C. While their C's may vary in size, they all have experienced being a racial minority in a white-dominated culture. Sitaram calls communication between C's *minority communication* (3). Since the terms "minority" and "majority" are so relative, based on one's system of classification, and since the term "minority" tends to cause abrasive reactions among those who regard themselves as a minority in the United States but a majority in the world, we would prefer to call communication between C's *interethnic communication.* Groups also to be included in the C classification of interracial communication in the United States are the American natives (Eskimos, Indians, and Hawaiians) who have been forced into C space by the white structure.

"Interracial communication," then, is communication between white and non-white in the United States and is characterized by strain and tension resulting from the dominant-submissive societal and interpersonal relationship historically imposed upon the non-white by the structure of white America. "Interethnic communication" is that which occurs between members of different non-white groups in America, groups which have in common the sharing of a peripheral societal and interpersonal space to which they have been relegated by the white structure.

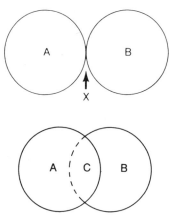

Figure 4

CONTRACULTURAL COMMUNICATION   Figure 4 shows that contracultural communication occurs when intercultural communication is transformed, by continued contact of cultures and the imposition of one culture upon the other, into interracial communication. In other words, what began as a simple egalitarian interaction between two strange but relatively equal cultures becomes a colonial relationship where one culture is forced to submit to the power of another. The X of the intercultural model, that area of shared or improvised means of communication, becomes the C of the interracial model, an area in which individuals are relegated to a position and their mobility to move out of that position is dictated by a dominant structure. When Columbus first landed on the shores of the New World, for example, he undoubtedly engaged in intercultural communication with the natives he encountered. He improvised a system (exchanged gifts, etc.). As the colonization progressed, however, the white Spaniards came to occupy A space and allowed certain of the Indians (from B) to form a C group. Had the Indians maintained control and enslaved the Spaniards, according to our theory, the Indians would then have occupied the A circle with the Spaniards relegated to C. (And those Spaniards remaining safely in Spain composing the B circle.)

The interracial diagram, then, also describes contracultural communication. As long as a power relationship exists between cultures, where one has subdued and dominated the other, a C circle exists, and as long as a C area exists, hostility, tension, and strain are introduced into the communication situation. Communication between an Englishman and an Indian, or between a Belgian and a Congolese, serves to exemplify what we mean here by contracultural communication.

Some Major Factors Influencing Interracial Communication

ECONOMIC AND/OR CLASS PARAMETER   To test the real extent to which racial and cultural differences influence communication between individuals, it is also interesting to hypothesize as to the effects of the introduction of economic and/or class parameters into interracial communication (Figure 5). Since in America class position is frequently determined by economic position, let us, for the sake of discussion, combine the two, and consider X the highest economic/social class, Y the middle economic/social class and Z the lowest economic/social class. An AX individual in our society would be someone occupying the position of Nelson Rockefeller or Richard Nixon (Nixon, a rather new member of X; Rockefeller, a comfortable inheritor of position X). A CX in our society might be Thurgood Marshall or Edward Brook. A BX would be a Japanese financier from Tokyo or a Prime Minister from Ghana.

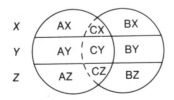

Figure 5

Several interesting questions arise from such a structure that could be translated into testable hypotheses for future research. For example, would Richard Nixon be more comfortable with and successful in eliciting a desired response from CX Edward Brook (a fellow Republican, though black), an AY (middle class clerk), or an AZ (poor coal miner)? (4) Would an American banker (AX) have a more successful business transaction with an African industrialist (BX) than he would with an American black capitalist (*CX*)? Do the tensions and strains in interracial communication resulting from the very existence of area *C* diminish as an individual member of *C* climbs the social/economic ladder from *Z* to *X*, or do tensions take other more subtle forms of expression? (It should be pointed out at this time, that a member of *C* has upward mobility in this model; he may move from *Z* to *X*, but he still has no lateral mobility to the left; that is, a *CX* can still not become an *AX*, or even an *AZ*, for that matter.) These are just a few of the many questions suggested by the introduction of an economic/social parameter.

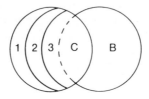

Figure 6

WHITE ETHNIC PARAMETER   One of the misleading assumptions of the interracial diagram (Figure 3) thus far has been in the classification of all members of *A* as one unit. From the non-white point of view, all whites are very much alike in the structure of our society. They do, by virtue of their color alone, enjoy many many benefits and advantages that non-whites do not. On the other hand, there are ethnic differences between those occupying the *A* space in our model. Attempting, for example, to place Jews within the model of interracial communication posed a problem. The majority of *C* members (Black Americans, for example) perceive Jews as white and as a part of the white power structure. In fact, much of black hostility against the white man is aimed at the Jew specifically, since often the Jew is spatially the closest to the black. Yet, the white society does not altogether regard the Jew as a member of the *A* group, and the Jew himself tends to identify with the more oppressed non-white groups. It seems appropriate, therefore, to add another dimension to the interracial communication model, that of white ethnic groups. For example, in Figure 6, we have arbitrarily divided *A* into three slices (it could conceivably be divided into as many slices as there are white ethnic groups in the United States). The closer the *A* slice is to *C*, the more tenuous is its position in the *A* circle. Jews, for example, would occupy position 3, the closest to the realm of *C*. Slice 2 might be occupied by Irish, Polish, and Italian Catholics, etc., and slice 1 would most likely be reserved for white Anglo-Saxon Protestants (5).

Figure 7, finally, is a rather complex attempt to include, in their various combinations, all the racial, ethnic, social, and economic variations that will influence the manner in which individuals in a complex society can interact. The *ABC* parameter represents racial groups. The *XYZ* parameter represents social/economic class. The *1234* notation in the *A* circle represents white ethnic groups (the higher the number, the less the group is regarded by the *A* circle). The *1234* notations in the *C* circle have no values placed upon them; they simply represent

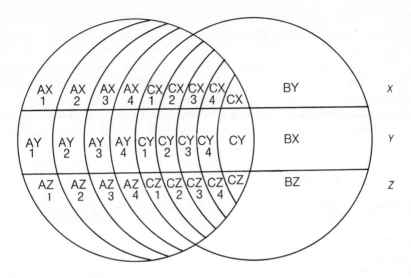

Figure 7

different non-white groups. (e.g., CX_1 would represent a wealthy black man, while CX_2 could represent a wealthy Japanese-American.) The numbers merely denote the difference between the two racial groups. Circle B is not divided into complex ethnic subdivisions, since the focus of this paper has been primarily upon racial and ethnic compositions that structure human interaction in the United States.

Conclusion

We have attempted, in this paper, to embrace the concepts of "intercultural" and "interracial" communication from a broad perspective. We first addressed ourselves to a discussion of the defining societal and interpersonal patterns and relationships that distinguish the various terms frequently used to apply to cross-group communication. In so doing, we sought to clarify and give meaning to these often loosely employed terms. Through our discussion of such societal and interpersonal relationships, we have defined "intercultural communication," "contracultural communication," "interracial communication," and "interethnic communication."

The second aim of our paper was to suggest some of the major factors that may influence patterns of interracial communication. Here we discussed how the dimensions of class and economic stratification and the multi-ethnic composition of the white and non-white populations of the United States further complicate the possibilities for interracial communication. Our exploration of a possible framework within which to view the many possible communication patterns arising in such an ethnically and racially diverse society has enabled us to propose certain interracial communication hypotheses and questions. For example: Are individuals more attracted to communication situations involving members of their own racial and/or ethnic group or to situations involving interaction with members of their own class and/or economic strata? Does tension in interracial communication diminish as the communicators ascend the economic and class ladders of the society?

These questions are a minute sample of the many relevant communication research areas suggested by the complex structure of our society. In asking such questions, and in attempting to provide a large framework within which we can view the multi-dimensional qualities of intercultural and interracial communication, we hope to gain a better understanding of the interaction between the various conflicting forces in our nation and our world.

References and Notes

1. K. S. Sitaram, "Intercultural Communication: The What and Why of It," International Communication Association, Division V: Intercultural Communication Division, Minneapolis, Minnesota, May 7–8, 1970, p. 2.

2. By "communication," we mean a process whereby a source elicits a response in a receiver through the transmission of a message, be it sign or symbol, verbal or nonverbal. We find it necessary for our purposes to include nonverbal and sign behavior in our definition of communication, since intercultural communication frequently occurs without the benefit of a symbolic system shared by the communicators.

3. Sitaram, *op. cit.,* p. 7.

4. Milton Rokeach, in *Beliefs, Attitudes, and Values* (San Francisco: Jossey-Bass, 1968), pp. 62–81, suggests in his findings on race, attitudes, and interpersonal choice, that individuals are more likely to choose as partners those who hold common beliefs with them rather than those who are of the same color. This study was conducted only in the North, which may have influenced its validity. Rokeach also states that discrimination is institutionally sanctioned.

5. Certain religions tend to be associated with given ethnic groups—Italian Catholics, for example. Though religion could be introduced as an entirely separate parameter, we have decided, for the sake of brevity, to combine ethnic background and religious affiliation into one graphic structure.

Cross-Cultural Studies
D. Price-Williams

In the same way that the study of individual differences shows to what degree particular person is similar to or different from others, so cross-cultural studies ocus on the similarities and differences of whole societies. Psychological cross-ultural studies provide an expansive background against which to plot information about any one society. For instance, when Freud's observations and nferences on the Oedipus complex were first propounded, the emphasis was laced on it as a universal biological phenomenon. The notion that it might be he product of a particular social structure operating in Central Europe, and that

From D. Price-Williams, "Cross-Cultural Studies," in Brian M. Foss, (ed.) *New Horizons in 'sychology,* pp. 396–416. Copyright © Penguin Books, 1966. Reprinted by permission of the publisher. The author is Professor of Psychology, Rice University.

in other cultures there might be variants of the situation or even that it might not exist, did not occur to anybody at the time. It is, of course, no criticism of Freud that this cultural aspect was lacking; the data were supplied only considerably later by the anthropologist Malinowski (1927) who noted that among the Trobrianders of Polynesia the social structure was such that the young boy had the repressed wish to marry his sister and was jealous of the maternal uncle, while in European society the picture is jealousy of the father and erotic desires towards the mother. In European society the genitor and the pater are usually the same person, and there are strong prohibitions against incestuous relationships between a boy and his mother. In Trobriand society the genitor and pater are two different people, the mother's brother taking on the role of pater, and there is a taboo against the brother's relationship with his sister. While there is a similarity in principle between the Trobriand and the European model, the different relationships enable us to view the Oedipus complex as a function of a social and not a biological factor.

Apart from the advantage of utilizing the differences between cultures as a buffer against generalizing from a comparatively small sample of the earth's population, cross-cultural work has the further asset of seeking out situations and influences which are either difficult to find in our own culture or are just nonexistent. For example, Zulus wean their children on a day set in advance; the weaning does not tail off gradually, but from this day the reliance on the mother's breast is terminated abruptly and permanently. This might conceivably be done by individuals in our own society, but it is not institutionalized. So that in the Zulu custom we are provided with an event which is rare, rather like finding an unusual specimen in the fields of botany and zoology. The event has more than just a curiosity value to the psychologist, because important issues related to theories about the effect of childhood experience on later life are bound up with the weaning experience. From this angle the Zulu case is more like a rare eclipse for astronomers; the theories can be tested empirically.

Unusual influences need not be related to social customs solely. They may be ecological, linguistic or occupational. Spatial perception can be studied in environments as markedly different as deserts and jungles. Linguistic differences in available words and phrases for the same object reveal much about perception and thinking. The Eskimoes, it is reported, have as many as thirty words for snow; some reindeer-herding people in Siberia have about the same number again for the patterns of reindeer hides; many West-African tribes use only three to five colour categories. How do these varying linguistic stores affect the perception and thinking of these people? These are legitimate cross-cultural questions and ones to which we have partial answers.

Perception

NATIVISM VERSUS EMPIRICISM   One of the purposes of studying perception cross-culturally is that it enables us to discover the extent to which perceiving is structured by the nervous system (which is common to the entire human race), and to what extent it is influenced by experience. The issue of nativism *versus* empiricism can be approached experimentally through application of various visual illusions. Two of these illusions, the classic Muller-Lyer (Figure 1) and the horizontal-vertical (Figure 2) are provided here. One of the first comprehensive attempts to apply visual illusions on a cross-cultural basis was that of the Cambridge Anthropological Expedition to the Torres Straits at the beginning of the century. One of the members of the expedition, W.H.R. Rivers, displayed these two and other illusions to the natives in that area (Rivers, 1901) and compared the results with English adults and children. He found that the Murray Island inhabitants were less prone to the Muller-Lyer than Europeans, which he attributed to the fact that the natives limited their attention strictly to the task they were asked to perform, paying attention to the horizontal lines of the figure, while European observers tended to regard the figure as a whole with the arrows. On the other hand, the horizontal-vertical illusion was more marked among the Murray Island men which, together with the pronounced character of the illusion in children, made Rivers feel that the source of the effect was to be found in some physiological condition or at least in a psychological condition of a simple and primitive character. The Cambridge expedition, in this respect, was a pioneer attempt and we require considerably more data than that taken from two or three tribes. A recent and more extensive approach has been carried out by Northwestern University, Illinois (Segall, Campbell and Herskovits, 1963; Campbell, 1964). Over a six-year period stimulus materials based upon the geometric illusions of the kind described were administered to samples of non-European children and adults, mainly in Africa, but including the Philippines, which were compared with South Africans of European descent and Americans in Illinois. There were thirty-nine items in all, which allowed for a comprehensive comparison between cultures. Rivers's finding with the Muller-Lyer is remarkably in agreement with these later and more extensive findings. If all the non-Europeans are compared with the Europeans, whether living in America or South Africa, the Europeans are much more prone to the illusion. If the illusion is measured by the percentage by which the upper line exceeds the lower line in Figure 1 when they are judged equal by any observer, it is found that the Europeans lie between fourteen to eighteen per cent (Campbell 1964; Figure 1), while all the remaining non-European people, except the Senegalese, lie below the ten per cent level of error. The Bushmen are lowest at four per cent. The horizontal-vertical illusion has a different cultural distribution. Here we have the Batoro and Bayankole people of Africa, who both live in high open country, at the top end of the percentage illusion dimension, while the Bete people, of jungle environment, are at the bottom. The European samples are intermediate, together with the Zulu. In this matter the ecology of peoples is probably crucial, a point which we shall return to after describing another illusion. This is a different kind from the geometric illusions and has its source in the 'transactionalist school' of perception which emphasizes the interaction between the perceiver and his environment. The illusion is generated by a figure cut in the form of a trapezoid which, when attached to a motor, revolves in a circle. Horizontal and vertical bars affixed to the trapezoid give the impression of a window. Most observers report the rotary figure as oscillating to and fro; seldom does it appear to them to revolve in a complete circle. Explanation of the phenomenon is given by the transactionalist school as a reconciliation by the observer of two sets of conflicting cues. On the one hand, the perceiver is accustomed to regarding longer retinal stimulations as coming from nearer objects. On the other hand, he regards this trapezoidal figure as a normal rectangular window. The longer edge of the figure is thus interpreted as being nearer and the window appears to oscillate rather than to rotate. The force of the illusion is thought to turn on the expectations which the observer brings to the figure. When the figure is altered to look less like a window by omitting the cross-bars, then the illusion is reduced. Similarly, it is reduced if it is presented binocularly rather than monocularly. The situation is thus perfect for showing the illusion to people who have had no experience with windows and who do not bring to it expectations of rectangularity. Allport and Pettigrew (1957) found such a case with Zulus, who do not live in towns and are not only not accustomed to conventional windows but also have a bias towards circularity, and not rectangularity, in their culture. Allport and Pettigrew then compared rural Zulu with urban Zulu and again with Europeans. The results were not entirely clear-cut as would be wished for any nativist-empiricist issue. Under optimal conditions for the illusion to be produced, that is monocularly at a longer distance, as many primitive Zulus reported the sway effect as urban Zulus and Europeans. However, under sub-optimal conditions (in which the effect is lessened) of binocular vision from a shorter distance, there was a tendency for the rural Zulus to report the effect less often than the urban Zulus. In particular, African subjects who held a preference for circles against a rectangle or trapezoid saw the illusion less often than those that expressed preference for rectangular figures.

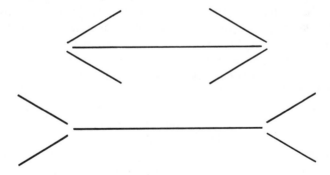

Figure 1   The Muller-Lyer illusion.

THE ROLE OF ECOLOGY   What lessons do these various cross-cultural studies on perceptual illusions contain? While there may not be completely unequivocal results supporting either side of the nativist-empiricist issue, the findings of both the early study of Rivers and the later Northwestern project indicate that there are functional differences in visual habits. If these habits are regarded culturally, then the clue to the differences might be sought in the varying habitats. This is not as simple to pin down as may appear, as within the same culture different occupations and interests may well have further influence, but certain broad trends can be distinguished. Campbell (1964) calls attention to what he calls the 'carpentered-world' hypothesis of the visual world of Western culture. 'We live in a culture in which straight lines abound and in which perhaps ninety per cent of the acute and obtuse angles formed on our retina by the straight lines of our visual field are realistically interpretable as right angles extended in space.'

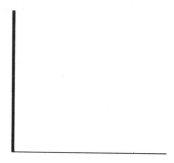

Figure 2   The horizontal-vertical illusion.

In a largely non-man-made environment, where the strict linearity of urban and Westernized features does not apply, there is less bias towards interpreting acute and obtuse angles as right angles extended in space. Campbell regards the cross-cultural findings on the Muller-Lyer and similar geometric illusions as well as the rotating trapezoid as supporting this idea. The horizontal-vertical illusion is similarly interpreted ecologically. The tendency here is to perceive the vertical line as longer than the horizontal, although both are of equal length. Campbell takes the ideal situation of a person who lives on a flat plain *versus* the person who lives in a rain forest. The former would have a much shorter retinal extension of vertical lines, that is lines that extended away from him, than those that crossed him from left to right. The latter who would have tree trunks and hanging vines extending vertically in front of him would be less likely to foreshorten the vertical. Europeans who had just as much familiarity with horizontal floors and vertical walls might provide intermediate cases. While the actual experimental data, as Campbell allows, do not completely fit this hypothesis, there is sufficient positive evidence to regard this line of thought as profitable. Being immersed in a single culture sometimes blinds one to the fact that apparently basic frameworks are in fact cultural artefacts. Two-dimensional representations of three-dimensional life as in drawings, photographs and motion pictures are examples of what we in our culture have mastered early in life and have grown accustomed to, so that we do not have to go through the inferential process of reconstructing the real world from the photograph. It can be quite otherwise with people not accustomed to such two-dimensional representations. Those that have attempted to show motion pictures to people totally unaccustomed to this type of representation have reported curious effects. Sellers (1941) who showed films to Nigerian audiences noted that a vertical 'tilt' shot of a building gave the impression that the building was sinking into the ground. Sellers inferred that his audiences were seeing the screen as flat, and not inferring a three-dimensional space. In an experimental situation Hudson (1960) compared literate and illiterate groups in South Africa in the perception of three-dimensional cues such as superimposition (one object partly obscuring another object), perspective and object size, in drawings and photographs. The literate sample perceived depth in the representations far more frequently than the illiterate group who had not been exposed to pictorial matter, and not one illiterate perceived a photograph as three-dimensional.

Cognition

In many ways it is extremely difficult to ascertain the thinking ability of non-European people, especially those in the under-developed regions of the world. Not only is it agreed by psychologists that formal tests of intelligence which have been constructed and standardized in Western society are inappropriate for evaluating results in these areas (Anastasi and Foley, 1949, 725–6; Cryns, 1962), but also tests of abstract reasoning have this difficulty of the bias of environmental factors (Jahoda, 1956). More fruitful approaches to cross-cultural cognition have consisted in comparing one particular cognitive process across various cultures, and investigating the special question of language.

SPECIFIC CULTURAL ELEMENTS   Choosing an element of a culture which can be examined from a cognitive point of view interests anthropologists as much as psychologists. Frake (1961) investigated the conceptual scheme of disease diagnoses in the Philippines. He describes his perplexity with the society's (the Subanun of Mindanao) diagnosis of an infectious swelling which he developed early in his field work. He received a variety of names for his disease and was not able at first to perceive clarity in the diagnosis by Subanun people. Further interrogation, however, showed that different people were speaking at different levels of contrast. One person was contrasting skin diseases with all other kinds of external diseases. Another informed him that he had an 'inflammation' and not some other skin disease. Yet another refined the concept of inflammation as 'an inflamed quasi bite' and not some other kind of inflammation. It is clear from his account that a cognitive examination of Subanun diagnostic criteria involved a good knowledge of the underlying levels of contrast against which the disease concepts were operating. In a similar manner Hallowell (1942), investigating the psychological aspects of measurement among the Salteaux (an American Indian group) noted that there did not exist common units of distance which applied to all classes of linear measurement. Distance-away or distance-apart with reference to places or objects in space belonged to quite a different category to the length of an object which could be manipulated, like a piece of string or a canoe.

COMPARATIVE THOUGHT PROCESSES   Such anthropological descriptions, although of extreme interest for the psychologist (but not all psychologists take sufficient note of them) probably do not go far enough as analysis to satisfy the cognitive psychologist. An early attempt to stratify cultural thought along some psychological dimension was formulated by Carmichael who worked with Greenlanders (Carmichael, 1940). He gave his subjects a problem in the form of a narrative. In the story three men were discussing what they should do to a fourth man whom they all hated, and especially what they would do to him if he should suddenly at the moment enter. Whereupon the detested man does (in the narrative) enter, exhausted and cold, and the question is: What would the subjects do if they were in the place of the three men? Carmichael combed the answers not so much for the logical scheme underlying the answers but for the effect of social influences. He found features which reflected quick, confident and stereotyped responses, generalizations which reflected a cultural conventional way of thinking, of the same kind which Bartlett found in his study of remembering (Bartlett, 1932) and which Nadel found in the comparison of retention and communication between two African tribes (Nadel, 1937). When one turns to the question of logical thinking a convenient framework is that of the Swiss psychologist Piaget, who in many publications (see Flavell, 1963, for best summary) has postulated a number of levels through which children progress in their thinking. He has provided the impetus for several cultural studies. The writer has studied concepts of conservation of quantities with bush African children, and found that although there may have been an age delay with these children as compared with European children, the same sequence, from reliance on perceptual attributes to a proper understanding of what conservation implies, was detected. Jacqueline Goodnow (1962) investigated judgments of space, weight and volume with Chinese children in Hong Kong, with varying degrees of formal schooling. She compared these Chinese children with European children of comparable age living in Hong Kong. Variables like schooling and socio-economic status showed little effect on such judgments. Indeed Chinese children with low socio-economic status and semi-schooling did better than those children that had more schooling, and up to the age of eleven the Europeans do no better than the Chinese. On the other hand Peluffo (1962), who studied the differences between children born and resident in Genoa with those immigrating to Genoa from the underdeveloped parts of Southern Italy did find differences in conceptual understanding of substance, weight and volume. Such studies go beyond the simple question of whether there is any difference between subjects of different national and linguistic stock; they also ask whether there is any difference within the same country and language, due to impoverished economic environment and exposure to formal schooling. The advantage of employing Piaget's methods is that they are not of the paper and pencil kind; familiar objects such as glasses, bits of clay and stones—objects which are familiar to the culture—are used, and cross-cultural equivalence is better assured than by using more formal tests of abstraction and intelligence.

Other frameworks than that used by Piaget are possible. An object-sorting task has been designed by Riley Gardner, consisting of seventy-three familiar objects which subjects are asked to cluster spontaneously into as many or as few groups as they prefer. An index of conceptual differentiation is made according to whether people form many groups, which represents a high degree of conceptual differentiation, or few groups, which represents a low degree. The use of this task in the United States with adults and with children has shown consistent differences in the manner in which objects are categorized. Application of this same test in Mexico (Mercado, Diaz Guerrero and Gardner, 1963) shows how unexpected light may be thrown on a culture through using a comparable technique across cultures. Whereas there were no differences between boys and girls in the American sample, there were found big sex differences in the Mexican population, boys performing at significantly higher levels of abstraction than girls. Such studies show that a major contribution of cross-cultural method lies not only in the gross comparison between cultures, but helps to illuminate the role of important variables such as sex, socio-economic status and the role of formal education.

LANGUAGE AND THINKING   Quite clearly any cognitive inquiry requires an examination of the linguistic features of the society being interrogated. Stimulated by the writings of Benjamin Lee Whorf (see Carroll, 1956) an important sub-field of psychology has emerged in the last few years aimed at understanding the influence of language—particularly languages not of the Indo-European stock— upon thinking. Much of this inquiry has been descriptive and inferential. For example, in the Hopi language there is no substantive noun for time and no tense system of past, present and future as in the English language. From considerations such as these Whorf questioned whether the Hopi thinking of time was similar to that of people who spoke of time events in the Indo-European languages. His thesis was that language acted as a mould to thought, forcing our thinking into the *a priori* linguistic categories; so that if a language exists which has, from our point of view, radically different ways of expressing time relationships, then thinking about it would be radically different also. Psychological experiments on this point are very difficult to carry out, as much of the thesis defies experimental design, but the Whorfian notion has stimulated some psychologists to probe into the question. Some idea of what has to be done is represented by a classic experiment by Brown and Lenneberg (1954), who worked with the English language throughout. The colour spectrum is divided into a small set of categories. There are, in fact, about seven and a half million 'just noticeable differences' in the colour solid, but in English we tend to use commonly only about eight colour names. In English some colours have a ready label, like red or green; others have to be eked out with two words, like 'royal purple' or 'shell-pink'. This difference in accessibility of labels has been called 'codability' by Brown and Lenneberg. The same colour in two different languages may be differentially codable. The contrast between the many terms used for snow in the Eskimo language with the almost single term of 'white' in the English language is a contrast in codability. To express shades of whiteness is easier if there exists in the language a range of terms to indicate them. The Brown and Lenneberg experiment consisted in initially finding out the codability factor for colours in the English language, and then correlating the colours for naming with their later recognition. In this the results proved positive; that is to say there did seem to be a relationship between the accessibility of linguistic terms and the psychological process of recognition. Particularly, the experiment showed the influence of language on the storage factor; simply, this means that it is easier to remember something if there is a term for it. This experiment was repeated in a cross-cultural framework with Zuni and English speakers. In Zuni orange and yellow

are given a single term. In their recognition test, Zuni speakers frequently confused the orange and yellow colours. English speakers never made this error,
while bilingual speakers of Zuni and English were intermediate.

An experiment with Navaho children further indicates the type of experiment in this field (Carroll and Casagrande, 1958). In the Navaho language verbs
of handling involve different forms according to the kind of object being handled.
A long flexible object, like a piece of string, has one verb form; a long rigid object,
as a stick, has another verb form; and an object like a piece of paper or cloth which
is flat and flexible has yet another verb form. Developmental psychologists have
found with Euro-American children that objects are first distinguished on the
dimensions of size or colour, and shape later. Contrasting, therefore, Navaho-
speaking children with English- or American-speaking children, there should be
a difference in the order of emergence of various concepts. Navaho children, if
the peculiar emphasis on form in their language made any difference, should be
able to distinguish form characteristics of objects earlier than American children.
The experiments were arranged so that a child was shown a pair of objects in
which the members differed significantly in two characteristics, and then was
shown a third object which resembled the others in one characteristic only, and
the child was asked which member of the original pair went best with the third
object. For example, a yellow stick and a same-sized piece of blue rope was shown
to the child; the child was then shown a yellow rope and asked to say which of
the former two objects the yellow rope went best with. He could either choose
on the basis of colour, that is he would choose the yellow stick, or he could choose
on the basis of form, in which case he would choose the blue rope. Three groups
were actually used in this experiment: Navahoes whose own language was dominant, Navahoes whose language was dominantly English, and white American
children, speaking, of course, no Navaho at all. If the first two groups are
compared alone, the results do seem to indicate that the linguistic factor is
operative; the saliency for shape or form, although higher in both groups for
shape over colour than the English group, is lower in the English-speaking
Navahoes than the Navaho-speaking Navahoes. On the other hand, when the
third group, the white American children from Boston, are considered, the overall impression is slightly marred by the fact that this group behaved like the
Navaho-speaking Navahoes, a fact which has to be explained. The authors considered that early and continued practice with toys of the formboard kind tended
to shift the importance of shape over colour in these fairly well-to-do children.
Be that as it may, the Carroll and Casagrande experiment is of the kind needed
to provide psychological and not just inferential evidence on this important issue.

Socialization

The majority of older cross-cultural studies are those which have considered
man in his cultural setting from the point of view of institutions. In this task the
sister disciplines of social and cultural anthropology and of sociology have made
heavy inroads into cross-cultural psychology. Many of the concepts used have

stemmed from anthropologists; many of the methods employed are those which have been traditional in the social sciences. With the study of socialization we make a transition from the general processes of psychology, such as perception and thinking, towards accepting the individual as a social unit.

UNIVERSALITY VERSUS RELATIVITY A simple inquiry of early work on socialization was to note whether 'growing-up' was more or less the same all over the world or drastically different. The notion had been held in psychological thought that the tribulations of adolescence were a feature of the muscular and glandular changes which occur during this period. The underlying assumption was that it was 'human nature' that adolescence should be a period of difficulty. It was part of the intentions of a cultural anthropologist like Margaret Mead to show by heavy and detailed documentation (Mead, 1928, 1930) that this model simply did not hold in the South Seas. In Polynesian society adolescence just did not have the sort of difficulties which European and American adolescents appeared to undergo. The emphasis, by psychologically minded anthropologists, on the cultural relativity of similar processes tended to shift attention away from the universal biological model towards the patterning of social institutions and their effect on the psychology of the individual.

INSTITUTIONALIZED GOALS Strictly speaking the term 'socialization' does not merely mean 'growing-up'; the term is properly used for the training of an individual towards certain sets of values which are dominant in any society. The units of socialization may be either descriptive or explanatory. This is to say the particular social unit taken for study may either be manifest in the society, like the emphasis placed on 'balance' in Balinese society (Belo, 1935), or the unit chosen may be explanatory in the sense that it is used to explain manifest behaviour in the individuals of the society. A variety of explanatory units exist, as they stem from different parent theories. Psycho-analytic theories tend to encourage usage of terms like orality and anality, which focus attention on the stages of nurturance by the mother and of preoccupations with toilet training, both of which are thought to be connected with later events in the individual's life. Achievement is a category which has issued from a different theoretical orientation and draws attention to the motive themes of a society and the effect of these on people: how achievement values are introduced to the child; the special institutions which encourage or discourage achievement, and so forth. With all such categories, in whatever way they are studied, there is the thesis that a longitudinal linkage exists whereby the values in a society are created and supported by events in childhood. Work on socialization has either been preoccupied with institutionalized values or actual individuals. The differing emphasis can best be described by indicating the methods used.

METHODS Anthropological observation has been the hallmark of early work on socialization. There has been a plethora of observational reports on varying aspects of childhood and puberty: dependence upon the mother, weaning, toilet training practices, early sexual behaviour with its restrictions and encouragements, aggressive behaviour, the tolerance of society for the child's independence, achievement themes, among others (see Child, 1954, for summary). Sometimes the observations are more narrowly psychological, concentrating on one aspect, as with the study of motor development in some African children (Géber, 1958). Many firsthand observational reports now exist from which the theoretically inclined psychologist finds sufficient data to build into his theories of child rearing. One school of thought (see Whiting, 1961, for summary) has utilized the ethnographic information collected in the Human Relations Area Files (which contain neatly categorized information pertaining both to social institutions and social processes such as child training) for engendering correlations between early events in childhood and adult practices. For example, it has been shown that exclusive mother and child sleeping arrangements are strongly associated with male initiation rites at puberty. This correlation has prompted different psychological interpretations. It is either taken to mean that sleeping arrangements increase the supposed Oedipal rivalry between the son and his father to an extent where open revolt at the time of puberty becomes dangerous to the maintenance of society, so that initiation rites have to be set up publicly to acclaim the youngster as an adult in his own right. Or it has been interpreted with respect to over-dependency on the mother; it is necessary to break this dependency sharply by some institutional practice at puberty. Or again while there may not be actual dependence on the mother there is an identification which must be broken. Further correlational studies appear to indicate the second or third interpretation rather than the first as being correct, but the evidence is still correlational. In this case the antecedent condition is ecological—sleeping arrangements; other correlational studies of the Whiting kind have selected personal behaviour as the antecedent and beliefs as the consequent condition. Spiro and D'Andrade (1958) established a connexion between parental treatment of children with attitudes towards supernaturals in the same society. Harsh parental treatment is associated with the belief that the spirit or supernatural world is also harsh and aggressive. On the other hand, gentle treatment of children is associated with the notion that gods can be propitiated. The specific argument is presented that people, who in their infancy and early childhood are treated kindly and with some indulgence by their parents or elders, grow up with the belief that supernatural forces or gods are not severe and aggressive beings like the Old Testament conception of Yahweh, but are beings that can be propitiated and perhaps controlled by ritual.

Although interesting and provocative, correlational studies probably do not meet the exact canons of experimentally minded psychologists who desire a more stringent observational design before drawing conclusions. Earlier the fact of sudden weaning among the Zulus was mentioned. This was taken as a central point for comparative study by Albino and Thompson (1956). They compared Zulu children who had been weaned in the traditional fashion with urban Zulu children who had been weaned earlier and not abruptly. The authors kept track of the immediate changes following the weaning experience and noted that the traditional Zulu child went through various changes. At first he became negativistic and aggressive, and often ignored the mother. Then he tried to get the attention of his mother, which in turn was followed by increasing independence with no signs of anger or other forms of disturbance. In short there were transitory effects of the kind which might have been predicted from psychoanalytic theories of weaning, but they proved not to be lasting. What could be counted as more permanent effects in the experimental group of Zulu children were due to the readjustments of the organism to the experience of weaning. These readjustments varied from child to child; and showed themselves in different attitudes towards the mother. In some cases the child renounced the mother, in others there was renouncement plus hostility, in others again there was an attempt to regain affection. The authors considered that although abrupt weaning created a tempo-rary disturbance in the child's emotional and social life, over a longer period it aided the development of qualities of self-reliance and sociability. Succinctly, it was thought to be an adaptive transition rather than a cause of permanent damage.

Personality

With the latter example we move in the direction of the thesis that the adult personality is in some way moulded by the experiences which are undergone in childhood. As these experiences vary from culture to culture the relativistic notion has arisen that each society contributes towards its own special personality type. This has been expressed under various headings in the literature.

CULTURAL PERSONALITY TYPES   In a useful article Singer (1961) has mar-shalled the various ideas of personality and culture. In all of them there is contained the belief that each culture has a typical personality which is distinctive of that culture and which, therefore, can be contrasted with the typical personal-ity of another culture. The key term 'typical', though, has different interpreta-tions. Ruth Benedict emphasized a configurational personality which reflects the dominant *ethos* in the culture. Concentrating on the American Indian groups, literary and psychiatric typologies were constructed to call attention to the differ-ing value patterns. Nietzsche's classical distinction of Apollonian and Dionysian types was attributed to the Zuni and Plains Indians respectively. While in later publications the Kwakiutl Indians were characterized as 'megalomaniac para-noid'. Benedict's personality typologies were impressionistic and built up from collective behaviour, such as rituals, rather than first-hand from actual individu-als. The idea of a Basic Personality Structure, which we owe to Abram Kardiner, is a postulated personality type which is thought to mediate between what Kar-diner called primary institutions such as family organization, subsistence tech-niques and child-rearing practices, and secondary institutions, by which Kardiner included art forms, folk-lore, mythology and religion. Under this scheme of cultural personality it is considered that once a set of nuclear trends could be identified, then the link between primary and secondary institutions could be made, and a causal sequence is implied in that the values inherent in the art and folk-lore of a society are influenced by early childhood techniques. This notion aims directly at the connexion between socialization and personality, and owes much to psychoanalytic theory. While both the models of Configurational Per-sonality and a Basic Personality Structure reflect preoccupation with institutions, the third theory of a Modal Personality, originated by Cora Dubois, attempts to put over the view that an examination of actual individuals who share a common culture should reveal a set of common characteristics. As is implied by the usage of the statistical term 'mode', the implication is that although there may be different kinds of individuals in any one culture there is a most frequent type which can be contrasted with the most frequent type of modal personality of another culture.

NATIONAL CHARACTER TYPOLOGIES   This leads on to a historically older notion, namely, that different nations produce different characters, symbolized often by stock cartoons such as John Bull. The idea of a national character can degenerate into the stereotypes which one nation has of another, but some prominence has been given to it through the writings of anthropologists, sociologists and psychiatrists. Much has been written about the American, English, German, Russian, Japanese and Hindu characters, among other national groups. Inkeles and Levinson (1954) have made the logical point that what we call national character should really be equated with the idea of modal personality, in which case all that we have learned of the latter can be applied to the former. In practice, however, the idea of a national character has been mostly connected with child-rearing practices, so that, to give an extreme example, swaddling-techniques in childhood for the inhabitants of the area called Great Russia are postulated as being associated with impassivity and the control of rage in the adults. The insistence on toilet-training habits among Japanese people in relation to the Japanese character belongs to the same class. A difficulty with the concept of national character is that it is too embracing: Inkeles (1961) has shown that it can be defined as institutional pattern, as cultural theme, as action and as racial psychology. When differently defined the kind of picture that is drawn depicting the national characteristic involved and the methods whereby this is found out can also be different. When national character is identified with an institutional pattern the picture chosen as exemplar is that of the dominant institution, particularly, as Inkeles goes on to state, that concerned with politics or economics. When identified with a cultural theme attention is drawn to folk-ways; themes in books and films would be examples of this identification.

METHODS   As with many other concepts in this field the validity of different personality and national character terms is based finally on the manner in which we can utilize them. Disregarding the analysis of child-rearing systems as constituting a special class of techniques, there are basically two methods generally employed (Inkeles and Levinson, 1954). The first is personality assessment of individuals, which leans heavily on the use of projective techniques. Rorschach and Thematic Apperception tests have been taken from Hindu, Javanese, Thai, Zulu and American Indians, and numerous other societies; the tests either being applied without any change to their original form or modified especially to fit in with the particular group studied. A genuine difficulty with this kind of personality test is that of confusing proper inference about personality characteristics with the factors of motivation and communication. Kaplan (1961) noted, with the Thematic Apperception Test responses from the records of Thai agricultural workers, that the subjects were not telling stories at all, but simply describing the picture and saying what appeared to be happening in them. Kaplan felt that one could not conclude from this that Thai people were literal-minded and that they lacked fantasy, only that the particular test did not elicit any fantasy material. This is not to dismiss all cross-cultural personality studies using projective techniques as being useless; only to mark that certain cultural factors completely outside personality enter into the inference that one might be led to draw from their application. Kaplan cautioned that one might be led into serious error if there was exclusive reliance placed on them. Many cross-cultural studies in the personality sphere also utilize interviews, questionnaires and other methods suitable for individual application.

The second method is to utilize collective adult phenomena—collective documents like folk-tales, films, popular journals; or collective behaviour, as in dramatic themes, or in rituals. In both of these groups dominant value patterns are traced which are supposedly spread among the individuals of the society. The collective behaviour and the themes which recur in documents are considered to be reflections of the tendencies of individuals making up the behaviour or producing the themes. The best-known case is that of Bateson and Mead (1942) in their study of the Balinese theme which is expressed in ceremonial dances. The female dancer transforms from a coquettish woman, leading on the responsive male, into a witch who violently frustrates the male. This theme or plot is found in other spheres of Balinese collective life and is found also in the relationship between mother and child. This is thought to reflect certain dominant personality tendencies in the Balinese individual.

Conclusions

Cross-cultural studies have both the advantage and disadvantage of belonging to a no-man's-land in which other disciplines, particularly cultural anthropology, have more salience than psychology. Different disciplines have their own language and their own theoretical framework. In the fields of perception and cognition the theoretical influence is basically psychological, with linguistics having a heavy bias. In the fields of socialization and personality the demarcation lines of disciplines are more difficult to lay down with complete clarity. Further cross-cultural work, which I have not had space to mention in this chapter, has been devoted to the study of dreams, emotions, expressive behaviour and, particularly, mental illness. Inasmuch as the world's the limit, there seems no stringency on what work can be done. A difficulty which faces the psychologist concerns the basis of comparison between cultures in the study of some psychological process. In order to assess, say, concept formation in two widely separate regions of the world, we have to be sure that the methods of interrogation can be equated for both regions. This is more difficult than it may superficially seem, for many psychological techniques are very sensitive to environmental influences, and to the way in which they are applied. The ability to create *transcultural* variables, so that they are measurable on an equivalent basis anywhere in the world, is a challenge which always faces cross-cultural research.

See original source for references.

Suggested Readings

Bryson, L., L. Finkelstein, and R. M. MacIver (eds.), *Approaches to Group Understanding* (New York: Conference on Science, Philosophy and Religion in Their Relation to the Democratic Way of Life, 1947; distributed by Harper & Row). Although the title specifies *group* understanding, this book could very well be titled cultural understanding. It contains 67 diverse essays directed to the understanding of cultural differences and the development of communication between societies.

Condon, J. C., and F. Yousef, *An Introduction to Intercultural Communication* (Indianapolis: Bobbs-Merrill, 1975). This book serves as an excellent introduction to the field of intercultural communication. The authors write in a casual manner that makes the book very readable. Besides having a pleasant style, the book treats the essential ingredients of intercultural communication such as values, language, nonverbal behaviors, and social organization.

Fischer, H-D., and J. Merrill, *International Communication* (New York: Hastings House, 1970). This book surveys the broad and varied aspects of international communication. Containing 49 diverse essays, the book covers the field of international communication with an emphasis on mass media.

Harms, L. S., *Intercultural Communication* (New York: Harper & Row, 1973). This introductory text focuses on the relationship between communication and culture, inter-community communication, international and world communication, and the future of intercultural communication.

Keesing, R. M., and F. M. Keesing, *New Perspectives in Cultural Anthropology* (New York: Holt, Rinehart and Winston, 1971). The authors introduce the concepts of culture with emphasis on the social aspects. Relationships between socio-cultural elements and communication are well defined.

Kluckhohn, C., *Culture and Behavior* (New York: Free Press, 1965). Kluckhohn was one of the most respected anthropologists in the world. This volume consists of a collection of his most famous essays. The early part of the book offers an excellent analysis of culture while the second half examines various aspects of Navaho culture.

Oliver, R. T., *Culture and Communication* (Springfield, Ill.: Charles C Thomas, 1962). An excellent approach to an understanding of rhetorical systems in different cultures is found in this volume. Oliver analyzes how differences in Oriental and Western cultures call for different "logics" and strategies of persuasion.

Prosser, M. H. (ed.), *Intercommunication among Nations and Peoples* (New York: Harper & Row, 1973). This collection seeks to define international and intercultural communication as a field of study. Prosser's selections cover a wide range of intercultural topics including attitude formation, leadership, conflict resolution, rights and censorship, and many others.

Rich, A., *Interracial Communication* (New York: Harper & Row, 1974). This book is well written and well researched. It describes various interracial interaction situations and explores possible reasons for the problems that occur when people from different races attempt to communicate.

Smith, A. G. (ed.), *Communication and Culture* (New York: Holt, Rinehart and Winston, 1966). Here is a comprehensive book in which the efforts of many disciplines are focused on communication. Especially useful is the paradigm used for arranging the readings because it helps clarify the relationships between various components of the communication process.

Smith, A. L., *Transracial Communication* (Englewood Cliffs, N.J.: Prentice-Hall, 1973). One major concern of this book is its attention to symbolism—how symbols that exist for one ethnic group alone influence multicultural communication. The book also offers a model of transracial communication that attempts to show effective communication between groups.

Additional Readings

"Americans Abroad," *The Annals of the American Academy of Political and Social Science*, 368 (November 1966).

Barnett, V. M., Jr., *The Representation of the United States Abroad* (New York: Frederick A. Praeger, 1965).

Bateson, G., *Steps to an Ecology of Mind* (Ballentine Books, 1972).

Brislin, R. W. (ed.), *Topics in Culture Learning*, vols. 1 and 2 (Honolulu: East-West Center, 1973, 1974).

Carroll, J. B., *Language and Thought* (Englewood Cliffs, N.J.: Prentice-Hall, 1964).

Cherry, C., *World Communication: A Threat or Promise? A Social-Technical Approach* (New York: Wiley-Interscience, 1971).

Doob, Leonard W., *Communication in Africa* (New Haven: Yale University Press, 1961).

Duncan, H. D., *Communication and Social Order* (Totowa, N.J.: Bedminster Press, 1962).

Gardner, G. H., "Cross Cultural Communication," *Journal of Social Psychology*, 58 (1962), 241–256.

Goodman, M. E., *The Individual and Culture* (Homewood, Ill.: Dorsey Press, 1967).

Hayes, A. S., "A Tentative Schematization for Research in the Teaching of Cross-Cultural Communication," *American Journal of Linguistics*, 28 (1962), 155–167.

Hymes, D., "The Anthropology of Communication" in *Human Communication Theory*, ed. F. E. X. Dance (New York: Holt, Rinehart and Winston, 1967).

Lerner, D. M., and W. Schramm (eds.), *Communication and Change in the Developing Countries* (Honolulu: East-West Center Press, 1967).

Mead, M., "A Case History in Cross-National Communications" in *The Communication of Ideas*, ed. L. Bryson (New York: Institute for Religious and Social Studies, 1948; distributed by Harper & Row).

Pye, L. (ed.), *Communication and Political Development* (Princeton: Princeton University Press, 1963).

Rogers, E., *Modernization among Peasants: The Impact of Communication* (New York: Holt, Rinehart and Winston, 1969).

Textor, R. B. (ed.), *Cultural Frontiers of the Peace Corps* (Cambridge, Mass.: MIT Press, 1966).

Sinauer, E. M., *The Role of Communication in International Training and Education* (New York: Frederick A. Praeger, 1967).

Concepts and Questions

1. In what ways are intercultural communication and communication alike? In what ways, if any, are they different?

2. With what cultures, other than your own, might you have occasion to interact? How did you arrive at your decision that these social groups constitute cultural groups?

3. What is the relationship existing between social perception and intercultural communication?

4. How are the terms "intercultural," "contracultural," "interracial," and "interethnic" alike? How are they different?

5. Are there any variables omitted from the models presented by Rich and Ogawa that should have been included?

6. How are economic and class factors related to intercultural communication?

7. Why is intercultural communication considered more difficult than other forms of communication?

8. What are some of the specific changes, both domestic and foreign, that have brought about an awareness of intercultural communication? How many of these changes have affected you personally?

9. What are the commonalities between definitions of communication and definitions of intercultural communication? Are there any differences?

10. What are the major factors we learn from our culture? How do they affect intercultural communication?

11. D. Price-Williams asks the following question: "How do varying linguistic stores affect perception and thinking?" What is your answer to that question?

12. What conclusions with regard to intercultural communication can be drawn from studies of socialization?

13. How does the following quotation relate to the study of intercultural communication? ". . . we move in the direction of the thesis that the adult personality is in some way moulded by the experiences which are undergone in childhood. As these experiences vary from culture to culture the relativistic notion has arisen that each society contributes toward its own special personality type."

14. What elements of the communication process are most likely to be influenced by culture?

Part Two   Socio-Cultural Factors: What We Bring to Intercultural Communication

One of the most important axioms found in human communication is that what the participants bring to a communication experience will affect their behavior during and after the encounter. Psychologists A. H. Hastorf and H. Cantril underscored this issue when they noted that all of us act according to the personal uniqueness we bring to the occasion. You need only reflect on those countless situations when you and some friends left a movie theater or lecture hall and found that there were major differences in your reactions to what you had all just shared. What you deemed dull your companions found exciting; what you considered pointless they found "meaningful." The messages being received were the same for all parties; yet because each of you has a unique personality you experience a variety of feelings, sensations, and responses. In short, you all brought different backgrounds to the event and therefore attributed different meanings to the messages.

It is our contention that to understand any communication encounter we must appreciate the idea that there is much more to communication than an analysis of messages. These messages, and the responses we make to them, are a product of our past experiences. The concept of past experience takes on added significance when we introduce the dimension of culture. For now the individual is influenced not only by personal experiences but by culture as well. As we suggested in Part One, culture refers to those cumulative deposits of knowledge, values, and behaviors that are acquired by a large group of people. In this sense our culture, in both conscious and subconscious ways, has taught us what we think is attractive and what we think is ugly. Our culture has also taught us such things as how close to stand to strangers and even the various ways we can demonstrate our anger. For instance, when we are interacting with others and become disturbed by their actions, we can cry, become physically violent, shout, or remain silent. Each of these behaviors, depending on our culture, is a manifestation of what we have learned—it is a cultural experience. These are experiences, ways of perceiving and acting, that each culture passes on from generation to generation. Because these behaviors are so much a part of our thinking, we might forget they shift from culture to culture. That is why the person from Japan might remain silent if disturbed by someone's actions. On the other hand, an Israeli or an Italian would most likely verbalize such displeasure.

Whatever the culture, we can better understand our behavior and the reactions of others if we realize that what we are hearing and seeing is a reflection of that culture. As you might predict, this understanding is greatly facilitated when our cultural experiences are similar to those of the people we are interacting with. Conversely, when we bring different and diverse backgrounds to communication, we often find it difficult to share internal states and feelings. This section attempts to focus on those difficulties by examining cultural *experiences* and *perceptions*.

2

Cultural Determinants of Experiences and Backgrounds

In this chapter we present seven essays that endeavor to highlight the many ways our cultural experiences influence communication. These selections are not intended to be a complete sampling of all experiences found in each culture. Such an undertaking would indeed be an impossible task. Instead, our purpose is to demonstrate a few of the characteristics found in some cultures that are apt to surface during communication. In Chapter 3, our treatment will discuss how these experiences relate to perception.

The family may well be the most dominant force shaping our cultural experiences. That is, what we bring to an encounter may well have its roots in the social organization of the family. Therefore, we begin our analysis of cultural experiences with a selection entitled "Cultural Variations in the Family" by Stuart A. Queen and Robert W. Habenstein. As we indicated, the family gives us our beliefs, values, goals, many of our attitudes, and countless modes of behavior. As you can imagine, ways of thinking and acting are different as we move from culture to culture. These variations are the main concern of Queen and Habenstein. To better understand these differences they survey various behaviors that can be traced to one's family background. For example, they investigate the nuclear and extended family, marital selection, descent and inheritance, child rearing, subordination of women to men, divorce, and sex mores. All of these factors help explain why people of dissimilar cultures are apt to communicate in ways that appear alien to us.

In the second essay, Dolores and Robert Cathcart explore how a culture's view of a specific concept can influence behavior. In this case, the concept is the Japanese philosophy and attitude toward groups. If our experiences with groups change from culture to culture, then it follows that each culture might well bring a different way of acting to a group situation. The Cathcarts investigate this very issue when they compare the Japanese concept of groups with that found in the United States. This article clearly illustrates the importance of what each of us brings to communication.

Thus far the bulk of our discussion has been concerned with foreign cultures, that is, cultures that exist beyond our immediate boundaries. There are, however, various subcultures in our society that often bring alien and diverse experiences to a communication encounter. Because these subcultures are much more visible than are foreign cultures, we often take their presence for granted. Yet a lack of understanding of these subcultural experiences can result in serious communication problems. Therefore, the next series of essays in Chapter 2 examines some of the cultural experiences found in five subcultures living within the United States. Admittedly there are more than five subcultures that could have been included in our analysis—subcultures that differ in such things as language, values, religion, diet, and style of life. However, we based our final selection on three considerations. First, the simple fact of space and efficiency precluded presenting a long list of subcultures. Second, we decided to include those subcultures that are often in conflict with the larger society. And third, we wanted to expose you to some of the subcultures that you are apt to be interacting with. Thus, we selected some of the dominant subcultures in the United States. It should be noted that in this section we excluded the "black experience." The reason for this determination is that the black culture is treated in numerous articles later in the book.

Recently we have been made aware of a subculture that had previously been taken for granted. Because women are so much a part of our perceptual field, and hence part of our daily life, we have never conceived that the experience of being female was a viable area of investigation. However, the resurgence of feminism in the last few years has forced all of us to reexamine what it means to be a member of that particular subculture. Betty Roszak pursues this issue in her essay "Masculine/Feminine." She reviews the experience of being female from a number of perspectives. After briefly sketching the historical causes behind the many roles women play in our society, she discusses the effects of these roles on both women and society. She also looks at some of the reasons why women have been forced into these behavioral patterns.

Simon and Gagnon, in their essay on homosexuality, offer us innumerable insights into the cultural experience of the homosexual. They support the position that homosexuals, because of their unique situation, face a series of problems that are quite different from other ethnic and occupational subcultures. So that we may better comprehend these problems, and hence the communication behavior of homosexuals, Simon and Gagnon suggest we examine "the complexity of the life cycle of the homosexual, the roles that mark various stages of this cycle, and the kinds of forces, both sexual and nonsexual, that impinge on the individual actor." In some detail they also consider problems of earning a living, maintaining a residence, and learning to live with one's family. All of these issues, which represent experiences that homosexuals bring to communication, will shape their behavior during interaction.

Most of us have been guilty of assuming that because the poor lived in America they shared a similar culture with the general population. Yet during the last decade sociologists have alerted us to the fact that the poor might well be a subculture living both within and apart from the rest of society. This idea serves as the central theme of Jack Daniel's essay, "The Poor: Aliens in an Affluent Society: Cross-Cultural Communication." In the article, he looks at values and experiences that are unique to the poor. He notes that the attitude of the poor toward education, authority, and the like is often quite different from the beliefs of the average American. In addition, he suggests that many of these attitudes are a result of the messages the poor are exposed to—messages that are often at variance with the rest of society. These and other examples demonstrate the large chasm between the poor and the main culture in the United States. Many of these differences are so great that effective communication is often impossible. Daniel maintains that we must understand these "divergent fields of experience" if we are to overcome many of the barriers that often stifle intercultural communication.

There have been a great many myths surrounding the culture of the American Indian. One of the reasons for these myths is that the American Indian, unlike the last three cultures we discussed, actually holds dual membership in two conflicting cultures—their own and that of the larger society. So that we can appreciate the problems inherent in dual membership Robert L. Faherty offers an essay entitled "The American Indian: An Overview." In his article Faherty develops two major ideas. First, he looks at some stereotypes of the Indian. These false assumptions are (a) Indians are savage, (b) they are a vanishing race, (c) they are all alike, and (d) they cannot change. Second, he examines some major differences that exist between the Indian culture and the larger culture it is asked to model and emulate. Although many variations could have been cited, Faherty compares Indian and white culture with respect to their conception of time, decision making, and "being." He concludes by saying that a "deeper and more accurate understanding of the Indian people is needed."

A somewhat different view of a cultural experience is offered by Arturo Madrid-Barela in his essay "Towards an Understanding of the Chicano Experience." Unlike the other selections in Chapter 2, this article does not examine the family, role behaviors, or other traditional areas of social organization. Instead, its thesis is that to understand the Chicano of the 1970s we must understand the historical roots of the movement and philosophy. It is Madrid-Barela's contention that what we bring to an encounter often has its antecedents far removed from the immediate situation. To document this view the author traces the beginnings of the Chicano experience from the early nineteenth-century to the present. Two important threads weave their way throughout his analysis. First, he shows how the proximity of Mexico to the United States has helped shape the Chicano experience. Second, he links the white economic system in the United States to the role played by Chicanos during the last hundred years.

Cultural Variations in the Family
Stuart A. Queen and Robert W. Habenstein

The family (described for the moment as a group of kinsmen living intimately together, its members mating, bearing and rearing offspring, growing up, and protecting one another) is rooted in the past, built on our prehuman, biological heritage as well as on our human experience. It is a way of life shared not only by mankind, but by many other species as well. It is a complex of impulses and habits imbedded in our very nature and an integral part of every culture. The living together of man and woman, of parents and children, in an intimate relationship is so firmly established that we need give little thought to the likelihood of its disappearance. Yet, as we have seen, this way of life has no single, uniform pattern. Despite some elements in common, it displays an enormous variety in structure, life cycle, controls, and functions.

One of the important variations has to do with the relation of the nuclear family (mates and their offspring) to the extended family (including grandparents, uncles, aunts, cousins, etc.). In our culture the nuclear family receives most attention. It usually has a separate residence; it is commonly a self-supporting unit. In fiction, in drama, and in everyday living it is accorded the place of honor. More distant relatives are considered, too, but they are usually outside the inner circle of our closest ties, our most intimate experiences, and our basic obligations. But in some other cultures it is very different. Among the Hopi, ancient Chinese, Hebrews, and Romans the wider, more inclusive kinship groups are dominant. Mating is arranged by the head of the kin, who continue to exercise some control over young people even after their marriage. Economic responsibilities are shared throughout the larger group. Often several married couples—elders, children and their spouses, and grandchildren—literally live together in the same household.

Bound up with these differences in the relative importance of the nuclear family and the extended family are the modes of marital selection. In contemporary North America it is not uncommon for a young man and a young woman to meet, woo, and marry almost without the knowledge of their respective kin. To be sure, their freedom is not absolute; in most states they must secure a license and go through a simple ceremony; if they are first-cousins, or, in some states, members of different races, they are forbidden to marry. But as compared with other cultures ours offers a wide range of choice and a minimum of control. Indeed, it appears that marriage in accordance with arrangements made by family heads is very common outside our system. Among the ancient Greeks and until recently among the Chinese many a bride and groom did not even see each other before their wedding. Romantic love as a basis for marriage is relatively new and

From *The Family in Various Cultures,* by Stuart A. Queen and Robert W. Habenstein. Reprinted by permission of the publisher, J. B. Lippincott Company. Copyright © 1967. Professor Queen formerly taught in the Department of Sociology, University of Arizona, Tucson, and is now retired. Professor Habenstein is a member of the Department of Sociology, University of Missouri, Columbia.

is dominant only in the Western world, chiefly in the United States and Canada. As we go from culture to culture, several of which are dealt with in this book, we find a wide variety of rules concerning who may marry whom. Among the Todas of South India cross-cousin marriages (e.g., daughter of a man to his sister's son) are preferred, while among the Manus of New Guinea they are forbidden.

Descent and inheritance are frequently patrilineal (in the male line from father to son), but among the Hopi, Crow, and Haida of North America they are matrilineal. In the Trobriands of the South Pacific a man inherits from his mother's brother. In many cultures personal effects are handed down, while land belongs to the kinship group. With us almost anything may be left to almost anyone by making a will. The line of descent and inheritance may or may not correspond to the place of residence. Thus the Chinese and Japanese families have been both patrilineal and patrilocal (living with the man's parents), but the Hopi are matrilocal (living with the wife's parents).

In most cultures, it appears that children are desired, but in others, such as the Marquesan, quite the opposite is indicated. Also among the Baganda the first child, after it is weaned, is sent to live with its father's brother. On the other hand, the birth of twins, considered a catastrophe in Toda society, is an occasion for great rejoicing among the Baganda. In the majority of cultures both "primitive" and "historical," their education is usually informal and acquired partly in the family and partly in the larger group. Adult authority may be concentrated, as in the Roman *pater familias,* or it may be diffused among all kinsmen older than the child, as in Samoa. Among many preliterate peoples lactation continues for several years, while with us babies are weaned within a few weeks or months. Discipline is mild in most preliterate groups, but among some of our European ancestors it has been harsh and severe. Infanticide is reported in many cultures, including the highly civilized Greeks and Romans.

In most of the cultures about which we have information, women are subordinate to men. Some of the most extreme cases are those of the Todas and the ancient Greeks. On the other hand, the status of women is relatively high among the matrilineal Haida and the patrilineal Kwoma. Among the Hopi, women might almost be described as dominant. Despite these varied patterns of domination and subordination and even plural marriage the relations of husbands and wives do not appear to involve much hostility; mutual affection is shown under conditions that would seem intolerable to us. But in some tribes, such as the Kwoma, there is a great deal of friction, and among the Manus marriage seems to be regarded as a necessary evil. Whether the status of the sexes is determined by their economic importance is a moot point. Toda men do practically all the work of any consequence, while the Mundugumor of New Guinea leave most of the work to their women; in both cultures women are definitely subordinate. Among the matrilineal Hopi, men do most of the gardening and herding, while "women's place is in the home." Yet the relative status of the sexes is not what would be expected in conventional "white" society in the United States. Likewise there is some question as to the possible relation between status of the sexes and breadth of the culture base (number and variety of traits which make up a culture). Curiously, there have been approaches to equality of the sexes in cultures as diverse as those of contemporary Scandinavia and the Crow Indians.

Some provision for divorce is made in almost every known culture. In this men usually initiate the proceedings, but in Dahomey and the United States the great majority of divorces are secured by women. Among the Hopi both men and women may seek divorce at will. Among the ancient Hebrews the husband could dispose of his wife by giving her a "bill of divorcement." The Roman husband had to call a family council before putting away his wife. Among the early Christians divorce was a private family affair. With us it is controlled by the state. The Catholic Church has forbidden complete divorce, while for a time Russia made it relatively free and easy.

In no culture do we find absolute promiscuity, but there are wide differences in the sex mores. Young people in Samoa and the Trobriand Islands enjoy great freedom and enter numerous liaisons, some of which lead to marriage. In the Israeli *kibbutz* there is also great freedom, but there are comparatively few liaisons. Against all this the Christian code is adamant. Among the Arunta and some of the Eskimos hospitality includes wifelending; among the early Romans extramarital relations of all kinds apparently were rare. Among the Crow Indians, as in Christian Europe and America, there has really been a double standard. Girls and women were expected to remain "pure" while boys and men "sowed their wild oats." Prostitution seems to be rare among the preliterates, but common in urban civilizations. Birth control has been practiced in many lands, but is still a matter of dispute in our country. The general attitudes toward sex range from the Samoan, where sex is a matter of art and recreation, to the early Christian, where all sex was vile and even marriage was looked down upon. Thus we find an amazing variety of practices, rules, and sentiments in the domestic institutions of different peoples, indicating that human nature is capable of adapting itself to and through a wide range of customs and controls.

But through all the varied forms of family life four facts stand out rather clearly. First, there is everywhere a relatively strong tie between mother and child, at least during the child's early years.

Second, some approximation to monogamy has been the dominant, if not the ideal, form of marriage; partly because of the near equality in numbers of the sexes, partly because of the smaller expense and fewer obligations involved.

Third, nowhere do we find evidence of unregulated promiscuity. From the standpoint of our mores the sex relations of some peoples seem to be indiscriminate and uncontrolled, but on closer study they are always found to be regulated. The rules may be very different from those in our culture, but there are always some rules, and they are often more effectively enforced than ours.

Fourth, in nearly all cultures about which we have information the institution we call the family is identified with four functions: procreation, orientation, division of labor between the sexes, and status-giving. To be sure, many children are born out of wedlock, and there are childless couples in many lands. But the great majority of families include the offspring of the adult members, and most children enter the world as members of families. It is also true that children learn a great deal about the world from persons outside their families, but for most children everywhere the initial orientation to life and its setting is acquired within the family. Likewise, status—particularly that involved in sex, age, familial relations, class, caste and "race"—is acquired from the family into which one is born.

Perhaps it is time we stopped to define some of the terms we have been using in our discussion. The term family itself has been employed in several different ways. In the simplest biological sense it consists of those individuals who are related by mating and descent, regardless of whether there be any other connection or not. But the biological conception of the family also takes account of a parent or parents caring for offspring. On the human level the interaction between man and woman, parents and children, is not only physical; it involves the development of feelings and ideas, attitudes and sentiments, mutual awareness, and a sense of belonging together. Hence in the sociological sense we think of the family as an intimate social group of persons, most of whom are usually related by ties of blood, and who are regarded by their associates as a distinctive social unit. The limited biological family and the sociological family usually coincide in our culture, but even with us such a procedure as adoption may remove an individual from one family group and attach him to another. He is still the offspring of his biological parents, but he becomes legally and socially the child of his foster parents. Adoption, incidentally, is found in a great many different cultures. Divorce is another procedure through which a biological family may cease to be one sociologically. Even without such legal action as we have mentioned persons who are not related by blood may live together in a manner that will give them the status of a family group. . . .

In cultures which, like ours, trace kinship and descent bilaterally, we may belong to three different kinship groups, the father's, the mother's, and the spouse's. But in many cultures one line of descent receives major, if not exclusive, attention. In such cultures one may be a member of only one kinship group, his mother's if the system be matrilineal, his father's if it be patrilineal.

Finally, *marriage* is a term often applied to the ceremonial which is appropriately called wedding. It is also applied to the relationship between spouses, referring either to a particular pair (a larger number of individuals in plural marriages) or to the institutionalized pattern of relationship, not the ceremonial, and we shall deal especially with the generalized pattern of relationships between mates rather than the specific adjustments made by particular couples.

Japanese Social Experience and Concept of Groups

Dolores Cathcart and Robert Cathcart

Deru kugi wa utareru ("the nail that sticks up is hit") is a well-known saying in Japan. Japanese children hear it continually from parents and teachers. It reflects an important cultural attitude. Japanese are fond of the saying because it suggests their abhorrence of egocentricity and their wish to avoid being singled out for praise or blame. More importantly, this saying reminds them of the pain experienced when one fails to blend harmoniously into a group. It is this great desire to lose oneself within the confines of a group that is most characteristic of the Japanese.

If we were to place Japanese concepts of self and group at one end of a continuum it would be possible to produce an almost perfect paradigm by placing American concepts at the other. This remarkable polarity in cultural variation makes the study of Japanese groups useful to those interested in intercultural communication.[1] In both cultures we find a similar social phenomenon, highly developed group activity, but the contrasting perceptions of group dynamics are so disparate they bring into sharp focus the divergent social values of Japanese and Americans. Understanding these cultural variances in perception and values can help us cross communication barriers, and more importantly, help us understand how our American concepts of group are cultural variants rather than universal theories. In other words, the ethnocentrism of American theories of group dynamics may emerge more clearly as we examine Japanese concepts standing in polar opposition to our own.

I

An American would most likely begin the examination of "group" by defining or categorizing groups. Questions would be asked like, "What is a group?" "Can two persons be a group?" "What are the main differences between a small group and a large group?" These questions reflect Western thought patterns and would represent one end of the cultural continuum. The Japanese would not begin in this manner. Groups are not defined, they simply "are." They are the "natural" or normal milieu in which human interaction takes place. There is no counterpart in Japan to that American thought process which produces long essays and collections of experimental data on "how best to define a group." Such attempts at defining and categorizing are typical of Western attitudes and values.

This original essay appears here in print for the first time. All rights reserved. Permission to reprint must be obtained from the publisher and the authors. Dolores Cathcart is a freelance writer. Robert Cathcart teaches at Queens College of the City of New York. This joint project grows out of a research sabbatical spent in Japan.

Another American approach to groups is to consider *the role of the individual* in the group. On this continuum the American position is represented by the attitude that the individual is the more important part of the group. In American culture each person is perceived of as having a unique identity, a "self" separate from but influenced by the other members of a group and by group norms. This leads to the view that a group is a *collection* of individuals in which a person has a great deal of freedom to choose individual roles or even to remain apart from the group if he so chooses. This belief carries with it the assumption that the individual can function, in theory at least, independent of the group, guided by a duty to self and obligated to do that which he sees as morally right no matter what course the group follows.

The Japanese view of "no-self" stands in opposition to this. In Japan it is believed society is composed of on-going groups in which individual identity is submerged. The Japanese approach to the group role is to perceive of oneself as an integral part of the whole. Sociologist Yoshiharu Matsumoto explains:

> The individual does not interact as an individual but as a son in a parent–child relationship, as an apprentice in a master–apprentice relationship, or as a worker in an employer–employee relationship. Furthermore, the playing of the role of son, apprentice, student or worker persists twenty-four hours a day. There is no clear-cut demarcation between work and home life.[2]

The identification through group rather than self can be observed in ordinary interactions. When Japanese family members converse, they address one another not by using their given names but by using names that denote the person's group functions. A daughter-in-law named Reiko will be called by a name that denotes her place in the family rather than "Reiko," which designates her individually. Should a father in a family die and be replaced by the eldest son as head of the family, the son would then be called "father" even by his own mother.

Groups in Japan are permanent and determinate. Individuals are temporary and have no existence, in theory, outside the group. This outlook does not negate the important functions and contributions of individuals within groups but it does subordinate the "self" to the group. Individual fulfillment of self is attained through finding and maintaining one's place within the group. If the group is successful, so is each part of it.

The American concept of individual responsibility based on a belief in individual morality stands in sharp contrast to the Japanese concept of *group* morality and ultimate group responsibility. The Japanese see all decisions and actions as the product of group consensus. The individual is not held morally responsible for such decisions. When a person commits a wrongful act, it is the group that is embarrassed and, in the final analysis, responsible for the misdeed. It is commonly accepted in Japanese law and practice that the group should make amends and pay damages resulting from individual misconduct. This embodiment of group can be carried to the point where, in extreme circumstances, those persons at the top of the group hierarchy feel constrained to answer for the misdeeds of individual group members by committing *hara-kiri* (suicide) in order to erase the blot on the group's honor. This act of *hara-kiri* reflects a total denial of self and a complete loyalty to the group.

The Japanese is relieved of the typical American moral struggle wherein each person must continually weigh the duty to self and individual rights against obligations to the group. On the other hand, the Japanese cannot escape the tremendous anxiety produced by having to insure that every thought and act enhances the group. As Kawashima Takeoyoshi states it,

> There is no place for the concept of the individual as an independent entity equal to other individuals. In (Japanese) culture, the social order consists of social obligations, which are defined not in specific determinate terms, but in diffuse, indeterminate terms. . . . The indeterminateness of social obligations hence the lack of concepts of equality and independent individual—does not allow the existence of [individual] "right" as the counterpart of social obligations.[3]

Americans seldom feel an all-consuming loyalty to one group. As a result, America has been called a nation of "joiners." There is a tendency to be on the lookout for new groups to join which can fulfill one's personal desires as well as provide a place for meeting social obligations. Americans readily form groups, dissolve them, and go on to form new groups. The motivation is the individual search for identity.

Japanese cannot imagine this kind of "joining." A person in Japan is part of particular groups because that is the way society is structured, and the individual does not believe he can "go it alone." To leave a group in Japan is to lose one's identity, and it decreases the chances of finding fulfillment. Leaving a group is not a matter of individual choice just as joining a group is not. In Japan necessary group transitions such as leaving the university to join a company are circumscribed by elaborate rituals constructed to serve group needs rather than individual desires.

II

The perceptual patterns and value systems that produce this extreme identification with group rather than self can be traced to the central role of family as a model for all Japanese interpersonal relationships. As in the West, the family is the primary group and is the place where most attitudes and values are learned. Unlike the nuclear family of the West, which functions primarily to protect the offspring while preparing them to leave and assume a role in the larger society (where it is expected they will replicate the family with another nuclear family), "the Japanese family is conceived of as existing from the past and into the future, unceasingly, independent of birth and death of its members."[4]

In Japan, the family does not prepare the child to leave it and enter the social order; the family, itself, is perceived as the *basis of all social order*. Within the family the child learns the intricate rituals and linguistic nuances that influence the Japanese personality and that are operative in all relationships in and outside the family. That is, the Japanese *replicate* the family group structure and process throughout their society.

The Japanese word for family is *ie,* which literally means "the house" or "the household." The use of the term *ie* emphasizes the organizational and functional aspects of family. Each household consists of the head of the house and all persons, whether related by blood or not, who share in the social and economic life of the family. This relationship is designated *keifu,* which means "bond" and which refers to the maintenance and continuance of the family as an institution. This is in contrast to the kinship that binds the Western family through blood and inheritance. Although strictly patrilinear in structure, the Japanese family can be headed by a member with no blood relationship to the other family members. This is possible through the traditional practice of "adoption." For example, if there is no son to take over as the head of the house, a family adopts a suitable "son" and he immediately takes on the role of eldest son, with all the rights and privileges entailed and with all the duties and obligations that a son born to the position would have. After adoption, he would no longer "exist" as a son in the family he left and he could never return to or make claims in his blood family. His name is literally erased from that family's records. He takes a new name and his former name and "self" disappear.

The ancient feudal household consisting of a lord and all his retainers, peasants, warriors, and craftsmen was considered *ie,* or family. In this arrangement the line between kin and non-kin is blurred, and loyalty and contribution to the group becomes the bond (*keifu*) that unifies and distinguishes the family. In modern Japan, this concept of *ritual kinship* prepares a person to enter a group outside the family or household. When a Japanese is chosen to work for a company or organization he sees himself as being *adopted into a family* and he carries with him the same kinds of loyalties and methods of interpersonal relationships that he has learned in his (*ie*) family.

An important characteristic of the Japanese family is the way in which it fosters and perpetuates *dependency.* This dependency produces "indebtedness" or *on,* which in turn governs interpersonal relationships. A Japanese child, like an American one, learns at a very young age that he must rely on others. Unlike American families, the Japanese family purposefully *fosters* dependency as the child matures. Dependency, in Japan, is considered a natural and desirable trait capable of producing warm human relationships. (See the following discussion of *amae.*) In America, on the other hand, dependency is considered a limitation on individual growth and fulfillment, and so the family and school teach the child to become *self-reliant.*

A Japanese, even as an adult, never escapes dependency. All his life he depends on others, and all his life he must seek to repay his indebtedness to those who have cared for him by providing for those beneath him. This is what is meant by *on.*

On should be viewed as part of group structure and not as a relationship between two persons only. Everyone in a group *is at the same time* an *on*-receiver and an *on*-giver. Each member of the group is indebted to all those above him on whom he has had to depend, and in turn he must repay this indebtedness by giving assistance to all those below him who are dependent on him. *On* works to bind persons to the group, for if they left the group they would have no way of repaying the indebtedness incurred while a member of the group. It also functions as a means of linking all persons in the group in an unending chain of indebtedness and obligation.

While the *on* relationship might appear to be a typical pecking order hierarchy to the Westerner, it is a hierarchy of a very different quality. It is based on the natural dependency inherent in human relationships rather than on inherent individual qualities or attributes that enable some human beings to assume superior positions to others. *On* requires that the Japanese sees himself as fitting into a hierarchy—a hierarchy that exists in every group of which he is a member.

The very strong personal relationships characteristic of this vertical dyadic order are fostered by the *oyabun–kobun* relationship, a companion dimension that exists along with *on*. The *oyabun* is a father, boss, or patron who protects and provides for the son, employee, or student in turn for his service and loyalty. Again, this is a part of the two-way dependency relationship. Every boss or group leader recognizes his dependence on those below him. Without their undivided loyalty he could not function. He is acutely aware of the double dimension of this dependency because he has had to serve a long period as a follower or *kobun,* working his way up the hierarchy. He has reached his position at the top by faithfully serving his *oyabun* who in turn has protected him and provided for him. Each *oyabun* has one or more *kobun* whom he looks after much as a father looks after his children. The more loyal and devoted the "children," the more he succeeds and the better he can care for them. In the Japanese business world the *oyabun* finds work for his *kobun,* places them where they are best suited, provides for them when they are out of work, and accepts responsibility for personal problems they have on and off the job. In turn, *kobun* must heed his advice, defend him, and depend on him for help. "Everyone gets some sort of reward for submitting to an *oyabun;* consequently followers remain faithful to their *oyabun* during difficult times in a way they never would for a man who has used sheer power to subordinate them."[5]

The *oyabun–kobun* relationship makes for a unique structure in Japanese groups, one not found in American groups, where relationships are dependent on changing role functions and where the ideal group is one in which every person is considered equal to every other, free to participate as he chooses. Relationships with a Japanese group are vertical: something like a chain, each person being a link in the chain. Each member has a direct relationship with the person above (one's *oyabun*) and the person or several persons directly below (one's *kobun*). Interaction is usually with one person at a time and never with more than one above. The *kobun* does not go over the head of his superior or *oyabun.* Indeed, it would be unnecessary ever to do so, because the *oyabun* would never make a decision without considering the needs, interests, and desires of the *kobun.*

On and *oyabun–kobun* stress dependency and loyalty of superior and inferior in the vertical hierarchy of Japanese society. Without some balance, however, these concepts would produce a highly factionalized system with little or no regard for the interests of the whole. The group or collective, to be strongly united, must demand a mutual regard or loyalty to something larger than one's faction or *oyabun–kobun* link. In Western societies the normal tendency toward factionalism is counterbalanced by individualism and by the individual's acceptance of a universalist ethic. An American, for example, might be a Republican or Democrat but he has a duty to all other American citizens that supersedes or at least holds in check excessive loyalty to his chosen party. Often times this is stated as one's duty to be a "good neighbor" or a "good Christian" and this requires the American to be helpful or understanding of others even though they may be members of competing organizations or factions.

Japanese adhere to no such universalist ethic. Instead, the Japanese have internalized the concept of *giri,* which serves a similar function in checking factionalism. *Giri* controls the horizontal relationships in this vertically organized society.

It is difficult to produce an easily understood translation of or definition of *giri.* The term is widely used in Japan and can be found in almost every discussion of Japanese behavior. John W. Hall and Richard K. Beardsley, in their book, *Twelve Doors to Japan,* offer the following explanation of *giri:*

> To some Japanese, *giri* is the blanket term for obligation between persons in actual situations as contrasted with a universalistic ethic of duty. Others see *giri* as the form of obligation to the group without superiority on one side and inferiority on the other as in the *on* relationship. In either case, *giri* connotes obligation and as such sets the tone of relationship toward specifiable other persons. ... One can recognize the inevitable tension between *giri* and *ninjo.* ... *Ninjo* refers to what one would like to do as a human being and equally to what one finds distasteful or abhorrent out of personal sentiment; *giri* pertains to what one must do or avoid doing because of status or group membership.[6]

Giri implies the self-discipline that must be used to repress or channel personal desires and feelings. One may not like, personally, the older members of the group or think they are particularly wise or competent, but one must show affection and humbleness toward them for the sake of the group. In this way the selfish impulses of an individual or faction are held in check, not out of a desire to be polite or to avoid confrontation but rather through an obligation not to embarrass the group by causing any member to lose face.

Giri is well-suited to this society, which produces lifelong relationships. Japanese spend most of every day in close proximity with the other members of their group, and without *giri* such an intense interaction over such an extended period of time would be impossible to bear. The highly ritualized mode of interpersonal relationships developed to accommodate *giri* prevent incidences that could produce hostility. It is not difficult to understand that American notions of group participation, such as "group communication should be characterized by frank, open, and candid statements expressing individual personal feelings, wishes, and dislikes," would be the antithesis of the Japanese concept of *giri.*

Family traditions, the concepts of *on, oyabun–kobun,* and *giri* confine the individual Japanese within a fixed group, keeping him there all his life and effectively cut him off from other groups. He naturally grows more and more dependent on his group and more distrustful of anyone "outside." In fact, the Japanese are often callously indifferent (although always polite) to anyone outside their own group.

It is difficult for a Westerner to imagine a culture that so totally submerges the individual within the group. There is a tendency for Westerners to account for what they see by attributing subjugation of self to political and economic pressures that force or coerce submission to authority. Such an explanation does not fit Japanese culture nor can it account for the widespread satisfaction the Japanese feel for their way of life. A *Japanese* explanation of this behavior is offered by the psychiatrist, L. Takeo Doi. He maintains that the Japanese desire for group identity can be found in the concept of *amae*. There is no English equivalent of the word *amae* or *ameru* (the verb form), but it can be translated to mean to depend on or presume upon another's love, or it can mean lovable, or it can even mean "spoiled" as in the case of a child spoiled by too much affection. It can also mean "sweet" as in the sweet warmth of a mother's love. According to Doi, "it (*amae*) carries a positive connotation related to the sweet and warm dependency that a child feels when surrounded by his parents and other loving kin."[7] Doi believes that the Japanese carry this notion with them both consciously and unconsciously throughout life, continually seeking this dependency status in all activities. This, he feels, would account for their desire to constantly subordinate themselves in a group. Each Japanese is attempting to recreate in each group that state of sweet bliss he first experienced in his family. Doi finds the concept of *amae* so pervasive, he claims that "*Amae* might be the very factor that distinguishes Japanese people from other nations. . . ."[8]

III

The ability of the Japanese people to maintain their basic value system and to readily adapt their cultural concepts to new and changing situations is one of the more intriguing aspects of Japanese studies. Nowhere is this more apparent than in the Japanese re-creation of the Western industrial corporation as the twentieth-century counterpart of the feudal system family.

Today, Japan is a modern industrial giant absorbed in a technological race with other industrial nations. Her cities are overcrowded, polluted, fast-paced, and impersonal. To the casual observer, a Japanese city is like any other "big city" in the world: surrounded with huge factories populated by persons isolated from the rural regions, living in an impersonal atmosphere, bent on material acquisition. But anyone who lives in Japan knows how persistently the concepts of *on, giri,* and *amae* remain central to Japanese life. For example, the big corporation occupies a central position in modern Japan, not only as a producer of economic strength and goods, but as the system in which the Japanese maintain their traditional values. Chie Nakane, in an excellent sociological study called *Japanese Society,* argues that the corporate group is the unit that forms the basis for modern Japanese society.[9] Suzuki and Mishubishi have replaced the feudal family, but the structure has remained the same.

In feudal Japan, and it is important to recall that the Japanese feudal era extended well into the nineteenth century, the family household—composed of the lord and his retainers, warriors, peasants, and craftsmen—was the basic social unit or group. The codes of behavior, loyalty, and honor that served the household then have been transformed in essentially the same form to the modern version of the *ie,* the corporate group. It also is organized in a strict hierarchial order. Seniority determines rank, and merit plays an insignificant part in the advancement of an employee. The *oyabun–kobun* concept governs company–employee interaction. Once a person enters employment with a company he becomes an integral part of that corporate community and usually remains with it the rest of his life. The new employee is indebted to all those above him and he repays *on* through his obligation to all those who come after him or are below him. He is totally dependent on his company and he finds pleasure and satisfaction in this institutionalization of *amae.* Unlike the American company, which is considered primarily a place of employment *apart* from one's family, religious, and social groups, the company in Japan is intimately involved in each member's life. It is the center of the individual's social and economic life. Off work hours are spent with one's fellow employees, vacations are taken at the company-owned retreat, health services and counseling are provided, even family matters like marriage and divorce are the concern of the company. The worker becomes emotionally involved with the company group, and group duty or *giri* governs his life.

Kaisha, meaning "company" or "enterprise" has become a familiar word in modern Japan. *Kaisha,* superimposed on *ie,* has become the symbol of group consciousness. Nakane describes the importance of this "new" group:

> *Kaisha* does not mean that individuals are bound by contractual relationships into a corporate enterprise, while still thinking of themselves as separate entities; rather *kaisha* is "my" or "our" company, the community to which one belongs primarily, and which is all-important in one's life. Thus in most cases the company provides the whole social existence of a person, has authority over all aspects of his life; he is deeply involved in the association.[10]

In less than one hundred years Japan has moved from a feudal, agrarian society to become a major industrial power. The startling changes necessitated by this quick transition have come about without markedly disrupting the basic patterns of human interactions or altering the fundamental group value orientations. The Japanese have had the ability to accept and absorb methods and ideas from western culture and yet keep their traditional ritual and ethic. It is clear that the concept binding each Japanese to his group has served to preserve these ancient patterns.

Notes

[1]See Richard E. Porter and Larry A. Samovar, "Communicating Interculturally" in *Intercultural Communication: A Reader,* 2d. ed., ed. Larry A. Samovar and Richard E. Porter (Belmont, Calif., 1976), pp. 4–24.

[2]Yoshiharu Matsumoto, "Contemporary Japan: The Individual and the Group," *Transactions of the American Philosophical Society,* 50:1 (January 1960), 60.

[3]Kawashima Takeoyoshi, "The Status of the Individual in the Notion of the Law, Right, and Social Order in Japan," in *The Japanese Mind,* ed. Charles A. Moore (Tokyo, 1967), p. 274.

[4]Kizaemon Ariga, "The Family in Japan," *Marriage and Family Living,* 16:4 (1954), 362.

[5]John W. Hall and Richard K. Beardsley, *Twelve Doors to Japan* (New York, 1965), p. 84.

[6]*Ibid.,* p. 94.

[7]L. Takeo Doi, "Amae: A Key Concept for Understanding Japanese Culture," in *Japanese Culture: Its Development and Characteristics,* ed. Robert J. Smith and Richard K. Beardsley (New York, 1962), p. 132.

[8]*Ibid.,* p. 133.

[9]Chie Nakane, *Japanese Society* (Berkeley, 1970).

[10]*Ibid.,* p. 3–4.

Masculine/Feminine

Betty Roszak

Recent years have seen a resurgence of feminism that has taken mainstream America by surprise. It began with the discontent of lonely middle-class suburban housewives, whose malady was given a name by Betty Friedan in her immensely influential book, *The Feminine Mystique.* But it didn't become what we know as a "women's liberation movement" until the growth of the New Left from the civil rights and peace movements of the early 1960's. It wasn't until then that hundreds of young women, many of whom were seasoned veterans of antiwar and antisegregationist activities, began to realize the anomaly of their situation. Here they were, radical women involved in a struggle for human equality and an end to oppression, willing to dedicate years of effort to effecting political change, and what were they being allowed to do? Typing, mimeographing, addressing envelopes, sweeping, providing coffee and sexual diversion for the vigorous young men who were making all the decisions. Far from going forward together to change the world, men and women were once more stuck (and this time with a vengeance) with their time-honored roles: the men to think and act; the women to serve and drudge. The last equality—that between women and men—was never even mentioned. In fact, movement women found that they were even worse off than apolitical women, because they were aware of and extremely sensitive to the hypocrisies of their male colleagues who talked idealistically of

equality, but who acted scornful of women in their everyday lives. The rhetoric
of equality was directed at black, brown, and Third World *men* only. The New
Left of the late sixties had begun to take on a tough, aggressively male tone, born
of the idolization of Ché Guevara, guerrilla warfare, and admiration for the
exaggerated, overcompensating manliness of the Black Panthers. As nonviolence,
exemplified by Martin Luther King, Jr., became discredited by revolutionary and
black militancy, so the tough style became a political requirement. In deference
to this new brutalism men found it easy to take the necessary traditional he-man
attitude toward women, the attitude of dominance and power. This left women
in a bewildering dilemma. Were they to remain in a movement which allowed
them to exist only as lackeys and silently submissive bedmates, or would they
refuse to accept a subordinate status?

As this dilemma is being resolved today, there sounds in the background the
laughter of contemptuous radical men: "Crazy feminist bitches!" The words
merely echo a shared male ridicule that knows no class lines. Women find themselves of necessity beginning to re-examine the traditions of misogyny that even
radical men have unknowingly inherited.

In our cultural past "Woman" was the symbol of sex; and sex, though
necessary, was at the same time known to be an abhorrent evil, a degrading
passion. In the Middle Ages, the masculine world view of the church dared not
make light of women. Church authorities of the fifteenth century, ever on the alert
for the malevolence of the devil, used a popular handbook on the identification
and treatment of witches, the *Malleus Maleficarum,* in searching out evil in the
form of women. "What else is woman," says this medieval antisubversive activities manual, "but a foe to friendship, an unescapable punishment, a necessary evil,
a natural temptation, a desirable calamity, a domestic danger, a delectable detri-
ment, an evil of nature painted with fair colors?" By the eighteenth century,
Rousseau, one of France's most prolific proponents of democratic equality, could
write with impunity, "Women have in general no love of any art; they have no
proper knowledge of any; and they have no genius," thus curtly dismissing half
of humanity to a status of hopeless inferiority. By mid-nineteenth century, the
"evil of nature" had turned into an object of scorn, and Schopenhauer's indict-
ment of women as "that undersized, narrow-shouldered, broad-hipped, and
short-legged race," denied women even their beauty, their "fair colors," along
with their intellectual capacity.

Today's predominantly male society no longer sees women as evil, at least
on the surface. The ambivalent fear and attraction of the Middle Ages has
changed along with the prevailing attitude toward sex. Now that sexuality has
lost its mystery, the once dangerous and seductive female can be safely ignored
and denied her power. The fear has turned to ridicule. One cannot ignore evil,
but one can pretend that the ridiculous does not exist. Men irritably ask the
rhetorical question (echoing Freud), "What do women want?" meaning, of
course, that anything women want is absurd. The question is asked not of individual women but of the world, and in an exasperated tone, as if women were dumb

and couldn't answer. The false barrier continues to be built: "We" cannot under-stand "Them." Why are "They" so restive? Further communication between the sexes seems useless. Always it is men talking to men about women.

The fact of ridicule is constantly with us. When it was proposed in 1969 in the British House of Commons that attention be paid to developing a contracep-tive pill for men, "the idea provoked hearty laughter," according to Paul Vaughan in the London *Observer.* Moreover, he tells us, the British government has rejected outright any allocation of funds for research on a pill for men. When the question was under discussion in the House of Lords, one Labour peer advised the government to ignore " 'these do-gooders who take all the fun out of life' (laughter)." Researchers explain their reluctance to tamper with the male germ cells. Yet the same researchers have not hesitated to tamper with the female germ cells in developing the pill for women. Nor have unpleasant side effects or hazards to women's health deterred them, while they quickly stopped research on a substance being tested on men because it was noted that when men drank alcohol while taking it, their eyes became reddened! Doctors have been known to laugh at the mention of labor pains during childbirth and in the not too distant past have been willing to stand by, calmly withholding anesthetics while women underwent great agonies in labor. So, too, male legislators have laughed at the idea of the legalization of abortion, hinting at unprecedented promiscuity (on the part of women, not men) if such a thing were allowed. Meanwhile, thousands of desperate women die each year as the direct result of male laws making abortion illegal.

Women are learning the meaning of this male laughter and indifference in the face of the most hazardous and serious biological enterprise women under-take, willing or not. And in cultural enterprises, whenever women attempt to enter any of the male-dominated professions (who ever heard of a woman chair-man of the board, a woman orchestra conductor, a woman Chief Justice, a woman President or a woman getting equal pay for equal work?), we again hear the familiar laughter of male ridicule. If we look at the image of woman men present to us in novels, drama, or advertising, we see a scatterbrained, helpless flunky, or a comical sex-pot, or a dumb beast of burden. Is this what they mean when they exhort us in popular song to "enjoy being a girl"? But women are beginning to relearn the old lesson: in this male-dominated world, it is a misfortune to be born female.

From the very moment of birth a higher value is placed by his society on the male infant, a value which accumulates and accelerates into his adult life. By the time the female infant has grown into adulthood, however, if she has learned society's lessons well, she will have come to acquiesce in her second-class status —to accept unconsciously the burden of her inferiority. No matter what honors she wins, what her exploits, what her achievements or talents, she will always be considered a woman first, and thus inferior to the least honored, talented and worthy male of that society—foremost a sexual being, still fair game for his aggressive sexual fantasies. As Albert Memmi puts it, ". . . every man, no matter how low he may be, holds women in contempt and judges masculinity to be an inestimable good."

Male society's disparagement of women has all the force of an unconscious conspiracy. It is even more subtle than the racist and colonial oppressions to which it is so closely allied, because it is softened and hidden by the silken padding of eroticism. We women grow to think that because we are wanted as lovers, wives, and mothers, it might be because we are wanted as human beings. But if by chance or natural inclination we attempt to move outside these male-defined and male-dependent roles, we find that they are, in reality, barriers.

For many women this is the first inkling of the fact of oppression. Pressed from birth into the mold of an exclusively sexual being, the growing girl soon develops what Sartre calls the "phantom personality"; she comes to feel that she is what "they" tell her she is. This other self envelops her like a second skin. When she begins to experience a natural sense of constriction (which is growth), her real feelings clash with what "they" say she should feel. The more forceful and vital she is, the more she will have to repress her real feelings, because girls are to be passive and manipulatable. She becomes frightened, suspicious, anxious about herself. A sense of malaise overcomes her. She must obey the social prohibitions which force her back into the mold of the sexual being. She is not to desire or act, but to *be* desired and acted upon. Many women give up the struggle right there and dully force themselves to remain stunted human beings. The butterfly must not be allowed to come forth from its chrysalis: her vitality is only allowed guilty expression in certain private moments or is turned into sullen resentment which smolders during all her unfulfilled life.

Family and home, which look like a refuge and a sanctuary, turn out to be the same kind of trap. Beyond the marriage ghetto there is outright rejection and exclusion. In the work world there are lower wages, union and employer discrimination, the prohibitive cost of child care. In the professions mere tokenism takes the place of acceptance and equality. The same is true in government and political activity. The single woman knows only too well the psychological exclusionism practiced by male society. She is suspect, or comic, if over a certain age. All men assume she would be married if she could—there must be something psychologically wrong with her if she isn't. And single women have the added burden of not being socially acceptable without an "escort"—a man, any man.

Further, women are the nonexistent people in the very life of the nation itself —now more so even than the blacks who have at last forced themselves into the nation's consciousness. The invisible man has become the invisible *woman*. William James called it a "fiendish punishment" that "one should be turned loose on society and remain absolutely unnoticed by all the members thereof." Yet that is the treatment male society metes out to those women who wish to escape from the male-defined erotic roles. Left out of the history books, not credited with a past worth mentioning in the masculine chronicles of state, women of today remain ignorant of women's movements of the past and the important role individual women have played in the history of the human race. Male historical scholarship sees the suffragists and feminists of the nineteenth century as figures of fun, worthy of only a paragraph here and there, as footnotes on the by-ways of social customs, far from the main roads of masculine endeavor: the wars, political intrigues, and diplomatic maneuverings which make up the history of power.

With the blacks and other oppressed minorities, women can say, "How can we hope to shape the future without some knowledge of our past?" If the historic heroines of feminism are ignored or treated trivially, today's women are hindered from dealing with their own repression. This undermining of self-confidence is common to all oppressed peoples, along with the doubts of the reality of one's own perceptions. Women's self-rejection as worthwhile human beings thus becomes an inevitable extension of the cycle of oppression.

But radical women have begun to rebel against the false, exclusively sexual image men have created for them. And in rebelling, many women are seeing the need for bypassing the marriage ghetto altogether. They are recognizing the true nature of the institution of marriage as an economic bargain glossed over by misty sentimentalizing. Wash off the romantic love ideal, and underneath we see the true face of the marriage contract. It is grimly epitomized by the immortal slogan found chalked on innumerable honeymoon getaway cars: "She got him today; he'll get her tonight." Or, as put more sophisticatedly by Robert Briffault, "Whether she aims at freedom or a home a woman is thrown back on the defense of her own interests; she must defend herself against man's attempt to bind her, or sell herself to advantage. Woman is to man a sexual prey; man is to woman an economic prey." And this kind of oppression cuts across all economic class lines, even though there may be social differences between streetwalker Jane X, housewife Joan Y, and debutante Jacqueline Z. One may sell her body for a few dollars to the likeliest passerby; one for a four-bedroomed house in the suburbs; and one for rubies and yachts. But all must sell their bodies in order to participate in the bargain. Yet if women were to refuse to enter into the sexual bargain, they not only would refute the masculine idea of women as property, but they also would make it possible to free men from the equally self-destructive role of sole breadwinner. Thus there would be a chance to break the predatory cycle.

Beyond marriage and the old, outmoded roles, radical women are seeking new ways of dealing with the oppressive institutions of society. No longer will they acquiesce in the pattern of dominance and submission. They are beginning to take control of their own lives, building new relationships, developing new modes of work, political activity, child rearing and education. Rejection of male exploitation must start with psychic as well as economic independence. The new female consciousness is going to develop cooperative forms of child care; women's centers as sanctuaries for talk, planning, and action; all-female communes where women can escape for a while from the all-pervading male influence; the sharing of domestic drudgery with men in cooperative living arrangements; the building up of competence and self-confidence in such previously male-dependent endeavors as general mechanical repair work, carpentry, and construction.

By rejecting the false self for so long imposed upon us and in which we have participated unwittingly, we women can forge the self-respect necessary in order to discover our own true values. Only when we refuse to be made use of by those who despise and ridicule us, can we throw off our heavy burden of resentment. We must take our lives in our own hands. This is what liberation means. Out of a common oppression women can break the stereotypes of masculine-feminine and enter once more into the freedom of the human continuum.

Women's liberation will thus inevitably bring with it, as a concomitant, men's liberation. Men, no less than women, are imprisoned by the heavy carapace of their sexual stereotype. The fact that they gain more advantages and privileges from women's oppression has blinded them to their own bondage which is the bondage of an artificial duality. This is the male problem: the positing of a difference, the establishment of a dichotomy emphasizing oppositeness. Men are to behave in this way; women in that; women do this; men do the other. And it just so happens that the way men behave and act is important and valuable, while what women do is unimportant and trivial. Instead of identifying both the sexes as part of humanity, there is a false separation which is to the advantage of men. Masculine society has insisted on seeing in sexuality that same sense of conflict and competition that it has imposed upon its relation to the planet as a whole. From the bedroom to the board room to the international conference table, separateness, differentiation, opposition, exclusion, antithesis have been the cause and goal of the male politics of power. Human characteristics belonging to the entire species have been crystallized out of the living flow of human experience and made into either/or categories. This male habit of setting up boundary lines between imagined polarities has been the impetus for untold hatred and destruction. Masculine/feminine is just one of such polarities among many, including body/mind, organism/environment, plant/animal, good/evil, black/white, feeling/intellect, passive/active, sane/insane, living/dead. Such language hardens what is in reality a continuum and a unity into separate mental images always in opposition to one another.

If we think of ourselves as "a woman" or "a man," we are already participating in a fantasy of language. People become preoccupied with images of one another—surely the deepest and most desperate alienation there is. The very process of conceptualization warps our primary, unitary feelings of what we are. Mental images take the place of the primary stimuli of sex which involve the entire organism. Instead of a sense of identification, we have pornographic sex with its restrictive emphasis on genital stimulation. This "short circuiting between genitals and cortex" as William E. Galt calls it (in a brilliant article, "The Male-Female Dichotomy," in *Psychiatry,* 1943) is a peculiarly modern distortion of the original, instinctual nature of sex. We are suffering from D. H. Lawrence's "sex in the head." In childhood we know sexuality as a generalized body response; the body is an erotic organ of sensation. To this Freud gave the nasty name of polymorphous perversity. But it is actually the restriction to localized genitality of the so-called "normal" adult that is perverted, in the sense of a twisting away from the original and primary body eroticism. Biological evidence indicates that the sex response is a primitive, gross sensory stimulation—diffused and nonlocalizable. Phallic man, however, wishes to assert the primacy of his aggressive organ. The ego of phallic man divides him off from the rest of the world, and in this symbolic division he maintains the deep-seated tradition of man *against* woman, wresting his sexual pleasure *from* her, like the spoils of war. The total body response must be repressed in order to satisfy the sharpness of his genital cravings.

But in the primary sexual response of the body, there is no differentiation between man or woman; there is no "man," there is no "woman" (mental images), just a shared organism responding to touch, smell, taste, sound. The sexual response can then be seen as one part of the species' total response to and participation in, the environment. We sense the world with our sensitive bodies as an ever-changing flow of relationships in which we move and partake. Phallic man sees the world as a collection of things from which he is sharply differentiated. If we consider the phenomenon of the orgasm in this light, we can see that its basic qualities are the same for male and female. There can be no real distinction between the feminine and masculine *self*-abandonment in a sexual climax. The self, or controlling power, simply vanishes. All talk of masculine or feminine orgasm misses this point entirely, because this is a surrender which goes beyond masculine or feminine. Yet how many men are there who are willing to see their own sexual vitality as exactly this self-surrender?

When men want desperately to preserve that which they deem masculine—the controlling power—then they insist on the necessity of the feminine as that which must be controlled and mastered. Men force themselves into the role of phallic man and seek always to be hard, to be tough, to be competitive, to assert their "manhood." Alan Watts wisely sees this masculine striving for rigidity as "nothing more than an emotional paralysis" which causes men to misunderstand the bisexuality of their own nature, to force a necessarily unsatisfactory sexual response, and to be exploitive in their relations with women and the world.

According to Plato's myth, the ancients thought of men and women as originally a single being cut asunder into male and female by an angry god. There is a good biological basis to this myth; although the sexes are externally differentiated, they are still structurally homologous. Psychologically, too, the speculations of George Groddeck are apt:

> Personal sex cuts right across the fundamental qualities of human nature; the very word suggests the violent splitting asunder of humanity into male and female. *Sexus* is derived from *secare*, to cut, from which we also get *segmentum*, a part cut from a circle. It conveys the idea that man and woman once formed a unity, that together they make a complete whole, the perfect circle of the individuum and that both sections share the properties of this individuum. These suggestions are of course in harmony with the ancient Hebrew legend, which told how God first created a human being who was both male and female, Adam-Lilith, and later sawed this asunder.[1]

The dichotomizing of human qualities can thus be seen as a basic error in men's understanding of nature. Biologically, both sexes are always present in each. Perhaps with the overcoming of women's oppression, the woman in man will be allowed to emerge. If, as Coleridge said, great minds are androgynous, there can be no feminine or masculine ideal, but only as the poet realizes,

> ... what is true is human,
> homosexuality, heterosexuality
> There is something more important:

---

1. *The World of Man* (New York, Vision Press, 1951).

to be human
in which kind
is kind.[2]

Homosexuality: The Formulation of a Sociological Perspective

William Simon and John H. Gagnon

The study of homosexuality today, except for a few rare and relatively recent examples, suffers from two major defects: (1) It is ruled by a simplistic and homogeneous view of the psychological and social contents of the category "homosexual." (2) At the same time it is nearly exclusively interested in the most difficult and least rewarding of all questions, that of etiology. While some small exclusions are allowed for adolescent homosexual experimentation, the person with a major to a nearly exclusive sexual interest in persons of the same sex is perceived as belonging to a uniform category whose adult behavior is a necessary outcome and, in a sense, reenactment, of certain early and determining experiences. This is the prevailing image of the homosexual and the substantive concern of the literature in psychiatry and psychology today.

In addition to the fact that sexual contact with persons of the same sex, even beyond the age of consent, is against the law in forty-nine of the fifty state jurisdictions of the United States, the homosexual labors under another burden which is commonly the lot of the deviant in this society. The process of labeling and stigmatizing behavior not only facilitates the work of legal agencies in creating a bounded category of deviant actors such as the "normal burglar" and the "normal child molester" as suggested by Sudnow, but also creates an image of large classes of deviant actors all operating out of the same motivations and for the same etiological reasons. The homosexual, like most significantly labeled persons (whether the label be positive or negative), has all of his acts interpreted through the framework of his homosexuality. Thus the creative activity of the playwright or painter who happens to be homosexual is interpreted in terms of his homosexuality rather than in terms of the larger artistic rules and conventions of the particular art form in which he works. The plays of the dramatist are scanned for the Albertine Ploy and the painter's paintings for an excessive or deficient use of phallic imagery or vaginal teeth.

2. Clayton Eshleman, from "Holding Duncan's Hand."

From *The Journal of Health and Social Behavior*, Vol. 8, No. 3 (September 1967), pp. 177–185. Reprinted by permission of the publisher and authors. Professor Simon is in the Department of Psychology, Long Island University. Professor Gagnon teaches in the Department of Sociology and Psychiatry, State University of New York, Stony Brook.

It is this nearly obsessive concern with the ultimate causes of adult conditions which has played a major role in structuring our concerns about beliefs and about attitudes toward the homosexual. Whatever the specific elements that make up an etiological theory, the search for etiology has its own consequences for research methodology and the construction of theories about behavior. In the case of homosexuality, if one moves beyond those explanations of homosexual behavior which are rooted in constitutional or biological characteristics—that is, something in the genes or in the hormonal system—one is left with etiological explanations located in the structure of the family and its malfunctions. The most compelling of these theories are grounded ultimately in Freudian psychology, where the roots of this behavior as well as the rest of human character structure are to be found in the pathological relationships between parents and their children.

As a consequence of our preliminary work and the work of others such as Hooker, Reiss, Leznoff and Westley, and Achilles, we would like to propose some alternative considerations in terms of the complexity of the life cycle of the homosexual, the roles that mark various stages of this cycle, and the kinds of forces, both sexual and nonsexual, that impinge on the individual actor. It is our current feeling that the problem of finding out how people become homosexual requires an adequate theory of how they become heterosexual; that is, one cannot explain homosexuality in one way and leave heterosexuality as a large residual category labeled "all other." Indeed, the explanation of homosexuality in this sense may await the explanation of the larger and more modal category of adjustment.

Further, from a sociological point of view, what the original causes were may not even be very important for the patterns of homosexuality observed in a society. Much like the medical student who comes to medicine for many reasons, and for whom the homogeneity that is professional behavior arises from the experiences of medical school rather than from the root causes of his occupational choice, the patterns of adult homosexuality are attendant upon the social structures and values which occur to the homosexual after he becomes, or conceives of himself as, homosexual, rather than upon original and ultimate causes.

What we are suggesting here is that we have allowed the sexual object choice of the homosexual to dominate and control our imagery and have let this aspect of his total life experience appear to determine all his products, concerns, and activities. This prepossessing concern on the part of non-homosexuals with the purely sexual aspect of the homosexual's life is something which we would not allow to occur if we were interested in the heterosexual, but the mere presence of sexual deviation seems to give the sexual content of life an overwhelming significance. Homosexuals, moreover, vary profoundly in the degree to which their homosexual commitment and its facilitation becomes the organization principle of their lives. Involved is a complex outcome which is less likely to be explained by originating circumstances than by the consequences of the establishment of the commitment itself.

Even with the relatively recent shift in the normative framework available for considering homosexuality—that is, from a rhetoric of sin to a rhetoric of mental health—the overweighting of the sexual factor is evident. The change itself may have major significance in the ways in which homosexual persons are dealt with; at the same time, the mental health rhetoric seems equally wide of the mark in understanding homosexuality. One advance, however, is that in place of the language of optimum man which characterized both the moral and the early mental health literature, we find a growing literature concerned with what are the psychological characteristics necessary for a person to survive in some manner within specific social systems and social situations. In this post-Freudian world, major psychic wounds are increasingly viewed as par for the human condition and —as one major psychiatric theoretician observes—few survive their parents without such wounding. The problem then becomes whether the wounds inflicted are exposed to social situations which render them either too costly to the individual or to the surrounding community.

Accompanying this trend toward reconceptualization of mental health has been a scaling down of the goals set for men; instead of exceedingly vague and somewhat utopian goals, we tend to ask more pragmatic questions: Is the individual self-supporting? Does he manage to conduct his affairs without the intervention of the police or the growing number of mental health authorities? Does he have adequate sources of social support? a positively balanced and adequately developed repertoire of gratification? Has he learned to accept himself? These are questions we are learning to ask of nearly all men; among the remaining exceptions is found the homosexual. In practically all cases, the presence of homosexuality is seen as prima facie evidence of major psychopathology. When the heterosexual meets these minimal definitions of mental health, he is exculpated; the homosexual—no matter how good his adjustment in nonsexual areas of life is—remains suspect.

Our own recently tabulated data, drawn from homosexuals interviewed outside of institutions, suggest that most homosexuals manage fairly well and particularly well when we consider the stigmatized and, in fact, criminal nature of their sexual interests. In a group of homosexuals with extensive histories of homosexuality, we found that about 80 percent reported no trouble with the police and an additional 10 percent had had minor contacts but were not arrested. Only 20 percent reported problems of managing relations with their parental families, and about 10 percent or under reported difficulties in school or work. Of those who had had military experience, only one fifth reported difficulties. And with reference to the military, it is important to note that in the military, possibly more than in civilian life, homosexuality is a difficulty which washes out all other considerations.

We do not want to appear to be saying that the homosexual life does not contain a great potential for demoralization, despair, and self-hatred. To the contrary, as in most deviant careers there remains the potential for a significant escalation of individual psychopathology. This also is suggested by other segments of these same data. For example, we found that over two fifths indicated some measure of regret about being homosexual, giving reasons such as fear of social disapproval or rejection, inability to experience a conventional family life, feelings of guilt and shame, or fear of potential trouble. About one half reported that 50 percent or more of their sexual partners were persons with whom the subject had had only one contact (one-night stand), and for about one quarter this was true for 80 percent or more of their contacts. For two fifths, their longest homosexual affair had lasted one year or less. For about one quarter, kissing occurred in one third or less of all their sexual contacts. About 30 percent had never made love in their own homes. To this we should add the proportion of homosexuals who report having been robbed (frequently after being beaten)—over 25 percent—and the proportion who have been blackmailed—almost 10 percent. These figures require more detailed analysis and there are also uncertainties about sample bias which must be considered. However, it is our feeling that these proportions would not be changed a great deal given a more complete exploration of these factors. These data, then, suggest a depersonalized quality, a driven or compulsive quality, to the sexual activity of many homosexuals, which cannot be reckoned as anything but extremely costly to them.

Obviously, the pursuit of a homosexual commitment—like most forms of deviance—makes social adjustment more problematic than it might be for a conventional population. What is important to understand is that consequences of these sexual practices are not necessarily direct functions of such practices. It is necessary to move away from an obsessive concern with the sexuality of the individual, and to attempt to see the homosexual in terms of broader commitments that he must make in order to live in the world around him. Like the heterosexual, the homosexual must come to terms with the problems which are attendant upon being a member of the society: he must find a place to work, learn to live with or without his family, be involved or apathetic in political life, find a group of friends to talk to and live with, fill his leisure time usefully or frivolously, handle all of the common and uncommon problems of impulse control and personal gratification, and in some manner socialize his sexual interests.

There is a nearly unnoticed diversity to be found in the life cycle of the homosexual, both in terms of solving common human problems and in terms of the characteristics of the life cycle itself. Not only are there as many ways of being homosexual as there are of being heterosexual but the individual homosexual in the course of living his life encounters as many changes and as many crises as the heterosexual. It is much too easy to allow the label, once applied, to suggest that the complexities of role transition and identity crisis are easily attributable to, or are a crucial exemplification of, some previously existing etiological defect.

An example of this is in the phase of homosexuality called "coming out," which is that point in time when there is self-recognition of one's identity as a homosexual and the first major entry into exploration of the homosexual community. At this point in time, the removal of inhibiting doubts frequently releases a great deal of sexual energy. Sexual contacts during this period are often pursued nearly indiscriminately and with greater vigor than caution. This is very close to that period in the life of the heterosexual called the "honeymoon," when coitus is legitimate and is pursued with a substantial amount of energy. This high rate of marital coitus, however, declines as demands are made on the young couple to take their place in the framework of the larger social system. In these same terms, during the homosexual honeymoon many individuals begin to learn ways of acting out a homosexual object choice which involves homosexual gratification, but which is not necessarily directly sexual and does not involve the genitalia.

It is during this period that many homosexuals go through a crisis of femininity; that is, they act in relatively public places in a relatively effeminate manner and some, in a transitory fashion, wear female clothing—known in the homosexual argot as going in drag. During this period, one of the major confirming aspects of masculinity—that is, nonsexual reinforcement by females of masculine status—has been abandoned, and it is not surprising that the very core of masculine identity should not be called into question. This crisis is partially structured by the already existing homosexual culture in which persons already in the crisis stage become models for those who are newer to their commitment to homosexuality. A few males remain in this commitment to pseudo-femininity, a few others emerge masquerading as female prostitutes to males, and still others pursue careers as female impersonators. This adjustment might be more widely adapted if feminine behavior by men—except in sharply delimited occupational roles—were not negatively sanctioned. The tendency is, then, for this kind of behavior to be a transitional experiment for most homosexuals—an experiment that leaves vestiges of "camp" behavior, but vestiges more often expressive of the character of the cultural life of the homosexual community than of some overriding need of individual homosexuals. Since this period of disorganization and identity problems is at the same time highly visible to the broader community, this femininity is enlisted as evidence for theories of homosexuality that see as a central component in its etiology the failure of sexual identification. The homosexual at this point of the life cycle is more likely to be in therapy, and this is often construed as evidence for a theory which is supported by a missampling of the ways of being homosexual.

Another life-cycle crisis that the homosexual shares with the heterosexual in this youth-oriented society is the crisis of aging. While American society places an inordinate emphasis on youth as a positive attribute, the homosexual community, by and large, places a still greater emphasis on this fleeting characteristic. In general, the homosexual has fewer resources with which to meet this crisis. For the heterosexual there are children whose careers assure a sense of the future, and a wife whose sexual availability cushions the shock of declining sexual attractiveness. In addition, the crisis of aging comes later to the heterosexual when sexual powers have declined and expectations concerning sexuality are considerably lower. The management of aging by the homosexual is not well understood but there are, at this point in time, a series of behavioral manifestations—symptoms—attendant to this dramatic transition which are misread as global aspects of homosexuality. Here, as with coming out, it is important to note that most homosexuals, even with fewer resources than their heterosexual counterparts, manage to weather the period with relative success.

A central concern underlying these options and the management of a homosexual career is the presence and complexity of a homosexual community which serves most simply for some persons as a sexual marketplace, but for others as the locus of friendships, opportunities, recreation, and expansion of the base of social life. Such a community is filled with both formal and informal institutions for meeting others and for following, to the degree the individual wants, a homo-sexual life style. Minimally the community provides a source of social support, for it is one of the few places where the homosexual may get positive validation of his own self-image. Though the community often provides more feminine or camp behavior than some individuals might desire, in a major sense camp behav-ior may well be an expression of the aggregate community characteristics without an equal commitment on the part of its members. Further, the camp behavior may also be seen as a form of interpersonal communication that characterizes persons during intra-community behavior and changes significantly for most during interaction with the larger society. The community serves as a way of mediating sexuality by providing a situation in which one can know and evaluate peers and, in a significant sense, convert sexual behavior into sexual conduct.

Insofar as the community provides these relationships for the individual homosexual, it allows for the dilution of sexual drives by providing social gratifi-cation in ways which are not directly sexual, and in consequence the homosexual with access to the community is more protected from impulsive sexual acting out than the homosexual who has only his fear and his knowledge of the society's prohibitions to mediate his sexual impulses.

It should be pointed out that in contrast to ethnic and occupational subcul-tures the homosexual community—as well as other deviant subcommunities—has very limited content. This derives from the fact that the community members often have only their sexual commitment in common. Thus, while the community may reduce the problems of access to sexual partners and reduce guilt by provid-ing a structure of shared values, often the shared value structure of the commu-nity is far too narrow to transcend other areas of value disagreement. The college-trained professional and the busboy, the WASP and the Negro slum dweller may meet in sexual congress, but the similarity of their sexual interests does not eliminate the larger social and cultural barriers. The important fact is that the homosexual community is, in itself, an impoverished cultural unit. This impoverishment, however, may only be partially limiting, since it constrains most members to participate in it on a limited basis, thereby reducing anxiety and conflicts in the sexual sphere and increasing the quality of performance in other aspects of social life.

Earlier we briefly listed some of the general problems that the homosexual —in common with the heterosexual—must face; these included earning a living, maintaining a residence, learning to live with family. At this point, we might consider some of these in greater detail.

First there is the most basic problem of all: earning a living. Initially, all the variables that apply to all labor force participants generally also apply to homo-sexuals. In addition there are the special conditions imposed by the deviant character of the homosexual commitment. What is important is that the occupa-tional activity of homosexuals presents itself as a fairly broad range. The differ-ences in occupational activity can be conceptualized along a number of dimensions—some of which would be conventional concerns of occupational sociology, while others would reflect the special situation of the homosexual. For example, one element would be the degree of occupational involvement; that is, the degree to which occupational activity or ancillary activity is defined as intrinsically gratifying. This would obviously vary from professional to ribbon clerk to factory laborer. A corollary to this would be the degree to which the world of work penetrates other aspects of life. The first of these elements—involvement—is important if only as part of a consideration of alternative sources of gratification available. In terms of influence upon a homosexual career, involvement very likely plays a constraining role during the acting-out phase associated with coming out, as well as serving as a source of alternative investment during the "crisis of aging." The second bears directly upon the issue of the consequences of having one's deviant commitment exposed. For some occupational roles disclosure would clearly be a disaster—the schoolteacher, the minister, the politician, to mention just three. There are other occupations where the disclosure or assumption of homosexual interests is either of little consequence or—though a relatively few—where it has a positive consequence. It should be evident that the crucial question of anxiety and depersonalization in the conduct of sexual activity can be linked to this variable in a rather direct way.

A second series of questions could deal with the effects of a deviant sexual commitment upon occupational activity itself. In some cases the effect may be extremely negative as pursuit of homosexual goals may generate irresponsibility and irregularity. Some part of this might flow from what we associate with bachelorhood generally: detachment from social structure and, on the sexual level, constant striving for what is essentially regularized in marriage. More simply stated this would be: too many late nights out, too much drinking in too many taverns, and unevenness in emotional condition. On the other hand, several positive effects can be observed. Detachment from the demands of domestic life not only frees one for greater dedication to the pursuit of sexual goals, but also for greater dedication to work. Also, the ability of some jobs to facilitate homosexual activity—such as certain marginal, low-paying white-collar jobs—serves as compensation for low pay or limited opportunity for advancement. There may be few simple or consistent patterns emerging from this type of consideration, yet the overdetermination of the sexual in the study of the homosexual rests in our prior reluctance to consider these questions which are both complex and pedestrian.

Similarly, just as most homosexuals have to earn a living, so must they come to terms with their immediate families. There is no substantial evidence to suggest that the proportion of homosexuals for whom relatives are significant persons differs from that of heterosexuals. The important differences rest in the way the relationships are managed and, again, the consequences they have for other aspects of life. Here also, one could expect considerable variation containing patterns of rejection, continuing involvement without knowledge, ritualistically suppressed knowledge, and knowledge and acceptance. This becomes more complex as several of the patterns may be operative at the same time with different members of one's family constellation. Here again it is not unreasonable to assume a considerable degree of variation in the course of managing a homosexual commitment as this kind of factor varies. Yet the literature is almost totally without reference to these relationships. Curiously, in the psychiatric literature

—where mother and father play crucial roles in the formation of a homosexual commitment—they tend to be significant by their absence in considerations of how homosexual lives are lived.

This order of discussion could be extended into a large number of areas. Let us consider just one more: religion. As a variable, religion (as both an identification and a quality of religiousness) manifests no indication that it plays an important role in the generation of homosexual commitments. Clearly, it does or can play a significant role in the management of that commitment. Here, as in other spheres of life, we must be prepared to deal with complex, interactive relations rather than fixed, static ones. Crucial to the homosexual's ability to "accept himself" is his ability to bring his own homosexuality within a sense of the moral order as it is projected by the institutions surrounding him as well as his own vision of this order. It may be that the question of bringing homosexuality within a religious definition is the way the question should be framed only part of the time, and for only part of a homosexual population. At other times—for other homosexuals—to frame the question in terms of bringing religiousness within the homosexual definition might be more appropriate. The need for damnation—that rare sense of being genuinely evil—and the need for redemption—a sense of potentially being returned to the community in good standing—can be expected to vary given different stages of the life cycle, given different styles of being homosexual, given varying environments within which the homosexual commitment is to be enacted. And our sense of the relation suggests that more than asking of the homosexual's religious production, how it expresses his homosexuality, we must also learn to ask how his homosexuality expresses his commitment to the religious.

The aims, then, of a sociological approach to homosexuality are to begin to define the factors—both individual and situational—that predispose a homosexual to follow one homosexual path as against others; to spell out the contingencies which will shape the career that has been embarked upon; to trace out the patterns of living in their pedestrian aspects as well as those which are seemingly exotic. Only then will we begin to understand the homosexual, and this pursuit must inevitably bring us—though from a particular angle—to those complex matrices wherein most human behavior is fashioned.

The Poor: Aliens in an Affluent Society: Cross-Cultural Communication

Jack Daniel

Introduction

> Give me your tired, your poor
> Your huddled masses yearning to breathe free,
> The wretched refuse of your teeming shore,
> Send these, the homeless, tempest-tossed, to me:
> I lift my lamp beside the golden door.

Emma Lazarus 1849–1887

In commemoration of the one hundredth year of American independence, the Statue of Liberty was placed in New York harbor bearing the above inscription. America received its share of the poor but in 1965 Michael Harrington saw fit to write that the poor are internal aliens in an affluent society. This paper is concerned with revealing some possible communication breakdowns resulting from the poor being aliens in an affluent society.

The General Problem of Cross-Cultural Communication

Within a given culture, even within the so-called primitive cultures, communication is a highly complex process. From culture to culture, the symbols differ, the channels differ, and messages are encoded and decoded in different fashions. When messages are sent across cultural boundaries, they may be encoded in one context and decoded in another. Wilbur Schramm has described the problem in the following diagram:(1)

Field of Experience   Field of Experience

                              Signal

Source Encoder   Decoder Destination

Schramm states that the source and the receiver are not "in tune" when they have different "fields of experience":

> Think of those circles as the accumulated experiences of the two individuals trying to communicate. The source can encode, and the destination can decode, only in terms of the experience each has had. If we have never learned Russian, we can neither code nor decode in that language. If an African tribesman has never seen or heard

From *Today's Speech,* Vol. 18 (Winter 1970), pp. 15–21. Reprinted by permission of the author and publisher. Professor Daniel is affiliated with the Black Studies Program at the University of Pittsburgh.

of an airplane, he can only decode the sight of a plane in terms of whatever experience he has had. The plane may seem to him to be a bird, and the aviator a god borne on wings. If the circles have a large area in common, then communication is easy. If the circles do not meet, if there has been no common experience, then communication is impossible. If the circles have only a small area in common, that is, if the experiences of the source and destination have been strikingly unlike, then it is going to be very difficult to get an intended meaning across from one to the other.(2)

Edward T. Hall and William Foot Whyte provide us with an example of cross-cultural communication in their description of North American-Latin American communication difficulties:

In North America, the "proper" distance to stand when talking to another adult male you do not know well is about two feet, at least in formal business conversation. (Naturally at a cocktail party, the distance shrinks, but anything under eight to ten inches is likely to provoke an apology or an attempt to back up).

To a Latin American, with his cultural traditions and habits, a distance of two feet seems to him approximately what five feet would to us. To him, we seem distant and cold. To us, he gives an impression of pushiness.

. . . We once observed a conversation between a Latin and a North American which began at one end of a forty-foot hall. At intervals we noticed them again, finally at the other end of the hall. This rather amusing displacement had been accomplished by an almost continual series of small backward steps on the part of the American, trying unconsciously to reach a comfortable talking distance, and an equal closing of the gap by the Latin American as he attempted to reach his accustomed conversation space.(3)

Communication between Professional and Poor People as a Problem in Cross-Cultural Communication

Concern for the problem of communication between professionals and the poor as a problem in cross-cultural communication manifests itself in the many community action programs which make use of "indigenous nonprofessionals."

In describing the indigenous non-professionals and discussing their usefulness, Riessman said:

The indigenous non-professional *is* poor, *is* from the neighborhood, *is* often a member of a minority group. His family *is* poor; *he* is a peer of the client and shares a common background, language, ethnic origin, style and group of interests which it would be impossible and perhaps even undesirable for most professionals to maintain.(4)

Edgar S. and Jean C. Cahn, writing in *The Yale Law Journal,* proposed the establishment of a neighborhood law firm in poor communities and expressed concern about the potential communication problems that might exist between the lawyer and the poor people in the community.(5)

Besides access to grievance, such an institution must be able to establish rapport and communication. Here, the middle class status of professional persons often constitutes an impediment to the development of confidence and identification. This problem has been dealt with by various kinds of outreaching social work carried on by the community organizer, detached worker and gang or street worker.(6)

It is held here that middle-class oriented professionals and poor people in the United States have such divergent fields of experience that communication between them is in fact a case of cross-cultural communication.

Oscar Lewis' study of poverty has focused primarily on families in Mexico, and recently Puerto Rican families in New York City. His methods consisted of anthropological-psychological field work with much of his time spent living with poor families.(7) According to Lewis:

> The culture of poverty is not just a matter of deprivation of disorganization, a term signifying the absence of something. It is a culture in the traditional sense in that it provides human beings with a design for living, with a ready-made set of solutions for human problems, and so serves a significant adaptive function. This style of life transcends national boundaries and *regional* and rural-urban differences within nations. Wherever it occurs, its practitioners exhibit remarkable similarity in the structure of their families, in interpersonal relations and in their orientation in time.(8)

In further describing the culture of poverty, Lewis offers the following information:

> The people do not belong to labor unions or political parties and make little use of banks, hospitals, department stores or museums. . . .
>
> People in a culture of poverty produce little wealth and receive little in return. Chronic unemployment, low wages, lack of property, lack of savings, absence of food reserves in the home, and the chronic shortages of cash imprison the family and the individual in a vicious circle. . . . Along with disengagement from the larger society, there is hostility to the basic institutions of what are regarded as the dominant classes. There is hatred of the police, mistrust of government and of those in high positions and a cynicism that extends to the church. . . . Yet on the whole it is a comparatively superficial culture. There is in it much pathos, suffering and emptiness. It does not provide much support or satisfaction; its pervading mistrust magnifies individual helplessness and isolation. Indeed, the poverty of the culture is one of the crucial traits of the culture of poverty.(9)

In addition to Oscar Lewis, other writers such as Ben H. Bagdikian(10) and Michael Harrington(11) are inclined to speak of the culture of poverty writes of the poor among the American Indian and Negro, and the poor city dwellers, while Harrington's focus is primarily on the poor in New York. From his many interviews with poor individuals, Bagdikian presents the following example of an estrangement between the two cultures:

> Middle-class assumptions of common sense and social responsibility often make no sense to the poor. What is prudent for the well-fed may be irresponsible for the poor. For most Americans there is something contemptible in the outlook of the impoverished: don't put off until tomorrow any gratification that can be achieved today. For the poor these rules are tried and true. For the poor the future is demonstrably treacherous.(12)

From his analytic description of the poor in New York, Michael Harrington concludes that poverty forms a culture. After vividly describing the poor intellectuals, the poor in the Bowery, and the poor in areas such as Albany and New York, Harrington states:

> Perhaps the most important analytic point to have emerged in this description of the other America is the fact that poverty in America forms a culture, a way of life and feeling, that it makes a whole. . . . Then, poverty is a culture in the sense that the mechanism of impoverishment is fundamentally the same in every part of the system. The vicious circle is a basic pattern. It takes different forms for the unskilled workers, for the aged, for the Negroes, for the agricultural workers, but in each case the principle is the same. There are people in the affluent society who are poor because they are poor; and who stay poor because they are poor.(13)

Advocates of the concept of the culture of poverty often will refer to divergent attitudes between the poor people and other parts of the dominant society. An example of this is a study by Ralph Segalman. The summary of the study done by Ralph Segalman appears in Figure 1. Segalman's data come from interviewing students at Texas Western College.

Consider Walter B. Miller's discussion of the differences in focal concerns.

> The dominant concern over "trouble" involves a distinction of critical importance for the lower class community—that between "law-abiding" and "non-law-abiding" behavior. There is a high degree of sensitivity as to where each person stands in relation to these two classes of activity. Whereas in the middle-class community a major dimension for evaluating a person's status is "achievement" and its external symbols, in the lower class, personal status is very frequently gauged along the law-abiding-non-law-abiding dimension. A mother will evaluate the suitability of her daughter's boyfriend less on the basis of his achievement potential than on the basis of his innate "trouble" potential.

It is being maintained here that the middle-class oriented professional and the poor person are sufficiently different that they can be thought of as representing diverging cultural backgrounds. Consider some of the communication problems of a middle-class oriented professional speaking to a group of sixth grade Negro youngsters who are attending an "inner city" school in Detroit, Michigan on the topic of good eating habits. If the professional speaks of the vitamins that one can get from cauliflower, eggplant, and broccoli, then there will probably be problems in communication stemming from the fact that "in their culture" the Negro youngsters eat mustard greens, collard greens, and occasionally turnips, kale, and spinach.

Some of the differences between middle-class oriented professionals and the poor, and the resultant communication difficulties might be illustrated by a few statements from a poor but highly verbal individual:

> They keep on telling us, those welfare ladies, to take better care of our money, and save it away, and buy what's the best in the stores, and do like them for dresses, and keep the children in school, and keep our husbands from leaving us. There isn't nothing they don't have a sermon on. They'll tell you it's bad to spend your money on a smoke or a drink; and it's bad to have your kids sleep alongside you in the bed

and you're not supposed to want television because you should be serious with your dollar, and it's wrong for kids, too; and it's bad for you to let them stay out after dark, and they should study their lessons hard and they'll get away ahead and up there.

Well, I'll tell you, they sure don't know what it's about, and they can't know if they come knocking on my door every week until the Lord takes all of us. They have their nice leather shoes, and their smart coats, and they speak the right order of words all right, so I know how many schools they been to. But us? Do they have any idea of what us is about? And let them start at zero the way we do, and see how many big numbers they can become themselves. I mean, if you have got nothing when you're born, and you know you can't get a thing no matter how you tries—well, then you dies with nothing. And no one can deny that arithmetic.

They just don't understand what it's like. You are born in a building where it's cold, and the rats keep you company all day and you are lucky if they don't eat you at night, because they're as hungry as you.

Figure 1. The Cultural Chasm (14)

The concept of	*in middle-class terms stands for*	*but in the lower class is*
Authority (courts, police, school principle)	Security—to be taken for granted, wooed	Something hated, to be avoided
Education	The road to better things for one's children and oneself	An obstacle course to be surmounted until the children can go to work
Joining a Church	A step necessary for social acceptance	An emotional release
Ideal Goal	Money, property, to be accepted by the successful	"Coolness": to "make" out without attracting attention of the authorities
Society	The pattern one conforms to in the interests of security and being "popular"	"The Man," an enemy to be resisted and suspected
Delinquency	An evil originating outside the middle-class home	One of life's inevitable events, to be ignored unless the police get into the act
The Future	A rosy horizon	Nonexistent, so live each moment fully
The Street	A path for the auto	A meeting place, an escape from a crowded home
Liquor	Sociability, cocktail parties	A means to welcome oblivion
Violence	The last resort of authorities for protecting the lawabiding	A tool for living and getting on
Sex	An adventure and binding force for the family—creating problems of birth control	One of life's few free pleasures
Money	A resource to be cautiously spent and saved for the future	Something to be used now before it disappears

Then the food, it's not always around when you want it, and you don't have money to buy what you do want. Then you go to those schools, and the teachers, they looks down on you, and makes you think you have done something wrong for being born. They shout and make faces, and they treat you like dirt and then tell you to be a doctor or a lawyer; if you just go to the library and stay in school and be neat, that's all it takes. Once in a while lately they want to take you on a trip crosstown, and show you a museum or something. They tell you that you haven't got any pictures at home. So there, take a look and now you own them, and man, you're rich.(15)

If as Oscar Lewis states slum children have usually adopted the attitudes and values of their culture by the time that they are six or seven years old, then one might expect to see cross-cultural communication problems between teacher and students in slum schools. If marked cultural differences exist, then the teachers' methods should be altered from those which are used in middle-class schools. The popular usage of the term "culturally deprived child" partially attests to the fact that such differences in culture do exist between the children who live in poverty and those who are brought up in middle-class homes.

Frank Riessman has defined "culturally deprived" as "those aspects of middle-class culture—such as education, books, formal language—from which these groups have not benefited."(16) By "these groups," Riessman refers to lower socioeconomic groups of people. In discussing the value of an understanding by the teacher of the culture of the underprivileged, Riessman states:

> A sound cultural understanding should enable the teacher to establish a much better relationship with the deprived child who is typically antagonistic toward the school and, on the surface at least, unmotivated to learn. Through an emphatic understanding of his culture, the teacher will begin to see why the deprived child is hostile, what he expects of her, why he wants her to prove herself. The teacher will come to learn why he needs a structured classroom, how she can utilize his in-group loyalty, informality, equalitarianism, humor, and the like. She will come to understand why he does not need love but respect.(17)

Through an understanding of the deprived child's culture, the teacher would not automatically begin to lecture to the child about "delinquency" and his moral character after he has several "unexcused" absences. The child might not have been in school because he has to share one bed with four other brothers and sisters and thereby is not able to sleep in the hot, stuffy, odorous apartment at night. He might not have been in school because his peer group exerts a powerful influence over him, and ascribes status to those who play "hooky." He might have been absent because he found himself in an institution that emphasizes feminine characteristics whereas his culture emphasizes masculinity. As Riessman explains, "Conformity, dependence, neatness, nonaggression—major values in a female school—are not consistent with the masculine stress on vigor and independence."(18). Through an understanding of the deprived child's culture, the teacher could foresee the failure of approaches that emphasized permissiveness and unstructured activity, since the deprived child's culture emphasizes values such as authority, structure, rules, and discipline.

Often teachers of deprived children at the high school level express confusion when they offer to help a student with some problem that exists outside the classroom. I knew a white middle-class teacher who sought employment in one of Pittsburgh's worst slum communities. The teacher desired such a placement because she wanted to "help the children beyond the normal responsibilities of the teacher." However, once she had secured such a position, most of her offers to help were rejected by the students. Had this teacher obtained more information about the attitudes and values of poor people, she would have realized that some poor people have so many needs that haven't been fulfilled for such a long period of time that walking up to them and saying "I've come to help you" is like trying to walk up to a wild lion and petting him. As soon as the offer is made to help, the poor person might become suspicious and begin to look for the "catch."

It is admitted here that the "culture of poverty" is not firmly established as a scientifically useful concept. However, regardless of the term that is used, i.e., *class* or *cultural* differences, *culture* versus *subculture,* etc., significant differences do exist between the "fields of experience" of poor and middle-class people in the United States and elsewhere. That *differences* exist is the major concern of this paper. It is further maintained that these differences, unless taken into consideration, can lead to communication breakdowns between poor and middle-class professionals in America.

As part of communication strategy, the would-be communicator might engage in an audience analysis to determine what channels are being used by his intended audience. If poor people and middle-class people have divergent fields of experience, then one might expect to find differences in channel usage. Researchers in mass communications have found differences in channel usage as a function of social class in America. In the first volume of the "Yankee City Series," Lloyd Warner and Paul S. Lunt described newspaper and magazine subscriptions, motion picture attendance, and book reading according to social class.(19)

Warner and Lunt reported that: (1) There was a high correlation between social class and magazine preference. For example, the *National Geographic* was read mostly by the two upper classes whereas the lower-lower class did not read it at all. (2) There was a definite class bias with regard to the selection of newspapers. Once again, lower classes did not subscribe to the newspapers selected by the upper classes and vice-versa. Warner and Lunt gave similar reports on book reading and movie attendance. In the Hill District of Pittsburgh a brief audience analysis would indicate that if radio is used as the channel for communicating with blacks then one should use radio stations WAMO and WZUM, not just WRYT and KQV. The Hill District is made up of at least 90% Negroes and is considered to be the worst poverty area in Pittsburgh. WAMO and WZUM feature Negro disc jockeys and pop and jazz music whereas WRYT is more of the "silent hour" type and KQV features white disc jockeys playing the "Rolling Stones," and "The Beatles."

In *Social Class In America,* W. Lloyd Warner gives the following account of the soap opera:

The soap opera is a product of contemporary radio. The average upper-middle class radio listener has little interest in soap opera; in fact, most of this group are actively hostile to these curious little dramas that fill the daytime air works. Yet millions and millions of American women listen daily to their favorite soap operas, and advertisers of certain commodities have found them invaluable in selling their products.

Research has shown that the soap opera appeals particularly to the level of the common man. (The common man level is headed by the lower-middle class). The problems raised in these folk dramas, their characters, their plot and values have a strong positive appeal to women of this class level whereas they have little appeal to women above the common man level.(20)

Just as Warner suggests that the soap opera is of little interest to the average upper-middle class radio listener, here it is hypothesized that poor, Negro, six year old Jack's and Jerri's have little or no interest in reading about white, six year old Dick's and Jane's, their Puff's and Spot's and the rest of their middle-class culture. This may contribute to Jack and Jerri becoming "slow readers" who lack motivation.

Margherita MacDonald, Carson McGuire and Robert J. Havighurst investigated the hypothesis that "Children of different social classes will belong to different clubs, form different after school play habits and vary in the movies they attend, the books they read, and the amount of time they spend with their families."(21) They reported that whereas upper-middle and lower-middle class children attend Boy and Girl Scouts, the upper-lower and lower-lower attended neighborhood clubs which were operated by social agencies for serving children who need recreational facilities. Likewise, it was found that the upper class children were more restricted in movie attendance, and that different kinds and numbers of books were read according to the social class of the children.

Lazarsfeld and Kendall(22) focused on variables such as newspaper and magazine reading, movie going, and radio listening of the average American. Again, class distinctions were found. Wilbur Schramm and David M. Whyte(23) found that comic reading declined with higher economic status.(24)

The above studies deal with mass communications in terms of listening and reading habits according to socio-economic status. It is the opinion of this investigator that the communication problems that exist between poor and professional people consist of more than differences in listening and reading habits but also differences in non-verbal forms of communication. In describing the non-verbal aspects of communication, Edward T. Hall says:

Those of us who keep our eyes open can read volumes into what we see going on around us. The citizens of a typical American farming community, for example, do not have to be told why old Mr. Jones is going to town. They know that every other Thursday he makes a trip to the druggist to get his wife a bottle of tonic and that after that he goes around to the feed store, visits with Charley, drops in to call on the sheriff, and then goes home in time for the noonday meal. Jones, in turn, can also tell whenever anything is bothering one of his friends, and the chances are that he will be able to figure out precisely what it is. He feels comfortable in his way of life because most of the time he "knows what the score is." He doesn't have to say very much to get his point across: a nod of the head or a grunt as he leaves the store is sufficient. People take him as he is. On the other hand, strangers disturb him, not because their mannerisms are different, but because he knows so little about them. When Jones meets a stranger, communication, which is normally as natural as breathing, suddenly becomes difficult and overly complex.(25)

Because of their cultural differences, the professional and the poor person might experience tremendous difficulties in communicating. When a professional makes a poor person wait for six hours in order to obtain a food order for hungry children, when a professional fiddles with papers on his desk while the poor person is talking to him, when the professional works in the poor neighborhood but lives in the suburbs, and when the professional comes to the poor person's home wearing a facial expression of fear and disgust, non-verbal messages are received by the poor person. Moreover, the translation of these messages, by the poor person, may lead to a break in the communication relationship between the poor and the professional person. When a poor person calls in for an emergency appointment but is one half hour late for the appointment, when a poor person claims that his relief check is insufficient yet he takes part of his check and plays the numbers, and when a poor Negro teen-ager walks into the employment office with his hair processed or natural, again non-verbal messages are received. Once again, depending upon how the professional translates these messages, there may be breaks in the communication relationship.

Summary and Conclusion

The more the overlap in life experiences, the easier it is for two individuals to communicate on an interpersonal basis. Conversely, as the respective source's and receiver's fields of experience have less in common, it becomes more and more difficult for the two individuals to have effective interpersonal communication. In the United States, the middle-class oriented professional and the poor person represent divergent fields of experience, and hence communication between them is very difficult. In one set of experiences one has three balanced meals per day and in the other one is lucky to get one daily plate of beans and a piece of bread. One has individual beds while the other has to share a single bed with a brother and a sister. One person goes in for regular dental and medical check-ups whereas the other views a doctor's bill as missed meals, two more months before you obtain a cheap, new pair of shoes, and one more month behind on the gas bill. The communication difficulties between professional and poor people are increased even more when two different ethnic groups are involved, i.e., Black-White, White-Puerto Rican, Chinese or Black. An essential step to overcoming these barriers will obviously involve people seeking understandings of the divergent cultures in America. On the college campuses this understanding can be enhanced by Black and other ethnic studies.

Notes

(1) Wilbur Schramm, *The Process and Effects of Mass Communication* (Urbana, Illinois, 1955), p. 6.

(2) *Ibid.*

(3) Edward T. Hall and William Foote Whyte, "Intercultural Communication: A Guide to Men of Action," *Human Organization,* XVIV (1960), pp. 9–10.

(4) Frank Riessman, "The Indigenous Nonprofessional—A Strategy of Change for Community Mental Health Programs," Report No. 3, National Institute of Labor, Education, and Mental Health Programs (November, 1964), p. 8.

(5) Edgar S. Cahn and Jean C. Cahn, "The War on Poverty: A Civilian Perspective," *Yale Law Journal* LXXIII (July, 1964), pp. 1334–1335.

(6) *Ibid.*

(7) Oscar Lewis, *Five Families* (New York, 1959).

(8) Oscar Lewis, "Culture of Poverty," *Scientific American* (October, 1966), p. 19.

(9) *Ibid.*

(10) Ben H. Bagdikian, *In the Midst of Plenty: A New Report on the Poor in America* (Baltimore, 1966), p. 49.

(11) Michael Harrington, *The Other America* (Baltimore, 1966). p. 156.

(12) Bagdikian, p. 49.

(13) Harrington, p. 22.

(14) Ralph Segalman, "The Cultural Chasm," *Harper's Magazine* (October, 1965).

(15) Robert Coles, "The Poor Don't Want to be Middle-Class," *Selective Reading Series,* No. 7, California State Department of Welfare (1965), p. 16.

(16) Frank Riessman, *The Culturally Deprived Child* (New York, 1962), pp. 7–8.

(17) *Ibid.*

(18) *Ibid.*

(19) Lloyd W. Warner and Paul S. Lunt, *The Social Life of a Modern Community* (Connecticut, 1941).

(20) Lloyd W. Warner, *Social Class in America* (New York, 1960), p. 31.

(21) Margherita MacDonald, Carson McGuire, and Robert J. Havighurst, "Leisure Activities and the Socioeconomic Status of Children, American Journal of Sociology, LIV (1949), pp. 505–519.

(22) Paul F. Lazarsfeld and Patricia Kendall, *Radio Listening in America* (New York, 1948).

(23) Wilbur Schramm and David M. Whyte, "Age, Education and Economic Status as Factors in Newspaper Reading," reported in *The Process and Effects of Mass Communication* (Urbana, Illinois, 1955), pp. 71–74.

(24) *Ibid.*

(25) Edward T. Hall, *The Silent Language* (Connecticut, 1959), pp. 33–34.

The American Indian: An Overview
Robert L. Faherty

For almost five centuries, the original inhabitants of what is now the United States and those people who have come to call themselves Americans have remained largely strangers. This situation is beginning to change, but years of

From *Current History,* Vol. 67, No. 400 (December 1974), pp. 241–244, 274. Reprinted by permission of Current History, Inc. Robert L. Faherty is the managing editor of the 20-volume *Encyclopedia of Indians of the Americas* and of the *Dictionary of Indians of North America.*

misunderstanding, suspicion, and mistreatment are not easily brushed aside. Misconceptions that have become deeply enrooted are difficult to eradicate.

Perhaps most devastating is the image of the Indian as savage, an image that has influenced the view of white society toward the Indian since the earliest days of contact. Either a nomadic, hostile brute impeding the civilizing process of advancing settlers or a noble, unspoiled child of nature symbolizing freedom for Rousseau and others, the Indian was stereotyped as uncivilized, and mentally, culturally, and religiously inferior to the white. Denied equal status as a person, he could be converted, removed, exploited.

Sometimes early writers stated bluntly that Indians were warlike, crude, lazy, simple, unreliable, or the like; at other times they used words that implied the same moral judgments. When Indians killed whites, it was a "massacre," but whites only "fought" or "battled" Indians. The whites farmed the land, while Indians were depicted essentially as hunters and gatherers. White people are pictured protecting their homes and families from the savage "menace" or "peril." But it is rare to find a description of the Indian defending his life or his homeland against the ever encroaching white. According to the whites, the westward-moving frontier was the manifest destiny of the white culture, and the Indians gave ground inevitably and deservedly to that superior culture.

This conception has colored the official relationship between the United States government and the Indian societies. During his Second Annual Message in December, 1830, President Andrew Jackson justified his signing of the Indian Removal Act some months previously in the following words:

> What good man would prefer a country covered with forests and ranged by a few thousand savages to our extensive Republic, studded with cities, towns, and prosperous farms, embellished with more than twelve million happy people, and filled with all the blessings of liberty, civilization, and religion?[1]

In 1871, Congress terminated the making of treaties with Indian tribes on the theory that it was degrading for Congress to give equal status to nations of primitive people. Government policy—whether it be the allotment policy legislated in 1887, whereby reservation Indians would be granted private property, or the reservation-termination policy of the 1950's, whereby Indians would be relocated to urban centers—has returned time and time again to the idea of civilizing the Indian by assimilating him into white society.

The image of the savage Indian has been subtly reinforced in other ways. Anthropological literature has concentrated almost totally on aspects of Indian life that could be thought of as "aboriginal" or "native." Anthropologists and ethnologists have tended to present not the dynamic, living, changing complex that is the Indian community under study, but only the more traditional elements in that culture. For example, one of the most often described ethnographic events among Indians in the southwestern United States is the Hopi snake dance. From

---

[1]Quoted in Roy Harvey Pearce, *The Savages of America* (Baltimore: Johns Hopkins Press, 1953), p. 57.

a survey of available literature, it would be natural for the casual reader to infer that the snake dance is the most significant event in the lives of the Hopi people. Instead, the focus on the snake dance only reflects the fascination that the handling of live rattlesnakes holds for members of the non-Indian culture.[2]

Popular literature, movies, and television have contributed to the stereotype. Even television documentaries that attempt to present the story of Indian people have inevitably shown little more than the poverty on a few reservations. Although these conditions certainly exist, their exclusive showing tends to label the Indian as someone who is not quite able to survive on his own.

In a recent article, Vine Deloria expressed great concern that at Wounded Knee, South Dakota, in 1972, the Indian activists had resorted to racing around on horseback before the television cameras like warriors of old. Thus the relevant social issues of the protest were lost and the worst suspicions of whites were reinforced at a time when the ancient image of the savage could have been buried once and for all.[3]

A second lingering misconception is that Indians are a vanishing race. This image, which gained prominence at the beginning of the twentieth century, was captured in James E. Fraser's statue of a bent and battered Indian sitting on an equally forlorn horse, both with heads bowed. According to the title of the statue, this was "The End of the Trail." At about the same time, in 1909, Joseph K. Dixon, working with the Bureau of Indian Affairs, arranged "The Last Great Indian Council." It included 21 representative Indian chiefs, scouts, and warriors, and was intended to be a farewell to a people on the verge of extinction.[4]

On the contrary, however, Indians are increasing in greater numbers than any other group in the United States, although the Indian population decreased dramatically by the end of the last century as a result of warfare, removal, disease, and the destruction of the buffalo. During the last decade, the rate of population growth in Indian communities on or near federal trust land averaged about 2.5 percent, although this figure seems to be tapering off.

Furthermore, the cultures of the native Americans have not withered and died through the process of assimilation. Indian cultures are changing, yet traditional values and institutions live on.

A third mistaken notion is that Indians are all alike. They were not alike in the past, and they are not alike today. There is no such creature as *the* American Indian. As Harold E. Fey and D'Arcy McNickle pointed out in their study, *Indians and Other Americans,* "There is no 'Indian language,' no 'Indian reli-

---

[2]See Bernard L. Fontana, "Savage Anthropologists and Unvanishing Indians in the American Southwest." Paper read at the 67th meeting of the American Anthropological Association (unpublished manuscript).

[3]Vine Deloria, Jr., "The American Indian Image," *Encyclopedia of Indians of the Americas,* vol. 1, 1974, p. 41.

[4]See Joseph K. Dixon, *The Vanishing Race: The Last Great Indian Council* (New York: Popular Library, 1972). This book was originally published in 1913.

gion,' no 'Indian character'—even the racial strain was a mixture of several physical types."[5]

At the time of the first contact between Indians and whites, there was far greater linguistic and cultural diversity in the New World than in Europe. The number of distinct languages depends upon the recognition of what constitutes a separate language. Some 200 languages have been claimed for aboriginal California alone. Anthropologists' estimates range from a conservative 200 to between 600 and 800 as the number of languages in use in the area that was to become the United States.

Besides speaking different languages, tribes varied widely in their philosophies, in their social, political, and religious institutions, and in their practices. Indian governments, for example, ranged from a loose grouping of family groups and village communities among California Indians to the complex Iroquois Confederation of highly organized tribes. The mode of obtaining food or of building homes, of raising children or of burying the dead varied notably from tribe to tribe. What is more, there was considerable diversity within most of the tribes.

Though it may take different forms, Indian cultural pluralism continues. Overlaid on the legacy of distinct tribal traditions is, of course, the reservation-urban dichotomy. Many Indians have moved off the reservations to urban areas. Yet even this distinction is not sufficient to explain the highly complex social-cultural character of the Indian people. Reservations are not all the same. On some reservations, per capita income is no more than a few dollars per year; on others, like the vast Navajo reservation, tribal organization, tourism, industry, government aid, utilization of resources, and so on have provided a fair source of income for much of the Indian population. Indians in the cities, though normally poor, show the same variation.

As a further complication, urbanism is moving into some reservations. Peter MacDonald, the tribal chairman, has announced the inauguration of a new Navajo nation, with a capital city that will be centered in a reservation as large as the states of Massachusetts, Vermont, and New Hampshire combined. MacDonald has indicated that the new state will reflect in all its aspects the character of Navajo culture. Other examples could be cited for what might be termed emerging new states and on-reservation urbanism.

The range and character of Indian organizations is another indication of the intricacy of the Indian community. National organizations include the National Congress of American Indians and the National Tribal Chairmen's Association. Such groups as the American Indian Movement, the National Indian Youth Movement, and numerous university student organizations represent the younger and often more activist elements among native Americans. Particular groups are represented by such organizations as the National Indian Physician's Association, the National Indian Education Association, the National Indian Women's

---

[5]Harold E. Fey and D'Arcy McNickle, *Indians and Other Americans* (New York: Harper & Row, 1970), p. 14.

Association, and others. Among the urban Indians, there are some 50 different organizations in the Los Angeles area alone.

A fourth stereotype is the belief that the Indian does not change; he is as unbending in the face of time as he is pictured to be in the face of torture. Indian cultures and societies are examined and understood as they once were, before contact with the white man. Subsequent changes, when they are noted, are attributed not to any internal, creative, adaptive dynamism on the part of the Indian communities but only to a passive acceptance of external relationships with, and influences from, the white culture. The post-contact history of a tribe thus becomes solely the story of Indian response to white stimulus, and there is virtually no account of the recent history of the tribe.[6]

Who and How Many?

Who, then, is the Indian? The answer to the question is both simple and complex. It is simple enough to say that an Indian is an individual who can trace his or her origins to the indigenous peoples of America. But to go beyond this involves consideration of a number of different factors.

Ethnologically, must an individual be a full-blooded Indian, or three-quarters, or half? Culturally, how much of the traditional life style or religion must he maintain? Sociologically, must he live on a reservation or, at the least, be enrolled in an Indian community?

In the legal sense, the question of who is an Indian is most important, because of the distinct rights and obligations of Indian citizens as opposed to non-Indian citizens. For example, an Indian may share in his tribe's land holdings, which may be quite extensive. Yet there is no clear-cut general legal definition of "Indian" in the United States. In each legal case, the question of whether or not an individual is an Indian must be sought in the applicable statutes, administrative decisions, and opinions. As a rule of thumb, however, there are two basic qualifications: (1) that some of the individual's ancestors lived in America before its discovery by the Europeans, and (2) that the individual is accepted as an Indian by the legally constituted Indian community in which he lives.[7]

The legal question actually becomes more social and political than biological. A full-blooded Indian can withdraw from a tribe and thereby, for all legal purposes, cease to be an Indian. On the contrary, an individual with only the most tenuous Indian ancestry can be accepted by the tribe and thus can be legally an Indian. It is interesting to note that a Wyandot tribal roll that was proposed to Congress in the 1930's listed a person with only 1/256 degree of Wyandot blood.[8]

This indicates the importance of two factors operating on a deeply internal, personal level. Does the tribe or community consider the individual to be one of

---

[6]See Robert F. Berkhofer, Jr., "Indian Americans and United States History," *National Council for Social Studies Yearbook,* 1973.

[7]See *Federal Indian Law* (Washington, D.C.: U.S. Government Printing Office, 1958), pp. 4–12. *Federal Indian Law* is a revision and updating through 1956 of the *Handbook of Federal Indian Law* prepared by Felix S. Cohen and first printed in 1940.

[8]*Federal Indian Law,* p. 986n2.

them? Does the individual consider himself to be part of the tribe or community? If an individual has left the reservation or village, how long can he stay away from the ceremonies, festivals, and major moments in the life of his people—that is, how long can he miss his "Indianness"—before either the tribe or the individual decides he no longer belongs? There are some traditionalists who believe that once an individual has left the community—even to take a professional or academic position—he has abandoned his Indianness. This is an extreme attitude, but most groups demand at least periodic contact.

All of this renders perplexing the question of how many Indians there are in the United States. Population estimates vary in accordance with the definition of Indian. Furthermore, accurate demographic figures are extremely difficult to obtain. Some Indians still live in remote areas that are difficult to reach, and many a census taker obtains his information about the numbers, names, and ages of families from a convenient trading post. The fact that an individual Indian may be known under a variety of names is a further hazard.

Bearing these observations in mind, we can note that according to the 1970 census the total number of Indians in the United States was 827,091; they constituted slightly more than 0.4 percent of the country's total population. Unofficial estimates place the Indian population as high as 15 million. It is safe to say that there are several million people in the country who, according to one or another valid definition, are Indians.

Despite the conservative nature of its population figures, the 1970 census provided interesting data. The state with the largest Indian population was Oklahoma, with 97,731 Indians; this was followed by Arizona (95,812), California (91,018), New Mexico (72,788), and Alaska (51,528). These five states account for almost one-half of the Indian population. The state with the highest percentage of Indian population was Alaska—where Indians constitute more than 17 percent of the total population—followed by New Mexico, Arizona, and South Dakota. A total of ten states have an Indian population that is one percent or more of their total population. These statistics show that, though Indians constitute a small minority of the total national population, they are highly concentrated in the Southwest, Oklahoma, the Dakotas, and Alaska. In these regions, the Indians can be a powerful social and political force.

Of the Indians reported in the census, 37 percent live in "Standard Metropolitan Statistical Areas." This metropolitan Indian group, however, is less than one-fourth of one percent (.22) of the total metropolitan population in the United States. The Los Angeles-Long Beach metropolitan area has by far the largest Indian population—numbering almost 25,000—followed in order by Tulsa, Oklahoma City, New York, San Francisco-Oakland, Phoenix, Minneapolis-St. Paul, Seattle-Everett, Chicago, and Tucson. According to these figures, Indians have moved in large numbers to metropolitan areas. The reasons for this shift are largely economic. The Indian is attracted by the idea of finding a job and making more money than he can on the reservation.

There are, however, some indications that a "return to the reservation" movement is also taking place. One Gros Ventre Indian, a recent graduate of the University of California at Berkeley who spent some time with the Indian community on Alcatraz, recently reported that perhaps as many as 80 percent of the Indians that he knew in the San Francisco Bay area were returning to their tribal communities. He himself was returning to work toward the establishment of a tribal museum and culture center on his reservation. According to this young man, many Indians who had moved to the urban area had made a fair living, but they were deciding that the violence, the cost of living, the hassle—in short, the quality of life—in the urban environment were not worth it. Even for those who periodically go to the city for a while, the reservation remains a sanctuary to which they can return, a sacred place where they can be at home with their families. According to him, this is something that neither the white, the black, the Puerto Rican, the chicano, nor any other group in the United States has.

If, indeed, non-Indians have been generally misinformed about the Indian peoples, what are some of the steps that might be taken to correct this situation? The following observations may provide some broad guidelines.

The non-Indian has to recognize that there are fundamental differences between the majority white culture and the cultures of the Indian peoples. Many differences could be cited, but the point should be sufficiently made by briefly examining how the two cultures differ in their conception of time, decision making, and being.

To the white culture, time is a regularized object whose symbol is the clock. Our schools, offices, means of transportation, television, and all our institutions are ordered according to arbitrarily established units. We speak of "saving" time, of "wasting" time, or of "spending" time. We pay people for their time rather than for what they do or how well they do it. Punctuality geared to the clock is a virtue and, in fact, a necessity in our highly industrialized society.

Set off against this is natural time, a fluid continuum that is geared to the rising and setting of the sun and to the changes in seasons. It is this sense of time that most Indians—many of whom have been reared in the essentially rural, non-industrialized environment of the reservation—have internalized. Indians joke among themselves about operating "on Indian time." This means, for example, that a community meeting will start this evening sharp. Whether the meeting starts at seven o'clock, eight o'clock, or nine o'clock, it will be held, and it will continue until everyone who wishes has had his or her say.

This leads into the next area of cultural difference. Within the white culture, decision making is based on a concept of authority that is exercised on a vertical plane. Power is exerted by those above on those below. We recognize that some people are more legitimately in power than others; someone makes decisions—usually after a certain amount of discussion or debate—and issues orders that others then act upon.

Authority in the Indian cultures is of a more horizontal type. The councils of many Indian tribes last for days because of the necessity of reaching unanimity on a decision. Orders are not issued; consensus agreements are reached.

Another cultural difference regards the identification of self and of how one regards self in relation to the world outside. Individuals who have been raised in the white culture have learned to think of themselves in a perpetual state of becoming. They are taught as children to live for the future—to be discontent with what they are and forever to plan to improve. A white American looks forward to being smarter, to having more money, to owning a larger house, to being the first or the most or the best.

In contrast, it makes little sense to ask an Indian child what he wants to be when he grows up. Indian children already are. They are children. They do not have to wait to be. And so it is through life. One is what one is; one is continually in a state of being rather than of becoming. One will become other things, of course, but the important thing is improving oneself as he is now.

Once the non-Indian accepts the fact that there are cultural differences, then he must appreciate the value of cultural pluralism in the United States. We must abandon the older national ideal of assimilation, the "melting pot" into which diverse peoples would be blended to lose their distinctive character. We must accept the idea that the United States is strong precisely because of its diversity; the contributions of each group should be honored, preserved, and enhanced in the enrichment of the whole.

The non-Indian must turn to the Indians themselves for more information about and appreciation of their history and their culture as it was and as it is. For far too long the dispensers of knowledge about the Indian have been the non-Indian explorer, soldier, missionary, government official, or scholar. The Indian has been described in various ways, sometimes not accurately, always from the non-Indian point of view. In most instances the Indian and his community have emerged as static and passive elements in society. The Indian's role in history and the reality of his continuity from the past to the present have been vague at best and often completely lost.

In recent years, several tribes (e.g., Zuni, Southern Ute, Nez Perce, Cheyenne-Arapaho, and Navajo) have begun systematically to gather and publish their own materials about their history, language, literature, music, and other elements of their culture. They have especially asked their old people to record on tape their memories of past years, ancient legends, and important leaders and events.[9]

For professionals in history, anthropology, and other appropriate disciplines, these projects can provide important insights into the past, present, and future of the Indian peoples. There is, however, discussion among these professionals about the merit of the projects because, for the most part, they are being conducted by non-academics. Questions have been raised about the validity of the use of oral history or whether these are "authorized" histories. Regarding oral history, it might be mentioned that Western civilization's grandest records began with oral history: the Iliad, the Odyssey, and the Old Testament attest to this fact. Regarding authorized history, it might be said that previous history written by outside parties about Indian people was unauthorized. This is not to say that

---

[9]See Dave Warren, "Concepts and Significance of Tribal History/Literature Projects." Paper prepared for the Research and Cultural Studies Development Section, Institute of American Indian Arts (Santa Fe, 1973).

every work that is written by an Indian will be a good work or even an accurate work; nonetheless, these projects should be welcomed with an open mind by the academic community.

Towards an Understanding of the Chicano Experience

Arturo Madrid-Barela

Until recently Chicano was a private word, used by people of Mexican ancestry living in the United States, in particular those of lower social and economic circumstances, to refer to themselves, *Soy Chicano,* and to identify each other in an alien and hostile environment, *Es Chicano.* What was a private word with limited use is now a public name used by the mexicanos de acá de este lado, *Somos Chicanos.* Chicano expresses the conflictive historical and cultural experience of a colonized people still politely and euphemistically referred to as Latins, Spanish, Latin Americans, Spanish Americans, Spanish-speaking Americans, Spanish-surnamed Americans, *never* Mexicans, and only recently Mexican Americans.

In the last ten years these hitherto ignored people have increasingly come to the attention of the United States. Recently, on August 31, 1972, the very prestigious periodical, *The New York Review of Books,* published a special supplement on the Chicanos by a distinguished historian of México, John Womack, Jr., of Harvard University. Honored as we may be by the recognition of a great publication and by the selection of a reviewer as knowledgeable about and sympathetic to Chicanos as Professor Womack, the appearance of his article is one more sad reminder of our colonial status and of a continuing colonial mentality even among the most progressive elements of the society. For despite *NYRB*'s liberationist and anti-colonialist sympathies it apparently never occurred to its editors that a Chicano should have written the review article.

John Womack has written a provocative and informative introduction to Chicanos for the readers of the *New York Review of Books,* and since the article has been reprinted in the Mexican journal *Plural,* it is reaching a similar Mexican public as well. Particularly worthy of praise are his comprehensive, eminently readable synopsis of the Chicano experience; his no-nonsense dismissal of the pretentious collections of readings which pass for anthologies of Chicano literature; his hardnosed critique of studies on the Chicano; his welcome puncturing of current Chicano myths; his sensitive treatment of the contributions of César

Reprinted from *Aztlán-Chicano Journal of the Social Sciences and the Arts,* 4: 1 (Spring 1973), 185–193. Aztlán Publications, c/o Chicano Studies Center, UCLA. Arturo Madrid-Barela is currently Director, Graduate Fellowships Program, Educational Testing Service, Berkeley, California.

Chávez and Ernesto Galarza. Unfortunately, despite Professor Womack's wealth and breadth of knowledge, his analysis of the "peculiar character" of Chicano existence is neither clear nor convincing.

As Womack views it, the Chicano minority is only one more "ethnic minority" which like all the others will dissolve into an "ethnic category." The Chicano movement, he says, is likewise "only another ethnic movement," at best providing "for its surviving professional and amateur chiefs their quota of revenge and power in America." To be sure many Mexicans are making it in lower middle-class America and may soon take their place alongside Italian, Polish, and even Greek-"Americans." The Chicano movement, for lack of a revolutionary ideology, may well become just another ethnic movement with more and more caciques selling out for less and less. What is neither clear nor convincing, on the contrary puzzling, deeply troubling, is Dr. Womack's view of Chicano history:

> From the beginning this has been a curious history. Never a melting into an American pot, or an assimilation to an American archetype, or an acculturation to an American civilization, or a preservation within America of a separate culture, it has become an ethnic history—like the histories of the Old Stocks, the Early Immigrants, the New Immigrants, the Blacks, the Indians, the Orientals, the French Canadians, the Puerto Ricans, and the Cubans here, like all American histories. But it remains as different from them as they have been from each other. And after fifty years of study, its peculiar character is still obscure. The reason is fear, of Mexico and America.
>
> In quiet dread of discovering too much pain in Mexico and too much promise in America, regular Americans have treated the "Mexicans," the "Spanish-speaking," the "Spanish-surnamed," and now the "Mexican Americans," as intruders in this country, whom they could always "send back to Mexico."

Surely in the United States of the 1970's it should be clearly recognized that there is a major difference between the histories of Native Americans, Blacks, Asian Americans, Puerto Ricans, and Chicanos on the one hand, and German, French, Irish-Americans, et al., on the other. Robert Blauner has recently described it very clearly as a difference between "colonized" and "immigrant" minorities in American society (In *Racial Oppression in America,* Harper and Row, 1972). Without exception the colonized groups are also the nation's racial groups. The nature of their *original* entrance into society, the types of labor to which they were and in many cases still continue to be restricted, the pervasive racism they experienced (socially, economically, educationally, politically, culturally) and which their descendants and more newly arrived brethren continue to experience makes the histories of the racial minorities *profoundly* different from those of the white immigrants, whether English, Irish, Scandinavian, East European or South European. Like Native Americans, Chicanos are historically a conquered population; like Blacks they have been subjected to dehumanizing bondage; like Asian Americans they have been recruited to labor in the U.S. and restricted when no longer needed; and like all of America's racial minorities they have been victims of racial exclusion, exploitation and violence.

The Chicano experience began not in the days of the mythical Aztlán of the Aztecs, nor in the centuries of the romantic New Spain of the Conquistadores, nor in the first decades of this century when the refugees from México's turmoil doubled, tripled, quadrupled the numbers of mexicanos de acá de este lado, but in the early 19th century when Anglo America began to encroach on the fur-trapping areas, the vast grazing lands, the endless forests, the mineral-laden hills and the fertile river valleys of the Spanish Borderlands. It began with the reports of those advance men of Anglo-American expansion about the population of Spanish-Mexican America, reports which initiated the character assassination and the cultural vilification which marks not only the Chicano experience but that of America's other racial minorities as well. Four aspects of Spanish-Mexican society were of prime interest to them: the distribution of wealth, the class divisions of the society, the religious practices of the population and the racial makeup of the masses.

The economic situation of the ricos, the "Spanish" among the population, was clearly worthy of their admiration and imitation, yet they were shocked by the misery of the mestizo and indian masses. Though moved by the hospitality and overwhelmed by the lifestyle of their rico hosts the puritan in them rankled at what they considered to be a degenerate Southern European aristocratic tradition with outmoded concepts of superiority based on blood and background, a tradition which was in direct conflict with the Anglo American values of individual industriousness and success. The Catholicism of the Spanish-Mexicans brought forth historically remote yet profoundly felt prejudices against a people the calvinistic Anglos considered to be practitioners of Popery. But it was the racial question which most preoccupied and bothered them. Heirs to centuries of the anti-Spanish Black Legend of the English and French Propagandists they viewed the "Spanish" among the population with jaundiced eye, but their hostility toward the inquisitors of the Indies did not translate into sympathy, respect, understanding or comprehension of the mestizo and indian masses. On the contrary, to the pobres, the "Mexicans" of the population, they attributed all the traits which ran counter to what they saw as superior in themselves: insensibility, cruelty, brutality, savagery, guile, falsity, deviousness, stupidity, incompetence, inferiority, backwardness, instability, immorality, cowardice and laziness. Their professed abhorrence of the institution of peonage sprang principally from economic and not moral or humanitarian considerations.

Thomas Jefferson Farnham, who visited California in 1841, dwelt at length on "the indian character of the lower class, the dull suspicious countenance, the small twinkling piercing eye, the laxness and filth of a free brute, using freedom as a mere means of animal enjoyment . . . dancing and vomiting as occasion and inclination appears to require." (*Travels in California and Scenes in the Pacific Ocean,* New York, 1844, pp. 356–357). Alfred Robinson wrote that " . . . the men are generally indolent and addicted to many vices, caring little for the welfare of their children, who like themselves, grow up unworthy members of society." (*Life in California during a residence of Several Years in that Territory,* San Francisco, 1891, pp. 83–84). An anonymous correspondent to the *National Intelligencer* in 1846 informed the Anglo-American world that " . . . the Spanish portion of the inhabitants are a thieving, cowardly, dancing, lewd people, and generally indolent and faithless."

And so when the Spanish-Mexicans of the Borderlands, in the middle of the 19th century, were invaded and conquered, a conquest which was conceptualized in *religious* terms (*Manifest Destiny*), expressed with *religious* sincerity ("We come as friends, to better your condition," said General Stephen B. Kearney to the assembled populace of Santa Fe in 1846), and pursued with *religious* zeal, the Anglo-American population which came down the valleys wild to lay claim to the vast territories their armies had conquered used these attitudes to justify the seizure of their lands, the exploitation of their labor, and the violence to their minds, and bodies, and culture. Reies López Tijerina, the messianic leader of Nuevo México's mercedistas (land grant heirs) would tell his followers a century later:

> They took your land away and gave you powdered milk.
> They took your trees and grazing away from you and
>   gave you Smoky the Bear.
> They took your language away and gave you lies in theirs.
> They took your manhood away and asked you to lie down
>   and be a Good Mexican.
> They told you you were lazy and cowardly and backward,
>   and you believed them . . .

While there were no Warner Brothers cartoons featuring Speedy González, no Walt Disney comic books depicting revolutionary buffoons, no television series starring the Cisco Kid and Pancho, no Madison Avenue commercials plugging Frito Banditos, no slick Hollywood movies projecting ragged, chili-eating, mono-syllabic Mexicans, there were the ubiquitous dime novels and Texas romances which made similar views available to everyone and created the image of the inferior Mexican in the consciousness of Everyman.

If the military phase was quite brief and relatively bloodless the actual occupation was lengthy and intensely violent. Anglo Americans, attracted to California by the discovery of gold, found themselves bested by the native Cali-fornios and Sonoran gambusinos. The small number of Californios (1300) who went to the goldfields extracted more gold in 1848 than the more numerous Anglo Americans, but by 1849 they were back on their ranchos, forcibly driven out of the diggings by the Anglo American miners, who then numbered 80,000. The gambusinos, who taught the neophyte 49ers how to pan, how to locate the veins, and how to mine and process the ore, were run out of the goldfields in 1850. The Sonoran peddlers who undersold their Yankee competitors in California paid a heavy price for their economic abilities. At the opposite end of the Spanish borderlands, Anglo Texas freight interests systematically and forcibly harassed their Mexican competition out of the million dollar trade between San Antonio and Chihuahua, México.

It was the occupation of the land, however, which was most indicative of the conquest. From the Matamoros haciendas near the Gulf of México to the Petaluma ranchos off San Francisco Bay the landholding ricos were forced off their holdings, pushed up against the technicolor canyon walls or run across the sometimes bloody waters of the muddy Rio Grande. Those who survived the armed violence fell victims to the Land Law of 1851, which permitted settlers to stake out claims on land which "to the best of one's knowledge" was unused. Those who resisted the squatters impoverished themselves in the courtrooms and backrooms of the new legal system, confused by judges and commissioners, outmaneuvered by plaintiffs, swindled by lawyers. Those who won the legal battles lost their lands to moneylending, taxmanipulating entrepreneurs who flooded the West after the Civil War. The few survivors, extended token and symbolic political and social recognition, became the models for the "fantasy heritage" of Silver Dons, gay caballeros and Spanish conquistadores created at the turn of the century by publicists for the railroads and land companies and nurtured by Helen Hunt Jackson, Charles Lummis and other romanticizers of the Southwest.

The majority of the conquered, peons on the large estates of the Southwest, continued their peonage under new masters as their old ones were dispossessed: on the winter and summer pastures of Nuevo México and Colorado; on the cattle ranches of Texas and Southern California; in the California goldfields they had so recently fled. But as their skills and expertise as sheepherders, cowboys and miners were appropriated by the new lords of the land, and the violence of Manifest Destiny was visited upon them ("Twenty-one, not counting Mexicans," as Billy the Kid numbered his victims), they were forced to withdraw. Those who did not flee to México huddled together for protection in small communities along the border; others clustered in the Chihuahuas, Zacatecas, Sonoras and other "Mextowns" adjoining the now Anglo-dominated towns of the West to work as cooks, servants and handymen for their new patrones. Still others retreated to the hidden mountain valleys and remote grassy plains of Nuevo México and Colorado to grow their beans and corn and chile and to tend their tiny herds of sheep on the land grants of their fathers' fathers, away from the gun-slinging cowboys, the ruthless Texas Rangers, the land-hungry cattlemen, away from the turbulence of the rapidly expanding gringo world . . . to disappear from sight, away from the hatred and contempt and violence of those who came "to better their condition." They became "forgotten people" as George I. Sánchez would refer to them almost 100 years later, remembered individually or collectively solely when they spoke the only language the United States has ever understood: the violence of Joaquín Murieta, Tiburcio Vásquez, Gregorio Cortez, Sóstenes L'Archeveque, Juan Cortina, Las Gorras Blancas, La Mano Negra.

The mental sets of their new masters, however, were to be passed on from generation to generation of "immigrant Americans," to be applied to all the succeeding generations of mexicanos de acá de este lado whether recent immigrants from México, refugees from Revolutionary or Pre-Revolutionary México, or sons of the sons of the original settlers of the Borderlands. The social, cultural, legal and economic legacy the dispossessed left behind, whether mining technology or mineral law, irrigation techniques or water rights, cattle-herding know-how or cattle-raising institutions, sheep-related skills or agricultural expertise, was to be forgotten, buried under the layers upon layers of myths which gild the Golden West.

But in the late 19th century those who were called unindustrious, unambi-
tious, incompetent, indolent, were once again to be found in the mines, the sheep
pastures and the cattle ranges of occupied México, having migrated once more
north from México to mine quicksilver at New Almadén, coal in Ratón, Gallup,
Madrid, copper at Santa Rita and Clifton, silver at Socorro, Kingston, and Silver
City; to cut cattle on the West Texas Chaparral, on the grasslands of the Llano
Estacado, on the thousand hills of Southern California; to herd sheep in South
Texas, on the eastern plains of Nuevo México, on the mountain pastures of the
Río Arriba; to shear sheep from San Antonio to Santa Paula; to haul freight,
heavy equipment, food and provisions from Guaymas and Sonora to the mines
of southern Nuevo México and Arizona; and finally to lay the tracks of those
railroads which would end the isolation of the Borderlands along those trails their
ancestors had established, from Santa Fe to Santa Clara, from El Paso to El
Cajón, from San Antonio to San Francisco.

And in the early decades of the 20th century, when their immigrant counterparts were organizing in the factories and foundries, Mexicans were passing from
small-scale peonage to large scale bondage at the hands of enganchistas who
sought them out in the small villages on both sides of the border and parcelled
them out to till the fields, gather the crops, work the mines and maintain the
railways of western America, which still attributes its economic development to
Anglo American ingenuity, superiority, and hard work. Rounded up in small
villages on both sides of the border and herded to ever larger railway centers,
Mexicanos were then bunched into boxcars and dispatched to man the section
crews and extra gangs of the Southern Pacific and Santa Fe, formerly the job of
the despised Chinese; to pick the cattle-displacing cotton of middle and west
Texas, a task abandoned by northward-moving Blacks; to do the risky, dirty
digging in the Gila Hills of southern Arizona, a job disdained by Anglo miners;
to harvest the crops of the Great Western Sugar Beet Co., which preferred them
to those immigrants permitted upward mobility, to develop the empires of California's agri-businessmen, ultimately to replace the Filipinos, who had before
replaced the Japanese, who previously had replaced the Chinese, all of whom had
become less manageable and therefore less desirable. For whatever expansionist
America may have thought of Mexicans, capitalist America needed their labor
and their skills; used them to depress the wages and suppress the organizational
efforts of the nation's other exploited minorities; and promoted the propaganda
of racial and cultural inferiority to justify their inferior wages, their miserable
working conditions and their wretched existence.

As Mexicans moved north along the tracks and into the slaughterhouses of
Kansas City and Chicago, into the iron and autoworks of Gary and Detroit, into
the packing plants of Minneapolis and Milwaukee, and into the steel mills of
Bethlehem and Lorain to replenish the war-depleted labor force in the 1920's, the
mexicanos de acá de este lado again became the objects of contempt, hatred, and
violence, this time around for Poles, Slavs, Hungarians, Czechs, Greeks and
Italians. For America's white immigrants, northern European or southern European, aristocrat or peasant, bourgeois or proletariat, rich or poor, successively

adopted the myth of "America for white Americans" and used it to push their own economic, political and social incorporation. And as America's industrialists started to use Mexicans to break strikes and lower the wages of their labor force, Mexicans found out they had to battle not only their white capitalist bosses but their white capitalist fellow workers as well.

In the 1930's, like other racial minorities, the mexicanos de acá de este lado were the first to feel the effects of the Depression, but unlike their colonized brothers they were shipped back to México, 500,000 of them, men, women, children, recent immigrants, long-time residents, native born, because those who had profitted from their labor were not disposed to provide for their welfare. The Mexicans were to return again, in the 1940's, as U.S. Government sponsored braceros to labor in the factories, in the fields of profit-hungry agri-businessmen, until the 1950's when once again people began to outnumber available jobs and the deportation squads of the U.S. Immigration Service again sent Mexicans packing to México (in smaller numbers yes, yet no less traumatically). To judge by the search and deport missions being carried out in the barrios and colonias of the U.S. at this very moment, the pattern is holding in the 1970's, for as John Womack has correctly stated, 'regular Americans' have always treated 'Mexicans' as expendable, to be returned to country of origin when no longer needed or no longer exploitable. The immigrant experience of incorporation into America by the second generation is not part of the experience of the great mass of Chicanos or other racial minorities. Instead the xenophobia and racism basic to this country have been visited upon the second, third, fourth, and fifth generations of colonized minorities and upon their recently immigrated brothers and sisters.

What makes Chicano history different from the histories of other immigrants is not "fear," as Professor Womack would have it, but a racist colonial experience which continues to this day. What gives the Chicano experience its "peculiar character," what makes Chicano history different from the histories of other racial minorities is the proximity of México and the never-ending pool of Chicanos its masses represent. The lengthy and arbitrary border which separates occupied México from neo-colonial México has never been an obstacle to the "merchants of labor." Mexicans—braceros or "green carders" if they have the U.S. seal of approval, "wetbacks" or "illegals" if they don't—have always been available to depress the wages and suppress the organizational efforts of their Chicano brothers and sisters, whether in the Mexican food packing plant of Romana Bañuelos, the western-clothing factory of Willie Farah, or the lettuce fields of Bud Antle.

The peonage of the past continues into the present. Chicanos continue to be concentrated, the colonial elite notwithstanding, in the most exploitive of Southwest enterprises: the agricultural, assembly, garment, service and food-packaging industries. Today, because of the American-owned industries and assembly plants which have sprung up along the border from Matamoros to Tijuana it no longer depends on which side of the border one is exploited to be Chicano. As the sensitive Mexican caricaturist, Rius, in an issue of his political comic book, *Los Agachados,* has said to all Mexicans: ¿Cuándo nos vamos a dar cuenta de que todos somos Chicanos?

Suggested Readings

Bahr, H. M., *Skid Row: An Introduction to Disaffiliation* (New York: Oxford University Press, 1973). The book deals with homeless skid row dwellers as a subculture. Bahr presents a detailed profile of the skid row individual. He also looks at the social organizations, both formal and informal, that are found on skid row.

Deloria, V., Jr., "Religion and the Modern American Indian," *Current History* (December 1974), pp. 250–253. This article discusses the problems that modern American Indians have in relating to the white majority culture because of the vast differences in spiritual orientation. Deloria suggests that Indians understand their conflict with the rest of society as a religious confrontation.

Goody, J. (ed.), *The Character of Kinship* (London: Cambridge University Press, 1973). This excellent collection deals with a number of cultural factors that are important in understanding the role of past experiences on communication. Issues such as kinship and family are explored. The essays in this book cover a wide range of cultures.

Hess, B., "Stereotypes of the Aged," *Journal of Communication*, 24 (Autumn 1974), 76–85. To better understand the myth and the reality of being old, Hess has reviewed the stereotypes of the aged and compared them to the real world. The factors that contribute to the stereotypes are also explained.

Hraba, J., and J. Siegman, "Black Consciousness," *Youth and Society*, 6 (September 1974), 63–90. The authors discuss the concept of black consciousness in light of recent black militancy. They argue that this militancy can be understood as an instance of consciousness formation.

Lebra, T. S., and W. P. Lebra (eds.), *Japanese Culture and Behavior: Selected Readings* (Honolulu: University Press of Hawaii, 1974). The editors of this volume have put together an outstanding collection of essays that offer insight into the experience of being Japanese. In four interrelated sections they treat concepts such as values and beliefs, patterns of interaction, socialization, and cultural stress.

Madsen, M., and K. Spencer, "Mother-Directed Achievement of Children in Two Cultures," *Journal of Cross-Cultural Psychology*, 4 (June 1973), 221–228. By comparing Mexican and Anglo child-rearing procedures the authors draw some conclusions regarding the impact and influence of cultural experiences on achievement.

Simmer, E., *Pain and Promise: The Chicano Today* (New York: Mentor Books, 1972). This book traces the history of the Mexican-American for the last 100 years. Through this historical review we can see what the Chicano of the 1970s is like and understand the roots of his behavior.

Tannenbaum, A. S., et al., *Hierarchy in Organizations: An International Comparison* (San Francisco: Jossey-Bass, 1974). This book reviews the effects of hierarchy on various organizations representing five different cultures. It is primarily concerned with breakdowns in communication, lack of motivation, jealousy, and resentment.

Warner, R. S., D. T. Wellman, and L. J. Weitzman, "The Hero, the Sambo and the Operator: Three Characterizations of the Oppressed," *Urban Life and Culture*, 2 (April 1973), pp. 53–84. The authors describe three characterizations of oppressed people—the poor, blacks, and women. These characteristics are described for their uniqueness and related to the appropriate oppressed group as ways in which these people have learned to cope with the majority society.

Westerman, J., "The Urban Indian," *Current History* (December 1974), pp. 259–262, 275. In this article Westerman describes the plight of the American Indians as they move into urban culture. She describes the problems of adjustment and retention of Indian culture in an urban society.

Witherspoon, G., "The Central Concepts of Navajo World View (I)," *Linguistics* (January 1, 1974), pp. 41–59. This article takes an anthropological approach to the Navajo experience. Four general categories of world view—universal categories, intuition, symbolic analysis, and ethnoscience—are discussed and applied to the Navajo.

Additional Readings

Bardwick, J., *The Psychology of Women* (New York: Harper & Row, 1970).

Bergman, P. N., *The Negro in America* (New York: Harper & Row, 1969).

Cahn, E. S. (ed.), *Our Brother's Keeper: The Indian in White America* (New York: World Publishing Company, 1969).

Chiu, Lian-Hwang, "A Cross-Cultural Comparison of Cognitive Styles in Chinese and American Children," *International Journal of Psychology,* 7 (1972), 235–242.

Curtis, J. C., and L. L. Gould, *The Black Experience in America* (Austin: University of Texas Press, 1970).

Freedman, M., *Homosexuality and Psychological Functioning* (Monterey, Calif.: Brooks/-Cole, 1971).

Gardiner, H. W., U. P. Singh, and D. E. D'Orazio, "The Liberated Woman in Three Cultures: Marital-Role Preferences in Thailand, India, and the United States," *Human Organization,* 33 (Winter 1974), 413–414.

Gaster, T. H., *Customs and Folkways of Jewish Life* (New York: W. Sloane, 1966).

Gault, U., and A. M. Wang, "Cultural Variations in British and Australian Personality Differentials," *British Journal of Social and Clinical Psychology,* 13 (1974), 37–40.

Giallombardo, R., *The Social World of Imprisoned Girls: A Comparative Study of Institutions for Juvenile Delinquents* (New York: John Wiley & Sons, 1974).

Goldstein, R. L., *Black Life and Culture in the U.S.* (New York: Thomas Y. Crowell, 1971).

Gomez, D. F., "Chicanos: Strangers in Their Own Land," *America,* 124 (June 1971), 649–652.

Gordon, D. F., "The Jesus People: An Identity Synthesis," *Urban Life and Culture,* 3 (July 1974), 159–178.

Grebler, L., J. W. Moore, and R. C. Guzman, *The Mexican-American People* (New York: Free Press, 1970).

Kaplan, H. R., and C. Tausky, "The Meaning of Work among the Hard-Core Unemployed," *Pacific Sociological Review,* 17 (April 1974), 185–198.

Lawton, M. P., and J. Cohen, "Environment and the Well-Being of Elderly Inner-City Residents," *Environment and Behavior,* 6 (June 1974), 194–211.

Lee, P. C., and N. B. Gropper, "Sex-Role Culture and Educational Practice," *Harvard Educational Review,* 44 (August 1974), 369–410.

Matthiasson, C. J., "Coping in a New Environment: Mexican Americans in Milwaukee, Wisconsin," *Urban Anthropology,* 3 (1974), 262–277.

Mead, M., *The Changing Culture of an Indian Tribe* (New York: Capricorn Books, 1966).

Mkalimoto, E., "Theoretical Remarks on Afroamerican Cultural Nationalism," *Journal of Ethnic Studies,* 2 (1974), 1–10.

Norton, E. H., "Affirmative Action for *Both* Minorities and Women: The Road to Real Reform," *Contact* (Fall 1974), pp. 12–15.

Ogawa, D., and T. A. Welden, "Cross-Cultural Analysis of Feedback Behavior within Japanese American and Caucasian American Small Groups," *The Journal of Communication,* 22 (June 1972), 189–195.

Pineo, P. C., and J. C. Goyder, "Minority Group Status and Self-evaluated Class," *The Sociological Quarterly,* 15 (Spring 1974), 199–211.

Powers, R. B., and D. G. Dean, "Cultural Contradictions and Sex Roles: Fact or Arti-Fact?" *Youth and Society,* 6 (September 1974), 113–120.

Short, J., *Group Process and Gang Delinquency* (Chicago: University of Chicago Press, 1974).

Snyder, P. F., "Social Interaction Patterns and Relative Urban Success: The Denver Navajo," *Urban Anthropology,* 2 (1973), 1–24.

Spaights, E., "Some Dynamics of the Black Family," *The Negro Educational Review,* 24 (July–October 1973), 127–137.

Stewart, V. M., "A Cross-Cultural Test of the 'Carpentered World' Hypothesis Using the Ames Distorted Room Illusion," *International Journal of Psychology,* 9 (1974), 79–89.

Strickland, R., "The Idea of Environment and the Ideal of the Indian," *Journal of American Indian Education,* 10 (October 1970), 8–14.

Vlahos, O., *New World Beginnings: Indian Cultures in the Americas* (New York: Fawcett World Library, 1970).

Weis, J. G., "Styles of Middle-Class Adolescent Drug Use," *Pacific Sociological Review,* 17 (July 1974), 251–285.

Wilcox, R., *Psychological Consequences of Being a Black in America* (New York: John Wiley & Sons, 1971).

Yorburg, B., *Sexual Identity: Sex Roles and Social Change* (New York: John Wiley & Sons, 1974).

Young, G., "You Can't Win if the Rules Won't Let You," *Nation's Business* (November 1974), pp. 66–70.

Concepts and Questions

1. Why is the study of the family important to the study of intercultural communication? What aspects of the family are most likely to be manifested in intercultural interaction?

2. Is the concept of family as important an element in the development of cultural experiences in the United States as in other countries?

3. How does the Japanese social experience in groups differ from your experiences in groups?

4. Do you believe that a Japanese would behave differently in an intercultural group than you would? In what ways?

5. How does the experience of being female in the United States differ from the female role in other cultures?

6. How would the role of female affect communication? How might it affect international aspects of intercultural communication? Would a woman be suitable as a government official representing the United States in all other countries? Why not?

7. What differences do you find between your value system and that of other cultures?

8. Why are values of such crucial importance in intercultural communication?

9. What do Simon and Gagnon mean when they talk about the social structure and values that occur among homosexuals? How do these structures and values differ from other subcultures? How are they reflected in intercultural communication?

10. How does the Schramm diagram, as presented in the Daniel article, relate to the experiences of the poor? In what ways do these experiences differ from "middle-class" experiences?

11. What does it mean to be poor in terms of the development of an experiential background?

12. Do you believe subcultural groups who seek the opportunity to live and practice their way of life ought to be permitted such freedom?

13. How have most of us received our image of the American Indian? How has that image been reinforced? What is the influence of that image on intercultural communication?

14. What is the relevance of the difference in which racial minorities and ethnic minorities have been treated in the United States?

15. Why does the history of a culture or subculture offer us insight into their communication behavior?

16. How does the experience of being Chicano affect the development of a cultural perspective?

3

Cultural Influences on Social Perception

In Chapter 2 we submitted the contention that our cultural orientation, which each of us learns, affects how we behave *during* a communication encounter. Perception, the main theme of Chapter 3, is yet another factor that we bring to the communication situation. Like our past experiences, perception plays a role when we interact with others. This influence and impact serves as the nucleus for Marshall Singer's article "Culture: A Perceptual Approach." He begins his analysis with two important premises. First, individual patterns of behavior are based on individual perceptions of the external world. Second, because these patterns are learned they are culturally based. These two ideas lead Singer through a model of culture and perception that helps explain why communication between members of contrasting cultures is often so difficult. The problem, as this essay suggests, is that our view of reality is shaped by our cultural experiences.

The second article, "Cultural Influences upon Perception," by Harry C. Triandis, looks at some specific ways culture can affect and alter our perceptions. Triandis seeks to document many of the assumptions advanced by Singer. After reviewing numerous experimental studies, he offers a summary of the relationship existing between culture and the following factors: (1) recognition and retention, (2) the perception of space, (3) illusions, (4) physiognomic perceptions, and (5) the perception of emotion. The results presented in each of these five categories clearly demonstrate how our cultural background helps determine what we perceive. The findings also underscore the main thesis of this section—our cultural experiences influence what we bring to an encounter, how we take part in communication, and even the way we respond.

Although the next article, by Frances F. Korten, examines only two cultures, its conclusions may be applied to nearly all cultures. The study deals with one of the most important ideas found in intercultural communication. It is also a specific treatment of a concept expressed by Singer and again by Triandis. What Korten attempts to do is experimentally verify the notion that culture is far more complex than the consistent patterns of behavior among a given group of people; it also must include the influences of these experiences on perception. To demonstrate this relationship Korten examines the role culture has on the perception of persons. In concluding the study she notes that "different cultural groups use different systems of categories in perceiving other people."

While Korten focused on the perception of a person, the final selection in Chapter 3 is concerned with how culture influences our perception of an abstract idea. Specifically, what is the impact of culture on the perception of shame? Anthony J. Marsella, Michael D. Murray, and Charles Golden examined three ethnic groups (Caucasian-American, Chinese-American, and Japanese-American) to discover how each of these groups sees shame. Their results, although confined to these three cultures, offer us some interesting generalizations regarding intercultural communication. As the authors point out, shame and its behavioral implications are not the same for all groups. To facilitate communication we must recognize that the meaning and interpretation of emotions often shift from culture to culture. Hence, the components of a specific emotion for one culture may not be the same when we move to another culture.

Culture: A Perceptual Approach[1]

Marshall R. Singer

The Perceptual Model[2]

It is a basic premise of this paper that man behaves as he does because of the ways in which he perceives the external world. By perception we mean here the process by which an individual selects, evaluates, and organizes stimuli from the external environment.[3] While individuals and the groups which they constitute can only act or react on the basis of their perceptions, the important point is that the "same" stimuli are often perceived differently by different individuals and groups. Whether or not an objective "reality" exists apart from man's perception of that reality need not concern us here. In terms of human behavior, however, there exists, for man, only subjective reality—i.e., the universe as individual men perceive it. The question then becomes: How does man form his perception of the external world and how do those perceptions affect his behavior?

From *Readings in Intercultural Communication,* Vol. 1, edited by David S. Hoopes, pp. 6–20. Reprinted by permission of the author. Professor Singer teaches in the Graduate School of Public and International Affairs, University of Pittsburgh.

[1]An earlier edition of this paper originally appeared in *Preliminary Report on the Suggested Training Program for Centre d'Exchanges Technologiques Internationaux* prepared by the Graduate School of Public and International Affairs, University of Pittsburgh, May, 1965.

[2]The perceptual model presented here, as well as several experimental applications of that model are currently being developed in considerable detail by the author and are scheduled to appear in a forthcoming work, tentatively entitled *Group Perception and Social Action.* Pages 1–6 of this paper are taken from an article "Perception and Social Change in Ceylon," soon to appear in a special issue of the *International Journal of Comparative Sociology.*

[3]Thus, our use of the term "perception" includes "memory" (in the cybernetic sense) and "cognition" in the interpretative sense.

We would argue (rather simplistically here, because it is not the main purpose of the paper) that man is inescapably a social animal. Particularly in his earliest years, but throughout his entire life as well, man must exist in relationship with other human beings. Each of the humans with whom he comes into contact brings to that relationship his own perceptual view of the universe. More important, perhaps, each of the groups in which he has been raised will have conditioned him to view the world from their perspective. Will he regurgitate or salivate at the thought of eating the flesh of a cow or of a kitten? It will depend on how thoroughly he has internalized the attitudes and values which he has been taught by his groups. Not only the languages he speaks and the way in which he thinks, but even *what* he sees, hears, tastes, touches, and smells are conditioned by the cultures[4] in which he has been raised.

Benjamin Lee Whorf, the noted linguist, has written: "We are thus introduced to a new principle of relativity, which holds that all observers are not led by the same physical evidence to the same picture of the universe, unless their linguistic backgrounds are similar, or can in some way be calibrated."[5] We would go a step further and substitute the word "perceptual" for the word "linguistic." We would argue that every culture has its own language[6] or code, to be sure, but that a language is the manifestation—verbal or otherwise—of the perceptions which the group holds. Language, once established, further constrains the individual to perceive in certain ways, but we would insist that language is merely one of the ways in which groups maintain and reinforce similarity of perception.

Specifically our model is based on the following set of premises, some of which are quite generally accepted; some of which are, at this stage, only hypotheses; and others of which are merely definitional. As the model is refined and further developed, some of these will undoubtedly be dropped, others will probably be rephrased, and still others may be added. While we believe that the approach is more important than the specific components, we present them here in order to make our model as explicit as is possible.[7]

1. Individual patterns of behavior are based on individual perceptions[8] of the external world, which are largely learned.

2. Because of biological and experiential differences, no two individuals perceive the external world exactly identically.

3. The greater the biological and experiential differences between individuals, the greater is the disparity in perceptions likely to be. Conversely, the more

---

[4]In our list of propositions presented below, we define each group as having its own culture.

[5]From *Collected Papers on Metalinguistics,* quoted by Franklin Fearing in "An Examination of the Conceptions of Benjamin Whorf in the Light of Theories on Perception and Cognition," in *Language in Culture* edited by Harry Hoijer, University of Chicago Press, Chicago, 1954, p. 48.

[6]Here we are using language in the broadest sense. This may include the jargon or symbols used by social scientists or mathematicians, for example, to express the concepts peculiar to their group.

[7]These premises draw rather heavily on the extensive literature produced by the cultural anthropologists, sociologists, psychologists, communications theorists and linguists. In particular the model is strongly influenced by the notion of perceptual constancies. See F. P. Kilpatrick (ed), *Explorations in Transactional Psychology,* New York University Press, NY, 1961.

[8]As used here perception includes attitudes and values.

similar the biological and experiential background, the more similarity are individuals likely to perceive.

4. A perceptual group may be defined as a number of individuals who perceive some aspects of the external world more or less similarly.[9]

5. A number of people who perceive some aspects of the external world more or less similarly, and recognize (communicate) that they share that similarity of perception, may be termed an identity group.

6. The higher the degree of similarity of perception that exists among a number of individuals, other things being equal: (a) the easier is communication among them likely to be; (b) the more communication among them is likely to occur, and (c) the more likely it is that this similarity of perception will be recognized—that an identity group will form.[10]

7. Ease of communications will allow for constant increase in degree of similarity of perception (through feedback mechanisms) which in turn allows for still further ease of communication. Thus, there tends to be a constant reinforcement of group identity.[11]

8. The greater the number and the degree of intensity of perceptual groups which individuals share—the more overlapping of important perceptual groups which exists among a number of individuals—the more likely they are to have a high degree of group identity.[12]

9. A pattern of perceptions and behavior which is accepted and expected by an identity group is called a culture. Since by definition each identity group has its own pattern of behavioral norms, each group may be said to have its own culture.[13]

10. Since communication tends to be easiest among individuals who identify most closely with each other, and most difficult among individuals who perceive more or less dissimilarly, this tends to reinforce and exacerbate awareness of

---

[9]While the terms "more" and "less" are vaguely quantitative, they are clearly inadequate for a precise science of social action. Unfortunately, they are often the best that the social scientist can produce, given the current state of our knowledge. A good deal of serious research being done by psychologists today, however, indicates that they are finding ways of measuring perceptions more and more precisely. For some suggestive approaches to this problem, see B. Berelson and G. A. Steiner, *Human Behavior: An Inventory of Scientific Findings,* Harcourt Brace and World, Inc., New York, 1964.

[10]The converse of this is also true.

[11]Where there is little or no communication among individuals there tends to be a decrease in similarity of perception which in turn tends to make further communications more difficult. See premise 10.

[12]In most societies the family enjoys the highest degree of group identity. Among the reasons that this is so is the fact that the family tends to combine a great many different perceptual groups simultaneously. Thus, with rare exception, all adult members of the family speak the same language, are from the same place of residence, are of the same religious persuasion, have approximately the same educational level, are of the same socio-economic class, are very likely to be employed in the same occupational grouping, and so on at incredible length. In other words, the family enjoys one of the highest possible degrees of group identity precisely because the members of that group are also concurrently members of so many other perceptual groups. Indeed, family identity as the superordinant identification for the individual tends to break down precisely in those more mobile societies (particularly in urban, industrial areas) where the family combines fewer similarities of perception.

[13]For a further discussion of this approach, see below.

group differences. Any "we" (identity group) comes into much sharper focus when juxtaposed against "they" (a different identity group).

11. An individual must inevitably be a member of a myriad of different perceptual and identity groups simultaneously, by definition. However, he shares a higher degree of similarity of perception, and a higher degree of group identity, with some groups than with others. Consciously or otherwise, he rank orders his various group identities.[14]

12. Because environmental and biological factors are ever changing, perceptions, attitudes and values are ever changing. Consequently, the rank ordering of group identities is ever changing and new perceptual groups are constantly being formed, while existing groups are constantly in a state of flux.[15]

We know from the study of genetics that no two individuals are physiologically completely identical. Certainly if the skin on the tips of the fingers is different for each individual then each person's sense of touch must be presumed to be individual and unique. Yet far more important for the way men view the universe are the still unanswered questions of physical variations in other sensory receptors. What about the configuration of cones and rods in the retina of the eye, or taste buds on the tongue, or fibers in the ear, or any of the other physical receptors of external stimuli? If no two individuals have identical receptors of stimuli, then it must follow, on the basis of physiological evidence alone, that no two individuals perceive the external world completely identically. Yet biological differences probably account for only the smallest fraction of the perceptual distinctions made by man.

Far more important in determining an individual's perceptions of the external world are the experiential factors involved in the incorporation, organization and processing of sensory data. Genetically, we inherit from our parents those physical characteristics that distinguish us as their offspring. Admittedly there is a good deal of individual variation biologically and environmentally, but there is also a good deal of similarity. Given two white parents the overwhelming probability is that the offspring will be white. Given two English speaking parents the

---

[14]It often happens that individuals and/or groups exist, having internalized elements of several differing or even conflicting value systems simultaneously. Individuals and groups are able to survive and function under these conditions primarily because: (a) they are able to identify in differing degrees —and at differing levels of consciousness—with each of the value systems with which they identify; and (b) because most group identities which are simultaneously held only rarely come into direct *conscious* conflict. When two equally held value systems do come into conflict, a high degree of personal and/or group anxiety (conscious or otherwise) may result. The individual and/or group often seeks some third identity which can accommodate, neutralize, rationalize and/or synthesize these conflicting value systems. For some individuals and/or groups it could produce an inability to act. For still others, it might mean rather erratic behavior, alternately overstressing one value system at the experience of the other. In any one of these cases, however, it would probably be diagnosed as ambivalence.

[15]Small, isolated and relatively undifferentiated societies may often seem to be almost totally unchanging and unchangeable just because there is a high degree of shared perceptions among most of the members of those societies. It is precisely because there is such a high degree of identity and such a high degree of reinforcement of similarity of perception that it is so difficult to introduce change into those societies.

overwhelming probability is that the offspring will speak English. The difference is that biologic identity is—within a given range of probability—fixed, while environmental identity is not. The son of two white parents will always remain white no matter what happens to him after birth, but the son of two English speaking parents may never speak English if immediately after birth he is raised by a totally non-English speaking group. Thus while biologic inheritance is relatively immutable, environmental inheritance is ever changing. The fascinating aspect of environmental conditioning, however, is that while there is theoretically, an almost infinite number of possibilities, in fact, the number of environmental factors to which most individuals are exposed is amazingly limited. Thus for example, while there may be a whole world to explore, if not an entire universe, the incredibly overwhelming majority of individuals who inhabit this planet never stray more than a few miles from their place of birth. Indeed each of us is a member of a finite, and comparatively small, number of different identity groups.

If, for biologic and environmental reasons, it is not possible for any two individuals to perceive the universe 100 percent similarly, neither is it possible—for the same reasons—for them to share absolutely no similarity of perception. Hence we are postulating here a continuum of similarity of perception among individuals. At one end we can approach—but never reach—zero; at the other we can approach—but never reach—100 percent. Actually, degree of similarity of perception can probably best be measured not as a point of a continuum, but rather as a range of points. Thus, for example,[16] two Catholics—one from a third generation wealthy Boston family, and the other from an illiterate and impoverished small village in the Congo—may share, as Catholics, no more than perhaps a 10 to 15 percent similarity of perception. Yet we would argue that to the degree that they share an identity (recognize a similarity of perception) as Catholics they are a part of the broad identity group called "Catholics." Teachers, considered as a group, may share an average range of 20–25 percent similarity of perception. If we narrow the group to include only college teachers, the range of similarity of perception may increase to from 40 to 50 percent. If we further specify that the group consists of only Catholic, male, heterosexual college teachers of quantum physics, with Ph.D.'s from M.I.T. between the ages of 35 and 40, the range of similarity of perception might well increase to perhaps 75 to 80 percent. Notice that while we have decreased the number of people who can be included in our group, we have increased the number of group identities which the members of the groups share. By doing so we have greatly increased the likelihood of their sharing still greater similarities of perception in the future. It is no wonder that the smaller the group the greater the group cohesion is likely to be.

By communication we mean here that one individual or a group of individuals more or less understands another's message. Since no two individuals perceive 100 percent similarly, it follows that no individual will perceive another's message 100 percent as the sender intended it to be understood. When we couple this with

---

[16]Any figures used in our examples are completely hypothetical, and are included merely to illustrate a concept. They are not based on any known research.

what Claude Shannon[17] has said about the ever present distortion in the communication process we recognize the potentially high degree of noncommunication inherent in the process. Fortunately, it is not imperative to the functioning of groups that communications be perceived 100 percent accurately. Fortunately too, there are corrective devices inherent in almost any communication system. One such device is the "feedback mechanism" which may allow for continuous testing of accuracy of perception.[18] Another is redundancy. Most verbal languages are themselves more than one-half redundant. Thus, if part of the message is lost, either due to differing perceptions or to distortions within the system, enough of the message usually gets through to convey the general meaning intended. At least in face to face communication and to some extent in television and movies, there is repetition of the same message over a number of channels. Thus, both audio and visual channels may simultaneously convey and reinforce the same message. Regardless of the type of media available in any society, however, face to face communications will remain the most effective form of communication.

But verbal communication comprises only a portion—and it may perhaps be the smallest portion—of the communication that goes on in any society. Far more important are the silent, non-verbal communications which we only half consciously or unconsciously transmit and receive. Perhaps a million persons intersect at the corner of Broadway and 42nd Street in New York City each day, and yet, the non-verbal communication process is so accurate that without a word being spoken they filter past each other in orderly fashion, only rarely touching. A glance, a shrug, time and spacial communication,[19] indeed an endless number of non-verbal cues which are often too subtle even to be conscious, may communicate far more than words. There is mounting evidence that within any given group non-verbal communications may account for the overwhelming majority of the communication which occurs. It is precisely because we communicate and perceive so well within our own groups that we feel so comfortable there. We can communicate effectively with a minimum of effort and frustration because the patterns of behavior of the members of our own groups are so predictable to us that a minimum of effort is required for effective functioning.

It is precisely such shared, often unarticulated, and sometime unarticulatable patterns of perception, communication, and behavior which are referred to as "a culture." But group identities do not necessarily recognize the integrity of national boundaries. In the hypothetical case of the college teachers of quantum physics cited above, no mention was made of nationality. To be sure, if we were to stipulate that they all be Americans, the percentage of their shared similarity of perception would probably rise still higher. But the fact is that there is a considerably higher degree of similarity of perception among college teachers of quantum physics—regardless of nationality—than there could possibly be be-

[17]See Claude E. Shannon and Warren Weaver, *The Mathematical Theory of Communication,* University of Illinois Press, Urbana, 1949.

[18]For a dramatic demonstration of the necessity of feedback for even partial similarity of perception between sender and receiver, see Harold Levitt, *Managerial Psychology,* University of Chicago Press, second edition, 1964, chapter 9.

[19]See Edward T. Hall, *The Silent Language,* Doubleday and Co., New York, 1959.

tween them and, let us say, uneducated sharecroppers or perhaps barbers in the same society. It is for this reason that we consider only each group as having its own culture, rather than attempting to consider only each society as having its own culture, and then being forced to consider deviations from the societal norms as "sub-cultural." This is not to say that societal cultures do not exist. On the contrary; to the degree that an entire society shares and communicates certain similarities of perception and behavior it may itself be considered as an identity group—and thus to have a common culture of its own.

But we would argue, there is greater analytical and operational utility in considering each society as the aggregate of the identity (cultural) groups which exist within it. From there we may proceed to compare and analyze whole societies to determine which identity groups are present in each and—

1. how the presence or absence of certain groups in a given society effects that entire society;

2. what other clusters of groups may always, often, rarely or never be found in societies containing certain groups;

3. the differences and similarities between the same groups in different societies[20]— why they are different; how they relate to the whole society and how the whole society is related to them.

4. the differences and similarities between different groups in the same society.

While we believe that the implications of this formulation of the problem to the study of the process of social change are indeed significant, they fall outside the scope of this paper.[21]

Implications for Cross-Cultural Operations

Implicit in the perceptual model outlined above is the proposition that an individual is in fact functioning somewhat "cross-culturally" whenever he communicates with another individual. The fewer group identities he shares (and the less intensely held the identities which exist) with the individuals with whom he must communicate the more "cross-culturally" he is operating. We are dealing here with a continuum and not with dichotomies. The important point to note, however, is that some *intranational* communications can be far more cross-cultural than other *international* communications.

Workers in various anti-poverty programs have sometimes been chagrined and shocked to find their well-intentioned plans utterly rejected by the very people whom they were intended to help. What they have often overlooked—and what any experienced social worker knows—is the fact that the white, urban, middle-class, well educated professional probably has a totally different set of perceptions

---

[20]For example, the family, students, businessmen, industrial workers, bureaucrats, the military, the clergy, etc., in different societies.

[21]To some degree this aspect of the problem has been discussed in the author's "Group Perception and Social Change in Ceylon," cited above.

(and hence values, attitudes, and modes of behavior) than his Negro, rural, lower-class, uneducated client.[22] Merely because the professional sees merit in a particular proposal in no way ensures that the client will view the proposal in the same way. Indeed, it would be nearly miraculous if he did. It is precisely because of this that the demand has grown for greater participation of clients in the planning of proposals intended for their benefit. To some degree this may alleviate the problem. But until the cause of the problem is reorganized clearly, it is doubted that significant progress will be made. Until one of the groups concerned (and it can only be the professional group) recognizes that their perceptions differ markedly from those of the other—and recognize that different is not the same as bad—and makes a concerted attempt to understand the others' perceptions, the incidence of friction and frustration is likely to continue. What is more, now that the Negro in the United States has begun to organize to defend the validity of his identity, the white population has begun to sense an urgency for understanding these perceptions.

International cross-cultural operations are often more complicated and more difficult than domestic cross-cultural operations—not necessarily because the individuals involved share fewer perceptions, but rather because it is often extremely difficult to adjust levels of expectation of communication in unfamiliar environments. Within our own society there are a multitude of familiar silent and/or subtle cues which tell us at which levels of sophistication we may communicate. When the physicist talks to his barber in the United States, he knows that he is expected to discuss baseball, the weather, and women. He also knows that it would be futile for him to attempt to discuss quantum physics. Thus he adjusts his communication expectations accordingly and leaves the barber shop a little wiser about the league standing of the home team, a little apprehensive about the impending winter, and a little titulated by the cover of *Playboy*. But he certainly has no feeling of frustration at not having been able to discuss physics. He knows his own society well enough to know with whom he may discuss baseball and with whom he may discuss physics. In a foreign environment, on the other hand, it is difficult—particularly for the newcomer—to assess at which level he may communicate. The same physicist operating outside of his own country may be pleasantly surprised to find that his foreign counterpart not only speaks his language, but *appears* to have the same problems, aspirations, and values as he himself has. He, therefore, expects to be readily understood, even when discussing the most complicated intellectual problems. If he later finds that he was not completely understood, he may feel hurt, cheated and frustrated. Because of the outward *appearance* of similarity based on common perceptions which the two share as quantum physicists, he may not have taken into account the fact that there are a myriad of other group identities—and consequently many other patterns of perception and behavior—which they do *not* have in common.

But there is another reason for the increased difficulty of international cross-cultural operations. While two individuals in the same society may be a cultural

---

[22]The extreme contrast is used here merely for illustrative purposes. Although perhaps in differing degrees the same holds true for clients from other groups as well.

world away from each other educationally, physically they may reside in the same city, in the same mass culture. If the physicist eats in the barber's home, he will know approximately what to expect and how to behave. When he leaves the barber's house he will drive down familiar streets, with familiar faces, places and smells to the security and comfort of his own home. In the home of another physicist in, say, Bombay, on the other hand, he will not only have to remember the specifics of not eating with his left hand (and any other specific cross-cultural data that he may have acquired) but he must be prepared for the totally unexpected. It is simply not possible to teach someone from one culture the perhaps hundreds of millions of discreet "bits" of information he would have to know to truly understand another culture. Yet it is precisely because he does not know what it is about another culture that he does not know that his anxiety level must perforce be high. Further, as soon as the hypothetical American physicist leaves the home of his counterpart in Bombay, he must wander through strange streets, with strange faces, places and smells. All the silent little cues which would come to him subliminally in the United States would be missing. In Bombay it would be necessary for him to expend an enormous amount of energy merely making explicit all of those myriad little cues which in his own culture can remain implicit and subconscious. But, obviously, the lack of reception of silent cues are not all that complicate international cross-cultural operations. The matter of adjusting to unfamiliar food, climate and other physical differences can be a very real problem. Further there is the additional real burden of functioning in a society in which one may be totally or partially unfamiliar with the spoken or written language.

There is one additional factor which tends to make international cross-cultural operations more emotionally taxing than most domestic cross-cultural operations. While we have argued that, analytically, all communications are to some degree cross-cultural, within our own society contact with significantly different groups can be kept to a minimum. At home we tend to spend most of our leisure time, at least, surrounded by individuals who perceive more or less as we do. Even if our work is of the nature which forces us to deal with people significantly different from ourselves during the day, in the evening we can retreat to the comfort and ease of our own groups. Internationally this is not always possible.[23] Aside from possible contact with fellow countrymen (the connotation of the term *landsmann* is significant here) when working or living in a foreign environment one can expect no relief from the strain of uncertainty—either until his task is accomplished and he returns home or until he has lived in that environment long enough to increase his own range of similarity of perception with those around him to the point where, if not everything, at least most things need no longer be made conscious and explicit.

In short, while some communications within the same society can be more cross-cultural than other international communications, international cross-cul-

---

[23]It does help to explain, however, the prevelance of the American, German, British, and other foreign ghettoes and clubs one finds abroad.

tural operations tend to be significantly more difficult because we tend to share a higher degree of similarity of perception with more groups in our own society than we do in a foreign environment.

Cultural Influences upon Perception

Harry C. Triandis

Physical energies impinge on an organism and are processed in such a way as to acquire meaning. The activation of the organism, in response to such energies, is called *sensation;* when meaning is added to sensation, the process is called *perception.* As Gibson (1963) pointed out, "to feel pain is not to feel the prick of a needle." All the evidence presently available suggests that there are not cultural influences upon sensation. However, cultural factors may provide some of the meaning involved in perception and are therefore intimately implicated with that process.

A. Recognition and Retention

The view that cultural factors are important determinants of perceptual responses is sometimes referred to as the "new look" in perception. Dukes (1955) reviewed the early experimental studies of the conditions under which cultural factors become implicated in perception. It appears, however, that many of the experiments which provided positive results (i.e., which showed the influence of such cultural factors) were subject to experimental artifacts, and well-controlled experiments (e.g., Dorfman and Zajonc, 1963) led to negative results. Eriksen (1963), after a review of 15 years of research, concluded that values, needs, and expectations affect only the responses that subjects make. Perceptual responses, according to Eriksen, are modified by both the frequency of occurrence of a particular stimulus (the more frequent stimuli are recognized more easily) and by the kind of previous reinforcements received in the presence of the stimulus. This view agrees with Doob's (1960) analysis of the effect of category codability on perception. The Luganda language compels its speakers to note whether an event occurred within or before the 24-hour period immediately prior to the time at which the event is described. Doob concluded that this has a small effect on what is perceived (what he calls the afferent function of language) but a substantial effect on response (efferent function).

From "Cultural Influences upon Cognitive Processes" in *Advances in Experimental Social Psychology,* Vol. 1, edited by Leonard Berkowitz (New York: Academic Press, 1964). Reprinted with permission of the author and publisher. Harry C. Triandis teaches in the Department of Psychology, University of Illinois, Champaign.

Eriksen's view of perception suggests that members of a culture may perceive object A rather than object B because of: (a) the greater meaning of A than of B (Bartlett, 1932); (b) the higher frequency of occurrence of A relative to B; and (c) the more pleasant associations with A than with B. Thus, previous cultural experience may enhance the availability of a category and depress the availability of another. In Bagby's (1957) study of perceptual predominance in binocular rivalry, Mexican and American subjects were given exposure with binocular vision to bullfight and baseball pictures. The results indicate that at tachistoscopic speeds, the Mexicans saw the bullfight and the Americans the baseball pictures. The relative availability of a category may have important consequences in problem solving (Cofer, 1951) and the regulation of behavior (Luria, 1961).

Retention is another cognitive process affected by category availability. The method of serial reproduction has been used in different cultural settings (Bartlett, 1932; Nadel, 1937; Talland, 1956; Goodman, 1962). Goodman compared the responses of 239 Japanese and 681 urban middle-class children in the fifth and sixth grades. She employed the same story used by Nadel with the Nupe and Yoruba 12- to 18-year-old West African adolescents. The story included the sentence "God will punish him." The Japanese, who were the least religious of the samples, recalled this in only 6% of the cases in contrast to 17% of the Americans, 25% of the Yoruba, and 50% of the Nupe.

B. The Perception of Space

In an interesting study by Hudson (1960), pictures constructed to provide self-evident responses of two- or three-dimensional perception were administered to white and African samples of school-going and non-school-going subjects. School-going subjects saw the pictures predominantly as 3D, while the non-school-going subjects saw them almost entirely two dimensionally. Evidently, it is necessary to learn to see pictures and photographs in three dimensions. Cultural isolation from pictures and photographs was proportionately related to difficulty of seeing three dimensionally.

C. Illusions

Experimental work with optical illusions has cast considerable light on cross-cultural differences in spatial perception. Allport and Pettigrew (1957) found that urban Zulus report the trapezoid illusion more often than rural Africans. Under optimal conditions (monocularly at twenty feet) no differences were observed between the Zulus and Europeans, but under suboptimal conditions the unacculturated subjects reported the illusion less frequently than did the acculturated. Bonte (1962) also found that the Bashi Africans were less susceptible to the Müller-Lyer illusion than a European sample.

By far the best study on this topic is Segall *et al.* (1963, 1964). The study is a model for cross-cultural research. The authors employed extremely careful procedures in standardization. A total of 1878 subjects representing 14 non-

European cultures and three European were tested. The test materials were versions of the Müller-Lyer, the Sander Parallelogram, and the Horizontal-Vertical illusion. The results strongly support the empiricist hypothesis that the perception of space involves, to an important extent, the acquisition of habits of perceptual inference.

Both Rivers (1905) and Segall *et al.* (1963, 1964) found that Europeans experience the Müller-Lyer and Sander Parallelogram illusions much *more* sharply than non-Europeans; but they experience the Horizontal-Vertical illusion *less* sharply than non-Europeans. The authors argued that subjects living in a highly carpentered world—more typical of Europeans than non-Europeans—will tend to perceive the "shorter" line of the Müller-Lyer as the "front edge" of boxes, while the "longer" line would be seen as the back edge along the inside of the box. Since they "know" that boxes have edges of the same size, they will infer that the "front" is shorter than the "back" edge. The carpentered world hypothesis, then, predicts that subjects living in tropical forests or other noncarpentered environments would be less susceptible to the Müller-Lyer illusion. The data generally support this prediction. They also point out that a short, vertical line in a drawing may represent a relatively long, horizontal line extending away from the observer. Subjects living on flat plains devoid of trees, posts, or poles tend to interpret vertical retinal extensions as greatly foreshortened lines in the horizontal plane extending along the line of regard. Thus, such subjects would be maximally susceptible to the Horizontal-Vertical illusion. The data again are consistent with this view. Segall *et al.* (1964) concluded that ecological and cultural factors operating in the visual environment create differences in visual inference.

D. Physiognomic Perception

The previous sections suggest that recognition, retention, the perception of space, and illusions depend largely on the physical characteristics of the stimuli being used. However, cultural factors provide significant modifications to the perceptual process, which can be accounted for by ecological determinants. As the ambiguity of the stimulus increases, the effect of the cultural variables increases. Thus, when the perception of aesthetic qualities is considered, cultural factors should control more variance than the characteristics of the stimuli. Nevertheless, there is evidence that even in the area of aesthetic preference some judgments are not influenced by culture.

Physiognomic perception (Ryan, 1938) appears to be free of cultural influences, although more evidence is needed before this can be regarded as definitely established. One technique for studying physiognomic perception employs nonsense words and abstract drawings and asks subjects from different cultures to match them. Davis (1961) showed that children in Tanganyika were similar to English controls in matching nonsense names and abstract drawings. Thus, some characteristics of visual and auditory stimuli suggest similarities among them. Voorhees (1954) found that American subjects could identify the moods intended in Bedouin, Indonesian, and other exotic music. This suggests that some sounds may have universal meaning.

The hypothesis of phonetic symbolism, that the sound of a word suggests its meaning, has interested social psychologists for some time, Klineberg (1954) reviewed several studies on this subject. In a recent review, Taylor (1963) described some of his own experiments, concluding that "people associate certain sounds with certain meanings, but the same sound is associated with different meaning in different languages" (p. 205). The speakers of a language may learn to associate a particular sound with a particular category because many of the words associated with that category utilize the sound. For instance, in English, G is associated with bigness—grand, great, grow, gain, gargantuan, gross. The Taylor position, however, is challenged by Miron (1961), who presented convincing evidence that certain materials have expressive value due to their inherent phonetic content.

Osgood (1960a) studied visual-verbal synesthetic tendencies with 40 Navahos, 10 Mexicans, 27 Anglos, and 20 Japanese. However, all subjects were bilingual to some extent. Concepts such as up, down, heavy, good, and pictorial alternatives depicting up-down, vertical-horizontal, thick-thin, near-far (Osgood, 1960a, Fig. 1) were employed. The experimenter would name one of the concepts and then show the series of cards with the pictorial alternatives. The subjects pointed to which of the alternatives in each card seemed most appropriate to that concept. The results indicated an impressive cross-cultural agreement in synesthetic tendencies. "Happy," for example, goes with colored, up and white; "sad" goes with uncolored, down, and black.

On the question of aesthetic judgments involving visual or auditory materials, there is little doubt that culture is a most powerful determinant (Lawlor, 1955). However, Pratt (1961) correctly observed that "cultural relativism has gone a bit too far." He reviewed a number of studies that suggest similarities in these judgments across cultures. For instance, Morris (1957) obtained judgments of preference for modern paintings from Chinese, Indian, and American subjects. Though many of the responses were culture-specific, there was enough cross-cultural agreement to suggest a panhuman factor in such judgments.

The evidence suggests, then, that panhuman generality can be demonstrated for physiognomic perception, synesthetic tendencies, and to a lesser extent, aesthetic judgments. This suggests that the same basic emotion mechanism is used by all humans, but ecological differences produce differences in conditioning to particular kinds of stimuli. The following section will develop this point.

E. The Perception of Emotion

Cultural differences seem to be widespread and quite significant in the definition of what situations are appropriate for what emotional expression (Klineberg, 1954). However, these must be considered in the same class as customs, rather than as fundamental differences in cognitive functioning.

The evidence concerning the judging of emotional expressions among various national groups indicates that there are no important differences among them.

Vinacke and Fong (1955) examined three racial groups in Hawaii and found no significant differences among them in the judgment of facial expression. Studies testing Schlosberg's (1954) theory of emotion with Greek (Triandis and Lambert, 1958), Dutch (Frijda, 1953; Frijda and Philipzoon, 1963), and Australian subjects (Gladstones, 1962) appear to agree.

Schlosberg (1944) attempted to reduce the dimensions required to order judgments of pictures that presumably reflect emotional states in the person photographed. He proposed that the classic Woodworth categories could be arranged in a two-dimensional space defined by (a) pleasant-unpleasant, and (b) attention-rejection. Later Schlosberg (1954) extended this theory to include a further dimension, tension-sleep. A recent study (Gladstones, 1962) with Schlosberg's pictures, employed Torgerson's method of complete triads for multidimensional scaling of the pictures. The pleasant-unpleasant dimension was the first factor, the tension-sleep dimension was the second, and a doubtful third factor also emerged. The contributions of these three factors to the observed variance in judgments were in the proportion 3:2:1. Thus, five sixths of the variance accounted for can be described by the pleasant-unpleasant and tension-sleep factors. The correspondence between these factors and Osgood's evaluative and activity factors was noted by Triandis and Lambert (1958), Osgood (1963), and others. Semantic differential studies involving judgments of pictures of emotional expression (Osgood, 1955, 1962) also agree with these results.

Given, then, that at least two of the three Schlosberg dimensions are well established, what evidence is there about their cross-cultural generality? Triandis and Lambert (1958) tested a number of hypotheses with two samples of Greek subjects. Fifteen subjects were young adults in an isolated village in the north of the island of Corfu, and 15 were sophisticated young adults from Athens. The choice of samples was an attempt to vary the movie attendance of the subjects, which might lead to stereotypic judgments of emotions.

Triandis and Lambert first tested the hypothesis that the Greek subjects would rate emotional expression in much the same way as American subjects (using the Schlosberg norms of Brown University students). The rank-order correlations for the 48 pictures ranged from .67 ($p < .0001$) (for the judgments of the Brown University students and the Corfu villagers on the sleep-tension dimension), to .91 (for the Brown and Athenian subjects on the pleasant-unpleasant dimension). Using the Thurstone successive intervals procedure, Triandis plotted the emotion solid for the Greek and American data (see Triandis and Lambert, 1958, Fig. 1). The two solids look similar, but the American subjects tended to make wider discriminations than the Greeks on the pleasant-unpleasant dimension for pictures that they judged as "tense." Analysis of the data revealed that, on the average, the Greeks (whether urban or village) gave more ratings toward "attention" and "tension" for the unpleasant pictures, while the Americans gave more ratings of this kind for the pleasant pictures ($p < .001$). One possible explanation is that the Americans are more activist and instrumentally oriented than the Greeks.

The same study hypothesized that the position of a picture in the Woodworth categories (love, surprise, fear, anger, disgust, contempt) can be predicted from its ratings on the pleasant-unpleasant and attention-rejection dimensions, in both cultures. The hypothesis was supported. The study further hypothesized that movie attendance makes the judgments of the urban Greeks more similar to judgments of American subjects than to judgments of the villagers. This hypothesis was also supported.

Although the results of the Triandis and Lambert study supported the hypothesis of generality in judgment of emotion, certain differences in the perception of particular pictures were observed. Thus, the villagers saw a picture which Schlosberg described as "intense anger in argument" as significantly more pleasant and less tense than the two urban groups did. In the village studied, verbal aggression is a traditional form of entertainment, with loud and angry debates the favorite pastime of the villagers. Similarly, the villagers judged pictures that depict physical strain as less tense and less pleasant than the urban samples. The villagers undoubtedly associated physical strain with work, whereas the college students associated it with athletics. Thus, while the frame of reference for the judgments remains the same across cultures, the specific judgments about the meaning of particular emotions may be quite different.

See original source for references.

The Influence of Culture on the Perception of Persons

Frances F. Korten

Culture is far more than the consistent patterns of behavior among a given group of people. The similar basic life experiences of the people of a cultural group shape similar cognitive structures which in turn cause that cultural group to perceive their environment in certain consistent ways. Triandis (1972) has called this cognitive aspect of culture "subjective culture" which he defines as a given group's characteristic way of perceiving its social environment. He suggests that to understand other peoples we must come to understand the cognitive structures which shape their perceptions and hence determine their behavior. He further notes that we must understand how these structures differ from culture to culture and how the environment influences the development of these structures.

Reprinted from the *International Journal of Psychology,* Vol. 9 (1974), pp. 31–44, by permission of the International Union of Psychological Science and Dunod Editeur, Paris, and by permission of the author. Frances F. Korten is currently consultant to The International Committee on the Management of Population Programmes, The Pathfinder Fund, Instituto Centroamericano de Administración de Empresas.

This paper discusses a particular type of cognitive structure—namely the system of categories which people draw on in perceiving other persons. Here the word "category" does not refer to some specific characteristic of the person that the perceiver notes—such as "smart." Rather, "category" refers to a class of attributes—in this case the characterization "smart" falling in the category of "ability." (See Table 1 for the complete set of categories used in this study.)

The present paper examines the categories of attributes which people use in describing other persons, and specifically examines how the frequency of use of these categories differs from the culture of Ethiopian students to that of American students, and from the sub-culture of American male students to that of American female students.

Psychologists have long been intrigued with cultural differences in perception, particularly emphasizing cultural differences in object perception (cf. Segall, Campbell and Herskovits, 1966). However, as Warr and Knapper (1968) have pointed out in their comprehensive review and integration of person perception studies, cross-cultural studies in person perception are less common, though some exist. A few examples include Hall's (1959, 1966) popularization of the concept of non-verbal cues and the intercultural misunderstandings that can result from their misinterpretation; Ekman and Friesen's (1969, 1971) recent work on cultural similarities and differences in the expression of emotions; the work of Dennis (1951) and of Martin (1964) regarding how bodily characteristics are evaluated differently from one culture to another; and Triandis's work (1967, 1968, 1972) with the influence of stereotypes and roles on cultural differences in perceptions of persons.

However, Warr and Knapper point out that there is a lack of research on the cultural determinants of the input of perception noting that in the future "it is very likely that differences will be observed in the way people from different cultures select input material" (1968, p. 41).

The question of determinants of perceptual input has been of interest to psychologists for some time, through primarily in regard to the perception of objects. Bruner (1957) proposed the concept of perceptual readiness, hypothesizing the processes that may determine a person's readiness to perceive particular stimuli. With regard to person perception, Kelley (1950) demonstrated the influence of expectancy on perceptual readiness showing that perceivers expecting a person to be "cold" had dramatically different perceptions of him than ones who expected that person to be "warm." If such a minor previous experience can significantly affect the perception of a person, we should expect culture—the accumulation of a multitude of previous experiences—to strongly affect the perception of persons. But through what mechanism might this influence be exerted? Bruner (1957) has suggested that one way in which previous experience exerts its influence on the cues attended to is by determining the categories the person is most in the habit of using. Thus, it might be expected that such habits would differ from one culture to another, and by examining which categories of attributes are most frequently used from one culture to another it should be possible to demonstrate systematic differences.

The present paper reveals such systematic differences in the frequency of category usage for different cultural groups and hypothesizes how the specific differences found might have come about. Such hypotheses provide initial input to the understanding of the determinants of subjective culture.

Method

FREE RESPONSE APPROACH   Since the purpose of the study was to reveal which categories subjects were in the habit of using most frequently in perceiving other people it was felt necessary to allow the subjects the greatest possible spontaneity in their responses. Beach and Wertheimer (1961) have pointed out that by requiring subjects to make judgments on scales provided by the experimenter, we may be getting judgments on scales which the subject would not have used in perceiving a particular person, making the results difficult to interpret. Thus, they stress that allowing the subject the greatest possible freedom in determining his own responses provides more valid results. It may be for this reason that in the study of sex differences in person perception, it has turned out that the methodology most reliable in capturing such differences is one that allows a free response (War and Knapper, 1968). Hence, for this study it was felt that to best capture cultural differences, a free response approach was most appropriate.

SUBJECTS   Ethiopian subjects consisted of male students enrolled in a psychology course in the College of Business Administration at the National University in Ethiopia. Only males were asked to volunteer to participate in the study as there were very few females enrolled in the school. American subjects consisted of undergraduate students, both male and female, enrolled in a statistics class at Stanford University.

THE BASIC TASK   The data for this study consist of the subjects' descriptions of persons they knew well and ones they knew little, with the experimenter specifying from what group these persons were to be chosen.[1] Thus, Ethiopians were asked to describe two persons that they knew well and two they knew little from each of three groups—University students, Uneducated City Dwellers, and Villagers. In fact, while all subjects described University students, some did not have time for the descriptions of City Dwellers and Villagers—hence the N for students is 39, while those for City Dwellers and Villagers are 19 and 14 respectively. The Stanford students were asked to describe persons they knew well and ones they knew little from among Stanford male premedical students and Stanford male under-graduate English majors. However, due to a time constraint instead of describing two people known well and two known little for each group, as the Ethiopians had, they described two known well and two known little for

---

[1]The groups were specified because the data were also used in an analysis of the process of stereotyping. A month prior to the collection of the subjects' descriptions of individuals reported here, subjects had described characteristics which they felt were common to each of the groups named as a whole. After describing the individuals, subjects then rated them on their own descriptions of the group as a whole. These data and the implications for stereotype theory are reported elsewhere (Korten, 1973).

one group and only one known well and one known little for the second group. Thus, a random half of the subjects described a total of four premeds and two English majors, while the other half described a total of four English majors and two premeds.

MEANS OF DESCRIPTION   Because the Ethiopians were unused to psychological research, it was decided to receive their descriptions orally while for the sake of speed, the Americans wrote their descriptions. Pretests indicated that Americans produced essentially the same content whether done orally or in written form. The Ethiopians' descriptions were tape recorded and then transcribed for analysis. The tape recorder did not appear to bother the subjects and in fact the author was frequently surprised at the openness with which the subjects responded to the task. In both cultures the instructions were the same. First the subject wrote down the initials of the persons known well and known little that he was going to describe for a given group. (This was done to prevent the process of the description to influence the subsequent choice of persons to describe.) He was then asked to describe each of those persons by reporting whatever spontaneously came to mind regarding the characteristics of that person —the only restriction being a requirement to use full sentences in describing the person rather than single words or phrases. The Ethiopians were allowed to continue to talk until they had made 14 statements about the person while the Americans were given five minutes to write about each of their individuals.

LANGUAGE   While normally for cross-cultural comparisons it is desirable to have each cultural group speaking their own language, in this study the use of two languages would confound any results. In using two languages any differences found in the frequency of use of the perceptual categories could be attributed to the differences in the structures or the availability of particular types of expressions in each of the two languages. Fortunately, with the Ethiopian students it was possible to hold these semantic factors constant by using English for both groups since the Ethiopians were completely fluent in English. At the time this study was done, English had been the students' exclusive language of instruction from the first grade right up through their current university classes. By using English for the Ethiopians it was assured that if language were to affect the types of perceptions made, it would be in the direction of greater similarity to the Americans. Thus, differences from the Americans would reflect cultural differences shining through the Western language being spoken.

THE CONTENT ANALYSIS   The subject's open-ended descriptions were subjected to a content analysis in which each perception was placed in one of twelve mutually exclusive categories, as listed in Table 1. The twelve-category system was based closely upon that devised by Beach and Wertheimer (1961) to content analyze open-ended descriptions of persons. The author modified this schema somewhat in ways which seemed to more meaningfully differentiate types of perceptions, resulting in the system outlined in Table 1. This coding system had the advantage of being independent of the behavior of the person being described, since all of the categories could be applied to any person (*i.e.,*

Table 1 The Twelve Category System used for the Content Analysis[a]

Category	Description
Actions and Desires Concerning Actions	
1. Interpersonal Interactions	Perceptions of O's actual interactions with others as well as his thoughts, feelings, and desires concerning interactions with others; includes how he gets along with others, his friendships and his feelings regarding others. Ex.: He likes to talk with his roommates.
2. Interests and Activities	Perceptions of O's (1) actual activities, such as studying and recreational activities; (2) interest in activities; and (3) general concerns, such as about his occupation, society, or money. Ex.: He studies very hard. He likes to ski. He is money-minded. Perceptions involving people—O's activities with, interest in, or concern about people—are classed under Interpersonal Interactions.
3. Others' Relations with Person Described	Perceptions of other people's interactions with O or their perceptions of him. Perceptions of O's popularity, etc. Ex.: His fraternity brothers like him.
Cognitions	
4. Opinions and Beliefs	Perceptions of the specific content of O's thoughts, such as his opinions, beliefs, values, and expectations. Ex.: He is against the country's present form of government.
5. Self-Concept	Perceptions of O's feelings, thoughts, or desires concerning himself. Ex.: He thinks he is intelligent.
6. Aspirations	Perceptions of O's desires, hopes, expectations, beliefs, or concerns about his own future. Ex.: He wants to earn a big income after he graduates.
Enduring Personal Characteristics	
7. Abilities and Knowledge	Assessments of O's competence or potential competence in any area. O's knowledge—its general scope or specific facts that O knows. Ex.: He is a good artist.
8. Cognitive-Emotional Style	O's personal style regarding his emotions and thinking—such as his temperament, approach to problems, sense of humor, and rigidity. Also, his cognitive-emotional states and personality dynamics. Ex.: He gets angry easily.
9. Interpersonal Style	Perceptions of O's manner or style of interacting with others. An actual interaction need not be mentioned. Ex.: He is friendly.
10. Global Characterizations	Perceptions which "sum up" O in a very general way. Ex.: He is an Ivy League Type.
Objective Information	
11. Appearance and Possessions	Perceptions which could be based on knowledge derived by simply looking at O, such as his dress, grooming, and physical stature. Perceptions of things O possesses. Ex.: He dresses neatly.
12. Background	Perceptions of objective, demographic facts about O, such as his membership groups, marital status, age, and family members. Ex.: He has two children.

[a] "O" here refers to the object of the perception, that is the person being described.

all persons have background characteristics, interactions with other persons, appearance and possessions, etc.). Thus, the categories used in describing another person did not depend on the nature of the target person but rather on what the perceiver chose to notice about him. This characteristic of the coding system was particularly important since the Ethiopians were describing other Ethiopians while the Americans were describing other Americans and it was important that the categories reflect the perceivers' habits rather than the targets' particular behaviors. The system proved to be successful both in terms of the suitability for classifying the perceptions produced and the reliability of those classifications. By suitability is meant that coders had little difficulty placing the perceptions in the categories available, seldom needing to resort to the "residual" category. Of the total of 10,551 perceptions produced by all subjects in the study only 61—or .6% —fell into the residual category. A reliability test was conducted by selecting a stratified random sample of 20% of the descriptions of all types of persons described. A second coder then independently coded each of these perceptions using the coding manual as a guide. For 92% of all the perceptions, the second coder placed the perception in precisely the same category as had the first coder.

Results

The raw data generated by the content analysis are the frequencies with which the subjects used any given perceptual category. Since the precise number of perceptions produced varied from subject to subject, these frequencies were treated entirely in terms of percentages. Because the category usage for descriptions of persons known well and those known little were not significantly different for either the Americans or the Ethiopians, these data are pooled. Further, the category usage for the Americans' descriptions of premedical students was not significantly different from that for English majors and again these data are pooled and will be referred to simply as University Students.

CULTURAL DIFFERENCES   Since both Ethiopians and Americans described university students, these data, shown in Table 2 are most directly comparable. The Ethiopian sample included only males, and hence Table 2 includes only responses of American males, and further, since each Ethiopian described only four university students, only the first four descriptions of university students by each American were used in the analysis.

The data in Table 2 reveal many highly significant differences in catagory usage demonstrating that each cultural group perceives its fellow university students in very different ways. When the American descriptions are compared to Ethiopians' descriptions of city dwellers and villagers, the differences in category usage remain significant and consistent, further confirming the very different perceptual habits of Americans and Ethiopians.

ETHIOPIAN-AMERICAN DIFFERENCES   The results revealed dramatic differences in the Ethiopians' and the Americans' use of the perceptual categories. While both groups used extensively the category "Interests and Activities," the Ethiopians stressed "Interpersonal Interactions" and "Opinions and Beliefs" far more than the Americans, and the Americans stressed the categories "Abilities and Knowledge," "Cognitive-Emotional Style," and "Interpersonal Style" far more than the Ethiopians.

Regarding these results the question arises of whether these particular cultural differences are peculiar to the descriptions of university students or reflect more generalized perceptual habits. Thus, would we find similar cultural differences if different groups were described? The Americans' descriptions are compared with the Ethiopians' descriptions of uneducated city dwellers and of villagers. Here we see the strong consistency of the cultural differences regardless of the particular groups being described. This is not to say that the descriptions themselves were the same—quite the contrary. Subjects said very different things about all the targets—but the categories used remained the same. Thus, an Ethiopian might say that a university student believes that the government should redistribute the land while he might say that the villager believes that education corrupts people—the content is completely different, but the category "Opinions and Beliefs" is used consistently. Thus, the data reveal that perceivers have particular categories of attributes that they habitually use in describing others regardless of the specific characteristics of the persons they are describing. This result was also found in a study by Dornbusch, Hastorf *et al.* (1965) showing that the categories used by a describer depended more on who the describer was than on who the target was. Further confirming this point is the fact that in the present study the perceptual categories used for persons known well did not differ significantly from those used for persons known little either for the Americans or for the Ethiopians. Thus it appears that perceivers have characteristic categories that they tend to draw upon regardless of whom they are perceiving, and that the

Table 2 Ethiopian Males' Compared to American Males'
Descriptions of University Students

Category	% for Ethiopians (N = 39)	% for Americans (N = 47)	Difference between Ethiopians and Americans			
			Diff.	s_{md}	t	p
Interpersonal Interactions	21.6	7.4	14.2	1.63	8.71	.001
Interests & Activities	37.3	29.4	7.9	2.38	3.31	.002
Others' Relations With	2.6	1.8	.8	.65	1.23	NS
Opinions & Beliefs	10.6	3.2	7.4	1.69	4.40	.001
Self-Concept	3.2	2.5	.7	.70	1.00	NS
Aspirations	1.2	1.7	− .5	.49	.96	NS
Abilities & Knowledge	3.9	12.5	−8.6	1.45	5.90	.001
Cognitive-Emotional Style	7.3	15.0	−7.7	1.44	5.35	.001
Interpersonal Style	7.4	10.2	−2.8	1.40	2.10	.05
Global Characterizations	.4	4.3	−3.9	.57	6.91	.001
Appearance & Possessions	1.9	6.7	−4.9	1.48	3.28	.002
Background Information	2.3	4.6	−2.4	.88	2.68	.01
Residual	.4	.7	− .3	.24	1.42	NS

choice of which categories are used is markedly influenced by the culture in which the perceiver is raised.

Given these cultural differences, it becomes interesting to speculate regarding the cultural forces at work causing the differences. Katz (1960) has suggested that a perceiver is likely to see what is in some way useful to him. In looking at differences between American and Ethiopian cultures from this functional viewpoint, a number of cultural forces become apparent which might be expected to produce these differences in category usage.[2]

The first cultural force regards the sources of status in the two societies. As with many traditional societies, in Ethiopia status has traditionally been ascribed rather than achieved. Both Levine (1965) and Korten (1972) have stressed the extreme degree to which one's rank in Ethiopian society is determined by the rank of one's parents rather than by one's personal achievements. In contrast, in American society status is to a much greater extent achieved. Thus we see with regard to the categories of perception that one of the most significant differences falls on the category "Abilities and Knowledge" with Americans perceiving these attributes far more often than the Ethiopians. This may be due to the fact that this category has little functional value for the Ethiopians since it is largely irrelevant to the important matter of status. In contrast, for the Americans, attributes in this category are highly relevant in assessing the qualities of a person.

A paradoxical aspect of the Ethiopian result is that the Ethiopians involved in the study were all students, almost all from humble backgrounds, who had arrived at their status as university students by passing a series of exams. They are part of a changing segment of Ethiopian society in which status is no longer simply ascribed but rather can be achieved through one's abilities. It is interesting to note that the category "Background Information" which would be most relevant to status determinations of the city dweller and villager is most used by the Ethiopians in describing these groups—while for the descriptions of students, who have essentially risen above their backgrounds, it is not. Thus it would appear that under changing circumstances, an irrelevant perceptual category may be dropped long before the new, more appropriate category comes into use.

A second cultural force possibly shaping the differences in category usage observed is the urgency of the need within the Ethiopian culture for getting along with other people in the environment. Korten (1972) documents and discusses the Ethiopians' obsessive fear of incurring the disfavor of another person and the potentially disastrous effects of so doing. The societies in Ethiopia have been traditionally closed, with a person being born and dying in the same village. The members of his village all knew him and had an important influence on his life. If, by any chance, he came into a disagreement with them that caused them to reject him, the resulting ostracism could be disastrous. Rejected by his own village, he would find it extremely difficult to settle in any other area, since he

---

[2]The nation of Ethiopia is comprised of a variety of tribes, religions, and cultures. However, the dominant culture has been that of the Amhara-Tigre and it is the characteristics of that culture which are referred to here.

would always be considered an outsider and treated with suspicion. In such a culture it would appear terribly functional to seek indices which might facilitate one's interactions with others. Back and Paramesh (1969) have suggested that such indices would include categories of perception pertaining to the beliefs of others and their interpersonal interactions. These two categories are precisely those used most heavily by the Ethiopians in comparison to the Americans.

A third cultural difference that can be noted from the category usage is the difference in the tendency to search for the enduring or dispositional properties of the person. Looking at the overall pattern of category usage, it can be noted that the Americans, with their greater use of the categories of "Abilities and Knowledge," "Cognitive-Emotional Style," "Interpersonal Style," and "Global Characterizations" display a preoccupation with the enduring aspects of the persons they perceive. These categories all involve the perceiver's taking the raw data of more concrete perceptions and making inferences concerning the individual's more lasting characteristics—the essense of his personality. The Ethiopians, in contrast, show low usage of these categories relating to enduring personal characteristics. Their perceptions fall primarily in categories involving concrete actions or desires concerning actions (Interpersonal Interactions, Other's Relations with the Person Described, or Interests and Activities).

This is not to suggest that the Ethiopians are not using any inference at all in their perceptions. A statement typical of the Ethiopian descriptions such as "He likes to play football" takes a certain amount of inference, but clearly it involves less than the more dispositional statement "He is aggressive" which would be more typical of the American descriptions. The cultural cause of this difference can only be conjectured. It may be that in a culture as stable, traditional, and technologically simple as that of Ethiopia, habits of inference are not as highly developed as they are in members of a rapidly changing and complex society such as that of the U.S. Hence perhaps one of the cultural forces shaping the structure of category usage involves the generalized cognitive habits regarding the use of inference.

These cultural explanations of the category differences found are, of course, only speculative. Further research—particularly with other cultures—could validate or invalidate the generality of these tentative hypotheses. Thus, is it true that in societies where status is ascribed that abilities are not salient perceptual attributes? Is it true that in societies where there is a high need for getting along with others that opinions and beliefs and interpersonal interactions become particularly salient perceptual attributes? Is it true that in stable, traditional societies there is less use of inference and hence less concern with the dispositional properties of the person? And finally, is it true that under conditions of change, inappropriate perceptual categories are dropped before newer, more appropriate ones come into use?

In analyzing the Ethiopian-American differences it was suggested that Ethiopians may not use the category "Abilities and Knowledge" as much as Americans because of its reduced relevance in determining status. Regarding the American male-female differences it might be suggested that abilities and knowledge are less important in determining the status of women than that of men.

While males are accorded status for the demonstration of abilities and knowledge (*e.g.*, in grades in school, ability in sports, etc.) for women the results of demonstrating such ability may be much more equivocal (*cf.* Horner, 1969). What then is a major source of status for women? Aside from beauty, which to some extent is fixed, one of her surest avenues to status is in terms of her interpersonal skills. In the Ethiopian-American analysis, the Ethiopian emphasis on the interpersonal interactions was suggested as due to a need to get along with others, and again for the American females such a need is proposed as the reason for the female emphasis on this category.

Conclusion

The study demonstrated that different cultural groups use very different systems of categories in perceiving other people. It was suggested that cultural needs affect the importance of particular perceptual categories and in this way shape the interpersonal perceptions of the culture's members. Specific hypotheses regarding how particular needs might affect category use were proposed, but only further cross-cultural research will indicate how these hypotheses need to be refined or changed so that it may be possible to predict the cues to which a cultural group will be most alert.

References

Back, K. W. & Paramesh, C. R. Self-image, information exchange, and social character. *International Journal of Psychology,* 1969, 4, 109–118.

Beach, L. & Wertheimer, M. A. Free response approach to the study of person cognition. *Journal of Abnormal and Social Psychology,* 1961, 62, 367–374.

Bruner, J. S. On perceptual readiness. *Psychological Review,* 1957, 64, 123–152.

Dennis, W. Cultural and developmental factors in perception. In R. R. Blake & G. V. Ramsey (Eds.), *Perception: An approach to personality.* New York: Ronald Press, 1951.

Dornbusch, S. M. & Hastorf, A. H., *et al.* The perceivers and the perceived: Their relative influence on the categories of interpersonal cognition. *Journal of Personality and Social Psychology,* 1965, I, 434–440.

Ekman, P. & Friesen, W. V. Constants across cultures in the face and emotion. *Journal of Personality and Social Psychology,* 1971, 17, 124–129.

Ekman, P., Sorenson, E. R. & Friesen, W. V. Pan-cultural elements in facial displays of emotions. *Science,* 1969, 164, 86–88.

Hall, E. *The silent language.* New York: Doubleday, 1959.

Hall, E. *The hidden dimension.* New York: Doubleday, 1966.

Horner, M. S. Fail: Bright women. *Psychology Today,* 1969, 3 (6), 36–38.

Katz, D. The functional approach to the study of attitudes. *Public Opinion Quarterly,* 1960, 24, 163–204.

Kelley, H. H. The warm-cold variable in first impressions of persons. *Journal of Personality,* 1950, 18, 431–439.

Korten, D. C. *Planned change in a traditional society: Psychological problems of modernization in Ethiopia.* New York: Praeger, 1972.

Korten, F. F. The stereotype as a cognitive construct. *Journal of Social Psychology,* 1973, 90, 29–39.

Levine, D. *Wax and gold.* Chicago: University of Chicago, 1965.

Martin, J. G. Racial ethnocentrism and judgment of beauty. *Journal of Social Psychology,* 1964, 63, 59–63.

Segall, M. H., Campbell, D. T. & Herskovits, M. J. *The influence of culture on visual perception.* Indianapolis: Bobbs-Merrill, 1966.

Triandis, H. C. *The analysis of subjective culture.* New York: Wiley, 1972.

Triandis, H. C. & Vassiliou, V. Frequency of contact and stereotyping. *Journal of Personality and Social Psychology,* 1967, 7, 316–328.

Triandis, H. C., Vassiliou, V. & Nassiakou, M. Three cross-cultural studies of subjective culture. *Journal of Personality and Social Psychology,* Monograph Supplement, 1968, No. 4, Part 2, 1–42.

Warr, P. B. & Knapper, C. *The perception of people and events.* New York: Wiley, 1968.

Ethnic Variations in the Phenomenology of Emotions

Anthony J. Marsella, Michael D. Murray, and Charles Golden

Since the dawn of human history, emotions have been of considerable interest and concern to man. While poets, artists, and musicians have sought to portray emotions in word, image, and song—offering us new vistas of insight and awareness—philosophers and scientists have sought rational knowledge about emotional development, expression, and change. But yet, in spite of the centuries of portrayal and study, man's emotions continue to remain a mystery to him.

One reason for this is the private nature of emotions. Each man's emotions are a function of his own subjective experience, and this privacy does not lend itself well to scientific efforts which seek to make the private public and the subjective objective. However, the need to understand emotions is critical, especially for investigators in the field of ethnopsychiatry. Ethnopsychiatric researchers are faced with two problems in their study of emotion: cross-cultural variations in emotional expression, and techniques to measure subjective experience.

Method

SUBJECTS   The Ss were 324 college students enrolled in undergraduate psychology courses at the University of Hawaii. Of these, 97 were of Caucasian-American ancestry (45 males and 52 females), 102 were of Chinese-American ancestry (43 males and 59 females), and 125 were of Japanese-American ancestry (65 males and 60 females). All Ss were volunteers and received extra class points for participation.

From *Journal of Cross-Cultural Psychology,* Vol. 5, No. 3 (Sept. 1974), pp. 312–328 by permission of the publisher, Sage Publications, Inc. Anthony J. Marsella and Charles Golden teach in the Department of Psychology, University of Hawaii.

PROCEDURE   All Ss were administered a 20-scale semantic differential which required them to rate eight concepts: shame, guilt, love, hate, anger, humiliation, pride, and envy. These concepts were rated on 20 7-point bi-polar scales. The scales were selected on the basis of previous work by Block (1957) and Osgood et al. (1957). Time for completion of the task was approximately 50 minutes.

ANALYSIS   The data were analyzed in two ways. First, means for each of the 20 scales on each concept were compared across the 3 ethnic groups, using a one-way analysis of variance. All scales with significant differences were then checked for ethnic group differences by paired comparison t-tests.

Second, the ratings of each ethnic group were submitted to a principal axes factor analysis and varimax rotation. Eigen-values of 1.00 were used to terminate factor extraction and loadings of .50 were used as a cutoff for assigning a scale to a factor.

Results

The results for the concept of "shame" are displayed in Tables 1 and 2. Table 1 contains the mean scores across all 20 scales for each of the ethnic groups and

Table 1   Ethnic Group Comparison of Mean Scores
for Concept "Shame"

| | Ethnic Group Means | | | | |
Scale	Caucasian	Chinese	Japanese	F-Value	t-tests[a]
High-Low	4.98	3.81	4.12	10.58[b]	C >Ch and J[b]
Weak-Strong	3.43	4.24	4.26	3.59[d]	Ch and J >C[b]
Rough-Smooth	3.40	3.15	3.36	NS	
Active-Passive	4.77	4.36	3.95	7.95[b]	C >J[b]
Empty-Full	3.24	3.55	3.56	NS	
Angular-Rounded	4.07	3.33	3.69	6.37[c]	C and J >Ch[b]
Cold-Hot	3.74	3.88	4.18	NS	
Clear-Hazy	4.69	4.43	4.02	9.54[b]	C >J[c]
Calm-Excited	4.37	4.85	4.90	NS	
Sick-Healthy	2.72	2.80	3.11	NS	
Tense-Relaxed	2.42	2.00	2.18	3.39[d]	C >Ch[d]
Sad-Happy	1.98	2.09	2.44	NS	
Soft-Loud	3.95	4.20	3.99	NS	
Beautiful-Ugly	5.51	5.41	5.39	NS	
Sharp-Dull	4.27	3.88	3.35	14.09[b]	C and Ch >J[b]
Fresh-Stale	4.73	4.32	4.43	4.60[d]	C >Ch[b]
Green-Red	4.33	4.83	4.87	NS	
Good-Bad	5.54	5.32	5.14	7.73[b]	C >J[d]
Humorous-Serious	5.49	5.49	5.02	9.53[b]	C and Ch >J[d]
Complicated-Simple	2.81	2.88	3.41	NS	

[a] Significance tests based on paired comparisons.

[b] = < .001   [c] = < .01   [d] = < .05

the results of the analyses of variance and paired comparison t-tests conducted to identify ethnic group differences. The results indicate that numerous differences exist among the mean scores for the different ethnic groups. Ten of the 20 scales yielded significant differences across the 3 ethnic groups.

Table 2 displays the results of the factor analyses. Differences were revealed both in the number and the type of factors which emerged. The Japanese-American factorial solution yielded four factors (% of variance = 55%), while both the Caucasian-American and Chinese-American factorial solutions yielded six factors, each accounting for 66% and 63% of the variance, respectively. Factorial interpretations were relatively similar for all groups; however, different scales comprised the factors in each group. The names assigned suggest that the connotative meaning of shame includes evaluative, dynamism, sensory synesthesia, awareness, arousal, and intensity elements. However, the various elements differ across ethnic groups.

Discussion

THE NATURE OF SHAME   Although shame has been the topic of numerous psychological and anthropological investigations (e.g., Piers and Singer, 1933; Ausubel, 1955; Hare, 1967; Lewis, 1971), it remains a difficult emotion to conceptualize. *The American Heritage Dictionary* defines shame as, "a painful emotion caused by a strong sense of guilt, embarrassment, unworthiness, or disgrace," and "a condition of disgrace, dishonor, and ignominy." *Roget's Pocket Thesaurus* lists shame under "personal affections" and cites the following words as synonyms for shame: disgrace, dishonor, tarnish, stain, blot, sully, taint, discredit, degrade, and debase. Clearly, these linguistic aids offer little clarification of shame, and what little they do offer seems to be primarily relevant to Western cultural traditions.

Lewis (1971: 37), who has written a major book on shame, wrote the following:

> In shame . . . there is an implosion of the self. The body gestures and attitudes include head bowed, eyes closed, body curved in on itself, making the person as small as possible. At the same time that it seeks to disappear, the self may be dealing with an excess of autonomic stimulation, blushing or sweating or diffuse rage, experienced as a "flood" of sensations. Shame is thus regarded by adults as a primitive reaction, in which the body functions have gone out of control . . . shame is a relatively wordless state. The experience of shame often occurs in the form of imagery, of looking or being looked at. . . . The wordlessness of shame, its imagery of looking, together with the concreteness of autonomic activity make shame a primitive, irrational reaction to which there is difficulty applying a rational solution.

We all know what shame is and yet we do not really understand it. We do know that it is a "felt experience" of some degree of discomfort which is typically associated with the violation of social norms or expectations. It is a major method of social control in many societies and in some instances may even find itself institutionalized in various forms or types of psychotherapy (e.g., *Naikan Therapy*). However, it does not necessarily have the same meaning or connotation in all societies. For examples, Bulatao (1964) discusses the concept of "Hiya" in Filipi-

Table 2 Factor Analysis of Scales According to Ethnic Group for the Concept of Shame and, in Parentheses, Factor Labels as Descriptive Guidelines

Caucasian-American		Chinese-American		Japanese-American	
I. (Evaluative)		I. (Evaluative)		I. (Evaluative Arousal)	
Good-Bad	+.85	Beautiful-Ugly	.78	Beautiful-Ugly	.80
Beautiful-Ugly	.82	Good-Bad	.76	Humorous-Serious	.74
Healthy-Sick	.74	Humorous-Serious	.74	Good-Bad	.74
Happy-Sad	.52	Simple-Complicated	.62	Happy-Sad	.74
II. (Sensory Synesthesia)		II. (Dynamism)		Healthy-Sick	.65
Angular-Rounded	.83	Active-Passive	.75	Fresh-Stale	.64
Rough-Smooth	.69	High-Low	.71	Relaxed-Tense	.53
Loud-Soft	.66	Strong-Weak	.71	II. (Dynamism)	
III. (Dynamism)		Full-Empty	.70	Cold-Hot	.79
High-Low	.88	Sharp-Dull	.60	Low-High	.78
Strong-Weak	.86	III. (Arousal)		Empty-Full	.68
Active-Passive	.53	Green-Red	.69	Passive-Active	.56
IV. (Awareness)		Cold-Hot	.67	Weak-Strong	.53
Clear-Hazy	.74	Calm-Excited	.53	III. (Sensory Synesthesia)	
Fresh-Stale	.68	IV. (Sensory Synesthesia)		Angular-Rounded	.73
Sharp-Dull	.65	Rough-Smooth	.81	Excited-Calm	.70
V. (Arousal)		Angular-Rounded	.66	Rough-Smooth	.59
Green-Red	.80	V. (Arousal Evaluative)		Loud-Soft	.55
Calm-Excited	.75	Tense-Relaxed	.76	IV. (Awareness)	
Relaxed-Tense	.52	Sad-Happy	.63	Clear-Hazy	.83
VI. (Intensity)		VI. (Awareness)		Sharp-Dull	.52
Humorous-Serious	.69	Clear-Hazy	.83		
Simple-Complicated	.59	Healthy-Sick	.62		

NOTE: To make all the above loadings positive, numerous scales from Table 1 have been reversed.

nos and notes that it is somewhat similar to shame in Americans but yet is something more because of the peculiar nature of the Filipino's "unindividuated ego." "Hiya" means a state of total insecurity or social isolation of the individual which extends far beyond the state of embarrassment which the Western world often associates with the word. In addition, for Filipinos, the term "Walang Hiya," which roughly translates as "You are without shame," is considered to be an extremely derogatory comment akin to saying that the person is unsocialized or unresponsive to social pressure.

In a society which emphasizes conformity to normative ideals and frowns upon autonomy or independence behavior, shame becomes a far different word from a society in which individuality and nonconformity are stressed. For example, Lebra (1971) observed that, in Japanese culture, there is a social sharing of shame, which produces strong pressures to conform to social expectations. Lebra suggests that shame is related to "status incongruency"; it is the feeling which arises when there is "exposure, actual or anticipated, to observers of an action or a state which is incongruous with the claimed and socially identified status" (1971: 248). Shame has different meanings and implications for different cultural groups; this is closely related to different senses of identity (group versus individual) which are conditioned by socialization processes.

Where values of conformity, dependence, group solidarity, and hierarchical authority are encouraged, shame assumes a particular meaning, while in societies where independence, autonomy, and equalitarian values are fostered, shame assumes a different meaning. In both cases, it functions as a social control mechanism which makes use of aversive stimulus properties. Let us examine some differences and similarities in the connotative meaning of shame among populations of different cultural heritages.

CAUCASIANS   The shame profile for Caucasians (Table 1) has a number of interesting aspects. For example, shame is rated as a low, passive, empty, hazy, sick, tense, sad, ugly, stale, bad, complicated, and serious experience. It is obviously an aversive state and one to be avoided. Factorially, it appears to be rather highly differentiated (six factors), suggesting it is experientially quite complex. This may be a function of a tendency among Caucasians to be intraceptive and to label emotional experiences verbally. For example, in Western cultures, great emphasis is placed on the verbalization of feelings and the labeling of emotional experience. Individuals are frequently encouraged to explain motives behind behaviors and to discuss why they behaved in a particular way. Indeed, one of the cardinal characteristics of most psychotherapy systems in the West is the teaching of emotional awareness and the direct labeling of feelings. For example, Rogerian (1951) therapy emphasizes the articulation of feelings and emotions by clients and facilitates this by its use of reflection, clarification, and encouragement by the therapist.

The picture of shame which emerges for Caucasians is one characterized by a judgmental process revolving around a strong, painful but rather nonspecific feeling. Its basic components consist of: evaluation, synesthesia, dynamism, awareness, arousal, and intensity. It is, of course, conceivable that the factors could be labeled differently. Similarly, it should be recognized that the factors are limited by the scales used in the analysis. The presence of other scales could conceivably yield a different picture although the authors feel satisfied that the present analysis makes good sense.

CHINESE-AMERICANS   The shame profile for Chinese-Americans indicates that shame is construed as rough, angular, sick, excited, tense, sad, ugly, red, bad, complicated, and serious. As was the case with the Caucasian-Americans, shame is clearly an aversive feeling. Of particular interest is the emergence of an inclination among the subjects to rate shame as red. In conjunction with the other scales of Factor III, one is tempted to conclude that shame has a rather interesting tactile or somatic property for Chinese-Americans. Factorially, the emergence of six factors in accounting for the data indicates that shame is highly differentiated. The basic factors identified include: evaluative, dynamism, arousal, sensory synesthesia, arousal evaluative, and awareness. The factor dimensions suggest that shame can be characterized as a state involving an evaluational process centered around a strong, aversive, and complex feeling which is difficult to articulate.

JAPANESE-AMERICANS   According to the shame profile for Japanese-Americans, shame is considered to be rough, tense, excited, sick, sad, ugly, sharp, red, bad, and complicated serious. All these imply that shame is a very unpleasant experience. Factorially, it is complicated but not as highly differentiated as it is for the Chinese; it consists of four dimensions which suggest a picture of a complex judgmental process revolving around an acute and aversive sensory feeling. The complexity is related to the integration of seemingly diverse components into a distinct factorial dimension.

In Factor I, shame appears to involve an evaluational process for the Japanese-Americans in which aesthetic, moral, and organismic dimensions emerge. The fact that these do not appear as separate components is rather interesting but puzzling. One speculation which might be offered is that shame is understood at a molar level in which many atomistic components are integrated rather than separated. We would speculate that the style for the Japanese-Americans is to seek harmony and integration of various dimensions rather than more atomistic analysis.

Cross-Cultural Differences

In the previous section an attempt was made to examine the results according to individual ethnic groups. A cross-cultural comparison is now offered. As Table 1 demonstrates, a comparison of mean scores across ethnic groups reveals a number of differences. We previously noted that all three groups appeared to see shame as an uncomfortable state; but the degrees of differences are not discussed. For example, all the groups rated shame as a serious rather than a humorous experience; however, the Caucasian-Americans and the Chinese-Americans rated it as significantly more serious than did the Japanese-Americans.

A closer examination of the differences reveals in several instances that the Caucasian-Americans rated scales differently from the two Oriental groups. The Caucasian-Americans rated shame as significantly more low, weak, and dull than did the two Oriental groups. Also, they rated it more passive, hazy, bad, and serious than the Japanese-Americans and more rounded, relaxed, and stale than the Chinese-Americans. The Japanese-Americans rated the scales as significantly more low, rounded, sharp, and serious than the Chinese-Americans. One conclusion which seems to emerge from these results is that shame is less clearly identifiable (or perhaps understood) for the Caucasian group. It does not appear to be as specific and identifiable, as seems to be the case for the Orientals. One interpretation of this is that shame may be used as a technique of social control more often in Oriental societies and children consequently learn to read the organismic and situational cues more readily. This does not mean that the authors are endorsing a position of "shame" versus "no-shame" cultures but rather that shame, as a social control mechanism, is simply implemented more frequently in certain cultures than in others.

Another interpretation is that the Oriental groups may be better able to read somatic cues associated with shame and thus experience it more clearly. In unpublished research on sensory abilities in imagery, the authors found that Japanese-Americans demonstrated significantly better scores in kinesthetic, somesthetic, and tactile areas of functioning than Caucasian-Americans. By being able to utilize information better in these modalities, all of which are involved in the somatic arousal which accompanies shame, it is conceivable that shame is more readily identifiable for the Japanese-Americans and is thus not perceived to be dull, hazy, and weak. In addition, shame may be more of an all-or-none phenomenon among Orientals. The situations in which it can occur may be more clearly identifiable, and the consequences of its occurrence may be more severe.

No effort was made to compare the factorial structures objectively in order to identify the amount of overlap and disagreement among the groups. However, a visual check of the factorial structures across the different groups indicates certain similarities. The factor labels are definitely the same, but it should be noted that there are often different scales which appear for the various ethnic groups. For example, all three groups have an awareness factor; however, for one group it consists of clear-hazy, fresh-stale, and sharp-dull, for another it consists of clear-hazy and healthy-sick, while for the last group it consists of clear-hazy and sharp-dull. Results such as these suggest that the awareness of shame is different from group to group; perhaps the cues are different in its perception. In some cases, the differences are large, while in others they are small, but they are different!

Variations also seem to be present in the degree of differentiation of shame among the three groups. Clearly, shame is less differentiated for the Japanese-Americans than for the Caucasian-American or Chinese-American groups. We have already noted that this may, in part, be a function of a cognitive style among the Japanese which seemingly harmonizes or integrates disparate dimensions more readily than the cognitive styles of either of the other two groups.

Another source of differences can be found in the types of factors which emerged across the groups. For example, the Caucasian-Americans evidenced an intensity factor (Factor IV) but neither of the other groups did; however, intensity scales (humorous-serious, simple-complicated) were interspersed in Factor I for both the Oriental groups. This suggests that the evaluative component involves intensity aspects for Oriental groups.

Some Implications for Ethnopsychiatry

Ethnopsychiatry is largely concerned with the problems of adjustment and disorder in different cultures. Of all aspects of this adjustment continuum, emotions are the most important to understand. Indeed, one might conclude that the nature of emotional development, expression, and control constitutes the fundamental problem for understanding psychological adjustment. In different cultures, these aspects of emotions differ. For example, in certain cultures emotional displays are minimized even in the face of major emotional stimuli; in others, emotional displays are continually encouraged even when emotional stimuli are barely identifiable. Clearly, the nature of the connotative meaning of emotions between these two cultures should differ! The semantic differential offers a suitable method for understanding the variations in meaning across cultures.

But variations in meaning are only part of the task. By understanding the nature of cultural differences in emotion, different approaches toward classification and diagnosis can be taken. For example, Marsella et al. (1973) demonstrated that depression is manifested differently among various ethnic groups. One aspect of these differences was concerned with the verbalization of mood states by different ethnic groups; Chinese-Americans are hesitant to say that they are depressed but do report that they are fatigued, tired, nervous, and suffering from numerous somatic complaints. Understanding of the connotative meaning assigned to different emotions by individuals from different cultures will permit new diagnostic alternatives to be considered and better treatment to be offered.

As we have seen, shame simply does not mean the same thing nor have the same behavioral implications for the different groups we have studied. To facilitate communication and increase a therapist's capacity for empathy and understanding, it is imperative that he comprehend the meaning of the patient's communications. By failing to understand the meaning of emotions in different cultures and the functional roles which they play in the maintenance and enhancement of the culture, the naive psychotherapist could actually increase deviance.

References

Ausubel, D. (1955) "Relationships between guilt and shame in the socializing process." *Psych. Rev.* 62: 378–390.

Block, J. (1957) "Studies in the phenomenology of emotion." *J. of Abnormal and Social Psychology* 53: 358–367.

Bulatao, J. (1964) "Hiya." *Philippine Studies* 12: 424–438.

Hare, R. (1967) "Cultural differences in the use of shame and guilt in child-rearing." Institute of Philippine Culture Paper 5: 35–77.

Lebra, T. (1971) "The social mechanism of guilt and shame: the Japanese case." *Anthropological Q.* 44: 241–255.

Lewis, H. (1971) *Shame and Guilt in Neurosis.* New York: International Universities Press.

Marsella, A. J., D. Kinzie, and P. Gordon (1973) "Ethnic variations in the expression of depression." *J. of Cross-Cultural Psychology* 4: 435–458.

———— and P. Tannenbaum (1957) *The Measurement of Meaning.* Urbana: Univ. of Illinois Press.

Piers, G., and M. Singer (1953) *Shame and Guilt.* Springfield, Ill.: Charles C. Thomas.

Rogers, C. (1951) *Client-Centered Therapy.* Boston: Houghton Mifflin.

Suggested Readings

Aspaturian, V. V., "Chinese and Soviet Perceptions of One Another," *The Journal of General Education,* 26 (Fall 1974), 219–240. Aspaturian details the perceptual images Chinese and Russians have of one another based on their cultural similarities and dissimilarities. He relates how common goals and purposes produce common and positive perceptions while conflict results in negative perceptions.

Bagby, J. W., "A Cross-Cultural Study of Perceptual Predominance in Binocular Rivalry," *Journal of Abnormal and Social Psychology,* 54 (1957), 331–334. Bagby reports a cross-cultural experiment involving American and Mexican children. His short and to the point article neatly demonstrates the significant relationship between culture and perception.

Eubanks, E. E., "A Study of Perceptions of Black and White Teachers in De Facto Segrated High Schools," *Education,* 95 (1974), 51–57. Eubanks studied 97 teachers from six de facto segregated high schools. Perceptions of job satisfaction, teacher–student relations, school status, attributes for success as a teacher, and behavioral, emotional, and social characteristics of students were considered.

Gardner, R. C., "Ethnic Stereotypes: The Traditional Approach, A New Look," *The Canadian Psychologist,* 14 (April 1973), 133–148. This paper views ethnic stereotypes as beliefs generally shared in the community about characteristics of various groups. Implications of this position are discussed and traditional assessment procedures criticized. An alternative measurement procedure is described, and its applications to the study of many aspects of the stereotyping process are summarized.

Klineberg, O., *The Human Dimension in International Relations* (New York: Holt, Rinehart and Winston, 1964). Here is an excellent application of social psychology to international communication. Various social–psychological factors, such as stereotypes, social perceptions, and roles, are seen as cultural variables in the international communication process.

Luce, T. S., "Blacks, Whites and Yellows: They All Look Alike to Me," *Psychology Today* (November 1974), pp. 105–106, 107. In this article, Luce describes studies he has conducted that reveal that the stereotype of members of other ethnic and racial groups all looking alike is widespread among racial and ethnic groups.

Taylor, D. M., and F. E. Aboud, "Ethnic Stereotypes: Is the Concept Necessary?" *The Canadian Psychologist,* 14 (October 1973), 330–338. A review of ethnic stereotypes reveals that there have been very few attempts to integrate stereotypes into the mainstream of psychological theory. The authors suggest that the classification of stereotypes as "bad" either because they are invalid or because they are the results of an inferior cognitive process has not significantly increased our understanding of psychological processes.

Toch, H., and H. C. Smith (eds.), *Social Perception: The Development of Interpersonal Impressions* (Princeton: D. Van Nostrand Co., 1968). This book brings together knowledge about the ways in which people perceive, appraise, classify, predict, evaluate, anticipate, and understand their fellows. The diversity of the readings make this volume an excellent sourcebook for social perception.

Wedge, B., *Visitors to the United States and How They See Us* (Princeton: D. Van Nostrand, Inc., 1965). In this volume, Wedge describes the problems foreign visitors to the United States have in reconciling their stereotypes and expectations about the United States and the reality of their perceptions. He details the effect prior conceptions have on the perception process.

Additional Readings

Bell, D., "The Disjunction of Culture and Social Structures: Some Notes on the Meaning of Social Reality," *Daedalus,* 94 (Winter 1965), 208–222.

Byrne, D., "Interpersonal Attraction and Similarity," *Journal of Abnormal Psychology,* 62 (1961), 713–715.

Delia, J. G., "Dialects and the Effects of Stereotypes on Interpersonal Attraction and Cognitive Processes in Impression Formation," *Quarterly Journal of Speech,* 50 (October 1972), 285–297.

Hartsough, W. R., and A. F. Fontana, "Persistence of Ethnic Stereotypes and the Relative Importance of Positive and Negative Stereotyping for Association Preferences," *Psychological Reports,* 27 (1970), 723–736.

Lambert, W., "A Cross-National Comparison of Ethnocentrism, Perception of Similars, and Affection Vis-a-Vis Other Peoples," *Acta Psychologica* (1961), pp. 612–619.

Lindgren, H. C., and J. Marrash, "A Comparative Study of Intercultural Insight and Empathy," *The Journal of Social Psychology,* 80 (1970), 135–141.

Lindgren, H. C., and A. Tebcherani, "Arab and American Auto- and Meterestereotypes: A Cross-Cultural Study of Empathy," *Journal of Cross-Cultural Psychology,* 2 (June 1971), 173–180.

Neimi, R. G., *How Family Members Perceive Each Other: Political and Social Attitudes in Two Generations* (New Haven, Conn.: Yale University Press, 1974).

Segall, M. H., D. T. Campbell, and M. J. Herskovits, *The Influence of Culture on Visual Perception* (Indianapolis: Bobbs-Merrill, 1966).

Stewart, E. C., "The Simulation of Cultural Differences," *Journal of Communication,* 16 (1966), 291–304.

Szalay, L., and D. A. Lysne, "Attitude Research for Intercultural Communication and Interaction," *Journal of Communication,* 20 (1970), 180–200.

Concepts and Questions

1. What is the relationship between culture and perception?

2. How does culture affect the perception of physical objects? Of people?

3. How would culture influence what you see and what you don't see in the world around you?

4. How do you suppose someone from a vastly different cultural background would respond to your city on a first visit? To your home?

5. In what ways would your cultural background influence what you would expect to encounter if you visited another country?

6. What stereotypic expectations have you developed and expect to perceive with regard to members of other ethnic or racial groups in your city?

7. What does Singer mean by "subjective reality?" How does this concept relate to intercultural communication?

8. Do you agree with the twelve steps found in Singer's analysis? Which ones, if any, do you find tenuous?

9. Can you, from your own experiences, think of additional cultural differences with regard to recognition and retention?

10. Why does Korten say we must understand how cognitive structures "differ from culture to culture and how the environment influences the development of these structures"?

11. Based on Singer's analysis, what are some reasons that tend to make intercultural communication more difficult than communication within the same culture or reference group?

12. What is implied by the phrase ". . . ecological and cultural factors operating in the visual environment create differences in visual inference?" In very practical terms, how does this relate to intercultural communication?

13. From your own experiences can you think of any cultural differences in the perception of persons? What factors (values, experiences, etc.) within that culture would tend to contribute to those differences?

14. Marsella, et al., base their study on the following rationale: "The study was stimulated by the work of Block (1957), who reported differences in the connotative meaning of emotions between Scandinavians and Americans and by the authors' interest in ethnocultural variations in emotions (e.g., Marsella, et al., 1973)." How does this concept relate to the study of intercultural communication?

Part Three

Intercultural Interaction: Taking Part in Intercultural Communication

If we seek to understand a people we have to put ourselves, as far as we can, in that particular historical and cultural background. . . . One has to recognize that countries and people differ in their approach and their ways, in their approach to life and their ways of living and thinking. In order to understand them we have to understand their way of life and approach. If we wish to convince them, we have to use their language as far as we can, not language in the narrow sense of the word, but the language of the mind.

—Jewaharlal Nehru

In this part we are concerned with taking part in intercultural communication. Our interest focuses on both verbal and nonverbal forms of symbolic interaction. As we pointed out while introducing Part Two, meanings reside within people and symbols serve as stimuli to which these meanings are attributed. Meaning-evoking stimuli consist of both verbal and nonverbal behaviors. Although we consider these forms of symbolic interaction separately for convenience, we hasten to point out their interrelatedness. As nonverbal behavior accompanies verbal behavior, it becomes a unique part of the total symbolic interaction. Verbal messages often rely on their nonverbal accompaniment for cues that aid the receiver in decoding the verbal symbols. Nonverbal behaviors serve not only to amplify and clarify verbal messages but can also serve as forms of symbolic interaction without verbal counterparts.

When we communicate verbally, we use words with seeming ease, because there is a high consensus of agreement about the meanings our words evoke. Our experiential backgrounds are similar enough that we share essentially the same meanings for most of the word symbols we use in everyday communication. But, even within our culture we disagree over the meanings of many word symbols. As words move farther from sense data reality they become more abstract, and there is far less agreement about appropriate meanings. What do highly abstract words like "love," "freedom," "equality," "democracy," or "good time" mean to you? Do they mean the same things to everyone? If you are in doubt, ask some friends; take a poll. You will surely find that people have different notions of these concepts and consequently different meanings for these words. Their experiences have been different, and they hold different beliefs, attitudes, values, concepts, and expectations. Yet all, or perhaps most, are from the same culture. Their backgrounds, experiences, and concepts of the universe are really quite uniform. When cultures begin to vary, much larger differences are found.

Culture exerts no small influence over our use of language. In fact, it strongly determines just what our language is and how we use it. In the narrowest sense, language is a set of symbols (vocabulary) that evoke more or less uniform meanings among a particular population and a set of rules (grammar and syntax) for using the symbols. In the broadest sense, language is the symbolic representation of a people, and it includes their historical and cultural backgrounds as well as their approach to life and their ways of living and thinking.

What comes to be symbolized and what the symbols represent are very much functions of culture. Similarly, how we use our verbal symbols is also a function of culture. What we think about or speak with others about must be capable of symbolization, and how we speak or think about things must follow the rules we have for using our language. Because the symbols and rules are culturally determined, how and what we think or talk about is, in effect, a function of our culture. This relation between language and culture is not unidirectional, however. There is an interaction between them—what we think about and how we think about it also affects our culture.

As we can see, language and culture are inseparable. To be an effective intercultural communicator requires that we be aware of the relationship between culture and language. It further requires that we learn and know about the culture of the person with whom we communicate so that we can better understand how his language represents him.

Another important aspect of verbal symbols or words is that they can evoke two kinds of meaning: *denotative* and *connotative.* A denotative meaning indicates the referent or the "thing" to which the symbol refers. For example, the denotative meaning of the word "book" is the physical object to which it refers; or, in the case of the set of symbols "*Intercultural Communication: A Reader,*" the referent is the book you are now reading. Not all denotations have a physical correspondence. As we move to higher levels of abstraction, we often deal with words that represent ideas or concepts, which exist only in the mind and do not necessarily have a physical basis. For example, much communication research is directed toward changes in attitude. Yet attitude is only a hypothetical construct used to explain behavior; we have no evidence of any physical correspondence between some group of brain cells and a person's attitudes.

The second type of meaning, the connotative, indicates an evaluative dimension. Not only do we identify referents (denotative meaning), we place them along an evaluative dimension that can be described as positive–neutral–negative. Where we place a word on the dimension depends on our prior experiences and how we "feel" about the referent. If we like books, we might place *Intercultural Communication: A Reader* near the positive end of the dimension. When we are dealing with more abstract symbols, we do the same thing. In fact, as the level of abstraction increases, so does our tendency to place more emphasis on connotative meanings. Most will agree that a book is the object you are holding in your hand, but whether books are good or bad or whether this particular book is good or bad or in between is an individual judgment based on prior experience.

Culture affects both denotative and connotative meanings. Consequently, a knowledge of how these meanings vary culturally is essential to effective intercultural communication. To make the assumption that everyone uses the same meanings is an invitation to *communication disaster.*

There are other ways in which culture affects language and language use. We tend to believe that our way of using language is correct and that any deviation is wrong or substandard. This belief can and does elicit many negative responses and judgments when we encounter someone from another culture whose use of language deviates from our own specifications.*

---

*See, for example, the findings of Lambert and his associates discussed in the first reading of this book, in addition to the readings in this chapter.

4

Verbal Interaction

The first selection in Chapter 4 introduces a generally accepted principle of language development, the Sapir–Whorf hypothesis, which states that language functions not simply as a device for reporting experience but also, and more significantly, as a way of defining experience for its users. In "The Sapir–Whorf Hypothesis," Harry Hoijer examines this classic theory of culture and language. If we accept this view, we can easily see how language plays a large and meaningful role in the totality of culture. To aid our understanding of this important theory, Hoijer reviews and classifies the Sapir–Whorf hypothesis, illustrating and adding to it from his own work with the Navajo language.

As we noted in the introduction to this part, language involves attaching meaning to word-symbols. If those symbols have to be translated, as in the case of a foreign language, numerous problems can arise. Without accurate translations we often end up simply exchanging noise or meaningless sounds. What usually happens is that our interpretations lack a common vocabulary and familiar referents. What is needed, therefore, if our goal is mutual understanding, are equivalencies in each culture. A search for this common ground is the main focus of a selection by Lee Sechrest, Todd L. Fay, and S. M. Zaidi. In their article, "Problems of Translation in Cross-Cultural Communication," they maintain that while equivalence in idiom, grammar, and syntax may be important, equivalence of experience and concepts is probably most important. With this notion as their central thesis, they attempt to point out some of the inherent problems of translation and also suggest some ways for overcoming these problems.

Edmund S. Glenn, in "Meaning and Behavior: Communication and Culture," further points out complexities of language and culture by introducing us to the concept of latent meanings. Glenn is concerned with what happens to meanings when languages are translated from one culture to another. For example, he wanted to know whether a *direct* semantic translation carries a *direct* meaning to the other culture; and to discover possible latent meanings, he conducted a study of semantic analysis based on a comparison between original statements and their translations. His results indicate that such meanings do exist and that they may act as a metalanguage indicating how messages are to be interpreted. From his work we can learn a great deal about sending verbal messages from culture to culture.

The next essay not only reflects Glenn's argument but demonstrates one of the major themes of this volume. We have noted that language and behavior are closely correlated, and that the way a culture uses language is, at times, an expression of a cultural value or orientation. This premise is given impetus by a selection written by L. Takeo Doi. In his essay, Doi endeavors to explain how the concept of *amae,* which describes a complex Japanese personality trait, influences both speech and behavior. It is Doi's contention that *amae* runs so deep in the Japanese culture that its effects are manifested in the linguistic character of the language. Doi points out that the Japanese fondness for hesitation and ambiguities of expression can be traced to the concept of *amae.* Even the fact that Japanese verbs come at the end of the sentence is related to this idea of *amae.* This article offers the student of intercultural communication a vivid example of how a culture's temperament and nature are mirrored through their language.

The article by Edith Folb, "Vernacular Vocabulary: A View of Interracial Perceptions and Experiences," is important for a number of reasons. First, as the title indicates, Folb extends her analysis to include perception, experience, and language. For her the three issues are inseparable. She notes, "What we think about and how we think about it are direct functions of our language; and what we think about and how we think about it in part determine the nature of our culture." To document this particular point of view, the study examined various terms that were used by black and white youths who, although not interacting with each other, were sharing the same experiences. This comparison demonstrates the interdependence existing between background and language. Second, the essay is important because it shows the influence subcultures often have on the majority culture. For example, a careful reading of this essay will give credence to the contention that black vernacular is a chief source of new words for the white community. Note how many of the expressions in this essay have found their way into the vocabularies of many white Americans.

It has long been assumed that we use speech as an indication of a person's prestige and status. In the final selection of this chapter, John Nist examines the concept of speech and prestige from the perspective of social class as a subculture. His essay, "The Language of the Socially Disadvantaged," is of vital concern to the student of intercultural communication. It helps us understand various subcultures, and we can also see from Nist's analysis how the language and dialect of a subculture can offer information regarding the characteristics of that group. He concentrates on three types of speech (acrolect, misilect, and basilect) as a means of determining the extent to which differences are found as one moves in and out of various social classes. There is also a subtle philosophical message found in this reading. The underlying theme is that we must not condemn people's cultural values or language simply because they are different from ours. Just as we see individual differences among individuals as something natural, so we should accept differences between cultures.

The Sapir-Whorf Hypothesis

Harry Hoijer

The Sapir-Whorf hypothesis appears to have had its initial formulation in the following two paragraphs, taken from an article of Sapir's, first published in 1929.

> Language is a guide to "social reality." Though language is not ordinarily thought of as of essential interest to the students of social science, it powerfully conditions all our thinking about social problems and processes. Human beings do not live in the objective world alone, nor alone in the world of social activity as ordinarily understood, but are very much at the mercy of the particular language which has become the medium of expression for their society. It is quite an illusion to imagine that one adjusts to reality essentially without the use of language and that language is merely an incidental means of solving specific problems of communication or reflection. The fact of the matter is that the "real world" is to a large extent unconsciously built up on the language habits of the group. No two languages are ever sufficiently similar to be considered as representing the same social reality. The worlds in which different societies live are distinct worlds, not merely the same world with different labels attached.
>
> The understanding of a simple poem, for instance, involves not merely an understanding of the single words in their average significance, but a full comprehension of the whole life of the community as it is mirrored in the words, or as it is suggested by their overtones. Even comparatively simple acts of perception are very much more at the mercy of the social patterns called words than we might suppose. If one draws some dozen lines, for instance, of different shapes, one perceives them as divisible into such categories as "straight," "crooked," "curved," "zigzag" because of the classificatory suggestiveness of the linguistic terms themselves. We see and hear and otherwise experience very largely as we do because the language habits of our community predispose certain choices of interpretation. [In Mandelbaum 1949: 162.]

The notion of language as a "guide to social reality" is not entirely original with Sapir. Somewhat similar ideas, though far less adequately stated, may be found in Boas' writings, at least as early as 1911. Thus we find in Boas' introduction to the *Handbook of American Indian Languages* a number of provocative passages on this theme, to wit:

> It seems, however, that a theoretical study of Indian languages is not less important than a practical knowledge of them; that the purely linguistic inquiry is part and parcel of a thorough investigation of the psychology of the peoples of the world [p.63].
>
> ... language seems to be one of the most instructive fields of inquiry in an investigation of the formation of the fundamental ethnic ideas. The great advantage that linguistics offer in this respect is the fact that, on the whole, the categories which are formed always remain unconscious, and that for this reason the processes which

lead to their formation can be followed without the misleading and disturbing factors of secondary explanation, which are so common in ethnology, so much so that they generally obscure the real history of the development of ideas entirely [pp. 70–71].

The Sapir-Whorf hypothesis, however, gains especial significance by virtue of the fact that both these scholars had a major interest in American Indian languages, idioms far removed from any in the Indo-European family and so ideally suited to contrastive studies. It is in the attempt properly to interpret the grammatical categories of an American Indian language, Hopi, that Whorf best illustrates his principle of linguistic relativity, the notion that "users of markedly different grammars are pointed by their grammars toward different types of observations and different evaluations of externally similar acts of observation, and hence are not equivalent as observers but must arrive at somewhat different views of the world" (1952: 11).

The purpose of this paper is twofold: (1) to review and clarify the Sapir-Whorf hypothesis, (2) to illustrate and perhaps add to it by reference to my own work on the Navajo language. . . .

The central idea of the Sapir-Whorf hypothesis is that language functions, not simply as a device for reporting experience, but also, and more significantly, as a way of defining experience for its speakers. Sapir says (1931: 578), for example:

> Language is not merely a more or less systematic inventory of the various items of experience which seem relevant to the individual, as is so often naively assumed, but is also a self-contained, creative symbolic organization, which not only refers to experience largely acquired without its help but actually defines experience for us by reason of its formal completeness and because of our unconscious projection of its implicit expectations into the field of experience. In this respect language is very much like a mathematical system which, also, records experience in the truest sense of the word, only in its crudest beginnings, but, as time goes on, becomes elaborated into a self-contained conceptual system which previsages all possible experience in accordance with certain accepted formal limitations. . . . [Meanings are] not so much discovered in experience as imposed upon it, because of the tyrannical hold that linguistic form has upon our orientation in the world.

Whorf develops the same thesis when he says (1952: 5):

> . . . that the linguistic system (in other words, the grammar) of each language is not merely a reproducing instrument for voicing ideas but rather is itself the shaper of ideas, the program and guide for the individual's mental activity, for his analysis of impressions, for his synthesis of his mental stock in trade. . . . We dissect nature along lines laid down by our native languages. The categories and types that we isolate from the world of phenomena we do not find there because they stare every observer in the face; on the contrary, the world is presented in a kaleidoscopic flux of impressions which has to be organized by our minds—and this means largely by the linguistic systems in our minds.

It is evident from these statements, if they are valid, that language plays a large and significant role in the totality of culture. Far from being simply a technique of communication, it is itself a way of directing the perceptions of its speakers and it provides for them habitual modes of analyzing experience into significant categories. And to the extent that languages differ markedly from each other, so should we expect to find significant and formidable barriers to cross-cultural communication and understanding. These barriers take on even greater importance when it is realized that "the phenomena of a language are to its own speakers largely of a background character and so are outside the critical consciousness and control of the speaker" (Whorf 1952: 4).

It is, however, easy to exaggerate linguistic differences of this nature and the consequent barriers to intercultural understanding. No culture is wholly isolated, self-contained, and unique. There are important resemblances between all known cultures—resemblances that stem in part from diffusion (itself an evidence of successful intercultural communication) and in part from the fact that all cultures are built around biological, psychological, and social characteristics common to all mankind. The languages of human beings do not so much determine the perceptual and other faculties of their speakers vis-à-vis experience as they influence and direct these faculties into prescribed channels. Intercultural communication, however wide the difference between cultures may be, is not impossible. It is simply more or less difficult, depending on the degree of difference between the cultures concerned.

Some measure of these difficulties is encountered in the process of translating from one language into another that is divergent and unrelated. Each language has its own peculiar and favorite devices, lexical and grammatical, which are employed in the reporting, analysis, and categorizing of experience. To translate from English into Navaho, or vice versa, frequently involves much circumlocution, since what is easy to express in one language, by virtue of its lexical and grammatical techniques, is often difficult to phrase in the other. A simple illustration is found when we try to translate the English phrases *his horse* and *his horses* into Navaho, which not only lacks a plural category for nouns (Navaho łį·? translates equally English *horse* and *horses)* but lacks as well the English distinction between *his, her, its,* and *their* (Navaho bilį·? may be translated, according to context, *his horse* or *horses, her horse* or *horses, its horse* or *horses,* and *their horse* or *horses.)* These Navaho forms łį·?, bilį·? make difficulties in English also because Navaho makes a distinction between a third person (the bi-in bilį·?) psychologically close to the speaker (e.g., *his* [that is, a Navaho's] *horse)* as opposed to a third person (the hà- of hàlį·?) psychologically remote (e.g., *his* [that is, a non-Navaho's] *horse).*

Differences of this order, which reflect a people's habitual and favorite modes of reporting, analyzing, and categorizing experience, form the essential data of the Sapir-Whorf hypothesis. According to Whorf (1952:27), it is in these "constant ways of arranging data and its most ordinary every-day analysis of phenomena that we need to recognize the influence . . . [language] has on other activities, cultural and personal."

The Sapir-Whorf hypothesis, it is evident, includes in language both its structural and its semantic aspects. These are held to be inseparable, though it is obvious that we can and do study each more or less independently of the other.

The structural aspect of language, which is that most easily analyzed and described, includes its phonology, morphology, and syntax, the numerous but limited frames into which utterances are cast. The semantic aspect consists of a self-contained system of meanings, inextricably bound to the structure but much more difficult to analyze and describe. Meanings, to reiterate, are not in actual fact separable from structure, nor are they, as some have maintained (notably Voegelin 1949: 36), to be equated to the nonlinguistic culture. Our interest lies, not in questions such as "What does this form, or form class, mean?" but, instead, in the question, "In what manner does a language organize, through its structural semantic system, the world of experience in which its speakers live?" The advantage of this approach to the problem of meaning is clear. As Bloomfield long ago pointed out, it appears quite impossible, short of omniscience, to determine precisely the meaning of any single form or form class in a language. But it should be possible to determine the limits of any self-contained structural-semantic system and the ways in which it previsages the experiences ot its users.

To illustrate this procedure in brief, let us turn again to Navaho and one of the ways in which it differs from English. The Navaho color vocabulary includes, among others, five terms: łigài, dìłxìł, łižìn, łičí·?, and dò·xìž, to be taken as one way of categorizing certain color impressions. łigài is roughly equivalent to English *white*, dìłxìł and łižìn to English *black*, łičí·? to English *red*, and dò·x̌ìž to English *blue* or *green*. Clearly, then, the Navaho five-point system is not the same as English white-black-red-blue-green, which also has five categories. English *black* is divided into two categories in Navaho (dìłxìł and łižìn), while Navaho has but one category (dò·x̌ìž) for the English *blue* and *green*. We do not, it should be noted, claim either that English speakers cannot perceive the difference between the two "blacks" of Navaho, or that Navaho speakers are unable to differentiate "blue" and "green." The difference between the two systems lies simply in the color categories recognized in ordinary speech, that is, in the ordinary everyday ways in which speakers of English and Navaho analyze color phenomena.

Every language is made up of a large number of such structural-semantic patterns, some of which pertain to lexical sets, as in the case of the Navaho and English color terms, and others of which pertain to sets of grammatical categories, such as the distinction between the singular and plural noun in English. A monolingual speaker, if his reports are to be understood by others in his speech community, is bound to use this apparatus, with all its implications for the analysis and categorization of experience, though he may of course quite often select from a number of alternative expressions in making his report. To quote Sapir again (Mandelbaum 1949: 10–11):

> . . . as our scientific experience grows we must learn to fight the implications of language. "The grass waves in the wind" is shown by its linguistic form to be a member of the same relational class of experiences as "The man works in the house." As an interim solution of the problem of expressing the experience referred to in this sentence it is clear that the language has proved useful, for it has made significant use of certain symbols of conceptual relation, such as agency and location. If we feel the sentence to be poetic or metaphorical, it is largely because other more complex types

of experience with their appropriate symbolisms of reference enable us to reinterpret the situation and to say, for instance, "The grass is waved by the wind" or "The wind causes the grass to wave." The point is that no matter how sophisticated our modes of interpretation become, we never really get beyond the projection and continuous transfer of relations suggested by the forms of our speech. . . . Language is at one and the same time helping and retarding us in our exploration of experience, and the details of these processes of help and hindrance are deposited in the subtler meanings of different cultures.

It does not necessarily follow that all the structural-semantic patterns of a language are equally important to its speakers in their observation, analysis, and categorizing of experience. In describing a language, we seek to uncover all its structural-semantic patterns, even though many of these exist more as potentialities of the system than in actual usage. For ethnolinguistic analysis we need to know, not only that a particular linguistic pattern exists, but also how frequently it occurs in everyday speech. We also need to know something of the degree of complexity of the pattern of expression. There are numerous patterns of speech, particularly among peoples who have well-developed arts of oratory and writing, that are little used by any except specialists in these pursuits. The patterns of speech significant to ethnolinguistic research fall clearly into the category of habitual, frequently used, and relatively simple structural-semantic devices; those, in short, which are common to the adult speech community as a whole, and are used by its members with the greatest ease.

Not all the structural patterns of the common speech have the same degree of semantic importance. In English, for example, it is not difficult to ascertain the semantic correlates of the structural distinction between singular and plural nouns; in most cases this is simply a division into the categories of "one" versus "more than one." Similarly, the gender distinction of the English third-person singular pronouns, as between "he," "she," and "it," correlates fairly frequently with the recognition of personality and sex.

In contrast to these, there are structural patterns like that which, in many Indo-European languages, divides nouns into three great classes: masculine, feminine, and neuter. This structural pattern has no discernible semantic correlate; we do not confuse the grammatical terms "masculine," "feminine," and "neuter" with the biological distinctions among male, female, and neuter. Whatever the semantic implications of this structural pattern may have been in origin, and this remains undetermined, it is now quite apparent that the pattern survives only as a grammatical device, important in that function but lacking in semantic value. And it is perhaps significant that the pattern is an old one, going back to the earliest history of the Indo-European languages and, moreover, that it has disappeared almost completely in some of the modern languages of this family, notably, of course, in English.

In ethnolinguistic research, then, it is necessary to concentrate on those structural patterns of a language which have definable semantic correlates, and to omit those, like the Indo-European gender system, which survive only in a purely grammatical function. The assumption behind this procedure is as follows: every language includes a number of active structural-semantic categories, lexical and grammatical, which by virtue of their active status serve a function in the everyday (nonscientific) analysis and categorizing of experience. It is the study of these categories, distinctive when taken as a whole for each language, that yields, or may yield, significant information concerning the thought world of the speakers of the language.

One further point requires emphasis. Neither Sapir nor Whorf attempted to draw inferences as to the thought world of a people simply from the fact of the presence or absence of specific grammatical categories (e.g., tense, gender, number) in a given language. To quote Whorf (1952: 44) on this point: the concepts of time and matter which he reports for the Hopi

> do not depend so much upon any one system (e.g., tense, or nouns) within the grammar as upon the ways of analyzing and reporting experience which have become fixed in the language as integrated "fashions of speaking" and which cut across the typical grammatical classifications, so that such a "fashion" may include lexical, morphological, syntactic, and otherwise systematically diverse means coordinated in a certain frame of consistency.

To summarize, ethnolinguistic research requires the investigator to perform, it seems to me, the following steps:

1. To determine the structural patterns of a language (that is, its grammar) as completely as possible. Such determination should include not only a statement of the modes of utterance but as well a careful indication of the frequency of occurrence of these modes, lexical and grammatical, in the common speech.

2. To determine, as accurately as possible, the semantic patterns, if any, that attach to structural patterns. This is a task neglected by most structural linguists who, as is repeatedly mentioned in the discussions that follow, are frequently content simply to label rather than to define both lexical units and grammatical categories. In this connection it is important to emphasize that the analyst must not be taken in by his own labels; he is to discover, where possible, just how the form, or form class, or grammatical category functions in the utterances available to him.

3. To distinguish between structural categories that are active in the language, and therefore have definable semantic correlates, and those which are not. It goes without saying that such distinction requires a profound knowledge of the language, and possibly even the ability to speak and understand it well. Mark Twain's amusing translation of a German folktale into English, where he regularly translates the gender of German nouns by the English forms "he," "she," and "it," illustrates, though in caricature, the pitfalls of labeling the grammatical categories of one language (in this case, German gender) by terms belonging to an active structural-semantic pattern in another.

4. To examine and compare the active structural-semantic patterns of the language and draw from them the fashions of speaking there evidenced. As in Whorf's analysis of Hopi (1952: 25–45), while clues to a fashion of speaking may be discovered in a particular grammatical category or set of lexical items, its

validity and importance cannot be determined until its range and scope within the language as a whole is also known. Whorf's conclusions as to the nature of the concept of time among speakers of English rest not alone on the tense distinctions of the English verb (mixed as these are with many other and diverse distinctions of voice, mode, and aspect) but as well on techniques of numeration, the treatment of nouns denoting physical quantity and phases of cycles, and a host of other terms and locutions relating to time. He says (1952: 33):

> The three-tense system of SAE verbs colors all our thinking about time. This system is amalgamated with that larger scheme of objectification of the subjective experience of duration already noted in other patterns—in the binomial formula applicable to nouns in general, in temporal nouns, in plurality and numeration.

5. Taken together, the fashions of speaking found in a language comprise a partial description of the thought world of its speakers. But by the term "thought world" Whorf means

> more than simply language, i.e., than the linguistic patterns themselves. [He includes] . . . all the analogical and suggestive value of the patterns. . .and all the give-and-take between language and the culture as a whole, wherein is a vast amount that is not linguistic yet shows the shaping influence of language. In brief, this "thought world" is the microcosm that each man carries about within himself, by which he measures and understands what he can of the macrocosm [1952: 36.]

It follows then that the thought world, as derived from ethnolinguistic studies, is found reflected as well, though perhaps not as fully, in other aspects of the culture. It is here that we may search for connections between language and the rest of culture. These connections are not direct; we see, instead, in certain patterns of nonlinguistic behavior the same meaningful fashions that are evidenced in the patterns of the language. Whorf summarizes this facet of his researches in a discussion of "Habitual Behavior Features of Hopi Culture and Some Impresses of Linguistic Habit in Western Civilization" (1952: 37–52).

It may be helpful to outline briefly some aspects of Navaho culture, including the language, as illustration of the Sapir-Whorf hypothesis. In particular, I shall describe first some of the basic postulates of Navaho religious behavior and attempt to show how these fit in a frame of consistency with certain fashions of speaking evidenced primarily in the morphological patterns of the Navaho verb.

A review of Navaho religious practices, as described by Washington Matthews, Father Berard Haile, and many others, reveals that the Navaho conceive of themselves as in a particular relationship with the environment—physical, social, and supernatural—in which they live. Navaho man lives in a universe of eternal and unchanging forces with which he attempts to maintain an equilibrium, a kind of balancing of powers. The mere fact of living is, however, likely to disturb this balance and throw it out of gear. Any such disturbance, which may result from failure to observe a set rule of behavior or ritual or from the accidental or deliberate committal of some other fault in ritual or the conduct of daily activities, will, the Navaho believe, be revealed in the illness or unexplained death of an individual, in some other personal misfortune or bad luck to an enterprise, or in some community disaster such as a food shortage or an epidemic. Whereupon, a diviner must be consulted, who determines by ritual means the cause of the disturbance and prescribes, in accordance with this knowledge, the appropriate counteracting religious ceremony or ritual.

The underlying purpose of the curing ceremony is to put the maladjusted individual or the community as a whole back into harmony with the universe. Significantly, this is done, not by the shaman or priest acting upon the individual and changing him, nor by any action, by shaman or priest, designed to alter the forces of the universe. It is done by re-enacting one of a complex series of religious dramas which represent, in highly abstract terms, the events, far back in Navaho history, whereby the culture heroes first established harmony between man and nature and so made the world fit for human occupation. By re-enacting these events, or some portion of them, the present disturbance, by a kind of sympathetic magic, is compensated and harmony between man and universe restored. The ill person then gets well, or the community disaster is alleviated, since these misfortunes were but symptoms of a disturbed relation to nature.

From these numerous and very important patterns of Navaho religious behavior, it seems to me we can abstract a dominant motif belonging to the Navaho thought world. The motif has been well put by Kluckhohn and Leighton, who also illustrate it in many other aspects of Navaho culture. They call it, "Nature is more powerful than man," and amplify this in part by the Navaho premise "that nature will take care of them if they behave as they should and do as she directs" (1946: 227–28). In short, to the Navaho, the way to the good life lies not in modifying nature to man's needs or in changing man's nature but rather in discovering the proper relation of nature to man and in maintaining that relationship intact.

Turning now to the Navaho language, let us look at some aspects of the verb structure, illustrated in the following two forms:

nìńtį *you have lain down*
nìšíńtį *you have put, laid me down*

Both these verbs are in the second person of the perfective mode (Hoijer 1946); the ń- marks this inflection. Both also have a prefix nì-, not the same but subtly different in meaning. The nì- of the first means *[movement] terminating in a position of rest,* that of the second *[movement] ending at a given point.* The second form has the causative prefix ł- and incorporates the first person object, expressed in this form by ši-. The stem -tį, common to both forms, is defined *one animate being moves.*

The theme of the first verb, composed of nì- . . . -tį, means *one animate being moves to a position of rest,* that is, *one animate being lies down.* In the second verb the meaning of the theme, nì- . . . -ł-tį, is *cause movement of one animate being to end at a given point* and so, by extension, *put an animate being down* or *lay an animate being down.*

Note now that the first theme includes in its meaning what in English we should call both the actor and the action; these are not, in Navaho, expressed by separate morphemes. The subject pronoun prefix ń- serves then simply to identify a particular being with the class of possible beings already delimited by the theme. It functions, in short, to individuate one belonging to the class *animate being in motion to a position of rest.* The theme of the second verb, by reason of the causative ł-, includes in its meaning what in English would be called action and goal. Again the pronoun ši-, as a consequence, simply identifies or individuates one of a class of possible beings defined already in the theme itself. It should be emphasized that the forms used here as illustration are in no sense unusual; this is the regular pattern of the Navaho verb, repeated over and over again in my data.

We are now ready to isolate, from this necessarily brief analysis, a possible fashion of speaking peculiar to Navaho. The Navaho speaks of "actors" and "goals" (the terms are inappropriate to Navaho), not as performers of actions or as ones upon whom actions are performed, as in English, but as entities linked to actions already defined in part as pertaining especially to classes of beings. The form which is glossed *you have lain down* is better understood you *[belong to, equal one of] a class of animate beings which has moved to rest.* Similarly the second form, glossed *you have put, laid me down* should read *you, as agent, have set a class of animate beings, to which I belong, in motion to a given point.*

This fashion of speaking, it seems to me, is wholly consistent with the dominant motif we saw in Navaho religious practices. Just as in his religious-curing activities the Navaho sees himself as adjusting to a universe that is given, so in his habits of speaking does he link individuals to actions and movements distinguished, not only as actions and movements, but as well in terms of the entities in action or movement. This division of nature into classes of entity in action or movement is the universe that is given; the behavior of human beings or of any being individuated from the mass is customarily reported by assignment to one or other of these given divisions. . . .

References

Boas, Franz (ed.) (1911). "Introduction," *Handbook of American Indian Languages,* Part 1. Washington, D.C.

Hoijer, Harry (1946). "The Apachean Verb, Part III: The Prefixes for Mode and Tense," *International Journal of American Linguistics* 12:1–13—(1953). "The Relation of Language to Culture." In *Anthropology Today* (by A. L. Kroeber and others), pp. 554–73. Chicago, University of Chicago Press.

Kluckhohn, Clyde, and Dorothea Leighton (1946). *The Navaho.* Cambridge, Harvard University Press.

Mandelbaum, David G. (ed.) (1949). *Selected Writings of Edward Sapir.* Berkeley and Los Angeles, University of California Press.

Sapir, Edward (1931). "Conceptual Categories in Primitive Languages," *Science* 74:578.

Voegelin, C. F. (1949). "Linguistics without Meaning and Culture without Words," *Word* 5:36–42.

Whorf, Benjamin L. (1952). *Collected Papers on Metalinguistics.* Washington, D.C., Department of State, Foreign Service Institute.

Problems of Translation in Cross-Cultural Communication[1]

Lee Sechrest, Todd L. Fay, and S. M. Zaidi

To at least some degree every cross-cultural research project must involve the use of language, if only to convey the instructions for a "non-verbal" procedure of some sort. Of course, some projects are far more dependent on linguistic communication than others, and some are exclusively verbal, or linguistic, in nature. We think that there are at least potential communication problems in *all* cross-cultural research, e.g., can one be *sure* that a Pashtun version of "Please do this as quickly as you can" is the same in its meaning as the English? Nonetheless, the problems do vary, and it is worthwhile to note the kinds of problems that are involved and the errors they may produce. We hope in this paper to achieve some clarification of the process of translating from one language into another for purposes of cross-cultural research. We will begin with a discussion of the types of materials which cause translation difficulties, go on to a discussion of the kinds of equivalences which are necessary, and then describe attempts which have been made to overcome translation difficulties. Along the way we will refer to our own work in connection with a comparative study to be carried out in several cultures. It will be evident that we have relied heavily on the work of Werner and Campbell (1970) and Brislin (1970).

Types of Translation Problems in Cross-Cultural Research

There are, generally speaking, four types of translation problems in cross-cultural studies although little attention has been paid to but one of them. First, nearly all instances of cross-cultural work require that some orientation to the research be given. Ordinarily those persons who are research subjects or informants must be given some rationale for the tasks set for them, and it would seem obvious that some attention would be paid to the equivalence of such introductions as made in different cultures. However, there are no instances known to us in which an investigator specifically mentions such a problem, let alone a solution to it. In any case, there often will be instances in which an investigator must "explain himself" to members of different language groups, and when that necessity arises, its companion necessity is for precision in translation.

The second type of translation problem involves the translation of instructions specific to different types of tasks or measures being used. Even though the response of a subject may require no verbal component, it is almost always

From *Journal of Cross-Cultural Psychology,* Vol. 3, No. 1 (March 1972), pp. 41–56 by permission of the publisher, Sage Publications, Inc. Professor Sechrest is in the Psychology Department, Northwestern University, Professor Fay is in the Psychology Department, University of Western Ontario, and Professor Zaidi teaches at Karachi University.

[1]The preparation of this article was supported in part by the Ateneo-Penn State Basic Research Program, sponsored by the United States Office of Naval Research, with the Pennsylvania State University as prime contractor (Nonr-656 37).

necessary that the nature of the task and of his response be explained in words (Anderson, 1967). And those words must be translated from one language to another when one crosses linguistic boundaries. Again, very few investigators seem to have paid much attention to this problem. It seems usually to be *assumed* that translations are adequate. Very few investigators can be described as having been sufficiently wary to make us totally confident in their findings. Rather paradoxically, it is probably the case that the briefer the instructions are, the greater the tendency to assume similarity. However, as Werner and Campbell (1970) make clear, it is, in fact, more difficult to get and to be sure one has gotten a satisfactory translation of a short passage than of a longer one. Such phrases as "Do your best," "Guess if you want to," "Take the one you like best," and "Make A the same as B" involve many translational pitfalls for the unwary. It is the lack of context in short phrases and sentences that makes the problem so difficult. Or, viewed in another way, the redundancy in short messages may be very limited. Recently we have been using the Rod-and-Frame Test to measure field dependence-independence in different cultures, and two of the most difficult problems we encountered were in finding a Tagalog (Philippine) word or phrase for "upright" or an Urdu word for "rod."

The third type of translation problem is the obvious one of phrasing questions or the other verbal stimuli in ways that are comparable in two or more languages. Interview questions, statements on personality inventories or attitude questionnaires, and verbal stimuli on projective tests such as incomplete sentences are all examples of the third type of translation problem. This is a problem to which many investigators have addressed themselves. In fact, the problem is so obvious that it is inescapable, and unlike the first two problems, there are almost no investigators unaware of the problem. However, we might point out that translation problems can and do arise even within cultures when different subcultures are being examined, and many investigators have ignored the likelihood that a particular verbal stimulus may not mean the same to a person in one subculture as to a person in another. Dialect differences, use of scholarly rather than vernacular language, and regional differences in colloquial speech and idiom all contribute to potential subcultural research problems. Odd as it may seem, English may at times need to be translated into English, and Urdu into Urdu.

The fourth type of translation problem involves translation of *responses* from one language or dialect to another so that comparisons may be made. Many questionnaires have limited response alternatives, e.g., true-false, agree-disagree, and the translation is made prior to the response. However, for open-ended questions, interviews, projective tests and the like, it may be necessary to translate the responses. When responses must be translated, the same problems exist as in translating other material. In many cases translation and its attendant expense and difficulties can be avoided by coding, categorizing, or scoring responses in the language in which they are given. If the coding system is easily communicated and relatively unambiguous, many difficulties can be obviated. To be sure, the coding system itself must be translated, but that is a decidedly simple task when compared to translation of responses, and especially when one has access to bilingual coders. It should be noted, though, that Ervin (1964) found that language of response could make a difference in the responses of bilinguals, and bilingual coders need to be checked for their consistency also.

Problems of Equivalence in Translation

As we stated earlier the major problem in translation is to determine that the translation is equivalent to the original language. There are, however, a number of different kinds of equivalence that have somewhat different effects and implications. We propose here to discuss several different aspects of equivalence which must be considered in transporting a research instrument from one linguistic area to another. While the problems vary somewhat in importance and are most serious when languages and cultures are maximally different, we think that all the problems exist in some measure even within cultures; they merely become increasingly troublesome with increasing-decreasing linguistic and cultural similarity.

VOCABULARY EQUIVALENCE   Perhaps the most obvious kind of equivalence is in vocabulary, in the words used in two or more translations. For example, an item such as "I am happy most of the time" could be translated rather directly into another language than English with the major vocabulary problem being, in most instances, finding an equivalent term for "happy." Or, in using a Semantic Differential (Osgood, Suci, & Tannenbaum, 1957), one would need to find comparable terms for such items as strong-weak, rich-poor, and fast-slow.

While it might seem that vocabulary problems could be solved with a good dictionary, and indeed, that is a valuable resource, the fact of the matter is that the problems are not by any means so simple. In the first place, dictionary language is often not the language of the people. In fact, we could make a parallel comment about the use of translators, who are often chosen from a population of highly educated persons who speak and write somewhat pedantically in both their languages. We have numerous instances of translations made with either dictionary or translator that proved unworkable because they did not have the right meaning to persons for whom the test was intended. Thus, a good first rule in translating is to use translators who have good acquaintance with the language *as used by the prospective test respondents.*

A second aspect of the problem of vocabulary equivalence in relation to dictionary translations is that most words in the dictionary are defined in a number of ways or by a number of terms. It is not easy to know which terms to select for the translation. The problem is to reflect in the term chosen the obvious meaning and the important nuances of the original term. Such terms as *responsible, suggestible, aloof,* and *tough* are all English terms with nuances that make it difficult to find just the right equivalent in other languages. On the other hand such Urdu terms as *sanjida, pakbaz, ameen* and *ghairat* (all indicating good and desirable personality traits in Pakistan) are also expressive of delicacies of thought that make the discovery of a vocabulary equivalent difficult.

There may, in fact, be terms in one language for which it is almost impossible to find an equivalent in another language. For example, we found that there is no really good Tagalog term for *feminine,* i.e., a term that makes it posssible to say "Maria is more *feminine* than Elena." Similarly, there was no Tagalog equivalent for *domestic* that we might apply in describing people, so as to say, "Mr. Santos is very *domestic* in his interests." On the other hand, *hiya* (related to shyness, embarrassment, shame, and deference) and *pakikisama* (related to getting along with others, acceding to wishes of one's peer group, and conformity) are Tagalog words difficult to translate into English because there just are not any equivalents. We found it somewhat difficult to find good counterparts for orderly, conforming and polite in Urdu, and *moonis, humdum,* and *habeeb* (all indicating differences in degree of friendship and closeness) are Urdu words without ready English equivalents.

A frequent attempted solution to problems of non-equivalence of terms, one recommended by Werner and Campbell (1970), is the use of several words in the target language to try to convey an idea expressible in one word in the source language. Although such a procedure will be discussed later in this paper, we would note here that differences in length of materials should be kept within fairly close limits.

Vocabulary equivalence is not necessarily equally difficult to achieve between all pairs of languages. We have no data on this but there are many reasons such as cultural differences, as well as linguistic traditions, for incomparability between two languages. To illustrate, however, we have been involved in considerable translation from English to Tagalog and back, and from English to Urdu and back. It is our distinct impression that it is easier to translate between English and Urdu than between English and Tagalog. At least a part of the difference in difficulty we attribute to the differential availability of words in the two languages which are comparable to English words. Tagalog does not seem to have very good words for a lot of English terms and vice versa. While there are obvious problems translating from English into Urdu, it seems to be richer in the kinds of words which are used in English texts. Brislin (1970) found substantial differences between languages in translation error rates (while he found Tagalog-English to be relatively easy, it is almost certainly the case that his Tagalogs were more nearly bilingual than his other linguistic assistants).

To the extent that words do not mean the same thing to respondents in different cultures, the responses are uninterpretable with respect to cultural similarities or differences. But, vocabulary equivalence is only part of the problem.

IDIOMATIC EQUIVALENCE   Frequently in translating one encounters problems that arise because idiomatic speech is employed in one language, and idioms never translate properly, if at all. In fact, one often becomes aware of idiomatic language only when one attempts to translate and realizes that a direct translation would not make sense at all. For example, the direct translation of the Tagalog adjectival expression *hipong-tulog* is "fish sleeping"; yet a more meaningful equivalent in English might be conforming, indecisive, or "following the present current of thought or action."

Although it might seem that one should avoid use of idioms in producing technical research material, and that is what Werner and Campbell recommend, idioms are so firmly embedded in our speech patterns that under most circumstances we are scarcely aware of them. Moreover, to attempt to avoid idioms completely in, for example, writing instructions or writing items, would probably produce a highly stilted, pedantic form of discourse which would be utterly unsuitable for research efforts with the general population in any culture. And, of course, if one is translating the responses of an informant or subject, idiom cannot be avoided. Therefore, the best that can be done is to attempt to insure that when idioms are used in a translation they are equivalent in meaning to the idioms used in the original, and that the general level of idiomatic speech in the two languages is approximately equivalent so that one does not seem more scholarly, more stilted, or in some other way different from the other. For example, the Tagalog idiom *galit-bulkan* is literally translated "angry volcano" and is interpreted to mean a sudden expression of anger. One might be able to use the English slang term "blow up" as an idiomatic equivalent. To "keep your mouth shut" can be translated into Urdu, but a better equivalent in terms of usage would be *tum chup raho,* which back translates as "you keep quiet."

GRAMMATICAL-SYNTACTICAL EQUIVALENCE   Still another equivalence problem arises from the fact that languages differ widely in their grammars and syntaxes and these differences are often critical to the meanings in various translations. While these problems are probably of somewhat greater importance with longer passages, they do occur even in relation to very short passages, perhaps even for single words. One of the reasons for a grammatical equivalence problem involving single words is that two languages may not have equivalent parts of speech. Thus, for example, if there is no gerund in a particular language there may be some problems in achieving good equivalence for the commonly used gerunds in English. (Urdu has no gerund quite like English). A fairly ordinary type of test item consists of asking an individual which of a list of activities he enjoys and the list is often couched in terms of such gerunds as singing, dancing, eating, playing, writing, and the like. While it is most certainly possible to develop an equivalent form for such items in most languages, there do arise some difficulties in specifying the exact linguistic form which is to be used in a language which lacks the gerund. Other parts of speech such as adjectives, adverbs, and the like, may be missing in particular languages and may pose some problems for translators.

Nonetheless, the more important problems in attaining grammatical syntactical equivalence involve longer passages. Probably one of the more common grammatical problems in achieving equivalence is in dealing with verb forms. Not all languages deal with the problems of verb mood, voice, or tense in the same way by any means, and it is sometimes very difficult in a given language to put expressions which have the same verb form or meaning in English. For example, in the Tagalog dialect there is no subjunctive mood. As a result, it becomes impossible to find literal equivalents and difficult to find conceptual equivalents for English conditional subjunctive expressions. The English sentence, "If I had

had the money, I would have bought the dress," can be translated in Tagalog to *Kung mayroon sana akong pera, nabili ko sana ang baro.* The literal translation of this Tagalog sentence into English would be "If I have the money (understood I have not), I bought the dress (understood I did not)." Needless to say, the tense and the conditional sense seem not to be the same as the original English.

The whole area of translation has been so little studied in the context of the field of psychology that it is difficult to cite specific instances of syntactic nonequivalence, although there is no question that they abound and that they can affect the meaning of translations.

The work of Whorf (1956) contains many examples such as the Hopi utilization of what we think of as nouns as verb or action forms. Thus *chair* is *chairing* or the act of sitting. Or, looking elsewhere one finds that in English it is obligatory to specify number in relation to nouns, nearly all of which are either singular or plural. However, in Yoruba (Nigeria) it is not at all obligatory that number be specified. And Arabic obliges that number be specified as singular, dual, or plural. Obviously such syntactical variations can very much affect meaning and the problems of translation.

EXPERIENTIAL EQUIVALENCE   There are two remaining equivalence problems which are of a somewhat different order than the ones we have discussed above, since the remaining two do not involve purely linguistic considerations. Nonetheless, they are important for translators to keep in mind and may constitute severe impediments to the development of adequate materials for studies in societies with different languages. The first of these is experiential equivalence, the second is conceptual equivalence.

By experiential equivalence we mean that in order for translations to be successful from one culture to another they must utilize terms referring to real things and real experiences which are familiar in both cultures, if not exactly equally familiar. Werner and Campbell call this "*cultural* translation" as distinguished from *linguistic* translation. If two cultures differ so greatly in the nature of their objects, in the nature of their social arrangements, in their overall ways of life, or that objects or experiences which are familiar to members of one culture are unfamiliar to members of another, it will be difficult to achieve equivalence in meaning of a variety of linguistic statements no matter how carefully the translation is done from the standpoint of the language involved. Let us take a perhaps trivial, but very obvious example. If the item "I would like to be a florist" appeared on a personality or interest measure for use with Americans it would probably be understood by most of them. That same item, however, would be incomprehensible to most people around the world, no matter how carefully it were explained to them. Flower shops simply are not found in most parts of the world and, in many cases, the idea of a flower shop where one has flowers made into fancy arrangements and the like would be totally foreign to the experience of most people. Consequently, if one wished to achieve experiential equivalence one would have to think about why the item involving doing the work of a florist is used in an American sample and then find an equivalent that is in terms of a local experience type of activity in the other culture being studied. Thus, if in an

American test the item is scored for femininity because it is thought to reflect an interest in feminine kinds of activities, then in another culture in which flower shops were missing one would have to look for a similar kind of economic activity primarily identified with females and thought to reflect an effeminate outlook even when it occurred among males. That might not be easy to do but, for example, in the Philippines most market vendors are women, and it is possible that Filipinos might think a male effeminate if he were a market vendor. In that case one could use the item "I would like to be a market vendor" as an experiental equivalent to "I would like to be a florist."

In some cases there may be no alternative but to eliminate items because a counterpart does not exist or would be of too uncertain equivalence in another culture. Animals, household objects, architectural features, terrain features, biological specimens, etc. are all examples of categories of concrete objects where cultures may differ so much in experience that the problem of attaining equivalence is difficult. No translation of "department store" into Urdu is possible because they are unknown in Pakistan, and the closest one could get would be "large shop."

However, it should not be thought that the problems of equivalence pertain only to such concrete aspects of cultures. They may also stem from differences between other cultural arrangements. One good example lies in the kinship patterns and social relations that differ so widely from one culture to another. The term "cousin," for example, means something very different in the Philippines than it means in the United States, and it means something else again in Pakistani culture. Or, to take another example, the typical school classroom or even university classroom is so very different in its meaning, in the way it is conducted, in the relationship among the students or in the relationship between the students and professors, that it is very difficult to insure that any items or statements about the university classroom as an experience can possibly be equivalent for members of cultures as diverse as, let us say, Pakistani and American. Such an item as "I seldom speak up in class" would undoubtedly have a very different meaning for American and Pakistani students because the experience of being in a class is so very different for the two groups. Again, achieving an adequate translation of the item would involve figuring out what the item was supposed to reflect in the way of a trait or response disposition in an American culture and then finding an equivalent lying within the experience of typical Pakistani students.

The position taken here is much akin to that of Przeworski and Teune (1970), who suggest that in most instances of the kind at issue here the important question concerns the *equivalence of inferences* rather than of stimuli. They indicate that inferences must be validated within rather than across social systems. "An instrument is equivalent across systems to the extent that the *results* provided by the instrument reliably describe with (nearly) the same validity a particular phenomenon in different social systems" (opus cited, p. 108). While we are perhaps somewhat more interested in and sanguine about achieving linguistic equivalence than Przeworski and Teune, and while we have some reservations about using similarity of factorial structure as the sole criterion of equivalence, we are in general agreement with their propositions.

CONCEPTUAL EQUIVALENCE   The final problem in achieving equivalence between measures to be used in two or more cultures is the problem of insuring that the concepts used in the measures, interview, or other translated materials are equivalent in the two cultures. This is somewhat apart from the previous kinds of equivalence problems for it may very well be that one has in two cultures a word which, when translated, mutually yields high agreement and yet it may not be that the concepts implied by the two words are, in fact, identical or particularly close in nature. For example, the item "I love a parade" might be quite easy to translate into other languages than English and, at least on a word-for-word basis there would be no problem in equivalence in such things as vocabulary and experience. Nonetheless, the concept "love" as used in that English item is far different in its implications from the concept which might be implicit in words used in other languages. English is, perhaps, not an especially rich language for expressing positive feelings about things and, consequently, the word "love" is used to mean several different things, or at least to connote varying degrees of positive affect toward some object.

A second aspect of the problem of conceptual equivalence is that a concept well understood and frequently employed in one culture may be lacking altogether in another culture, or it may appear at least in such varied different fragmented forms that it is very difficult to construct materials that treat the true concepts equivalently. For example in the Philippines it proved to be very difficult to find even a concept, let alone words, which had the same connotations as the common American concept of homosexual. The available Philippine words are used in a variety of ways which suggests that the concept simply does not exist in the same highly developed form as it does in the American culture (Sechrest & Flores, 1969). In fact, it is our feeling that doing translations in both directions in two or more cultures is an excellent way of coming to understand the divergent ways of thinking about problem areas in different cultures.

THE PARADOX OF EQUIVALENCE   We have gone into some detail concerning the problems of achieving equivalence across two or more languages as if equivalences were the fundamental problem. Actually, in certain respects it is not, for there may be a distinct paradox involved in translation for the sake of achieving equivalence. The paradox is that if one demands that a form of a test or other measure yield comparable results in two cultures in order to demonstrate equivalence, then the more equivalent two forms become the less the probability of finding cultural differences. On the other hand, if one looks predominantly for cultural differences and ignores the problem of equivalence, then the less attention that is paid to the problem of equivalence the greater the probability of finding cultural differences. For example, in his work on the comparison of Japanese and American college students responses to the Edwards Personal Preference Schedule, Berrien (1967) argued that differences found between the two samples stemmed from different concepts of social desirability for the two cultures. If that were done, however, it is entirely possible that important cultural differences would be obliterated, or at least obscured, by the attempt to achieve what is a rather misleading form of equivalence. Obviously, we are not thinking here of the kinds of questions for which prior knowledge can be used to justify expectations either of differences or similarities between cultures, e.g., proportion of Roman Catholics in a culture. The paradox is troublesome for more complex issues for which prior expectations are uncertain or a poor guide, e.g., "What is the true cause of personal misfortune?"

The resolution of the equivalence paradox is not a simple one, but our feeling is that it probably lies in some method of triangulation whereby measures are subjected to increasingly more severe tests of equivalence, and we determine what sort of convergence in the responses of two cultures we may be able to obtain. The more rapidly the findings from two cultures converge in terms of the degree of effort required to achieve equivalence, the smaller the differences between the two cultures probably are. In any case, we can never know for sure what the absolute differences between cultures are and can probably only guess at their relative magnitude. Thus, we may be able to say that the members of two cultures are more similar with respect to one area of functioning than with respect to another, or that they are more or less similar to each other than they are to members of some third culture. There are, of course, some measures for which diminishing returns of equivalence manipulations are likely to be achieved at a very rapid rate. For example, in the case of the Rod-and-Frame test it seems scarcely likely that any real differences, for example between men and women, are simply a function of equivalence of instructions to the two groups.

Obviously in research the aim of producing versions of some communication which are equivalent in two or more languages has a pragmatic justification. One does not labor over translations for the sake of art. The aim of equivalence is that the specific influence of language on responses may be removed. It is, as we have suggested, difficult to know when equivalence has been achieved, but Werner and Campbell and Brislin have proposed several very useful criteria. However, in his empirical study of translation equivalence Brislin had monolingual raters examine an original English version and one translated back into English in order to detect "errors that might make differences in the meaning people would infer." That process when followed by correction of the errors produced reasonably good translations although pretesting of instruments revealed some additional errors.

DIRECT TRANSLATION   The most common procedure by which an attempt to achieve equivalent forms of questionnaires, interview, and the like for cross-cultural research has been the direct translation. That is, a translator or translators who are bilingual attempt to translate as best they can from one language into the other. This translation procedure, as a matter of fact, is still characteristic of a great deal of work of a cross-cultural nature and it is particularly likely to be used in relation to brief sets of materials, orientation, instructions, and the like. The method has also been used for the development of adjective check lists and similar materials. However, as Werner and Campbell have pointed out it is exactly for such brief materials that a method of direct translation is likely to be most inadequate. To be sure, it is probably rare that a translator works without any check at all on the adequacies of his efforts, but in a great many instances the checking is likely to be unsystematic and inadequate.

There are several problems with direct translation, the most important of which is that idiosyncrasies may be introduced by the translator himself. The translator himself may not be sufficiently skilled on one or the other of the languages in which he is working, he may not be culturally representative of the group for which the materials are to be used, and he may, by reason of his own experience, have peculiarities of word understanding or word use which will not be shared by persons for whom the materials are intended.

Obviously, it would be going beyond the realm of reason to assert that all translations made by a single translator are inadequate, but we feel that the probability of inadequacies of translations may go undetected. Therefore, we believe that the method should be rejected out of hand, particularly when in nearly all instances there are better, if not perfect, alternatives. We would, however, point out that the method of direct translation is still quite common and, in fact, it is probably still characteristic of the large bulk of all anthropological translation.

BACK TRANSLATION   Werner and Campbell have described a method of translation which is distinctly superior to the method of direct translation even though it may not be the ideal solution in many instances. In the method of back-translation a translation is first made from one language to another, for example, from English to Urdu, by one or more translators. The translated material is then back translated, for example, from Urdu to English, by another translator or set of translators. The two versions of the original can then be checked for the adequacy of the translation. For example, if a statement in English such as "I get tense before examinations," is translated into Urdu and then comes back into English translated from the Urdu as "I get excited before examinations,"[2] the discrepancy between the two versions would suggest to the experimenter that the further translation is required. Presumably, by successive translations and back translation a better and better approximation to the original can be obtained, and the final version of the translated material should be satisfactory.

However, we would suggest that not all problems in translation are quite so easily solved as might be suggested by the foregoing. For one thing, when a back-translation is accomplished there are almost inevitably some discrepancies between the original English version and the back-translated version. It then requires a judgment on the part of someone whether the two versions are, in fact, equivalent. There may be a number of reasons for nonequivalence which have to be treated quite differently in the process of developing a satisfactory research instrument. For one thing discrepancies may occur because the original translation was inadequate, and if that is true the only solution is improvement of the translation. However, the inadequacy may have stemmed from different sources. It may have been the result of an idiosyncratic translation by the translator. For example, a translator may himself not know the difference between the words "tense" and "excited," or may not regard the distinction as important. A second possibility is that since the translation and back translation are done by different people, the two separate English versions may be more equivalent than they seem

---

[2]There is no good Urdu equivalent for tense, and the likely substitute, Tanao, might be backtranslated as excited, upset, or even embarrassed.

because of idiosyncratic habits in the use of English words. Thus, if the word "annoyance" is translated into Urdu and then comes back translated into English as "pain" it is entirely possible that the discrepancy is attributable to faulty knowledge of English rather than to any inadequacies in Urdu. In any case, in such an instance the experimenter would have to make a decision as to whether the translation was inadequate or not, that is, whether "pain" is a reasonable English synonym for "annoyance," e.g., as in "waiting in line is a pain."

A second source of difficulty in producing equivalent back translations is that the lack of equivalence may in fact stem from the absence of a satisfactory word, or at least from the lack of equivalence of concepts in the two languages. Thus, the word "homosexual" when translated into Tagalog usually becomes "bakla" which, when translated back into English might come out as "sissy" or something of that sort. The problem lies not in the idiosyncracy of the translator or in the failure to use the best term, but simply in the fact that there is no equivalent in Tagalog for the English term "homosexual." Such problems of nonequivalence can only be resolved by having available a number of bilingual speakers who can be consulted with respect to the problems involved. Preferably the bilingual speakers should come from different backgrounds of the subjects who are to respond to the instrument being developed. For example, we have found that many of the persons who are most readily available as translators are persons who are considerably higher in education than the subjects who will be using the instrumental and they therefore produce stilted, academic versions of a questionnaire which are not readily understood by the subjects. In fact, an additional problem arose in the Philippines where, since there are many different dialects, many potential translators were not in fact native-speakers of the dialect into which they were making translations. Because of the movement toward development of a national language in the Philippines there has been a considerable increase in the number of students who are studying the national language, Pilipino, in school. Such speakers of Pilipino may actually be superior in terms of grammatical knowledge and in terms of formal linguistic knowledge of Pilipino or Tagalog to native speakers, but in fact their language is different from that of the native speaker of Tagalog, and if one is to use a questionnaire with native speakers then the versions produced by the academically trained persons may be quite inadequate. For example, the Tagalog word for science, *agham,* is not familiar to many native speakers who do use the English word. We believe that the only solution is to have available as translators, or at least as informants, persons who are native speakers of the language to which the translation is to be done.

Actually the process of back-translation, when properly done, is literative, i.e., an initial translation is made, back-translated, examined for errors, corrected, again back translated, etc. At every stage improvement depends upon a rather critical set being taken by the translator working at that stage. Brislin has shown that the pretesting is an important addendum to the back-translation process, for he found a number of meaning errors that had previously gone undetected. Errors may well go undetected for any of a number of reasons mentioned above, e.g., translators of different subculture than subjects, conventions in translating that are not completely legitimate (*bakla*=homsexuality), etc. Fortunately, despite the problems with back-translation as a technique, Brislin has shown that very good results may be obtained when it is carefully done.

The major advantage of back-translation is that it operates as a filter through which non-equivalent terms will not readily pass. If there is not an appropriate word or phrase in a target language for one in the source language, that fact has a high probability of being discovered. For example, if there is no equivalent in a target language for the American expression "take advantage of someone," it will probably be back-translated as "boss someone around," "cheat someone," etc. The investigator will be able to decide fairly accurately just what concepts he can employ in the two languages. He need not speculate; he can act on the basis of the back-translation results.

References

Anderson, R. B. W. On the comparability of meaningful stimuli in cross-cultural research. *Sociometry,* 1967, *30,* 124–136.

Berrien, F. K. Japanese and American values. *International Journal of Psychology,* 1966, *1,* 129–141.

Brislin, R. W. Back-translation for cross-cultural research. *Journal of Cross-Cultural Psychology,* 1970, *1,* 185–216.

Ervin, S. M. Language and TAT content in bilinguals. *Journal of Abnormal and Social Psychology,* 1964, *68,* 500–507.

Osgood, C. E., Suci, G. J., & Tannenbaum, P. H. *The Measurement of Meaning.* Urbana, Ill.: Univ. of Illinois Press, 1957.

Sechrest, L., & Flores, L. Homosexuality in the Philippines and the United States: the handwriting on the wall. *Journal of Social Psychology,* 1969, *79,* 3–12.

Werner, O., & Campbell, D. T. Translating, working through interpreters, and the problem of decentering. In R. Naroll & R. Cohen (Eds.) *A handbook of method in cultural anthropology.* New York: The Natural History Press, 1970, pp. 398–420.

Whorf, B. L. *Language, thought, and reality.* New York: John Wiley & Sons, 1956.

Meaning and Behavior: Communication and Culture

Edmund S. Glenn

Levels of Meaning

To attempt to define "meaning" is to attempt the impossible. But it can be said that two expressions have the *same* meaning if their utterance results in the same change of behavior. For example, we assume that the English "Good

From the *Journal of Communication,* Vol. 16 (December 1966), pp. 248–272. Reprinted by permission of the author and publisher. The author is Professor of Intercultural Communication, University of Delaware.

morning, Sir" and the French "Bonjour, Monsieur" have the same meaning for
a considerable range of subjects, because it is our impression that many people
would react in similar manners if so addressed—even though the range of situations in which the deferential "Sir" is used in English may be narrower than that
of the French "Monsieur."

Such an approach to meaning brings in the possibility of observing meaning,
i.e., observing behavior brought about by communication. Yet one should not
oversimplify: assuming that one begins to observe behavior at the moment of
utterance, when can one safely terminate observation? I may approach a man on
campus and say "Excuse me, Dr. Jones, my watch has stopped. Could you tell
me the time?" I can also say "Hey, buddy, got the time?" The chances are that
Dr. Jones will react by telling me the time—in either case. Thus what might be
called the *immediate* meaning of the two expressions may be the same. However,
if my name comes up at some later date in a conversation in which Dr. Jones
participates, his attitudes may differ according to the expression I have used. We
may call *latent* the level of meaning which may give rise to specific behavior at
a later moment. To have identical meaning, expressions must coincide in both
their immediate and their latent effects.

A Procedure of Semantic Analysis

The purpose of this paper is to present an example of semantic analysis based
on a comparison between original statements and their translations with the
purpose of discovering possible latent meanings (7, 8, 5, 3).

The corpus we shall use in this analysis is made up of some parts of the
printed record of the meetings of the Security Council of the United Nations,
which is suitable because it is a document with the same immediate meaning in
several languages—although only its English, French, and Russian versions will
be analyzed.

Obviously, a number of divergencies between the different texts must remain:
strictly literal translations are seldom possible and almost never acceptable. If
such divergencies as exist expressed differences in immediate meaning, the different language versions would not have been accepted as equivalent. Since they
have been so accepted, the remaining divergencies must either be meaningless, or
else reflect deeper, possibly subconscious, linguistic necessities or stylistic preferences.

The question is, therefore, whether the remaining divergencies between
different language versions are meaningless, or whether they can provide some
indications as to the ways in which work the minds of people speaking or writing
the different languages, and also whether there are nuances of meaning which are
easily expressed in some languages, and only with difficulty or not at all in other
ones.

The first step in seeking an answer to this question is to see whether divergencies form patterns: Translation is not a science but an art, and it is always possible
that isolated divergencies represent nothing more than a situational difficulty
encountered by one translator. The situation is different in the case of repeated

patterns: such patterns represent genuine differences, on a linguistic or a stylistic level.

The interpretation of the meaning of such patterns of divergencies (if and when found) is something else again. We may expect that the meaning of the patterns which may be found will be somewhat obscure. The criterion to determine whether patterns of divergencies are meaningful will be a comparison between such patterns and certain models developed by the author for general cultural analysis (7, 9, 4, 14, 13). Three such models will be used here:

1. UNIVERSALISM   The basis of this model is explicit or implicit trust in pure reason. This entails two characteristics on which much of the analysis below is based:

> a. Explanations and descriptions "point outwards," i.e., through the reference of particular situations to general standards; and
>
> b. The field is subdivided into broad units (quasi-universals), and attention is drawn to items of comparatively broad scope.

2. CASE-PARTICULARISM   The basis of this model is an explicit or implicit mistrust of pure reason, and trust in experience and action. This leads to two characteristics in polar opposition to the ones above:

> c. Explanations and descriptions "point inwards" to the observable particularity of the situation at hand; and
>
> d. The field is subdivided into small units, and attention is drawn to immediately perceptible elements small in scope.

3. RELATIONALISM   The gist of this model is a preoccupation with bringing together, and if need be reconciling, reason and experience. Hence two basic characteristics:

> e. The field is likely to be subdivided into units intermediate in scope between the ones expected under (b) and (d); and
>
> f. Attention is likely to be directed towards the relations joining universals and particulars.

In seeking patterns of expression corresponding to the characteristics above, it is useful to bear in mind that most expressions contain an element which is assumed by the speaker to be as obvious to the listener as it is to himself (th element upon which mutual intelligibility is *based*), and an element to be imparted to the listener, who is assumed to be unaware of it (and which makes up the purpose of the expression) (11, 1). The manner in which the first element— the apparently non-controversial one in the eyes of the speaker—is selected, throws a great deal of light on his subconscious assumptions.

"Pointing Inwards" and "Pointing Outwards"

The following examples (each of which is representative of a group of similar divergencies) show how the choice of words on the part of a speaker or a translator shows whether his preoccupations lead him to "point inwards" to the particularity of a situation, or to "point outwards" towards a general frame of reference:

1. The word "proper," in the sentence "it is within the province of each member to make such move as he may deem proper at the time," is translated in French by *"utile"* (useful) and in Russian by *"nuzhnyi"* (somewhere between useful and needed).

The meaning of this divergence may be sought by the method of substitution, classical in linguistic analysis. Let us take a fairly simple sentence in which the word under scrutiny has the same semantic value as in the original: "The delegation deemed it *proper* to present a proposal in writing." A translation such as: "La délégation jugea *utile* de présenter une proposition par écrit." appears acceptable. Let us now modify the sample sentence into: "The professor deemed it *proper* to call on the dean." A translation such as: "Le professeur jugea *utile* de faire une visite au doyen." would carry connotations entirely different from those of the original.

It would, of course, be absurd to suggest that French and Russian carry connotations of utilitarianism, whereas English does not. Yet this is what the example above would appear to signify, if it were taken in isolation—as it shouldn't be. It is, however, one of a series.

It may, for instance, be compared with another item, namely the translation of "like this" by *"de ce genre"* and *"takovo roda"* (of this kind). It is possible to say "the situation is like this, and it is unique." It is not possible to say that something described as "of a kind" is unique (the expression "the only one of its kind" notwithstanding). "Like this" may refer to a description the form of which is dictated entirely by the particular circumstances of the moment; *"de ce genre"* or *"takovo roda"* imply the classification of the entity described *with* others of a like kind.

Let us return to "proper." It carries in the example above the connotations of its etymology, that is to say, the meaning of "belonging to the situation," or "determined by standards proper to the situation." As such (a) it can be compared to "like this" and opposed to *"de ce genre"* and *"takovo roda";* and (b) it could be used equally well in the case of the professor and in that of the delegation, precisely because it referred to standards determined solely by the immediate context, and thus changed its meaning with a change in the context. On the contrary *"utile"* refers to a general standard of "usefulness," which fits in with one case, that of procedure, but does not with the other, that of a social or an ethical relationship.

This interpretation may be further explored by two more substitutions: "Le professeur jugea qu'il était *de son devoir* (he was obligated) de faire une viste au doyen." is an acceptable rendition of the English sentence dealing with the professor. On the contrary: "La délégation jugea qu'il était *de son devoir* de présenter une proposition par écrit" says more than does the corresponding English sentence; moreover, the context shows that the interpretation it adds is erroneous.

Thus, as the models lead us to expect, in the examples above, the expressions used in English pointed to standards of *explanation* internal to the situation, i.e., they asked the listener to seek understanding by comparing the various aspects of the situation with one another. On the contrary, the expressions used in French and Russian pointed to standards of explanation of a more general nature, external to the situation, i.e., they asked the listener to seek understanding by comparing the situation to notions of a more general nature. This difference in *methodology of reasoning* does not affect the immediate meaning, as it is possible to find general notions—usefulness in this case—equivalent to the particular notions involved. At the same time, there is no reason for believing that different methodologies of approach will lead to identical results when the subject matter is complex and compound—such as the accumulation of mental processes leading to the elaboration of a world-view.

The question now arises as to the degree of prevalence of the two contrasting practices.

2. Another example is that of the translation of "he should be given a chance" by *"il devrait avoir de droit"* (he should have *the* right) and *"yemu dolzhnabyt' pryedostavlyena vozmozhnost' "* (to him must be presented possibility; there are no articles in Russian). The syntactical form of the translations will be discussed in connection with other groups of examples; for the moment I shall concentrate on a comparison between "*a* chance," *"le droit,"* and *"vozmozhnost'."*

"Chance" is precisely something which resists codification, which varies from occurrence to occurrence. Let us take the expression "he has had his chance": It puts an end to the story to which it relates—but at the same time it hints nothing about the future. This connotation of particularity in "a chance" is still strengthened by the use of the indefinite article. It is *a* chance for a man to avail himself of the circumstances, whereas *the* right is a definite right which he always has.

"Droit" means not only "right" but also *"law."* What is right and is wrong is not made to depend upon particular circumstances but upon general principles: What is right, or what is lawful, in a given concrete case can be determined only by a comparison of the particular circumstances to general standards. The very use of the same word for "right" and for "law" cannot but derive from an implicit belief that what is right can be described with a satisfactory degree of fullness: This is, in a nutshell, the question of codified versus common law. The use of the definite article further strengthens the connotation derived from the lexical choice.

As for *"vozmozhnost' "* (possibility), it seems to be somewhere in between, closer, if anything, to the French: We may oppose "impossible" to "possible," as "wrong" can be opposed to "right"; whereas, no binary scheme of opposition is possible with chance. It follows that the use of "chance" leads away from any general schemes of organization of reality based on two-valued logic, whereas the French and Russian expressions either point to such schemes or at least admit them.

3. "To deal with" is translated as *"discuter," "examiner,"* or *"traiter,"* and in Russian by *"rassmotryet' "* (to examine in detail) or *zanyat'sya"* (to busy oneself with).

Six native speakers of English were asked to describe their interpretations of "to deal with." They came up with "to take action," "to handle in an appropriate manner," "to take care of," "to study and then take appropriate action," etc. In all cases they expressed a connotation of "getting it over with" or of obtaining a closure. Considered in such a light, all of the translations would appear woefully inadequate.* If they were made in this form, and if, indeed, they render adequate the immediate meaning of the utterances of which they are part, it is because the Security Council deals with problems precisely through examination and discussion.

Thus, contrarily to the first example where the English expression derived its meaning from the context, in this case it is the French and the Russian translations which lean on the context.

Yet there is a difference between the two cases: In the first example the context appeared as the subject matter of the statement. Conversely, in the present case the context is general and legal knowledge and is not mentioned in any statement. In the first case, the context was that of a particular situation. In the second one, it was that of the general procedures of the Council.

Thus in this example, as in the others, the English carries a suggestion of "pointing inwards," whereas the French and the Russian "point outwards," towards a general scheme of comparison.

Furthermore, the English expression points towards closure ("dealing with"), whereas the French and Russian ones point towards the continuing operations of the Council.

4. The question of "pointing inwards or outwards" may be further clarified by an example taken from elsewhere.

In teaching English syntax, a generally used method is that of diagramming sentences, that is to say of determining and picturing the inner relationships, to a large extent *particular to each sentence,* which tie together its various words. On the contrary, in French and Russian schools what is taught is to distinguish in the analysis of a sentence the various *general syntactic categories* into which its words fall. Thus, for nouns alone, a fifth and sixth grade French textbook distinguishes the following functions: Subject, attribute, apostrophe, apposition, direct or indirect object, and the complements of noun, adjective, attribution, agency, place, time, instrumentality manner, cause, comparison, company and purpose; every noun used in the discourse must belong to one of these categories. Such a scheme of categorization is simplified and strengthened in Russian by the system of declension: what may be for the French a matter of didactic preference, becomes for the Slavs a matter of linguistic necessity.

Circumscribing Cases

Indications quite similar to those derived in preceding paragraphs from lexical examples may also be derived from syntactical and stylistic data. For instance, the verb "to be," particularly in the third person singular of the present indicative, is used much more frequently in English than it is in French and Russian translations. Out of a total of 620 divergencies, there are sixteen times

---

* *"Rassmotryet"* is perfective and thus stands for completed action. Yet the action to be completed is merely that of examining; there is no hint of anything beyond.

when "to be" appears in the English original and is eliminated from the French, as against one case where this verb is used in French without having appeared in English (the use of "être" as an auxiliary of tense is not counted). There are twenty cases where "to be" is eliminated from the Russian translation of English sentences in which it appeared; there are no instances of the contrary.*

Let us look into the possible latent meanings which might be attached to the presence of "is" in the English phrases and its absence from the corresponding French and Russian ones:

1. "The suggestion of 'X' is that ..." is translated into French by " 'X' propose que. ..." It is clear that the English construction makes "the suggestion" somewhat independent of its author: Constructions such as "the suggestion is that ...," leaving out the identification of the person responsible for it, and, in fact, leaving implicit the very fact of an authorship, are not only possible, but often used in this text. One can easily imagine (though not within the Security Council) an admonition such as "forget the personality of 'X,' think only of his suggestion," or "take the suggestion on its own merits."

If we remember that verbs, in principle, describe relations, we see that the French construction describes a relation between "X" and the phrase following *"que."* The English construction expresses two relations: a minor one—minor because the sentence could stand without it—expressed by "of" and tying "suggestion" with "X," and a major one joining "suggestion" to the phrase following "that." The latter one is particularly interesting: it places a phrase in a relationship of equality (not only apparent, for the "is" here is one of identity) with a noun, an *ens* or a thing by definition: it thus entifies the content of the suggestion. Such a style gives a permanent, thing-like appearance to a set of circumstances. It is in this manner that *cases* are defined: for example, a case such as "Jones and Loughlin *vs.* the NLRB" is a set of circumstances which acquires a permanent thing-like character within the mind of a lawyer.

Universals are also often obtained through the entification of abstractions. The difference is that universals are also (in general) expressible by single words; their number is limited and their system amounts to the subdivision of the field into a (comparatively) small number of large units. In contradistinction to this, cases are often unnamed; even those which receive an identification are numerous, and the area of influence of each is usually small. Thus the entification of cases through the frequent use of "is" as in the example above, amounts to the subdivision of the field into numerous small units.

Where "X," the subject of the French construction, is both durable and to a large extent independent of any action of the Council, "suggestion," the subject of the English construction, is immediately and fully subject to such an action. This fits in with the "action" characteristic of case-particularism.

Here again English, contrarily to French, draws attention to a particular context, that of the proposal before the Council at the moment, and away from a more general one (the delegate), while the French draws attention to the

---

*"To be" is seldom used in the present indicative in Russian; it is generally ellipticized and the sign zero, obtained as a result of the ellipse, has the same semantic value as "to be"; these sign zero situations are *not* counted as equivalent to the elimination of "is" in the total above.

individual delegate whose overall attitude should be evaluated not on the basis of one proposal only, but rather on the basis of all of the positions he takes.

2. "The matter is before the Council . . . ," appears in Russian as "Vopros, stoyashchiy pyeryed Sovyetom. . . ." There could have been a full stop after the English clause. Not so after the Russian one, which literally means "the question, standing before the Council. . . ." Thus the Russian draws attention to the clause which must necessarily follow, while the English draws attention away from it. Let us see how this looks in the context of the complete sentence: "The matter is before the Council to decide" is the English text, and "Vopros, stoyashchiy pyeryed Sovyetom, Sovyet dolzhen razryeshit' sam" (the question "standing" before the Council, the Council must decide itself) is the Russian one. The English text draws attention to the situation or the circumstances, and merely identifies the substance involved—a decision to be taken by the Council; the Russian merely identifies the circumstances and insists on the substance. Once again, a sentence such as "The matter is before the Council," with a full stop, would have had approximately the same semantic value as the actual English, while a sentence such as "Etot vopros Sovyet dolzhen razryeshit' sam" ("this question, etc.") would have approximately the same semantic value as the actual Russian.

Thus what the Russian places in the principal clause and at the principal center of attention, is a decision of a political nature, possibly with far reaching consequences and doubtless connected with the broad picture of the political organization of international life; what it places in the secondary clause is the procedural facts which govern the immediate actions of the Council. What the English places in the principal clause are precisely those immediate considerations connected with the means of action; what it places in the subordinate clause is the reference to a more distant and broader goal.

3. ". . . That the Council be free . . ." is translated into French by ". . . que le Conseil ait toute liberté . . . ," where the verb "have" is used instead of "to be." This example may be put in parallel with an example taken from another group, in which the original French "chacund'entre nous aura . . . la volonté d'y participer" (everyone of us will have the will to participate) is translated into English by ". . . everyone of us will be anxious to help"—here a French "have" is replaced by an English "be."

There is in the verb "to be" a suggestion of completeness and of permanency which the verb "to have" lacks. It is possible to say that "something is x, *and* y, *and* z . . . ," but this is seldom done: the locution tying an attribute to a subject is in general sufficiently compelling to leave other attributes unmentioned. In addition "is" carries a suggestion that what one is, one is all the time. On the contrary, one has this and that and the other. One has something one day, and not the next. Compare "I am cold" with "I have a cold." Background knowledge tells us that I am not cold all the time, but the expression has a compelling strength which eliminates past, future and almost everything else from the pertinent range of thought: "I am cold," that is the whole situation, perhaps something better be done about it. "I have a cold," on the contrary, implies a passing situation and a partial description—even in cases such as "I have cancer," where it may well be final. It suggests incompleteness: "I have a cold, so I am staying home today."

The statement, "the Council is free to . . . ," or "everyone is anxious to . . . ," in a parliamentary debate, is likely to be referring to some particular situation. The use of the verb to be, with its connotations of completeness and permanency, has for effect to isolate that situation, to make it self-sufficient within thought. On the contrary the "have" constructions of the French version draw attention to the Council as such, more than to the situation: the impermanency of this verb does not isolate the particular situation with which it deals, but rather subordinates it to the continuing aspects of the Council's activities.

To sum up: "Is," because of its frequent use in situations where it stands for identity, carries connotations of "full" explanation or description—that is to say of closure. It is immediately clear that the Council is not fully described by a statement that it "is free," or that "everyone of us" is not fully described by saying that he "is anxious to help." Yet these descriptions may appear as equivalent to full statements when appearing in the precise context of a situation in regard to which they describe the role played by the entity concerned. Thus attention is drawn, once again, to the situation, that is to say to something circumscribed, limited and particular; furthermore, this something is entified, as in the concept of a "case."

In contradistinction, "to have" describes a relation. Where applied to the Council, or to a group of delegates, it performs the same function as the active form, "le délégué propose . . .": it relates people to items on the agenda or to opinions, and ties together various stands through emphasizing the people involved. What is obtained is thus a system of relations.

4. Another case is that of the translation of "we are under an obligation to . . ." by "nous devons" (we must, also we owe) in French (and "nasha obyazannost' " (our duty) in Russian). Here again the English construction sets out the fact that it is dealing with one particular situation.

The subject is the same in English and French: "we." But the construction through "are" of the English suggests an equality between the subject and the nominative predicate, which is obviously occasional: let us discharge the obligation defined by the phrase following "to" and obtain closure. The French version does not carry such a connotation: "we must" may refer to a permanent as well as to an occasional obligation. One can say "we must be honest," but to say "we are under an obligation to be honest" would sound funny.

Choice of Subject

An important pattern of recurrence is one of inversion of subject and predicate between English and Russian. Thus for instance: "The important point is 'X' " becomes: "vazhnym obstoyatyel'stvom yavlyayetsya 'X' " ("X is the important point"). "The . . . method . . . would be 'X'," becomes: "Sposobom . . . bylo by 'X' " ("X would be the method"). "That conveyed the idea that 'X'," becomes: "Iz etogo slyeduyet 'X' " ("X follows from that"). (The lexical implications of this example will be considered later.) "There are a number of delegations which have 'X'," becomes: "U ryada delyegatsiy imyeyutsya 'X' " ("There is 'X' by a number of delegations").

Even in the case mentioned earlier, where the somewhat punctual English expression, "we are under an obligation," becomes the timeless Russian, "nasha obyazannost'," the latter does not appear as subject but as predicate. Thus: "We are under an obligation to 'X'," becomes: "Nashey obyazannostyu yavlyayetsya 'X' " ("X is our duty"). (The predicate in Russian is identified in many cases not by its position in the sentence but by a case ending.)

If the English subjects, the translation of which appears as predicates in Russian, are examined in the light of the context, it appears that all of them perform the function of tying what is about to be said—"X"—to the background of the debate. In all cases they refer to a situational and immediate element. As for "X," the Russian subject, it stands for (1) the position taken by several countries, (2) the question of a postponement of the discussion, a controversial point at the moment, (3) the date of a debate, again the very subject of controversy, (4) political statements in regard to the question under consideration, and (5) dealing with a political proposal. In all cases these subjects contain the overall substance under consideration.

It does not *necessarily* take a noun to make a subject, yet most often subjects are nouns. Thus, making something the subject of a sentence has an effect of reification or at least entification. It has also an effect of emphasis.

In the present pattern English entifies and emphasizes immediate situations, while Russian places the stress on the substance.

Furthermore, in situations such as those in the Security Council, the substance is invariably something more extensive in time and space, less tangible and more abstract, than is immediate procedure; it is obviously also a question of goals and programs, and not one of means.

Here again the Russian text exhibits a characteristic expected from the universalistic model, and the English text one expected from the case-particularistic one.

Statements as Such,
Versus the Content of Statements

The patterns described previously may be compared with a different group of divergencies.

We find—as an example of a group—the Russian sentence "vmyeshatyel'stvo . . . nye sootvyetstvuyet dyeystvityel'nostiyi" (the interference . . . does not correspond to reality) translated into English by "the allegation of interference . . . was not in accordance with the facts."

The word "allegation" was added by the translators, obviously to eliminate a connotation which would have been only too obvious in English—and in French, where the translation is, "réfutait les allégations selon lesquelles . . . s'immisceraient."

Elsewhere the French, "la conclusion présentée par le représentant . . . précise que . . ." ("The conclusion of the representative . . . clearly states") becomes in Russian, "Iz slov predstavityelya . . . stanovitsya yasnym" (from the words of the representative . . . it becomes clear). In this case the translation seems to imply that saying, "the statement is clear"—with no connotation as to the acceptance or rejection of the statement on the part of those to whom it is addressed—is the equivalent of, "the statement makes it clear," which suggests acceptance on the part of the audience.

Still elsewhere the French, "le Gvt. . . . a exprimé les mêmes préoccupations que . . ." (The Gvt. . . . has expressed the same concern as . . .) is translated into Russian by, "pravityel'stvo ozabocheno . . . v toy zhe myerye kak . . ." (The Gvt. *is* concerned to the same degree as . . .).

In all of these cases the Russian, either original or translation, fails to observe the distinction, expressed carefully in the other two languages, between fact and statement about fact, or between object language and meta-language.

There is even a case where the Soviet delegate speaks of *"otritsaniye faktov"*—the "refutation of facts." The English and French translators carefully add "allegations," as above.

The attitude found in these Russian expressions appears less strange if viewed against the background of the universalistic model than it does within the usual frame of reference of the English-speaking cultures. Let us think of Plato: Statements may be mere opinions, but the observables, which we nowadays tend to call facts, are mere approximations. Both can be refuted and careful distinguishing between them is pedantry. Only reason gives truth.

Preoccupation with Precision in French

A hierarchical organization of ideas implies a relational neatness: The same neatness may be found in the careful search for *"le mot juste,"* exhibited by the French both in the case of the original and in that of the translations.

In the case of translations from French, we see very often that the original uses words just slightly more precise than either the English or the Russian translations. Thus, for instance, a delegate presents *"des explications"* in French, while he merely makes "remarks" in English; the positions of two parties are *"réciproques"* in French, and "relative" in English ("relative" could apply to more than two); looking at the text of the Charter a delegate *"constate"* in French, but merely "finds" in English, etc.

Turning now to translations into French, we find that if there are two Articles of the Charter instead of one to justify an invitation being sent for a non-member Country to join the Council in its debate, that Country's "case is much stronger" in the original English; this becomes, *"sa participation . . . a plus de raison d'être,"* in French. Such an invited delegation would participate, "in the work, in the sittings (?)" in the original English, but *"à l'examen de la question"* in the French translation.

The French translators can be pitiless with suspected redundancies. For instance, "the placing of this item, the application" is cut down to *"la question";*

when a delegate says, "but my attitude is such that I . . . ," this becomes simply, *"mais je. . . ."*

(In all of these cases of translation from English, the Russian follows the original. This may be merely the result of the fact that translators tend to follow the original whenever they can: In any case, it seems that Russian translators do not share the preoccupation with precision which is that of their French colleagues.)

Although the English in the examples above does not show the precisionist approach of the French, it presents no ambiguity to anyone even slightly familiar with the background circumstances. It might be said that the motivation in the choice of words in English is to be understood at the time and place of the utterance. French seems to be attempting something more than that: Perhaps to present a "true picture of the real situation." It thus implies that reason is capable of grasping reality, and words of depicting it.

It might be objected that many French expressions (outside of this corpus) seem particularly irrational and redundant. Such is, for example, *"qu'est-ce c'est que cela?"* for "what is this?" Bally explains such constructions, particularly frequent in negations and interrogations, as being part of an evolutionary struggle between inversions and the French tendency towards progressive sequence (1). This progressive sequence is often called *"l'ordre logique"* by the more conservative among French grammarians: While I would be among the first to reject the claim of any construction to a "true" or logical status, the fact of calling a sequence "logical" implies a preoccupation with and a belief in rationalism.

It seems hard to deny that while "a red rose" suggests a so-called concrete sequence of sensation-recognition, *"une rose rouge"* follows a more abstract sequence of principal classification sub-class (6).

Russian, while also emphasizing ideas in preference to tangible facts, does not show a comparable preoccupation with the precise definition of relations. The latter, as it was noted, is indicative of relationalism rather than of pure universalism.

Actor-Action Relationship

A considerable number of English sentences, such as (1) "The suggestion of 'X' . . . is that . . . ," where "to be" stands for identity; or (2) "Are there any observations to be made?", where "to be" stands for existence; or (3) "A . . . matter . . . to be determined when . . . ," where "to be" is an auxiliary of the passive voice; or (4) "(Powers) conferred on the Council by the Charter," in the passive voice without "to be"; or (5) "It (a question) needs more time to study," where the grammatical subject is a "false" subject from the point of view of the actor-action relationship, are translated into French by sentences or clauses where the subject is also the actor. In most cases a transitive verb with a direct complement is used; to wit: (1) *" 'X' propose que . . . ,"* (2) *"Quelqu'un a-t-il des observations à formuler?",* (3) *"Une question sur laquelle nous pourrons nous prononcer lorsque . . . ,"* (4) *"(Pouvoirs) que la Charte confère au Conseil,"* (5)

"Il nous faudra davantage de temps pour étudier cette question" (a "false" subject also, but with greater emphasis on *"nous,"* the actors), etc.

There is a similarity between this pattern and the one studied earlier in regard to Russian: In both cases there is a change of subject. There is, however, an important difference: In many cases the French could have followed the English construction. For instance, (2) *"Y a-t-il des observations?"* or (4) ". . . *conférés par la Charte au Conseil,"* without a change of subject, are acceptable French.

We are dealing, therefore, not with a choice imposed by the language itself (*"langue"* according to the de Saussure terminology [2]), but with a stylistic preference on the part of the people responsible for the translation.

Eight native speakers of French were interviewed and asked which they found more idiomatic of seven sentences taken from the French translations in the corpus or of the corresponding sentences following the original English in construction. Seven of the informants agreed with the translators in all cases, while one agreed with them in four cases out of seven, and declared both constructions to be equally good in one case.

The informants were also asked to give a reason for their preference. Here the pattern didn't seem particularly informative, *"c'est plus direct"* and *"c'est plus naturel"* being among the most frequent answers.

The fact remains that the result of the style selected by the translators, and approved of by the informants, is to set out clearly the actor-action relationship. Such a style is called analytical and historiographic by both Bally and Mathesius (1, 11); it draws attention to the principle of causality, to that of responsibility, and it tends to deal, though somewhat statically with lengthy spans of time, as the cause; for instance the adoption of the Charter, may be quite remote from the effect which alone is pertinent to the situation being discussed, as are the powers of the Council in the situation with which the fourth example above is concerned. It should also be noted that such a style is more relational than entifying, as the subject is in general a real entity, often a person, and much of the meaning is carried by a verb.

Summing up the choices of subject in the three languages, we see in Russian a preference for abstract entities of great scope, in French for individual actors, and in English for "cases," i.e., situations or sets of circumstances, in general fairly specific and limited in scope. Between the three preferences, the French one leads to the selection of subjects intermediate in scope (for example in probable extension in time, and in importance) between the other two. Furthermore, the insistence on the individual (in preference to either broad principle or specific circumstances) has for effect drawing attention to the manner in which each individual relates generalities to particulars.

Subjectivity in English

This investigation uses for data only cases of divergencies between original statements and their translations within the corpus. In consequence, expressions of individualism, including those of its manifestations appearing in the form "I" sentences will be noted only if and when there is a divergence between original and translation. This does not mean that "I" sentences are never used in any different way in the language of the original statement; it only means that a particular way in which they are used seems to create difficulties in translation into the target languages. Clearly this doesn't exhaust the question: Other techniques, such as frequency counts in the language of origin, may also lead to data relevant to the general problem of patterns of thought.

Three examples of divergencies in the case of English "I" clauses, appear particularly significant.

1. "I am very anxious that . . ." appears in Russian as, *"Ya schitayu kraynye zhelatyel'nym"* (I deem it very desirable). (The case of the French translation will be examined further down.) Several things are immediately apparent: (a) The emphasis, as expressed by "very" or *"kraynye"* is transferred from the modus to the dictum (or from the speaker to the substance of the statement). (b) The word "desirable" introduces an ambiguity: From whose point of view is it desirable? From the point of view of a "me" or from that of an "us"? Or is it *pro bono publico?* Or again, in order to satisfy some abstract ideal of justice?

The English original openly expresses a personal (or, given the circumstances, a national) position. The usual means for resolving difficulties deriving from differences in personal wishes is compromise. The Russian version, however, introduces a pretense or a semblance of objectivity. The normal manner for resolving difficulties resulting from differences of opinion about an objectively knowable state of affairs is through bowing to superior knowledge.

2. There are many cases in which the phrasing of English shows that the knowledge or the understanding of the speaker is not something entirely divorced from his intentions, but rather that it is combined with them in a transactional whole. On the contrary, the French and Russian versions strive to separate knowledge or understanding from will or intention: "I understand that . . ." is translated by *"Je tiens à faire connaître . . ."* (I wish to make known) and, *"Ya dolzhen dolozhit' . . ."* (I must communicate).

The situation here is as follows: The speaker is in the Chair and the clause after "that" announces that a delegate wishes to make a declaration. The English construction implies that awareness leads to action—this is also shown by the expression, "I recognize the delegate of . . ."—and that an official having a definite function makes his intent known by stating his awareness.

3. The example below shows again French and Russian preference for the "objective" over the volitional: In another case, "as long as I understand that . . ." is translated as, *"s'il s'agit de . . . ,"* and *"poskol'ku ryech idyet o . . ."* (both are idioms meaning, more or less, "if what is being dealt with is . . .").

Here again the context is interesting: The speaker intimates that he will take a certain attitude "as long as I understand that . . ." He does not say "as long as." He predicates his attitude on his understanding, not on a hypothetical objective state of affairs, and gives the other parties the opportunity—but not the obligation—to challenge his interpretation.

4. With a "government" for subject, "believes" becomes *"estime"* and *"schitayet."* Elsewhere "I feel" becomes *"je crois"* (I believe), and, again, *"schitayu."* In the other direction, *"schitayu"* becomes *"j'estime"* in French and "I think" in English.

There seems to be a regular gradation of certainty: The Russian is certain, the English merely advances an opinion. As for the French, it also advances an opinion, but in a manner which strongly suggests that this opinion is based on careful reasoning.

Is there anything in common between the volitional aspect of the expressions in the first three cases, and the hypothetical tone of the purely modal ones in the last one?

One might venture to say that both are indications of a case-particularistic or empiricistic approach. According to this school of thought, reason may only suggest hypotheses, only experience, ergo action, may lead to certainties. Hence the identification of hypothesis with suggestion for action and the reluctance to use expressions connoting certainty on the theoretical plane.

5. The French expressions under (4) in the preceding paragraph were on the whole stronger than the corresponding English ones. On the contrary, the expression, "I am very anxious . . ." under (1) becomes in French, *"je serais très désireux,"* with its strength diluted by the use of the subjunctive.

One might venture to say that relationalistic or simply rationalistic usage in French leads to strength in the affirmation of opinion, while empiricistic usage in English leads to strength in the affirmation of intent.

Determinism in Russian

French draws attention to causal relations through the intermediate state of setting out actor-action relationships, that is to say, in a manner suggesting the complementary notions of responsibility, free will, and possible diversity of opinion. The situation is different in Russian.

1. An expression such as, "that conveyed the idea" (in French: *"ce qui signifie"*—"which means"; characteristically more positive) becomes in Russian, *"iz etogo slyeduyet,"* or again, "there is a question" (in French, *"il s'agit de savoir"*—the point is to know) becomes *"voznikayet vopros."* The first Russian expression means, "it follows," the second one means "a question follows therefrom." Yet the two Russian verbs are different from one another. Indeed, Russian is extremely rich in verbs meaning "to follow from," in the abstract sense: Thus in translations from Russian we find *"pryedlozheniye nye vytyekayet"* (translated by "this proposal is not based . . ."), *"mogut vozniknut' oslozhnyeniya"* (difficulties may arise), *"iz etogo slyeduyet"* (this shows), *"iskhodit iz"* (has in view), *"na odnom iz poslyeduyushchikh zasyedaniyi"* (one of the later meetings). Yet all four of the Russian verbs, as well as the participial adjective in the last example, mean literally "to follow from," except perhaps *"iskhodit','"* in the case of which "to proceed from" seems better.

2. There is also a group of divergencies in which the English subject, generally but not always of a verb in the passive voice, becomes in Russian an indirect complement in the dative. For instance, "the Council has been called upon to act ..." becomes *"Sovyetu prikhoditsya dyeystvovat'..."* (to the Council it comes to act) and "Do I take it that ...?" becomes *"Schitat' mnye, chto ...?* (which differs from the English in placing the first person pronoun in the dative rather than the nominative).

Now the dative in such cases is described by Roman Jakobson as characterizing "the recipient of happening" *(Empfänger des Geschehens)* (10).

Taken together, the two groups carry a strong suggestion of determinism or fatalism: The first group suggests that things follow ineluctably one from another; the second group suggests that man is somewhat passive in the face of circumstances.

Determinism fits in well with the universalistic ideal of omniscience. Fatalism is a more archaic trait of culture, fitting in somewhere between *mana* and the universalistic idea of lawfulness in the universe: Occasional failure of magical manipulations may be explained at first by greater *mana* operating against the self. An unpredictable mixture of successes and failures then comes to suggest a "fate" beyond all manipulation. The next step is to find out what the fate is: hence the search for laws. A belief in total lawfulness is the essence of determinism.

Synthetic Character of Russian

A deterministic attitude calls for a certain rigidity: Such a rigidity may be found in several patterns of divergencies in the corpus. For instance, in cases where a copular construction is carried over from English into Russian, the transparent English "to be" is generally replaced by more precise verbs such as *"sostoyat'"* (to consist in) or *zaklyuchat'sya"* (to be delimited or defined by). It should be noted that while sentences such as " 'A' is 'B' " are neutral in respect to the Aristotelian categories of accident and essence, these two Russian verbs unavoidably introduce essences. (Verbs such as *"slyedovat',"* *"iskhodit',"* or *"yavlyat'sya,"* which also are often used for "to be," were discussed earlier.)

Another convergent pattern may be found in a tendency in Russian to use nouns where the other two languages use verbs—thus implying rigidity and permanency for the relationships described—and to still strengthen the impression created by introducing such nouns by non-transparent and rather uncompromising verbs. For instance: *"nye podlyezhit rassmotryeniyu Sovyetom,"* although translated as "should not be considered by the Council" (in French, *"le Conseil ne doit pas examiner,"* with a characteristic interversion of the actor-action type), literally means "is not subject to consideration by the Council." Or again, *"takomu analizu ya dolzhen podvyergnut'...,"* although translated as "I must analyze" *(je vais analyser),* literally means "I must submit ... to such an analysis." Still elsewhere, the Russian uses the noun *"otritsaniye"* where the English and French translators use the corresponding verbs "to refute" and *"réfuter."* Characteristically enough (as it was noted earlier), what is thus refuted are not statements, but "facts"— *"v otritsaniye faktov."*

Such a frequent use and abuse of nouns leads, according to both Bally and Mathesius (1, 11), to a strongly synthetic character of expression: *"Rassmotryenie voprosa Sovyetom"* (the consideration of the question by the Council) is a unit, while "the Council examined the question" may be divided into subject and predicate. Again, Russian presents as indivisible, large "chunks" of experience which the other two languages tend to subdivide.

Behavioral Correlates

The moment has come to present some examples of nonlinguistic behavior correlating with the styles of expression analyzed above.

Two spheres of activity will be arbitrarily selected out of many available ones, for purposes of illustration: politico-economic organization and inter-personal relations.

Universalism leads to an expectation of politics directed towards the implementation of broad ideologies, and of a tendency towards centralism. Both have characterized Russian political life, not only under Communism, but before it as well.

Case-particularism leads to an expectation of decentralization, of the carrying out of necessary policies by ad hoc bodies, and of a political life directed mainly at the reconciliation of the interests of individuals and of common-interest groups. Roughly, such a description applies to the political life of the United States, of Britain, and of the other English-speaking countries.

Relationalism leads to an expectation of a compromise between the two tendencies above. An example may be the French economic plan, with its elaborate procedures for reconciling governmental desires with private decisions. Another example is that of a centralized civil service, whose influence is tempered —but only tempered—by grass-root politicking.

In the sphere of the organization of inter-personal relations, American behavior is characterized by numerous friendships, each of which takes up only a small fraction of the time of the individuals concerned. Furthermore, interaction between an individual and each of his friends tends to be specialized: the American has friendships centering around work, around children, around political opinions, around charities, around games, around various occasions for sharing food and alcohol, etc.; it is relatively seldom than any two individuals carry out their relations through many of these compartments. In the case of married people, there are male interactions, female interactions, and couple interactions; all relatively independent among themselves. This fits in with the case-particularistic expectation of a subdivision of the field into numerous small units or cases.

The habitual behavior of Russians in the same area is characterized by a few deep friendships, carrying with them an obligation of almost constant companionship, and the rejection of any reticence or secretiveness among friends. Where an American tends to become interested in another one because of some special point of common interest, and tends to limit mutual relationship to such a point, a Russian tends to embrace the whole person. This fits in with the universalistic pattern of subdividing the field into small number of large units.

Here again, French patterns of friendship occupy an intermediate place. Friendships are specialized, but they also tend to be organized in patterns of long duration, often with an expectation of family friendships extending over more than one generation. Where Americans are competitive even within the group of friends, for Frenchmen as for Russians friendship excludes competitiveness; the co-existence of cooperation with competition, so natural to Americans, appears incomprehensible to French and Russian informants. The divergent demands of privacy, independence and long and close friendships are reconciled by the French through the institution of the *brouille* (15): friendship is put in abeyance but not broken, the individuals concerned are not on speaking terms, but expect a reconciliation and stand ready to resume mutual help under some grave circumstances, such as death in the family. Under similar circumstances Americans would quietly drift apart, and Russians seek immediate resolution through a stormy scene.

Cross-Cultural Communication

Examples such as those above could be multiplied, almost ad infinitum. There is little point in doing so, because even many examples are not enough to constitute proof, and a few examples are enough to present an illustration. However, let us suppose that the hypotheses advanced on the basis of the first stage of the analysis hold up under further scrutiny. What can one say about the efficiency of the communication process itself?

It seems that immediate meanings were properly transmitted, but that latent meanings were not. Immediate meanings (in the case of the sample) deal with the processes of diplomacy. Latent meanings may correlate with broad patterns of national behavior, including collective processes of decision making. It is the differences between such decisions (for example between Russian Communism and American Democracy) which underlie the gravest world problems, in particular those which diplomatic intercourse is trying to resolve.

It thus appears that the very gist of the underlying causes of conflict correlate with the communication that doesn't take place. As for the communication that does take place, it apparently correlates only with the immediate and the superficial. The latter may at times be enormously important, but the failure to communicate the former may have much to do with the impression of futility one often obtains when observing the debates of the world's highest council.

References

1. Bally, Ch. *Linguistique Française et Linguistique Générale.*

2. de Saussure, F. *Cours de Linguistique Générale.*

3. Gastil, R. D. "Language and Modernization: A Comparative Analysis of Persian and English Texts." Cambridge, Massachusetts, Harvard University, Center for International Affairs, mimeographed, 1959.

4. Glenn, E. S. "The Concept of Cultural Regression," xviiith International Congress of Psychology, 1963.

5. Glenn, E. S. "Languages and Patterns of Thought." Washington, D.C., Georgetown University, mimeographed, presented at the vth International Congress of Anthropology and Ethnology, 1956.

6. Glenn, E. S. A presentation at the Symposium on Psycholinguistics, APA Convention.

7. Glenn, E. S. "Semantic Difficulties in International Communication." *ETC.* 1954.

8. Glenn, E. S. "Translation as a Tool of Research," *Report of the Sixth Annual Round Table Meeting on Linguistics and Languages Teaching.* ed. R. H. Weinstein, Washington, D.C., Georgetown University, 1955.

9. Glenn, E. S. "The Use of Epistemological Models in the Analysis of Cultures," *Proceedings of the vith International Congress of the Anthropological Sciences.* Paris, Musée de l'Homme, 1960.

10. Jakobson, R. "Beitrag zur allgemeinen Kasuslehre," *Travaux du Cercle Linguistique de Prague* No. 6.

11. Mathesius, J. *"Reč A Sloh."* Prague.

12. Mead, M., and R. Métraux. *"Themes in French Culture."* Stanford, 1954.

13. Northrop, F. S. C. *The Meeting of East and West.* New York: Macmillan, 1953.

14. Pribram, K. *Conflicting Patterns of Thought.* Washington, D.C.: Public Affairs Press, 1945.

15. Wylie, L. *Village in the Vaucluse.* Harvard, 1957.

The Japanese Patterns of Communication and the Concept of *Amae*

L. Takeo Doi

I think some of you are already familiar with the concept of *amae,* but for those who are not I shall first quote the relevant passage *from an earlier paper:*

> *Amaeru* [*amae* is its noun form] can be translated as "to depend and presume upon another's love." This word has the same root as *amai,* an adjective which corresponds to "sweet." Thus *amaeru* has a distinct feeling of sweetness, and is generally used to express a child's attitude toward an adult, especially his parents. I can think of no English word equivalent to *amaeru* except for "spoil," which, however, is a transitive verb and definitely has a bad connotation; whereas the Japanese *amaeru* does not necessarily have a bad connotation, although we say we should not let a youngster *amaeru* too much. I think most Japanese adults have a dear memory of the taste of sweet dependency as a child and, consciously or unconsciously, carry a lifelong nostalgia for it (p. 92).

Thus it is true that *amaeru* has its primary locus in childhood, but it can be applied to any interpersonal relationship between adults, if that is known to contain the same kind of longing for dependency or belonging as a child must

From *The Quarterly Journal of Speech,* Vol. 59, No. 2 (April 1973), pp. 180–185. Reprinted by permission of the author and publisher. Dr. Doi is Professor of Mental Health at the University of Tokyo.

have. It dawned on me then that the visibility of accessibility of such a basic desire as *amae* might be the very factor that distinguishes Japanese people from other nations. So I wrote "*Amae*—A Key Concept for Understanding Japanese Personality Structure,"[1] when I was asked to participate in the symposium on culture and personality, a program of the Tenth Pacific Science Congress held in Honolulu in 1961. In this paper I stressed the central importance of *amae* for the Japanese patterns of emotion, which seemed to find a linguistic confirmation in the existence of a rich vocabulary in the Japanese language centering around the theme of *amae* with its multifarious shades. I argued that this fact must be indicative of the characteristics of Japanese society, that in Japan parental dependency is fostered and its behavior pattern institutionalized into the social structure. Today I am not going to elaborate upon the structural aspect of Japanese society that bears out *amae,* the area which should be better reserved for Prof. Nakane to discuss. Instead I shall try to demonstrate how the psychology of *amae* pervades and actually makes the Japanese patterns of communication.

Let me state at the beginning that the existence of the rich vocabulary centering around the theme of *amae* indicates foremost the awareness, not the fulfillment, on the part of Japanese people of the all-powerful desire to *amaeru*. They of course would like to gratify such a desire if they can, but since this is not always feasible, they have to develop a special sensitivity as to when and where they can gratify it and a capacity to endure the painful frustrations that would invariably occur. In other words, the rich vocabulary concerning *amae* attests to the appreciation of dependency needs in Japanese society as well as to the attempt at controlling such needs. Surely such controlling mechanisms are called for, for the desire to *amaeru* is entirely contingent upon others for its gratification. Namely, one cannot conjure its gratification by a verbal magic as sometimes can be done in the case of "I love you." In fact, Japanese seldom say "I *amaeru* on you," though they may say something like that when they are much obliged. Still, the gratification of *amaeru* stands as the norm in Japanese society, or perhaps it is better to say, as the principle of mutuality which alone guarantees a smooth transaction.

This being so, suppose that all interpersonal communications in Japanese society have the emotional undertone of *amae*. Then, would it be surprising that Japanese tend to have many short breaks in their conversation? Apparently during those breaks they try to feel out one another and assess the situation. Because what is most important for Japanese is to reassure themselves on every occasion of a mutuality based upon *amae*. One could say then that for Japanese verbal communication is something that accompanies non-verbal communication and not the other way around. In other words, they are very sensitive to the atmosphere pervading human relationships. Either they will try to soften the atmosphere or they are afraid to spoil it. No wonder that they often look pensive, smile unnaturally, at any rate are not properly communicative; the vices of which Japanese are often accused by foreign observers.

---

[1] In *Japanese Culture: Its Development and Characteristics,* ed. Robert J. Smith and Richard K. Beardsley, Viking Fund Publication in Anthropology, No. 34 (New York, 1962), pp. 132–139.

To explain this point further, let me introduce to you a very interesting comparative research done by Dr. William Caudill and Mrs. Helen Weinstein. They selected a matched sample of 30 Japanese and 30 American three-to-four-months-old infants and studied the interactions of those infants with their mothers. The conclusion the authors draw from this study is astounding:

> American infants are more happily vocal, more active, and more exploratory of their bodies and their physical environment, than are Japanese infants. Directly related to these findings, the American mother is in greater vocal interaction with her infant, and stimulates him to greater physical activity and exploration. The Japanese mother, in contrast, is in greater bodily contact with her infant, and soothes him toward physical quiescence, and passivity with regard to his environment. Moreover, these patterns of behavior, so early learned by the infant, are in line with the differing expectations for late behavior in the two cultures as the child grows to be an adult.[2]

One can see easily from this that Americans are conditioned from the very beginning of life to associate human contact with verbal communication, whereas Japanese, more with nonverbal empathic communication.

In this connection I would like to tell you my first reaction to Americans when I went to the United States in 1950. I was greatly surprised, almost perturbed, by the fact that Americans love to talk incessantly whenever they get together, even during the meal. As a matter of fact, they sounded to me almost hypomanic. This impression was undoubtedly at least partly due to the language barrier I was then painfully aware of, partly due to the difference in customs between the United States and Japan; because, when we were growing up, we used to be chided if we chatted during the meal. But I thought there was more to it, for I could not help feeling that Americans hate silence, whereas Japanese can sit together comfortably without saying a word to one another. To tell you the truth, even though I no longer feel the pinch of the language barrier now, it is still a strain for me to keep pace with Americans during a social evening. I cannot hide behind the couch so to speak, as when I am acting professionally. At any rate, I often bless myself for being a psychiatrist because of the privilege of keeping silence except for occasional "wise" comments!

One more example to prove the point. I know one Japanese simultaneous interpreter who recently served at three international conferences held in Tokyo and Kyoto. He told me it was simply amazing that Japanese participants did not communicate much vis-à-vis Americans. I remind you that they didn't have to speak English, as they could count on the ample service of simultaneous interpreters. Still, according to my informant, they didn't talk much, looking most of the time stiff and stony-faced. Don't think that they were simply awed by the presence of dignified Americans, though this might have played a role. Because Japanese don't talk much even at conferences of Japanese only, this even when they are congenial with one another. They usually spend a long time fishing for clues as to where each of them stands on the question at issue, so that they can somehow reach unanimous agreement, which they are so eager to have on any occasion.

---

[2]"Maternal Care and Infant Behavior in Japan and America," *Psychiatry,* 32 (Feb. 1969), 42.

Speaking of unanimous agreement, it has a very important social function for Japanese. It is a token that the mutuality of all the members has been preserved. In other words, it is a token satisfaction of *amae*. For Japanese hate to contradict or to be contradicted, that is, to have to say "no" in the intercourse. Since they don't want to have divided opinions in the first place, if such an outcome turns out to be inevitable, they get so heated and emotional that it becomes almost impossible to have reasoned discussions. I think this explains why the Japanese Diet or any intra-group strife in Japan becomes violent. The greater the power of cohesiveness, the more violent the effect of breaking up. It is like splitting the atom.

Now the well-known Japanese fondness for hesitation or ambiguities of expression can also be explained along the same line. Japanese hesitate or say something ambiguous when they fear that what they have in mind might be disagreeable to others, that is to say, when they have to say no. To impress you how deeply ingrained this trait runs in Japanese people from immemorial time let me cite from Manyoshu, the oldest anthology of Japanese poems, composed in the eighth century. The story behind the poems in question is as follows: A beautiful girl was sued by two boys, who fought fiercely over her. She apparently could not let her mind be known as to whom she loved, and lamenting for the fact that a humble maid as she was, she became the cause of two boys' fight, she killed herself. Hearing of the death of the girl, one of the two boys at once killed himself and the other left behind was much grieved that the one who at once followed her to death might have beaten him. He couldn't swallow his defeat, however, so he killed himself also soon after. The villagers deeply mourned over the deaths of three young people and built monumental mounds for each with the one for the girl in the middle. Several years passed. The tree planted in front of the girl's mound stretched its branch toward one of the other two mounds. The villagers then said, "Now we know for sure which of the two the girl loved, as the tree stretched its branch." Please note in this story that there is no condemnation of suicide, nor of the girl's apparent indecisiveness. If anything, she is appreciated for having been so modest and tenderhearted that she could not bear seeing two boys fighting over her. This is Japanese! I have been told that nowhere else in world literature is found such a story, horrendous yet very moving.

Concerning the Japanese ambiguity I have more things to say. That the Japanese language is so constructed as to be particularly conducive to the effect of ambiguity is well known. For instance, Japanese verbs come at the end of the sentence. Therefore, unless and until you hear the whole sentence, you wouldn't know where the speaker stands. This apparently gives him a psychological advantage, as he can change his position in anticipation of your possible reaction to it. However, it may happen that you are often left wondering whether he really means what he says. Also, there is the case of numerous auxiliary words in the Japanese language which primarily function as adhesives of other words and sentences. Since I am not a student of the Japanese grammar, I cannot adequately explain them except that they roughly correspond to conjunctives, interjections, or auxiliary verbs in English. Contrary to English, however, those Japanese equivalents have a very unique feature of faithfully reflecting the speaker's reaction to the changing situation. That is why we can do without pronouns in everyday conversation, a fact which may occasion ambiguity at times. Other factors, too, create ambiguity. Take conjunctives, for instance. In English they provide logical connections. Not necessarily so in Japanese. Rather, more often they serve only to cement and induce the speaker's free associations. At the same time they may help to hold the audience's attention. So, whether spoken or written, Japanese communication is usually quite loose in logical connections. You can go on talking for hours, even gracefully, without coming to the point. That is why it is sometimes extremely difficult to render a Japanese speech or article into English.

The Japanese fondness for unanimous agreement may also contribute to the effect of ambiguity. Curious as it may seem, for Japanese the form of unanimous agreement is not strictly binding, even if obligatory to respect it, which in itself, I am afraid, is an ambiguous statement. What I mean is this. Since the unanimous agreement is a token that the mutuality of all the members has been preserved, it is all right as long as one does not openly challenge its being a *fait accompli*. In other words, it doesn't prevent individual members from harboring their own thoughts or feelings. Here comes the famous Japanese double standard of *tatemae* and *honne*. The former can be translated as "principle" and the latter "true mind." But all of this is rather misleading. Because it looks then as though Japanese espouse hypocrisy as their morality, which is not at all the case. *Tatemae* is any rule of conduct which Japanese accept by unanimous agreement and it would be wrong if you think that Japanese don't take it seriously. It is like a valuable license that secures them membership in a coveted group. Still it is a formal front rather than a principle, behind which one may safely and continuously entertain one's *honne*. The discrepancy between the two is born, if not so bravely, with a good conscience. So for Japanese themselves there is nothing ambiguous about the double standard of *tatemae* and *honne*. It is even quite rational, as it seems that this is the only way things can be done given the nature of Japanese society. As a matter of fact, it is deemed the measure of maturity in Japan to acknowledge the existence of such a double standard and to adjust one's life accordingly. Incidentally, the distinction between *tatemae* and *honne* corresponds in the Japanese mind to the distinction between the public and the private, a topic which Professor Barnlund has taken up this morning.[3] These two pairs of concepts, however, are not really the same. This should be clear, if you trace historically the meanings given to the public or the private.

I am wondering if I have succeeded so far in making the Japanese patterns of communication intelligible to you. If I have, then hopefully you will find the notorious Japanese ambiguity no longer annoying. Writing this paper, I often fancied its title to be "In Defense of the Japanese Ambiguity," if not "In Praise of the Japanese Ambiguity." Of course I am not defending ambiguity as such. I am only saying that ambiguity has a meaning. Only if we know it, ambiguity

---

[3] *Editor's Note:* Dean Barnlund's study of these concepts in Japan will soon be published in Japanese. (*The Public and Private Self in Japan and the United States,* Tokyo: Simul Press.) Publication in English has not yet been arranged.

disappears for all practical purposes. But if we don't, ambiguity may even increase. Such a result is likely to happen when and where two cultures meet. That is, ambiguity in a foreign culture is not appreciated for its hidden meaning, instead is condemned in the name of one's own culture, thus making it even more difficult to understand. I think such danger is particularly great for Japanese culture, for it abounds in ambiguity, even makes a virtue of it as can be seen from its moral code, as I hinted above, or its cultivation of Zen Buddhism or its literary sensibility of which the best example is *haiku*. Unfortunately, nowadays it is not just foreigners who misunderstand Japanese culture, but Japanese as well who fall under the spell of Western ideas. So one may see many Japanese youth denouncing the double standard of *tatemae* and *honne* as adult hypocrisy to the great consternation of the older generation.

Only if they know what they are doing! Because it seems to me that they really don't know either Japanese culture or Western culture. They are only mixing up two cultures and getting mixed up themselves as a result. Please note that I am not just trying to save Japanese culture from contamination by Western culture. Intercultural communication is here to stay, and I shall be doomed if I fight it. I am only saying that for intercultural communication to be really fruitful each culture has to be understood from its roots. To get back to Japanese youth who feel compelled to denounce their own tradition, first they have to rediscover Japanese culture within themselves. Then they have to study Western culture more objectively. For instance, do they know why Western idealism, either in the form of democracy or communism, insists that the ideal is something that can be truly realized on this earth? It is so different from the concept of *tatemae*. Where does that belief come from? It is only because of this belief that one who does not live up to one's professed ideal is denounced as hypocritical. Or perhaps in the latter-day West is this belief being undermined? So much so that Western people do not suffer from the sense of guilt as they used to and have acquired the sense of being realistic. But then, isn't this contemporary sense of being realistic, which is not related at all to the original meaning of realism either in philosophy, literature or fine arts, similar to the Japanese double standard of *tatemae* and *honne?* If so, what does it mean, since they couldn't have borrowed it from Japan? Would it be rather that what appears to be peculiarly Japanese is really a universal human trait and Western people come to appreciate it only at this late date?

Vernacular Vocabulary: A View of Interracial Perceptions and Experiences

Edith A. Folb

Students of intercultural communication are aware of the intimate reciprocity of language with cultural perceptions and experiences. As Porter and Samovar have observed in the introductory essay in this volume, "culture and language are inseparably intertwined. What we think about and how we think about it are direct functions of our language; and what we think about and how we think about it in part determine the nature of our culture" (p. 18). However, when two groups of people—even within the same culture—share a language, this does not necessarily mean that vocabulary is used to characterize similar or identical experiences. One of the greatest barriers to effective communication, whether it be intracultural or intercultural, is the lack of shared experiences and a common vocabulary to define them. In American society, this sociolinguistic chasm between racial and ethnic subcultures and the dominant culture is still apparent. In his discussion of linguistic hostility as a factor in intracultural conflict, Maurer (1969) pointed out that "the so-called ghettos constitute sub-cultures within sub-cultures in many parts of the United States. . . . In these areas the break with the mores and the language of the dominant culture is of such proportions that several generations will be required to bring them together" (p. 606).

If we are to understand how intracultural and intercultural tensions can be reduced, we must look at the kinds of cultural experiences that are designated as important within and between groups of people. Because vocabulary is the part of language that is most immediately under the conscious manipulation and control of its users, it provides the most accessible place to begin exploration of shared and disparate experiences.

This paper focuses on a subset of the American lexicon, here referred to as *vernacular vocabulary* (nonstandard, unconventional, and so-called deviant words and phrases that have been variously labeled slang, argot, lingo, and jargon). The discussion deals with a selected body of vernacular expressions that were elicited from a cross section of black youths living in the greater Los Angeles area, and subsequently presented to a cross section of white youths also living in Los Angeles. The paper explores how those terms were defined, used, and talked about by the black and white youths interviewed.

This original essay appears here in print for the first time. All rights reserved. Permission to reprint must be obtained from the publisher and the author. Dr. Folb teaches at the University of California at Irvine. A portion of this research was done as part of a Ford Foundation Grant with the Afro-American Studies Center at the University of California at Los Angeles.

Background

The findings presented here are drawn from my continuing work on intracultural and intercultural vernacular vocabulary use (see Folb, 1972, 1973a, 1973b). Over the past six years, I have participated in some 200 taped interviews and numerous informal conversations with black and white youths from low- and middle-income backgrounds, living in diverse residential areas of Los Angeles. All youths were 15 to 20 years old. A background questionnaire and a glossary of vernacular vocabulary items were administered in the taped interviews in order to compare informant responses. During informal conversations, the same format was essentially used. As additional lexical items were elicited from black youths, they were presented to white youths for their definition and response.[1] All interviews were oral and personally conducted in a face-to-face informal context. The interview itself usually took place in the youth's neighborhood.

The lexicon covered a wide range of topics that labeled and identified important areas of youthful black interest and concern. These "interest categories" dealt with such matters as covert and overt forms of verbal and physical manipulation; male–female relations; sex; the care, maintainance, and display of one's car; drugs and so on.[2]

The Drug Experience

SHARED DRUG EXPERIENCES   Though there were several interest categories represented in the lexicon, only one area clearly linked youths from different racial, economic, and residential backgrounds—namely, drugs and drug-related activities. Fully 50 percent of the drug terms elicited from black informants were known by some portion of the white population.[3] Aside from this one area of interracial usage, virtually none of the other terms were shared by blacks and whites.

The drug lexicon can be divided into subsections that relate to specific kinds of drugs and drug behavior. Shared informant knowledge of these subsets of drug terms is of particular significance, since it tells us what aspects of the drug experience were most consistently perceived as important to both black and white youths.

The largest body of shared drug vernacular revolved around the use of pills, such as barbiturates and amphetamines, and marijuana. The number of synonyms known and used by black and white youths to describe each of these drugs was extremely elaborate and reflected the attention and importance assigned to them.

---

[1]To date, the lexicon includes over 2,000 entries. It forms part of a larger work on black vernacular vocabulary that I am presently engaged in writing.

[2]See Folb (1972), Chapter Six, "A Comparative Study of Urban Black Argot," for a full explanation and discussion of these interest categories.

[3]The total number of drug-related entries was 280.

Barbiturates, known in the vernacular as *downs, downers, stums,* and *stumblers,* are commercially distributed under various trade names. The most popularly used barbiturates were sometimes called by the name of their manufacturer or by their commercial identification number, but most often by their color. For example, Amytal (amabarbital marketed by Eli Lilly and Company) was called *blue, blue angel, blue heaven;* Nembutal (pentobarbital, Abbott Laboratories), *yellow, yellow jack, yellow jacket;* and Tuinal (amobarbital and secobarbital, Eli Lilly and Company), *rainbow, Christmas tree.* By far the most commonly used commercial barbiturate,[4] among both black and white informants, was secobarbital, known by the trade name Seconal (Eli Lilly and Company). Its popularity was attested to by the proliferation of vernacular expressions identifying it—*r.d., red, red devil, Lilly, Lilly F40* (manufacturer and commercial identification number), *F40, bullet,* and *bullethead.*

Though a number of commercially prepared amphetamines (known in the vernacular as *ups, uppers,* and *pep-'em-ups*) were used by both black and white informants, the one that was most often referred to was the compound Benzedrine, variously labeled *white, benny, chalk,* or *wake-up.* Interestingly, the amphetamine Methedrine, which was extremely popular among white youths, proved to have limited appeal among blacks. Only two vernacular terms—*speed* and *meth*—were elicited from black informants to describe the drug. Though some black youths had taken *speed,* Methedrine was generally considered to be a "white trip."

Shared vernacular was used to identify not only pills but the quantity or unit of measurement in which they could be gotten. For example, a single pill was referred to as an *ace;* two pills, a *deuce;* three to ten pills of varying or similar strength or type, a *roll;* and a bottle of 500 to 1,000 pills, a *jar.* A common way of asking for a given quantity of pills was *throw me out an* (*ace, deuce, roll,* and so on).

Without question, the most popular and widely used substance among both black and white informants was marijuana. Its immense popularity was reflected in the striking number of terms used to identify it—*grass, gani, weed, gauge, maryjane, juana, boo, shit, bush, tea, pot, smoke*—to a name a few. Furthermore, youthful "connoisseurs" of marijuana further classified it according to assumed place of origin and degree of potency. So, for example, informant discussion would often move from general terms for marijuana to detailed comparisons of the various types available, like *Acapulco gold, Chicago green, Mexican green,* or *Panama red.*

---

[4]Not all pills were commercially prepared compounds. In the case of barbiturates, some were secured through prescriptions; many others were purchased from drug dealers who, in turn, got the barbiturates through black market contacts in Mexico and Canada. Though these illegally secured pills were often extracted from commercial drug companies, they were extracted from their original capsules and mixed with a variety of substances, such as baking soda or sugar, to dilute them before they reached the streets. Knowledgeable informants, in fact, made a vernacular distinction between commercially prepared barbiturates, such as secobarbital, and dealer compounds. The former were called *prescription reds;* the latter, *border reds.*

Corollary to this intense interest in marijuana was the detailed vernacular attention given to the quantity or unit of measurement in which it could be obtained. Again, marijuana connoisseurs demonstrated detailed knowledge of such matters. The following conversation between a black and a white youth illustrates some of the fine points (and particularized vernacular) surrounding a purchase.

B: Man, in them olden days you could *score* (purchase) a *match* (a matchbox full of marijuana). No more. Don't even see no more *cans* (one ounce container of marijuana) or *lids* (one ounce container of marijuana)! It be *baggies* (plastic food bags used to hold various quantities of marijuana) now!

W: Yeah, me and my partner tried to *cop* (purchase) a *five cent bag* (five dollars worth of marijuana) last night. Dude told us he don't sell no more five cent bags. "Inflation, man"—that's what he told us. It's *ten cent* (ten dollar) or *quarter* (twenty-five dollar) bags nowadays. And shit, you're not getting any more weed than before! I'm gonna start *dealing* (selling drugs) myself! I have this friend who deals and he said he'd turn me on to his *connection* (source of drugs). Make some bread.

B: I hear ya, man. Next time, Ima get me a whole fuckin' *key* (approximately two pounds of marijuana)! Me an' some brothers gon' trip on down to *T.J.* (Tijuana) and score a righteous *brick* o' *shit* (approximately two pounds of marijuana). Yeah, then I'm gonna have a righteous *stash* (supply) *for days* (for a long time)! Can you dig it! (Mutual laughter.)

Finally, the ritual surrounding the preparation, paraphernalia and act of smoking a marijuana cigarette (*J, joint, dubee, stick, smoke, number*) carried its own extended vernacular description. When I asked a white middle-class informant to describe the ritual, he provided the following narrative:

Well, man, I get high every day, so I guess I'm an expert in that field. First, I get out my stash and my *papers* (cigarette papers used to roll a marijuana cigarette)— usually me and my partner *light up* (light up a marijuana cigarette) after school— then I roll two or three numbers. It depends on how good the shit is, you know. Like with *gold* (*Acapulco gold*), you take four or five *hits* (puffs) and you can get loaded pretty fast. That is some fine grass! Anyway, I roll some numbers. (What kind of papers do you use?) *Zig-Zag whites* (a particular brand of cigarette papers used to roll a marijuana cigarette; they come in brown and white). But this dude turned me on to some licorice papers—you know they come in all flavors and colors now. They're okay. Anyway, depending on my mood and how much grass I've got, I may roll a regular j or a couple of *bombers* (fat marijuana cigarettes). So then, anyway, we *fire up* (light up) and just sit back—get some wine—listen to some music maybe and just get stoned! (How many terms can you think of that describe being under the influence of marijuana or pills?) Shit, there's so many of them—*stoned, loaded, high, wired, ripped, wasted, ruined.* If you really get loaded, like you're *really fucked up* (profoundly under the influence), you just *flake out* (fall asleep).

Though the interracial drug vocabulary indicated a keen awareness of and interest in barbiturates, amphetamines, marijuana, and the behavior surrounding their use, the same was not true for so-called hard drugs—opium and its derivatives (morphine, codeine, and heroin) or cocaine. Only the most common vernacular terms for heroin (*H, smack, boy, stuff, skag*) and cocaine (*coke, girl, snow*) were elicited from black informants. No vernacular terms were offered for either codeine or morphine. Though white informants were encouraged to provide additional vernacular to describe hard drugs, none contributed any items other than those elicited from blacks. Similarly, terms describing the preparation, handling, and effects of hard drugs were infrequently brought up in conversation. When statements were made about the effects of getting high, they invariably centered on pill- or marijuana-induced behavior. Though some youths had *chipped* (occasionally used one or another of the hard drugs), they were not habitual users. Of the total informant population, less than 5 percent admitted to frequent or habitual use of hard drugs.

A variety of reasons were offered for an informant's lack of involvement with these drugs—lack of opportunity, lack of money, lack of accessibility, lack of interest, fear of becoming hooked. One black youth, who lived in Watts, provided a graphic statement about why he did not use hard drugs that rather clearly summarizes informant feelings:

> Pills and *weed*—da's fo' me. Nice high, cheap high. I kin git 'em—one way or d'other. *Irvine* (police) ain' gon' *swoop* (suddenly appear) and bust me fo' none o' dem *tracks* (needle marks) on my arms. Don' need that shit. *Green ain't never gonna be long enough* (money is never going to be sufficient) to support *dat* habit. Ain' gon' break my momma's heart wid a few little ole pills and shit. Junkie he a fool, a sucker! He got a hunger he ain't *never* gonna fill—til he *dead!*

Whether as the result of circumstance or choice, hard drugs did not figure importantly in informant conversations or the vocabulary they shared.

DIVERGENT DRUG EXPERIENCES   Thus far, no mention has been made about the whole class of consciousness-altering drugs popularly known as *psychedelics* or *hallucinogens*. Popularized vernacular terms for the most commonly known psychedelic drugs—lysergic acid diethylamide (*acid, LSD*), mescaline (*cactus*), peyote (*button*), and psilocybin (*magic mushroom*) were virtually nonexistent in the vocabulary elicited from black informants. Fewer than ten terms referred to this whole area of drug use and related behavior; and then only *LSD, acid, to trip* (when used specifically to refer to the effects of hallucinogens) and *psychedelic* (of or pertaining to the psychedelic experience) were used with any frequency.

Yet, if one were to glance through Landy's *The Underground Dictionary* (1971), which deals extensively with contemporary drug terms and their use, one will find a substantial number of entries describing and defining psychedelic drugs and related behavior. Why? Simply put, hallucinogenic drugs were not a viable part of the black drug experience. The psychedelic experience that fueled so many anti-Establishment actions and attitudes on the part of the so-called *flower chil-*

dren, hippies, long hairs, and countercultural *drop-outs* of the sixties was preeminently a white middle-class phenomenon.[5]

Black informant response to the use of psychedelics was overwhelmingly negative. Their use was seen as part of "whitey's trip," and provoked responses of disdain, outright dismissal, and most significantly, apprehension and fear. Less than a dozen blacks had experimented with any of the psychedelic drugs. The experiences of two black youths who had *dropped acid* (taken LSD) are worth recounting. They provide some insight into possible cultural reasons for the aversion to these drugs. One young woman told the following story about her experience with acid:

> I've taken one acid trip, you know, to see what it was like, but I didn't like it. I was at home, there was this party going on, and me and my old man dropped some acid. It was a real bad scene. I started talking a whole lotta *trash* (nonsense) and then I started crying because my brother would't be my friend. . . . He got mad at me. And, I said, "Just say that you'll be my friend!" And he wouldn't. He just looked at me like I was crazy. Kept telling me, "C., be cool, you ain't acting' right, be cool! Your *mind is weak* (not in control of yourself). You talking' like one o' them crazy hippies! Get yourself together, girl!" Then, I started crying. I really started crying.

Another story was told by a young man who lived in South Central Los Angeles:

> Me an' my partner we was *trippin' on some acid* (feeling the effects of *LSD*). Went over to the projects (Hacienda housing project in Watts) lookin' for a party. But, my head wasn't right. Started seein' things—polices everywhere. Heard sirens, and man, I *freaked* (lost control)! Started runnin' through the projects, yellin', "Pigs after me! They after me! Gon' *jack me up* (beat me up)! They gonna *blow me away* (kill me)!" Spent the whole fuckin' night hidin' from the police an' "Bear" (a member of a rival gang who had threatened him), hidin' from everybody! . . . Acid jus' ain't my bag. Mind gets crazy with that stuff! Gimme some *reds!* Gimme some *weed!* Gimme some *pluck* (wine)! Now, da's a nice high. Relax you, make you feel mellow. World look good den.

Generally, black informant response gave support to two important cultural factors, implicit in the two narratives, that mitigated against the use of psychedelics. One was the possibility of losing one's "cool" (losing control over one's environment and personal behavior, a negatively valued psychological stance in black culture). Another was the accompanying fear and paranoia brought on by becoming physically and psychologically vulnerable to a world which, for many

---

[5]The power and mystique of psychedelics gave birth to a whole generation of middle-class white rebels who—along with Timothy Leary, the guru of mind expansion—"tuned in, turned on and dropped out." However, blacks did not "tune in" to the white drug prophets, nor did they "turn on" to psychedelics. As far as "dropping out," many of them had been forced or chose to reject mainstream white values long before any of the psychedelic savants appeared on the scene. If anything, blacks during the sixties were marching to the tune of different drummers—Huey Newton, Rap Brown, Stokely Carmichael, and Malcolm X.

black youths, is already sufficiently distressful and dangerous without its being exacerbated by mind-altering drugs.

When black experiences are compared with white responses to taking psychedelics, we begin to see where culture-specific experiences and perceptions determine not only what drugs one uses and enjoys, but why one enjoys them. The experience of one white youth may highlight this point.

> Yeh, I drop reds and I smoke grass. It's alright, if you wanna *kick back* (relax) and do some *lightweight tripping* (mild consciousness expansion). But mostly, my bag is acid and mescaline. I dropped some acid this weekend—some *Sunshine* (a particular type of LSD that comes in yellow or orange tablets). Me and some friends went over to the park back of my house and really got into nature. Cops came by, we just waved. No hassle, just went on. We spent the day there, just trippin'. No cares, no hassles, just trippin'.

Nathan Kantrowitz (1969), in his discussion of the vocabulary of race relations used by prisoners to characterize fellow inmates, observed that "if a phenomenon is important, it is perceived, and, being perceived, it is named" (p. 24). As I have noted elsewhere (Folb, 1972), that supposition can be carried one step further:

> It may be said that those who have identified the phenomenon as important, and consequently, have named it, will come to share that name with others whom they [may] encounter and with whom they [may] interact in the pursuit of shared activities of which the phenomenon is a part (p. 13).

There is no doubt that most informants, whether black or white, perceived drugs to be an important phenomenon—whether in their own lives, the lives of their peers, or in both. The heavy drug users[6] among black and white youths, regardless of socioeconomic background, knew the greatest number of terms related to drugs and their use. Their superior knowledge of the drug lexicon was understandable, given their self-admitted, deep involvement in the drug experience. But the influence of the so-called drug culture was so far-reaching (and still is), that even the *lame* (socially inexperienced or naïve person) knew many of the vernacular terms used by his or her drug-savvy peers. The profundity of the drug experience was so keenly felt across barriers of race, economics, and geography, that significant portions of informant conversations were given over to discussing this phenomenon. If youths took drugs, they talked at length about their experiences; if they didn't take drugs, they rationalized about why they didn't; if they were undecided, they weighed the alternatives in light of the experiences of others. And consistently, they talked about drugs in the vernacular vocabulary used by their friends and acquaintances—a drug vocabulary that, as this paper points out, was shared in some significant measure interracially.

---

[6]The designation "heavy drug user" was applied to those youths who (1) admitted to repeated use of drugs, (2) used a variety of drug terms not represented in the glossary, (3) displayed intimate knowledge of the ritual activities surrounding the taking of drugs, as well as knowledge of the effects these drugs produced, and/or (4) had school or police records (or both) of extensive drug use.

Semantically Differentiated Lexical Items and Interracial Concerns

The following conversation took place at a bus stop, where two young men —one white, the other black—were "hanging out."

> *Young white man:* Hey, man, see that dude over there (points across the street), he's a real *punk!*
>
> *Young black man:* I hear ya. Don't be messin' with me, 'lessen he wanna be *blowed away* (killed)!
>
> *Young white man:* Yeh, dude tried to hustle my old lady—right in front of me too!
>
> *Young black man:* What you talking' 'bout, man? Thought you said he a *punk.* No punk gon' hustle a young lady.
>
> *Young white man:* Whadda you mean? I *saw* him *do* it, man. (Two look at each other with puzzled expressions.)

Despite the proprietary tone of the conversation, the exchange points up an important feature of vocabulary use. Though a word or phrase may be phonetically realized as, for example, *punk,* the semantic reading assigned to that expression may be primarily or totally different for two people. The fact that in the white youth's vernacular *punk* meant someone you dislike or have little regard for, while in the black youth's vocabulary, it referred to a male homosexual, indicates that we are dealing with semantically different lexical items that happen to take an identical phonetic form. It is apparent from the preceding example that if two people—or two cultures—do not share the same experiential referent for a given expression, communicative confusion is inevitable.

As already suggested, one of the primary functions served by vernacular vocabulary is to provide nonstandard or unconventional words and phrases to characterize new or important experiences in our lives. More often than not, these words and phrases are not newly coined, but are borrowed, directly or circuitously, from various subcultures within the larger culture, where they may be used to label significantly different phenomena. Therefore, the potential for interracial miscommunication, for example, is likely to be magnified.

In the present context, the potential for miscommunication becomes apparent if we look at the number of phonetically identical lexical items that were assigned different semantic readings by black and white youths. They are of particular importance, since they point up divergent interracial experiences. In white usage, these expressions were invariably associated with drugs; among black youths, they identified a whole range of cultural experiences, many of which were specifically tied to being black.

A number of verbs and verb phrases differentiated black nondrug from white drug usage. The expression *to bogart* meant to smoke more than one's share of a marijuana cigarette in the white vernacular;[7] among blacks, its primary mean-

---

[7]In fact, the expression *to bogart* was part of the opening line of a popular song of the late sixties that was often aired on white rock radio stations: "Don't bogart that joint, my friend, pass it over to me."

ings were more generalized: to physically assert one's presence or to physically accost another. The phrase *to burn someone* also had a drug-specific meaning for the white youths who knew it: It meant either to accept money for drugs that were never delivered or to sell diluted or "phony" drugs. Within the black vernacular, the primary meaning was to "steal" the affections of another's spouse or lover. The expressions *to be clean* and *to kick* had drug-related meanings among white youths. *To kick* was an abbreviated version of *to kick the habit,* to stop using drugs. *To be clean* meant the same thing, but had an additional semantic reading —to be free of drugs on one's person. In black vernacular, *to kick* meant to depart from somewhere, while *to be clean* referred to the state of being well-dressed.

To bust a cap and *to flash* both related to the psychedelic experience in the white vernacular. *To bust a cap* meant either to ingest a capsule containing *LSD* or to share a capsule of *LSD* with a friend. *To flash* had two primary meanings: to experience the first effects of a drug—especially a psychedelic and to hallucinate. For some white informants, it had a third meaning: to vomit. In the black vernacular, the expressions were totally unconnected with drug use. *To bust a cap* meant to shoot a gun, and *to flash* meant to show off what one possessed—one's clothes, car, lover, money, and so forth.

A number of black vernacular nouns were used to positively or negatively characterize or classify a person's manner, appearance, or behavior. One such set of these black "classification names" related to the evaluation of women. In the white vernacular they again related to drugs. For example, the white semantic reading for *stuff* was drugs—often heroin. Though the term has long been used by blacks to refer to heroin, the primary black definition here connoted a sexually desirable woman. In a similar vein, the expression *main stuff,* among whites, referred to the principal drug one used; among blacks, the phrase identified one's number-one woman, one's woman friend, or the woman with which one regularly had sex. Again, the black pejoratives *chippy* (prostitute or sexually promiscuous woman), *dog food* or *skag* (an unattractive woman), and *peach* (a woman with extremely short hair, an unkempt woman) meant, respectively, an occasional drug user; heroin; and an amphetamine in the white vernacular.

A number of classification names in the black vernacular characterized black people from a decidedly intraracial perspective. Such terms as *cotton* (a black person who has recently arrived from the South); *monkey* (an obsequious black person who curries favor with whites); *Sam* (abbreviation for *Sambo*—a "country hick," or an obsequious black person); and *head* (a black male—usually one who makes trouble or is unruly) all reflect culture-specific usage. In the white vernacular these expressions all revolved around the drug experience. *Cotton* referred to the wad of cotton used to absorb a liquefied drug; a hypodermic needle is then stuck into the drug-soaked cotton, and the drug is drawn into the syringe in preparation for *shooting up* (injecting the drug). *Monkey,* an abbreviation for *monkey on one's back,* referred to a drug habit—usually an addiction to heroin. *Sam* identified a federal narcotics agent. Finally, *head* referred to someone who frequently uses a particular drug, such as *acidhead* (a habitual user of LSD), *pothead* (a habitual user of marijuana), *pillhead* (a habitual user of pills), and so on.

The terms *hippy* and *freak* were used by both blacks and whites to character-ize a given person, but the respective characterizations were decidedly different. In the white vernacular, the terms carried a positive connotation; in black usage, the connotation was unquestionably negative.

Hippy actually had a number of meanings in the black vernacular. It referred to a black person who was uninformed, naïve, or dated in dress or manner. It also meant a black person who emulated whites in various ways. Finally, the term referred to a trouble-maker, particularly someone who provoked fights. On the other hand, the *hippy* was embraced by white informants as a counter-culture ideal, and was predominantly characterized as a white middle-class youth who had dropped out of mainstream society. That is, he or she seldom worked, invariably took drugs, grew long hair, dressed unconventionally, and often lived in a communal environment.

Similarly, the term *freak* had a generally positive association in the minds of white informants. Like *hippy, freak* designated one who had rejected main-stream American values and defied the Establishment by his or her shocking appearance and/or behavior. In additiona, the term meant one who demonstrated a strong preference for a particular drug, for example, *acid freak.* For the major-ity of blacks interviewed, a *freak* was one who engaged in so-called deviant sexual activity. Most often, the reference was to homosexuality, a sexual preference that was viewed with particular repugnance—especially among black males.

Observations

The comparative vernacular vocabulary data suggest that interest in drugs and drug use was the single most important experiential bridge between the black and white youths interviewed. This preoccupation with drugs was particularly apparent among white informants—especially those from middle-class back-grounds. As a group, middle-class whites provided the greatest number of drug-related semantic readings for nondrug black vernacular expressions.

Conversations with informants indicated that a variety of drugs had long been available in the black community. But, the widespread smoking of *dope* (marijuana) and the taking of various pills for "kicks" was a phenomenon that developed during the sixties among white youths—particularly among affluent white youths living in Los Angeles County.[8] Therefore, it is congruent with their keen and new-found interest in drugs that they should not only use more drug terms in the course of the interviews, but provide the greatest number of drug-related semantic readings for nondrug stimulus terms.

The fact that a negligible number of terms elicited from black informants were known by whites or assigned the same semantic readings by them suggests that a well-formed black vernacular vocabulary exists that is largely a private part of the black experience. As Kochman (1972) has noted: "That black people in general should possess and use a different vocabulary from whites is understand-

---

[8]"The Incidence of Drug Use among Los Angeles County Youth: A Profile," Department of Probation, County of Los Angeles (1968).

able, given the respectively different nature of the black and white experiences in this country" (p. 140).

In this paper, I have explored only one aspect of interracial vocabulary use and its relationship to shared and disparate life experiences. Much additional comparative information is needed to provide answers to questions about the origin, nature, and function of vernacular vocabulary in intercultural contexts. Certainly, the study of vernacular usage promises to provide a rich and relatively unmined source of data about social interaction. As Kochman (1972) has stated:

> one of the best ways to get to know a group is to identify and examine the vocabulary (names, terms and expressions) habitually used within the group. . . . It is this "other" world, oral, vernacular, induced and unsanctioned, that is the antithesis (and at times the antidote) to the formalized, academic, imposed, and legitimated world of adults and institutions, one from which adults can learn a great deal about culture, learning, and life." (p. 109)

References

Folb, Edith A. (March 1972). "A Comparative Study of Urban Black Argot." *Occasional Papers in Linguistics,* No. 1. Los Angeles: UCLA.

Folb, Edith A. (1973a). "Black Vernacular Vocabulary: A Study in Intra-Intercultural Concerns and Usage." *Afro-American Monograph Series,* No. 5. Los Angeles: Afro-American Studies Center, UCLA.

Folb, Edith A. (August (1973b). "Rappin' in the Black Vernacular." *Human Behavior.* Reprinted in Spain, ed. (1975). *The Human Experience: Readings in Sociocultural Anthropology.* Illinois: The Dorsey Press.

Kochman, Thomas, ed. (1972). *Rappin' and Stylin' Out: Communication in Urban Black America.* Urbana: University of Illinois Press.

Landy, Eugene E. (1971). *The Underground Dictionary.* New York: Simon and Schuster.

Maurer, David W. (1969). "Linguistic Hostility as a Factor in Intra-Cultural Conflict." *Papers of the Tenth International Congress of Linguistics.* Bucharest, Roumania.

The Language of the Socially Disadvantaged
John Nist

The various versions of Modern American English spoken in Hawaii today illustrate the linguistic fact that within every geographical dialect area of the United States there are at least three different social-class lects in current use (see Nist, 1973, Ch. 4): the educated *acrolect,* the vernacular *mesilect,* and the uneducated *basilect* (see Stewart, 1964, 1967, Spring 1967, Spring 1968, and Spring/

Summer 1969). In the Hawaiian Islands themselves, for example, college graduates of the younger generation generally tend to speak acrolect; with maximum prestige attached to the use of their code, these socially advantaged Americans are fashioning the so called "standard" English of Hawaii. By way of contrast, however, their middle-aged parents, usually native born, who grew up with Hawaiian creole as their preferred resonant lect and then moved on to partially master some form of mainland American English, generally tend to speak mesilect; with medium prestige attached to the use of their code, these somewhat socially advantaged Americans of high school education are lending their moral support to the fashioning of the so-called "standard." By way of further contrast, however, their old-aged parents, usually immigrants to the Islands, who were adult learners of one of the pidgins simply because they grew up with some foreign tongue as their preferred resonant language, generally tend to speak basilect; with minimum prestige attached to the use of their code, these socially disadvantaged Americans of no more than grade school education are little better than "innocent bystanders" on the linguistic scene. Simplistic as this analysis may be, it implies an important relationship between the term *different* and the term *inferior* as each applies to the linguistic phenomenon known as social-class lects—namely, the relationship of *prestige*.

American Social-Class Lects

THE PROBLEM OF PRESTIGE   When a linguist says that "everybody talks funny," he is merely making a popular assessment of the linguistic facts about the major speech varieties of every natural language on earth. These linguistic facts, in turn, mean that no living language is ever *completely uniform* in such formal characteristics as vocabulary and meaning, morphology and syntax, segmental phonology and intonation patterns (see Bloomfield, 1933, 1962, Ch. 19). Hence the characteristic differences among British English, American English, and the various kinds of Commonwealth English (see Nist, 1966, pp. 21–27). When the same linguist says that not everybody speaks some variety of his language with the same amount of prestige, however, then he is not making so much a linguistic assessment as he is a sociological one. But facts are facts, whether linguistic or sociological. And this is a fact: the same amount of prestige does *not* apply to all the speech varieties of a language.

Because of the vast amount of variety within its some thirty-eight geographical dialects, for example, present-day British English (see Nist, 1973, Ch. 4) has made a virtue of necessity by accepting the historical emergence of its *Received Pronunciation Standard* (known in acronym abbreviation as *RPS*) as the most prestigious of its current versions. Accepting both Scots and Irish English as regional standards to supplement its RPS (see Francis, 1963, 1965, p. 234), contemporary British English is nevertheless characterized by the enormous range of its dialect variants. Indeed as Nist (1966, p. 25) has said,

No version of the language in the United States [and Canada, or anywhere in the Commonwealth for that matter] can imitate the whine of Suffolk, the clipping of

Yorkshire, the guttural throatiness of Northumberland, the glottal stopping of Lancashire, the bardic pitch patterns of Wales, or the Gaelic thickness of the Scottish Highlands. A simple question in South Staffordshire, for example, betrays ancient Germanic influence on syntax and Middle English control of pronunciation: "*Bist tha bi guwin' uwt?*" ("Are you to be going out?") A fundamental command by a Cockney, on the other hand, might run to such incomprehensible limits as these: "*Pu' th' 'ud i' th' o'!*" ("Put the wood in the hole!"—i.e., "Shut the door!")

As contrasted with RPS, the acrolect of the universities and the BBC, the geographical dialects of present-day British English exemplify the key lesson in Shaw's *Pygmalion*—namely, that failure to master the *RPS* places terrible social, educational, and financial limitations upon the individual. Why? For one reason, because since RPS exists as the educated version of British English, any departure from that code, except for Irish English and Scots, marks the speaker as confined to either the vernacular of mesilect or to the "folk speech" of basilect or to both these rather nonprestigious forms of the language. In other words, except for Irish English and Scots, *geographical dialects in present-day British English automatically become social-class lects.* Within the linguistically elitist system of Great Britain, therefore, the term *different,* with the two exceptions noted, does tend very markedly to mean "inferior."

But what of the seemingly egalitarian linguistic system of the United States? Here the equation of *different* with *inferior* is not so easy to make. Why? Because no equivalent of RPS has emerged as an ideal code form for Modern American English; *acrolect* versions of the various geographical dialects of the United States have never impeded communication. In other words, in direct contrast to British English, Modern American English continues to maintain a rather high level of uniformity among the *well-educated* speakers of its various geographical dialects or regionalisms. This relatively high level of uniformity in well-educated versions of American English has been inherited from colonial days, and was praised in 1791 by the British editor of David Ramsey's *History of the American Revolution* as follows (see Nist, 1966, p. 365):

> It is a curious fact that there is perhaps no one portion of the British Empire in which two or three millions of persons are to be found who speak their mother tongue with greater purity or a truer pronunciation than the white inhabitants of the United States. This was attributed, by a penetrating observer, to the number of British subjects assembled in America from various quarters, who, in consequence of their intercourse and intermarriages, soon dropped the peculiarities of their several provincial idioms, retaining only what was fundamental and common to all—a process which the frequency or rather the universality of school-learning in America must naturally have assisted.

The relatively high level of uniformity seen in educated American English by the British editor in 1791 has been increased in the past two centuries, of course, by means of population mobility (both geographical and social), rapid transportation, mass-media communication, and universal education. This relatively high level of uniformity among *acrolect* versions of Modern American English means, moreover, that insofar as geographical dialects or regionalisms are concerned, in the language of the United States *different* does not necessarily mean "inferior."

The qualifier *necessarily* in the preceding value judgment applies, however, only to *acrolect* versions of Modern American geographical dialects. Insofar as *mesilect* and *basilect* versions of these same dialects are concerned, *different* does indeed mean "inferior," if in no other attribute than that of prestige. This attribute of prestige, in turn, depends in large measure upon the *principle of correctness,* indeed one might say in the words of Donald J. Lloyd (1952) the "national mania for correctness," in Modern American English. This principle may be depicted as follows:

The Principle of Correctness in American English

Correctness = linguistic usage + social acceptability

The social-acceptability part of the equation means that in addition to the *horizontal* dimension of the language, known as regional speech varieties or geographical dialects, there is also the *vertical* dimension, known as social-class lects. And it is precisely in this vertical dimension that the problem of prestige obtains.

In the coined terminology of William A. Stewart (1964, etc.), Co-director of the Education Study Center in Washington, D.C., *acrolect* corresponds with the educated or so-called "standard" version of a dialect; *mesilect,* with the vernacular; and *basilect,* with the uneducated vulgar or "folk speech." Thus speakers of acrolect tend to fit the cultural patterns of Hans Kurath's (see Kurath *et al,* 1939–43; Kurath, 1949; Kurath and McDavid, 1961) Type III of informants (see Atwood, 1970, p. 183)—that is, these speakers tend to enjoy a superior education (usually college), together with a culturally enriched background that includes wide reading and/or extensive social contacts and travel. Speakers of mesilect, by way of contrast, tend to fit the cultural patterns of Kurath's Type II of informants (see Atwood, 1970, p. 183)—that is, they tend to enjoy a formal education (usually high school), together with the social advantages of some reading and/or travel. Speakers of basilect, finally, tend to fit the cultural patterns of Kurath's Type I of informants (see Atwood, 1970, p. 183)—that is, this last group tends to suffer from the social disadvantage of little formal education, little reading, and restricted travel and contact with other people.

Using Stewart's terms for their scientific accuracy and their general lack of unpleasant connotations and emotional overtones, a linguist may relate these three social-class lects of Modern American English with the amount of prestige which they confer upon their speakers as follows:

Prestige and the Social-Class Lects of
Modern American English

Acrolect $\longrightarrow$ *maximum* amount of prestige for its speakers.
Mesilect $\longrightarrow$ *medium* amount of prestige for its speakers.
Basilect $\longrightarrow$ *minimum* amount of prestige for its speakers.

Above and beyond their relationship with the phenomenon of prestige, these three social-class lects are so important within the various geographical dialects of Modern American English that they must be characterized in some measure of detail. Hopefully, from that characterization will come a firmer basis upon which to build an answer to the question, "Does *different* = *inferior?*"

ACROLECT   First of all, there is the *acrolect,* or the most prestigious form of any speech variety within the language. Without fully defining the form, a linguist may nevertheless list some of the most outstanding characteristics of this present-day American social-class lect as follows (see Nist, June 1969, p. 20):

Characteristics of the Acrolect *in Modern American English*

1. Speakers of acrolect American English tend to be well-educated, culturally advantaged, socially adroit, and highly competent in performance.

2. Acrolect American English has a very extensive vocabulary, fully responsive to the discourse demands placed on the cultural levels of usage (standard, nonstandard, substandard) and the functional varieties of the language (e.g., colloquial, commercial, technical, literary).

3. Acrolect American English operates skillfully in all the styles or keys of discourse (see Joos, 1961, 1962, 1967; Gleason, 1965, Ch. 15)—intimate, familiar/casual, consultative, deliberative, rhetorical/oratorical—and appears frequently in published formal writing.

4. Acrolect American English is generally free of so-called "grammatical errors" and of stylistic lapses that violate mood, tone, or attitude.

5. Acrolect American English shows an extreme sensitivity to the immediate context situation and tends to keep emotive function at a pleasant level, usually positive in mood, tone, and attitude.

6. Acrolect American English is recognized for the foregoing five reasons, among others, as the "standard" and therefore the most prestigious version of its speech variety, regionalism, or geographical dialect.

In the sociolinguistic theory of Basil Bernstein (1970, pp. 45–46), speakers of acrolect Modern American English almost always come from families that foster intrapersonal methods of learning, open systems of communication, personal-appeals modes of control, and hence elaborated codes (i.e., rhetorical means of mastering the message, both in transmission and in reception).

Drawing upon the wealth of *belles lettres* available in the language, and thereby avoiding any embarrassment that may be attached to the use of any "real-life" models, a linguist may illustrate the acrolect in Modern American English by means of the following passage from Chapter 40 of Thomas Wolfe's *Look Homeward, Angel* (1929):

"What happens, Ben? What really happens?" said Eugene. "Can you remember some of the same things that I do? I have forgotten the old faces. Where are they, Ben? What were their names? I forget the names of people I knew for years. I get their faces mixed. I get their heads stuck on other people's bodies. I think one man has said what another said. And I forget—forget. There is something I have lost and have forgotten. I can't remember, Ben."

"What do you want to remember?" said Ben.

A stone, a leaf, an unfound door. And the forgotten faces.

"I have forgotten names. I have forgotten faces. And I remember little things," said Eugene. "I remember the fly I swallowed on the peach, and the little boys on tricycles at St. Louis, and the mole on Grover's neck, and the Lackawanna freight-car, number 16356, on a siding near Gulfport. Once, in Norfolk, an Australian soldier on his way to France asked me the way to a ship; I remember that man's face."

He stared for an answer into the shadow of Ben's face, and then he turned his moon-bright eyes upon the Square.

Although the diction in the preceding passage remains fairly simple, the magnificent prose-poetry of its rhythm and the lack of any grammatical or stylistic blemish mark the language as unmistakably acrolect. The narrator and his characters achieve both an adequate segmentation of reality and an appropriate image of the self and the language roles which that self must assume.

MESILECT   Second, there is the *mesilect,* or the most pervasive version of any speech variety within the language. Again without fully defining this version of Modern American English, a linguist may nevertheless list some of the most outstanding characteristics of the mesilect as follows (see Nist, June 1969, pp. 20–21):

Characteristics of the Mesilect in Modern American English

1. Speakers of mesilect American English tend to have no more than a high school education, to be neither very culturally advantaged nor very socially adroit, and to be only fairly competent in performance.

2. Mesilect American English has a rather restricted vocabulary, only partially responsive to the discourse demands placed on the cultural levels of usage and the functional varieties of the language (see Kenyon, 1948).

3. Mesilect American English operates only fairly skillfully through the three lower or more informal styles or keys of discourse (i.e., intimate, familiar/casual, and consultative) and appears most frequently in the writing of personal letters and very seldom in published form, except in the dialogues and *dramatis-persona-mask* narrations of Modern fiction.

4. Mesilect American English is generally full of *hyperurbanisms* (mistakes by over-correctness) like to *whomever stays* and *between you and I;* of stylistic lapses that violate mood, tone, or attitude; of hackneyed expressions, sententious clichés, and modish slang.

5. Mesilect American English is not very sensitive to the immediate context situation, is often inadequate in public gatherings, and frequently steps emotive function up to an unpleasant level, whether positive or negative in mood, tone, and attitude.

6. Mesilect American English is not recognized as the "standard" and prestigious version of its speech variety, regionalism, or geographical dialect, but rather for the foregoing five reasons, among others, as the most representative and "average" manifestation of it.

In the sociolinguistic theory of Bernstein (1970, pp. 45–46), speakers of mesilect Modern American English usually come from families that foster interpersonal methods of learning (with emphasis on role obligation and differentiation), prefer closed systems of communication to open (though permitting open), and emphasize positional modes of control over personal-appeals and restricted codes over elaborated.

The following passage from Chapter 5 of Sinclair Lewis's *Babbitt* (1922) offers an excellent example of the mesilect in Modern American English:

> During the game of duck-pins, a juvenile form of bowling, Paul was silent. As they came down the steps of the club, not more than half an hour after the time at which Babbitt had sternly told Miss McGoun he would be back, Paul sighed, "Look here, old man, oughtn't to talked about Zilla way I did."
>
> "Rats, old man, it lets off steam."
>
> "Oh, I know! After spending all noon sneering at the conventional stuff, I'm conventional enough to be ashamed of saving my life by busting out with my fool troubles!"
>
> "Old Paul, your nerves are kind of on the bum. I'm going to take you away. I'm going to rig this thing. I'm going to have an important deal in New York and—and sure, of course!—I'll need you to advise me on the roof of the building! And the ole deal will fall through, and there'll be nothing for us but to go on ahead to Maine. I—— Paul, when it comes right down to it, I don't care whether you bust loose or not. I do like having a rep for being one of the Bunch, but if you ever needed me I'd chuck it and come out for you every time! Not of course but what you're——course I don't mean you'd ever do anything that would put——that would put a decent position on the fritz but——See how I mean? I'm kind of a clumsy old codger, and I need your fine Eyetalian hand. We——Oh, hell, I can't stand here gassing all day! On the job! S'long! Don't take any wooden money, Paulibus! See you soon! S'long!"

In this passage, of course, Lewis as narrator uses acrolect, while letting his characters speak in mesilect. Paul, for example, steps emotive function up to a rather unpleasant level with such unit tacts as *sneering at the conventional stuff, ashamed of saving my life,* and *busting out with my fool troubles.* His slangy use of *old man* as a vocative of friendship is matched by his casual omission of *have* in the unit tact *oughtn't to talked about.* Even more important, however, is the fact that Paul Riesling, unhappily married as he is, has become a victim of his own interpersonal methods of learning. His own moral emphasis on role obligation has trapped him in an inadequate segmentation of reality—an inadequacy which is reinforced by the inept and closed code that will not permit him to achieve an appropriate image of himself and of the language role he must assume, if possible, with Babbitt.

And what about Babbitt? Emotionally incapable of handling intimate subject matter in familiar or casual key, Babbitt embarrasses himself into breaking off the conversation with his friend Paul Riesling, who has just "bared his soul" concerning his tragic marriage with Zilla. Babbitt's slangy use of unit tacts like *kind of on the bum, rig this thing, bust loose, the Bunch, chuck it, come out for you, on the fritz, kind of a clumsy old codger, gassing all day,* and *on the job* marks the language as unmistakably mesilect. As an implicit note of warning to all purist sticklers for the importance of a so-called "grammatical correctness," Babbitt's grammer is impeccable; it is his atrocious diction and his stylistic lapses that violate mood, tone, and attitude which are so reprehensible. Joining mild profanity (*Rats, Oh, hell*) with syntactical ellipses (*See how I mean? On the job! See you soon!*) and morphological clippings (*rep, S'long!*), Babbitt uses his brand of Modern American English like an irresponsible teen-ager sent out on an adult's mission. His ultimate failure may be heard in the banally inappropriate *Don't take any wooden money, Paulibus!* Babbitt, in short, is "cute" without really being funny. As a matter of linguistic fact, he is pathetic.

Pathetic because Babbitt, like his friend Paul Riesling, has become a victim of his own interpersonal methods of learning. Trapped in his own emphasis on role obligation, Babbitt is even more handicapped in his mesilect than is Paul. Why? Because Paul at least does not try to fool himself; Babbitt does. The courage of his personal loyalty to Paul is constantly being vitiated by his cowardice in the face of public opinion. Thus the tension between "I don't care whether you bust loose or not" at one pole of assertion and "I do like having a rep for being one of the Bunch" at the other can find only a partial release in this totally inept attempt at mixing explicit exoneration and its attendant self-justification with implicit exhortation and its attendant imperative mode of control: "Not of course but what you're——course I don't mean you'd ever do anything that would put ——that would put a decent position on the fritz but——See how I mean?" Paul sees. Sees that despite Babbitt's sterile attempt at humor, which merely serves to betray his provincial prejudice in the insulting pronunciation of *Eyetalian* and his cultural insecurity in the immature wit of Latinized *Paulibus,* Zenith's ace realtor is fundamentally an arch-hypocrite who suffers unknowingly from his own inadequate segmentation of reality and his own inappropriate image of himself and the language role he should assume, but has failed to assume, in mature compassion for his friend. What Paul sees, so eloquently indicated by his silence, is what Lewis intends for the reader to see—namely, this: *what Babbit cannot express he cannot experience.* And so his mesilect has become for him a kind of pernicious anemia of the soul.

BASILECT   Third, there is the *basilect.* As the generally recognized standard form of any speech variety, regionalism, or geographical dialect, the basilect in Modern American English constitutes its own form of cultural deprivation and social disadvantage (see Evertts, 1967). Once again without fully defining this most nonprestigious version of the language, a linguist may nevertheless list some of the most outstanding characteristics of the basilect as follows (see Nist, June 1969, pp. 20–21):

Characteristics of the Basilect in Modern American English

1. Speakers of basilect American English tend to have no more than a grade school education, if that, to be both culturally disadvantaged and socially nonadroit, and to be very noticeably poor in both competence and performance.

2. Basilect American English suffers from an extremely restricted vocabulary, which is very inadequately responsive to the discourse demands placed on the cultural levels of usage and the functional varieties of the language.

3. Although no form of Modern American English is completely monostylistic (see Labov, 1970b, p. 19), the basilect does tend to operate most of the time by means of one key of discourse—a confusing blend of intimate, familiar/casual, and consultative —with the result that its speakers tend to look upon more sophisticated users of the language as outsiders and therefore as emotionally suspect. In its almost exclusively oral manifestation (except for its ubiquitous printed appearance in modern fiction), the basilect seldom appears even in personal letters, for the simple fact that at times it borders on illiteracy—indeed, at times it is illiteracy.

4. Basilect American English is generally full of such grammatical and stylistic lapses as these: faulty references, wrong verb forms, double or multiple negatives, pleonastic subjects (*My brother he*), preference for the vulgar historical present tense, misuse of personal-pronoun forms and of *them* as a demonstrative, and an indiscriminate use of *ain't* and the so-called "flat" adverbs (see Mencken, 1963, Ch. IX). Shot through with malapropism, the basilect nevertheless varies grammatically from region to region, depending upon such factors as these: ethnic origin of its speakers, degree of their social isolation, amount of interference from *native* (as distinct from *national*) language, and relative prestige of *ancestral* tongue (i.e., that spoken by one's forebears of more than two previous generations).

5. Basilect American English is usually, though not always, insensitive to the immediate context situation, is generally inadequate in public gatherings, and has a strong tendency to step emotive function up to an unpleasant level, usually negative (though not always) in mood, tone, or attitude. Many black ghetto speakers of the basilect, understandably but unfortunately, tend to have a rather high and negative emotive function as addressers and a rather low and negative conative function as addressees.

6. Basilect American English is recognized, even stigmatized, precisely for the foregoing five reasons, among others, as the substandard and therefore the nonprestigious version of its speech variety, regionalism, or geographical dialect. Unless militantly alienated from the mainstream of present-day American culture, speakers of the basilect usually want their children to linguistically "get more out of life" than they have got.

In the sociolinguistic theory of Bernstein (1970, pp. 45–46), speakers of basilect Modern American English usually come from families that foster hierarchy methods of learning (with emphasis on authority and status), develop closed systems of communication rather than open, prefer imperative modes of control over both positional and personal-appeals modes, and produce, therefore, restricted codes instead of elaborated ones.

The following passage from Chapter 8 of John Steinbeck's *The Grapes of Wrath* (1939) serves as a splendid illustration of the basilect in Modern American English:

The preacher said, "I don't recollect that John had a fambly. Just a lone man, ain't he? I don't recollect much about him."

"Lonest goddamn man in the world," said Joad. "Crazy kind of son-of-a-bitch, too —somepin like Muley, on'y worse in some ways. Might see 'im anywheres—at Shawnee, drunk, or visitin' a widow twenty miles away, or workin' his place with a lantern. Crazy. Ever'body thought he wouldn't live long. A lone man like that don't live long. But Uncle John's older'n Pa. Jus' gets stringier an' meaner ever' year. Meaner'n Grampa."

"Look a the light comin'," said the preacher. "Silvery-like. Didn' John never have no fambly?"

"Well, yes, he did, an' that'll show you the kind of fella he is—set in his ways. Pa tells about it. Uncle John, he had a young wife. Married four months. She was in a family way, too, an' one night she gets a pain in her stomick, an' she says, 'You better go for a doctor.' Well, John, he's settin' there, an' he says, 'You just got stomickache. You et too much. Take a dose a pain killer. You crowd up ya stomick an' ya get a stomickache,' he says. Nex' noon she's outa her head, an' she dies at about four in the afternoon."

"What was it?" Casy asked. "Poisoned from somepin she et?"
"No, somepin jus' bust in her. Ap-appendick or somepin. Well, Uncle John, he's always been a easy-goin' fella, an' he takes it hard. Takes it for a sin. For a long time he won't have nothin' to say to nobody. Just walks aroun' like he don't see nothin' an' he prays some. . . ."

Several key features in the preceding passage from Steinbeck's great novel mark its two lower-class characters as speakers of basilect American English: the markedly "slurvian" patterns of their pronunciation, as in *fambly* for *family, on'y* for *only, ever'body* for *everybody, older'n* for *older than, meaner'n* for *meaner than, a* for *at, outa* for *out of, nex'* for *next, somepin* for *something, jus'* for *just, fella* for *fellow, nothin'* for *nothing, aroun'* for *around,* and *an'* for *and;* their use of wrong verb forms like *don't* with the third-person singular subject, *et* for *ate, settin'* for *sittin',* and *bust* for *burst;* Joad's preference for the vulgar histori- cal present tense as the emotive function of his narrative rises; the use of double and triple negatives like *he don't see nothin'* and *he won't have nothin' to say to nobody;* the inability to articulate properly the learned word *appendix;* the use of *ain't;* the repetition of pleonastic *he* with *Uncle John* and *John;* and above all else, the unconscious saturating of the discourse with highly emotive unit tacts like *lonest goddamn man, crazy kind of son-of-a-bitch, stringier an' meaner, dose a pain killer, crowd up ya stomick, outa her head,* and *takes it for a sin.* Despite its lack of prestige, the basilect of this passage proves that Labov (1970b, p. 54) is right when he claims that nonstandard Modern American English is generally effective in its brevity and clarity. Indeed as many American writers have shown, because of the drama inherent in its high emotive function, basilect is often the linguistic stuff from which great literary art is made.

Great literary art not withstanding, the semantic deficiency inherent in basi- lect Modern American English clamors for attention in the passage quoted from Steinbeck's novel. Uncle John, the subject of Casy and Joad's discussion, is now a demented widower because of his own inadequate segmentation of reality and its attendant corollary: the inappropriate image which he once had of himself and of the language role he should have assumed with his then-pregnant but now-dead wife. Incapable of dealing with ambiguity (or plurisignificance) and multivalence, Uncle John diagnosed the cause of his young wife's sudden pain by means of an immature wishful-thinking pleasure principle rather than by a mature fact-facing reality principle. More annoyed than alarmed by his wife's potentially dangerous indisposition, Uncle John resorted to his own hierarchy methods of learning, with their emphasis on authority and status, and came up with the wrong remedy— a remedy which treated merely a symptom rather than the illness. Abysmally ignorant of the exact location of the stomach in the human anatomy (a sign of his inadequate segmentation), Uncle John recommended his wrong remedy with- out the slightest trace of mitigation or politeness (a sign of his inappropriate image of himself) and in a very ugly and vulgar version of the imperative mode (a sign of his inappropriate image of the language role he should and must assume), a version which placed the unjust moral onus of gluttony and stupidity upon his young wife, who knew that her painful condition called for the professional care of a physician.

Implicit in Joad's account of the incident, of course, is the fact that such a physician's services will cost money. Reacting out of fear-boundedness rather than out of love-freedom, Uncle John covered his own insecurity with the mask of his position and therefore power within the family—i.e., the older and more experienced husband and head of the household. Behind that authoritarian mask of his status, Uncle John humiliated his young wife by reducing her role to that of a child, devoid of discretion, and permitted therefore only three possible external channels of expressive behavior (see Bernstein, 1970, p. 41): rebellion, withdrawal, or acceptance. From that reduction, death was inevitable. Although neither Joad nor Casy is fully aware of the dimension of the tragedy, their author most certainly is. And Steinbeck demonstrates, with an implicit vengeance, that the old saying "What a man doesn't know won't hurt him," is a lie. What a man doesn't know may *kill* him—or those about him. Truly "set in his ways," as Joad says, Uncle John is the tragic victim of his basilect American English and the terrible semantic deficiency which it entails. Dominated by the closed system of communication inherent in his painfully restricted code, Uncle John unintentionally lets his own avarice and stupidity kill his young wife and therefore destroy his own life. Insofar as his own basilect is concerned, the term *different* unquestionably *does* mean "inferior." The inferiority which springs from that "differentness" is the psychological murderer of Uncle John.

Suggested Readings

Bernstein, B., and D. Henderson, "Social Class Differences in the Relevance of Language to Socialization," *Sociology,* 3 (1969), 1–20. This study discusses class differences between middle and working classes in England. Emphasis is placed upon the different uses of language as it applies to socialization of children in the areas of interpersonal relationships and the acquisition of basic skills.

Burgest, D. R., "The Racist Use of the English Language," *The Black Scholar,* 5 (1973), 37–45. Burgest portrays language as a potent force of our society that goes beyond being merely a communicative device. He suggests that language not only expresses ideas and concepts but may actually shape them. Although the process is completely unconscious with the individual concerned, the influence of the spoken or written expression is cultural.

Bosmajian, H. A., "Defining the 'American Indian': A Case Study in the Language of Suppression," *The Speech Teacher,* 21 (March 1973), 89–99. Professor Bosmajian shows how language has functioned as a force suppressing the American Indian. He asserts that the first act an oppressor does linguistically is to redefine the oppressed victims he intends to jail or eradicate so they will be seen as creatures warranting suppression.

Burr, E., S. Dunn, and N. Farquhar, "Women and the Language of Inequality," *Social Education,* 36 (1972), 841–845. The authors assert that language goes beyond being merely a means of communication. They show that it is also an expression of shared assumptions that transmits implicit values and behavioral models to all who use it. The authors suggest certain changes in language designed to eliminate phraseology that reflects outdated assumptions about women.

The Florida FL Reporter (Spring/Summer 1969). This special issue is devoted to the problems of cultural differences in language and language use in the United States. Emphasis is placed on teaching problems and practical methods for improving intercultural understanding.

Kemnitzer, L. S., "Language Learning and Socialization on the Railroad," *Urban Life and Culture,* 1 (1973), 363–378. Kemnitzer discusses how linguistic competence serves as a socialization experience for entrants into new speech communities. The paper discusses the author's experience as a brakeman, conductor, and member of a grievance committee on three railroads. He details the socialization of the railroad worker through the acquisition and development of competence in the linguistic structures peculiar to the railroads.

Key, M. R., "Linguistic Behavior of Male and Female," *Linguistics* (August 15, 1972), pp. 15–31. Key discusses the linguistic behavior of male and female and approaches the topic as a linguist. She holds the basic assumption that there is system in language, and data gathered can be studied, analyzed, and described.

Kramer, C., "Women's Speech: Separate but Unequal?" *Quarterly Journal of Speech,* 60 (February 1974), 14–24. Kramer, in this very interesting article, seeks to discover differences in the ways men and women use the English language. She maintains that "sex roles are important to our culture." Specifically she focuses on differences in grammatical, phonological, and semantic aspects. Language differences in verbal skills, instrumental uses of language, and the relationship between verbal and nonverbal dimensions are also explained.

Labov, W., "The Logic of Non-Standard English," *Georgetown Monograph Series on Languages and Linguistics,* 22 (1969). Labov discusses the various forms of English used in the United States and shows that each is a definite language rather than a substandard variant. He further points out why nonstandard forms should not be discouraged or corrected to white, Anglo, middle-class standards.

Norton, D. E., and W. R. Hodgson, "Intelligibility of Black and White Speakers for Black and White Listeners," *Language and Speech,* 16 (1973), 207–210. This study investigated the auditory discrimination ability of black and white listeners. No significant differences were found between the discrimination ability of the two groups of listeners. However, both groups obtained better discrimination scores when listening to white rather than black speakers.

Rosen, H., "Language and Class: A Critical Look at the Theories of Basil Bernstein," *The Urban Review,* 7 (1974), 97–114. Rosen critically examines the sociolinguistic theories advanced by Basil Bernstein, pointing out their usefulness as well as their shortcomings.

Sapir, E., *Language* (New York: Harcourt Brace Jovanovich, 1949). The author's main purpose is to show what he conceives language to be rather than to assemble facts about it. A complete coverage of various aspects of language is included, with sections dealing with interaction between languages and the relationship of language, race, and culture.

Stevens, J. H., K. F. Rucer, and R. Tew, "Speech Discrimination in Black and White Children," *Language and Speech,* 16 (1973), 123–129. The authors examine the effect of dialect on speech discrimination scores of black and white adolescents. Results showed that both black and white students did significantly better in their performances on speech discrimination tests when white teachers served as speakers.

Additional Readings

Bentley, R., and S. Crawford, *Black Language Reader* (Glenview, Ill: Scott, Foresman & Co., 1973).

Bosmajian, H. A., "The Language of Sexism," *ETC.,* 29 (1972), 338–344.

Brennan, E. M., and E. B. Ryan, "Reported Language and Verbal Fluency of Bilingual Mexican American Adolescents," *Anthropological Linguistics,* 15 (December, 1973), 398–405.

Carpenter, C., "The Eskimo Language," *ETC.,* 15 (December 1968), 467–473.

Carter, T. P., "Cultural Content for Linguistically Different Learners," *Elementary English*, 48 (February 1971), 162–175.

Cohen, R., "The Language of the Hard-Core Poor: Implications for Culture Conflict," *The Sociological Quarterly*, 9 (1968), 19–28.

Dillard, J. L., "Lay My Isogloss Bundle Down: The Contribution of Black English to American Dialectology," *Linguistics*, 119 (January 1974), 5–14.

Foster, H. L., *Ribbin', Jivin' and Playin' The Dozens* (Cambridge, Mass.: Ballinger Publishing Co., 1974).

Friedman, P., and G. M. Phillips, "Toward a Rhetoric for the Poverty Class," *Journal of Communication*, 17 (1967), 234–249.

Goodwin, C. D., and I. B. Holley, Jr., "Toward a Theory of the Intercultural Transfer of Ideas," *Southern Atlantic Quarterly*, 67 (1968), 370–379.

Innis, H. R., *Bilingualism and Biculturalism: An Abridged Version of the Royal Commission Report* (Canada: McClelland and Stewart, Ltd., 1973).

Kantrowitz, M., "The Vocabulary of Race Relations in Prision," *Pads*, 51 (April, 1969), pp. 23–34.

Kirch, M., "Language, Communication, and Culture," *Modern Language Journal*, 57 (November, 1973), 340–343.

Labov, W., *Language in the Inner City* (Philadelphia: University of Pennsylvania Press, 1972).

Mark, Y., "The Yiddish Language: Its Cultural Impact," *American Jewish Historical Quarterly*, 59 (December 1969), 201–209.

Reed, I. K., *Esperanto: A Complete Grammar* (Metuchen, N.J.: The Scarecrow Press, Inc., 1968).

Smith, A. L., *Language, Communication and Rhetoric in Black America* (New York: Harper & Row, 1972).

Stanley, J. P., "Homosexual Slang," *American Speech*, 45 (Spring-Summer 1970), 45–59.

Toliver-Weddington, G., "The Scope of Black English," *Journal of Black Studies*, 4 (December 1973), 107–114.

Turner, P. R., "Why Johnny Doesn't Want to Learn a Foreign Language," *The Modern Language Journal*, 58 (1974), 191–196.

Vetter, H. J., "Special Language: The Psychedelic Subculture," in *Language and Behavior* (Itasca, Illinois: F. E. Peacock Publishers, Inc., 1969), Chapter 11.

Weldon, P. D., "Indonesian and Chinese Status and Language Differences in Urban Java," *Journal of Southeast Asian Studies*, 5 (March 1974), 37–54.

Williams, F., *Language and Poverty: Perspectives on a Theme* (Chicago: Markham Publishing Company, 1970).

Concepts and Questions

1. Can you think of examples that would demonstrate the validity of the Sapir-Whorf hypothesis?

2. What is meant by the phrase "Language is a guide to social reality"?

3. Can you think of some arguments that would tend to disprove the Sapir-Whorf hypothesis?

4. How do the types of translation problems discussed by Sechrest, Fay, and Zaidi apply to everyday intercultural encounters?

5. Some people have suggested that the problems associated with translation could be solved if everyone spoke the same universal language. Evaluate this view in light of the influence culture has on language.

6. What does Wedge mean by "latent meanings"?

7. Drawing from your experiences with a foreign language, try to think of words and phrases not discussed by Wedge that contain latent meanings.

8. Does Folb's essay offer support for the Sapir-Whorf hypothesis? If so, in what ways?

9. What groups, in addition to Blacks, have developed a subset of words and phrases? Can you think of some examples that would represent that subculture's vernacular vocabulary?

10. What forms of vernacular language are common among you and your friends? How does this usage differ from that of your parents or other members of the community?

11. In addition to social class, what other traits do we often infer from dialect and vocabulary?

12. Do you believe that the problems of the urban poor could be solved by introducing changes in their language behaviors?

13. How does the Glenn article relate to the Sechrest, *et al.*, article? How do these articles help us overcome translation problems?

14. Suggest ways that people might learn about the experiential aspects of other cultures that lead to unique language differences.

15. Does the Japanese concept of *amae* have any equivalent in the United States?

5

Nonverbal Interaction

Successful participation in intercultural communication requires us to be more than familiar with culture's influence on verbal interaction. It requires that we recognize and have knowledge of the influence culture has on *nonverbal interaction* as well. Nonverbal behaviors constitute messages to which people attach meaning just as verbal behaviors do. Because nonverbal symbols are derived from among such diverse behaviors as body movements, postures, facial expressions, gestures, eye movements, physical appearance, the use and organization of space, and the structuralization of time, these behaviors often vary from culture to culture. Therefore, an awareness of the role of nonverbal communication is crucial if one is going to appreciate all aspects of intercultural interaction.

Nonverbal behavior is largely unconscious. We use nonverbal symbols spontaneously, without thinking about what posture, what gesture, or what interpersonal distance is appropriate to the situation. These factors are critically important in intercultural communication because, as with other aspects of the communication process, nonverbal behaviors are subject to cultural variation, and this variation can be categorized in two ways.

In the first, culture tends to determine the specific nonverbal behaviors that represent or symbolize specific thoughts, feelings, or states of the communicator. Thus, what might be a sign of greeting in one culture could very well be an obscene gesture in another. Or what might be a symbol of affirmation to one culture could be meaningless or even signify negation in another. In the second, culture determines when it is appropriate to display or communicate various thoughts, feelings, or internal states, and this is particularly evident in the display of emotions. Although there seems to be little cross-cultural difference in the behaviors representing various emotional states, there are great cultural differences in what emotions may be displayed, by whom, and when or where they may be displayed.

As important as verbal language is to a communication event, nonverbal communication is just as important if not more important. Nonverbal messages can tell us how other messages are to be interpreted. They can indicate whether verbal messages are true, joking, serious, threatening, and so on. Gregory Bateson* has described these "second-order messages" as meta

---

*Gregory Bateson, "A Theory of Play and Fantasy," *Psychiatric Research,* 2 (1955), 39–51.

communication, which we use as frames around messages to designate how they are to be interpreted. Its importance can be seen from communication research, which indicates that as much as 90 percent of the social content of a message is transmitted paralinguistically or nonverbally.†

In Chapter 5 we deal with nonverbal interaction. The readings examine the influence of culture on various aspects of nonverbal behavior in order to demonstrate the variety of culturally derived nonverbal behaviors and the underlying value structures that produce these behaviors.

To begin Chapter 5, Weston LaBarre, in "Paralinguistics, Kinesics and Culture," introduces the concept of nonverbal communication by pointing out cultural differences in the use of our body, limbs, and eyes. As a means of demonstrating cultural kinesics, LaBarre explains how various cultures engage in greeting, kissing, gestures of contempt, politeness, and beckoning. We see, for example, that kissing in the Orient is an act of private lovemaking and often arouses only disgust when performed publicly. These, and many other examples, are used to show that simple movements can elicit entirely different meanings as we move from culture to culture. Awareness of these cultural differences is indeed one sign of the successful intercultural communicator.

How cultural variance in nonverbal communicative behavior can lead to serious communication errors or misunderstandings is detailed by Fathi S. Yousef in "Nonverbal Behavior: Some Intricate and Diverse Dimensions in Intercultural Communication." Yousef cites three examples in which misinterpretation of nonverbal behaviors led to intercultural misunderstandings. He then examines the underlying cultural value systems and structures that produced the misinterpreted nonverbal behaviors. Clearly, the major implication to be found in this analysis is that people do not realize that misunderstandings of nonverbal behavior have occurred. Rather, they interpret the behaviors in accordance with their own experiences and value systems and when the behaviors conflict with their expectations, they draw false conclusions about the intentions and attitudes of the people with whom they are interacting.

The influence culture has on nonverbal behavior is further demonstrated by Roman Jakobson's article "Nonverbal Signs for 'Yes' and 'No'." In this article, Jakobson describes how the nonverbal expression of yes and no varies among three European cultural groupings. The extent of this difference is so great that a head motion taken to signify approval in one culture can indicate disapproval in another. Such distinctions are crucial to the intercultural communicator seeking successful interactive outcomes.

The characteristics of Japanese nonverbal behaviors are described and explained in terms of the historical and social factors peculiar to Japan by Helmut Morsbach in his article "Aspects of Nonverbal Communication in Japan." This article is a nonverbal counterpart to Doi's article about the Japanese concept of *amae*, which appeared in the preceding chapter. Not

---

†Albert Mehrabian and Morton Wiener, "Decoding of Inconsistent Messages," *Journal of Personality and Social Psychology,* 6 (1967), 109–114.

only are body movements and facial expressions important nonverbal
behaviors but, for the Japanese, the nonverbal silences that accompany verbal
behavior can be equally important. In other words, what isn't said may be
more meaningful than what is said.

Further insight into nonverbal aspects of intercultural communication
may be found by examining cultural variations in nonverbal behavior found
among cultural minorities in the United States. As an example, Kenneth R.
Johnson, in "Black Kinesics—Some Non-Verbal Communication Patterns in
Black Culture," presents a detailed account of nonverbal behaviors as they
are practiced by many Black Americans. In this article Johnson traces the
development of Black kinesic behavior and relates how it has come to be
expressive of such social conditions as stress or conflict situations. He
describes specific nonverbal behaviors such as "rolling the eyes," the "limp
stance," and the "rap stance" and compares these to white nonverbal
behaviors that reflect the same or similar social situations.

Not only does movement have different meanings from culture to culture,
other nonverbal elements send divergent messages when used by various
cultures. Lawrence K. Frank, for example, investigated the constituents of
touch (tactile experiences) between different cultures. He believed that
cultures differ in the kind, amount, and duration of tactile experiences given
to children, and that these differences lead to a variety of tactile approaches
and responses as we engage in communication. Granting that touch can have
meaning, the various interpretations we give to these experiences are directly
related to our cultural backgrounds.

The final selection demonstrates the relationship between perception,
attitudes, values, and *actions.* John Horton's "Time and Cool People"
illustrates that our attitudes and values eventually find their way into our
behavior, and the person who understands intercultural communication can
appreciate the axiom that "our culture helps determine our behavior." The
conception of *time* in one specific culture is the focus of this essay. We are
shown that participants in the "street culture" of the low-income ghetto not
only behave differently but may well do so because of their notion of time.
By knowing something of the "cool peoples's" conception of time we can,
suggests Horton, understand something of the people themselves.

Paralinguistics, Kinesics, and Cultural Anthropology

Weston LaBarre

Though man is everywhere a notably "handed" animal, pointing with the forefinger and other fingers curled palmward is a limitedly cultural phenomenon, probably of Old World origin and dispersion (American Indians, on both New World continents, point with the lips, as also do Shans and other Mongoloid peoples; in other groups, pointing is done with eye-movements, or nose-chin-and-head movements, or head-movements alone). As for negation and affirmation kinemes, bahaviorists and other psychologists have sought to explain our "yes" nod as the movement of the infant seeking the breast, the "no" as avoiding it. But here the psychologists have reckoned without their cultural hosts: they have an elegantly universalistic explanation for a phenomenon which is not humanly universal, a common pitfall for any social scientist who ignores culture. Cultural anthropologists can supply us with many alternative kinemes for "yes" and "no" in various cultures (1). For example, shaking the hand in front of the face with the forefinger extended, is the Ovimbundu sign of negation, while Malayan Negritos express negation by casting down the eyes. The Semang thrust the head forward in affirmation. In fact, there are even regional "dialects" of affirmation in the Indic area: crown of the head following an arc from shoulder to shoulder, four times, in Bengal; throwing the head back in an oblique arc to the left shoulder, one time, somewhat "curtly" and "disrespectfully" to our taste, in the Punjab and Sind; curving the chin in a downward leftward arc in Ceylon, often accompanied by an indescribably beautiful parakineme of back-of-right-hand cupped in upward-facing-palm of the left hand, plus-or-minus the additional kineme of a crossed-ankle curtsey.

Greeting kinemes vary greatly from culture to culture. In fact, many of those motor habits in one culture are open to grave misunderstanding in another. For example, the Copper Eskimo welcome strangers with a buffet on the head or shoulders with the fist, while the northwest Amazonians slap one another on the back in greeting. Polynesian men greet one another by embracing and rubbing each other's back; Spanish-American males greet one another by a stereotyped embrace, head over the right shoulder of the partner, three pats on the back, head over reciprocal left shoulder, three more pats. In the Torres Straits, the old form of greeting was to bend the right hand into a hook, then mutually scratching palms by drawing away the right hand, repeating this several times. An Ainu, meeting his sister, grasped her hands in his for a few seconds, suddenly released his hold, grasped her by both ears and gave the peculiar Ainu greeting cry; then they stroked one another down the face and shoulders. Kayan males in Borneo

From *Approaches to Semiotics*, ed. Thomas Sebeok (The Hague: Mouton Publishers, 1964), pp. 198–202, 216–220. Reprinted by permission of the author and publisher. The author holds the chair of James B. Duke Professor of Anthropology at Duke University.

grasp each other by the forearm, while a host throws his arm over the shoulder of a guest and strokes him endearingly with the palm of his hand. When two Kurd males meet, they grasp one another's right hand, raise them both, and alternately kiss the other's hand. Andamanese greet one another by one sitting down in the lap of the other, arms around each other's necks and weeping for a while; two brothers, father and son, mother and daughter, and husband and wife, or even two friends may do this; the husband sits in the lap of the wife. Friends' "good-bye" consists in raising the hand of the other to the mouth and gently blowing on it, reciprocally. At Matavai a full-dress greeting after long absence requires scratching the head and temples with a shark's tooth, violently and with much bleeding. This brief list could be easily enlarged by other anthropologists.

Kissing is Germanic, Graeco-Roman and Semitic (but apparently not Celtic, originally). Greek and Roman parents kissed their children, lovers and married persons kissed one another, and friends of the same or different sexes; medieval knights kissed, as modern pugilists shake hands, before the fray. Kissing relics and the hand of a superior is at least as early as the Middle Ages in Europe; kissing the feet is an old habit among various Semites; and the Alpine peasant kisses his own hand before receiving a present, and pages in the French court kissed any article given them to carry (2). Two men or two women exchange the "holy kiss" in greeting before meetings, in the earlier Appalachian-highland version of the snake-handling cult of the Southeast; the heterosexual kiss is a secular one, not used in public. Another admired gambit is to move the rattlesnake or copperhead back and forward across the face, and closer and closer, until the communicant's lips brush the flickering-tongued mouth of the snake; one Durham minister once offered to kiss the police officers who had raided a snake-handling meeting, to show "no hard feelings", but this offer was not accepted. Kissing, as is well known, is in the Orient an act of private lovemaking, and arouses only disgust when performed publicly: thus, in Japan, it is necessary to censor out the major portion of love scenes in American-made movies. Tapuya men in South America kiss as a sign of peace, but men do not kiss women (nor women, women) because the latter wear labrets or lip plugs. Nose-rubbing is both Eskimo and Polynesian. Djuka Negroes of Surinam show pleasure at a particularly interesting or amusing dance step by embracing the dancer and touching cheek to cheek, now on one side, now on the other—the identical attenuation of the "social kiss" (on one cheek only, however) between American women who do not wish to spoil each other's make-up. And one of the hazards of accepting a decoration in France is a bilateral buss in the name of the republic. Ona kissing in Tierra del Fuego is performed only between certain close relatives and young married couples or lovers; and not lip-to-lip, but by pressing the lips to the hand, cheek, or arm of the other, accompanied by a slight inward sucking (3).

Sticking out the tongue is a kineme with indisputably diverse significance in varied cultures. In Sung Dynasty China, tongue protrusion was a gesture of mock terror, performed in ridicule; the tongue stretched far out was a gesture of surprise (at the time of the novel, *Dream of the red chamber);* in modern south China ·at least (Kunming), a quick, minimal tongue-protrusion and -retraction signifies embarrassment and self-castigation, as at some social *faux pas* or misunderstanding; it can vary in context from the humorous to the apologetic. Among the Ovimbundu of Africa, bending the head forward and sticking out the tongue means "you're a fool". In India, the long-protruding tongue in the statues of the goddess Kali signifies a monumental, welkinshattering rage, a demon-destroying anger as effective as a glance from the Saivite third eye in the forehead. In New Caledonia, in wooden statues of ancestors carved on houses, the protruded tongue means wisdom, vigor, and plenitude, since the tongue "carries to the outside the traditional virtues, the manly decision, and all the manifestations of life which the word bears in itself". Perhaps this is the meaning, in part, of similar New Zealand carvings, although here there may be other overtones of ancestral fertility, etc. (the meaning of the connecting of the elongated nose and mouth to umbilicus and genitals in Melanesian carvings is unknown to me). In the Carolines, however, the gods are disgusted at the lolling tongues of suicides by hanging, and for this reason refuse entry to the souls of such among the deities. In at least one of the eighteen "Devil Dance" masks in Ceylon, specialized for the exorcistic cure in specific illnesses, the black mask has a protruding red tongue, probably synergistic (to judge from other cognates in the India area) with the extremely exophthalmic eyes which are characteristic of all eighteen of these masks: to frighten out the demons regarded as causing the specific diseases. In Mayan statues of the gods, the protruded tongue signifies wisdom. In Tibet, the protruded tongue is a sign of polite deference, with or without the thrust-up thumb of the right hand, scratching the ears, or removing the hat (4). Marquesans stick out the tongue as a sign of simple negation. In America, of course, sticking out the tongue (sometimes accompanied by "making a face") is a juvenile quasi-obscene gesture of provocative mockery, defiance, or contempt; perhaps the psychiatrists can explain why this is chiefly a little girl's gesture, though sometimes used playfully by adult women, or by effeminate men. One might also conjecture a European "etymology" behind this gesture in American child-culture, based on this chronological sequence: apotropaic (a stone head with thrust-out tongue and "making a face" on a Roman fort in Hungary, although this etymon may also include a note of defiance as well), protective-defiant (gargoyles with thrust-out tongue on Gothic cathedrals), mock-affirmative (the subordinates of the demon Malcoda in Dante acknowledge a command by sticking out their tongues and making a rump-trumpet)—all with an obscure overtone of the obscenely phallic—whence the modern child-gesture of derision (and there comes to mind a similar "shame on you gesture", using the left-hand pointing gesture and using the similarly held right hand in an outward whittling movement, repeated). But such precarious kinemic "etymologies" must await more adequate ethnographic documentations, and these we largely lack. The Eskimo curl up the tongue into a trough or cylinder and protrude the tongue slightly, but this is not a kineme; it is rather a motor habit, used to direct a current of air when blowing a tinder into flame.

Gestures of contempt are a rich area for study also. A favorite Menomini Indian gesture of contempt is to raise the clenched fist palm downward up to the level of the mouth, then bringing it downward quickly and throwing forward the thumb and the first two fingers. Malayan Negritos express contempt or disgust by a sudden expiration of breath, like our "snort of contempt". Neapolitans click the right thumbnail off the right canine in a downward arc. The *mano cornudo* or "making horns" (first and little fingers of the right hand extended forward, thumb and other fingers folded) is primarily used to defy the "evil eye". The *mano fica* (clenched right fist with thumb protruding between the first and second fingers) is an obscene kineme symbolizing the male genitals; in some contexts its meaning is the same as the more massive slapping of the left biceps with the right hand, the left forearm upraised and ending in a fist (5); a less massive, though no less impolite, equivalent is making a fist with all save the second ("social finger") and thrusting it upward. Mediterranean peoples are traditionally rich in such gestures; I believe, though with admittedly unsatisfactory evidence, that the "cocked snout" came from Renaissance Italy as a gesture of contempt about the same time as the fork arrived in England in the reign of Elizabeth.

Beckoning gestures have been little collected. In a restaurant, an American raises a well-bred right forefinger to summon a waiter. To express "come here!", a Latin American makes a downward arc with the right hand, almost identical with an American jocular gesture of "go away with you!" The Shans of Burma beckon by holding the palm down, moving the fingers as if playing an arpeggio chord. The Boro and Witoto beckon by moving the hand downward, not upward, as with us, in our face-level, wrist-flexing, cupped-hand "come here!" signal.

Gestures of politesse are equally sparse in ethnographic sources. The Hindu palms-together, thumbs about the level of the chin, is a greeting, a "thank you", and a gesture of obeisance, depending on the context. A Shan, on being done a kindness, may bend over and sniff the sleeve of the benefactor's coat; the meaning is "how sweet you smell", not entirely unlike the Indian "shukriya" (sweetness) meaning "How sweet you are!" Curtseys and bows (almost infinitely graded in depth of bend in the Orient, to express a wide gamut of deference or mock-deference, depending on the social context) are both European and Asiatic. Indic and Oceanic peoples sit down to honor a social superior; Europeans stand up. In both Africa and Melanesia, hand-clapping is a gesture of respect to chiefs and kings. Covering and uncovering the head in deference to gods, kings, and social superiors, is complex, and sometimes contradictory in nature, in Europe and Asia. Taking off or putting on articles of clothing is also full of subtleties of politesse: in classic south India a woman uncovers the upper part of her body in deference, but in America a man puts on his coat to show respect to a lady. The psychology of clothes (6) and the motor habits in handling one's clothing can benefit from much more study: a Plains Indian warrior, for example, could express a wide variety of emotional states, simply through the manner in which he wore his outer robe or cloak. Quite as many gentlemen object to ladies hiking down their skirts or girdles, as ladies object to gentleman hiking up their pants; and I once witnessed the interview with a young psychiatrist of a female hysteric in which a lively and wholly unconscious colloquy was carried on: she with various tugs at her bodice, skirt-hem, and other parts of her dress and underclothing, he with corresponding "business" with his tie, trousers, etc. (7). . . .

The Chinese have a complex gestural language of assignation, and most of the courtesans are very expert in their interpretation. A forefinger rubbed below the nose means that a man finds a woman attractive and would like to make a more intimate acquaintance; a forefinger tapping the tip of the ear means "No!" while the right hand slapping the back of the left hand means the same. Closed fists, but with the forefingers and second fingers of both extended and rubbed together as if sharpening knives, or putting the two hands together and shaking them like castanettes, have meanings easily imagined. The most infamous of these signs would only be used by the most vulgar of coolies: shoving the right forefinger in and out of the closed palm of the left hand. By means of signs the price and the hour of meeting are also communicated; or else the fan is used to indicate the appropriate information. I have no doubt that similar signs are used on the Spanish Steps in Rome, but I do not know these; the "language of the fan" was known to all coquettes in eighteenth-century court circles in France. In Calcutta I was taught a gesture which effectively got rid of the beggars that besiege Americans as insistently as flies, but unfortunately I never learned what it means.

In advertising, the hand symbol for a well known beer (to indicate "Purity, Body, Flavor" by touching forefinger and thumb, the last three fingers extended) is a gesture equally well known to kinesiologists as an ancient and obscene European gesture for coitus. Kinsey has also made a minor contribution to kinesiology in the following passage:

> The toes of most individuals become curled or, contrariwise, spread when there is erotic arousal. Many persons divide their toes, turning their large toes up or down while the remaining toes curl in the opposite direction. Such activity is rarely recognized by the individual who is sexually aroused and actually doing these things, but the near universality of such action is attested by the graphic record of coitus in the erotic art of the world. For instance, in Japanese erotic art curled toes have, for at least eight centuries, been one of the stylized symbols of erotic responses (8).

The erotization of body parts (foot, nape of neck, ear, etc.), on the other hand, appears to vary ethnographically quite widely (9).

To my mind, the artist William Steig has an uncanny ability to portray psychiatric syndromes (especially in his classic, *The lonely ones*) largely through the postural tonuses of his figures (10). From a study of daily column-wide wordless cartoons entitled "Tall Tales" that have appeared during the last two years, I am prepared to give, with exhaustive proofs, and in the appropriate context, a fairly complete psychiatric profile of the artist, Jaffe; I would venture the same, on the same grounds, for Gladys Parker of the series "Mopsy", and for Charles M. Schulz of "Peanuts". One of my students, expert in the Goodenough "Draw-a-Man" projective technique, applied this to the study of "Little Orphan Annie" with extraordinary results; and another has done a brilliant study on the psychological complexes of Pablo Picasso, through a study of his paintings.

The gesture language of the Japanese "tea ceremony" has been adequately described by ethnographers, but never sufficiently analyzed by kinesiologists.

A study of the approved stances and motor modalities in various sports might well be made from the point of view of kinesiology. Particularly absorbing to me has been the observation of the motor "business" and mannerisms of baseball, as observed in the Little League playing of my second son. Various athletes, I maintain, can be matched with their sport, by merely noting the way they sit in classrooms or walk across the campus; and like many other local fans I particularly admire the walking style of the Duke runner, David Sime, especially after he gave up football.

The Abbé Dubois made an exhaustive study of the motor acts of an orthodox Brahman, in connection with attendance to excretory acts (11). Sex-dichotomized motor habits of this sort for men and women are well known to everyone in our society; but these are by no means the same for the appropriate sex in all societies.

Spitting in many parts of the world is a sign of utmost contempt; and yet among the Masai of East Africa it is a sign of affection and benediction, while the spitting of an American Indian medicine man is one of the kindly offices of the healer. The enormous variety and flexibility of male punctuational and editorial-comment spitting is especially rich, I believe, in Southern rural regions. Urination upon another person (as in a famous case at the Sands Point, Long Island, country club, involving the late Huey P. Long) is a grave insult among Occidentals (12), but it is a part of the transfer of power from one medicine man to another in Africa, or to the patient in curing rituals and initiations.

Hissing in Japan (by sudden breath-intake) is a *politesse* to social superiors, implying the withdrawal of the subject's inferior breath in the presence of the superior person thus complimented. The Basuto applaud by hissing; but in England hissing is rude and public disapprobation of an actor or a political speaker.

The extraordinary complexity of motor and paralinguistic acts involved with drinking liquids in Africa is the subject of an article by A. E. Crawley (13). The elaborate modesties of eating are also known to ethnologists with respect to India, Polynesia, and Africa.

The kinesic use of interpersonal physical distance will be familiar to this audience from the work of Edward T. Hall's indispensable text for all kinesiologists and paralinguists (14).

Applied Kinesiology

It is easy to ridicule (15) kinesiology as an abstruse, pedantic, and unimportant study by pure scientists. But I believe kinesiology is, on the contrary, one of the most important avenues for better understanding internationally. Consider, as one small example, how Chinese hate to be touched, slapped on the back, or even to shake hands; how easily an American could avoid offense by merely omitting these intended gestures of friendliness (16)! Misunderstanding of nonverbal communication of an unconscious kind is one of the most vexing, and unnecessary, sources of international friction. (Consider, for example, the hands-over-the-head self-handshake of Khrushchev, which Americans interpreted as an arrogant gesture of triumph, as of a victorious prize-fighter, whereas Khrushchev seems to have intended it as a friendly gesture of international brotherhood.)

Gregory Bateson taught me in Ceylon the great value of attending Indian-made movies as an inexpensive kind of easily available fieldwork; and I have since, gratefully, assiduously attended foreign movies of all kinds. I should like to conclude, as a penultimate example, with some conjectures based on the Russian movie, "The Cranes are Flying", which I believe explain somewhat the famous United Nations episode of Khrushchev's banging his shoe on a desk in the presence of that august body. I do not understand Russian, so that my comments are based entirely upon observation of the motor acts of the characters in two scenes of this movie. First scene: a soldier in a military hospital receives news that his sweetheart has married another man. Much uncontained total emotion, kinetically; raging, tearing at bandages with the teeth, so that there is potential danger to his war wounds; hospital manager is summoned in person to quell the one-man riot, and bring the social situation back to normal. No stiff-upper-lip Anglo-Saxonism here! The assumption seems to be that the mere feeling of an emotion by a Russian is sufficient legitimation for the expression of it (17). Anyone, even the highest authority in the context, it is assumed, can legitimately be called upon to help contain it, since the experiencer of the emotion cannot, need not, or is not expected to. (In this connection one recalls the finding of Gorer that the Russian infant is swaddled because, despite his small and unthreatening size, he is regarded as a center of dangerous and uncontained emotion; whereas Polish swaddling is done because the human being is an infinitely precious and fragile thing, in need of this protection.)

Second scene: a little raggamuffin boy, quite self-contained and stolid as a street-urchin alone in the snow, comes into a warm canteen full of Russian women; some minor contretemps in which the little boy's wish is crossed, then: not merely a simple temper tantrum in the child (panhuman phenomenon) *but* all the women begin running around, dropping everything else, as if it were the most natural and necessary things in the world to help the exploding individual contain his emotion through attention and pacification. Hypothesis: if this is the expectancy of the Russian child in the enculturation experience and evidenced both in his behavior and in that of the soldier, is it possible that Khrushchev was unconsciously using a coercive modality, plausible and understood and unconsciously taken for granted in Russian culture, that wholly missed its mark, certainly for the Anglo-Saxon expectancies of Americans and British present? My reasoning is tenuous; it needs to be supported by masses of ethnographic fact before even being respectfully listened to. But the point I wish to make is that such kinesic and paralinguistic communication is of paramount importance in international relations. Would Pearl Harbor have occurred if we had been able to read the "Japanese smile" of the diplomats as they left their last fateful meeting with Secretary of the State Cordell Hull?

My last example has to do with a more modest and homely matter, the act of dunking doughnuts. During the last War there appeared in the North African edition of *Stars and Stripes* a news picture, purporting to portray an American GI teaching an Arab the gentle art of dunking doughnuts. The American is obviously much self-amused, and the whole context of the picture is "See how good Americans make friends with anybody in the world!" by teaching the foreigner a homely aspect of the American's own culture. But, protests the cultural anthropologist, is this what is actually happening here? Is the GI really teaching, or even essentially teaching, the Arab *all there is to know* about doughnut-dunking? For doughnut-dunking also evokes Emily Post, a male vacation from females striving for vertical social mobility, Jiggs and Maggie, the revolt of the American he-man from "Mom" as the modern introject-source for manners in a neomatriarchate—and much else besides. The archly bent little finger (some obscure kineme? wonders the Arab) is an American lampoon of the effete tea-drinking Englishman and reminds us of 1776—and who, after all, won *that* war. It implies the masculine frontier, class muckerism, and effeminately tea-drinking Boston versus the coffee-drinking rest of the country. There may even be an echo of a robust Anglo-Saxon parody of Norman-French manners in Montmorencys and Percivals, and thus recall 1066 and all that. Underlying it all is the classless American society—in which everyone is restlessly struggling to change his social status, by persuading others that he is a "good guy" and a good average noncom-formist-conformist. Doughnut-dunking is all this—and more!

Is the Arab, in fact, actually being "taught" all these intricate culture-historical implications of an alien tradition—about which, in all probability, our GI (who only finished high school) is neither conscious nor articulate? On the contrary, the Arab brings to the event his own cultural apperceptions and inter-pretations. To be sure, Arabs know all about coffee (and sugar too, for that matter) and knew it long before Europeans; in fact, the common European names for these two substances are all derived from the Arabic. The Arab is far more likely to be worried about another matter: is this oddly shaped breadstuff perhaps cooked (O abomination!) in pork-fat; thus is this eating not so much naughty-humorous as filthily blasphemous! But perhaps he may be reassured that the cooking fat does not derive from an unclean animal, and the Arab can be happy that it is cottonseed oil from good old South Ca'lina, or peanut oil, possibly laced with Tay-ex-us beef suet—none of which were prohibited by the Prophet. Where, then, can he search for an explanation of the GI's manifest amusement at himself in his doughnut-drinking? Ah! At last it is clear: the doughnut is an obscene symbol for the female (such as is common in Arab life), with coffee "black as night, hot as hell, and sweet as a woman," as the Arab prefers it. Now, perhaps, in universal male confraternity, the Arab can join with his GI friend in tasting the sweetness of women (O, of course, that powdered sugar is intended to symbol-ize the face powder of those obscenely bare-faced Christian women!). But these outlandish paynim kaffirs are certainly peculiar buzzards in their symbolisms! However, let us be reassured, for these are the Arab's ratiocinations, not ours. For all that we have been doing, the whole time, is sitting quietly here, with the best of good intentions, purely and simply dunking doughnuts!

References

1. A number of examples are given in LaBarre, *Cultural basis,* pp. 50–51.

2. E. Crawley has a chapter on "The nature and history of the kiss", in his *Studies of savages and sex* (New York, n.d.), 113–136.

3. Cooper, J. M., "The Ona", 143 *Bulletin, Bureau of American Ethnology,* 1, 107–125, esp. p. 118.

4. The desirability of multiple sources on such a matter is indicated here: R. D. Mallery (ed.), *Masterworks of travel and exploration* (New York, 1948), p. 271 (Tibetans put out their tongue in polite deference to a police official in Lhasa investigating their provenience and purposes); p. 275 (Tibetans scratched their ears and put out their tongues at Europeans when they break out their

pictures, microscopes, etc., some with mouths open in awe); Hayes, *op. cit.*, p. 223 ("In Tibet, customary greeting to a fellow traveller: thrust up thumb of right hand and thrust out the tongue"); H. Bayley, *The lost language of symbolism*, 2 vols. (London, 1912), 2,128, noted in Hayes, p. 226: "In Tibet a respectful salutation is made by removing hat and lolling out the tongue." See also: A. Sakai, *Japan in a nutshell*, 2 vols. (Yokohama, 1949), 1,131 - "Formerly every *Sambaso* [a kind of prologue in a classical play, Kabuki as well as Bunraku] doll or mask had its tongue thrust out in accordance with the greatest obeisance performed in Tibet, from which, according to the late Rev. Ekai Kawaguchi, *Sambaso* was introduced."

5. The Boro and Witoto of Amazonia have a sign to express desire for coitus, but this is a mere jest or ribald suggestion: the right elbow is grasped with the left hand, the elbow being flexed so as to have the right hand extend upwards; it is, in fact, the letter Z of the deaf-and-dumb alphabet. Note that this is somewhat the opposite of the American obscenity, so far as right and left are concerned.

6. The British psychoanalyst, J. C. Flügel has shown an exquisite sensitivity to meanings in his monograph, *The psychology of clothes* (London, 1930). I have not seen E. B. Hurloch, *The psychology of dress*, 1929, or F. A. Parsons, *Psychology of dress* (1921).

7. In this same psychiatric clinic, at another time, I also observed a self-justifying male patient giving a long song-and-dance about himself, while slightly to his rear beside him, his psychiatrist (of German origin) gave a complete editorial comment on his patient's story, entirely through facial gestures and motions of his head—fully as skillful a performance as John O'Hara's in the original short story version of "Pal Joey" in which a self-justifying heel condemns himself out of his own mouth.

8. Kinsey, A., *et al., Sexual behavior in the human female* (Philadelphia-London), p. 620.

9. LaBarre, W., "The erotization of body parts in various cultures", address to the Yale Anthropology Club (1936).

10. LaBarre, W., "The apperception of attitudes, responses to *The lonely ones'* of William Steig", *American Imago*, 6 (1949), 3–43.

11. Dubois, Abbé J. A., *Hindu manners, customs and ceremonies*, 3rd ed. (Oxford, 1906).

12. See, in this connection, the paper by Karl Abraham, comprising chapter XIII of his *Selected papers* (London, 1927), pp. 280–298; and also the references on the urethral personality in W. LaBarre, *They shall take up serpents: Psychology of the southern snake handling cult* (Minneapolis, 1962), p. 197, note 120.

13. Crawley, A. E., "Drinks and drinking", *Hastings encyclopedia of religion and ethics*, 5:72–82.

14. Hall, E. T., *The silent language* (New York, 1959).

15. *Horizon* Magazine, in 1959–1961, in a reference I cannot locate.

16. Consider, indeed, that the atomic bomb need never have been dropped, if an interpreter had only properly translated the Japanese word *mokusatsu* (W. LaBarre, *The human animal*, pp. 171, 348 [p. 360 in 4th and later printings]).

17. Is there any remote connection here with the Siberian "olonism" that S. M. Shirokogoroff *Psychomental complex of the Tungus*, London, 1935) writes of: when the underprivileged underdog expresses the most violent and psychotic emotions, and the whole society turns out to recapture the run-away "wild man" in the forest and then attempts to pacify him? If he succeeds in influencing the people, he may become a shaman; if not, he is a psychotic, in need of cure by an established shaman.

Nonverbal Behavior: Some Intricate and Diverse Dimensions in Intercultural Communication

Fathi S. Yousef

Funny People

John Smith has just returned to New York from a vacation in Puerto Rico. John told his friends that since he understood and spoke Spanish he had no problems communicating with people over there. John also said that he wasn't surprised that the area was rather underdeveloped. "After all, people there have no sense of organization. Even their business behavior is quite chaotic," John elaborated. "For instance, once, I walked to a counter in one of the largest department stores in San Juan, the capital, around noon. The salesman was talking to a couple of native customers; however, as soon as I arrived, he greeted me and asked what he could do for me. I thanked him and told him to attend first to those he was already serving. The salesman smiled and continued the transaction with his customers. In the meantime, other people arrived, interrupted, were served, and left while I stood quietly fuming and waiting for my turn, which, incidentally, the salesman never acknowledged. I tell you these people don't have any sense of order or business." At the same time in Dammam, Saudi Arabia, Jim Ralph was flown from the U.S. Head Office to conduct a management seminar for the native personnel in the branch of one of *Fortune Magazine*'s 500 corporations. In commenting on the seminar members to the North American Branch Manager, Jim said, "These people are strangely nervous and jerky. Every time I come close or talk to one of them, the man's body bolts up and tenses in his seat. I wonder what kind of managers they will be." While in Compton, California, white, Anglo-Saxon, Protestant Miss Mary Moore in her elementary school classroom was shouting angrily at little black Johnny, "For the hundredth time, you look at me and listen when I talk to you! Is that clear?" Johnny, meanwhile looked up at her, down at the floor, turned and looked sideways while the teacher stood burning, helpless, and frustrated as she later told a friend.

Who's Funny

In all of these examples there is a communication breakdown based primarily on misunderstanding and unawareness of the subtle cultural nonverbal cues in each context. John Smith, in Puerto Rico, though linguistically competent, when faced with a different concept of time reverted to his own cultural behavior

This original essay was written especially for this volume. All rights reserved. Permission to reprint must be obtained from the publisher and the author. Professor Yousef teaches in the Speech Communication Department, California State University, Long Beach.

patterns[1] and found Puerto Ricans having no sense of order or business. John Smith, in that department store, misunderstood the interactional cycle of behaviors in terms of the culture's temporal etiquette. John Smith expected a monochronic pattern of interpersonal communication where one customer at a time was attended to, and every customer was to be served in the order of his arrival. What happened was that John Smith was faced with a polychronic concept of time where the salesman did not serve one customer at a time but rather tried to serve all customers at the same time. John Smith acted and reacted according to his North American cultural expectations: Time is structured in monochronic segments. Things are attended to one at a time. In this instance, customers should expect to be served in the order of their arrival or they are owed an apology or an explanation. Or, to be charitable, it is simply an inefficient and failing organization. On the other hand, from the salesman's cultural perspective he felt he had done his duty and was quite courteous. As soon as John Smith walked in, he was greeted and his presence was acknowledged while the transactions with other customers were continuing efficiently. John Smith, however, was quiet and seemed to want to wait, or maybe he wanted to look around for a while before he made up his mind. Anyway, he never mentioned what he wanted while many other customers arrived, were served, and left.

The salesman's behavior reflects a polychronic segmentation of time in interpersonal relations where interaction at several different levels is carried on simultaneously. The same behavior can be observed here for example, in Any Town, U.S.A., in ethnic Armenian, Greek, Lebanese, or Syrian grocery stores where we see the "foreign" sales person trying to serve several customers simultaneously and regardless of the order of their arrival. In social or business interactions involving a North American and a Latin American or a Middle Easterner, or sometimes certain Southern Europeans, the North American may be talking or listening to the other party when the "foreigner" may "interrupt inappropriately" to acknowledge the presence of another individual. In no case is either party's business or social behavior inefficient, slighting, or insulting or intended to frustrate, irritate, or aggravate. It is simply a different cultural structuring and meaning of temporal cycles in interpersonal interactions.

On the other hand, Jim Ralph's description of the behavior of his management trainees was quite accurate. His interpretation, however, was off base. What Ralph viewed as nervous, jittery behavior was a native manifestation of attention, deference, and courtesy. Jim Ralph was regarded by the seminar members as the North American expert from overseas. He was a man accorded an especially distinguished and superior rank. Jim Ralph was in a status-conscious society whose members' interactions are marked by formalized rituals in which the nonverbal dimension is very important. Contexts involving superior–subordinate, instructor–student, or trainer–trainee interactions in the Middle East, as in many traditional societies, are usually of a formal nature where role, status, and rank are clear and definite. In the Middle East, when a party of a higher status or rank

---

[1]F. S. Yousef, "Cross-Cultural Testing: An Aspect of the Resistance Reaction," *Language Learning*, 18 (1968), 227–234.

approaches or addresses another, the verbal response of the other party is usually preceded or accompanied by a reshuffling and a straightening of the body posture whether one is standing or sitting. To a native that nonverbal message simply denotes respect, courtesy, and attention. In other words, what Jim Ralph saw according to his North American cultural perspective as peculiar nervous reflexes were conscious and deliberate native cultural nonverbal behaviors meant to convey messages of deference and interest. They were intended by the Middle Eastern management trainees to enhance an atmosphere for communication and understanding.

By the same token, in Compton (near Los Angeles), Mary Moore, the elementary school teacher, was in a strange baffling environment. As a dedicated and responsible teacher she felt it her duty to straighten out untowardly behaviors in her young charges in this almost all black school. Yet, at times, it seemed like a most frustrating, irritating, and exasperating task. She thinks the kids don't seem to listen to her. When she was talking to little black Johnny, from her WASP perspective the kid seemed listless, inattentive, and uninterested. On the other hand, Johnny was confused and helpless. He cast his eyes downward as a sign of respect when the teacher spoke to him, as a "good kid" should do according to his Mom and Dad at home, yet that seemed to infuriate the teacher and make her shout at him. Both the teacher and the student in this instance were victims of conflicting cultural nonverbal behavior expectations that caused a communication breakdown. Mary Moore expected that with clear demonstrations of anger and admonition Johnny's insolent manners or irresponsible nonverbal behavior will adjust to "proper North American standards." In the meantime, Johnny expected that by behaving politely and casting his eyes downward when spoken to, Miss Moore will conform and respond according to the "proper North American standards" that he sees and hears about at home. The two "proper North American standards" are obviously those of white middle-class America and black ghetto America, where nonverbal communication is often reflected and manifested in sets of different behaviors. In this case, little black Johnny sent a message of respect and attention, while Mary Moore from a WASP cultural perspective saw in the same message insolence and inattention.[2]

Value Systems: Isolates, Sets, and Patterns

As a discrete academic field of study, cross-cultural nonverbal behavior is a relatively new subject. Its dimensions are as varied as the interests of students of human behavior. In a way, the field may be easier to delineate by what it does not include than by what it includes.[3] In a given culture, however, nonverbal behavior patterns are usually an extension and a reflection of the culture's value

---

[2]R. D. Abrahams, "Black Talk and Black Education," *The Florida FL Reporter,* 7 (Spring/Summer 1969), 10–12.

[3]J. C. Condon and F. S. Yousef, *Introduction to Intercultural Communication.* Indianapolis: Bobbs-Merrill, 1975.

system. However, concentration and study of singled out sets of nonverbal behavior or their componential isolates can mislead foreign individual observers or interactants into all sorts of fallacious assumptions that cause communication breakdowns.[4]

After the discovery of the North Sea oil, Henry Kissinger, the U.S. Secretary of State, on his way back from a trip in the Middle East, stopped in London for consultations with the British government. The next day, the media reported that as Kissinger and the British Prime Minister Harold Wilson were shaking hands Wilson said that he thought that with the new discovery of British oil Kissinger would greet him with a hug and a kiss! The allusion was to greeting behaviors in the Arab countries, where Kissinger was met with friendly hugs and kisses on the cheek by the heads of states there. Fortunately, the joke had no political repercussions. In the Middle East as well as in Latin America, male friends, especially when they haven't seen each other for a while, usually exchange greetings with hugs and kisses on the cheek, contrary to the usual norms of greeting behavior in the United States, where maximum tactility in such contexts is reflected in a warm handshake, a pat, or a shadow boxing gesture that touches the shoulder. The same Middle Eastern greeting behavior is engaged in by the peoples of many Latin American, Southern European, and Mediterranean countries. Another dimension or extension of that category is the commonly reported observation from visitors to these areas of the world that males are often seen there walking arm in arm in the streets or standing up closely talking and holding hands. Females too are observed indulging in the same behaviors with each other, though to some people in the United States that female behavior may be understandable and may be expected, excused, and dismissed because women are supposed to be affectionate and demonstrative creatures.

A mere description of any such a set of greeting behavior or interaction with an analysis of its component isolates, no matter how thorough and detailed, cannot lead to any meaningful information about the behaviors involved. Unless the whole pattern is constructed, analyzed, and understood—unless the combination of sets of behavior that make up the pattern are seen and understood in their contextual relationships—the studies can amount to no more than pleasant or different descriptions of sometimes bizzare behaviors of some funny, strange people. Consider, for example, the concept of chaperonage which, simply phrased, is the notion that a "good" girl shouldn't be allowed or shouldn't allow herself to be alone with a boy without the presence of a third party. Behavioral reflections of the concept are again observed in Middle Eastern, Latin American, Southern European, and Mediterranean countries. A picture from any such a country could be presented with an accompanying detailed analysis of its nonverbal dimensions, ranging from the kinds and degrees of tactility and the paralinguistic, kinesic, and proxemic behaviors of all interactants to their sensory and physiological reactions to each other and to their surroundings. In the same manner, contrasting behaviors in similar situations from different countries or

---

[4]E. T. Hall, *The Silent Language*. New York: Doubleday, 1959.

cultures may be efficiently presented and studied without an understanding of the underlying meaning of the behaviors manifested. For example, in the Middle East, in Latin America, and in Southern European and Mediterranean countries, patterns of interpersonal relationships are governed by the dictates of a value system largely derived and centered around women's sexual behavior.[5] The female's behavior in the nuclear or extended family and in society at large is a strong determinant of individual feelings of honor and shame. Male friends may greet each other with hugs and kisses on the cheek, but they only shake hands with the women present. Men may greet women relatives by hugs and kisses on the cheek, but under *no circumstances* are kisses exchanged on the lips in public, except sometimes by spouses or fiancés in airports or train stations. In similar contexts in the United States, however, male and female friends and relatives often greet each other with a short kiss on the lips. By the same token, because of the cultural high premium and investment in the legal purity of female sexual behaviors, males may hold hands or walk arm in arm in public, as do females, without offending any cultural sensitivities. Male–female tactility in public, however, is frowned upon. The implications and assumptions are that such behaviors are of a sexual and hence private nature. In the same manner, contexts involving a male and a female alone smack of sexual connotations that could jeopardize a female's reputation and bring shame and disgrace to her, her family, and her clan. By the same token, in such cultures there is a pervasive tendency to view societies where female behavior is less inhibited as dissolute and immoral. However, with the spread of urbanization, coeducation, and female participation in the professions, business, and some social interactions, situations that might involve the presence of a male and a female alone are now being drained of taboo sexual implications and are gaining in acceptability. Social behavior, though, and the notions of honor and shame in such societies are still governed to a large extent by the role expectations and sexual behaviors of the female in the culture. In these expectations and behaviors lie the need and meaning of chaperonage and the implications and nature of male–female and female–female observable tactility as opposed to male–female public tactility in the United States, for instance.

Conclusion

In this essay I tried to illustrate some of the diversity and intricacies of the study of nonverbal cross-cultural behavior. My basic premise is that serious undertakings in that area require meaningful study and analyses of the target cultures that go beyond the anecdotal narration of bizzare behaviors or the presentation and quantification of isolates of nonverbal behavior in sets singled out and studied in the abstract. The emphases should be on structuring related behavioral sets into meaningful patterns whose study would reveal the cultural underlying value systems of the areas studied.

---

[5]J. G. Peristiany, (ed.), *Honor and Shame: The Values of the Mediterranean.* England: Widenfeld & Nicolsen, 1965.

Bibliography

Abrahams, R. D., "Black Talk and Black Education," *The Florida FL Reporter,* (Spring/Summer 1969), 10–12.

Condon, J. C., and F. S. Yousef, *An Introduction to Intercultural Communication* (Indianapolis & New York: Bobbs-Merrill Company, 1975).

Hall, E. T., *The Silent Language* (Greenwich, Conn.: Fawcett Publications, 1959).

Hall, E. T., "Adumbration as a Feature of Intercultural Communication," *American Anthropologist (The Ethnography: Special Publication),* (1964), 154–163.

Hall, E. T., and G. L. Trager, *The Analysis of Culture* (Washington, D. C.: American Council of Learned Societies, 1963).

Hall, E. T., and W. F. Whyte, "Intercultural Communication: A Guide to Men of Action," *Human Organization,* 19 (1960), 5–12.

Peristiany, J. G. (ed.), *Honor and Shame: The Values of the Mediterranean* (England: Weidenfeld and Nicolson, 1965).

Stewart, E. C., *American Cultural Patterns: A Cross-Cultural Perspective* (Pittsburgh: Regional Council for International Education, 1971).

Yousef, F. S., "Cross-Cultural Testing: An Aspect of the Resistance Reaction," *Language Learning,* 18 (1968), 227–234.

Yousef, F. S., *Cross-Cultural Social Communicative Behavior: Egyptians in the U.S.* (Ann Arbor, Mich.: University Microfilms, 1972).

Yousef, F. S., "Cross-Cultural Communication: Aspects of Contrastive Social Values between North Americans and Middle Easterners," *Human Organization,* 33 (1974), 383–387.

Yousef, F. S., and N. E. Briggs, "The Multinational Business Organization: A Schema for the Training of Overseas Personnel in Communication," paper presented at the International Communication Assn. Convention, Chicago, 1975.

Nonverbal Signs for 'Yes' and 'No'[1]

Roman Jakobson

Since the domain of certain conventional gestures and head motions often encompass a wider area than linguistic isoglosses, a naïve notion about the universality of certain meaningful gestures and movements of the head and facial muscles arises very easily.[2] When Filippo Tommaso Marinetti visited Moscow in the beginning of 1914, the painter Mixail Fëdorovič Larionov, who had at first greeted the Italian futurist with hostility, soon struck up friendly relations with him, although at the time Larionov did not know a single foreign language and his new friend did not understand a single word of Russian. Larionov treated his

From *Language in Society,* Vol. 1 (1972), pp. 91–96. Reprinted by permission of Cambridge University Press and the author. Dr. Jakobson is a member of the Slavic Languages and Literatures Department, Harvard University and Institute Professor, Emeritus, Department for Literatures and Linguistics, Massachusetts Institute of Technology.

[1]The Russian text of this article has been published in *Jazyk i čelovek,* memorial volume for Professor P. S. Kuznecov (1899–1968), Moscow University Press, 1970.

[2]Giuseppe Cocchiara in an interesting book (1932), poses the question, 'Il linguaggio del gesto è un linguaggio universale?' (p. 20).

guest alternately to paintings done by himself and other members of his team and to Russian vodka. Once Mixail Fëdorovič was impatiently awaiting the end of the debates in French between Marinetti and Russian writers at a meeting of the Moscow Literary–Artistic Circle, and suddenly took the Italian by surprise, coming up close to him and twice flicking himself on the neck above the collar with his finger. When the attempt to remind the foreigner in this way that it was time to go drinking—or, speaking metonymically, 'to pour [a drink] behind the collar'[3]—turned out to be manifestly unsuccessful, Larionov remarked acidly, 'A real jerk! Even *that* he cannot understand!'

Russian soldiers who had been in Bulgaria in 1877–8 during the war with Turkey could not forget the striking diametrical opposition between their own head motions for indicating 'yes' and 'no' and those of the Bulgarians. The reverse assignment of signs to meanings threw the parties to a conversation off the track, and occasionally led to annoying misunderstandings. Although facial expressions and head motions are less subject to control than speech, the Russians could, without great effort, switch over to the Bulgarian style for the signs of affirmation and negation; but the main difficulty was contained in the uncertainty of the Bulgarians over whether a given Russian in a given instance was using his own code of head motions or theirs.

Such juxtaposition of two opposite systems of motions signifying 'yes' and 'no' easily leads to a new false generalization, namely the conviction that the distribution of the two semantically-opposed head motions is a purely arbitrary convention. A careful analysis, however, reveals a latent imagery—'iconicity', to use Charles Peirce's semiotic terminology[4]—underlying these symbols, seemingly entirely devoid of any connection or similarity between their outward form and their meaning. 'Our' binary system of signs for affirmation and negation belongs to the code of head motions used by the vast majority of European peoples, including, among others, the Germanic peoples, the East and West Slavs (in particular, the Russians, Poles, and Czechs), the French and most of the Romance peoples, etc. Moreover, similar signs in the same function are in general widespread, though by no means universal, among various peoples of all parts of the world. A nod of the head serves here as an expression of agreement, in other words, as a synonym for the word 'yes'.

Like certain forms of affirmative hand motions, this head motion has a close analog in the particular welcoming ritual which is used in the same ethnic environment.[5] The movement of the head forward and down is an obvious visual representation of bowing before the demand, wish, suggestion or opinion of the other participant in the conversation, and it symbolizes obedient readiness for an

---

[3]A common colloquial metonymic expression in Russian meaning 'to have a drink'—cf. English 'to down a few'.

[4]Peirce (1932). Efron (1941) uses the term 'pictorialism'.

[5]Arnold H. Landor (1893) remarks that for affirmation and negation the Ainu do not use head motions, but only hand gestures: 'Both hands are gracefully brought up to the chest and prettily waved downwards—palms upwards—in sign of affirmation. In other words, their affirmation is a simpler form of their salute, just the same as with us the nodding of the head is similarly used both ways' (p. 234).

affirmative answer to a positively-worded question.[6] The direct opposite of bend-ing the head forward as a sign of obedience ought to be throwing the head back as a sign of disagreement, dissent, refusal—in short, as a sign of a negative attitude. However, such a straightforward opposition of two motions of the head is obstructed by the need for insistent emphatic repetition of both the affirmative and the negative head motions; cf. the vocal repetitions 'yes, yes, yes!' and 'no, no, no!'[7] The corresponding chain of head motions in the first case would be the alternation 'forward-backward-forward-backward-forward-backward' etc., and in the second case the reverse set 'backward-forward-backward-forward-back-ward-forward' etc., i.e. two similar series; the entire difference between them comes down to the initial movement forward or backward and easily slips by the addressee, remaining beyond the threshold of his perception.

The semantically opposite signs of affirmation and negation required percep-tibly-contrasting forms of head motions. The forward-bending movement used in an affirmative nod found its clear-cut opposite in the sideward-turning movement which is characteristic of the head motion synonymous with the word 'no'. This latter sign, the outward form of which was undoubtedly constructed by contrast to the affirmative head motion, is in turn not devoid of iconicity. Turning the face to the side, away from the addressee (first, apparently, usually to the left),[8] symbolizes, as it were, alienation, refusal, the termination of direct face-to-face contact.[9]

If in the system of head motions for 'yes' and 'no' under discussion the sign for affirmation appears to be the point of departure, then in the Bulgarian code, which also has parallels among a few ethnic groups in the Balkan Peninsula and the Near East, it is rather the sign for negation which serves as the point of departure for the system. The Bulgarian head motion for 'no', appearing at first glance visually identical to the Russian head motion for 'yes', under close observa-tion displays a significant point of difference. The Russian single affirmative nod is delimited by a bending motion of the head forward and its return to the usual vertical position. In the Bulgarian system, a single negative sign consists of

---

[6]The analysis of affirmative and negative hand gestures does not enter into the present analysis. A copious, but rather mechanical and unsystematic compendium was made by Garrick Mallery (1881). In connection with numerous examples of the hand—with the fingers held touching each other—moving forward and downward as a sign of agreement, the author refers to sources interpreting the hand in the yes-gesture of the Dakota and Iroquois Indians as a metaphor for an affirmative nod of the head (p. 455). Cf. Tomkins (1926), p. 58.

[7]'Puede reforzarse por la iteración simple o múltiple', as G. Meo-Zilio puts it (1961), p. 129. Cf. also Meo-Zilio (1960). p. 100.

[8]This kind of negative movement of the head specifically to the left has been observed, e.g., among the Indians of Terra del Fuego (see Gusinde (1937:1447) and among the Persians (Phillott (1908:619ff.).

[9]Among many peoples in both hemispheres the iconic gesture accompanying or replacing the head motion for 'no' consists of raising the palms—open and with fingers extended—in front of the addressee, as if in a sign of rebuff or defense. The hands in this gesture move either forward and back, as if parrying the other party, or from side to side, as if shutting oneself off from him, brushing him aside or pushing away from him. These two variants can be compared to two varieties of the gesture of threatening which are related to them in both form and meaning: the movement of the raised index finger perpendicular to the line of the shoulders in Eastern Europe or parallel to the shoulders in the Central European region.

throwing the head *back* and the consequent return to the vertical position. However, emphatic intensification makes the return to the normal position into a slight bending of the head backward in our 'yes' or forward in the Bulgarian 'no'. Frequently, because of emphasis, the same head motion undergoes immediate repetition—once or many times—and such repetition, as had already been noted above, more or less obscures the difference between our sign for affirmation and the Bulgarian sign for negation.

In the pure form of the Bulgarian negation, the head—thrown back, away from the addressee—bespeaks departure, disagreement, discord, a rejected suggestion, refusal of a positive answer to a given question, while the Bulgarian sign for affirmation—turning the head from side to side—represents an obviously secondary form, a derivative from its negative antonym. In keeping with Saussure's formula (1916: I, ch. I, § 2), observations of the structure of the Bulgarian head motion for 'yes' and of its basic core of inalienable properties should reveal even in this visual sign a certain degree of iconicity. With the initial turn of the head—usually to the right—and with each further turn, the addressor of this affirmative cue offers his ear to the addressee, displaying in this way heightened attention well-disposed to his words; cf. such Bulgarian figures of speech as 'Az s"m celijat v usi' ('I'm all ears'); 'davam uxo/nadavam uxo' ('I give [you my] ear', cf. 'lend me your ears').

Systems of head motions for affirmation and negation are represented in Europe by both types considered above—'ours' and the 'Bulgarian' type, as I label them—and also by a third type, occurring in certain parts of the Mediterranean area, consisting of bending the head forward for affirmation and backward for negation. I have observed that this kind of opposition is consistently used by the Greeks in Athens, and the same system is preserved in certain regions of Southern Italy, for example among the Neapolitans and Calabrians.[10] Nevertheless, the fact that it is difficult to perceive the difference between the two sets of repeated noddings of the head—forward and backward—is completely corroborated, even in the present case. Both of these head motions are in fact accompanied by two mutually-contrasting movements of the pupils, eyeballs and eyebrows—downward as a sign of agreement and upward as a sign of negation. But even these movements, just like the aforementioned movements of the head, turn out to be nothing more than concomitant, redundant phenomena, while the role of the autonomous, distinctive signal in this case is played by the furrow between the eyebrows and the cheekbones, especially the right eyebrow and cheekbone; this furrow is narrowed as a sign of affirmation and is, in contra-distinction to this, widened as a sign of negation.[11]

The work of the facial musculature, causing the movement of the eyebrow either towards or away from the cheekbone, creates a kind of synecdoche: the

---

[10]As Mallery states, 'The ancient Greeks, followed by the modern Turks and rustic Italians, threw the head back, instead of shaking it, for "no"' (p. 441). It is interesting that in the cases of cooccurrence of both forms of negation—vertical and horizontal—the selection of the first of these two gesticulatory synonyms in Southern Italy is interpreted in the same way as a look meekly directed upwards in avoidance of a bold, unseemly, categorical denial or of an impolite, point-blank refusal.

[11]A similar correlation has been observed among the Persians (cf. the above-mentioned article by Phillott) and the Polynesians (see Métraux (1940:33)).

lowered or raised eyebrow becomes a meaningful, valid substitute for the submissively-bent-down or obstinately-thrown-back head. Another signal for specifying the head motion for negation—used, for example, among those Arabic tribes which have a similar opposition built around bending the head forward or backward—is a click sound, which accompanies the basic movement of the negative sign, i.e., the initial bending of the head backwards.

Several other motions of the head and face are connected in form and meaning with the signs for 'yes' and 'no' of 'our' type. A question is contrasted to an affimrative nod in which the head is thrown back by having the chin thrust forward and up. The head either remains set in this position or the questioner moves it slightly from side to side. In addition, opening the eyes wide signals a puzzled question, while squinting is characteristic of an encouraging attitude on the part of the questioner. As has been already noted above in another connection, the key role here is played by the widened or narrowed space between the eyebrows and the cheekbones.

Amazement, as if removing the capability of an unambiguous reply ('neither yes nor no'), is expressed by rocking the head from side to side, usually from left to right. An inclined movement of the head relates this sign to the head motion for 'yes', and the direction from side to side relates it to the motion for 'no'. Shrugging the shoulders signifies doubt ('perhaps yes, perhaps no'). Reducing the angle between the head and the shoulders brings together the signs of surprise and doubt; but in the case of the former the head is bent toward the shoulders, which remain stationary, and in the case of the latter the head remains stationary while the shoulders are raised toward it.

It is necessary to subject the formal makeup and semantics of various systems of motions to thorough analysis, eliciting the invariants of the sign within each of them. The ethnological and geographical distribution of individual systems, as well as the role assigned to them in the processes of communication (the hierarchical significance of gesture, motion, facial expression, and speech, and the degree of their interconnection) are subject to investigation. In such an investigation the linguist ought to take into account the highly instructive indigenous terminology, both nominal and verbal, used for referring to the customary gestures, head motions and facial expressions.

The exciting questions about the interrelation of naturalness and conventionality in these motor signs, about the binary, 'antithetical' principle of their construction, and, finally, about the ethnic variations and universal invariants—for example, in signs for affirmation and negation—raised almost 100 years ago in Darwin's searching study *The expression of the emotions in man and animals* (1872) demand a comprehensive and systematic examination.[12]

References

Cocchiara, G. (1932). *Il linguaggio del gesto.* Torino.

Darwin, C. (1965 [1872]). *The expression of the emotions in man and animals.* Chicago.

---

[12]I would like to thank Claude Lévi-Strauss for the valuable bibliographical references which he —
kindly provided to me.

Efron, D. (1941). *Gesture and environment.* New York.

Gusinde, M. (1937). Die Yamana: vom Leben und Denken der Wassernomaden am Kap Hoorn. *Die Feuerland-Indianer II.* Wien.

Landor, A. H. (1893). *Alone with the Hairy Apes.* London.

Mallery, G. (1881). Sign language among North American Indians. *Bureau of Ethnology, Annual Report,* I, 263–552. Washington.

Meo-Zilio, G. (1960). *El lenguaje de los gestos en el Rio de la Plata.* Montevideo.

———— (1961). El lenguaje de los gestos, en el Uruguay. *Boletín de Filología* 13. Santiago de Chile.

Metraux, A. (1940). *Ethnology of Easter Island.* Honolulu.

Peirce, C. S. (1932). Speculative grammar. *Collected papers II.* Cambridge, Mass.

Phillott, D. C. (1908). A note on sign-, gesture-, and secret-language amongst the Persians. *Jnl and Proc. Asiatic Society of Bengal* (n.s.) 3, n 9, 619–622.

Saussure, F. de (1916). *Cours de linguistique generale.* Paris: Payot.

Tomkins, W. (1926). *Universal Indian sign language.* San Diego.

Aspects of Nonverbal Communication in Japan

Helmut Morsbach

Nonverbal communication plays an important role in Japanese social interaction. The Japanese language gives a hint of this: while the commonly used ideograph for "face" is pronounced *kao,* there is another ideograph, pronounced *men,* which can mean either face *or* mask. Indeed, some masks worn by the main performer in Noō plays can convey various nonverbal shades of emotion to the audience, depending on the angle at which they are tilted in relation to the lighting.

The Importance of Nonverbal Communication

Some Historical Factors

RACIAL AND CULTURAL HOMOGENEITY   There is no archeological evidence that large waves of immigrants came to Japan after about 500 A.D. The small numbers who did come afterward were speedily absorbed by the native population (20th century Korean immigrants excepted).

Combined with the isolated island nature of Japan, this racial homogeneity, undisturbed for over 1400 years, allowed a culture to develop which is remarkably uniform in many of its major aspects for a modern nation numbering more than 100 million. This, in turn, makes for good interpersonal understanding in numer-

From the *Journal of Nervous and Mental Disease,* Vol. 157. Copyright 1973, The Williams & Wilkins Co. Reproduced by permission. Professor Morsbach teaches in the Department of Psychology, Glasgow University, Glasgow, Scotland.

ous situations. Many intentions do not need words for their fluent transmission. By contrast, Great Britain shows far greater intracultural diversity, *e.g.*, due to the Celtic minority groups, and more recent influential immigration from the Continent.

THE INFLUENCE OF ZEN BUDDHISM   Zen Buddhist teaching places great value on silence and on the communication of ideas and feelings by nonverbal means. True enough, Zen Buddhism never claimed a very large proportion of the Japanese as adherents. However, it was adopted by the small but very influential samurai class during the Kamakura period (1185 to 1333). Samurai behavior, in turn, became the ideal for many who belonged to the lower classes, and thus certain aspects of Zen Buddhist-inspired behavior became relatively common.

In Zen Buddhist teaching a large amount, often the essential part, is left unsaid. Great importance is attached to the concept of *kan,* which can be translated as "perception," "intuition," or "the sixth sense." Indeed, *satori* (enlightenment) can quite specifically *not* be attained by talking about it.[1]

The teaching of traditional arts (*e.g.,* tea ceremony, archery, calligraphy) in Japan is strongly influenced by Zen ideals. The task of the pupil is to imitate the *sensei* (master) faithfully; no long explanations are given, and the master does not expect questions to be asked (20).

Young boys, wanting to become monks in a Zen monastery, often have to demonstrate their sincerity of intent by kneeling motionlessly near the entrance for several days. Nonverbalization and "nonobviousness" in Zen are related to a refinement of form, and to concepts such as *sabi* ("patina") and *wabi* ("quiet taste") which have no real equivalents in Western languages, but refer to subtlety and indirection (4, p. 174).

THE TOKUGAWA PERIOD, 1603 TO 1867, AND AFTER   For over 260 years Japan was ruled by a highly centralized authority which was harsh and authoritarian. This, together with the virtually complete cutting off from the outside world, greatly assisted further development of cultural homogeneity and led to highly prescribed and predictable behavior in social interaction, much of which was nonverbal.

Lafcadio Hearn (19), in a chapter called "The rule of the dead" discussed the enforced discipline before the Meiji Restoration. After presenting some findings of the historians J. H. Wigmore and D. B. Simmons concerning the legal status of the masses during the Tokugawa period, he wrote as follows about nonverbal behavior:

> Demeanour was most elaborately and mercilessly regulated, not merely as to obeisances, of which there were countless grades, varying according to sex as well as class —but even in regard to facial expression, the manner of smiling, the conduct of the breath, the way of sitting, standing, walking, rising. Everybody was trained from infancy in this etiquette of expression and deportment. At what period it first became

---

[1]The word *satori* is derived from the verb *satoru,* to comprehend or see. According to R. Frager (personal communication) one can interpret *satori* as the kind of immediate and holistic comprehension obtained through the visual mode-in seeing a picture, for example.

a mark of disrespect to betray, by look or gesture, any feeling of grief and pain in the presence of a superior, we cannot know; there is reason to believe that the most perfect self-control in this regard was enforced from prehistoric times. But there was gradually developed—partly, perhaps, under Chinese teaching—a most elaborate code of deportment which exacted very much more than impassiveness. It required not only that any sense of anger or pain should be denied all outward expression, but that the sufferer's face and manner should indicate the contrary feeling. Sullen submission was an offence; mere impassive obedience inadequate; the proper degree of submission should manifest itself by a pleasant smile, and by a soft and happy tone of voice. The smile, however, was also regulated. One had to be careful about the quality of the smile: it was a mortal offence, for example, so to smile in addressing a superior, that the back teeth could be seen. In the military class especially this code of demeanour was ruthlessly enforced. Samurai women were required, like the women of Sparta, to show signs of joy on hearing that their husbands or sons had fallen in battle: to betray any natural feeling under the circumstances was a grave breach of decorum. And in all classes demeanour was regulated so severely that even today the manners of the people everywhere still reveal the nature of the old discipline. The strange fact is that the old-fashioned manners appear natural rather than acquired, instinctive rather than made by training.

An edict was passed that no one was allowed to involve himself in the troubles of strangers. Pretending that nothing had happened became the safest kind of behavior, especially when samurai were around. The latter had the right to behead anyone who displeased them. Commoners could suffer great injustice without their families being able to appeal (3). Keeping quiet became a virtue, and since most things in daily life were tightly regulated anyhow, language could be amplified, changed, or replaced by nonverbal communication.

Fischer and Yoshida (15) investigated Japanese values about speaking and language by analyzing proverbs. They concluded, "Basically, the most ubiquitous lesson about speech in Japanese proverbs is 'Shut up' " (p. 36). This is shown in the following examples, "One treats one's mouth like a guarded jar;" "A mouth is to eat with, not to speak with;" or, "To say nothing is a flower" (*i.e.,* it is a good idea to leave many things unsaid).

This hesitancy to speak out and the resulting use of nonverbal ways to transmit one's thoughts were very much evident before (and during) World War II. Richard Storry (28), who lived in Japan just before World War II, remarked:

> The condition of the *kurai-tanima* ("dark valley") made me appreciate the significance of oblique, indirect criticism. At that period the Hawks seemed to dominate the scene. The Doves were silent. Yet their silence, correctly understood, was quite eloquent. . . . indicative of fearful anxiety about the future course of Japan (p. 368).

Today silence still retains much of its appeal, even for advertisers. Toshiro Mifune, prototype of the strong, brooding, male Japanese hero, could be seen on television during 1972, exhorting all virile males with his command, "Men, keep quiet, and drink Sapporo Beer!"

Some Social Factors

THE EMPHASIS PLACED ON RANKING AND HIERARCHY   Bruno Lewin (22), studying the Japanese language, paid special attention to the many polite forms (*keigo*) which can indicate interpersonal distance as well as ranking. Since they had already been found in the first existing records of the language, (around 800 A.D.), Lewin concluded that they did not develop during historical times, but instead were inherent elements of the language. Strict observance of ranking and hierarchy was strengthened further by the adoption of Confucian ethics from the early 7th century onward (18). The importance of ranking on nonverbal communication will be discussed in the conclusion of this paper.

MOTHER-CHILD RELATIONS   A careful and important study was carried out by Caudill and Weinstein (10) who investigated the relationship between maternal care and infant behavior in Japan and America. Close observation of 30 Japanese mothers with their babies and 30 matched Americans was carried out when the babies were 3 months old. The authors found strong cultural differences concerning nonverbal communication—the Japanese mothers showed significantly less vocal interaction with their babies, but had greater bodily contact with them and tended to soothe them more often in attempts to keep them quiet. Such differences were not found in comparable studies with Japanese and American infants 1 month old (10; Wolff and Okada, personal communication). Neither were differences found when comparing 3-month-old American infants with Japanese American infants from the third generation to be born in the U.S. (8). These two findings indicate that it seems to be the culture which shapes the level of activity at the age of 3 months, and not genetic factors. The pattern of greater nonverbal communication between Japanese mothers and their children was found to continue until the age of 2½ years and beyond (6). Caudill (10) put forward the following explanations for this consistent difference: watching mother-infant interaction (by an observer making a check on a score sheet once every 15 seconds for a prescribed time), it was found that Japanese mothers in his sample interacted mainly with their children with the object of keeping them quiet and making them go to sleep. Therefore, when a Japanese child cried, it was usually taken up, fed, or played with, and then put down again once it became drowsy. Now this had a powerful conditioning effect: soon after it had been put down it wanted to be with the mother again. It therefore started crying once more so that the mother would pick it up, and the cycle was repeated several times until at last the child fell asleep. In the American sample, on the other hand, the mother usually played with the child if it was awake, and left it alone when it wanted to sleep. And it was allowed to cry for a short time before going to sleep, but this did not cause the mother to pick it up again. In the American sample the mother was much more in and out of the room, in contrast to the Japanese mother who usually stayed with the child, whether it was awake or asleep. In several cases the Japanese mother would even lie down with the baby, breastfeed it, and go to sleep at the same time. Therefore, American babies had more chances to make differentiated noises at an early age because there was: a) more crying and calling for an absent mother; and b) more often a chance for the mother to say "hello" and "goodbye." In this way, American babies made an earlier and clearer differentiation between negative crying and positive gurgling sounds.

Far closer physical contact between parent and child (and therefore greater ability to communicate nonverbally) is possible in Japan because mothers usually sleep together with the youngest child, and the father sleeps with the second youngest one. This pattern usually persists until a child is 10 years old (10).

Wagatsuma (personal communication) added:

> American mothers tend to create a physical distance between themselves and their child and 'bridge over' this gap by talking to them. This is far less necessary in Japan. Americans, on the whole, are much more verbal. In their culture it is a good thing to speak up, be articulate, be self-expressive. Traditionally in Japan talkativeness was sign of a person's 'shallow character.' Many American women need to be constantly told that they are loved—they tend to feel lonely without verbal assurances. Japanese lovers, when happy, remain silent, Americans TALK!

INTRAGROUP SOLIDARITY   In contrast to most Western cultures, the average Japanese adult is first and foremost a member of *one* specific group and tends to show great loyalty toward it. For a female this group usually consists of her family (with special emphasis on her own children). For an adult, urbanized male the most important group tends to be located at his place of work. According to Nakane (24) members have relatively few contacts outside their group, which makes in-group interaction, reciprocal obligations, and expectations all the more intense. Since members tend to be inside such a group from the time of entry in their late teens or early 20s until their retirement, they get to know each other exceedingly well—their family life, love affairs, capacity for drink, *etc.*

> Among fellow-members a single word would suffice for the whole sentence. The mutually sensitive response goes so far that each easily recognizes the other's slightest change in behaviour and mood and is ready to act accordingly (p. 121).

Such sensitivity is, of course, also discernible among group members of other cultures. The difference is a quantitative, not a qualitative one.

Nakane emphasized the importance of nonverbal communication in the Japanese situation as follows:

> The high degree of involvement in interpersonal relationships of both positive (allies) and negative (enemies) kinds within such small groups must surely be allied to, though perhaps not be the cause of, the development of the extremely sensitive manners, phraseology (virtually incapable of translation), facial expressions and postures of the Japanese. The delicacy tends to be couched in ambiguity of expression, which is used to avoid confrontation, for self-defence and to conceal hostility. The flattery, the insinuation and the smile are used to gain advantages, while at the same time they conceal the precise nature of desire or feeling. . . .
>
> The acquisition of these extremely delicate ways of conducting personal relations requires considerable social training, though most Japanese achieve them through their social life from childhood onwards. Not only foreigners but even those Japanese who spend their teens or twenties abroad face considerable difficulty in meeting all the complicated techniques of personal relations, which do not require much intellectual manoeuvre but demand highly sensitive and nervous procedures (pp. 123–124).

From the foregoing it can be expected that nonverbal communication in Japan is in many cases quite different, both qualitatively and quantitatively, from that found in most Western cultures. The following section attempts to discuss specific aspects of nonverbal communication in Japan.

Specific Examples of Nonverbal Communication

Duncan (13) suggested the division of nonverbal communication modalities into six sections:

Body-motion or kinesic behaviour: gestures and other body movements, including facial expression, eye movement, and posture;

paralanguage: voice qualities, speech nonfluencies, and such nonlanguage sounds as laughing, yawning, and grunting (p. 118);

proxemics: use of social and personal space and man's perception of it (16, p. 1);

olfaction;

skin sensitivity;

use of artefacts . . . such as dress and cosmetics (13, p. 118).

Since little or no work has been published on olfaction and skin sensitivity concerning Japan, these points will not be considered in the present paper, except to mention that many centuries ago perfume identification contests were popular among the nobility, as described in Lady Murasaki's *Tale of Genji.*

Body Motion

Asch (2) pointed out that there is a basic repertoire of expressions occurring, without exception, in all human societies. This includes crying when in pain, trembling when fearful, and smiling or laughing when happy. Eibl-Eibesfeldt (14) carried out extensive unobserved filming in various cultures and concluded that, among others, the following body motions were to be found universally: crying, smiling, stamping of feet in anger, grimacing in anger, flirting behavior (showing an "eyebrow flash" and then turning the head away), greeting by raising of the hand or arm, nodding, shaking of the head to say "no," *etc.* By and large these body motions are to be found in Japan, although several are present in young children but suppressed or changed in later life.

GESTURES   With virtually no contact between Japan and the West until a century ago it is not surprising that only a few gestures have exactly the same meaning in both areas. On the other hand, some gestures are shared, but have different meanings. Finally, some Japanese gestures seem to have no equivalent in the West.

Apart from emphasizing points made while speaking, or being useful when two persons are trying to communicate when out of earshot, some gestures allow ideas to be transmitted which would be too direct, and thus possibly offensive, if verbalized, *e.g.,* they can convey ideas (usually negative ones) about a third person able to overhear a conversation.

Some gestures are readily understood by Westerners, *e.g.,* an invitation to join a male drinking session by miming the holding of a sake cup and making a

slight "throwing-away motion" with the wrist. This kind of gesture is called
temane in Japanese, which can be translated as "hand imitation."

A vigorous scratching behind the ear among males shows that one is komatta
(perplexed); and making a counterclockwise circling motion with the index finger
pointing toward the temple (*hidarimaki,* to wind counterclockwise) indicates that
the person being discussed is regarded as eccentric or "mad." Finally, Westerners
readily understand the sign for "I" or "myself" where the index finger is pointed
at the nose (and not at the heart, as is common in the West).

Gestures which can be misunderstood in the West include the following:

Making a circle with one's index finger and thumb in Japan was traditionally
a reference to money (*okane*). In Western countries it usually means "O.K.,"
"good," "delicious," *etc.,* and this is now also encountered among some Japanese,
giving rise to possible confusion.

Holding both fists, one before the other, in front of the nose indicates that
the person referred to is "long-nosed" (*Hana ga takai*), *i.e.,* overconfident.

Calling a person toward oneself in Japan is achieved by extending one's arm
slightly upward, palm downwards, and fluttering the fingers. This can lead to
amusing misunderstandings among Westerners, as Seward (27) recounts:

> One day in Hakone, I was watching a Japanese girl-guide whose American tourist
> charges had become separated from her by a considerable distance and saw her use
> this gesture to try to gather her flock of about twenty elderly, bewildered-looking souls
> about her. The diverse effects were amusing. Some thought they had been abandoned
> by their girl-guide and began to mill about like worried sheep. Others appeared to
> think that it was a signal for a drink and started to straggle back toward the bar of
> the hotel. Still others apparently interpreted it to mean that they were now on their
> own and began to disperse through the town (p. 42).

The Western "thumbs up" sign also has quite a different meaning in Japan
—it is a discreet reference to some male, *e.g.,* a boy friend, husband, patron or
oyabun (a boss, usually of gangsters or gamblers).

The following signs are unknown in most Western countries: A sign complementary to the Japanese "thumbs up," mentioned previously, is the little finger
pointed straight up. This can mean girlfriend, wife, or mistress. Seward (27)
remarks:

> An advantage of this finger gesture is that you can use it to refer to the woman you
> saw Mr. Moribe out with last night when you are afraid to hazard a guess at the exact
> relationship between them. If you want to know if she will be in Mr. Moribe's
> company again tonight, you should point your little finger toward the ceiling, like a
> caricature of a prim tea drinker, and say: '*Konya mō* (finger up) *irrashaimasuka?*'
> (Will the lady come with you again tonight?) (pp. 42–43).

Discreet reference to somebody suspected of stealing can be made by lifting the
right hand, with all fingers mostly bent, except for the index finger which is half
bent. This indicates that the person in question has an unfortunate habit of
"hooking onto" things not his own.

Similarly, a fast crossing of the index fingers alludes to *chanbara* (sword
fighting) or *kenka* (an argument). When this gesture follows an unfinished sen-

tence such as, "Mr. and Mrs. Suzuki. . . ." it implies that they are having a fight. It can also indicate personal struggle inside the speaker.

Guarded reference to a member of the outcaste group in Japan can be made by bending the thumb onto the palm and spreading out the other four fingers. This gesture refers to four-legged animals such as cows, *etc.*, which only the outcastes slaughtered and skinned in pre-Meiji times (*i.e.,* before 1868), since Buddhism forbids the killing of animals. Wagatsuma (personal communication) suspects that this gesture is still widely used, especially by older people.

Instead of saying outright that someone is suspected of being a liar, use can be made of the gesture called *mayutsuba* (eyebrow-saliva). Here, the index finger is briefly licked with one's tongue and then stroked over an eyebrow. (Originally it was a magical protection against being cheated by a fox.) According to Wagatsuma (personal communication), this has become old fashioned. However, it is interesting to note that the gesture is now being verbalized. By uttering the word *"mayutsuba"* in the appropriate context, Japanese are now able to imply dishonesty in someone without actually using the word "liar."

To mention a female's jealousy, both hands can be put to the forehead, with the index fingers sticking up and angling forward (27, p. 43). This represents a woman's "horns of jealousy" which, incidentally, a Japanese bride hides on her wedding day with the special headdress called *tsunokakushi* (horn-hider). The latter is intended to keep her from becoming jealous, but in view of the prevailing double standard in marriage it is unlikely to be of much protection.

The right hand waved limply in front of one's face, with the thumb nearest to it, indicates a desire to pass closely in front of a person. It is accompanied by a slight bending of the body, as if bowing.

MOVEMENTS WITH THE WHOLE BODY   One of the most important nonverbal communications in hierarchy-conscious Japan is the bow (*o-jigi*). Its first task is to establish a certain condition of communication. Okawa[2] quotes the article "Greetings and social life" (*Aisatsu to Shakai*) in the journal "Language Life" (*Gengo Seikatsu*), 1968, No. 196, p. 97, which states, "Bowing is the beginning of human relations." Furthermore, it enhances and augments many civilities mentioned during a conversation between people and can finally be used to end the interaction.

Of course its basic meaning is readily understood by Westerners who also use it to some extent, especially in Germany.

However, bowing is usually a far more intricate procedure in Japan because it may involve several repeats, and the angle at which the torso moves downward from the vertical position is of great importance. Befu (personal communication) remarks that doctoral dissertations could be written on all variations of bowing and their social, situational, and ecological determinants. This is clearly not within the scope of the present paper. Suffice it to say that reciprocal bowing is largely determined by rank: the social inferior bows more deeply and the superior decides when to stop bowing. Where the relative social standing is not clear-cut,

---

[2]Okawa, Hisashi. Case studies of communication in department stores. Unpublished thesis. International Christian University, Tokyo, 1971.

these decisions may be difficult for both. Here an especially close watch must be kept on the other person to gauge depth and duration of the other's bow. Frequently one tries to be the more polite one, and this can result in a "bowing contest" which Wagatsuma calls "one-downmanship." When bowing deeply, one should bend slightly to one's right so as to avoid hitting the other's head with one's own. Some female department store employees have the sole function of bowing to customers at department store escalators, while smiling and politely saying *"Irasshaimase"* ("Welcome"). However, life-sized animated bowing dolls with tape recorded voices are beginning to take over this welcoming function at smaller establishments, such as *pachinko* (pin-ball) parlors.

That bowing has become a largely automatic movement is evidenced by the fact that many Japanese can be seen to bow repeatedly to invisible partners at the other end of a telephone line.

Quite by accident I found this "bowing reflex" most useful when shopping in Japan: If a salesgirl saw me approaching her counter she frequently pretended not to notice me—after all, most foreigners cannot make themselves properly understood and are likely to cause her no end of trouble. However, due to her inquisitiveness, this pretence at "not noticing" was not kept up all the time, and at intervals there was the rapid glance to see what the foreigner was up to. This was the precise moment I would wait for: looking her in the face I would bow quickly, thereby invariably eliciting her "bowing reflex." Now that she had "officially" taken notice of me, she was also under obligation to treat me as a customer.

The handshake, however, is very much a Western import, and the dilemma whether to bow or to shake hands with Westerners can be rather great, especially if a cosmopolitan Japanese meets a foreigner in love with Japanese customs. One compromise often seen is to shake hands while bowing at the same time—a procedure fraught with the danger of knocking heads together, apart from looking quite hilarious. According to Wagatsuma (personal communication) this is very common among Japanese male immigrants in the U. S.

Kirkup (21) cites a newspaper report which highlights the importance of the bow as a sign of deference:

> An official of the Prime Minister's Office has a distinction unique in all Japanese history—he has shaken hands with the Emperor. It later turned out that the Imperial handshake was a mistake.
>
> Jitsuzo Tokuyasu, director of Administrative Affairs in the Prime Minister's office, was standing near the line of foreign diplomats at the beginning of the Imperial banquet given by Their Majesties the Emperor and Empress on Tuesday for King Bhumibol Adulyadej and Queen Sirikit of Thailand. Their Majesties, in accordance with traditional procedure, went down the line, shaking hands with members of the diplomatic corps.
>
> They then came to Mr. Tokuyasu. He was deeply tanned after a summer vacation and was wearing a Thai medal on his chest. The Emperor and Empress evidently thought he was a foreign diplomat and shook hands with him. Since the Emperor

Jimmu, no Japanese has ever before shaken hands with the Emperor. Mr. Tokuyasu was greatly reassured when protocol experts told him that to have refused a proffered hand would have been a much more flagrant impropriety than this breach of centuries of Imperial tradition by shaking hands with the Emperor (pp. 181–182).

FACIAL EXPRESSIONS   *Smiling and laughing.* While smiling and laughing are signs of joy in all humans, they can also be used in Japan to hide displeasure, anger or sorrow. Lafcadio Hearn's comments concerning this behavior in Tokugawa Japan have already been cited in the section on the Tokugawa period.

A breach of etiquette causes anxiety in any culture. While Westerners mainly respond by withdrawal, or with a show of anger, Japanese are more apt to smile, giggle or laugh nervously. The trained observer can distinguish between the latter and the laugh caused by something pleasant, and modifies his behavior accordingly. Asch (2) hypothesized that the tendency to smile in adverse conditions is due to the major concern with maintenance of control and showing respect to superiors, evident in Japan.

> Japanese learn . . . that it is necessary to keep a reserve of strength in the face of crisis in order not to be naked and exposed. The smile in this context has the significance of resisting the shock of pain and sorrow by a summoning of inner strength (p. 199).

Control of an outward show of pleasant emotions in public is also rarely relaxed in Japan. Women tend to cover their mouth while laughing, and males show true merriment (but also true anger) mainly after hours when their culture allows them greater freedom of behavior while drinking alcohol.

Eye contact. While many Western societies regard a person as being a slightly suspicious or "shifty" character if he does not make a certain amount of culturally prescribed eye contact with his partner when talking face-to-face (1), Japanese children are taught in school to direct the gaze at the region of their superior's Adam's apple or tie knot.

Wagatsuma (personal communication), who has lived outside Japan for many years, comments as follows:

> I am notorious for my habit of looking straight into a person's eyes when I am talking to him. This, I have been told, annoys or makes the person feel uneasy or threatened in Japan. I therefore try not to do that so often when talking to Japanese as I do talking to Americans. Older people, like my father, try not to look at the Emperor's eyes too long (when being presented to him), which means they look slightly downward, psychologically bowing to him.

> I recently read in a Japanese newspaper that a Japan Air Lines stewardess, who had accompanied the Emperor on his trip to Europe, started sobbing when she reported to the newspaper reporters after the Emperor had returned to the VIP-room, "The Emperor did not say a word to us when deplaning, but he momentarily stopped in front of me and looked straight into my face—such an honour!"

The ideal of an expressionless face. Self-control, thought of as highly desirable in Japan, demands that a man of virtue will not show a negative emotion in his face when shocked or upset by sudden bad news; and, if successful, is lauded as *taizen jijaku to shite* (perfectly calm and collected), or *mayu hitotsu ugokasazu ni* (without even moving his eyebrow). A short story by the novelist Akutagawa (1892 to 1927), entitled *"Hankechi"* (Handkerchief), illustrates this point very well: A mother visits her son's professor and tells him that her son is dead, without showing any emotional disturbance on her face. She is even smiling faintly. All of a sudden the slightly puzzled professor discovers that a handkerchief is held tightly between the mother's hands, almost on the point of being torn. The author commented, "She was crying with her two trembling hands."

The idea of an expressionless face in situations of great anxiety was strongly emphasized in the *bushido* (way of the warrior) which was the guideline for samurai and the ideal of many others. The saying "A samurai holds his toothpick high" (*Bushi wa kuwanedo taka yōji*) implies that in spite of great hunger a warrior should always pretend that he just had a satisfying meal.

In public settings, the poker-faced ideal is common in present day Japan. Very often the occupants of a Japanese bus or train will pretend not to notice a foreigner who is seated among them. The latter might even think that he is not the object of particular interest. However, I often noticed that most Japanese passengers are slowly but constantly oscillating their heads from left to right through a 90 degree arc, so that the foreigner can be watched briefly but regularly, once every few seconds. This poker-faced "lighthouse look" is, of course, often accompanied by verbal remarks which, it is confidently expected, the foreigner will not (and usually does not) understand.

A personal experience of witnessing the controlled facial expressions of Japanese came when a suburban train, in which I was standing, traveled through the Kanda area of Tokyo where many universities are situated. A violent student demonstration had been in progress for some time which caused the riot police to be very liberal in their use of tear gas. As the train entered the "battle zone," tear gas wafted into the carriage and caused my eyes to smart and fill with tears. As I grabbed for my handkerchief, I saw through streaming eyes that none of the passengers standing near me seemed to be affected in the slightest. To my admiration all of them kept up a poker face. However much I tried, I could not stop crying, and made an undignified but speedy exit at the next station to get out of the tear-gassed carriage.[3]

Paralanguage

When comparing the Japanese language with, say, English or German, it quickly becomes apparent that one can be much more vague in Japanese. Sentences left unfinished or ending with a *desho* (perhaps?) or *desu ga* (. . . but) are

---

[3]This explanation seems improbable to some Japanese friends whom I told about it. After all, it is unlikely that there are large racial differences in people's physiological reactions to tear gas, and the self-control required to keep one's tears back in such a situation would be beyond most people's ability. But I *did* have to cry, and the others seem unperturbed. Since I was traveling by myself, I have no witnesses but I still would like to recount this experience in the hope that someone can corroborate it.

quite common. Even nouns can be used in a vague way—a lot depends on the context in which they are used, *e.g.,* the word *hito* can have six meanings: "person," "persons," "a person," "some persons," "the person," "the persons." It is quite possible in Japanese to utter a long sentence, which has a certain meaning; and then to use the identical sentence on another occasion, changing only the major verb from positive to negative—and the listener's interpretation can still be the same. Furthermore, distinct changes in paralanguage (as well as language) occur, depending on: a) whether one talks *to* a superior, an inferior or an equal; and b) whether one talks *about* a superior, inferior, or equal.

Nakane (24) cites an interesting example:

> I was asked one day by a French journalist who had just arrived in Tokyo to explain why a man changes his manner, depending upon the person he is addressing, to such a degree that the listener can hardly believe him to be the same speaker. This Frenchman had observed that even the voice changes (which could well be true, since he had no knowledge of Japanese and so was unable to notice the use of differentiating honorific words; he sensed the difference only from variations in sound) (pp. 30–31).

Furthermore there is a large degree of polite patter in Japan which, compared to English, one might call " oververbalization" since the primary aim is to convey a few simple ideas in a certain way with as many polite variations as possible. This is mainly found in women's speech, of which Miller (23) gives an example,

> *A:* "My, what a splendid garden you have here—the lawn is so nice and big, it's certainly wonderful, isn't it!"
>
> *B:* "Oh no, not at all, we don't take care of it at all anymore, so it simply doesn't always look as nice as we would like it to."
>
> *A:* "Oh no, I don't think so at all—but since it's such a big garden, of course it must be a tremendous task to take care of it all by yourself; but even so, you certainly do manage to make it look nice all the time; it certainly is nice and pretty any time one sees it."
>
> *B:* "No, I'm afraid not, not at all . . ." (pp. 289–290).

Miller also remarks that it is pointless to ask for a "male speech" translation in this case:

> *A* might say "It's a nice garden, isn't it" (*ii niwa da na*) and that would be the end of it; to this *B* might reply (if at all) with a sublinguistic grunt, as a sign of acknowledgement or polite denial (p. 290).

Among the sublinguistic utterances, hissing (by inhaling one's breath) is perhaps the most perplexing to Westerners, since in Japanese it denotes a sign of deference and/or simply gives the speaker time to think (rather like "er . . ." in English). The use of "*hai*" (literal translation, "yes," "certainly," "all right," "very well") can also create problems in cross-cultural understanding, since the real meaning is frequently, "I understand what you are saying," but not necessarily implying agreement. A rapid succession of "*hai*" exclamations can therefore be heard when someone is listening on the telephone—it simply indicates to the speaker that the listener is still on the line.

Misunderstandings such as the following can therefore occur:

> American camera importer (speaking through an interpreter): "Can you ship by the end of this month?" Japanese camera manufacturer (speaking Japanese): "*Hai,* we can ship about the twentieth of next month." The American importer, knowing enough Japanese to think that he knows that *hai* means yes, smiled brightly when he heard the word *hai,* but his reaction switched to puzzlement and then irritation when the interpreter went on to explain that the shipment would be effected around the twentieth of next month. In this case, *hai* meant only, "I have heard and understood your question" (27, p. 36).

THE ROLE OF SILENCE IN LANGUAGE   It was mentioned earlier that in Japanese it can be quite proper to leave words hanging in the air, sentences unfinished. Schinzinger (26) observed that a great amount, often the essential part, is frequently left unsaid during conversations. He compared this to the Japanese ink drawings where the white paper of the background is often more expressive than the black shape of it. While most Westerners, according to Schinzinger, want to come to the point rather quickly in a conversation, the average Japanese first needs to get a "feel" for his partner and is not hesitant to let long silences develop.

These silences are frequently misunderstood by Westerners, who tend to interpret them as noncomprehension, and therefore try to shorten the silence by explaining their point once again, or by moving on to the next topic. Well meaning attempts to make the Japanese partner(s) "speak up" often tend to cause silent frustration and resentment since, from the Japanese viewpoint, the Westerners are often seen as being the culprits who should rather be taught how to "shut up."

Since most conversation in Japan is patterned in such a way that the response to a question can be in the affirmative, the word *iie* (no) need hardly be used. Indeed, silence in response to a question may already signify nonacceptance, and this again is easily misunderstood by most Westerners as being noncomprehension of their question.

Hall (17) tried to explain this different attitude toward silence and toward time as follows.

> "Monochronism" means doing one thing at a time. . . . American culture is characteristically monochronic. North Europeans and those of us who share this culture distinguish between "active" and "dormant" phases of everything. . . . Just plain sitting, trying to capture a sense of self, is not considered to be doing anything. . . . In a number of cultures (including Japan) just plain sitting is doing something. The distinction between being active or not is not made. . . . With us, you have to work to get ahead. We don't get ahead automatically. In the cultures mentioned above, this is not nearly so important (pp. 178–179).

Proxemics

An important way to communicate nonverbally is through the use of space, either between persons and objects, or between persons themselves. Japanese-

Western differences have been described by Hall (16), concerning the traditional use of space between persons and objects:

> (The Japanese) . . . were particularly ingenious in stretching visual space by exaggerating kinesthetic involvement. Not only are their gardens designed to be viewed with the eyes, but more than the usual muscular sensations are built into the experience of walking through a garden. The visitor is periodically forced to watch his step as he picks his way along irregularly spaced stepstones set in a pool. At each rock he must pause and look down to see where to step next. Even the neck muscles are deliberately brought into play. Looking up, he is arrested for a moment by a view that is broken as soon as he moves his foot to take up a new perch.
>
> In the use of interior space, the Japanese keep the edges of their rooms clear because everything takes place in the middle. Europeans tend to fill up the edges by placing furniture near or against the walls. As a consequence, Western rooms often look less cluttered to the Japanese than they do to us (pp. 49–50).

Living in a Japanese house can have a pervasive influence on interpersonal relationships. Hall (16) cites an old priest who told him:

> To really know the Japanese, you must have spent some cold winter evenings snuggled together around the *kotatsu*[4] Everybody sits together. A common quilt covers not only the *kotatsu* but everyone's lap as well. In this way the heat is held in. It's when your hands touch and you feel the warmth of their bodies and everybody feels together —that's when you get to know the Japanese. That is the real Japan! (p. 140).

But an American female student (personal communication) who lived with a Japanese family found this touching of feet in the *kotatsu* almost unbearable.

The use of space between persons in Japan also shows considerable differences from the West.

The major subdivision in this case is the use of space between in-group members in a private setting (*e.g.*, family, work group, *etc.*) on the one hand, and between persons in a public setting on the other.

In a private setting there is frequently very close proximity as around the *kotatsu* in winter time, mentioned previously. The physical closeness, especially between parents and young children in cosleeping arrangements, has also been mentioned already. Caudill and Plath (9) investigated the cosleeping arrangements in 323 Japanese households. From an American viewpoint, Japanese sleeping arrangements are usually thought of as showing a high degree of "overcrowding" which is commonly regarded as being due to lack of space in "densely populated" Japan. But the authors found that most three-person households did not tend to use more than a single room for sleeping, even if extra space was freely available. In larger households some dispersal was evident, but

---

[4]The *kotatsu* is a charcoal brazier (or, in modern times, an electric heater) at the bottom of a square hole about 18 inches deep in the middle of the room. A table is usually placed over the hole, allowing several persons to sit around it.

availability of space only accounted for 22 per cent of the variance. They concluded:

> We argue that this apparent overcrowding in the bedroom is only in part a function of lack of space: it derives more directly from the strength of family bonds. We argue further that the frequency with which children cosleep with parents expresses a strong cultural emphasis upon the nurturant aspects of family life and a correlative deemphasis of its sexual aspects (p. 344).

Dore (12) also emphasized the intrafamilial closeness.

> It would be very rare, for example, to find a family which used the living-room for sleeping in order to avoid having adult brothers and sisters sleep together in the same room, even in upper-class families. Modesty does not forbid uncovering the body in the presence of members of the opposite sex within the family, and, in any case, when the partitions between rooms are no more than sliding wood-and-paper doors, the difference between sleeping in the same room (in a separate set of bed-clothes) and sleeping in adjoining rooms is not very great. Incest is not unknown and it does appear occasionally as a subsidiary theme in novels, but it is far from being a general preoccupation. Generally speaking, sleeping in the same room with a member of the opposite sex is not defined as a sexually significant situation to anything like the same extent in Japan as in the West. It is common after late-night parties, either family parties or *geisha* parties, for all the assembled company, men and women, to sleep in the same room. The valued feature of this 'mixed sleeping' (*zakone*) is the sociability it affords; the opportunity for conversation in fuddled comfort for as long as one feels like staying awake. There is no assumption that anything improper will take place, though it sometimes does. . . . Beyond the limits of actual cramped discomfort, crowded sleeping seems to be considered to be more pleasant than isolation in separate rooms. The individual gains a comforting security and it is a sign that a spirit of happy intimacy pervades the family. A widow living with a 30-year-old son and a 27-year-old daughter in a two-roomed house, said, when asked whether they made any division of rooms, "No, we all sleep together, we are a happy family all together, sharing everything and keeping nothing from each other. It's happier that way." There is much to be said for the theory that this low evaluation of individual privacy is linked with the general preference for group, over individual, action and responsibility which characterizes Japanese society if compared with the "individualistic" West. A Japanese newspaper writer once remarked that Japan will never be democratized or the principle of individual responsibility established until Japanese are brought up in separate bedrooms with solid sound-proof walls and locks on the doors (pp. 48–49).

Similar closeness is found when bathing together in the nude in public baths or *onsen* (hot springs). Here again, sexuality is deemphasized. Separation of the sexes in public baths was ordered a century ago, mainly because the prudish Western model was seen as "more modern" at the time; but even today there are hot springs in Japan where this separation is not enforced. According to Befu (personal communication) there is a complex set of rules to establish and respect privacy in the bath house. A Westerner who remarked, "In Japan the nude is seen, but not looked at" was only scratching the surface of this nonverbal interaction pattern.

Most bathtubs in private homes are too small for two adults to sit inside it at the same time, but from birth onward, babies and little children are taken into the hot water by their mothers or grandmothers. Caudill (7) remarked:

The difference in emphasis between the two cultures (Japan and U. S.) in these regards is one of "closeness," or perhaps how such closeness is expressed. In Japan the relation between mother and child is for a long time almost a symbiotic one where words are not necessary since emotions are communicated in actions (p. 417).

Of course, physical closeness between family members in a private setting is by no means confined to the Japanese. Indeed, their treatment of interpersonal space is probably in line with most other cultures, and it is really the North European and U.S. middle-class culture which "deviates" in this respect, with its insistence on separate bedrooms, even for small babies.

However, in Japan there is also a sphere in which physical closeness (in a nonsexual sphere) is permitted between nonrelated persons; and this is during times of illness. Caudill (5) investigated the roles of subprofessional nurses in mental hospitals, called *tsukisoi,*

> . . . who act as motherly servants for both male and female patients. The relation with the patient is of a one-to-one nature, with each patient having his personal *tsukisoi* in the private psychiatric hospital. The *tsukisoi* is with the patient 24 hours a day, 7 days a week. They sleep in the same room as the patient and serve as housekeeper and companion. Hospitals in Japan consider these women largely in terms of their domestic services, but a meaningful relationship (in either a positive or a negative sense may develop between *tsukisoi* and patient with the limits set by the relative status positions of the two roles. These women are paid by the family of the patient and live most of their lives within the hospital and yet are not formally part of the hospital staff even though, next to the patients, they are the most numerous role group in the organization (p. 205).

The author also remarked that being cared for by a *tsukisoi* in Japan is not a novel situation because the patient is used to the close presence of others to a far larger degree than in the West.

The stronger separation between Japanese in-groups and out-groups is highlighted by the tendency to have high walls screening one's house from its surroundings, to entertain formal guests preferably in public restaurants and not at home, and, if they do enter the house, to keep then in the *okyakuma* (parlor), well away from the other rooms which are usually not regarded as being in a presentable state.

Further screening and distancing from the out-group is evident in the often elaborate wrapping of articles carried and presented in public, such as gifts.

Public display of affection between adults beyond the hand holding stage is still rare—boys and girls mostly keep a "proper" distance. On the other hand, babies and small children receive widespread attention and can be touched easily, even by complete strangers. It is not uncommon for maids in a *ryokan* (Japanese inn) to take a baby away without saying much to the parents and to play with it for long periods.

Even the etiquette rules of 90 years ago described by Dixon (11) can sometimes still be observed, such as that in public the wife should walk one to two paces behind her husband.

In an uncrowded situation touching between most adults in public is minimal —even the brief Western handshake is absent.

The situation changes drastically, however, when crowdedness occurs. With overcrowded trains and buses, especially in the Tokyo and Osaka areas, involuntary touching of strangers is an everyday experience for rush-hour commuters. Whereas the Western way of defense against anonymous intrusion often consists of hiding behind a newspaper, this is less frequent in Japan. In any case, there is rarely enough space to unfold one. Dozing off while sitting or hanging onto a strap is a favorite way of creating interpersonal distance and making the situation tolerable. At the same time, however, involuntary touching of limbs and bodies is frequently not evaded, even when one could conceivably move away a little. Time and again it happened that someone would doze off while sitting next to me, and his (or her) head often came to rest on my shoulder. Sometimes I was even acting as "cushion" for sleepers on both sides! I always felt very rude when I had to wriggle away on reaching my destination.

THE USE OF ARTIFACTS   The hierarchical structure of Japanese society, described so well by Nakane (24), governs social interaction to a large extent. When two Japanese meet for the first time with the desire to communicate, it is of great importance that they establish their social ranking vis-à-vis each other. Only when this has been achieved to some degree can dialogue begin at the appropriate level of politeness.

Easy nonverbal recognition of status is facilitated by the frequent wearing of some badge, costume, or uniform.

Richie (25) has paid special attention to the importance which Japanese, traditional as well as modern, have attached to katachi (form, shape). He comments:

> Japan is one of the last countries to wear costumes. Not only the fireman and the policeman, but also the student and the labourer. There is a suit for hiking, a costume for striking; there is the unmistakable fashion for the boy who belongs to a gang and the indubitable ensemble of the fallen woman.
>
> In old Japan, the pattern was even more apparent, a fishmonger wore this, a vegetable seller, that; a samurai had his uniform as surely as the geisha had hers. The country should have resembled one of those picture scrolls of famous gatherings in which everyone was plainly labelled, or one of those formal games—e.g. shōgi (Japanese chess) where each piece is marked (p. vii).

Many young hoodlums hanging around the amusement districts at night (e.g., the Shinjuku area of Tokyo) and who live from bribery and extortion, wear sunglasses as "insignia." Sunglasses and gangsters were until recently associated in the mind of the general public. The Tokyo salesman of the German Zeiss Optical Company told me in 1968 that because of this there was no market to speak of for his firm's sunglasses.

In the modern world of the sarariman (translation of "salary man," i.e., white-collar employee of a large firm), the "uniform" consists of the invariable white shirt and dark suit. A small company badge frequently worn on the lapel identifies the wearer as belonging to a firm with a certain status in the Japanese business hierarchy. However, even if worn, this badge does not indicate the rank of the wearer inside his organization. A second artifact thus becomes indispensable when meeting for the first time, especially in the business world: the *meishi* (name or business card). After the introduction by a third party and before a conversation starts, *meishi* are mutually exchanged and studied assiduously. While Western visiting cards would list, in order, one's given name, family name, address, and possibly one's occupation, a different order is followed in Japan. Since the most important criterion of rank in Japan is determined by the organization one belongs to, this is given first, followed by one's position inside that organization. The academic degree (if any) comes next, then the family name, the given name, and finally the address. After suitable exclamations of respect concerning what one has read, the conversation can start at the "proper" levels of politeness and distance.

Problems are encountered if the most important information is withheld, as Seward (27) relates,

> As a casual experiment, I once had printed a batch of *meishi* that gave only my name and Tokyo telephone number in English on one side and the Japanese equivalent on the back. At the time I was quite active around Tokyo and must have passed out at least a dozen of these *meishi* daily. At first I was astonished, then amused, and finally intrigued by the consternation they caused. To those who asked, I explained that these *meishi* gave my name, in both English and Japanese, and told how to communicate with me. Was that not sufficient? Indeed not, they protested. A name and telephone number were far from being enough. Just what was I? What was my position, my company, my sphere of influence? The truly important data, they clamoured, were not written on the card at all.
>
> What they wanted, of course, was a title or *Katagaki* (lit., writing on the shoulder) (p. 56).

Conclusions

An attempt has been made to list examples of Japanese nonverbal behavior and to explain some of the differences found, in terms of historical and social factors peculiar to Japan.

I believe that many misunderstandings in cross-cultural communication between Westerners and Japanese are not only due to linguistic problems, but also to mis- or noncomprehension of nonverbal cues. It seems highly desirable that students of the Japanese language and culture should acquaint themselves with important aspects of nonverbal communication accompanying, supplementing, and/or replacing Japanese verbal communication. A most promising start has already been made at the University of Hawaii, where Professor Harvey Taylor developed a video tape introductory course to the Japanese language. Here special attention is paid to nonverbal cues, and it is explained how these influence the social interaction between the Japanese speakers acting out certain situations in front of the TV camera.

This approach, together with more objective research (*e.g.,* unobserved filming) and perhaps a guide book sensitizing Westerners to nonverbal cues in the Japanese culture might contribute a little toward a better understanding of a fascinating social system which is in so many ways different from the Western one.

Final Remarks

An American professor at a Japanese university with an excellent command of Japanese language told me the following:

One day he had attended a faculty meeting where he fully participated in the lengthy discussions, using Japanese throughout. On leaving the meeting, he remarked to a Japanese colleague that, in his opinion, the meeting had finally arrived at a particular conclusion. Had not Professor X spoken in favor? His Japanese colleague agreed. And other professors, too? (going down the list one by one). Again, his Japanese colleague agreed, but finally remarked "All this may be so, but you are still mistaken. The meeting arrived at the opposite conclusion: You have correctly understood all the words spoken, but you didn't understand the silences between them."

References

1. Argyle, M. *The Psychology of Interpersonal Behaviour.* Penguin Books, Harmondsworth, 1967.

2. Asch, S. E. *Social Psychology.* Prentice-Hall, Englewood Cliffs, New Jersey, 1952.

3. Asō, I. Japanese humour. Jap. Q., *13:* 84–90, 1966.

4. Befu, H. *Japan—An Anthropological Introduction.* Chandler, San Francisco, 1971.

5. Caudill, W. Around the clock care in Japanese psychiatric hospitals: The role of the *tsukisoi. Am. Sociol. Rev., 26:* 204–214, 1961.

6. Caudill, W. Psychiatry and Anthropology: The Individual and His Nexus. Paper presented at the Conference of Mental Health and Anthropology, Stanford University, Palo Alto, 1971.

7. Caudill, W. Some problems in transnational communication (Japan-United States). In Group for the Advancement of Psychiatry. *Application of Psychiatric Insights to Cross-Cultural Communication.* Symposium No. 7, New York, 1961.

8. Caudill, W., and Frost, L. A comparison of Maternal Care and Infant Behavior in Japanese-American, American, and Japanese Families. Presented at the Stanford Conference on Mental Health and Anthropology, Palo Alto, 1971.

9. Caudill, W., and Plath, D. W. Who sleeps by whom? Parent-child involvement in urban Japanese families. Psychiatry, *29:* 344–366, 1966.

10. Caudill, W., and Weinstein, H. Maternal care and infant behavior in Japan and America. Psychiatry, *32:* 12–43, 1969.

11. Dixon, J. M. Japanese etiquette. Trans. Asia. Soc. Jap., *13:* 1–21, 1885.

12. Dore, R. P. *City Life in Japan.* University of California Press, Berkeley, 1958.

13. Duncan, S. Nonverbal communication. Psychol. Bull., *22:* 118–137, 1969.

14. Eibl-Eibesfeldt, I. *Grundriss der vergleichenden Verhaltensforschung.* Piper and Co., Munich, 1967.

15. Fischer, J. L., and Yoshida, T. The nature of speech according to Japanese proverbs. J. Am. Folklore, *81:* 34–43, 1968.

16. Hall, E. T. *The Hidden Dimension. Man's Use of Space in Public and Private.* Doubleday and Co., Inc., New York, 1966.

17. Hall, E. T. *The Silent Language.* Doubleday, Garden City, New Jersey, 1959.

18. Hall, J. W., and Beardsley, R. K. *Twelve Doors to Japan.* McGraw-Hill, New York, 1965.

19. Hearn, L. *Japan: An Attempt at Interpretation.* Macmillan, London, 1904.

20. Herriegel, E. *Zen in der Kunst des Bogenschiessens.* O. W. Barth, Munich, 1948.

21. Kirkup, J. *Japan Behind the Fan.* J. M. Dent, London, 1970.

22. Lewin, B. Die geschichtliche Entwicklung des japanischen Soziativs. In Lewin, B., Ed. *Beitraege zum interpersonalen Bezug im Japanischen,* pp. 18–63. Otto Harrassowitz, Wiesbaden, 1969.

23. Miller, R. A. *The Japanese Language.* University of Chicago Press, Chicago, 1967.

24. Nakane, C. *Japanese Society.* Weidenfeld and Nicholson, London, 1970.

25. Richie, D. Introductory essay. In Iwamiya. Takiji. *Katachi: Design and Craftsmanship of Japan; Stone, Metal, Fibers and Fabrics, Bamboo.* Abrams, New York, 1965.

26. Schinzinger, R. Maske und Wesen. Mitteilungen der Deutschen Gesellschaft für Natur-und Völkerkunde Ostasiens. Tokyo, *44:* 1–44, 1963.

27. Seward, J. *Japanese in Action.* John Weatherhill, Inc., New York, 1968.

28. Storry, R. A life-long affair. Jap. Q., *13:* 366–371, 1966.

Black Kinesics: Some Non-verbal Communication Patterns in the Black Culture

Kenneth R. Johnson

Although much research has been written on *verbal* communication patterns of Black People, little research has been directed toward their non-verbal communication patterns. The research of Bailey, Baratz, Dillard, Fasold, Kochman, Labov, Shuy, Stewart, Wolfram and others on the verbal communication patterns of Black people has demonstrated that many Black people speak a variety—or dialect—of English that differs from other varieties of English. The existence of Black dialect or Black English or Nonstandard Negro dialect (it has been given these labels) has been conclusively demonstrated; thus, it can be expected that non-verbal communication patterns in the Black culture, too, differ from those in the dominant culture or other American sub-cultures. Indeed, many of those who have researched verbal patterns (particularly Kochman and Stewart) have commented on this difference. The purpose of this paper is to describe some of these non-verbal communication patterns of Black people and the meanings these patterns convey.

Bailey, Dillard and Stewart have suggested that Black dialect did not evolve from a British or American variety of English, but that it evolved through a pidginization-creolization process. Further, they suggest that its evolution has been influenced by the African languages Black people originally spoke. Turner's monumental study of the dialect of the Gullahs, or Geechies, demonstrated the

Reprinted with permission of the *Florida FL Reporter,* from Vol. 9, Nos. 1 & 2, Spring/Fall 1971, pp. 17–20, 57; Alfred C. Aarons, editor. The author is Associate Professor of Education and Ethnic Studies at the University of California, Berkeley.

survival of "Africanisms" in the Gullah dialect. (The Gullahs—or Geechies, as most Black people call them—are a group of Black people who live mainly on the islands off the coast of South Carolina and along the coasts of South Carolina and Northern Georgia and who speak what is clearly a creolized variety of English which, most likely, is the prototype of Black dialect.) Black dialect, however, is much more like standard English (and other varieties of English) than the Gullah dialect. Still, its evolution—according to some researchers—has been influenced by the former African languages Black people originally spoke.

The hypothesis that Black dialect has a different base of development from other varieties of American English (even though it is similar to other varieties of American English and it shares many common features) can be extended to non-verbal communication patterns. That is, non-verbal communication patterns in the Black culture that are not commonly exhibited by other Americans possibly have their origins in African non-verbal communication patterns. This does not mean that all non-verbal communication patterns of Black people differ from those of other Americans. As with language patterns, Black people share many non-verbal patterns with other Americans. On the other hand, those unique non-verbal patterns of Black Americans don't necessarily have to be identical to African non-verbal communication patterns in order for them to have an African origin. Years and years of separation of Black Americans from their original African cultures could have produced alterations in these original non-verbal patterns, and separation could have produced entirely new patterns unrelated to African patterns.

Some support for the hypothesis that Black non-verbal communication patterns have an African base can be gained through observing Africans. For example, the non-verbal patterns—specifically, body movement—of a touring dance troupe from a West African country which visits the United States periodically are remarkably similar to those of Black Americans. This dance troupe includes a street scene in its repertoire and except for the props and, to a lesser extent, the costumes, the spirited talk ("lolly-gagging," "jiving," signifying" and "sounding") accompanied by body movements (especially walking) and gestures is not very different from what can be seen on any busy ghetto street during a hot summer evening. The similarity is too great to be due to chance.

Much research to support this hypothesis needs to be done. The purpose of this paper is not to establish the link between African non-verbal communication patterns and those of Black Americans. Instead, the hypothesis is suggested to provide a possible theoretical base to explain the differences between Black non-verbal communication patterns described here and the non-verbal communication patterns of other Americans.

A second hypothesis is that the isolation of the Black population from other Americans produced some differences in non-verbal communication patterns within the Black culture. Perhaps research will establish the validity of both hypotheses—that is, non-verbal communication patterns in the Black Culture could be a result of former African patterns and also a result of patterns that have evolved out of the indigenous conditions of Black Americans.

The focus of this paper will be on those non-verbal patterns that have been labeled *kinesics* by Birdwhistell. Specifically, kinesics refers to how people send messages with their bodies through movement, expressions, gestures, etc. Birdwhistell has pointed out that these non-verbal patterns are a learned form of communication which are patterned within a culture, and that they convey a particular message. Some of these patterns that are unique to the Black population and the messages they convey are described below.

Not every Black person exhibits every feature in his non-verbal behavior. However, these features occur with such great frequency in the Black population that they can be considered patterned behavior. (The same is true of Black dialect features. Not every Black person who speaks Black dialect will have all the features of this dialect in his speech.)

In stress or conflict situations, particularly when one of the participants is in a subordinate position (for example, a conflict situation involving a parent and child or a teacher and student), Black people can express with their eyes an insolent, hostile disapproval of the person who is in the authority role. The movement of the eyes is called "rolling the eyes" in the Black culture.

"Rolling the eyes" is a non-verbal way of expressing impudence and disapproval of the person who is in the authority role and of communicating every negative label that can be applied to the dominant person. The movement of the eyes communicates all or parts of the message. The main message is hostility. The movement of the eyes—rolling the eyes—is performed in the following way. First, the eyes are moved from one side of the eye-socket to the other, in a low arc (usually, the movement of the eyes—that is, the rolling—is preceded by a stare at the other person, but not an eye-to-eye stare). The lids of the eyes are slightly lowered when the eye balls are moved in the low arc. The eye balls always move *away* from the other person. The movement is very quick, and it is often unnoticed by the other person, particularly if the other person is not Black. Sometimes, the eye movement is accompanied by a slight lifting of the head, or a twitching of the nose, or both. Rolling the eyes is more common among Black females than it is among Black males.

This movement of the eyes is different from the movement of the eyes which is called "cutting the eyes" in the dominant culture. In "cutting the eyes" the movement of the eyes is always *toward* another person. Furthermore, after the eyes are focused on the other person (following the cutting) they usually remain focused in a stare. In other words, the stare follows the cutting action.

Black people (particularly females) will often roll their eyes when being reprimanded or "lectured to" about some infraction of a rule. After the person who is in the authority role has continued the lecture for a while, the Black person in the subordinate role (the "receiver" of the lecture) will roll the eyes. Rolling the eyes can also be used to express a kind of general disapproval. For example, if two Black women are together and a third woman enters their social sphere wearing a dress that the other two Black women know costs $5.95 and obviously giving the impression that she not only looks good but that the dress is much more expensive, then one of the two Black women will roll her eyes. In this situation the message communicated is "She sure think she cute but she don't look like nothing, 'cause that dress cost $5.95."

Rolling the eyes is probably partly responsible for the saying used by many Black people: 'Don't look at me in that tone of voice." In fact, one of the indications that rolling the eyes is a hostile impudent non-verbal message is that when it is done the Black person in the authority role will stop lecturing and say, "Don't you roll your eyes at me!" (The implied meaning of this command is, "I know what you're thinking and I know the names you're calling me." Sometimes, this command is punctuated by a slap "up-side the head".

Often, white teachers (who are in an authority role and who have contact with Black children) will miss the message communicated by Black children when they roll their eyes. It's just as well, because rolling the eyes gives the Black child an opportunity to non-verbally release his hostility and endure the reprimand with a minimum amount of conflict. Black teachers, on the other hand, usually recognize the action and properly interpret the message. As mentioned before, this sometimes causes them to punish the child, thus escalating the conflict and worsening the situation.

It is not known whether or not rolling the eyes is a non-verbal pattern in Western African cultures. It would be interesting and also a test of the hypothesis presented above if this could be determined.

Another eye behavior used by many Black Americans is found in many West African cultures. I am referring to the "reluctance" of Black Americans to look another person (particularly, another person in an authority role) directly in the eye.

Thus, the stereotyped view of many whites (particularly in the South) has some truth. That is, many Blacks (especially Black males) don't look another person in the eye, if the other person is in an authority role. To look another person in the eye (in the context of the dominant culture) is a non-verbal way of communicating trustworthiness, forthrightness, masculinity, truthfulness, sincerity, etc. In the Black cultural context, avoiding eye contact is a non-verbal way of communicating a recognition of the authority-subordinate relationship of the participants in a social situation.

Many Black children are taught not to look another person (particularly older persons) in the eye when the older person is talking to the younger person. To do so is to communicate disrespect.

In the South Black males were taught—either overtly or covertly—not to look a white male in the eye because this communicated equality. Thus, not to look white males in the eye was really a survival pattern in the South.

Note how "culture clash" can occur because of the avoidance of eye contact: in the dominant culture, eye contact is interpreted one way, while it is interpreted in another way within the Black culture. Avoidance of eye contact by a Black person communicates, "I am in a subordinate role and I respect your authority over me," while the dominant cultural member may interpret avoidance of eye contact as, "Here is a shifty unreliable person I'm dealing with."

Avoiding eye contact to communicate respect and acknowledgement of one's being in a subordinate role is a common pattern in Western Africa. (This pattern is also found in other cultures for example, in the Japanese culture.) It could well be that this particular pattern within the Black culture has its origins in former African cultures of Black Americans.

Reinforcing the avoidance of eye contact is a stance that young Blacks take in a conflict situation (this stance sometimes is taken by adult Blacks, too). Often, in a conflict situation Black youngsters (particularly, males) will slowly begin to take a limp stance as the reprimand from the person in the authority role goes on and on. The stance is as follows: the head is lowered, the body becomes extremely relaxed and the Black person stands almost as if he is in a trance. The stance is not taken immediately, but slowly evolves as the reprimand proceeds.

Young white males usually stand very rigid, with their legs spread and their arms extended stiffly down the sides of their bodies (fists balled up) as the reprimand is delivered.

The limp stance is a defense mechanism which non-verbally communicates: "I am no longer a person receiving your message of reprimand; I am only an object." Or, it communicates: "My body is present, but my mind is completely removed from the present encounter." In any case, when a Black person adopts this stance in a conflict situation, the best thing to do is to terminate the reprimand —the Black person is not receiving the message. The person in the authority role —the person delivering the reprimand—can be sure whether or not this is the non-verbal message if he notices the way the Black person walks away from him after the reprimand.

Before describing the walk away from a conflict situation, it is necessary to describe the "Black walk". It communicates non-verbal messages in other situations besides conflicts.

Young Black males have their own way of walking. Observing young Black males walking down ghetto streets, one can't help noticing that they are, indeed, in Thoreau's words "marching to the tune of a different drummer." The "different drummer" is a different culture; the non-verbal message of their walk is *similar* to the non-verbal message of young white males, but not quite the same.

The young white males' walk is usually brisk, and they walk on the balls of their feet with strides of presumed authority. Both arms swing while they walk. The non-verbal message is: "I am a strong man, possessing all the qualities of masculinity, and I stride through the world with masculine authority."

The young Black males' walk is different. First of all, it's much slower—it's more of a stroll. The head is sometimes slightly elevated and casually tipped to the side. Only one arm swings at the side with the hand slightly cupped. The other arm hangs limply to the side or it is tucked in the pocket. The gait is slow, casual and rhythmic. The gait is almost like a walking dance, with all parts of the body moving in rhythmic harmony. This walk is called a "pimp strut", or it is referred to as "walking that walk".

The walk of young Black males communicates the same non-verbal message as that of young white males. In addition, the Black walk communicates that the young Black male is beautiful, and it beckons female attention to the sexual prowess possessed by the walker. Finally, the Black walk communicates that the walker is "cool"; in other words, he is not upset or bothered by the cares of the world and is, in fact, somewhat disdainful and insolent towards the world.

The young Black male walk must be learned, and it is usually learned at quite a young age. Black males of elementary school age can often be seen practicing the walk. By the time they reach junior high school age, the Black walk has been mastered.

The description of the walk is a general description, and it includes all the components that can be present in the walk. All the components are not always present in each individual's walk, because each individual must impose a certain amount of originality onto the general pattern. Thus, some young Black males will vary the speed or swing of the head or effect a slight limp or alter any one or a number of the components of the Black walk to achieve originality. The general "plan" of the walk, however, is recognizable even with the imposed originality. This imposed originality also communicates the individualism of each young Black male.

The Black walk is used for mobility (as any walk is) and to arrive at a destination. Sometimes, however, one gets the feeling that *where* the young Black male is going is not as important as *how* he gets there. There is a great deal of "styling" in the walk. The means are more important than the end.

The walk is also used as a hostile rejection of another person in a conflict situation. For example, after a person in an authority role has reprimanded a young Black male, the person with authority can tell whether his reprimand has had positive effects (e.g., the young Black male follows the dictates of the reprimand, he is sorry for the offense, etc.) by the way the young Black male walks away from the authority figure. If the young Black male walks away in a "natural" manner, then the reprimand was received positively; if he walks away with a "pimp strut" it means that the young Black male has rejected the reprimand and in fact is non-verbally telling the authority person to "go to hell."

Young Black females communicate the same non-verbal message when walking away from a person in an authority role after a conflict situation by pivoting quickly on both feet (something like the military "about face") and then walking briskly away. Sometimes the pivot is accompanied by a raising of the head and a twitching of the nose.

When either the young Black male or the young Black female walks away from the authority person in the above manners, the knowledgeable authority person (particularly if he or she is Black) will angrily tell the young Black person to "come back here and walk away right." To walk away "right" means to walk away without communicating the negative, disrespectful, insolent message. This is proof that these walks are sending a message.

The Black walk is reflected in the stance young Black males take while talking in a group. For example, when talking in a group, the participants (say, four or five young Black males) will often adopt a kind of stationary "pimp strut." This means that while the young Black males are talking, they stand with their hands half-way in their pockets, and they move in the rhythmic, fluid dance-type way (without actually walking) to punctuate their remarks. The arm that is free will swing, point, turn and gesture as conversation proceeds. It's almost as if they are walking "in place." This kind of behavior always accompanies a light or humorous conversation, or a conversation about masculine exploits. It never accompanies a serious discussion about more general topics (planning something, difficulties with parents, political issues, etc. However, if these kinds of topics are discussed in terms of the young Blacks' masculinity or if they are "styling" while discussing these topics, the stationary "pimp strut" stance *will* be taken).

Often, when this stance is taken, *how* one says something—the style—is more important than *what* one says.

Another interesting thing that happens when a group of young Black males talk in a group is that the periphery of the group continually fluctuates. That is, the group moves in and out toward and from the center. (Young white males, when they are talking in a group, usually maintain a tight circle during the discussion.) When something particularly interesting or funny is said (if the statement reflects a use of language that is unique, creative and "styled") one or more of the participants will turn his back to the center of the group and walk away—almost dance away—with great animation to non-verbally communicate his confirmation of what has been said and his recognition of the creative way in which it was said. In other words, when young Black males are discussing a "light" or humorous topic, the observer can expect a great deal of movement and fluctuation in the periphery of the circle of discussants.

Another non-verbal behavioral pattern easily noticed in Black male group discussion is the way males punctuate laughter. Often, when something especially funny is said by a Black, the audience (either one or more other Blacks who are in the audience or group) will raise a cupped hand to the mouth and laugh. The hand is not actually placed over the mouth; instead, it is held about six inches away from the mouth as if to muffle the laugh. Sometimes this action is accompanied by a backward shuffle. This action—the cupped hand in front of the mouth —is common among West Africans. The non-verbal message is that the audience has acknowledged the particularly witty statement of the speaker.

The above description of Black group discussion always applies to a topic being discussed that is not serious. When a serious topic is being discussed, these behavioral patterns are not present in the group's behavior. Thus, we know that the topic is light when the group is "jiving" or "styling" or just playing verbal games. (Blacks play a verbal game of using language in a unique, creative, humorous way for the purpose of seeing how they can "mess up" the English language for comical effects.)

The Black walk is also carried over into the "rapping stance" of young Black males. A "rapping stance" is the stance a young Black male takes when talking romantically to a young Black female. (The word "rap" originally referred only to romantic talk to a female. When it was adopted by the young white population, the word took on an added meaning, to refer to any kind of aggressive talk on any topic.) The "rapping stance" of young Black males is a kind of stationary "pimp strut". When young Black males are talking romantically to young Black females—particularly when they are making the initial "hit", or when they are making the initial romantic overtures to a Black female that preludes a romantic relationship—they stand a certain way that non-verbally communicates: "Look at me. I am somebody you can really "dig" because I am beautiful and I am about to lay my 'heavy rap' on you and you can't resist it. Now listen to my 'rap' and respond."

The "rapping stance" is as follows: first, the Black male does not stand directly in front of the Black female but at a slight angle; the head is slightly elevated and tipped to the side (toward the female); the eyes are about three-fourths open; sometimes, the head very slowly nods as the "rap" is delivered; the arms conform to the "pimp strut" pattern—one hand may be half-way in the pocket, while the other arm hangs free; finally, the weight of the body is concentrated on the back heel (in the "rapping stance" the feet are not together but are positioned in a kind of frozen step). The Black female will listen to this "rap" nonchalantly with one hand on her hip.

The young white male "rapping stance" is different: the female is backed up against the wall, while the young white male extends one arm, extends the fingers and places his palm against the wall to support himself as he leans toward the female with all his weight placed on the foot that is closest to the female. Sometimes, both arms are extended to support his weight, thus trapping the female between his two extended arms.

It has been pointed out that Black males often turn their backs to another participant in a communication situation. This action always communicates a very friendly intimate message. This action—turning one's back to another—can be observed when Black males greet each other. One of the most friendly greetings that can be given to another Black is to walk up to him and verbally greet him with a warm statement (often, this verbal statement is delivered in a falsetto voice, the friendly level or "game" level) and then, after the verbal greeting is delivered, one (or both) of the participants will turn his back to the other and walk away for a few steps. This is probably the friendliest greeting Black males can give to each other. The non-verbal message is probably: "Look, I trust you so much that I unhesitatingly place myself in a vulnerable position in greeting you."

Another pattern that is common when Black males greet each other is for one to approach the other person, verbally greet him, and then stand during the initial stages of the greeting with the one hand cupped over the genitals. This stance is sometimes maintained throughout the subsequent conversation, particularly if the subsequent conversation pertains to sexual exploits or some kind of behavior which is particularly masculine.

This stance—the cupped hand over the genitals—can even be observed, sometimes, when the young Black male is in his "rapping stance". The non-verbal message here is not clear; perhaps, the young Black male is communicating non-verbally that he is so sexually potent that he must subdue or "rein in" his sexual potential.

The action of turning one's back on another person in a group discussion or greeting always non-verbally communicates trust or friendliness. It also non-verbally communicates confirmation of what another Black has stated. For example, when one Black makes a statement that another Black particularly confirms, the Black who wants to non-verbally communicate his confirmation will turn his back to the other. Often, this action is preceded by a "slap" handshake—that is, both Blacks will execute the "soul" handshake that consists of one Black holding his palm in an upward position while the other Black slaps the palm with his own, usually in a vigorous manner.

Turning the back can often be seen in a Black audience. When listening to a speaker (a preacher, teacher, etc.) members of the Black audience will often shift their positions in their seats to slightly turn their backs to the speaker to non-verbally communicate confirmation and agreement with the speaker's remarks (before this action, members of the Black audience will slightly bend forward in their seats to non-verbally communicate that they are concerned about or perhaps not quite sure of what the speaker is saying. At that moment when they understand what the speaker is saying or they agree with the speaker, they will shift in their seats to slightly expose their backs).

It was indicated that when listening to a "rap" of a Black male a Black female will often stand with one hand on her hip. Whenever a Black female places one hand on her hip, it non-verbally communicates an intense involvement with or concern about the situation. But the hand-on-hip stance non-verbally communicates a more specific meaning in other communication situations: it usually communicates intense aggression, anger, disgust or other hostile negative feelings toward the speaker.

In a conflict situation, or when a Black female delivers a hostile verbal message, the verbal message is often accompanied by the hand-on-hip stance. This is the most aggressive stance that Black females take, and it is executed in the following manner: first, the feet are placed firmly in a stationary step, with the body weight concentrated on the heel of the rear foot; the buttocks are protruded; and, one hand is placed on the extended hip (the hip is extended because of the weight concentration on the rear foot and the protrusion of the buttocks); the hand either rests on the hip supported by the fingers being spread, or it is supported by making the hand into a fist and resting the knuckles against the hip. Sometimes, the body of the Black female will slowly rock to and fro during the stance, particularly while she is listening to the other person. If the stance is not taken while the Black female is listening, it is quickly taken when she delivers her hostile verbal message. The stance can also be accompanied by a rolling of the eyes and a twitching of the nose to further punctuate the hostility of the Black female. (Flip Wilson, in his Geraldine characterization, often assumes this stance. In fact, Flip Wilson is a very good illustrator of Black female non-verbal aggressive behavior because the behavior is distorted for comical effects and easily noticed.)

Most Black people know to "cool it" when Black women take this stance. The non-verbal message communicated when a Black female takes this stance is: "I'm really mad, now. You better quit messing with me." (Chicano females often stand with both hands on their hips with their feet spread wide and their heads slightly raised to non-verbally communicate a similar message.)

The non-verbal behavior described in this paper provides some illustrations of the non-verbal communication patterns of Black people that are different from those of white people and other cultural groups in this country. *Why* they are different is a question that must be answered by research. The purpose here, again, has not been to explain the *why,* but to describe some of these patterns that are different. Hypotheses were presented to provide a basis on which this research can be conducted.

It is important (particularly, for people who work with Blacks—school teachers, social workers, industry personnel) to recognize these patterns and the messages they convey because it helps one to better understand the communications of Black people. In some ways, non-verbal communication patterns are more important than verbal communication patterns because they are often unconscious—a person cannot easily hide his true feelings when this is the case. The importance of non-verbal communication is indicated in the adage: "Your actions speak so loudly, I can hardly hear what you say."

Cultural Patterning of Tactile Experiences
Lawrence K. Frank

Cultures differ in the kind, amount, and duration of tactile experiences people give the infant. Thus the parents in each culture activate or limit initial tactile communication with the infant and provide such tactile communication in and through the patterns and relationships which are prescribed or permitted by tradition (4).

Since it is impossible to give an adequate statement of this cultural patterning of tactile experiences in this paper, the focus will be upon those tactile approaches and responses which seem to be more significant in human communication, remembering that at every moment the individual is communicating with the environment, receiving tactile stimuli and responding thereto more or less automatically or without awareness (e.g., pressure on sole of feet, on buttocks, changing atmospheric pressures, wind, etc.).

Thus we should note that color of skin is highly significant as a message which serves as a visual identification. While skin color is visual, it elicits responses which are often tactile, in the sense of avoiding contacts or in evoking approaches and contacts which would be inappropriate or prohibited to a person of another skin color. Insofar as an infant may have a nurse of another skin color, and young children apparently play together with little or no awareness of differ-

From *Genetic Psychology Monographs,* Vol. 56 (1957) pp. 209–225. Reprinted by permission of The Journal Press and the author's estate. The author was the late Director of the Caroline Zachry Institute for Human Development.

ences in skin color, these discriminatory responses to skin color may be considered as patterned. But within a group of people with similar skin color, there may be degrees of acceptance and rejection, of approval and dislike, as in the light-dark skin of Negroes, the blonde versus brunette, etc.

The skin has many potentialities, some of which are actively recognized, cultivated, refined or coarsened, and selectively utilized by each culture. The exposure of the skin is the most obvious patterning of tactile experiences since the amount and kind of clothing, the covering of specific parts, genitals, breasts, face, and exposure of hands, legs, navel, etc., differ widely and may alter according to the time, place, and occasion, e.g., ceremonial appearance, masks and headgear may also be used to disguise the skin and provide a different kind of communication according to rôle.

The body arts, which include all the varied kinds of ornamenting, painting, tattooing, incising, use of cosmetics generally, are significant as ways of enhancing the appearance of the skin or intensifying tactile communication where the skin and its decorations serve as messages which are then perceived visually as a sign or symbol, or sometimes as a signal to evoke a direct physiological response.

Grooming the skin, bathing of all kinds, anointing, oiling, perfuming the skin, plucking hair, shaving, are patterns for modifying communication by the skin, again relying upon visual cues to indicate tactual readiness for communication (actual or symbolic). Such grooming and decorating may also serve as signs of rank, caste, prestige, authority which others recognize and respond to with appropriate conduct. Indeed, these skin decorations and coverings are of large significance in the assumption and performance of the various roles when not only the individual assuming a rôle must act in a prescribed manner, but others must respond appropriately if the rôle performance is to be completed. Here the skin serves like a carrier wave upon which the particular message is imposed as a modification or patterning of that wave, as in telephoning.

Thus admiring glances, indicating approval of the individual's clothing, body arts, and grooming, serve as surrogates for invitations to actual tactile contacts. This is often elaborated in the customary public exhibition of the self through which courtship is conducted openly and directly, or indirectly as in public strolling or dancing.

The masculine and feminine roles are defined in large part by these different patterns of exposure of skin, body arts, clothing, grooming, and the kinds of tactile approaches and contacts allowed or forbidden to the male and female. Since masculinity and femininity are more or less polarized positions and relations which the boy and girl must learn, each may develop a kind of complementary tactile communication in which the intent may be, not primarily to transmit a message, but to evoke a response by a variety of tactual approaches or exhibition of signs and symbols of tactile significance. If these responses are evoked, then the initiator may offer more direct tactile communications, with degree of intimacy of direct tactual contacts.

It is significant, too, that the dead may be decorated and anointed (sacramental oils), and that bathing the feet has been a traditional ceremony of hospitality to the strangers.

Each cultural group has a conception of the skin and of tactile experiences which may not be explicitly recognized or stated, but is implied in its prescriptions for covering, exposing, decorating, making and avoiding tactile communication. Thus, modesty, in the sense of covering certain portions of the body and prohibiting or approving even symbolic tactile communication, with shame for violation of these prescriptions, blushing or pallor when discovered, are forms of tactile communications which serve to maintain the social order by regulating human conduct and especially interpersonal communication.

The patterning of direct tactile communication may be considered as one of the early and most significant social inventions (2). Among most infra-human species (apart from social insects), the individual can have and can keep his own food, lair, nesting place, etc., only by incessant vigilance, warding off intruders by force, or show of violence or by auditory signals like bird calls. Likewise, the individual organism may enjoy little or no personal safety and freedom from attack or invasion except by continual defensive-offensive activity to repel attackers. This exposure to other approach may be limited in herds or other animal aggregations where the individual is merged in the group and acts as a constituent member of the aggregate.

The establishment of inviolability of things and the person under penalties for unsanctioned approach made social order possible since each member of the group became the guardian of all others' property and person. Each child learns to respect these inviolabilities by refraining from approaching, touching, striking, taking or otherwise invading the private property or the person of others, or the sacred places or objects, always as defined by his culture. Since these inviolabilities are barriers to tactile contacts as well as motor approaches, we may consider private property and the sanctity or integrity of the person as forms of patterned tactile communication. Each object, animal, place, and person gives off a variety of cues, visual, auditory, which have become established initially through tactile contacts, or signs and symbols to which each member of the group exhibits the learned conduct of avoidance.

These lessons in recognizing and respecting the inviolability of objects and persons occur early in life when the child first explores the world, touching, taking, handling whatever he can reach. While learning this space-time orientation, he is blocked, diverted, often punished, with verbal admonitions to stop, "don't touch," etc. Gradually the child transforms these parental prohibitions into self-administered inhibitions by learning to perceive things and persons as signs or symbols for avoidance. His formerly eager exploratory touching is relinquished and he now responds with the prescribed conduct of avoidance when no adult is present to stop him or caution him. As he grows older, he learns to employ the group-sanctioned ceremonies, rituals, symbols for approaching persons, relying upon negotiating, barter, sale, contract, courtship, seduction, marriage, for setting aside the inviolability of the object, animal, or person with which he seeks to make direct tactual contacts or to establish tactual communication of intimacy.

Probably the most widely occurring and most rigidly maintained culture inviolability is the incest taboo which again may be violated, as we know, but is usually accepted and upheld not only by the law and threats of punishment, but by the learned conduct of avoidance that is established in the child. This incest taboo is a uniquely human cultural pattern since among infra-human mammals it does not seem to appear and in human breeding of domestic animals this taboo is deliberately violated in order to maintain certain hereditary strains.

Here we see very clearly how early tactile experiences provide the bases for transformation into learned symbolic conduct and participating in social order. It is as if the child who naïvely responds to the tactile communication received from objects and persons learns to recognize these provocative objects or persons as emitting a communication to negative action or inhibition. Instead of "come on," their message is now "don't touch me," which indicates that the child has a new awareness or altered perception of the world and has developed a pattern of conduct which is relevant and appropriate to that new perception. This is usually called repression, as if it were wholly "internalized," but obviously involves communications from things and persons. The wide array of property rights and of inviolability of persons according to kinship, rank, caste, age, marital, occupational, and professional status may be seen as transformations or elaborations of the basic tactile communications which each culture has utilized in its own way for maintaining its traditional way of life (3).

It would take too much time and space to do more than mention the cultural patterning of person-to-person tactile communications, such as handshake, with removal of glove, close contacts in social dancing which are not permitted elsewhere, rubbing of noses or foreheads or cheeks, clasping of arms around shoulders or waist, embracing the knees, and all the varied other tactile-motor contacts which have been established as signs or symbols for interpersonal communication. Kissing among some people has a special significance of intimacy and affection but it is prohibited by others. The laying on of hands as a ceremonial ritual for transmission of authority or of special powers and healing, such as the shaman touching the body, the king's touch as a cure of skin diseases, are also to be noted. Then too each culture sets certain patterns of what kinds of tactile experiences, especially pain, individuals must learn to accept, such as spanking a child, slapping the face or toleration of pain in fire walking, lying on a bed of nails, gashing and scarifying the skin and genitals in initiation ceremonies or ritual performances, stoical acceptance of sharpened objects in the skin (Plains Indians) and the exposure of the skin to heat and extreme cold (Indian all face!).

Likewise it is to be remembered that the elaboration and refinement of erotic arts, as portrayed, for example, in the Kama Sutra and similar manuals, provide a variety of practices for tactile stimulation of various parts of the body, especially the genitals and erogenous zones, but also of concomitant stimuli, pressure, often painful, with rhythmic patterns designed to build up to an intense climax of orgasm, or prolonged non-consummating intercourse, such as the Karezza of the original Oneida community. Caressing and manual, digital manipulation is usually associated with intercourse.

The stimulation of the genitals either by the individual or by others may be accepted and encouraged by some groups who manipulate the infant's genitals, and prohibited by others who may punish even a baby for such activity. Communication with the self by masturbation is probably universal, but sanctioned only by some. Other forms of tactile communication with the self are exhibited in various tics, and rubbing or patting areas of skin or hair, scratching, pressing against objects and utilizing various forms of bathing. In medicine the physician usually examines the patient by touching him, exploring for tender spots, for painful areas, for the various signs of neurological disorders such as disturbed reflexes, e.g., patellar, Babinski. Therapy may involve tactile manipulation as in osteopathic treatment and physical medicine. Massage or other manipulation of the body involving tactile contacts are also frequent and may be the focus of professional practices.

Each culture fosters or specifically trains its young as children and as adolescents to develop different kinds of thresholds to tactile contacts and stimulation so that their organic, constitutional, temperamental characteristics are accentuated or reduced. As adults they are more susceptible and vulnerable, or are anesthetic and indifferent to various kinds of tactile communications, as is evidenced by the clinical material on the number and variety of tactual idiosyncrasies, including sexual. Moreover, each culture builds upon the early tactile experience of the infant and child a more or less elaborate series of patterns of adult conduct in which tactile surrogates and symbolic fulfillments are provided.

We may say, therefore, that tactile experiences seem to be basic to many of the crucially important patterns of a culture, that tactile communication takes place on the level of signals, direct tactual stimulation, and on the level of signs and symbols which have been established as surrogates for tactile communications, both for sending and receiving. As in other forms of communication, tactile communication is highly susceptible to interference by noise (any kind of disturbance in transmission, or confusion and conflict in sender or receiver), is peculiarly ambiguous, often redundant and liable to frequent errors in coding and decoding. Without tactile communication, interpersonal relations would be bare and largely meaningless, with a minimum of affective coloring or emotional provocation, since linguistic and much of kinesic communication are signs and symbols which become operative only by evoking some of the responses which were initially stimulated by the tactile stimuli for which these signs and symbols are surrogates. Tactile communications are largely reciprocal transactions between two persons, each of whom in responding to the other, provides the stimulus for a response to him that will in turn initiate his response in a tactile dialectic of greater or less duration. These interpersonal communications may become increasingly symbolic as individuals learn to use words and gestures for sending and receiving such messages as culturally patterned (1).

Severing tactile communications, especially those which have involved intimacy, often creates a crisis for one or both participants for which some cultures provide rituals, ceremonies, and special sanctions (such as legal separation or divorce), or puberty rites. Likewise, as indicated earlier, specific rituals, like betrothal and marriage, are provided in some cultures as public sanction for establishing tactile communications, while others permit premarital relations which eventually lead to marriage.

In ritual and ceremonial activities, the tactile communications play a large rôle, but often on a symbolic level where there is no actual tactile contact, but every action implies or indicates as in the dance some tactile communication, a threat or invitation, and its patterned response. This is apparent in much of the kinesic activity and communication and in linguistic communication where the message may originate in a tactile context, be coded in verbal symbols, and decoded into tactile experiences.

The elaboration and refinement of cultures may be interpreted in part as the provision of signs and symbols as surrogates for tactile communications which, being more elementary and ambiguous, are superseded by more discriminatory symbols, just as writing offers more scope and subtlety than hieroglyphics or a rebus. Abstractions, concepts, generalizations would seem to be impossible through tactile communication, but tactile experiences transformed into signs and symbols may become abstracted and conceptualized as in finger language used by the blind, as Helen Keller has shown.

It should be emphasized that the establishment of signs and symbols has been a very difficult and often precarious undertaking. Every culture has been dependent upon gifted individuals who could perceive the world in new ways and imaginatively create the symbols which then were accepted and utilized by others. Since this is the kind of world in which many events are occurring more or less simultaneously, and every event, object, and animal appears in a context of greater or less complexity (5) that is, with many other existents, it is not at all easy or simple to recognize which particular signal belongs to or is emitted by a specific event, object, or animal to be identified. We speak of data, which literally means that which is given, but the whole history of science shows that these so-called data or signals are rarely or ever given; they must be laboriously and often painfully discovered, isolated, and established as unequivocal indicators of whatever is the focus of inquiry. Indeed, we might say that the progress of science takes place in large part through the recognition that what have been considered as valid data are not reliable and unequivocal indicators and must be replaced by other indicators that seem to be more nearly reliable signals.

References

1. Bateson, G., and M. Mead. *Balinese Character.* New York: Academy of Sciences, 1941.
2. Frank, L. K. "Concept of Inviolability in Culture." *Amer. J. Sociol.,* 1931, 36, 607–615.
3. Hallowell, I. "The Self and the Behavioral Environment." In *Culture and Experience.* Philadelphia: Univ. Pennsylvania Press, 1955.
4. Mead, M., and F. C. MacGregor. *Growth and Culture.* New York: Putnam's, 1951.
5. Weaver, W. "Science and Complexity." *Amer. Sci.,* 1948, 36, 536–544.

Time and Cool People

John Horton

Street culture exists in every low income ghetto. It is shared by the hustling elements of the poor, whatever their nationality or color. In Los Angeles, members of such street groups sometimes call themselves "street people," "cool people," or simply "regulars." Whatever the label, they are known the world over by outsiders as hoods or hoodlums, persons who live on and off the street. They are recognizable by their own fashions in dress, hair, gestures, and speech. The particular fashion varies with time, place, and nationality. For example, in 1963 a really sharp Los Angeles street Negro would be "conked to the bone" (have processed hair) and "togged-out" in "continentials." Today "natural" hair and variations of mod clothes are coming in style.

Street people are known also by their activities—"duking" (fighting or at least looking tough), "hustling" (any way of making money outside the "legitimate" world of work), "gigging" (partying)—and by their apparent nonactivity, "hanging" on the corner. Their individual roles are defined concretely by their success or failure in these activities. One either knows "what's happening" on the street, or he is a "lame," "out of it," "not ready" (lacks his diploma in street knowledge), a "square."

There are, of course, many variations. Negroes, in particular, have contributed much to the street tongue which has diffused into both the more hip areas of the middle class and the broader society. Such expressions as "a lame," "taking care of righteous business," "getting down to the nitty-gritty," and "soul" can be retraced to Negro street life.

The more or less organized center of street life is the "set"—meaning both the peer group and the places where it hangs out. It is the stage and central market place for activity, where to find out what's happening. My set of Negro street types contained a revolving and sometimes disappearing (when the "heat," or police pressure, was on) population of about 45 members ranging in age from 18 to 25. These were the local "dudes," their term meaning not the fancy city slickers but simply "the boys," "fellas," and "cool people." They represented the hard core of street culture, the role models for younger teenagers. The dudes could be found when they were "laying dead"—hanging on the corner, or shooting pool and "jiving" ("goofing" or kidding around) in a local community project. Isolated from "the man" (in this context the man in power—the police, and by extension, the white man), they lived in a small section of Venice outside the central Los Angeles ghetto and were surrounded by a predominantly Mexican and Anglo population. They called their black "turf" "Ghost-town"—home of the "ghost-

From *Trans-action*, Vol. 5, pp. 5–11. Copyright © April 1967 by Transaction, Inc., New Brunswick, New Jersey. Reprinted by permission of the author and the publisher. Professor Horton is with the Department of Sociology, University of California at Los Angles.

men," their former gang. Whatever the origin of the word, Ghost-town was certainly the home of socially "invisible" men.

The Street Set

The set can be described by the social and attitudinal characteristics of its members. To the observer, these are expressed in certain realities of day to day living: not enough skill for good jobs, and the inevitable trouble brought by the problem of surviving. Of the 25 interviewed, only four had graduated from high school. Except for a younger set member who was still in school, all were dropouts, or perhaps more accurately kicked-outs. None was really able to use or write formal language. However, many were highly verbal, both facile and effective in their use of the street tongue. Perhaps the art of conversation is most highly developed here where there is much time to talk, perhaps too much—an advantage of the *lumpen*-leisure class.

Their incomes were difficult to estimate, as "bread" or "coins" (money) came in on a very irregular basis. Of the 17 for whom I have figures, half reported that they made less than $1,400 in the last year, and the rest claimed income from $2,000–4,000 annually. Two-thirds were living with and partially dependent on their parents, often a mother. The financial strain was intensified by the fact that although 15 of 17 were single, eight had one or more children living in the area. (Having children, legitimate or not, was not a stigma but proof of masculinity).

At the time of the interview, two-thirds of them had some full- or part-time employment—unskilled and low-paid jobs. The overall pattern was one of sporadic and—from their viewpoint—often unsatisfactory work, followed by a period of unemployment compensation, and petty hustling whenever possible and whenever necessary.

When I asked the question, "When a dude needs bread, how does he get it?" the universal response was "the hustle." Hustling is, of course, illegitimate from society's viewpoint. Street people know it is illegal, but they view it in no way as immoral or wrong. It is justified by the necessity of surviving. As might be expected, the unemployed admitted that they hustled and went so far as to say that a dude could make it better on the street than on the job: "There is a lot of money on the street, and there are many ways of getting it," or simply, "This has always been my way of life." On the other hand, the employed, the part-time hustlers, usually said, "A dude could make it better on the job than on the street." Their reasons for disapproving of hustling were not moral. Hustling meant trouble. "I don't hustle because there's no security. You eventually get busted." Others said there was not enough money on the street or that it was too difficult to "run a game" on people.

Nevertheless, hustling is the central street activity. It is the economic foundation for everyday life. Hustling and the fruit of hustling set the rhythm of social activities.

What are the major forms of hustling in Ghost-town? The best hustles were conning, stealing, gambling, and selling dope. By gambling, these street people meant dice; by dope, peddling "pills" and "pot." Pills are "reds" and "whites" —barbiturates and benzedrine or dexedrine. Pot is, of course, marijuana— "grass" or "weed." To "con" means to put "the bump" on a "cat," to "run a game" on somebody, to work on his mind for goods and services.

The "woman game" was common. As one dude put it, "If I have a good lady and she's on County, there's always some money to get." In fact, there is a local expression for getting county money. When the checks come in for child support, it's "mother's day." So the hustler "burns" people for money, but he also "rips off" goods for money; he thieves, and petty thieving is always a familiar hustle. Pimping is often the hustler's dream of the good life, but it was almost unknown here among the small-time hustlers. That was the game of the real professional and required a higher level of organization and wealth.

Hustling means bread and security but also trouble, and trouble is a major theme in street life. The dudes had a "world of trouble" (a popular song about a hustler is "I'm in a World of Trouble")—with school, jobs, women, and the police. The intensity of street life could be gauged in part by the intensity of the "heat" (police trouble). The hotter the street, the fewer the people visible on the street. On some days the set was empty. One would soon learn that there had been a "bust" (an arrest). Freddy had run amok and thrown rocks at a police car. There had been a leadership struggle; "Big Moe" had been cut up, and the "fuzz" had descended. Life was a succession of being picked up on suspicion of assault, theft, possession, "suspicion of suspicion" (an expression used by a respondent in describing his life). This was an ordinary experience for the street dude and often did lead to serious trouble. Over half of those interviewed claimed they had felony convictions.

The Structure of Street Time

Keeping cool and out of trouble, hustling bread, and looking for something interesting and exciting to do created the structure of time on the street. The rhythm of time is expressed in the high and low points in the day and week of an unemployed dude. I stress the pattern of the unemployed and full-time hustler because he is on the street all day and night and is the prototype in my interviews. The sometimes employed will also know the pattern, and he will be able to hit the street whenever released from the bondage of jail, work, and the clock. Here I describe a typical time schedule gleaned through interviews and field observation.

Characteristically the street person gets up late, hits the street in the late morning or early afternoon, and works his way to the set. This is a place for relaxed social activity. Hanging on the set with the boys is the major way of passing time and waiting until some necessary or desirable action occurs. Nevertheless, things do happen on the set. The dudes "rap" and "jive" (talk), gamble, and drink their "pluck" (usually a cheap, sweet wine). They find out what happened yesterday, what is happening today, and what will hopefully happen

on the weekend—the perpetual search for the "gig," the party. Here peer socialization and reinforcement also take place. The younger dude feels a sense of pride
when he can be on the set and throw a rap to an older dude. He is learning how
to handle himself, show respect, take care of business, and establish his own
"rep."

On the set, yesterday merges into today, and tomorrow is an emptiness to
be filled in through the pursuit of bread and excitement. Bread makes possible
the excitement—the high (getting loaded with wine, pills, or pot), the sharp
clothes, the "broad," the fight, and all those good things which show that one
knows what's happening and has "something going" for himself. The rhythm
of time—of the day and of the week—is patterned by the flow of money and
people.

Time is "dead" when money is tight, when people are occupied elsewhere—
working or in school. Time is dead when one is in jail. One is "doing dead time"
when nothing is happening, and he's got nothing going for himself.

Time is alive when and where there is action. It picks up in the evening when
everyone moves on the street. During the regular school year it may pick up for
an hour in the afternoon when the "broads" leave school and meet with the set
at the corner taco joint. Time may pick up when a familiar car cruises by and
a few dudes drive down to Johnny's for a "process" (hair straightening and
styling). Time is low on Monday (as described in the popular song, "Stormy
Monday"), Tuesday, Wednesday, when money is tight. Time is high on Friday
nights when the "eagle flies" and the "gig" begins. On the street, time has a
personal meaning only when something is happening, and something is most
likely to happen at night—especially on Friday and Saturday nights. Then people
are together, and there may be bread—bread to take and bread to use.

Human behavior is rational if it helps the individual to get what he wants
whether it is success in school or happiness in the street. Street people sometimes
get what they want. They act rationally in those situations where they are able
to plan and choose because they have control, knowledge, and concern, irratio-
nally where there are barriers to their wants and desires.

When the street dude lacks knowledge and power to manipulate time, he is
indeed irrational. For the most part, he lacks the skills and power to plan a move
up and out of the ghetto. He is "a lame" in the middle class world of school and
work; he is not ready to operate effectively in unfamiliar organizations where his
street strengths are his visible weakness. Though irrational in moving up and out
of the street, he can be rational in day to day survival in the street. No one survives
there unless he knows what's happening (that is, unless he knows what is available, where to get what he can without being burned or busted). More euphemistically, this is "taking advantage of opportunities," exactly what the rational
member of the middle class does in his own setting.

To know what's happening is to know the goods and the bads, the securities,
the opportunities, and the dangers of the street. Survival requires that a hustling
dude know who is cool and uncool (who can be trusted); who is in power (the
people who control narcotics, fences, etc.); who is the "duker" or the fighter
(someone to be avoided or someone who can provide protection). When one

knows what's happening he can operate in many scenes, providing that he can "hold his mud," keep cool, and out of trouble.

With his diploma in street knowledge, a dude can use time efficiently and with cunning in the pursuit of goods and services—in hustling to eat and yet have enough bread left over for the pleasures of pot, the chicks, and the gig. As one respondent put it, "The good hustler has the know-how, the ambition to better himself. He conditions his mind and must never put his guard too far down, to relax, or he'll be taken." This is street rationality. The problem is not a deficient sense of time but deficient knowledge and control to make a fantasy future and a really better life possible.

The petty hustler more fully realizes the middle class ideal of individualistic rationality than does the middle class itself. When rationality operates in hustling, it is often on an individual basis. In a world of complex organization, the hustler defines himself as an entrepreneur; and indeed, he is the last of the competitive entrepreneurs.

The degree of organization in hustling depends frequently on the kind of hustling. Regular pimping and pushing require many trusted contacts and organization. Regular stealing requires regular fences for hot goods. But in Ghosttown when the hustler moved, he usually moved alone and on a small scale. His success was on him. He could not depend on the support of some benevolent organization. Alone, without a sure way of running the same game twice, he must continually recalculate conditions and people and find new ways of taking or be taken himself. The phrase "free enterprise for the poor and socialism for the rich" applies only too well in the streets. The political conservative should applaud all that individual initiative.

Clock Time vs. Personal Time

Negro street time is built around the irrelevance of clock time, white man's time, and the relevance of street values and activities. Like anyone else, a street dude is on time by the standard clock whenever he wants to be, not on time when he does not want to be and does not have to be.

When the women in school hit the street at the lunch hour and he wants to throw them a rap, he will be there then and not one hour after they have left. But he may be kicked out of high school for truancy or lose his job for being late and unreliable. He learned at an early age that school and job were neither interesting nor salient to his way of life. A regular on the set will readily admit being crippled by a lack of formal education. Yet school was a "bum kick." It was not his school. The teachers put him down for his dress, hair, and manners. As a human being he has feelings of pride and autonomy, the very things most threatened in those institutional situations where he was or is the underdeveloped, unrespected, illiterate, and undeserving outsider. Thus whatever "respectable" society says will help him, he knows oppresses him, and he retreats to the streets for security and a larger degree of personal freedom. Here his control reaches a maximum, and he has the kind of autonomy which many middle class males might envy.

In the street, watches have a special and specific meaning. Watches are for pawning and not for telling time. When they are worn, they are decorations and ornaments of status. The street clock is informal, personal, and relaxed. It is not standardized nor easily synchronized to other clocks. In fact, a street dude may have almost infinite toleration for individual time schedules. To be on time is often meaningless, to be late an unconsciously accepted way of life. "I'll catch you later," or simply "later," are the street phrases that mean business will be taken care of, but not necessarily now.

Large areas of street life run on late time. For example, parties are not cut off by some built-in alarm clock of appointments and schedules. At least for the unemployed, standard time neither precedes nor follows the gig. Consequently, the action can take its course. It can last as long as interest is sustained and die by exhaustion or by the intrusion of some more interesting event. A gig may endure all night and well into another day. One of the reasons for the party assuming such time dimensions is purely economic. There are not enough cars and enough money for individual dates, so everyone converges in one place and takes care of as much business as possible there, that is, doing whatever is important at the time—sex, presentation of self, hustling.

Colored People's Time

Events starting late and lasting indefinitely are clearly street and class phenomena, not some special trait of Afro-Americans. Middle class Negroes who must deal with the organization and coordination of activities in church and elsewhere will jokingly and critically refer to a lack of standard time sense when they say that Mr. Jones arrived "CPT" (colored people's time). They have a word for it, because being late is a problem for people caught between two worlds and confronted with the task of meshing standard and street time. In contrast, the street dudes had no self-consciousness about being late; with few exceptions they had not heard the expression CPT. (When I questioned members of a middle class Negro fraternity, a sample matched by age to the street set, only three of the 25 interviewed could not define CPT. Some argued vehemently that CPT was the problem to be overcome).

Personal time as expressed in parties and other street activities is not simply deficient knowledge and use of standard time. It is a positive adaptation to generations of living whenever and wherever possible outside of the sound and control of the white man's clock. The personal clock is an adaptation to the chance and accidental character of events on the street and to the very positive value placed on emotion and feeling. (For a discussion of CPT which is close to some of the ideas presented here, see Jules Henry, "White People's Time, Colored People's Time," *Trans-action,* March/April 1965).

Chance reinforces personal time. A dude must be ready on short notice to move "where the action is." His internal clock may not be running at all when he is hanging on the corner and waiting for something to do. It may suddenly speed up by chance: Someone cruises by in a car and brings a nice "stash" of "weed," a gig is organized and he looks forward to being well togged-out and throwing a rap to some "boss chick," or a lame appears and opens himself to a quick "con." Chance as a determinant of personal time can be called more accurately *uncertain predictability.* Street life is an aggregate of relatively independent events. A dude may not know exactly what or when something will happen, but from past experience he can predict a range of possibilities, and he will be ready, in position, and waiting.

In white middle class stereotypes and fears—and in reality—street action is highly expressive. A forthright yet stylized expression of emotion is positively evaluated and most useful. Street control and communication are based on personal power and the direct impingement of one individual on another. Where there is little property, status in the set is determined by personal qualities of mind and brawn.

The Variety of Time

Time in industrial society is clock time. It seems to be an external, objective regulator of human activities. But for the sociologist, time is not an object existing independent of man, dividing his day into precise units. Time is diverse; it is always social and subjective. A man's sense of time derives from his place in the social structure and his lived experience.

The diversity of time perspectives can be understood intellectually—but it is rarely tolerated socially. A dominant group reifies and objectifies its time; it views all other conceptions of time as subversive—as indeed they are.

Thus, today in the dominant middle class stereotype, standard American time is directed to the future; it is rational and impersonal. In contrast, time for the lower class is directed to the present, irrational and personal. Peasants, Mexican-Americans, Negroes, Indians, workers are "lazy"; they do not possess the American virtues of ambition and striving for success. Viewed solely from the dominant class norm of rationality, their presumed orientation to present time is seen only as an irrational deviation, something to be controlled and changed. It is at best an epiphenomenon produced in reaction to the "real, objective" phenomenon of middle class time.

Sociologists have not been completely exempt from this kind of reified thinking. When they universalize the middle class value of rational action and future time and turn it into a "neutral" social fact, they reinforce a negative stereotype: Lower classes are undependendable in organized work situations (they seek immediate rewards and cannot defer gratification); in their political action, they are prone to accept immediate, violent, and extreme solutions to personal problems; their sense of time is dysfunctional to the stability of the economic and political orders. For example, Seymour Martin Lipset writes in a paper significantly entitled "Working Class Authoritarianism":

> This emphasis on the immediately perceivable and concern with the personal and concrete is part and parcel of the short time perspective and the inability to perceive the complex possibilities and consequences of action which often results in a general readiness to support extremist political and religious movements, and generally lower level of liberalism on noneconomic questions.

To examine time in relation to the maintenance or destruction of the dominant social order is an interesting political problem, but it is not a sociology of time; it is a middle class sociology of order or change in its time aspect. Surely, a meaningful sociology of time should take into account the social situation in which time operates and the actor's as well as the observer's perspective. The sociologist must at

The importance of emotion and expression appears again and again in street tongue and ideology. When asked, "How does a dude make a rep on the set?" over half of the sample mentioned "style," and all could discuss the concept. Style is difficult to define as it has so many referents. It means to carry one's self well, dress well, to show class. In the ideology of the street, it may be a way of behaving. One has style if he is able to dig people as they are. He doesn't put them down for what they do. He shows toleration. But a person with style must also show respect. That means respect for a person as he is, and since there is power in the street, respect for another's superior power. Yet one must show respect in such a way that he is able to look tough and inviolate, fearless, secure, "cool."

Style may also refer to the use of gestures in conversation or in dance. It may be expressed in the loose walk, the jivey or dancing walk, the slow cool walk, the way one "chops" or makes it" down the street. It may be the loose, relaxed hand

---

least entertain the idea that lower class time may be a phenomenon in and of itself, and quite functional to the life problems of that class.

Of course, there are dangers in seeking the viewpoint of a minority: The majority stereotypes might be reversed. For example, we might find out that no stereotype is more incorrect than that which depicts the lower classes as having no sense of future time. As Max Weber has observed, it is the powerful and not the powerless who are present-oriented. Dominant groups live by maintaining and expanding their present. Minority groups survive in this present, but their survival is nourished by a dream of the future. In "Ethnic Segregation and Caste" Weber says:

"The sense of dignity that characterizes positively privileged status groups is natural to their "being" which does not transcend itself, that is, to their beauty and excellence. Their kingdom is of this world. They live for the present by exploiting the great past. The sense of dignity of the negatively privileged strata naturally refers to a future lying beyond the present whether it is of this life or another. In other words it must be nurtured by a belief in a providential "mission" and by a belief in a specific honor before God."

It is time to re-examine the meaning of time, the reality of the middle class stereo-

type of itself, as well as the middle class stereotype of the lower class. In this article I explore the latter: the meaning of time among a group most often stereotyped as having an irrational, present sense of time —the sporadically unemployed young Negro street corner population. I choose the unemployed because they live outside of the constraints of industrial work time; Negroes because they speak some of the liveliest street language, including that of time; young males because the street culture of the unemployed and the hustler is young and masculine.

To understand the meaning of street time was to discover "what's happening" in the day-to-day and week-to-week activities of my respondents. Using the middle class stereotype of lower class time as a point of departure, I asked myself the following questions:

In what sense is street time personal (not run by the clock) and present oriented?

What kind of future orientation, if any, exists?

Are street activities really irrational in the sense that individuals do not use time efficiently in the business of living?

I have attempted to answer the questions in the language and from the experience of my respondents.

rap or hand slap, the swinger's greeting which is used also in the hip middle class teen sets. There are many refined variations of the hand rap. As a greeting, one may simply extend his hand, palm up. Another slaps it loosely with his finger. Or, one person may be standing with his hand behind and palm up. Another taps the hand in passing, and also pays his respect verbally with the conventional greeting "What's happening, Brother." Or, in conversation, the hand may be slapped when an individual has "scored," has been "digging," has made a point, has got through to the person.

Style is a comparatively neutral value compared to "soul." Soul can be many things—a type of food (good food is "soul food," a "bowl of soul"), music, a quality of mind, a total way of acting (in eating, drinking, dancing, walking, talking, relating to others, etc.). The person who acts with soul acts directly and honestly from his heart. He feels it and tells it "like it is." One respondent identified soul with ambition and drive. He said the person with soul, once he makes up his mind, goes directly to the goal, doesn't change his mind, doesn't wait and worry about messing up a little. Another said soul was getting down to the nitty-gritty, that is, moving directly to what is basic without guise and disguise. Thus soul is the opposite of hypocrisy, deceit, and phoniness, the opposite of "affective neutrality," and "instrumentality." Soul is simply whatever is considered beautiful, honest, and virtuous in men.

Most definitions tied soul directly to Negro experience. As one hustler put it, "It is the ability to survive. We've made it with so much less. Soul is the Negro who has the spirit to sing in slavery to overcome the monotony." With very few exceptions, the men interviewed argued that soul was what Negroes had and whites did not. Negroes were "soul brothers," warm and emotional—whites cold as ice. Like other oppressed minorities these street Negroes believed they had nothing except their soul and their humanity, and that this made them better than their oppressors.

The Personal Dream

Soul is anchored in a past and present of exploitation and deprivation, but are there any street values and activities which relate to the future? The regular in the street set has no providential mission; he lives personally and instrumentally in the present, yet he dreams about the day when he will get himself together and move ahead to the rewards of a good job, money, and a family. Moreover, the personal dream coexists with a nascent political nationalism, the belief that Negroes can and will make it as Negroes. His present-future time is a combination of contradictions and developing possibilities. Here I will be content to document without weighing two aspects of his orientation: *fantasy personal future* and *fantasy collective future*. I use the word fantasy because street people have not yet the knowledge and means and perhaps the will to fulfill their dreams. It is hard enough to survive by the day.

When the members of the set were asked, "What do you really want out of life?" their responses were conventional, concrete, seemingly realistic, and—given their skills—rather hopeless. Two-thirds of the sample mentioned material aspirations—the finer things in life, a home, security, a family. For example, one said, in honest street language, "I want to get things for my kids and to make sure they have a father." Another said, jokingly, "a good future, a home, two or three girls living with me." Only one person didn't know, and the others deviated a little from the material response. They said such things as "for everyone to be on friendly terms—a better world . . . then I could get all I wish," "to be free," "to help people."

But if most of the set wanted money and security, they wanted it on their own terms. As one put it, "I don't want to be in a middle class bag, but I would like a nice car, home, and food in the icebox." He wanted the things and the comforts of middle class life, but not the hypocrisy, the venality, the coldness, the being forced to do what one does not want to do. All that was in the middle class bag. Thus the home and the money may be ends in themselves, but also fronts, security for carrying on the usual street values. Street people believed that they already had something that was valuable and looked down upon the person who made it and moved away into the middle class world. For the observer, the myths are difficult to separate from the truths—here where the truths are so bitter. One can only say safely that street people dream of a high status, and they really do not know how to get it.

The Collective Future

The Negro dudes are political outsiders by the usual poll questions. They do not vote. They do not seek out civil rights demonstrations. They have very rudimentary knowledge of political organization. However, about the age of 18, when fighting and being tough are less important than before, street people begin to discuss their position in society. Verbally they care very much about the politics of race and the future of the Negro. The topic is always a ready catalyst for a soul session.

The political consciousness of the street can be summarized by noting those interview questions which attracted at least a 75 percent rate of agreement. The typical respondent was angry. He approves of the Watts incident, although from his isolated corner of the city he did not actively participate. He knows something about the history of discrimination and believes that if something isn't done soon America can expect violence: "What this country needs is a revolutionary change." He is more likely to praise the leadership of Malcolm X than Lyndon Johnson, and he is definitely opposed to the Vietnam war. The reason for his opposition is clear. Why fight for a country which is not mine, when the fight is here?

Thus his racial consciousness looks to the future and a world where he will not have to stand in the shadow of the white man. But his consciousness has neither clear plan nor political commitment. He has listened to the Muslims, and he is not a black nationalist. True, the Negro generally has more soul than the white. He thinks differently, his women may be different, yet integration is preferable to separatism. Or, more accurately, he doesn't quite understand what all these terms mean. His nationalism is real as a folk nationalism based on experience with other Negroes and isolation from whites.

The significance of a racial future in the day to day consciousness of street people cannot be assessed. It is a developing possibility dependent on unforeseen conditions beyond the scope of their skill and imagination. But bring up the topic of race and tomorrow, and the dreams come rushing in—dreams of superiority, dreams of destruction, dreams of human equality. These dreams of the future are salient. They are not the imagination of authoritarian personalities, except from the viewpoint of those who see spite lurking behind every demand for social change. They are certainly not the fantasies of the hipster living philosophically in the present without hope and ambition. One hustler summarized the Negro street concept of ambition and future time when he said:

> The Negro has more ambition than the whites. He's got farther to go. "The man" is already there. But we're on your trail, daddy. You still have smoke in our eyes, but we're catching up.

Suggested Readings

Bennett, D. C., "Interracial Ratios and proximity in Dormitories," *Environment and Behavior,* 6 (June 1974), 212–232. Bennett explores spatial and social separation of blacks and whites in the United States. At Indiana University, he surveyed interracial experiences and attitudes as reflected in spatial separation of blacks and whites in the dormitory situation.

Bond, M. H., and D. Shiraishi, "The Effect of Body Lean and Status of an Interviewer on the Non-Verbal Behavior of Japanese Interviewees," *International Journal of Psychology,* 9 (1974), 117–128. The authors studied nonverbal communication in Japanese subjects. Body status and body lean variables were found to affect a variety of dependent measures.

Boucher, J. D., "Display Rules and Facial Affective Behavior: A Theoretical Discussion and Suggestions for Research," *Topics in Culture Learning,* vol. 2 (Honolulu: East-West Center, 1974). Boucher develops a theory of facial affective behavior in interpersonal intercultural interaction. Display rules for facial affective behavior were defined as a set of norms that the individual internalizes during socialization processes. Examples of behavior in an interpersonal interaction sequence are discussed, with emphasis on the identification of contextual characteristics of people and setting.

Brislin, R. W., "Seating as a Measure of Behavior: You Are Where You Sit," *Topics in Culture Learning,* vol. 2 (Honolulu: East-West Center, 1974). Seating is viewed as one measure of behavior useful in understanding the cross-cultural situation. Emphasis is given to where people sit as an important index of how they feel about others.

Efron, D., *Gesture, Race and Culture* (The Hague: Mouton, 1972). Here, Efron presents results of his study of some of the spatio-temporal and linguistic aspects of the gestural behavior of eastern Jews and southern Italians in New York City. This book, first published in 1941, has become a classic in its field.

Eisenberg, A. M., and R. Smith, Jr., *Nonverbal Communication* (Indianapolis: Bobbs-Merrill, 1971). Chapters 6 and 7 of this book deal with nonverbal communication and culture. The authors review numerous studies that compare and contrast the various ways different cultures use and interpret nonverbal communication. Such areas as movement, posture, proxemics, eye movement, and gestures are examined.

Ekman, P., "Communication through Nonverbal Behavior: A Source of Information about an Interpersonal Relationship," in S. S. Tompkins and C. E. Izard (eds.), *Affect, Cognition, and Personality* (New York: Springer Publishing Company, 1965), pp. 391–442. This book discusses basic concepts in nonverbal communication behavior; and how nonverbal expressions provide additional information for the interpretation of verbal systems.

Hall, E. T., *The Hidden Dimension* (Garden City, N.Y.: Doubleday & Co., 1966). Man uses space to communicate in very much the same way he uses words or gestures. In this volume, Hall sets forth his theory of proxemics, or how man structures and uses space; and he describes and discusses cultural variance in proxemic behavior.

LaBarre, W., "The Cultural Basis of Emotions and Gestures," *Journal of Personality,* 16 (1946), 49–68. Specific emotional expressions and gestures have their basis in culture, both in the appropriateness of the expression and the manner of expression. LaBarre discusses variations in these forms of nonverbal behaviors that result from cultural differences; he cites numerous examples and describes how different cultures have different nonverbal expressions for the same meaning.

Mehrabian, A., *Silent Messages* (Belmont, Calif.: Wadsworth Publishing Company, 1971). Much of this book is concerned with cultural differences in the performing and perceiving of nonverbal communication. In nearly all classes of nonverbal behavior, Mehrabian has included the role of culture.

Nisan, M., "Perception of Time in Lower-Class Black Students," *International Journal of Psychology,* 8 (1973), 109–116. Time perception is often viewed as a basic determinant of important behavioral patterns, such as long-range planning and willingness to delay gratification in expectation of future rewards. As such, it is of considerable potential value in understanding a number of cultural differences. This study investigated the effects of temporal distance from a goal upon expectancy that a goal will be attained.

Rich, A. L., "Interracial Implications of Nonverbal Communication," in *Interracial Communication* (New York: Harper & Row, 1974). In Chapter 7 of her book, Rich explores the importance of nonverbal communication to interracial interaction. Most dimensions of nonverbal communication are examined in this selection—environment, proxemics, clothing, physical characteristics, posture, gesture, eye contact, facial expression, and paralanguage.

Watson, M. O., and T. D. Graves, "Quantitative Research in Proxemic Behavior," *American Anthropologist,* 68 (1966), 971–985. Watson and Graves report an experimental study between Americans and Arabs that tested the hypothesis that Arabs interact closer physically than do Americans. This study is important because it not only supports proxemic theory; it also gives insight into cross-cultural research methodologies.

Additional Readings

Birdwhistel, R. L., *Introduction to Kinesics* (Washington, D.C.: Foreign Service Institute, Department of State, 1952).

Birdwhistel, R. L., *Kinesics and Context* (Phila.: University of Pennsylvania Press, 1970).

Duncan, S., Jr., "Nonverbal Communication," *Psychological Bulletin* 72 (1969), 118–137.

Ekman, P., and W. Friesen, *Emotion in the Human Face* (New York: Pergamon Press, 1972).

Ekman, P., R. Sorenson, and E. Friessen, "Pan-Cultural Elements in Facial Displays of Emotion," *Science,* 164 (1969), 86–88.

Hall, E. T., "The Silent Language of Overseas Business," *Harvard Business Review,* 39 (1960), 87–96.

Mehrabian, A., *Nonverbal Communication* (Chicago: Aldine-Atherton Press, 1972).

Montagu, A., *Touching: The Human Significance of the Skin* (New York: Columbia University Press, 1971).

Sebeck, R., and E. Cervenka, *Colombian and North American Gestures* (Bogota, Colombia: Centro Colombo-Americano, 1962).

Sommer, R., *Personal Space* (Englewood Cliffs, N.J.: Prentice-Hall, 1969).

Sommer, R., "The Distance for Comfortable Conversation: A Further Study," *Sociometry,* 22 (1959), 247–260.

Willis, F. N., Jr., "Initial Speaking Distance as a Function of the Speaker's Relationship," *Psychonomic Science,* 5 (1966), 221–222.

Concepts and Questions

1. From your personal experiences can you think of additional ways various cultures greet, kiss, show contempt, or beckon?

2. Are cultural differences based on linguistic problems harder or easier to overcome than the problems related to nonverbal actions?

3. In what ways do nonverbal behaviors reflect the values, history, and social organization of a culture?

4. How does culture affect the display of emotion?

5. What are some of the dangers of overgeneralizing from nonverbal communication?

6. Have you experienced situations where the nonverbal behavior of someone didn't meet your expectations? How did you react? Could this have been a cultural problem?

7. From your personal experiences would you say that the examples cited by Yousef are typical or atypical of the cultures that you have come in contact with?

8. How do we develop a theory of nonverbal behavior if we go beyond the anecdotal narration of bizarre behaviors?

9. Can you think of any cultural examples that would tend to support the notion that a culture's history influences its use of nonverbal communication?

10. What are the relationships between verbal and nonverbal forms of communication?

11. How might cultural differences in time conceptualization lead to intercultural communication problems?

12. Frank noted that "the skin has many potentialities, some of which are actively recognized, cultivated, refined or coarsened, and selectively utilized

by each culture." If we grant the validity of this statement, how does it relate to intercultural communication? What examples seem to come to mind?

13. How could a knowledge of "street time" offer insight into interracial communication?

14. How would you prevent the occurrence of intercultural communication problems brought about by the unconscious and unintentional performance of nonverbal behavior that deeply offends members of another culture?

Part Four   Intercultural Communication: Becoming More Effective

In a sense, this entire volume has been concerned with the practice of intercultural communication. We have looked at a variety of cultures and a host of communication variables that are in operation when people from different cultures attempt to interact. However, our analysis, thus far, has been somewhat theoretical. Previous selections have concentrated primarily on the issue of understanding intercultural communication. We have not, at least up to this point, treated the act of practicing intercultural communication. In this final section we shall slightly modify our orientation so that we can include a discussion based on the activity of communication. For although the readings in this portion of the book will increase your understanding, their main purpose is to improve your behavior *during* intercultural communication.

The motivation for this particular section grows out of an important precept found in the study of human communication. It suggests that human interaction is a behavioral act in which people engage for the purpose of changing their environment. Inherent in this notion is the idea that communication is something people *do*—it involves action. Regardless of how much we understand intercultural communication, when we are communicating with someone from another culture we are part of a behavioral situation. We, and our communication counterpart, are doing things to each other. This final part of the book deals with that "doing." In addition, we are concerned that your communication be as effective as possible.

As you might well imagine personal contact and experience are the most desirable methods for improvement. Knowledge and practice seem to work in tandem. The problem is that we cannot write or select readings that substitute for this personal experience. Therefore, our contribution by necessity must focus on the observations of those who have practiced intercultural communication with some degree of success.

6

Communicating Interculturally

This chapter offers the experiences and perceptions of those who are effective practitioners and teachers of intercultural communication. Through their personal observations and suggestions we will learn something about potential intercultural communication problems and the resolution of those problems.

The first essay in Chapter 6 looks at both problems and solutions. In her article "Intercultural Communication Stumbling Blocks," LaRay M. Barna attempts to deal with some specific reasons why intercultural communication often fails to bring about mutual understanding. She has selected five important causes for communication breakdown across cultural boundaries: (1) language problems, (2) nonverbal misunderstanding, (3) the presence of preconceptions and stereotypes, (4) the tendency to evaluate, and (5) the high anxiety that often exists in intercultural encounters.

The title of the next selection, written by Jean Marie Ackermann, clearly previews the scope and purpose of the essay—"Skill Training for Foreign Assignment: The Reluctant U.S. Case." Ackermann begins her essay with a vivid description of some real life problems that have arisen because of poor intercultural communication. As a professional trainer in overseas communication she deems it best not only to talk about problems but also to explore possible solutions for these problems. To this end the essay looks at (1) paradoxes that work against the acceptance of intercultural training, (2) approaches arising from American strengths and values that might make training acceptable and useful, and (3) some models for the conduct and content of intercultural communication training.

Howard F. Van Zandt deals with one cultural group (Japanese), yet he is actually talking about problems and solutions related to most cross-cultural situations. Van Zandt is very specific in treating the issues of successful intercultural communication. By examining the features of Japanese behavior, he offers insight into how our messages and our actions may be received and interpreted by the Japanese. Van Zandt also gives some concrete advice for dealing with interpreters in intercultural communication. Since much intercultural communication takes place through interpreters, Van Zandt's suggestions offer sound counsel.

After looking at a specific culture, we turn to "American Advisors Overseas" by Edward C. Stewart. Here we consider the problems of situations where co-workers speak a different language and have different customs and preferences. Stewart suggests some ways of overcoming, or at least working with, these differences. For him the first step is for the communicator to understand and be aware of the concept of cultural differences. He also believes that many problems can be traced to the incongruities between American and foreign cultural patterns. Stewart highlights some of the most common incongruities and offers ways of minimizing them.

Arthur L. Smith looks at communication from the standpoint of race. In "Interpersonal Communication within Transracial Contexts," he not only describes what transracial communication is, he also offers us some principles derived from communication theory and discusses the relationship of these principles to culture. He maintains that, by understanding what transracial communication is and how it operates, we will be better able to communicate across ethnic and racial lines. Smith also offers four suggestions for improving intercultural communication.

Intercultural Communication Stumbling Blocks

LaRay M. Barna

There are many viewpoints regarding the practice of intercultural communication but a familiar one is that "people are people," basically pretty much alike; therefore increased interaction through travel, student exchange programs, and other such ventures should result in more understanding and friendship between nations. Others take a quite different view, particularly those who have done research in the field of speech communication and are fully aware of the complexities of interpersonal interaction, even *within* cultural groups. They do not equate contact with communication, do not believe that the simple experience of talking with someone insures a successful transfer of meanings and feelings. Even the basic commonalities of birth, hunger, family, death, are perceived and treated in vastly different ways by persons with different backgrounds.[1] If there *is* a universal, it might be that each has been so subconsciously influenced by his own cultural upbringing that he assumes that the needs, desires, and basic assumptions of others are identical to his own.[2]

It takes a long time of noninsulated living in a new culture before a foreigner can relax into new perceptions and nonevaluative thinking so that he can adjust his reactions and interpretations to fit what's happening around him. The few who

Adapted from *Kentucky Speech Arts Journal,* November 1971. All rights reserved. Permission to reprint must be obtained from the author. Professor Barna teaches in the Department of Speech Communication, Portland State University, Portland, Oregon.

achieve complete insight and acceptance are outstanding by their rarity. After nine years of monitoring dyads and small group discussions between U.S. and international students, this author, for one, is inclined to agree with Charles Frankel, who says: "tensions exist within nations and between nations that never would have existed were these nations not in such intense cultural communication with one another."[3] The following typical reactions of three foreign students to one nonverbal behavior that most Americans expect to bridge gaps—the smile —may serve as an illustration:

> Japanese student: On my way to and from school I have received a smile by nonacquaintance American girls several times. I have learned they have no interest for me; it means only a kind of greeting to a foreigner. But if someone smiles at a stranger in Japan, especially a girl, she can assume he is either a sexual maniac or an impolite person.

> Korean student: An American visited me in my country for one week. His inference was that people in Korea are not very friendly because they didn't smile or want to talk with foreign people. That's true because most Korean people take time to get to be friendly with people. We never talk or smile at strangers.

> Vietnamese student: The reason why certain foreigners may think that Americans are superficial—and they are, some Americans even recognize this—is that they talk and smile too much. For people who come from placid cultures where nonverbal language is more used, and where a silence, a smile, a glance have their own meaning, it is true that Americans speak a lot. The superficiality of Americans can also be detected in their relations with others. Their friendships are, most of the time, so ephemeral compared to the friendships we have at home. Americans make friends very easily and leave their friends almost as quickly, while in my country it takes a long time to find out a possible friend and then she becomes your friend—with a very strong sense of the term. Most Americans are materialistic and once they are provided with necessities, they don't feel the need to have a friend. Purposes of their friendships are too clear, and you can hardly find a friendship for friendship's sake.

An American girl in the same class gives her view:

> In general it seems to me that foreign people are not necessarily snobs but are very unfriendly. Some class members have told me that you shouldn't smile at others while passing them by on the street. To me I can't stop smiling. It's just natural to be smiling and friendly. I can see now why so many foreign people stick together. They are impossible to get to know. It's like the Americans are big bad wolves. How do Americans break this barrier? I want friends from all over the world but how do you start to be friends without offending them or scaring them off—like sheep?[4]

One reason for the long delay in tackling the widespread failure to achieve understanding across cultures might be that it is not readily apparent when there has been miscommunication at the interpersonal level. Unless there is overt reporting of assumptions such as in the examples above, which seldom happens in normal settings, there is no chance for comparing impressions. The foreign visitor to the United States nods, smiles, and gives affirmative comments, which the straightforward, friendly American confidently translates as meaning that he has informed, helped, and pleased the newcomer. It is likely, however, that the foreigner actually understood very little of the verbal and nonverbal content and was merely indicating polite interest or trying not to embarrass himself or his host with verbalized questions. The conversation may even have confirmed his stereotype that Americans are insensitive and ethnocentric.

In a university classroom U.S. students often complain that the international members of a discussion or project seem uncooperative or uninterested. The following is a typical statement from the international's point of view:

> I had difficulty with the opinion in the class where peoples in group discuss about subject. I was surrounded by Americans with whom I couldn't follow their tempo of discussion half of the time. I have difficulty to listen and speak, but also with the way they handle the group. I felt uncomfortable because sometimes they believe their opinion strongly. I had been very serious about the whole subject but I was afraid I would say something wrong. I had the idea but not the words.[4]

Typically, the method used to improve chances for successful intercultural communication is to gather information about the customs of the other country and a smattering of the language. The behaviors and attitudes are sometimes researched, but almost always from a secondhand source. The information is seldom sufficient and may or may not be helpful. Knowing "what to expect" too often blinds the observer to all but what is confirmatory to his image or preconception. Any contradictory evidence that does filter through is likely to be treated as an exception.[5]

A better approach is to study the history, political structure, art, literature, and language of the country if time permits. But more important, one should develop an investigative nonjudgmental attitude and a high tolerance for ambiguity—which means lowered defenses. Margaret Mead suggests sensitizing persons to the kinds of things that need to be taken into account instead of developing behavior and attitude stereotypes, mainly because of the individual differences in each encounter and the rapid changes that occur in a culture pattern.[6] Edward Stewart concurs with this view.[7]

One way to reach an improved state of awareness and sensitivity to what might go wrong is to examine five variables in the communication process that seem to be major stumbling blocks when the dyad or small group is cross-cultural. The first is so obvious it hardly needs mentioning—*language*. Vocabulary, syntax, idioms, slang, dialects, and so on, all cause difficulty, but the person struggling with a different language is at least aware when he's in this kind of trouble. A worse language problem is the tenacity with which someone will cling to *"the"* meaning of a word or phrase in the new language once he has grasped one, regardless of connotation or contest. The infinite variations, especially of English, are so impossible to cope with that they are waved aside. The reason the problem is "worse" is because each thinks he understands. The nationwide misinterpretation of Khruschev's sentence "We'll bury you" is a classic example. Even "yes" and "no" causes trouble. When a Japanese hears, "Won't you have some tea?" he listens to the literal meaning of the sentence and answers, "No," meaning that he wants some. "Yes, I won't" would be a better reply because this tips off the hostess that there may be a misunderstanding. In some cultures, also, it is polite to refuse the first or second offer of refreshment. Many foreign guests have gone hungry because their U.S. hostess never presented the third offer.

Learning the language, which most foreign visitors consider their *only* barrier to understanding, is actually only the beginning. As Frankel says, "To enter into a culture is to be able to hear, in Lionel Trilling's phrase, its special 'hum and buzz of implication.' "[8] This brings in *nonverbal areas* and the second stumbling block. People from different cultures inhabit different nonverbal sensory words. Each sees, hears, feels, and smells only that which has some meaning or importance for him. He abstracts whatever fits into his personal world of recognitions and then interprets it through the frame of reference of his own culture.

An Oregon girl in an intercultural communication class asked a young man from Saudi Arabia how he would signal nonverbally that he liked her. His response was to smooth back his hair which, to her, was just a common nervous gesture signifying nothing. She repeated her question three times. He smoothed his hair three times and, finally realizing that she was not recognizing this movement as his reply to her question, automatically ducked his head and stuck out his tongue slightly in embarrassment. This behavior *was* noticed by the girl, and she interpreted it as the way he would express his liking for her.

The lack of comprehension of obvious nonverbal signs and symbols such as gestures, postures, and vocalizations is a definite communication barrier, but it is possible to learn the meaning of these messages (once they are perceived) in much the same way a verbal language is learned. It is more difficult to correctly note the unspoken codes of the other culture that are further from awareness, such as the handling of time and spatial relationships, subtle signs of respect or formality, and many others.

The third stumbling block is the presence of *preconceptions* and *stereotypes*. If the label "inscrutable" has preceded the Japanese guest, it is thus we explain his constant and inappropriate smile. The stereotype that Arabs are "inflammable" causes U.S. students to keep their distance when an animated and noisy group from Libya is enjoying lunch in the cafeteria. A professor who "knows" of the bargaining habits of natives of certain countries may unfairly interpret a hesitation by one of his foreign students as a move to "squirm out" of a commitment. Stereotypes help do what Ernest Becker[9] says the anxiety-prone human race *must* do, and that is to reduce the threat of the unknown by making the world predictable. Indeed, this is one of the basic functions of culture: to lay out a predictable world in which the individual is firmly oriented. Stereotypes are overgeneralized beliefs that provide conceptual bases from which to "make sense" out of what goes on around us. In a foreign land they increase our feeling of security and are psychologically necessary to the degree that we cannot tolerate ambiguity or the sense of helplessness resulting from inability to understand and deal with people and situations beyond our comprehension.

Stereotypes are stumbling blocks for communicators because they interfere with objective viewing of stimuli. Unfortunately, they are not easy to overcome in others or in ourselves by demonstrations of the "truth," hoping to teach a lesson of tolerance or cultural relativity. They persist because they sometimes rationalize prejudices or are firmly established as myths or truisms by one's own national culture. They are also sustained and fed by the tendency to perceive selectively only those pieces of new information that correspond to the image. The Asian or African visitor who is accustomed to privation and the values of denial and self-help cannot fail to experience American culture as materialistic and wasteful. The stereotype for him turns into a concrete reality.

Another deterrent to an understanding between persons of differing cultures or ethnic groups is the *tendency to evaluate,* to approve or disapprove, the statements and actions of the other person or group rather than to try to completely comprehend the thoughts and feelings expressed. Each person's culture, his own way of life, always seems right, proper, and natural. This bias prevents the open-minded attention needed to look at the attitudes and behavior patterns from the other's point of view. A midday siesta changes from a "lazy habit" to a "pretty good idea" when someone listens long enough to realize the midday temperature in that country is 115° Fahrenheit.

The author, fresh from a conference in Tokyo where Japanese professors had emphasized the preference of the people of Japan for simple natural settings of rocks, moss, and water, of muted greens and misty ethereal landscapes, visited the Katsura Imperial Gardens in Kyoto. At the appointed time of the tour, a young Japanese guide approached the group of twenty waiting American strangers and remarked how fortunate it was that the day was cloudy. This brought hesitant smiles to the group who were less than pleased at the prospect of a light shower. The guide's next few sentences included mention that the timing of the midsummer visit was particularly appropriate in that the azalea and rhododendron blossoms were gone and the trees had not yet turned to their brilliant fall colors. The group laughed loudly, now convinced that the young man had a fine sense of humor. I winced at his bewildered expression realizing that, had I come before attending the conference, I would have shared the group's inference that he was not serious.

The communication cut-off caused by immediate evaluation is heightened when feelings and emotions are deeply involved; yet this is just the time when listening with understanding is most needed. It takes both awareness of the tendency to close our minds and courage to risk change in our own values and perceptions to dare to comprehend why someone thinks and acts differently from us. As stated by Sherif, Sherif, and Nebergall, "A person's commitment to his religion, politics, values of his family, and his stand on the virtue of his way of life are ingredients in his self-picture—intimately felt and cherished."[10] It is very easy to dismiss strange or different behaviors as "wrong," listen through a thick screen of value judgments, and therefore fail miserably to receive a fair understanding. The impatience of the American public over the choice of the shape of the conference table at the Paris Peace talks and their judgment of a "poor reception" for the President of the United States because there were no bands or flag-waving throngs waiting for Nixon as he was driven through towns in New China on his historic visit are two examples.

The following paragraph written by an international student from Korea illustrates how a clash in values can lead to poor communication and result in misunderstanding and hurt feelings:

> When I call on my American friend, he had been studying his lesson. Then I said, "May I come in?" He said through window, "I am sorry. I have no time because of my study." Then he shut the window. I thought it over and over. I couldn't understand through my cultural background. In our country, if someone visits other's house, house owner should have welcome visitor whether he likes or not and whether he is busy or not. Then next, if the owner is busy, he asks to visitor, "Would you wait for me?" Also the owner never speaks without opening his door.[11]

This example also illustrates how difficult it is to bring one's own cultural norm into awareness. It is unlikely the "American friend" ever knew that he insulted the young Korean.

The fifth stumbling block is *high anxiety,* separately mentioned for the purpose of emphasis. Unlike the other four (language, illusive nonverbal cues, preconceptions and stereotypes, and the practice of immediate evaluation), the stumbling block of anxiety is not distinct but underlies and compounds the others. The presence of high anxiety/tension is very common in cross-cultural experiences because of the uncertainties present. An international student says it well:

> During those several months after my arrival in the U.S.A., every day I came back from school exhausted so that I had to take a rest for a while, stretching myself on the bed. For, all the time, I strained every nerve in order to understand what the people were saying and make myself understood in my broken English. When I don't understand what American people are talking about and why they are laughing, I sometimes have to pretend to understand by smiling, even though I feel alienated, uneasy and tense.
>
> In addition to this, the difference in culture or customs, the way of thinking between two countries, produces more tension because we don't know how we should react to totally foreign customs or attitudes, and sometimes we can't guess how the people from another country react to my saying or behavior. We always have a fear somewhere in the bottom of our hearts that there are much more chances of breakdown in intercultural communication than in communication with our own fellow countrymen.[12]

The native of the country is uncomfortable when talking with a foreigner because he cannot maintain the normal flow of verbal and nonverbal interaction to sustain the conversation. He is also threatened by the unknown other's knowledge, experience, and evaluation—the visitor's potential for scrutiny and rejection of himself and his country. The inevitable question, "How do you like it here?" which the foreigner abhors, is the host's quest for reassurance, or at least the "feeler" that reduces the unknown and gives him ground for defense if that seems necessary.

The foreign member of the dyad is under the same threat, with the added tension of having to cope with the differing pace, climate, and culture. The first few months he feels helpless in coping with messages that swamp him and to which his reactions may be inappropriate. His self-esteem is often intolerably undermined unless he employs such defenses as withdrawal into his own reference group or into himself, screening out or misperceiving stimuli, rationalizing, overcompensating, even hostility—none of which leads to effective communication.

Since all of the communication barriers mentioned are hard to remove, the only simple solution seems to be to tell everybody to stay home. This advice obviously is unacceptable, so it is fortunate that a few paths are being laid around the obstacles. Communication theorists are continuing to offer new insights and are focusing on problem areas of this complex process.[13] Educators and linguists are improving methods of learning a second language. The nonverbal area, made familiar by Edward T. Hall in his famous books, *The Silent Lanuage* and *The Hidden Dimension,* is getting a singular amount of attention.[14] The ray of hope offered by Hall and others is that nonverbal cues, culturally controlled and largely out-of-awareness, can be discovered and even understood when the communicator knows enough to look for them, is alert to the varying interpretations possible, and is free enough from tension and psychological defenses to notice them.

In addition, textbooks are appearing and communication specialists are improving means for increasing sensitivity to the messages coming from others in an intercultural setting.[15] Professional associations are giving increased amounts of attention to intercultural communication, and new societies such as the Society for Intercultural Education, Training and Research are being developed. The International and Intercultural Communication Annual [16] has a complete listing of these.

What the interpersonal intercultural communicator must seek to achieve can be summarized by two quotations. The first is by Roger Harrison, who says:

> . . . the communicator cannot stop at knowing that the people he is working with have different customs, goals, and thought patterns from his own. He must be able to feel his way into intimate contact with these alien values, attitudes, and feelings. He must be able to work with them and within them, neither losing his own values in the confrontation nor protecting himself behind a wall of intellectual detachment.[17]

Robert T. Oliver phrases it thus: "If we would communicate across cultural barriers, we must learn what to say and how to say it in terms of the expectations and predispositions of those we want to listen."[18]

References

1. Marshall R. Singer, "Culture: A Perceptual Approach," in *Readings in Intercultural Communication,* Vol. I (Regional Council for International Education, University of Pittsburgh), and Edward T. Hall, *The Hidden Dimension* (New York: Doubleday and Company, Inc., 1966), p. 2.

2. Edward T. Hall, *The Silent Language* (Greenwich, Conn.: Fawcett Publications, Inc., 1959).

3. Charles Frankel, *The Neglected Aspect of Foreign Affairs* (Washington, D.C.: Brookings Institution, 1965), p. 1.

4. Taken from student papers in a course in intercultural communication taught by the author.

5. For one discussion of this concept, see Daryl J. Bem, *Beliefs, Attitudes, and Human Affairs* (Belmont, Calif.: Brooks/Cole Publishing Co., 1970), p. 9.

6. Margaret Mead, "The Cultural Perspective," in *Communication or Conflict,* ed. Mary Capes (Association Press, 1960).

7. Edward C. Stewart, *American Cultural Patterns: A Cross-Cultural Perspective* (Pittsburgh, Pa.: Regional Council for International Education, University of Pittsburgh, April 1971), p. 14.

8. Frankel, *The Neglected Aspect of Foreign Affairs,* p. 103.

9. Ernest Becker, *The Birth and Death of Meaning* (New York: Free Press, 1962), pp. 84–89.

10. Carolyn W. Sherif, Musafer Sherif, and Roger E. Nebergall, *Attitude and Attitude Change* (Philadelphia: W. B. Saunders Co., 1965) p. vi.

11.&12. Taken from a student's paper in a course in intercultural communication taught by the author.

13. An early book, now in its second edition, which adapted the language of information theory to communication and stressed the influence of culture, remains one of the best sources: *Communication: The Social Matrix of Psychiatry* by Jurgen Ruesch and Gregory Bateson (New York: W. W. Norton & Co., 1968).

14. See for example: *Silent Messages* by Albert Mehrabian (Belmont, Calif.: Wadsworth Publishing Co., 1971).

15. Sources include: Edward D. Stewart, "The Simulation of Cultural Differences," *The Journal of Communication,* Vol. 16, December 1966; Alfred J. Kraemer, *The Development of Cultural Self-Awareness: Design of a Program of Instruction* (George Washington University, Human Resources Research Office, Professional Paper 27–69, August 1969); David Hoopes, ed., *Readings in Intercultural Communication,* Vols. I-IV. (Regional Council for International Education, University of Pittsburgh).

16. *International and Intercultural Communication Annual,* Vol. 1, December 1974, published by Speech Communication Association, Statler Hilton Hotel, New York.

17. Roger Harrison, "The Design of Cross-Cultural Training: An Alternative to the University Model," in *Explorations in Human Relations Training and Research* (Bethesda, Md.: National Training Laboratories, 1966), NEA No. 2, p. 4.

18. Robert T. Oliver, *Culture and Communication: The Problem of Penetrating National and Cultural Boundaries* (Springfield, Ill.: Charles C Thomas, 1962), p. 154.

Skill Training for Foreign Assignment: The Reluctant U.S.[1] Case

Jean Marie Ackermann

Differing expectations between managers from different countries lead at best to emotional foot-shuffling, tight-smiled chagrin, and rage. At worst, they lead to violence. Two extremes: The left-hand lead headline in *The Wall Street Journal* for May 8, 1974 read:

> GM DISCOVERED TRUST
> CAME SLOWLY, WARILY
> AT ITS ISUZU AFFILIATE

and went on to detail the two-year waiting period between Japanese "wariness and acceptance" of their U.S. affiliates. General Motors executives learned the hard way that "my time isn't your time" and that preliminaries are not prelimi-

---

[1] Adapted from *Training,* July 1974. All rights reserved. Permission to reprint must be obtained from the author. Dr. Ackermann is Director of Transcultural Training, Organizational Consultants Inc., Chicago, and teaches part-time at Governors State University.

nary at all but an integral, indispensable, and major part of Japanese negotiating and planning.

The Problems

But consider the U.S. engineering firm that in 1972 began mining operations on a Pacific island. The project manager hired island tribesmen for manual jobs. One worker was so good, he was promoted to foreman. Three months later he was found murdered in the company mess hall. By singling him out for special notice and advancing him above his peers—a U.S. tradition, but one that ignored the tribal code of group equality—the company had marked him for retribution —in this case, death. These are two extremes of the spectrum of woes that erupt —or smoulder—when people from different cultures meet. More common are upsets like the following, drawn from recent experiences privately reported by businessmen.

A U.S. bank executive lost a promised lease on a desirable headquarters when he kept his dealings "strictly business" instead of "working" on the continued personal association needed in the host country's tradition of negotiation. A Western manager who critized a Middle Eastern ruler in full hearing of host country colleagues was deported within 48 hours. He had imported his own version of freedom of speech into a land that interpreted it otherwise. A U.S. contracts officer gave his stateside headquarters a green light based on a promised letter of intent, which after six months and extensive preparation had not yet materialized. That is, an apparent "yes" may mean anything from "agree" to "disagree" to "acknowledge your words"; a handshake may imply welcome, or distance, or delay. And, while violence is rare, common results of transcultural misreadings are mistrust, anger, and pulling out of "sure" deals—that is, ultimate personal and corporate loss.

Yet, as U.S. companies expand overseas operations, they are transferring more and more untraveled staff, often on short notice. Unlike their predecessors, cadres of seasoned "career" cosmopolites—some current transferees have small interest in, background of, or aptitude for dealing comfortably and effectively with foreign nationals. They were tapped for foreign assignment hastily and perhaps arbitrarily. What should the company do? Obviously, careful screening of those who go abroad is a first option, demanding serious study—but even the outlining of such a process is beyond the scope of this paper. Orientation of staff to the new setting before transfer is another option whose scope we shall here suggest. In the United States, such training is often rushed, scanted, or missing. Two paradoxes within the U.S. tradition suggest why—and also suggest seminal solutions to problems of transcultural business dealings. Let us inspect briefly (1) paradoxes that work against the acceptance of such training, (2) approaches arising from American strengths and values that might make training acceptable and useful, and (3) some models for the conduct and content of such training. Meanwhile, please be aware, as I am, that this very paper is "American" in approach—optimistic, problem-solving, prescriptive, and so forth—and in the fact that it has been written at all.

Paradox 1: The Problems are Privately Known, Publicly Denied

In one sense, the murder tale recounted above is typical. It is well known in management circles, but it cannot be documented and is publicly denied. In contrast, the GM story is unusual in candor and detail. Most journalists or scholars researching multicultural business dealings are put off with unverified assertions. The statistics are up for grabs. For example, a third of North American executives working abroad return home before completing their assignments, says *Commerce Today* (February 21, 1972). Our own sales force reports that personnel directors confidentially up this to one-half. And, according to Adams and Kobayashi,[2] four out of five foreign representatives in Japan don't complete their missions.[3] Can these allegations be clarified or documented? Why are they neither confirmed nor refuted in interviews with top U.S. business leaders? In part, the reason is that some Americans can't bear to admit that "soft," cultural differences can have clout in "hard" business negotiations—or even that such differences exist. But most of the reluctance stems, I suggest, from a second seeming contradiction.

Paradox 2: U.S. Success Patterns Breed Overseas Failure

Those very behaviors that spell success at home for a U.S. businessperson may spell disaster abroad. So they need to be modified. And, while any change can be a threat to one's equilibrium, proposed changes in behavior that hitherto have produced high rewards for the person and the bottom line tend to be particularly bitterly resisted, or better, ignored. What are some such styles on which U.S. business people pride themselves, but which may rub others wrong? Let's focus on four:

1. PRAGMATIC THINKING   "What works?" "How much?" These are cherished questions that get to the heart of the matter—if achievement is the matter. But in some countries, achievement is secondary to the welfare of employees, or to meeting one's social obligations. Thus, the most "practical" American approach may in fact not work. For instance, some Americans transferring ask us for a list of Dos and Don'ts to read on the flight to their new post. There's surely nothing wrong in memorizing facts about how long a first business call should last, or who gets invited to what. But a list can give a sense of false security. For culture is not a show window with its wares on easy display but an apparent maze, which, when understood, can become a negotiable and enjoyable network.

Successful adaptation to another culture is not only knowing that one stands lower than one's superior (as in Thailand) or close to one's companion (as in Latin America), but where one stands in the total social context. Only then can one act confidently in unexpected situations. Simple rules like "Bring calling cards to Japan" are a start, sure, but they may let one think (s)he knows the way inside a culture when (s)he's only skating on its surface. A deeper grounding would stress the etiquette and attitude of presenting the card, the information it must contain in both languages, the manner of accepting and consulting a proffered card, the card's role in honoring each person, why all these things are so, and how they relate to and are paralleled in the rest of the Japanese system.

2. STRAIGHT TALK   "Telling it like it is" is greatly honored, at least ideally, in the United States. Yet other countries find such "openness" amazing and alarming, if not incredible. For instance, a favorite Iranian proverb advises: "Conceal thy gold, thy destination, and thy creed." And it is implicit in Iranian etiquette that one does not state opposition or refusal, but instead cloaks one's response in elegant and truly courteous language that may convey or suggest agreement where none exists. Here, traditional emphasis on maintaining a facade of harmony and peace in the midst of a troubled and troubling life and world often leads to misunderstandings, with Americans calling "lies" what are to Iranians simply elegant avoidances of giving offense.

3. SEPARATING WORK AND LIFE   Stemming in part from our rigid work ethic is an implicit assent to use others and to be used, strictly for work and profit. The split implies that relationships start and end at the office, with no resentment at the lack of outside socializing with colleagues. This pattern seems cold and inhuman to those countries where the "whole person" is the focus and where business and social life, particularly at higher levels, are closely joined. As noted above, one style is the Japanese, where a foreigner must be known over time before a company will share its secrets and negotiate, but this style exists also in the Middle East and Latin America. If (s)he's prepared for such preliminaries, a U.S. businessperson can ride them out with patience and good will, and substitute pride in learning how to operate comfortably and effectively in a whole new network for pride in a quick closing. But such learning does not come easily.

4. A SENSE OF INEVITABILITY   Many peoples believe that "our way is the natural way." Yet the American way is only one of many ways of organizing life or business. For instance, our value of "doing" not "being" is far from universal. And within achievement, goals differ. A U.S. manager may stress profit; his Japanese counterpart may focus on employee welfare; an Indonesian may emphasize family well being; and a Latin may look to enjoying life and respecting his network of obligations. While our superb technology and material stuffs have indeed seemed a standard for much of the world, not so the cultural freight they bear with them. Many U.S. businessmen find it hard to accept this rejection. Yet such arrogance in any people is inevitably, eventually, self-defeating. Arnold Toynbee sums it up: "As for the egocentric illusion all that need be said is that we Westerners have not been its only victims."[4] Overcoming the sense of being the world's standard is surely one of the hardest transcultural tasks.

Thus, some American styles seem to work against effective, comfortable transcultural business dealings. Yet, there are other American styles of thinking and acting that hold within themselves seeds of transcultural facility and expertise. A few of these:

1. *Problem-solving perspective.* The very problem-solution orientation that irritates some non-Americans can be harnessed for a positive purpose. Americans have a well-developed ability to define a trouble area and then take steps to solve it. Once transcultural dealings are recognized as a source of possible difficulty, and once we scrap the gentlemen's agreement to disregard or play down transcultural mishaps, we can better accept the need for specific preparation for working in a second culture, and can refine techniques already designed to handle this problem.

2. *Skill training.* Tied in with problem-solving is an American tendency to isolate and teach specific skills, especially those that can be measured. While cosmopolitan ease is hard to quantify, there are skills and facts that can be taught to reach specific goals in transcultural dealings. Again, as we shift from hiding the problem to dealing with it, new, effective, specific training techniques will be refined and adopted.

3. *Success-failure split.* There is an American habit of comparing, quantifying, and ranking things, people, and ideas, and especially of judging them successes or failures. As our weak points in transcultural dealings become freely discussed public knowledge, there will be a reactive tendency to develop further means of building these into strengths leading to successful encounters. Already, however, there exists a nucleus of transcultural training techniques. Let me outline goals and techniques I have found useful and congenial to American business personnel transferring abroad, in programs developed for various client populations (ranging from technicians to executives) and their accompanying families.

What Training Can Achieve

Transcultural training works to change basic perspectives, teach survival and enjoyment skills, and build a positive mental set toward oneself and the transfer-environment. The last is a prerequisite to the first two, and all three goals are integrated into every training module, some of which are outlined below.

Countering Culture Shock

Some American families adjust to living in a new culture with a minimum of discomfort. Others do not. By anticipating the possibility of anxiety, or even of mute terror at living and working on alien turf, transcultural orientation helps to surface awareness that distress is a possibility and a legitimate cause of concern but not alarm. Transcultural orientation also gives specific steps that can help to alleviate the distress. A few examples will suggest the scope.

First, studying the host-country language can reduce overall strangeness and focus energies on a discrete task and away from pain. However, learning language without its accompanying cultural baggage is risky, and can make one seem a "fluent fool," for if one knows the right words, he is presumed to know the behaviors and context they reflect. Exploring the levels and significance of language learning and deciding on one's investment in this are first goals of thoughtful transcultural training.

Second, training needs to meet personal needs and strengthen resources relative to living in a second culture. Such reinforcement can build on the trainee's existing strengths—one's essential nature does not change upon transfer. For example, transferring staff and families may want to bring with them favorite books, games, and sports equipment, as well as meaningful personal belongings such as curtains and small familiar items like ashtrays—family "security" blankets. Discussion of recreational needs and customs helps illuminate an area sometimes overlooked by Americans accustomed to easily available and often passive recreation.

Third, transcultural training needs to offer specific guidelines on "getting into" the host culture in constructive, rewarding ways, building on others' experiences and creating new ones. Taking pictures to document a specific aspect of a culture, such as transportation or shopping, or studying in depth or taking instruction in a national art, craft, or hobby, are ways to cope and learn. The very efforts are tonic, whatever the learnings.

Expanding Horizons

Beyond preparing transferring personnel for basic social and personal change, training for assignment overseas should be directed toward reinforcing three key attitudes that are indispensable for well-being abroad.

First, a cosmopolitan perspective is needed. This is a sense that, to rephrase Kipling, "we are only a kind of they," depending on who's doing the looking. This perspective is not easy to achieve. It involves first knowing one's own background —and that's far harder to recognize than the "strange" culture one is going to —and realizing that one's own way of seeing the world and its people is only one of many. Hardest of all, it means admitting that other ways of viewing may be just as valid and useful as one's own. What the perceptive historian Daniel Boorstin has called our "wholesome fear of the exotic" needs to be transformed to a clear-eyed, nonjudging outlook on our new next door neighbor.

Reassessing Strengths

This calls for training that further builds on participants' own strengths and potentials for dealing with minor upsets and crises—such as the ability to wait, the ability to take needed action, the ability to make new acquaintances on short notice or to refrain from doing so when this is not the custom. Contrasting American styles of coping with those of the host national places both in sharp relief. Incorporating the experiences of recently returned businesspeople and their families keeps this aspect of training current.

Accepting the Host Culture

Acceptance should be based on two sets of information: specific guidelines, including do's and don'ts, on appropriate behavior, competition and attitudes, and a larger network of cultural values, beliefs, goals, and life styles into which the guidelines fit. Armed with such a network of understanding, one is prepared to deal with—or at least not be thrown by—the unexpected and the unique occurrence, even if it has not been spelled out in the overseas transferee's training.

Skill Training

A third training essential for a satisfying overseas transfer is practice in the actual skills of intercultural dealings. Such practice may include taking part in simulated incidents, as reported by returned colleagues; acting out personal apprehensions; developing flexible alternatives of viewing a given person, act, or context; role-playing host nationals and other nationals; and handling ad hoc encounters with host-national trainers. Practice within theoretical frameworks leading to pre-set goals makes learning meaningful and likely to last. Programmed learning is a variant of such practice—useful both during and outside of training.

How Training Works

There are guidelines and goals, but training should be tailored to needs of participants, corporations, and host-countries. Some staff may prefer one-family counseling, where all members can air questions, work through anxieties, and get personal factual and emotional introductions to their new home. Marsh Associates of Honolulu specializes in this kind of intimate exchange on Japan. Some companies prefer programs for all personnel anticipating transfer within the year; for example, a midwestern store chain had us set up one intensive briefing for fifteen families anticipating transfer to France and Italy. Or a training group may advertise a country-specific briefing open to the business (or educational) community. Such was a recent series of Iran briefings I led, attended by transferring staff, trainers, and personnel directors. Most usually, however, experienced companies contract for briefings for from ten to twenty of their staff and families transferring abroad on a specific project; ideally, briefing precedes departure by six to eight weeks, but, in fact, lead time has been as short as ten days. Flexibility seems at least as crucial as expertise in providing a transcultural cushion for overseas crash programs.

Training design, duration, intensity, and size vary. Participants vary. Countries of destination vary. Indeed, I find only one constant in transcultural training —the acute, reluctantly admitted need. And from that builds my conviction that this most challenging of challenges—helping man relate to unknown man— deserves extraordinary, inventive modes of teaching.

Matching Methods to Challenge

Accordingly, we seek methods from both traditional and unorthodox sources. For example, we find that the arts uniquely excite, illuminate, suggest, and make personal the basic stuffs of strange encounters. To illustrate use of the arts, here is an outline of a briefing I recently conducted on Indonesia for an American aircraft company. We try to suit training not only to those who attend, but to the country they study. Thus for Indonesia, to complement presentations of business and social styles, community, daily living, and so forth, and to dramatize Indonesian concern for pattern, tradition, subtlety and balance, we wove the program together with films and poetry. For irreverent contrast, we opened with an Ogden Nash poem[5] on "we" and "they," "we-ness" deriving from who's eyeing whom. After exercises to strengthen alternative perception, we moved on to life in Indonesia via two contrasting poems, both celebrating love of one's native land. One was by a much loved Javanese poet, Todo Sudarto Bachtiar, the other by the American writer Paul Goodman (known most for his criticism of his country—another fact of patriotism). Integrated into presentations of Indonesia today, we underscored the perils of miming the West through a satiric poem by Benny Quay, citizen of Sabah and Canada, and followed this with Rudyard Kipling's warning to *his* countrymen, on the perils awaiting those who try to "hustle the East." The poems and the "solid" sessions counterpointed to make an effective training unit.

Others arts too have unique contributions. Novels can give the new resident the larger canvas, the scope and sweep of a country. Charles Wagley notes: "Brazilian fiction . . . is so closely related to Brazilian society that it provides indispensable documents for an understanding of that nation."[6] We agree, and in a Brazil briefing, we draw generously from scenes and characters in contemporary novels. Arts, cartoons, games—indeed, any expressions of a people's style and values—can be superb balances to factual and logistical core data which, while equally necessary for preparation, sometimes scant or cloud deeper determining social realities. The two are intertwined, of course; knowing the etiquette of hailing an orange taxi in Tehran helps both to get one around the city and to know where one is in the country. The languages of custom are at least as important as those of words.

Implications for Corporate Action

Lest all this seem deceptively facile, let us sound and examine some notes of cautious realism. First, the guidelines for transcultural training are by no means set or agreed on, and accepting the need for training is but the first step of many. After the decision is made, these operational questions must be confronted: What training to offer? For how long? Intensive or over time? During the work week or weekend? Shall we train in culture without language, language without culture, or culture with language? Shall we train in-house or externally? How shall we gauge the effects of training? How much shall we budget? Will different countries take different amounts of preparation? Such questions must arise to management as the decision to train gets implemented. How to handle them raises another question, the most important: Who shall take such training?

Multi-Level Training Needs

It is our considered view that transcultural orientation is an over-all organizational concern, and that training such as we outline above is but one facet of essential corporate (or organizational) action. Running a plant in Djakarta simply is not the same as running one in Waukegan or Danville, and the matter needs total top-level attention. Training for foreign-bound staff, while necessary, is not sufficient, a fact that was constantly and forcibly drawn to our attention by participants in our briefings, who commented about company disinterest or lack of knowledge and sophistication about transferring personnel. We therefore urge and offer consulting and training for foreign orientation in a multi-level unit that includes learnings for (1)top management involved in international decision making, (2)personnel departments involved in transfer operations, (3)back-up professional and technical staff who will be in touch with transferred staff, and of course, (4)the transferring staff and families.

Here are a few instances to illustrate the kinds of variables that may be involved at these different levels. Decision makers need to know actual likely lead time for concluding contracts in X country (as opposed to the official estimate of same). Proposal writers need to know what colors are acceptable to a host country: I phoned a Middle Eastern attaché regarding a proposal folder and was told emphatically, "Don't use red, use green." Personnel departments need to lean on decision makers to get firm, reasonable dates for staff so they can sell their homes without panic. And transferring staff need all the help they can get— including sharp understanding of their new emotional and professional situation by the stateside colleagues they will be interacting with long distance.

As I think further about what I have just written, two absolutes come to mind. The first is that transcultural preparation for organizations and their staff is viewed most accurately not as an expense but as an investment, with discrete and eventually measurable consequences. The second is that Band-aid measures such as 'do and don't' lists, which purport to orient, but in fact do not, are dishonest and damaging to the staff to whom they are applied.

Finally, I realize that the concerns we have been examining above are neither meaningful nor congenial to many U.S. nationals, nor are they in the mainstream style that shuns theory and rewards quick action. But they are in the best "American" tradition of admitting, defining, and studying a problem, and then mounting practical steps for its solution. As our mobility stretches across the globe, we must learn to put down strong roots in unfamiliar soil, even as our ancestors did three hundred years ago, in a strange and promising new land. But, one hopes, the rooting may be done with grace, not violence, and with a clear vision of both ourselves and those whose homelands we approach.[7]

References

1. "U.S." is preferred, if awkward, over "American" here, for the latter has many meanings, including South American. Even "U.S." is sprawling and inexact, and I ask readers to consider it as conveying a cluster of changing tendencies and traditions, and surely not a sense of national absolutes.

2. T. F. M. Adams and N. Kobayashi, *The World of Japanese Business* (Tokyo, 1969), p. 147.

3. Cf. Howard Van Zandt's "How to Negotiate in Japan," p. ___ in this volume.

4. Arnold Toynbee, *A Study of History.* Abridgement of Vols. I-VI by D. C. Somervell. (New York, 1946), p. 37.

5. I first encountered the poem in Seymour Fersh, *Learning about Peoples and Cultures/A Guide for Teachers* (Evanston, 1974), p. 18.

6. Charles Wagley, *An Introduction to Brazil* (New York, 1971), p. vii.

7. I am indebted to Steve Cottrell for the comment that led to the last sentence.

How to Negotiate in Japan

Howard F. Van Zandt

Trade between the United States and Japan can best be described in superlatives. Except for Canada, no other nation sells so much to, or buys so much from, the United States as Japan does. This trade is growing at a rapid rate, too. Exports and imports in 1970, estimated at $10 billion, will be approximately 80% above what they were just four years ago. . . .

Thanks to these changes in government policies, opportunities for Americans to serve the Japanese market will soon be freer of restrictions than at any time since the 1920's. . . .The success or failure of U.S. businessmen will be determined by a myriad of negotiations with Japanese businessmen and government officials. Although Americans can fairly quickly learn how to sell, invest, and operate in European countries, this is not the case in Japan with its unique East Asian type of culture. In order to deal constructively with the Japanese, considerable sophistication will be required. Thus it will be desirable to study such things as their sensitivities, preferences, behavioral patterns, and psychology.

Features of Behavior

Let us begin by looking at distinctive behavioral characteristics of the Japanese that influence their negotiations with U.S. executives. In my experience, 13 such characteristics need to be singled out for attention.

1. EMOTIONAL SENSITIVITY   The Japanese possess a greater emotional sensitivity than do we Americans. For example:

> Recently a friend came to my office, bringing a small potted Chinese bamboo. He explained that in his garden was a large bamboo which had had a baby. He carefully nourished the little one until it was big enough to put in a pot and bring to me. He advised me on its care.

Whenever I look at it, I think of the fine man who gave it to me, and of the thousands of acts of kindness I have received at the hands of Japanese. The sons of Nippon appreciate it when foreigners show emotional sensitivity, too.

2. HIDING OF EMOTIONS   Professor Chie Nakane of Tokyo University, after years of studying Europeans, Indians, and Americans, reports that Japanese are as emotional as the Italians, but that Japanese emotion is directed toward or

From *Harvard Business Review.* (November-December 1970), pp. 45–56. Copyright © 1970 by the President and Fellows of Harvard College; all rights reserved. Reprinted by permission of the publisher. The author is Senior Officer, International Telephone and Telegraph, in Japan.

against others, whereas the emotions of an Italian may only reflect his feelings at the time and have no relationship to others. What is more, the Japanese go out of their way to conceal their sentiments.

Although personal feelings play a significant role in Japanese behavior, a stranger from overseas may never realize it. The proverb, *No aru taka wa tsume wo kakusu* ("An able hawk hides his talons"), illustrates the point:

> One evening at a party in Tokyo, the host, the president of a large Japanese company, remarked to me in his language that an executive from Lucerne, with whom he had been chatting cordially in English, did not like Japanese people. My host added, "I will not do business with a man who does not like us." The visitor from Lucerne had concealed his dislike during his stay—or thought he had—but the president saw behind the mask. Even though the deal proposed by the Swiss would have been mutually profitable, the Japanese executive refused to proceed.

Unless hungry indeed, Japanese are unwilling to do business with someone they think may prove to be arrogant or unpleasant.

3. POWER PLAYS   Japanese dislike the bold use of power and try to avoid situations where this takes place. Many foreigners wondered in the 1960's why the government, which had a huge majority in the Diet, did not vigorously punish the rioters who had caused disruption of so many universities. Instead the Prime Ministers took a low posture and waited for public opinion to turn against the radicals. When at last the police were called in, the rioters were suppressed without brutality and without splitting the country politically.

The Japanese do not like naked displays of power in business either and have developed a remarkable ability to conciliate. They go to court only about one fiftieth as often as do Americans, since in making a decision a judge will perforce display public power nakedly, so someone must lose face. Foreigners should, if at all possible, avoid going to court to settle differences in Japan.

4. AMAERU AND PATERNALISM   Notable among the many Japanese characteristics of behavior that differ from those common in the Occident is one which is called *amaeru.* It may be defined as a longing to be looked after and protected. The greatest single cause of difficulty for foreign managers in Japan is personnel relations, and a lack of understanding of *amaeru* is at the root of much of the trouble.

This trait is one of the forces that have led to the lifetime employment system so widely followed. When a young man joins a good sized company, government agency, or university faculty, he expects to remain until he reaches retirement age. He develops a feeling of dependence on his employer, and realizes that his fate and that of the organization are interrelated.

The implications of the lifetime employment system should be kept in mind by Americans when negotiating. Japanese employees are completely loyal to the organizations for which they work, whether foreign or native, and will go to great lengths to defeat competitors. Also, if the deal an American is proposing will require recruitment of many new employees, the Japanese will want to be reasonably sure that those to be hired will be given steady employment. Many a scheme fails to materialize because such assurance is lacking.

5. GROUP SPIRIT   The Japanese prefer to work as members of groups rather than individually. This characteristic is often cited as one of the most important in explaining Japan's economic success. When negotiating, one should remember that it is not sufficient to convince just one person—the whole group must be won over. The instinct for group rather than individual action is carried over into politics. Few nations have spawned such a small number of dictators as Japan has.

The preference for group rather than individual action may be attributed in part to the Buddhist teaching called *shujo no on,* or feeling of obligation to the world and all living things for one's success. A man who has this belief attributes his good fortune to the assistance and joint efforts of others, rather than to his own wisdom, intelligence or hard work.

The proverb *Deru kugi wa utareru* ("The nail that sticks up is hit") reflects the preference for group action. In the lifetime employment system, it is desirable that no one makes a conspicuous mistake. If decisions are made by a group, there is no danger of a single person having to be struck down like a nail when a decision proves to have been wrong.

6. 'RINGI' PROCESS   Well over 90% of all large Japanese companies, and many small ones, follow a decision-making system known as *ringi.* Government agencies also follow it. The system is based on the principle that decisions will be made by groups, in accordance with a free consensus. Usually it is formalized by a sort of buck slip, or *ringisho,* which carries pertinent facts and a recommendation prepared by someone at the middle-management level. The proposal is passed upward and horizontally to all who are concerned. Each man who sees the *ringisho* is expected to study the proposal and affix his seal to it. Ultimately it reaches the president of the company, and when his vermilion seal is stamped, the policy is officially adopted. The fact that many men—perhaps 20 or more—will have sealed the proposal has the effect of taking the responsibility away from any one individual.

If a person's reaction to a proposal is negative, his best chance to stop—or change it will come in the many conferences that may be called to consider the proposal. However, once a consensus has been reached in conference, it is awkward to block the decision, for a unilateral disapproval offends the Japanese group spirit. Some men, however, do so by pigeonholing the *ringisho.* Others show their objection by affixing their seals upside down. In some organizations, a man may pass the buck by stamping his seal sidewise, which, by custom, means that he has seen the proposal but not passed judgment on it.

Since the *ringisho* is originated fairly well down in an organization—usually by the section specifically assigned responsibility for the subject—it might seem that top management would lose its authority. But, in actual fact, a proposal may be conceived by the president, his directors, or his department heads. The task of drawing it up and documenting it, however, is usually referred to someone at a less lofty level.

In some companies, *ringisho* are brought before the executive committee meetings attended by the president, vice presidents, and inside directors and are freely discussed. This helps resolve differences of opinion.

In comparing American and Japanese decision-making processes, one soon learns that, whereas in the United States a considerable proportion of management ideas are conceived in the executive suite and imposed from the top down, in Japan the reverse is true. More often than not, proposals start from somewhere down the line.

7. SPECIAL INTERESTS   Besides the normal influences, decision making in Japan is sometimes swayed by cliquism and sectionalism just as in many other countries. Before World War II, for example, the military clique was the most powerful single force in establishing governmental policy. In the past 20 years, business and agricultural interests have exercised considerable influence in the government.

In Japan, as in other Oriental countries, "face" is a factor. Sometimes an organization will decide on a certain course, not because of economic or political reasons, but in order to save face for some important person.

8. DELAYS IN DECISIONS   Unfamiliarity with decision-making practices is at the root of many misunderstandings between Japanese and Occidentals. To illustrate:

In one case I recall, a Pennsylvania company insisted that certain action be taken by a Tokyo company because it was covered by a contract. The Japanese agreed to study the matter. When, two months later, nothing apparently had happened, the Philadelphia officers were sure that the president of the Tokyo company did not intend to carry out the agreement.

Actually, this was not the case at all. The management had referred the matter to lower levels, where a *ringisho* had been drawn up with a proposal to proceed as the Americans desired. The proposition was so complicated, and involved so many different levels and departments of the organization as well as government agencies, however, that to move it and arrange for the necessary conferences on the way required over 60 days. During the whole time that Philadelphia was steaming, the local representative knew precisely each day where the *ringisho* was, and saw to it that it was acted on as speedily as was possible.

It has been my experience—sitting in the middle, as it were, of correspondence between Japan and North America, Europe, and Australia—that the Japanese run into long delays when government approvals are required. When governments are not involved, however, the time required for decision making is not much different from ours.

9. THREE-CORNER TALKS   Foreigners soon discover that at least three parties are involved when an agreement is being negotiated, viz., the Japanese company, the foreign company, and the Japanese government. It is complicated

enough for two companies to reach a decision between themselves; it is several times more difficult when a political body must also be satisfied.

The participation of the government may at times be a convenience to the Japanese company. If the foreign company's terms are severe, the government will doubtless demand that they be softened. If the Japanese company wishes to delay its decision, the government will be blamed. If at last the Japanese concern decides against the joint venture, the government may play a face-saving role and deny the application.

Sometimes a fourth party, the Japanese company's bank, will also become a party to the negotiations. Should it oppose the proposition, however, this will usually be kept from the foreigners lest they think that the Japanese company's credit is poor.

10. BUREAUCRATIC PROBLEM   Cabinet ministers and members of the permanent bureaucracy are all subject to pressures from trade associations, Diet members, university professors, private businessmen, and countless domestic lobbying groups, each arguing in its own interest. Except for advice from the Foreign Ministry, foreign embassies and governments, international trade associations, and a handful of internationally minded businessmen, government officials are not subject to much urging that they give a balanced view to international as well as domestic consideration.

The slowness with which the government has removed restrictions on imports and foreign equity investments is a reflection of this imbalance of pressures. The government recognizes the problem, however, and is trying to broaden thinking by sending junior officers of ministries besides Foreign Affairs to overseas posts for assignments of up to three years.

11. AVOIDANCE OF 'NO'   The next trait of the Japanese is another one that most Occidentals find hard to understand.

As professor Chie Nakane of Tokyo University states:

> Expression of *no* is virtually never used outside of completely reciprocal relationships, and from superior to inferior. You rarely receive a *no* from a Japanese, even when he means *no* he would use *yes* in the verbal form (1).

Foreigners long resident in Japan learn to recognize cues which mean *no*. For example, if, when pressed for an answer, a Japanese draws breath through his teeth and says "sah" (it has no meaning), or says, "It is very difficult," the chances are strong he means *no*.

Short-time visitors, when dealing with Japanese who forget that foreigners don't know the cues, are often misled. Typically, the stranger from overseas, after presenting his ideas and assuming that agreement has been reached, will enplane for home, satisfied with himself and the Japanese. The local representative of the U.S. company then has to find out if the agreement was really reached—or if the Japanese merely gave that impression in accordance with the ancient Oriental custom of telling high-level people what they *want* to hear rather than the real facts. For instance:

> I recall well a case where a visitor obtained a commitment from a Japanese concern to take some action. But, after the visitor had boarded his plane for Honolulu, the president of the Japanese company told me: "I know of course that we cannot carry out our promise, but I didn't want to hurt his feelings and spoil his trip. Now you must cable him and explain it can't be done!"

The practice of telling people what they want to hear, rather than the facts, causes trouble, even with resident foreigners. The best way I have found to avoid being misled is to conceal, if I can, what answer I want to receive. Even when soliciting opinions from my Japanese subordinates, I make it a policy to try not to give a clue to what answer is desired.

12. VALUE OF FRIENDSHIP   Friends are often called on in Japan to give help. The more good friends a man has, the more secure he feels. There are degrees of friendship, however. Professor Chie Nakane makes the following observation:

> The relative strength of the human bond tends to increase in proportion to the length and intensity of actual contact. The reason the newcomer in any Japanese group is placed at the very bottom of the hierarchy is that he has the shortest period of contact. This is a primary condition of the seniority system, which dominates Japan. Therefore, the placement of an individual in a social group is governed by the length of the individual's contact with the group. In other words, the actual contact itself becomes the individual's private social capital . . . (2).

One of the principal handicaps under which foreign companies operate is that only rarely do they have on their staffs Westerners who have the private social capital—old friendships—to which Professor Nakane referred. The longer the contact, the greater its value. The average resident Occidental stays about two years. If, during this time, there is frequent contact with certain Japanese businessmen or government officials, there would be opportunity to make meaningful friendships. Unfortunately, too few Westerners find these opportunities, and most complain on leaving that they have no close Japanese friends.

13. NO ARGUMENTS, PLEASE   Among the characteristics that confound visitors when negotiating is the Japanese reluctance to enter into arguments. When challenged, a Japanese usually will not retort, argue, or even discuss a point when he feels he is right. He just remains quiet. A Japanese authority has compared children's quarrels in Japan and Europe and reports that a prompt retort is not expected in Japan but is in Europe (3). In both areas the characteristic develops early.

When negotiating, Occidentals should remember this innate trait and should not consider the Japanese as stubborn or closed-minded because of it.

Art of Negotiating

Negotiating in Japan, whether for the purpose of concluding a joint venture agreement, selling a product, or some other task, usually involves a predictable series of steps and actions. What are these steps? How should the U.S. businessman try to take them?

PLANNING THE TALKS   Once a U.S. company has decided to go to Tokyo, it should prepare its representatives for a long stay and arm them with exhaustive explanations of what is to be offered. Plans should also be made to undertake thorough investigations of local circumstances in Japan. On the average it takes about six times longer, and is three times harder, to reach an agreement on the other side of the Pacific than in the United States. There are many reasons for this, including the need to use interpreters and the fact that neither Americans nor Japanese know much about each other's thinking processes.

Since interpreters will be required from the first day on, it will be wise to learn some basic rules for using them before commencing negotiations. I recommend the following:

1. Brief the interpreter in advance about the subject and give him a copy of the presentation to study and discuss.

2. Speak loudly, clearly, and slowly. (Some Americans try to talk with a cigar in the mouth—an egregious mistake.)

3. Avoid little-known words, such as "arcane," "heuristic," or "buncombe."

4. Maintain a pleasant attitude.

5. Explain each major idea in two or three different ways, as the point may be lost if discussed only once.

6. Do not talk more than a minute or two without giving the interpreter a chance to speak.

7. While talking, allow the interpreter time to make notes of what is being said.

8. Assume that all numbers over 10,000 may be mistranslated. Repeat them carefully and write them down for all to see. The Japanese system of counting large sums is so different from those of the West that errors frequently occur. Also, the number billion should be avoided, as it means 1,000,000,000,000 in Europe, and 1,000,000,000 in the United States.

9. Do not lose confidence if the interpreter uses a dictionary. No one is likely to have a vocabulary of 40,000 words in each of two languages, and a dictionary is often essential.

10. Permit the interpreter to spend as much time as needed in clarifying points whose meanings are obscure.

11. Do not interrupt the interpreter as he translates. Interrupting causes many misunderstandings, usually leaves the visitor from overseas only half informed, and gives the Japanese side a feeling that the foreigner is too impatient to be competent.

12. Do not jump to conclusions, as Japanese ways of doing things are often different from what foreigners expect.

13. Avoid long sentences, double negatives, or the use of negative wordings of a sentence when a positive form could be used.

14. Don't use slang terms, as, for example, "If you will let me have half a "G" at six bits a piece, it'll be gung ho with me." Rather, state simply, "I want 500 at 75 each."

15. Avoid superfluous words. Your point may be lost if wrapped up in generalities.

16. Try to be as expressive as possible by using movements of hands, eyes, lips, shoulders, and head to supplement words.

17. During meetings, write out the main points discussed, in this way both parties can double check their understanding.

18. After meetings, confirm in writing what has been agreed to.

19. Don't expect an interpreter to work for over an hour or two without a rest period. His work is exhausting and a nervous strain.

20. Consider using two men if interpreting is to last a whole day or into the evening, so that when one tires the other can take over.

21. Don't be suspicious if a speaker talks for five minutes and the interpreter covers it in half a minute. The speaker may have been wordy.

22. Be understanding if it develops that the interpreter has made a mistake. It is almost impossible to avoid making some errors, because Japanese and European languages are so dissimilar.

23. Be sure the Japanese are given all the time they want to tell their side of the story. If they hesitate, ask the interpreter for advice on what next to say or do.

GOOD PERSONAL RELATIONS   The Japanese go to great lengths in establishing the right emotional basis for business. In their eyes, emotion is often more important than cold facts in decision making. For instance:

An employee of a Japanese trading company who was assigned to Latin America was told, before leaving Tokyo, "Don't engage in business for one year —just get acquainted with people." He did exactly that, learning to play the guitar and to sing native folk songs. He also learned the local language. Later, in a critical stage in a negotiation, he impressed officials of the host country during a period of relaxation by playing the guitar and singing folk songs. He was so much appreciated for his personal warmth that in time he was decorated by the Latin American government. His company got many orders, too. Occidentals who do business with Japanese may not have time to learn how to strum a *samisen* or sing *joruri* dramatic ballads, but in some way they should try to find out-of-office ways of relating to local people.

Entertainment affords opportunities to get acquainted away from the strain of the conference table and is much used by Japanese businessmen in promoting goodwill. A term commonly used to describe the process is *Naniwabushi,* which means to get on such good personal terms with someone that he will agree to do you a favor when called on. A person gets on these good terms in various ways, one of which is entertainment. Advertising agencies and movie makers spend about 1.8% of sales proceeds on entertainment. The construction and real estate businesses spend about 1%. Popular types of entertainment are golf, geisha parties, and invitations to see sumo matches, kabuki, and other forms of amusement.

Gift giving is also customary and is a factor in negotiating. The gifts may be expensive, including such articles as mink coats, but in most cases they are worth not over 10,000 yen ($27.78). Many government officials receive cases of soft drinks in the summer and salted salmon in the winter. There is no bribery in giving such gifts, as the value of any one is insignificant. Sometimes more soft drinks or fish are received than can be consumed at home, so disposers are called, who buy the surplus at discounts of 30% to 40% and then sell it in turn to housewives at 10% to 20% below the market price.

MAKING A PRESENTATION   Normally the first person a Westerner will meet in a Japanese organization will be of high status, perhaps the director in charge of the foreign affairs division. Executives of this department, although they open the door to the U.S. company, usually do not possess the power to influence decisions. Therefore, they will arrange meetings with concerned internal departments, such as manufacturing, marketing, finance, purchasing, engineering, and research and development.

If the proposition proves interesting to the appropriate internal departments, meetings will be scheduled two or three times a week for a month or more, depending on the complexity of the subject. In one important case in which I was involved, I attended meetings three or four hours a day, six days each week, for nearly two months! The results of this lengthy presentation justified the effort.

There are several reasons why so much time must be spent in conferences:

1. The Japanese desire thorough explanations of every point. In describing and explaining new products and ideas, it will be found that the employment of visual aids is of especial value, for the eyes can supplement what is being said by the interpreter. Samples, models, photographs, maps, sketches, diagrams, catalogs, pamphlets, books, leaflets, blueprints, and so on are indispensable.

At the end of meetings, it may be desirable to give the conferees copies of printed matter and photographs to take back to their offices for further study. Where a formal presentation is made, it is also helpful to use slide films with synchronized recordings, 35mm slides with recordings, or talking motion pictures. The sound should, of course, be in Japanese. It is often beneficial to lend the audio-visual material to the Japanese so that they may then repeat the showings before other groups within their own organization and, if appropriate, to the government officials concerned. If a presentation has aroused enthusiasm, the borrowers will in effect assist in the selling by showing the material.

2. The Japanese use meetings in order to size up their visitors. They study not only what the Occidentals say, but also the character of the strange people from beyond the seas. Since the Japanese spend so much effort in studying the personalities of those around them and comparing notes with one another, they seem to have developed considerable skill in judging people. It should be kept in mind that they rarely do business singly; they usually go in twos and threes in accordance with the group concept.

STYLE OF APPROACH   One thing that they particularly look for is sincerity. Some Japanese, to show their honesty and sincerity, will go so far as to mention a few of the good qualities of competing products during their presentations. A study of reactions of Japanese university students to persuasive communications revealed that two-sided, rather than one-sided, arguments were most effective with those who were, at the outset, opposed to the position being advocated(4).

One test of sincerity is whether a man shows something in print to support his presentation. The Japanese feel that when a man is willing to put his case in print, where all may challenge what he has said, it is likely that he will be accurate so as not to lose face. Also, because their own spoken language is overfull of homonyms, oral statements are often misunderstood. When something is written in Japanese-Chinese characters or in English, the homonym misunderstandings disappear.

Occidentals coming to Japan should bring with them published material describing their company and its products. If some of this material has appeared in the respected technical or trade publication of general circulation, its credibility increases.

When dealing with visitors or resident foreigners, a Japanese will often request copies of cables and correspondence they have received from home offices in response to questions that have been asked during negotiations. The requests test the sincerity of the foreigners as well as reflect the high respect given by Japanese to written material. Also, the requests imply that the Japanese feel that the visitors or residents are working as middlemen who seek to solve problems and bring to fruition a mutually beneficial transaction, rather than as adversaries. It is desirable to establish such rapport.

Since the Japanese prefer a low-pressure sales approach and value sincerity so highly, Westerners are advised to build up their case a step at a time, using modest language rather than making extravagant claims. This strategy gives the Japanese opportunities to ask questions that would be missed if the visitors told their whole story in one lengthy, uninterrupted outflow of eloquence. The Japanese like to feel that the parties to a negotiation work together to establish the facts both pro and con.

In making a presentation, it should be remembered that Japanese and Americans have different objectives in doing business. The former continually stress growth, steady jobs for their own employees, full employment in the nation as a whole, and superiority over competitors. Profit, as a motive, falls behind these needs. But U.S. executives are motivated only by profit—or, at least, that is the way Japanese businessmen see it. When negotiating in Japan, Americans do well to appeal first to the four popular local objectives, and only then discuss profit.

OVERCOMING OPPOSITION   At some time during the negotiations, a crisis usually arises. It is liable to last for several weeks, and, during this period, the Japanese side may not wish to continue conferences. Westerners should keep channels open with the Japanese company during this time, even if there are no formal meetings.

One step that may be taken is to make discreet inquiries of men at lower levels who are known to be friendly, asking who is opposing the deal and why. The inside friends, with their company's best interests foremost, may even go so far as to suggest what approach is likely to be most effective. If the Japanese company president or some other high officer is in favor of the proposition, he may arrange for a private luncheon at which the chief opponents of the plan will explain their views to the perplexed visitors.

A Japanese businessman, when confronted with opposition, often follows a practice of what is called "selling one's face." He will drop in on his customer or the government official—whoever is blocking him—for a casual talk from time to time without making an appointment. He will just say, "I was passing by and dropped in to say hello." I know of men who have made 15 or 20 calls of this kind before they were able to get things moving forward.

It is not uncommon, during the crisis stage, to enlist the aid of a common friend and ask him to find out what is holding up the negotiations and to do what he can to get things moving again. If the go-between is someone who is a member of a club or other group to which an opponent belongs, or is an alumnus from the same university or high school, he is likely to have considerable influence. The old school tie has great worth in Japan.

DRAWING UP THE CONTRACT   After the crisis has passed, conferences have been resumed, and it becomes apparent that the Japanese, in general, are willing to go ahead with the proposition, a "Heads of Agreement" should be drawn up and initialed by both parties.

Often Occidentals make the mistake of presenting a detailed, one-sided, lengthy legal contract at this stage. This frightens the Japanese and immediately identifies the foreign negotiators as adversaries. Of course, a written contract should be made. But it should be developed jointly in the course of negotiations and be little more than a statement of the points that have been agreed to and understood.

Westerners usually want the contract to indicate commitments, conditions, and restrictions in precise language which will not be liable to later misinterpretation. On the other hand, the Japanese feel that the written agreement should be a declaration of intention and deal in specifics only where it describes the technology or services which the foreign company is expected to provide. Each may find it necessary to make some concessions to the other's viewpoint in this respect.

CLOSING THE DISCUSSIONS   When the contract is being drawn up, there will come a time when agreement must be reached on unclosed points which have, until then, been put aside. It is at this stage that—because of the American desire to "get on with it" and the Japanese custom of being silent for what is too long a time by U.S. standards—tactical errors are liable to occur.

Americans often don't know how to cope with silence. They can't understand what is going on. Briefly, this is what is happening:

When a pause or impasse in the discussions develops, the Japanese remain quiet, not feeling a compulsion to say anything. Many Japanese can even refrain from answering when a question is asked them, responding to it by drawing air through their teeth and then sitting back as though pondering what to say. When a couple of minutes have passed, and no comment is forthcoming, Americans become uneasy and feel that they must make some sort of statement. It is at this point that they often voluntarily give in on a disputed point or say something they should not say, just to get the conversation going again. There will, at all stages of the negotiations, but particularly near the end, be occasions when it is desirable to reach a compromise. The Japanese, though good conciliators, like to do it in such a way that neither side appears to have made a forced concession. Therefore, they object to frank, clearly defined compromises or to agreements to split the difference when the problem concerns something like price, delivery, or quantity. Instead, they like to develop a formula based on whatever facts and ideas can be bent to conform to the objective.

It is also common, near the end of negotiations, for the Japanese to insist on a large amount of data to justify the action that is being taken. Some of this will be needed for internal company use, but a considerable amount will be required to satisfy the government. If the Westerners refuse to supply the information requested, thinking it unnecessary, the Japanese may find it impossible to go through with the deal.

One of the reasons for demanding so much supporting data—all in visual forms—is that, should the venture fail, no one can then be rebuked; that is, no one will be blamed for recommending that his company proceed on a project if all the known evidence justified it.

When, at last, all the data have been assembled and the agreement has been put in form for signing, the time for final executive decision making comes. The *ringisho* decision document referred to earlier will be drawn up and the papers forwarded upward to the executive committee.

Conclusion

As this short exposition indicates, negotiating with the Japanese involves complications unknown in the Americas and Europe. The culture is an old one, and, since the Japanese politico-economic system is so successful, there is little likelihood it will be rapidly changed.

The nation is in sound fiscal condition, as nations go, despite the high debt ratio of its corporations. The national debt is small; individual indebtedness is inconsiderable; the economy is well balanced, not dependent on any one product, and therefore not as subject to boom or bust as it was in the early part of the twentieth century, when silk was so important. In addition the stated objectives of Japanese business—to achieve growth, to improve the livelihood of the public, and to benefit the nation generally—appeal to the idealism of most young people.

What is more, there are many economists in Japan who believe that within 15 years the per-capita annual income will rise to $10,000. This would mean that the average family would have over $20,000, after taxes, to spend each year. Should Japan's income rise as forecast, it would be by far the richest market in the world.

References

1. "Analysis of Japanese Social Structure," in *Lectures on Characteristics of Japanese Management,* International Management Program for Foreign Executives in Japan, International Management Association of Japan, 1st Session, July 30 to August 1, 1964, Hakone, Japan.

2. "An Analysis of Japanese Social Structure," *Management Japan,* October–December 1967, p. 34.

3. Kanji Hatano, "Children's Quarrels," as quoted by Muchitaro Tada, "A Content Analysis of 'Yakuza' Fiction," *Japanese Popular Culture,* edited and transcribed by Hidetoshi Kato (Tokyo, Charles Tuttle, 1959), pp. 182–183.

4. Eliott McGinnies, "Some Reactions of Japanese University Students to Persuasive Communications," *The Journal of Conflict Resolution,* December 1964, p. 486.

American Advisors Overseas
Edward C. Stewart

The difficulty in cross-cultural communication and cooperation for U.S. advisors overseas lies primarily in the disparity and conflict between the advisor's own cultural pattern and that of his foreign counterpart, and only secondarily in the strangeness of the foreign ways. It certainly appears that the cross-cultural performance of the U.S. advisor would be enhanced if his area training included instruction on the U.S. cultural pattern as well as on the foreign pattern.

Cultural Awareness

The need for the U.S. advisor to understand his own cultural pattern, as well as that of the host country, does not mean that his insight must be explicit and articulate. His cultural understanding may often be implicit, as when an advisor

From *Military Review,* Vol. 45 (February 1965), pp. 3–9. Reprinted by permission of the Editor-in-Chief, *Military Review,* U.S. Army Command and General Staff College. The author is a Research Scientist with the Human Resources Research Office, George Washington University.

gears his actions to existing cultural differences, even though he is not necessarily able to describe the relevant aspects of either his own or the foreign culture. In this circumstance, the advisor perceives the cultural disparities at some intuitive level and acts accordingly.

Direct Participation

In other instances, although lacking cultural understanding, the advisor is successful through serendipity. A fortunate and accidental combination of cultural factors on one hand, and personality and behavior of the advisor on the other, may produce a result that would usually be expected only on the basis of cultural insight. The average American's facility in establishing social relationships frequently creates favorable circumstances for giving advice, especially when it is followed by the American's willingness to work with those at the lowest levels of an organization or group. Thus, in non-Western countries, U.S. officers are often more effective in working with the enlisted men than with the officers. Part of the reason for the success of the Americans rests with their greater willingness—in comparison to non-Western officers—to work with all ranks, even the lowest.

Success through serendipity may take strange forms; the experienced advisor learns not to count on it, for unwitting failure is probably far more frequent than unplanned success. An example of this type of success was given by an Ecuadoran administrator who supervised several Peace Corps volunteers in social welfare work. Because the volunteers did not speak Spanish fluently on arrival, they were forced to demonstrate rather than to give lectures, working directly with the Indians instead of supervising them.

The actions of the volunteers influenced their Ecuadoran counterparts to work along the same line. Although the Ecuadoran administrator recognized that demonstration and direct participation are typical American methods of instructing and influencing others, he pointed out that many Americans overseas become like their local counterparts, giving lectures and remaining aloof. In this instance, he felt that the Peace Corps volunteers' lack of fluency in Spanish contributed, in part, to their success.

Cross-Cultural Incongruity

Many problems of U.S. advisors overseas can be traced to the incongruities between American and foreign cultural patterns. When the U.S. advisor is confronted with unusual cultural patterns, his lack of familiarity with them may lead to misunderstanding and friction. Americans, like members of any other culture, have their own cultural patterns which provide them with a comprehensive system of perceiving and understanding the world, and with preferred modes of action.

Whenever the individual finds the strangeness of life in a foreign country leading to uncertainty, he adopts hypotheses derived from his own cultural pattern to fit the new situation. Since these interpretations—based on his own cultural pattern—dominate, he is not likely to suspend judgment and action until he can fully understand the strange ways. Because his own ways seem to him normal and natural, he is likely to regard those of another culture as undesirable, unnatural, or immoral.

Consequently, the individual's own pattern comes into conflict with that of the foreign culture. Any contingency he may meet, no matter how strange, is likely to lead to an interpretation according to his own pattern. Since the cultural pattern itself is not precisely articulated, the tentative hypotheses are likely to be imprecise. The individual will, accordingly, spawn a crude interpretation and thereby reduce the ambiguity of cross-cultural differences.

Examples of Incongruity

The ways in which people act toward each other reveal many instances of cross-cultural incongruity, since each culture has preferred standards which govern social interactions. American men, for instance, have well-marked norms of displacement in space in regard to other people. When sitting in an audience, an American man does not ordinarily lean against or touch persons sitting next to him, because the act carries emotional or sexual meaning. In conversation, he stands at least an arm's length from the other person. If he comes closer, the distance is charged with significance. Thus, the intensity of a cocktail party, the intimacy of a small, crowded restaurant, and the camaraderie of people jamming a parade route, are all partly a result of the necessary proximity of the persons involved.

The inexperienced American overseas may become very uncomfortable when he talks to an Arab or a Latin American whose face is only a short distance from his own. Their proximity merely expresses a more personalized manner of interacting with other people; it is a custom, however, that is incompatible with American habits.

Another practice that may shock the American when he first observes it is the custom in many parts of the world—in Vietnam, for instance—for men to hold hands as an expression of friendship. While the American knows that the practice has no sexual significance for the Vietnamese, he cannot regard it with equanimity because his own cultural pattern gives him an interpretation of holding hands contrary to the Vietnamese meaning of the act. Both the Americans and the Vietnamese may well understand these different ways, yet each is likely to feel that his own way is the normal one.

An aspect of interpersonal relations found in U.S. culture, which contrasts with non-Western ways, is the depersonalized manner of dealing with other people. The American places a high value on equality, informality, and depersonalized business relations. He takes an objective approach to his job, trying to remove his feelings from his work. Preferring standard and predictable ways of interacting with other people, he is unprepared for the personal mode of social interaction in other parts of the world. In the Middle East, in southeast Asia, and in other areas of the world, the business dealings that take place over a purchase are seen as a personalized way of doing business. The price of an article is not standardized, but is subject to bargaining between the seller and the buyer.

In non-Western countries, bargaining is a transaction between persons who, because they have about the same control over the situation, may be considered equals. Gift giving, especially a gift of money, is a personalized way of conducting affairs in which reciprocity is incomplete or nonexistent. The person who received money may reciprocate with his usual services, or he may not be expected to make any return at all.

Personalization in unequal situations—between superiors and subordinates —may be regarded as graft, corruption, influence peddling, or nepotism by the American. He tends to react with moral indignation forgetting similar instances in his own country. His sense of outrage prevents his recognizing that personalized superior-subordinate relationships are expected in many non-Western cultures. His anticipation that U.S. money and material overseas will yield goods, services, or at least will not go into someone's pockets is not necessarily shared by his counterpart. U.S. money or goods, or even the advisors themselves, may mean to the counterparts a personalized gesture of good will from the U.S. Government which does not require an accounting.

Area of Application

Various aspects of interpersonal relations in U.S. culture provide precedents for understanding graft in other parts of the world. The tip, in some instances, has functions similar to graft. The main difference between the two is in the area of application. Whereas for Americans the tip is usually confined to personal services given by nonprofessional persons, people in other parts of the world extend the same kind of personal consideration to most activities.

This parallel between graft and the tip is not suggested to induce the American to regard graft as inevitable, but only to avoid reactions that will subvert his own purposes. For instance, he will anger many non-Westerners if he reacts to graft with moral indignation, because they accept what Americans call graft as part of social existence. They feel it is something not to abolish but only to curb. When an American reacts indignantly, as if graft can and should be eradicated, the non-Westerners may become angry, for they consider the American unrealistic and hypocritical.

Finding the Right Concept

The task of the U.S. advisor is much easier if he can find a concept that is meaningful to him and that can be effectively translated into the language of his counterpart without causing confusion. Transferring concepts from one culture to another is more than the translation of words. Culture differences exist even when members of both cultures speak the same language, as in the case of

Americans and the British, and require the same tact and understanding that is needed between the Americans and, say, the Chinese or Iranians.

The conflict between different cultural patterns can be so subtle that it may lead to misunderstandings difficult to unravel. Because the British and American cultures are very similar in most respects, no great difficulty arises in reducing the amount of discord between the two when translating the cultural items of one culture into the patterns of the other. When two cultures are very different, however, additional complications are introduced. The patterns of the two differing cultures may not be parallel and hence may lack analogous focal points.

Fortunately for the U.S. military advisor, he is working in areas of activity for which his own culture offers clear parallels. In most military matters, the advisor's activities can be considered as efforts to impose certain Western patterns of organization and action upon a different culture environment. Quite often it may be possible for the advisor to translate U.S. concepts into familiar terms dealing with generalized ideas or acts and thereby produce the desired results.

Some time ago in Laos, a U.S. military advisor attempted to motivate Lao soldiers by describing the squad, platoon, and company in terms of the family. This officer apparently recognized that the Lao might not have a national identification, that he could not readily identify himself with the army, and that he might not be motivated by a spirit of competition. The officer took advantage of the Lao soldiers' attachments to their own large and extended families to supply the motivation which, with the American, is usually derived from competition, personal rewards, and satisfactions.

Basic Differences

In each cultural pattern, experiences are organized by means of certain concepts. Western European and U.S. cultures, for instance, employ a subject-predicate relationship, clearly separating the agent both from his actions and the context in which they occur. These cultural focal points allow for the development of separate abstractions such as the individual, his feelings, and various kinds of activities in which he may engage.

Practically speaking, in the case of the military profession, the American can readily separate tactical and logistical problems and consider each problem by itself. An even more fundamental distinction can be made between military and political or social problems in a war like that being fought in Vietnam.

The Chinese, however, do not have clear parallels for such abstractions. They do not recognize the subject-predicate relationship, and do not clearly distinguish between the individual and his thoughts and feelings, the individual and his actions, and the context in which these occur. The Chinese mind is concrete and he is situation-centered to a degree unbelievable to the Westerner. He does not derive laws and principles that presumably govern events in the way that the Westerner does. In the writings of Mao Tse-tung we read that the laws of war are different according to the character of the war, its time, its place, and the nation.

Misunderstandings

Perhaps it is the Chinese trait of concrete thinking that induced one American writer to state that Mao's: ". . . theory has universal applicability only in its repeated warnings that every situation must be considered in the frame of its historic development and geographic setting."

Even though a word may be found to translate a concept from one cultural pattern to another, there is no assurance that an accurate and viable concept has been chosen in the second pattern that is equivalent to the original one. When two cultures are not parallel in their focal points, misunderstandings can occur and inaccuracies can be perpetrated by the application of familiar concepts in a foreign environment. Americans and other Westerners have taken political and social concepts such as nationalism, militarism, and the democratic system of elections, which are native to Western countries, and have attempted to apply them to the underdeveloped countries where they have different meanings.

The process of translating these ideas from one language to another is likely to fail of the desired intent. As an example, the Lao do not constitute a political entity in the sense that the Americans or Frenchmen do. The Lao villager, who identifies solely with his family and village, does not have the sense of being a national of his country in the same way as the American or the Englishman.

In regard to militarism, an officer in a Middle Eastern country is likely to represent the conservative feudal element of the society with an outlook and manner of life typical of his class. Elsewhere, as in Brazil, the military officer often represents the liberal intellectual whose attitude and position in his own society resemble that of militarists in other countries only in the uniform that others wear. Finally, an election in many non-Western cultures is more like a festival and celebration than a political campaign.

Serious Obstacles

Cross-cultural incongruities present serious obstacles to the U.S. advisor, because he may not have the principles and concepts readily available that will help him understand his situation. He may become puzzled and confused if he does not recognize the cultural disparities; more likely, since his own cultural pattern provides him with possible interpretations, he will derive erroneous conclusions about the meaning of the situation.

Advisors in Laos, when faced with the tactics of their Lao commanders—which they call a game of tag—suspected the Lao officers of cowardice and, in some cases, of collusion with the *Pathet Lao.* They apparently were not aware that one pattern of warfare in that part of the world is, in the American view, a matter of bluster, evasion, and deception, and hence such tactics do not necessarily represent cowardice or collusion.

Although the misunderstandings that can occur are many and varied, the instructor in area training who prepares advisory personnel for overseas work does not face an impossible task in giving advice and training. Interviews with advisors who have been overseas serving in various countries show certain similarities in the problems and difficulties that they regularly meet. The U.S. cultural pattern, shared by all U.S. advisors, provides one constant factor among all the competition and friction that develop between the American and the foreign ways. And although the widely separated countries to which Americans are sent each possess unique characteristics, they often differ from the American or Western culture in the same directions.

The primary objectives of the area trainer should not be limited to coping with information about the many different countries to which military personnel may be assigned. Rather, he should concentrate upon the development of concepts and principles that will help the student first to understand his own cultural pattern and then be able to translate it satisfactorily into the patterns of any country to which he may be assigned.

Sometimes the necessary interpretations can be carried out at a superficial level, but when the differences between the cultures are profound, the tactics of finding a common ground may be beyond the scope of common-sense concepts. It may require psychological or social analysis to discover the means for transforming the understanding of one cultural pattern into effective performance in another.

Interpersonal Communication within Transracial Contexts

Arthur L. Smith

Assuming that in the next few years you will interact verbally with many persons of a different racial background than yours, we have prepared this chapter on the premise: *The understanding of transracial communication barriers and the will to interact will greatly facilitate your ability to communicate meaningfully across ethnic and racial lines.*

Transracial Communication

We use "transracial communication," either dyadic or mass, to refer to the understanding that persons from different ethnic or racial backgrounds can

From Larry L. Barker and Robert J. Kibler, Editors, *Speech Communication Behavior: Perspectives and Principles* © 1971. Reprinted by permission of Prentice-Hall, Inc., Englewood Cliffs, New Jersey. Professor Aseti Asanti (Arthur L. Smith) is Chairman of the Department of Speech-Communication at the State University of New York, Buffalo.

achieve in a situation of verbal interaction. By defining "transracial" as including both *racial* and *ethnic* groups, we have sought to differentiate it from the much used term, "interracial," which usually denotes race only. After all, significant problems in communication exist between ethnic groups that may be anthropologically classified as of the same race. "Transracial" communication is also delineated from "intercultural" communication, which usually refers to political goals and diplomatic missions in an international context. "Transracial," in this chapter, refers, for the most part, to communication intra-nationally. You should also note that when we use the word "race" without also using "ethnic," and vice versa, both terms are meant, inasmuch as both "race" and "ethnic" are encompassed in our definition of *transracial communication.*

Such communication, more often than not, simultaneously takes place interculturally and intraculturally, in the sense that two or more ethnic cultures meet under the umbrella of what is for the most part a general culture, even though it might be synonymous with one of the ethnic cultures. Referring to minority ethnic groups as "culturally deprived" has been shown to be exceedingly erroneous (Allen and Hernandez, 1969), especially when groups such as Afro-Americans and Mexican-Americans consider themselves to be culturally advantaged.

The term "ethnic group" usually refers to those who possess a shared tradition, an idea of common destiny, and a feeling of spiritual togetherness, all of which may exist even if they possess no common territory or political organization. It has probably occurred to you that America is a nation of varied ethnic groups: Mexican-Americans, Afro-Americans, Jewish-Americans, Armenian-Americans, and so on. These groups tend to express an inner unity which often has semibiological undertones. In Black communities the term "soul" has come to express what is felt but cannot be transmitted to others. Growing out of a feeling of shared traditions and aspirations, this concept seems to name the semibiological experience of Black people.

Intra-ethnic expressions and aspirations identify common goals, beliefs, and anticipations which serve to cement the group. But group solidarity based on shared experiences need not become a barrier to intergroup communication. Sensitivity to others dissolves most walls that humans erect to keep from talking to others. Feeling into the peculiar set of experiences which sets another person apart from us can help to eliminate barriers while providing both parties with a shared experience: communication. This requires a concentrated effort.

An essential quality for the would-be transracial communicator is what Rokeach (1960) calls "open-mindedness." This is not a new concept to you. How many times have you responded to a friend's refusal to "see" your point with the words, "Oh, why can't you be open-minded?" Opposite to open-mindedness is closed-mindedness, and both are pervasive character traits found in varying degrees in each person, depending upon his system of beliefs. There are certain things that we are more open-minded about than others. Each person has a "central-intermediate-peripheral" continuum which structures his beliefs (Rokeach, 1960). "Central beliefs" are the fundamental beliefs a person has about himself, the physical world and the "generalized other." These beliefs are characterized by the intensity with which they are held. "Intermediate beliefs" are those which are based upon a person's view of authority, and upon the persons he depends for a picture of his world. These beliefs are usually strongly held, but not so strongly maintained, as central beliefs. Finally, "peripheral beliefs" are those derived from authority, which help a person complete his idea of the world. The openness of a person's system of beliefs can be determined by discovering his interest in and willingness to assess new information. This is particularly relevant in transracial communication, inasmuch as persons might hold central or intermediate beliefs about interaction between different racial or ethnic groups.

Open-mindedness in an individual produces an optimistic outlook (Bettinghaus, 1968) about the way things happen in society, and causes a person to view information from an historical perspective. In contrast, a closed-minded person compartmentalizes the beliefs he holds and is reluctant to compare various beliefs. While it is nearly impossible to always predict the responses of persons involved in transracial communication, it can be asserted that open-minded individuals will enter into more harmonious interpersonal communication with persons of a different race than dogmatic or closed-minded individuals. This does not mean, however, that other factors will not affect the interactive process. Again, a person might be less open-minded about some issues than about many others, which means that the content of the communication will influence the communicators. When two closed-minded individuals confront each other, the possibility of effective communication is substantially reduced.

On the other hand, open-minded persons will receive and evaluate messages on their merit. This means that it is possible for two open-minded persons to disagree about the merit of an idea. In fact, transracial communication is only truly accomplished when verbal interaction is normalized to the extent that people of different races can disagree, evaluate each other, and express deep feelings without the matter of their racial difference entering into the conversation. *Normalization* is the end of effective interracial communication. It is not normal for Blacks and whites to be denied the opportunity of communicating their disagreements and dissatisfactions with each other as individuals. Abnormal interaction is characterized by dishonesty and lack of candor; normal interaction is characterized by openness and maturity. Thus, the *normalization* of interpersonal relations through verbal interaction is the end of effective transracial communication.

The selection following this essay is an article which demonstrates the diversity of language in the American society. Our approach to these different styles of language and communication should be based upon a mature respect for effective interaction. In a multi-ethnic society it is essential that we understand and accept diversity. Perhaps Gittler (1956, p. 139) puts the issue best when he states:

> The basic problem is not diversity, but acceptance of diversity. Most thoughtful men realize that group diversity is a part of our world. How we learn to live with and accept diversity will determine the future of civilization as we have known it.

In fact, a more harmonious society than we have known can be based upon the acceptance of American diversity while simultaneously reaching across barriers to communicate with persons of different ethnic backgrounds.

In preparing this chapter we have assumed that most people, particularly college students, freed from some of the encapsulating racial stereotypes and prejudices of a few years ago, will want to know how they can have more harmonious communication with persons of another racial group. Obviously many of the obstacles to this type of communication are fundamental to all communication. Yet there is evidence (Ratcliffe and Steil, 1970), which suggests that race may be a more important determinant of attitudinal differences toward social issues than sex, class rank, age, or geographical location. On the basis of this analysis we believe that race can play a potent role in how you interact verbally with persons of another racial background, even though it does not have to. The traditional communication barriers are often amplified in a transracial context, particularly when you have already based an opinion or a judgment of the other person upon his race.

We have organized this chapter under three basic headings: (1) an overview of theory and research; (2) principles derived from theory; and (3) a selected reading. The first section is an attempt to put interpersonal communication between persons of different races into focus by viewing related theoretical formulations and research. Under the heading of Principles Derived from Theory we discuss some of the key concepts of interpersonal communication in transracial contexts and demonstrate their applicability to your own communication with persons of other races. Finally, the reading provides you with additional discussion of our subject.

Overview of Theory and Research

It is generally accepted by communication scholars (Westley and MacLean, 1957; Schramm, 1954; Berlo, 1960; and Bettinghaus, 1968) that interpersonal communication is liable to be more difficult to achieve, and is less likely to occur, the greater the contextual differences between source and receiver. This is to say, when communicators share a similar verbal code, are mutually available, and have similar values, their chances for understanding each other are immensely increased.

The paucity of literature directly related to interracial communication argues for more sensitive conceptual schemes for interpersonal analysis. Although several studies of intercultural communication have already been made, few if any recent research articles have contributed to our understanding of interracial communication intra-nationally. While this may appear exceedingly strange considering the enormity of our racial problems, it is not inconsistent with the lack of pluralism which has so often characterized academic research. It is highly likely that studies in interracial communication could prove equally as rewarding to the society as intercultural studies have proved. Furthermore, inasmuch as interpersonal communication in transracial contexts, particularly in America, must often be considered intercultural, a brief look at some pertinent research in this area might help us understand what might be referred to as "transracial communication."

Since the appearance of Franz Boas's (1940) collection of articles, a variety of cultural anthropologists, speech communication scholars, and sociolinguistic experts have studied language and culture (Carroll, 1964; Hall, 1959; Hoijer, 1954; Lado, 1963; A. G. Smith, 1966; Van Nieuwenhuijze, 1963; Weinreich, 1964). Even so, the employment of research designs and methodologies similar to Boas's has not provided the theoretical framework needed to make this research applicable to transracial contexts. In *Race, Language and Culture,* Boas attempted to demonstrate the relevance of his research to everyday problems. However, the section on language is primarily classificatory, dealing with the various traits and attributes of Indian languages, and little effort is expended to draw any implications about inter-ethnic communication. It is therefore doubtful that Boas accomplished his goal.

With perhaps more currency for interpersonal communication, Edward Hall (1959) suggested the possibility of a silent language operating between people of different cultures, and even later (1966) analyzed the perception of space and time dimensions as possible factors in intercultural relationships. Although verbal language is the essential medium of interpersonal communication in that words and sentences are the means of *connecting* one person to another, nonverbal signs play extremely significant roles in communication. Perhaps, in communication across racial lines, an understanding of the nonverbal signs is even more important than an understanding of the verbal code. Nonverbal signs can often serve as double-cutting edges when we are trying to communicate in transracial contexts. In one situation, a speaker might unintentionally use an "attack" word while speaking to a member of another race and be "rescued" by his unmalicious, perhaps, friendly appearance as reflected in countenance, ease, and gestures. In another, a person might misunderstand certain intergroup signs (Black handshake, Soul fingers, Victory walk, and so on) even when such "signs" are accompanied by rather innocent words. While Edward Hall (1959) does not discuss the domestic situation, his general treatment of cultural differences is a perceptive look at communication problems between people who view time and space differently.

A variety of books (Dance, 1967, Smith, 1966, Sereno and Mortensen, 1970; and Berlo, 1960, among others) concerned with theory and process have added to our knowledge of interpersonal communication. Berlo (1960) in writing about the characteristics of the "source-encoder" identified four factors which are valuable for our discussion. According to Berlo, the factors within the source capable of increasing the fidelity of his communication are his: (1) communication skills; (2) attitudes; (3) knowledge; and (4) sociocultural position. "Communication skills," his first factor, include writing, speaking, reading, and listening, the first two being "encoding" capacities and the latter two being "decoding" capacities. A fifth communication skill crucial to both encoding and decoding is thought. To be a fuzzy thinker is to run the risk of being misunderstood.

Berlo's second factor was "attitudes." Let us assume an attitude to be a predisposition, favorable or unfavorable, toward some object. Now it is possible to conceptualize what Berlo means by: (1) attitude toward self; (2) attitude toward subject matter; and (3) attitude toward receiver.

The third factor contributing to the source-encoder's credibility is his knowledge. Effective interpersonal communication requires both knowledge and understanding. The source must know what it is he wants to communicate and he must understand what communication skills can best be brought to bear on specific issues. You may possess sharp insight into inter-ethnic or interracial problems and yet not be able to communicate effectively because you do not understand how to use your communication skills. The person who enters such an interaction technically knowledgeable, but lacking understanding of communication skills, could possibly offend the receiver. Such situations can be avoided if the source-encoder concentrates on content and skill jointly; they are both indispensable to effective interpersonal communication in transracial contexts.

Perhaps more closely related to some of the concepts to be explored more thoroughly in this chapter is the factor of sociocultural position. Every person who communicates is a captive of his cultural environment. Berlo does not see this concept in relationship to interracial communication, although he gives general guidelines which he explains in terms of international differences (Berlo, 1960) and status. But it is still possible to speak of the source's sociocultural system *in re* transracial communication as well *in re* the corresponding system within the receiver. Actually, all that has been said above about the source can be applied to the "receiver-decoder." Later we shall discuss principles of communication applicable to transracial interaction, at which time specific concepts will be discussed.

From the foregoing discussion of related literature, several fundamental principles of interpersonal communication in transracial contexts can be stated. The principles derived from the body of knowledge about transracial communication behavior are placed in four categories: (1) common codification; (2) sender-receiver proximity; (3) perspective; and (4) general communication skills.

Principles Derived from Theory

1. Interracial Communication Is Facilitated When the Communicators Share a Common Coding System

Much conflict, interracial and otherwise, could be resolved and indeed prevented if people had some knowledge of each other's verbal code. When source and receiver share a codification system, their chances of achieving understanding are considerably improved. "Code" refers to the verbal and nonverbal signs of communication. It therefore serves as the primary link between source and receiver, and, if it is significantly impaired in any way, the communication process is less likely to succeed. Thus interpersonal communication depends upon a common code, and effective transracial communication requires that the communicators understand the essential elements of each other's code.

Fairly recent studies into the value of categorization (Hayek, 1952; Bruner, Goodnow, and Austin, 1956; and Triandis, 1960) have revealed that persons who categorize objects, events, and concepts in a similar manner should be able to communicate effectively. Accordingly, the work of several scholars (Homans, 1950; Runkel, 1956; and Newcomb, 1956) indicates that if persons possess cognitive similarity and have opportunity for interaction, then communication will be rewarding. These research findings may be taken as presumptive evidence that a common coding system facilitates interpersonal communication in transracial contexts.

OVERLAPPING CODES   Often, in interpersonal communication between different ethnic groups, the source and receiver have overlapping codes, i.e., codes which provide an area of commonality but which also contain areas of unshared codification. A factor contributing to this situation is the relative ease with which members of minority ethnic groups learn the code of the majority society. This means that most white communicators have had limited experience in integrated communication, except for peripheral relationships with maids, gardeners, and so on, and that most white communicators do not understand Black community language. Blacks and other minority-group members have also had limited experience with integrated communication, but they have developed functional communication behavior in the native language of the majority society. Few whites have developed functional communication behavior in the language of the Black community. Usually the Black, or minority person, acquires the majority's code formally but finds great resistance to its adoption among his peers, in his home, and at play. The white communicator has usually acquired his code informally, as a matter of course. A reason for this, of course, is that the language of the majority is the language of trade, commerce, education, politics, and services, and minority groups must therefore adopt this language to some extent, even if only in their daily intercourse with the external world and not in more immediate surroundings. The figures below represent some possibilities of code overlapping.

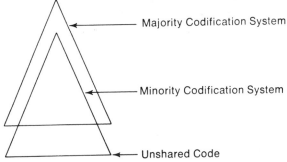

Majority Codification System

Minority Codification System

Unshared Code

Figure 1

Figure 1 shows one possibility of code overlapping and an unshared area of codification. This figure might represent the Black-white codification pattern in many areas of American society. You will notice that the Minority codification system is largely enclosed by the Majority codification system. This makes it possible for interracial communication to occur when it would otherwise be impossible, as when a Black communicator reverts to the use of community language while supposedly communicating with a white receiver. Community language, consisting of Black English, slang, and communication subtleties as reflected in the nonverbal code, is represented by the area labeled "Unshared code." It is usually reserved for communication between ethnic peers and family members, and during social occasions.

Figure 2 shows the commonality of code in the case of a minority whose cultural language is foreign to the general American codification system. This figure might represent the codification structure of many Spanish-speaking Americans, who share a small area of commonality with the larger codification system by virtue of limited participation in the society in search of employment and other necessities. Because the majority of Americans with whom they come into contract do not speak Spanish, the minority group has to learn the utilitarian words of English in order to provide for their families and get an education. Often they use Spanish in their churches, at home, and at play, much like Blacks use Black English and slang when not constrained by the formalities of the major culture.

NONVERBAL CODE   Nonverbal signs comprise a major portion of the code in effective interracial communication. Nonverbal codification, which is often used unconsciously, is indispensable to meaningful communication in transracial contexts. In order to achieve a measure of understanding, persons who communicate must possess the capacity to respond to nonverbal as well as verbal cues. It has been estimated that 65 per cent of the social meaning of communication is carried by nonverbal communication. "Action speaks louder than words," according to one adage. None of you would ever think seriously of saying "up" and simultaneously pointing a finger downward. The reason is that most Americans share a common nonverbal codification system for "up" and "down." Yet in inter-ethnic communication it is possible that a source might employ a word you think you understand, only to confuse you because the word employed and the accompanying nonverbal communication do not coincide as they should in your

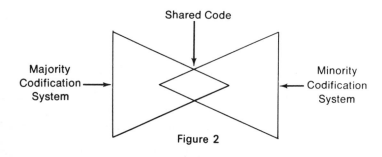

Figure 2

experience. When the word "beautiful" is used in reference to a girl you consider homely, you may have second thoughts about the exactness of the source's code especially when he says "beautiful" but recoils instead of being attracted by the girl's physical presence. Perhaps "beautiful" means something other than the receiver thinks it should, and the nonverbal communication often helps to point that out.

Ruesch and Kees (1956) identified three kinds of nonverbal communication: sign language, action language, and object language. "Sign language" is the conscious substitution of a gesture for words, numbers, or punctuation. Most Americans share·a similar sign language, which means that even in interracial communication there are many areas of shared meaning. "Action language" refers to all bodily movements that are not consciously meant to communicate, but nevertheless do: Certain unintended facial expressions might lead to interracial misunderstanding. In fact, it is possible for an observer to decode the action messages of another person and arrive at an unintended conclusion. This means that close attention must be paid to the implications of action language. In a certain medical school, an experiment was conducted on the ability of minority patients to identify doctors with racial prejudice. The results showed that although each doctor performed the same tasks, the patients were consistently able to identify those who were judged to have prejudicial attitudes. Finally, "object language" refers to material and physical displays, intentional and unintentional, which communicate. Thus object language can range anywhere from sartorial outfits like the berets and leather jackets of the Black Panthers to a display of the United States Flag. Given the complexities of this phenomenon, our brief discussion has not exhausted the subject, nor was it meant to, but we hope it has provided you with some guidelines in understanding how a common code facilitates interracial communication. For additional information regarding language differences, see Frederick Williams' article on "Acquisition and Performance of Communication Behaviors" in Chapter 3 of this volume.

2. Meaningful Communication in Transracial Contexts Requires the Proximity of Source and Receiver

All communication events require that the participants become available to each other inasmuch as there are physical limits to the transmitting of codes, whether verbal or nonverbal. In transracial communication, where availability is more difficult, access to some of the characteristics of each other's experience determines the effectiveness of our communication. Mistakes are often made when persons of different ethnic backgrounds fail to comprehend each other's perceptions and visualizations. Minority persons often have access to white perceptions because of the necessity to function within a majority society, while whites do not often reciprocate by learning what the minority's perceptions are. Of course, there are exceptions when the majority's society is threatened by minority group protests, demonstrations or violence; during such a time the survival of the white society appears at stake and efforts to understand minority complaints are in the best interest of the majority community. In writing this essay, however, we have become more than ever convinced that transracial communication can take place in the absence of pressure for survival upon the parties involved.

SINCERITY   Some of the mistakes of perception can be corrected if the communicators sincerely want to transcend boundaries. Nothing can happen if genuine willingness to become available to the other person is lacking. You can become available through research into the cultural background, the issues of interest, and the historical contributions of the persons you seek to understand. But more importantly, you must become geographically available. Transracial communication implies contact between the races. Reading the history of a race is not talking face to face with a member of that race. Availability is putting yourself where there can be contact. Enthusiasm about learning another's culture cannot substitute for personal availability. Proximity, of course, requires willingness. Transracial communication increases in more meaningful ways as the interaction among whites and minority groups increases as a result of open housing and open-mindedness. Willingness to send a message must be balanced by willingness to respond to a message, and the coordination of stimulus-and-response sensitivities will reduce the human distance between communicators.

PROPINQUITY   In several studies (particularly Byrne, 1961) propinquity has been well documented as a significant variable in interpersonal attraction and repulsion. These studies, for the most part, have concentrated on intraracial groups. We can assume from our earlier discussion of ethnic groups that the subjects generally held similar well-established aspirations and sentiments, and had similar learned drives. In fact those who seem deficient in the general values of the group are often defined as "incongruents" by consensual judgment.

Persons of different ethnic groups are also often defined as "incongruents" by virtue of their heritage, skin color, or religion. Incongruence works two streets, however. It is always possible for the describer to appear deficient in the eyes of the described. And once we have defined other persons as "incongruents" we seek to avoid them or escape them when we find ourselves in their presence. Many whites and Blacks feel their incongruence so intensely that they refuse to make themselves available for communication. A few studies have verified this reaction in a converse manner, by showing that a relationship exists between similar attitudes and interpersonal attraction (A. J. Smith, 1957; Jones and Daugherty, 1959). Thus even if a "stranger" exhibited attitudes similar to those of a group, it felt more attraction to him than to someone with dissimilar attitudes (Byrne, 1961). The results strongly suggest the need for the propinquity of source and receiver if interracial communication is to be effective. Incongruence and dissimilarity of attitudes can only be overcome when we make ourselves available to each other.

3. Interpersonal Communication with Transracial Contexts Often Fails Because the Sender and Receiver Do Not Share nor Seek Each Other's Point of View

Human beings come together into close identification and interact sensibly with each other primarily because of the commonality of their aspirations, dreams, fears, and anxieties. Transracial communication can be constrained by the diverse points of view of the communicators, who are sometimes unable and often unwilling to view issues and arguments from another's standpoint.

The attitude that "My people must win no-matter-what" seriously endangers communication between different ethnic groups. What is required in interracial communication is the ability to predict the speech-communication behavior of the participants. The sensitivity to others will allow one communicator to empathize with another. It is only then that interpersonal communication within transracial contexts ceases to be haphazard because it is only then that foresight and expectations of another's response prove to be reasonably accurate. The matter of viewpoint can be illustrated by the varying uses of language by whites and Blacks in given situations. Some whites may think of the ghetto conflagrations between 1965 and 1968 as "riots," but Blacks speak of them as "rebellions." Furthermore, many whites may perceive the participants as "hoodlums" while their Black counterparts may speak of "freedom fighters." In such cases, the use of language becomes mostly, if not totally, a matter of standpoint. For communication to take place, Blacks and whites must be flexible enough to aggressively seek to know the other's viewpoint, which may be defined as the particular perspective, partly characterized by emotional attachments, aspirations and cultural biases, which a person has of the society. Acceptance of another's viewpoint does not commit you to agreement with that person's position; it simply opens the way for possible interracial understanding by putting you into the other's place (Mead, 1934).

Obviously, we have not exhausted the concept of perspective in the above discussion. What is significant for transracial communication is that once we grasp an appreciation for another's viewpoint, our ability to see relationships and to make judgments can be strengthened. In fact the willingness to accept the possibility of a perspective other than our own relates to the earlier section on open-mindedness.

4. There Is Little to Suggest that Changing the Grammar of Blacks Will Make for Substantially More Effective Inter-ethnic Communication

It is argued in some circles that the major problem in interpersonal communication between Blacks and whites is the use of "bad English" or "substandard English" by Blacks. According to this theory, if all Blacks used standard American speech, we would not have interracial conflicts. While it is true that a common code contributes to interpersonal communication, it is not true that the Black users of Black English are not generally understood. Of course, there are Black English words which the average user of English might not grasp, but the same is true of English itself. There are few masters of every word in the English language, and to that extent most of us have limited vocabularies, but no one would dare suggest that we cannot communicate because we do not understand all the words that are used.

In addition, foreign speakers of English, even from Western nations, have little difficulty communicating although they possess exotic accents, often speak haltingly, sometimes have extremely basic vocabularies, and use incorrect grammar. Clearly, the principal trouble is not grammar but viewpoint.

It has been argued before that mankind is separated more by cultural difference than language (Oliver, 1962), and that thought patterns are more important than vocabulary and grammar. This is certainly the case between Blacks and whites. Grammar is an instrument used to promote clarity and understanding, but often the problems between Blacks and whites do not suffer as much for clarity as for the ability to look beyond the words to the source of the other person's ideas and to his frame of reference.

The foregoing discussion suggests that interpersonal communication between people of different races is possible, but at the same time that it does not often occur without effort. Beginning with sensitivity to the other's viewpoint and acceptance of the fact that his possibly different viewpoint grows out of peculiarly ethnic traditions and aspirations, the communicator must move beyond connection to communication. It is perfectly possible to be sensitive and yet not communicate, for this step involves committing oneself to interaction. When messages are transmitted between communicator and communicatee, they interact. And as we pointed out initially in this essay, the aim of transracial communication is understanding between persons of different races.

If sensing another individual's point of view is important, then the person who would communicate within transracial contexts should approach interaction humbly, feeling, "I do not know all I should know about this person's peculiar problems, fears, and aims." Knowing more, however, entails learning more about the person's ethnic background and point of view. As an outgrowth of sensitivity, not sentimentality, one develops a grasp of essential concepts, images, and philosophies.

Additionally, the codification system of the person with whom you want to communicate must be respected in the light of his ethnic aspirations. The importance of respecting the other's codification system is illustrated by a conversation I overheard. Two students, one white and one Black, stood in the front of the classroom discussing slavery just before class began. The white student said, "Slavery was good for the Africans because as savages they were introduced to Christianity." The Black student became exceedingly angry and retorted, "You're too stupid to talk to." At that point, the white student was dismayed and wanted to know what had he said. I explained to him that the word "savage" does not relate to the Black man's concept of himself or his ancestors. Blacks would argue that many Africans probably considered Christians to be barbarians and savages. So, in the same sense that whites do not consider their Christian ancestors savages, Blacks cannot consider their pagan ancestors savages. It is a matter of perspective. How we perceive ourselves and our roles in history and society greatly affects how we relate to others. Thus, scrutiny of one's own perceptions should always precede any extensive participation in transracial communication.

The task is challenging but rewarding, and a possible answer to intergroup conflict particularly when such conflict threatens our society. A final note—in this article, while we have sought to provide you with some fundamental principles of interpersonal communication in transracial contexts, we have not attempted to treat the subject exhaustively.

References

Allen, A., and D. Hernandez. Mexican American: Culturally Deprived? Anglo: Ethnocentric? Los Angeles: (unpublished), 1969.

Berlo, D. K. *The Process of Communication.* New York. Holt, Rinehart and Winston, 1960.

Bettinghaus, E. *Persuasive Communication.* New York. Holt, Rinehart and Winston, 1960.

Boas, F. *Language, Race and Culture.* New York: Macmillan, 1940.

Bruner, J. S., J. J. Goodnow, and G. A. Austin. *A Study of Thinking.* New York. John Wiley & Sons, 1956.

Byrne, D. "Interpersonal Attraction and Similarity." *Journal of Abnormal Psychology,* 1961, 62, 713–715.

——, and McGraw. C. "Interpersonal Attraction toward Negroes." *Human Relations,* 1964, 17, 201–213.

Carroll, J. B. *Language and Thought.* Englewood Cliffs, N.J.: Prentice-Hall, 1964.

Dance, F. E. X. *Human Communication Theory.* New York: Holt, Rinehart and Winston, 1967.

Gittler, J. *Understanding Minority Groups.* New York: John Wiley & Sons, 1956.

Hall, E. T. *The Hidden Dimension.* Garden City, N.Y.: Doubleday, Inc., 1956.

—— *The Silent Language.* Garden City, N.Y.: Doubleday, Inc., 1959.

Hayek, F. A. *The Sensory Order: An Inquiry into the Foundations of Theoretical Psychology.* Chicago: University of Chicago Press, 1952.

Hoijer, H. *Language in Culture.* Chicago: University of Chicago Press, 1954.

Homans, G. C. *The Human Group.* New York: Harcourt, Brace & World, 1950.

Jones, E. E., and B. N. Daugherty. "Political Orientation and the Perceptual Effects of an Anticipated Interaction." *Journal of Abnormal Psychology,* LIX 1959, 59, 340–349.

Lado, R. *Linguistics across Cultures.* Ann Arbor: University of Michigan Press, 1963.

Mead, G. H. *Mind, Self, and Society.* Chicago: University of Chicago Press, 1934.

Newcomb, T. M. "The Prediction of Interpersonal Attraction." *American Psychology,* 1956, 11, 575–586.

Oliver, R. *Culture and Communication.* Springfield, Ill.: Charles C. Thomas, 1962.

Ratcliffe, S. A. and L. K. Steil. "Attitudinal Differences between Black and White Students." *The Speech Teacher,* 1970, 19, 190–198.

Rokeach, M. *The Open and Closed Mind.* New York: Basic Books, 1960.

Ruesch, J., and W. Kees. *Nonverbal Communication: Notes on the Visual Perception of Human Relations.* Berkeley: University of California Press, 1956.

Runkel, P. I. "Cognitive Similarity in Facilitating Communication." *Sociometry,* 1956, 19, 178–191.

Schramm, W. "How Communication Works." In W. Schramm (ed.); *The Process and Effects of Mass Communication.* Urbana, Ill.: University of Illinois Press, 1954. Pp. 3–26.

Sereno, K. K., and C. D. Mortenson. *Foundations of Communication Theory.* New York: Harper & Row, 1970.

Smith, A. G. (ed.) *Communication and Culture.* New York: Holt, Rinehart and Winston, 1966.

Smith, A. J. "Similarity of Values and Its Relation to Acceptance and the Projection of Similarity." *Journal of Psychology,* 1957, 43, 251–260.

Triandis, H. C. "Cognitive Similarity and Communication in a Dyad." *Human Relations,* 1960, 13, 175–183.

Van Nieuwenhuijze, C. A. O. *Cross-Cultural Studies.* The Hague: Mouton, 1963.

Weinreich, U. *Languages in contact.* The Hague: Mouton, 1964.

Westley, B. H., and M. S. MacLean, Jr. "A Conceptual Model for Communication Research." *Journalism Quarterly,* 1957, 34, 31–38.

Suggested Readings

Amir, Y., "Contact Hypothesis in Ethnic Relations," *Psychological Bulletin,* 71 (1969), 319–342. Amir explores the assumption that ethnic contact will reduce ethnic prejudice and intergroup tension and improve relations between various ethnic groups. His findings suggest that specific conditions are necessary if contact is to result in tension reduction. Practical applications are also considered.

Banks, J. A., "Teaching for Ethnic Literacy: A Comparative Approach," *Social Education,* 37 (1973), 738–750. Banks argues that knowledge only about one's own ethnic group is insufficient to help students attain a liberating education and to fully grasp the complexity of the experience of their own ethnic group or the total human experience.

Cormack, M. L., "American Students in India," *International Studies Quarterly,* 17 (September 1973), 337–357. In this article, Cormack describes the life and experiences of American university students attending school in India. Her description includes the problems faced by the students in adapting to the Indian life style and the effect of their intercultural experience on defining their own lives.

Gregg, R., J. A. McCormack, and D. Pedersen, "A Description of the Interaction between Black Youth and White Teachers in a Ghetto Speech Class," *The Speech Teacher,* 19 (January 1970), 1–8. Although this article deals primarily with black students in a speech class, there are a number of valid conclusions that are generalizable to other cultures and other environments. They discuss the kinds of behaviors that are most appropriate for teaching ghetto youth.

Gupta, K. P., "Chinese Tradition of International Relations," *China Report,* 7 (July-August 1971), 2–11. In this article, the author relates a history of the methods and strategies of the Chinese approach to international relations. The concept of "Maoist metaphysics" is introduced as a means of explaining the Chinese approach to international relations. The article, written by an Indian, does reflect a bias favorable to India in terms of international relations between China and India; however, this bias does not prevent the reader from gaining considerable insight into international communication and behaviors that differ significantly from a western approach.

Kraar, L., "The Japanese are Coming—With Their Own Style of Management," *Fortune,* 91 (March 1975), 116–121, 160–161, 164. Louis Kraar, a staff writer for *Fortune,* has written an excellent account of Japanese management techniques in manufacturing plants opened in the United States. Stark differences between the roles of management in the United States and Japan are described, and the effect of the Japanese management concepts applied to American workers is discussed.

Logue, C. M., "Teaching Black Rhetoric," *The Speech Teacher,* 23 (1974), 115–120. Professor Logue describes his experiences in having taught a course in black rhetoric over seven times. His experiences, knowledge, and insights will prove useful to anyone who may be approaching such a teaching experience and to those who are interested in black/ white relationships generally.

Merritt, R. L. (ed.), *Communication in International Politics* (Urbana, Ill.: University of Illinois Press, 1972). Merritt has edited an excellent collection of readings in the area of international political communication. This volume is comprehensive and attempts not only to define the area of international communication but to examine some of its main concerns.

Mithun, J. S., "Cooperation and Solidarity as Survival Necessities in a Black Urban Community," *Urban Anthropology,* 2 (1973), 25–34. This paper explores the cooperative networks in an urban Afro-American community to discover the extent of cooperation and solidarity necessary for the survival of a community. Cooperation is viewed in the larger context of cultural adaptation. Some cultural traits such as etiquette and polite codes of behavior, larger family and friendship networks, mutual aid associations, and the behavior suggested in the concept of "soul brother" are described and analyzed.

Oliver, R. T., "Asian Public Address and Comparative Public Address," *The Speech Teacher,* 23 (1974), 101–108. In this article, Oliver analyzes the Asian approach to public address. In making this analysis, Oliver develops a case for the comparative study of public address cross-culturally as a means toward understanding communicative interaction patterns of other cultures.

Sinauer, M., *The Role of Communication in International Training and Education* (New York: Frederick A. Praeger, 1967). This book evaluates various training and educational programs for foreign students. In so doing, the author discusses a number of very practical training methods.

Trifonovitch, G. J., "On Cross-Cultural Orientation Techniques," *Topics in Culture Learning,* vol. 1 (Honolulu: East-West Center, 1973). This article deals specifically with cross-cultural orientation techniques used by the author in the last eight years with American personnel who were preparing to assume duties and responsibilities in Micronesia. Although the cultural orientation is limited in its scope, the techniques and methods are generalizable to training programs for a variety of cultures.

Yeh, E., A. A. Alexander, K. Tseng, M. H. Miller, M. H. Klein, F. Workneh, and H. Chu, "The American Student in Taiwan," *International Studies Quarterly,* 17 (September 1973), 359–372. This paper discusses the problems of American students attending school in Taiwan—their difficulties in adjustment, adapting to a new culture, and coping with cultural differences.

Additional Readings

Atkeson, P., "Building Communication in Intercultural Marriage," *Psychiatry,* 33 (1970), 396–408.

Baseman, G. E., and J. L. Simonelli, "Management Policy toward Task Environment Agents: A Cross-Cultural Study," *Management International Report* (June 1973), 121–126.

Brown, I. C., *Understanding Other Cultures* (Englewood Cliffs, N.J.: Prentice-Hall, 1963).

Gentry, J. E., and J. F. Watkins, "Organizational Training for Improving Race Relations," *Education and Urban Society,* 6 (May 1974), 269–283.

Goodwin, C. D. W., and I. B. Holley, Jr., "Toward a Theory of the Intercultural Transfer of Ideas," *The South Atlantic Quarterly,* 67 (1968), 370–379.

Grandjean, B. D., "The Division of Labor, Technology, and Education: Cross-National Evidence," *Social Science Quarterly,* 55 (1974), 297–309.

Hall, E. T., "Listening Behavior: Some Cultural Differences," *One Bridge,* Occasional Paper #2, March 1970.

Hawkins, H. C., and T. S. Gunnings, "Bi-Cultural Education: A Necessity," *The Journal of Afro-American Issues,* 1 (1973), 267–272.

Heisey, D. R., "A Swedish Approach to International Communication," *Topics in Culture Learning,* vol. 2 (Honolulu: East-West Center, 1974), pp. 41–49.

Hesseling, P., "Studies in Cross-Cultural Organization," *Columbia Journal of World Business,* 1973, pp. 120–134.

Hoffman, A. S. (ed.), *International Communication and the New Diplomacy* (Bloomington: Indiana University Press, 1968).

Kim, S. D., "The Night Clubs of Seoul, Korea: Plurality and Synthesis of Traditional and Modern Values in Organizational Structure," *Urban Life and Culture,* 2 (October 1973), 314–330.

Peace Corps Reader (Washington, D.C.: Office of Public Affairs, Peace Corps, 1969).

Rana, S., "China's Low Profile at the United Nations," *China Report,* 9 (May–June 1973), 6–10.

Record, J. C., and W. Record, "Ethnic Studies and Affirmative Action: Ideological Roots and Implications for the Quality of American Life," *Social Science Quarterly,* 55 (1974), 502–519.

Uberoi, P., "Culture, Personality and the Explaination of Revolutionary Change," *China Report,* 9 (September-October 1973), 72–81.

Weinshall, T. D., "Changing the Effects of Culture on Problem-Solving in Management Education," *Management International Report,* 4–5 (1973), 145–155.

Worpole, K., "The School and the Community: Towards a Common Culture," *The Urban Review,* 7 (1974), 84–96.

Concepts and Questions

1. If you were going to travel abroad, what preparations would you make to ensure the best possible opportunity for effective intercultural communication?

2. What specific suggestions can you make that could improve your ability to interact with other ethnic or racial groups in your community? How would you go about gaining the necessary knowledge and experience?

3. Does Barna's assertion that "people are pretty much alike" seem to conflict with one of the basic themes of this collection?

4. Can the 13 characteristics discussed by Van Zandt be used to analyze cultures other than the Japanese?

5. What does Stewart mean by cross-cultural incongruity? Can you think of any examples?

6. Have you observed specific instances that would prove the correctness of Smith's four categories? How can these four categories best be put into practice?

7. What is implied by the phrase "scrutiny of one's own perceptions should always precede any extensive participation in transracial communication"?

8. How would a "nonjudgmental attitude and a high tolerance for ambiguity" help intercultural communication? Is there such a thing as a "nonjudgmental attitude"?

9. Stewart mentions that we must understand our own cultural pattern as well as that of the host country. Why is this introspection important to intercultural communication?

10. Can you think of any mannerisms, behaviors, or styles that the U.S. businessperson reflects that are apt to stifle intercultural communication?

11. What kind of training program could be developed that would foster favorable attitudes toward other cultural groups? How would you get others to enroll in such a program? What do you suggest be done for those who refuse to enroll (they may need it the most)?

12. Can you think of any situations where businesspeople from other cultures are facing the problem of doing business in the United States? How would you suggest these people prepare themselves for intercultural communication in the United States?

7

Prospects for the Future

It has been the goal of this book to help you understand intercultural communication and to assist you in appreciating the issues and problems inherent in an interaction involving people from foreign and alien cultures. To this end we have presented a series of diverse essays that exposed you to a variety of variables that are in operation during an intercultural encounter. But what we have been looking at up to now is what we know about intercultural communication. Now we shift our emphasis to discussing the prospects for the future. What do we need to accomplish, what may we expect to accomplish, what philosophical issues must we deal with, and what kind of personalities must we develop if we are to improve the art and science of intercultural communication during the remainder of this century? Before introducing the essays in this final chapter, we believe a brief review of some of the factors we have already presented is appropriate, and we wish to set forth our philosophy toward intercultural communication in the future.

We introduced the topic of intercultural communication by pointing out both its boundaries and its territory. By looking at what intercultural communication is and is not, we were able to establish some guidelines for our investigation. In general terms, we suggested that intercultural communication occurred whenever a message sender is a member of one culture and a message receiver is of another culture. Once this broad definition was presented we were able to survey some specific refinements. We noted that culture was the sum total of the learned behavior of a particular group, and that these behaviors (attitudes, values, language, and so forth) were transmitted from generation to generation. Differences among international, interracial, and cross-cultural communication were also examined.

The next portion of the book focused on one of the conceptual threads that have been woven throughout this collection. It suggests that to understand intercultural communication we must realize the impact and influence of past experience. Anyone who has observed human interaction will have little trouble accepting the notion that where we come from, our cultural histories, are crucial to communication. Our past experiences, which have been structured by our culture, will help determine what we value, what we see, and how we behave. In short, what our culture has taught us, in both conscious and subconscious ways, will be manifested during intercultural communication. For example, Navaho Indians believe that the universe is full of dangers and that illness is a price to be paid for disorder and disharmony. These particular views are bound to be reflected in intercultural interaction. Or take people from cultures that deem men more important than women. Their behavior toward each sex will be influenced by this orientation. Even our backgrounds color what we perceive. The judgment of beauty is a case in point. In America, the slim, statuesque female represents the cultural stereotype of beauty. Yet in many Eastern European countries a heavier and stockier body reflects the ideal. What we see with these examples, and there are countless others, is the fact that culture gives us the framework for our experiences and our values. They, in turn, define our view of the world and dictate how we interact within that world.

Because we share cultural experiences in a symbolic manner, we explored our two most common symbol systems—verbal and nonverbal. Having symbols represent our ideas and feelings is a complex and complicated procedure at best. However, when we add the dimension of culture to the encoding and decoding process, the act of sharing internal states becomes even more intricate. To bring what understanding we could, we sought to demonstrate the relationship between three closely related axioms: (1) language helps shape our thoughts and perceptions (the Sapir-Whorf hypothesis), (2) diverse cultures have *different* words with *similar* meanings (foreign languages), and (3) cultures can have the *same* word with vastly *different* meanings (subcultural use of the vernacular and argot). We noted that the problems of coding systems plague actions as well as words. Even a simple hand motion can convey a host of unrelated meanings and interpretations. The hand gesture used by a hitchhiker in the United States is apt to produce a punch in the nose in Ghana. In short, the symbols we employ to share our cultural experiences may often be subject to confusion and ambiguity.

The next section of the book sought ways that contribute to successful intercultural communication. We proceeded on the assumption that intercultural communication is, by its very definition and nature, an action and an overt activity. Intercultural communication is, in short, something people do to and with each other. Because of advances in technology, such as increased air travel and communication satellites, we all seem to be engaging in more and more of this activity. In addition to increased communication between foreign cultures, the late 1960s and 1970s revealed that there were a number of subcultures and countercultures within our own boundaries. Subcultures such as the urban poor, women, the gay community, youth, and Chicanos wanted and demanded contact and dialog with the main culture. Consequently, we all are engaging in intercultural communication at an accelerating rate. If this interaction is to be significant, and if intercultural communication is to foster increased understanding and cooperation, then we must avoid potential problems. These potential problems and their resolution served as the core of the previous section. Now, in this final part, "Intercultural Communication in the Future," we have extended our analysis toward improvement. This is due, in part, to the fact that most of our interactions and meetings we have yet to face. The success of these communication experiences may well depend on our philosophy and attitude towards intercultural communication. The way we behave around others is often a reflection of our philosophy toward life and toward ourselves. Yet each of us is capable of change from day to day and from situation to situation. As free agents, individual alterations represent a gift that accompanies personal liberty. As Plutarch noted over two thousand years ago, "all things are daily changing." If we consider our intercultural exchanges worthy of our time and energy we must begin to realize that each of us is capable of this change. But change, as we all know, is not a simple matter. Many of our attitudes and behaviors are deeply engrained. And many of them are subject to ethnocentrism. By this we mean that as we learn a cultural pattern of behavior we are, in both obvious and subtle ways, acquiring a corresponding subjective and normative value judgment associated with that behavior. Many of us are guilty of assuming that our cultural group, whatever it may be, is superior to all other groups. We therefore judge other cultures by our own standards. How often do we hear people say, "Our way is the only right way"? Or we may foolishly assume that our ideas and solutions to problems are the only correct ones. This is often manifest in such ideas as are expressed by the statement "If you are not part of the solution you are part of the problem." This short-sighted notion fails to recognize that most social problems are complex and must be solved by many ideas and many approaches. The danger of this philosophy should be self-evident. It is indeed difficult to achieve mutual understanding if we place our culture in a central position of priority or worth. How foolish we are to assume that because one culture prays on Saturday, while another worships on Sunday, that one is superior to the other. Or take the cultural values of competition and "winning." Because these are important values to Americans, many of us assume that all cultures ought to strive to win and be first. However, there are many cultures where competition and winning are unimportant. On the contrary, cooperation and sharing are highly valued. If we are guilty of ethnocentrism, we can be assured that intercultural communication is doomed to failure.

Our new mode of behavior should not only be void of ethnocentrism, but it ought to reflect an attitude of mutual respect and trust. We urgently note that intercultural communication will not be successful if, by our actions or our words, we appear to be condescending. Every individual and every culture wants to believe they are as worthy as any other. Actions that manifest the opposite will diminish that worth and tend to stifle meaningful interaction.

The changes required of us are not easy. They require that we possess a willingness to communicate, have empathy toward foreign and alien cultures, be tolerant of views that differ from our own, and develop a universalistic, relativistic approach to the universe. If we have the resolve to adopt these behaviors and attitudes and the desire to overcome ethnocentrism and feelings of superiority, we can begin to know the feelings of exhilaration that come when we have made contact with someone far removed from our own sphere of experiences. Intercultural communication offers the arena for this interpersonal contact. Our ability to change, to make adjustments in our communication habits, give us the potential tools to have that contact be successful.

It might be well to view the three selections in Chapter 7 as only a sampling of the many issues that face intercultural communication. The field is so new and the challenges so varied it would be impossible to predict future directions with any degree of assurance. Therefore, our intent is to simply introduce you to a few of the issues and concepts that await us.

Samuel L. Becker begins by talking about intercultural research. Noting the need for such research he suggests fourteen important areas or directions for such research. These areas raise vital questions about intercultural interaction that must be answered before we can begin to develop any sort of sophisticated intercultural communication theory. Becker concludes by suggesting some issues and problems of conceptualizing and carrying out research that will deal with the questions raised in his paper.

In the next essay, anthropologist Margaret Mead is concerned with a number of practical and philosophical issues that are currently unresolved: (1) the way in which communicaton systems are related to given cultural values, (2) the particular ethical problems of responsibility raised by our current use of communication systems, and (3) problems of communicaton when cultural boundaries have to be transcended. As with all of the selections in this book, we must use the process of analogy to draw generalizations from this article and the cultures discussed in it to other cultures and other situations. When we do this we can easily see the significance of the problems raised by Mead.

We have selected as our final article one that not only expresses our philosophy toward intercultural communication but gives us a bright perspective for the future. Here Peter S. Adler introduces us to the concept of *multicultural man.* We find this notion highly attractive because multicultural man is a person whose identifications and loyalties have transcended the boundaries of nationalism and ethnocentrism and whose commitments are based on a vision of the world as a global community. Multicultural man is a person of the world—an international person who feels and is at home anywhere in any culture—who may be the prototype of the individual most suited to successful intercultural communication and, if the need should ever arise, interstellar or intergalactic communication.

Directions for Inter-Cultural Communication Research

Samuel L. Becker

The Speech Association of America, with the aid of the U.S. Office of Education, recently held an interdisciplinary colloquium on communication research. Four clear implications for our thinking about inter-cultural communication research emerged from that colloquium.

1. We must stop thinking of communication problems in terms of a particular mode of address, such as platform speaking, small group discussion, drama, or mass media communication. This is as fruitless as beginning one's research by deciding to do an attitude change study or a diffusion study or a study involving the semantic differential technique. In inter-cultural communication research, as in any other kind, we need to begin with the analysis of problems and then see whether and how communication might be made more effective to alleviate the problem.

2. The second implication of the SAA colloquium is that much more of our research must be relevant to our society Those of us in communication talk much about the importance of communication to society, and then take pride in the fact that our research is "basic" rather than "applied" which, unfortunately, we too often define as meaning that the research is useless rather than useful. Communication scholars certainly have no special wisdom in determining goals for society, but we do have a responsibility to acquire a sophisticated knowledge of existing goals and needs and then to design research consistent with those needs. This is not to say that we must forego theoretical research; far from it. The theoretical research, though, must have relevance to the society and, when developed in the laboratory, must be tested in the field. Dr. Rene J. Dubos, professor of environmental medicine at Rockefeller University, among others, has talked about this necessary feedback between practical and theoretical problems. He has even suggested that this feedback should be accelerated by the creation of institutions in which relevant theoretical ideas are taken to the field for the "acid test" and for the uncovering of new theoretical problems (1).

3. The third implication of the SAA project, one that was made clear at the inter-disciplinary colloquium by philosopher Richard Rudner, is that the important and practical theoretical task facing us—and it is far more difficult than it may appear—is the identification and clarification of the key concepts in our field.

4. The fourth major implication is that we must depart from the traditional ways of treating communication problems—we must stop trying to study every

From *Central States Speech Journal,* Vol. 20 (Spring 1969), pp. 3–13. Reprinted by permission of the Central States Speech Association and the author. Professor Becker is Chairman, Department of Speech, The University of Iowa.

problem with the same cookie-cutter methods, we must stop assuming that the ways we have always taught people to communicate are the best ways now, and that the ways we have taught people to communicate in this country are the best ways for all countries. I will return to this last point in a moment.

Because of the variety of purposes for which cross-cultural communication is important and the variety of cultures within which those purposes might be pursued, it is difficult to move from these general implications to more specific statements about research in inter-cultural communication, but I will try to be as specific as I can. In doing so, though, I may overlook many areas that should be discussed.

There are a number of ways to classify needed research. I will suggest only three. First of all, there is a key distinction which must be made between research on the communication processes *within* various cultures (the sort of work many linguists and cultural anthropologists and diffusion scholars are doing) and research on communication processes *across* various cultures. For many types of cross-cultural communication problems, something of within-culture communication processes must be known in order to develop hypotheses and methods for attacking the cross-cultural problem. I am not sure this is a necessary precondition for all cross-cultural communication research though. I do believe some thought needs to be given to this problem and strategies laid out for coordinating intra- and inter-cultural communication research and for deciding which most needs doing when.

Another important distinction must be made between research on intended and on unintended communication effects, as, for instance, research about the effect of Voice of America broadcasts on the image of America and research about the effect of the Beverly Hillbillies television series on the image of America when it is shown by television stations abroad. (Obviously, these effects are not always separable. For example, the same individuals may be exposed to both the Voice of America and the Beverly Hillbillies.)

My third distinction is of a somewhat different order than these first two, but important nonetheless. We in the United States tend to look at inter-cultural communication as a one-way circuit; when we hear this term, we think about the effect of stimuli from this country on the people of other countries. We seldom think of the equally important question of the effect of stimuli from other countries on us. I believe that one could make a good case for the proposition that one of the world's critical problems today is the image that people in the United States have of what is going on in a little country in southeast Asia. Closely related to this distinction between the effects of what is coming in and what is going out, is the interaction between these effects. Communication scholars have just about overcome their conception of inter-personal communication as a simple, one-way stream. We have even overcome this conception in large part when thinking about mass communication within our own country. We forget, however, that inter-cultural communication also involves feedback or interaction. For example, it seems to me that one important area for research is the ways in which our perceptions of another nation affect the sorts of information we send to them. This is clearly not a static process. As they respond, our perceptions change, which affects additional information that we send, etc.

Forgetting these various distinctions for a moment, I want to suggest a few of the inter-cultural communication research areas in which scholars from our field could make important contributions.

1. Just as we have recognized the importance of developing indigenous leadership and participation by all community members in deprived neighborhoods within this country, so we must recognize the need for the development of leaders and wide-spread participation in decision-making in other countries. If this leadership and participation are to be other than through force or fear, a high degree of skill in communication is required for the people in these countries. One of the great contributions that scholars in our field could make is to study the specific kinds of communication skills and understanding needed in various sorts of cultures and the best methods for helping natives of the culture to develop these skills and understandings. As I said earlier, I believe it would be incredibly naive to assume that we can transfer our purposes and methods for the teaching of speech and other communication skills directly to other countries. The immediate problems to which we need to give attention are the methods to use in searching for answers to these questions and the criteria to be used in assessing "needs" and "best" teaching methods.

2. There is a rapidly increasing body of knowledge from research in this country and, to a lesser extent, from a few other countries, about the diffusion of information, ideas, and practices. We are making great progress in pinning down patterns of diffusion and influence. However, there are still many unanswered questions. We have far from enough knowledge about the extent to which the generalizations from the research done to date are applicable in other types of countries, for other types of information or practice, and for influence between as well as within countries. We need to understand the differences among cultures in the ways in which different types of information are diffused—the role of print, the role of electronic media, the role of people. In the United States, the availability of most information is roughly equivalent for all men. We tend to forget that this is not so in all cultures. We also tend to forget that the patterns of leadership in some countries are, in part, dependent upon this differential availability of information. We have little knowledge of the institutions in various countries which inhibit or facilitate diffusion. ... These unique institutions within each culture must be understood if we are to intelligently plan inter-cultural communication, or even understand it as it occurs. In addition to differences across cultures, we need to study the ways in which the patterns of diffusion are changing within cultures over time. For example, it is possible that, in a culture which is shifting from a patriarchal or traditional state, where the young or the females are becoming disenchanted with the status quo (undoubtedly one of the necessary conditions for substantial social change), the mass media have a more direct effect on these disenchanted. On the other hand, it is possible that these disenchanted simply find new sorts of mediators or opinion leaders. Which is the case when? In addition, what happens to these patterns of mediation or leadership if we

broaden the availability of information through various programs of inter-cultural communication, such as Voice of America?

3. We need to study the ways in which the media and individual diffusion agents in each type of culture screen or supplement or distort the information that comes through. We know that, in this country, where we take pride in the relative objectivity of the news, the media badly distort many events largely because of a screening process. For example, the front pages and the headlines of newspapers have not accurately reflected the national, or even the southern progress in school desegregation which in most cases has proceeded very quietly. Because the media in this country equate news with conflict, peaceful integration is less "newsworthy" than non-peaceful integration, and so the latter receives relatively more play in the press. This treatment does not reflect racial prejudice on the part of newsmen; it reflects rather their definition of news. We need to discover the extent to which this same conception of news exists in other countries, both among individuals in the media and person-to-person information diffusers, if we are to understand the ways in which our communication efforts are distorted or buried as they cross national lines.

4. Up to now, I have been discussing research on the communication transmission lines within and between cultures. It is also extremely important for intercultural communication to understand the behaviors and drives of the receiver—what Herbert Menzel at the SAA research colloquium labelled "the culture of information seeking."

> We may assume that individuals regard some of the needs for information or counsel that come up in their daily lives as matters of general wise decision making, and still others as matters of taste; we may also assume that individuals have different tendencies to seek counsel from authoritative experts, from general or specialized opinion leaders, from technical literature, and so on. We do not know how these different types of information seekers are distributed over educational, class, or other groupings, nor do we know of the cultural uniformities with regard to areas of content that are regarded as matters of expertise, matters for general wisdom and so on. Worst of all, we know extremely little about the possible interlinkages between the different types of information seekers in any given area (2).

To summarize these questions on originators, diffusers, and seekers of information within and between cultures, I would say that we ought to be asking *who* within each of the cultures involved in each type of communication transaction, uses *what information* from that transaction *in what way and with what purpose.* In other words, to understand the processes and effects, we need to see what functions the information is serving for individuals in each culture.

5. A related problem area is the extent to which and the ways in which the traditions, political structure, family structure, etc. interact with what seem to be essentially the same communication events. . . . We need to pinpoint and describe these and related relationships in other cultures. We also need to study differences in the relationship of reference groups to communication processes in different

countries, and whether different types of reference groups tend to be salient for inter-cultural communication than are salient for intra-cultural communication.

6. As one aspect of the question of reference groups and diffusion, we in communication need to do far more research on informal and non-institutionalized forms of communication. That this is tremendously important in all cultures is evident from some of the research on the diffusion of birth control practices. In all of the family planning programs in countries where some research on diffusion has been possible, it is clear that a major contribution has been made by informal discussions among neighbors, relatives, friends and acquaintances. In one study in Taiwan, three out of four acceptors of a method of birth control had had no contact with the official communicators (or field workers) and, by the end of a year, a fourth of the acceptors came from areas not even being reached directly by the formal campaign. In one town in Thailand, over half of the women who accepted the use of contraceptives were brought to this acceptance through conversations with friends who used them (3).

A suggestion that has been made to the United States Information Agency is closely related to this point. This proposal is that the communication efforts of USIA can be most effective if they are used not for direct persuasion but to strengthen existing organizations whose objectives serve United States interests and help to create new organizations whose goals parallel our own (4). For example, one might simply put people with similar values in touch with each other so that each knows something about what the others are doing and thus can, to a degree, coordinate activities.

7. Another question that has been raised about the communication and acceptance of some method of family planning, which also has relevance to a range of other inter-cultural communication problems, is whether different communication factors are involved in the acceptance of an idea by individuals and by nations. James Fawcett of the Population Council hypothesizes that

> acceptance of family planning by *individuals* has been facilitated by a visible core group of users and by open discussion via mass media, acceptance by *nations* has been facilitated by the emergence of a group of developing countries with national programs and by spread of information about national programs via news media and particularly international exchange visits and conferences among high government officials (5).

Since many of the purposes of inter-cultural communication involve the acceptance of ideas by both nations and individuals, Fawcett's hypothesis deserves exploration to see (a) if it is so and, if it is, (b) the extent to which it is generalizable across cultures and across types of ideas.

8. There is at least one hypothesis that has been advanced by Daniel Lerner that deserves serious study. It grew out of Lerner's study of the role of communication in the social changes of developing countries. His hypothesis is that the mass media provide the people of these countries with the capacity to conceive

of situations and ways of life quite different from those which they have experienced. This is an important state for social change. Until men can conceive of something different than their existing situation, it is difficult for them to become sufficiently motivated to change (6). Again it seems to me that there are two questions here. One is whether the hypothesis is true. If it is true, then we wonder what effect messages from other cultures, such as the United States, have on this process.

9. Not only may cross-cultural communication aid in the process of learning to project oneself into non-experienced situations, but this projective or empathic ability is also important in order that individuals may comprehend many of the messages which they receive from other cultures. We need to learn what factors in individuals are associated with this empathic ability and what means can be employed to increase this ability.

10. In inter-cultural communication, as in intra-cultural communication, many scholars are interested in the question of the effects of different kinds of media on the audience. A question at least equally important for the communication scholar is the question of the effects of different kinds of audience on the media. We know that in this country the nature of the audience has a great deal of impact on the medium or the source. Whenever one attempts to reach a very large audience, for example, he becomes in a very real sense a captive of that audience. The tastes and interests of this audience set limits within which a medium must operate to stay in business. What effect does the nature of the audience in different countries have upon the mass media or the communication institutions of any sort in those countries? What effects do a source's perceptions of different cultures have upon his communication transactions with that country? As a part of this question, it would be interesting to know the perceptions that USIA people have of different countries and how these perceptions affect the messages they send to each country.

11. Another important problem has to do with the factors that affect the image which individuals in various countries have of other countries, and the effect that this image has, in turn, upon their behaviors with respect to other countries and their policies. Related to these questions, we need to know what the processes are by which information about one country is gathered, screened, altered, distributed, and used in other countries.

12. One interesting cross-cultural communication problem is that faced by the government agencies and industries of the United States which have offices in other countries staffed, in whole or in part, by individuals from those countries (7). The problems of organization and communication within these organizations, as some of these agencies are discovering, are completely different than the organization problems encountered and widely studied within organizations in this country. This could be a very important field of research.

13. Communication satellites have now made ready communication across countries and continents feasible. However, the particular nature of the broadcasting systems within each country and the apparent inability to achieve the

international cooperation necessary for such a system to truly work seems to be blocking optimum development of such communication. I think it important for those concerned with inter-cultural communication to do some applied research on how the barriers to such cooperation might be brought down. (By the way, we do not need to look far afield for some of these barriers. One might ask what the appeals would be that would cause those who control communication satellites in this country to give other nations an equal amount of control. One might ask what the appeals would be that would get networks and station licensees to agree to direct satellite to receiver communications.) Even more revealing than a study of the issue itself may be a study of the *debate* within each country *about the issue.*

14. We ought to discover and study the barriers to other forms of inter-cultural communication. For example, we ought to know what the issues are which determine the proportion of films or radio or television programs from one country that are imported and distributed in another country. Have you ever stopped to wonder about the fact that, although many American television programs are distributed throughout the world, you have seen television programs from relatively few other countries transmitted here? What are the means for setting these proportions? In some countries, it is done by government or regulatory agency fiat. In other countries, the only control is an economic one. Are there patterns which can be detected and studied?

There are certainly other research questions in inter-cultural communication. However, I believe that we must also attend to another type of problem—the problem of conceptualizing and carrying out the research to answer these questions. This is a problem which needs to be worried about at a number of different levels. We need to worry, for example, about the most appropriate type of question to study at this point in time. To what extent is there a need for hypothesis testing—for striving for generalizations or laws of inter-cultural communication which have some scope? To what extent is the major need at this time simply for descriptive data—to understand what is going on—or for work on individual, immediate, applied problems? The answers to these questions will vary somewhat with the problem area to be studied. For example, there has already been a good deal of laboratory research by Deutsch and others on modes of conflict resolution (8). It seems to me that we now have a body of generalizations from that research which needs to be tested in field situations, both intra- and inter-cultural.

Such research poses difficult methodological problems. It is relatively easy to set up and test problems of conflict with games in a room on a college campus: it is more difficult, but necessary, to test these matters in the field. We need to know to which kinds of conflicts the laboratory generalizations are relevant and to which they are not, if we hope to improve our ability to resolve such conflicts.

Another important strategy question is who will do the research or data collection: what should be the relationship of researchers to practitioners. That this is a problem is clear from at least one study done by the United States Information Agency in which sharp differences were found in the conclusions about the effectiveness of a United States exhibit at a trade fair in Yugoslavia drawn by an official of the exhibit and by an independent research group. The official observed that the U.S. exhibit outdrew all others; the independent survey showed it was outdrawn by both the Yugoslav and Soviet pavilions. The official observed that it was "winning loads of kudos"; the independent survey showed it produced more negative than positive impressions of this country (9).

Not only is there a question of the relationship of researcher to communication practitioner, there is the question of the relationship of researcher to the cultures involved in the research. For many kinds of problems, most notably the observation and study of informal communication, observers native to the culture must be trained in tasks requiring familiarity with the language and other aspects of the culture as well as the ability to observe without one's presence causing unnatural changes in the events observed. We must resolve the problem of how to select and train these research associates.

We must also resolve the problem of identifying the variables in inter-cultural communication situations which are most likely to be the important—or even relevant variables. One cannot collect all information on all cultures. Nor is it always profitable to collect data on the most exotic or unique aspects of a culture. Such data are often extremely interesting—they make for interesting anecdotes in one's reports and at cocktail parties—and they are often important if one is trying to understand a *culture*. They are not always important when one is trying to understand *communication* within or between cultures. A good starting place may be the set of variables which have proved fruitful in the study of communication within our culture.

An extremely difficult problem that must be resolved before many kinds of intercultural communication research can be done is that of assessing equivalence of meanings and responses. At this point, we cannot even get agreement on what equivalence of meaning is—how to operationally define it. In transactions, we are generally agreed that literal translation does not produce equivalent meaning. The question is, what does? One might define equivalence in terms of some behavioral responses. The only problem is that the responses to all terms or messages do not have visible components and the same manifest response may be indicative of quite different meanings, especially when compared across cultures.

Psychologist George Thompson, in the SAA colloquium, noted the need for procedures to measure "the less obvious meanings of words for individuals of different socialization backgrounds if we are to hope to understand some perennially important social issues" (11). He noted this problem for those communicating across social classes or across the generation gap (a problem which parents of teenagers can appreciate). The problem is greater when attempting to communicate across cultures—or when trying to study in some precise way this communication across cultures.

In attempting to resolve this problem, we must not fall into the error of many linguists and other communication scholars and think only of the equivalence of meaning of words. We must go far beyond the analysis of words. One cannot understand, for example, what is going on in debates at the United Nations if one

only analyzes the words spoken; just as one cannot understand the message of
the Viet Nam policy dissenters on American college campuses if one only analyzes what they say or even, literally, what they do. Their acts are symbolic, and
must be analyzed as such. With the rising importance of visual rhetoric—film,
television, and even the still photograph—we must find means to analyze the
process by which these stimuli work their effects. I suspect that the attitudes of
individuals in other countries regarding the United States have been affected at
least as much by the visual images of aspects of our culture to which they have
been exposed as by the verbal images. Again, as with verbal stimuli, much of our
research on intercultural visual communication is dependent upon the resolution
of the problem of equivalence of meaning across cultures.

There has been some research in the United States on the variance in meaning
of symbols when they are received through different sensory channels. It seems
to me that before many kinds of intercultural communication research can be
done, we need some idea of whether the same types of differences are found in
other cultures, or whether there is an interaction between type of difference and
type of culture.

The last difficulty with conceptualizing or carrying out inter-cultural communication research that I want to mention is one that was pinpointed by historian
Wilcomb Washburn at the Speech Association's recent colloquium when he was
talking about recent race riots in American cities.

> Politicians, social scientists and ordinary citizens were surprised by the location and
> intensity of the recent riots. Why? The ordinary citizen can be pardoned his igno-
> rance. But when the professionals miss, something has been overlooked. I suspect that
> one of the factors overlooked by the professional observers has been the growing
> personal, or social, distance which separates them from the objects of their study (12).

How much greater the distance when the objects of study are segments of other
cultures! Not only do we have the problem of not being able to perceive what is
happening in these cultures, we have the problem of Western values getting in
the way when we define the problems that need to be studied. Just as we have
the difficulty of the White not being close to the Black in American society, and
therefore not seeing the major questions, so Western man may not see the important questions in many developing countries. As we define change or progress,
we must guard against assuming that the only positive change—the only progress
—is that change which moves a culture toward a United States or Western model.
We must accept the fact that the ideals of all cultures may not coincide with the
ideals of our culture. If one accepts this fact, and I fail to see how it is possible
not to, one is faced with the interesting problem of how one operationally defines
"success" for many classes of inter-cultural communication (13).

I hope that these comments will stimulate fresh thought about inter-cultural
communication and communication research. As a start, I believe that there are
at least three questions which should be raised:

1. With what sort of research should we begin? Which questions about intercultural communication are most critical and, equally important, with which

are we in communication best prepared to make unique and meaningful contributions?

2. What must we do to develop communication scholars with the background and motivation to do important research in this area? In other words, what are the implications of the problems raised here for the graduate programs in our field?

3. Do we have any substantive knowledge and skills to contribute to other cultures or to inter-cultural communication now? If so, what are the best mechanisms through which we can make our contributions?

One last point. Most of my comments have been directed at the extreme complexity of the task of inter-cultural communication and inter-cultural communication research. It would be completely understandable if everyone threw up his hands and said that we might as well forget it; there really is not much we can do or discover. However understandable, this response cannot be tolerated. The task is too important—the need is too great. I believe that we must follow the advice of one of the great men in the field of speech, my good friend A. Craig Baird. Whenever a graduate student of Craig's would encounter a seemingly impossible problem in his research, Professor Baird would say, "That's all right; just keep with it. Just do the best you can." This seems to me to be good advice.

References

1. Rene J. Dubos, "Scientists Alone Can't Do the Job," *Saturday Review,* December 2, 1967, pp. 68–71.

2. Herbert Menzel, "Communication Through Institutions and Social Structures" (paper prepared for the Interdisciplinary Colloquium sponsored by the Speech Association of America, Racine, Wisconsin, October 10–11, 1967).

3. Bernard Berelson. "National Family Planning Programs: Where We Stand" (paper prepared for the University of Michigan Sesquicentennial Celebration, November 1967), pp. 15–16. (Mimeographed.)

4. W. Phillips Davison, paper presented to the U.S.I.A. seminar on communication problems, January 4, 1967.

5. Berelson, p. 3.

6. Daniel Lerner, "Comfort and Fun: Morality in a Nice Society," *The American Scholar,* xxvii (Spring 1958), 153–165; "Enlightenment and Communication," in *Comparative Theories of Social Change,* ed. Hollis W. Peter (Ann Arbor, Michigan: Foundation for Research on Human Behavior, 1966), pp. 221–225.

7. There is a good discussion of this problem in Edward T. Hall and William Foote Whyte, "Intercultural Communication: A Guide to Men of Action," *Human Organization,* xix (Spring 1960), 5–12.

8. Morton Deutsch, "Conflict and Its Resolution" (paper prepared for the Interdisciplinary Colloquium sponsored by the Speech Association of America, Racine, Wisconsin, October 10–11, 1967).

9. "Proceedings of the Seminar on [USIA] Effectiveness. Airlie House, Warrenton, Virginia. October 6–8, 1966" (Washington: United States Information Agency Office of Policy and Research, R-121-66. November 7, 1966), p. 11. (Mimeographed.)

10. These problems are explored in two excellent papers: Edmund S. Glenn, "Semantic Difficulties in International Communication," in *The Use and Misuse of Language,* ed. S. I. Hayakawa (New

York: Premier Books, 1962). pp. 47–69: "The Semantics of Socialism and Capitalism" (Washington: USIA Research and Reference Service. R-64-64. May, 1964). (Mimeographed.)

11. George C. Thompson. "Notes and Comments for SAA-USOE Interdisciplinary Colloquium" (paper prepared for the Interdisciplinary Colloquium sponsored by the Speech Association of America, Racine, Wisconsin, October 10–11, 1967).

12. Wilcomb E. Washburn, "Speech Communication and Politics" (Paper prepared for the Interdisciplinary Colloquium sponsored by the Speech Association of America, Racine, Wisconsin, October 10–11, 1967).

13. This idea of unique models of development for non-Western nations has been discussed at some length by Inavatullah, "Toward a Non-Western Model of Development," in *Communication and Change in the Developing Countries,* ed. Daniel Lerner and Wilbur Schramm (Honolulu: East-West Center Press, 1967), pp. 98–102. A different point of view on this issue is expressed in the same work by Daniel Lerner, "International Cooperation and Communication in National Development," pp. 103–125.

Some Cultural Approaches to Communication Problems

Margaret Mead

The great contemporary concern with communication problems must be laid not only to the enormous advance in technology and the resulting shrinking of the world into one potential communication system, with all the attendant difficulties of communication across cultural boundaries, but also to the increase in social awareness on the one hand, and the disintegration of the institutionalized centers of responsibility on the other. It is true that, through the centuries, expanding movements and nations have used various methods of propaganda (1) to advance their causes, to convert the unconverted, bring in line the recalcitrant, reconcile the conquered to their lot and the conquerors to their conquering role. It is also true that secular and religious hierarchies have consciously used these methods to advance their avowed and unavowed ends. But the addition of modern technological methods, by which the ownership of one radio station may decide the fate of a local revolution, and a single film or a single voice may reach the whole of the listening and watching world, has changed the order of magnitude of the whole problem.

At the same time development of social science is making it possible for communications to change their character. Instead of the inspired voice of a natural leader, whose zestful "We shall defend our Island, whatever the cost may be. We shall fight on the beaches, we shall fight on the landing ground, we shall fight in the fields and the streets, we shall fight in the hills; we shall never

From pp. 17–26 of "Some Cultural Approaches to Communication Problems" by Margaret Mead in *The Communication of Ideas,* edited by Lyman Bryson. Copyright, 1948 by Institute for Religious and Social Studies. Reprinted by permission of Harper & Row, Publishers, Inc. Professor Mead teaches in the Department of Anthropology, Columbia University.

surrender. . . ." galvanizing people to action, the appeals can be, to a degree, calculated and planned. Instead of the politician's hunch as to how some program is going over, polls and surveys can be used to bring back accurate information to the source of the propaganda and introduce a corrective. Theories of human nature which are no longer the inexplicit emphases of a coherent culture, but instead the partly rationalized, partly culturally limited formulations of psychological research, can be used as the basis of planned campaigns (2).

The thinking peoples of the world have been made conscious, during the past quarter of a century, of the power of organized and controlled communication, glimpsing that power both from the point of view of the victim or "target" and of the victimizer, he who wields the powerful weapon. Dissection of the methods of the enemy, the conscious cultivation of an immunity against appeals to one's own emotion, desperate attempts to devise methods appropriate to a democracy, while we envied totalitarian propagandic controls, have all contributed to the growth of this consciousness in the United States.

But consciousness of the potential power of communication has peculiar implications in the United States, in a country where no institution, neither Church nor State, has any monopoly of the organs of communication. The American, during the past twenty-five years, has seen systems of propagandic control develop in other countries, and even when propagandic moves of extreme importance have actually been promoted within the United States, they have usually been phrased as inspired by Berlin or Tokyo, London or Moscow, rather than as the expression of American attitudes.

The local American emphasis has thus been on resisting high powered communication pressures, and this has been congruent, not only with the Americans' fear of playing the sucker role *vis-à-vis* other nations, more skilled in international necromancy, but also with the great importance of advertising in the United States. Those European peoples which have felt the impact of modern totalitarian communications had as a background for the experience a past in which Church and State traditionally controlled and manipulated the symbols which could move men to feel and to act. The American on the other hand has experienced instead the manipulation of the same sorts of symbols, of patriotism, religious belief and human strivings after perfection and happiness, by individuals and groups who occupied a very different and far less responsible place in the social hierarchy.

In our American system of communications, any interest, wishing to "sell" its products or message to the public, is able to use the full battery of available communication techniques, radio and film, press and poster. It is characteristic of this system that the symbols used to arouse emotion, evoke attention, and produce action, have come into the hands of those who feel no responsibility toward them. In a society like Bali there is simply no possibility that such a symbol as "The Village," also spoken of as "Mr. Village" and as "God Village," could be used by a casual vendor or rabble rouser. The symbols which evoke responses are used by those whose various positions in the society commit them to a responsible use. But in the United States, most of the value symbols of American tradition are ready to the hand of the manufacturer of the most trivial debased product, or the public relations counsel of the most wildcat and subversive organizations.

The American is used to experiencing the whole symbolic system of his society, in a series of fragmented and contradictory contexts. These beget in him a continually heightened threshold to any sort of appeal (with a recurrent nostalgia for a lost innocence in which his tears could flow simply or his heart swell with uncomplicated emotion) and a casual, non-evaluative attitude toward the power wielded through any communication system. As he straightens his tie and decides not to buy the tie which is being recommended over the radio, or in the streetcar ad, he gets a sense of immunity which makes him overlook the extent to which he is continually absorbing the ad behind the ad, the deutero (3) contexts of the material which he feels he is resisting.

We may examine the types of learning which result from the various uses of symbols in the United States in terms of: Whose symbol is used? What is the order of relationship between the symbol-possessing group and the group which is using the symbol? What is the nature of the product or message for which the symbol is being used? Who benefits by its use?

As examples of various types of symbol usage, let us consider the use of the symbol of Florence Nightingale, devoted ministrant to suffering and dying humanity. In the first position, a maker of white broadcloth might put out an advertisement which said, "In the great tradition of Florence Nightingale, American nurses are to be found ministering to the suffering. And, needing the very best, in order to fulfil their devoted mission, they use *Blank's* broadcloth for their uniforms, because it wears—through sickness and death." The reader of this advertisement learns that Florence Nightingale is a name to conjure with, that she was admired and respected, and that *Blank's* broadcloth are using her to enhance *their* prestige. To this degree the value of Florence Nightingale's name is increased. But at the same time the reader or listener may also add a footnote, "Trying to tie their old broadcloth on to Florence Nightingale's kite," and the sense of a synthetic, temporary quality of all symbol associations is strengthened in his mind.

In the second case, the advocates of a dishonest correspondence course in nursing might use the name of Florence Nightingale in a plea to individuals to rise and follow the lamp once carried aloft by the great Nurse, and prepare themselves, in only twenty lessons, money down in advance, to follow in her footsteps. Here, to the extent that the listener realized that the correspondence course was phony, Florence Nightingale's name would also be shrouded with some of the same feeling of the phonyness, bedraggled and depreciated.

In the third case, a nurses' association might decide to put themselves back of a public education program in chest x-rays for tuberculosis control, and develop a poster in which they placed their great symbol, Florence Nightingale, beside an appeal for support for the local anti-tuberculosis committee. The reader and listeners here recognize that Florence Nightingale is a great and valuable symbol, because those to whom she is a value symbol have themselves used her name to advance some newer and younger cause. This last type is of course characteristic of the historical use of symbols in society. Even when groups which represented religious or political subversion from the point of view of those in power have appropriated to themselves the sacred symbols of those against whom they were fighting, such moves have been made seriously and responsibly by those who believed that their subversion and their heresy were neither subversion nor heresy but political justice and religious truth. Symbols which change hands between orthodox and heterodox, between conservative and liberal, do not suffer by the change as long as each group of users acts responsibly. Instead such exchange is an invaluable ingredient of continuity and consistency within a changing society.

But the advertising agency, the public relations counsel, as institutionalized in our culture, has no responsibility of this sort. An advertising agency, whatever the personal sense of conscientious rectitude of its staff, has one set of functions to perform, to sell the product successfully while keeping within the law. With sufficient sophistication, a refusal to spoil the market, either for the same product in the future, or for other products, might be included within its functions. But our society has no higher jurisdiction to which such agencies owe allegiance. The regulations formulated by patriotic societies to protect the flag have to be respected, or you get into trouble. Religious symbols can be used only if you are sure the churches will not get in your hair. Claims must be muted to the sensitivities of the Pure Food and Drug Administration. If you expect to keep the contract a long time, do not overplay a line which may go sour. If you do not want trouble from your other clients, or other agencies, do not take too obvious a crack at other products or organizations or causes. It is upon such disjointed rules of thumb that the day by day manipulation of the responsiveness, the moral potential of the American people, depends.

The National Nutrition Program, administered under Federal auspices during the war, was one interesting attempt to deal with this contemporary situation. Agreements were worked out by which advertisers were permitted to use the name of the National Nutrition Program, if, and only if, they acceded to certain conditions, the final ethical sanction for which came from the best scientific knowledge of nutritionists. Advertisers were not permitted to misquote, quote in part, or add to, the gist of the Nutrition theme which had been agreed upon, nor could they use it in association with products of no nutritional value. In spite of the many small expediencies which clouded the issues, this was a genuine attempt to supply an ethical sanction, rooted in science and administered by government, to a whole mass of communications on the subject of food and its uses. On a very simple level, this program represented one possible direction in which a country like the United States might move to give ethical form to the almost wholly unregulated mass of communications which now serve the interests of such a variety of groups—one way in which control can be vested in those to whom the symbol belongs.

A continuation of the present state of irresponsibility is exceedingly dangerous because it provides a situation within which steps backward rather than steps forward are so likely to occur. One possible response to the confused state of our symbolic system and the dulling of our responsiveness is an artificial simplification, a demand for the return of control to central authorities who will see to it that there is no more of the haphazard and contradictory use of important symbols. If the only choice open to us appears to be this increasing immunization against any appeal, this increasing apathy and callousness, so that photographs of a thousand murdered innocents no longer have any power to move us, the temptation to swing back to authoritarianism may become increasingly great. If, however, we can go on and formulate a system of responsibility appropriate to the age in which we live, a system which takes into account the state of technology, the type of mixed economy, the democratic aspirations, and the present dulled sensibilities of the American people, we may prevent such a reaction and, instead, move forward.

Any theory of the way in which responsibility for communications must be developed must deal with the problem of intent, with the beliefs that the communicator has about himself, and about his audience, as well as with the particular constitution and situation of that audience. This facet of the problem is particularly important in America, where the average citizen still identifies his position as a minority one, and so always thinks of power as wielded by THEM, and not by himself or a group to which he belongs. All discussions of the locations of responsibility for the communication stream, in any positive or constructive sense, are likely to stumble over this feeling that responsibility means power, and power is always in the hands of someone else. A set of negative controls, such as the rule that a radio station must discuss both sides of a situation, no matter how imperfectly and destructively each side is presented, is more congenial than any set of positive controls. So also were the teachings of propaganda analysis; the American felt safer in learning how not to respond to a false appeal than in permitting any effective development of appeals which would be so good that he would respond to them.

It therefore seems that it is important to arrive at a phrasing of responsibility which will meet this fear of misused power and develop an ethic of communications within a democracy such as ours. Once a climate of opinion expressing such an ethic begins to develop, appropriate institutional forms may be expected to emerge, either slowly or under intensive cultivation.

Such an ethic might take the form of an insistence that the audience be seen as composed of *whole* individuals, not artificial cut outs from crowd scenes, such as are represented on the dust jacket of a recent book (4) on radio. It might take the form of insisting that the audience be seen as composed of individuals who could not be manipulated but could only be appealed to in terms of their systematic cultural strengths. It might include a taboo on seeing any individual as the puppet of the propagandist, and focussing instead on the purposeful cultivation of directions of change. It would then be regarded as ethical to try to persuade the American people to drink orange juice, as a pleasant and nutritional drink, by establishing a style of breakfast, a visual preference for oranges, and a moral investment in good nutrition, but not by frightening individual mothers into serving orange juice for fear that they would lose their children's love, or their standing in the community.

Probably the closest analogue for the development of such sanctions can be found in medical ethics, legal ethics, etc., in which a group of self-respecting practitioners constitute themselves as a final court of appeal upon their own behavior. To the extent that advertising, public relations, market research, and the various communication media experts come to hold themselves and be held by the public in greater respect, such internally self-corrective systems might be developed.

If the contention is justified that democratic institutions represent a more complex integration of society, in which greater or different possibilities are accorded to each individual, we must expect corresponding differences between the communication ethics of societies representative of different degrees of feudalism and capitalism in different political combinations. The wholly feudal state may be said to have localized responsibility for communications within a hierarchical status system, and avoided the problem of power over individuals or trends by regarding that system as fixed and immutable. The totalitarian system which has lost the sanctions of feudalism and cannot depend upon the character structure of its citizens, develops monopolistic communication systems which seek to establish a direction in the society, but which in the interval are seen as operating on identified individuals, playing upon their most vulnerable points to bring them in line with a dictated policy. Whether it is claimed that the availability of concentration camps influence the propagandist or merely makes the audience members vulnerable, the interrelationship is there.

Political democracies have, to date, by insisting on negative sanctions, maintained systems in which the individual was the target of many sorts of propagandic themes but in which he was protected by the existence of contradictions in the appeals made to him. Such negative sanctions are better than none, but the target of American advertising is not a dignified human figure (5). The target of political campaigns in the United States is not a dignified human figure. The limitation on the sense of power of the advertising agency copy writer or the campaign manager has merely been the knowledge that there were opponents in the field, free to act just as irresponsibly as he and free to present an equally contradictory and destructive set of counter appeals.

This negative approach is challenged whenever the country goes to war and wishes to mobilize its citizens toward common goals. It is doubly challenged when branches of the United States Army or the United States Government are charged with the task of reeducating peoples who have lived under totalitarian regimes. The resistance of the Germans (6), for example, to the sort of protection of freedom which is implied in the cultivation of a two party system, challenges American culture to the development of a more positive ethic.

References

1. Margaret Mead, "Our Educational Emphasis in Primitive Perspective," in *Education and the Cultural Process,* ed., Charles S. Johnson. Papers presented at Symposium commemorating the 75th Anniversary of the founding of Fisk University, April–May 1941. Reprinted from the *American Journal of Sociology,* 48, May 1943, 6, pp. 5–12.

2. Ernest Kris, "Some Problems of War Propaganda," *Psychoanalytic Quarterly,* 12, 3, pp. 381–399 (for a discussion of the way in which Nazi propaganda methods drew upon LeBon's psychology of the crowd).

3. For a discussion of the concept of deutero learning see: Gregory Bateson, "Social Planning and the Concept of 'Deutero-Learning'," *Science, Philosophy and Religion, 2nd Symposium,* Conference on Science, Philosophy and Religion, New York, 1942, pp. 81–97.

4. Paul F. Lazarsfeld and Harry Field, *The People Look at Radio,* University of North Carolina Press, Chapel Hill, 1946.

5. Constantin Fitz Gibbon, "The Man of Fear," *Atlantic Monthly,* January 1947, pp. 78–81.

6. Bertram Schaffner, *Father Land, A Study of Authoritarianism in the German Family.* Columbia University Press, New York, 1948.

Beyond Cultural Identity: Reflections on Cultural and Multicultural Man

Peter S. Adler

Introduction

The idea of a multicultural man* is an attractive and persuasive notion. It suggests a human being whose identifications and loyalties transcend the boundaries of nationalism and whose commitments are pinned to a vision of the world as a global community. To be a citizen of the world, an international person, has long been a dream of man. History is rich with examples of societies and individuals who took it upon themselves to shape everyone else to the mold of their planetary dream. Less common are examples of men and women who have striven to sustain a self process that is international in attitude and behavior. For good reason. Nation, culture, and society exert tremendous influence on each of our lives, structuring our values, engineering our view of the world, and patterning our responses to experience. No human being can hold himself apart from some form of cultural influence. No one is culture free. Yet, the conditions of contemporary history are such that we may now be on the threshold of a new kind of person, a person who is socially and psychologically a product of the interweaving of cultures in the twentieth century.

We are reminded daily of this phenomenon. In the corner of a traditional, Japanese home sits a television set tuned to a baseball game in which the visitors, an American team, are losing. A Canadian family, meanwhile, decorates their home with sculptures and paintings imported from Pakistan, India, and Ceylon.

From *Topics in Culture Learning,* Vol. 2 (August 1974), pp. 23–40. Reprinted with permission of the author and the East-West Center. Dr. Adler is with the Office of Participant Affairs, The East-West Center, Honolulu, Hawaii.

*Despite the fact that men and women share an equal investment in psychological developments of our time, it is virtually impossible to express certain concepts in language that is sexually neutral. The idea of a multicultural "man" and other references to the masculine gender are to be considered inclusive of men and women alike.

Teenagers in Singapore and Hong Kong pay unheard of prices for American blue-jeans while high school students in England and France take courses on the making of traditional, Indonesian batik. A team of Malaysian physicians innoculates a remote village against typhus while their Western counterparts study Auryvedic medicine and acupuncture. Around the planet the streams of the world's cultures merge together to form new currents of human interaction. Though superficial and only a manifestation of the shrinking of the globe, each such vignette is a symbol of the mingling and melding of human cultures. Communication and cultural exchange are the pre-eminent conditions of the twentieth century.

For the first time in the history of the world, a patchwork of technology and organization has made possible simultaneous interpersonal and intercultural communication. Innovations and refinements of innovations, including mass mail systems, publishing syndicates, film industries, television networks, and newswire services have brought people everywhere into potential contact. Barely a city or village exists that is more than a day or two from anyplace else; almost no town or community is without a radio. Buslines, railroads, highways, and airports have created linkages within and between local, regional, national, and international levels of human organization. The impact is enormous. Human connections through communications have made possible the interaction of goods, products, and services as well as the more significant exchange of thoughts and ideas. Accompanying the growth of human communication has been the erosion of barriers that have, throughout history, geographically, linguistically, and culturally separated man from man. As Harold Lasswell (1972) has recently suggested, "the technological revolution as it affects mass media has reached a limit that is subject only to innovations that would substantially modify our basic perspectives of one another and of man's place in the cosmos." It is possible that the emergence of multicultural man is just such an innovation.

A New Kind of Man

A new type of person whose orientation and view of the world profoundly transcends his indigenous culture is developing from the complex of social, political, economic, and educational interactions of our time. The various conceptions of an "international," "transcultural," or "interculture" person have all been used with varying degrees of explanative or descriptive utility. Essentially, they all define a type of person whose horizons extend significantly beyond his or her own culture. An "internationalist," for example, has been defined as a person who trusts other nations, is willing to cooperate with other countries, perceives international agencies as potential deterrents of war, and who considers international tensions reducible by mediation (Lutzker, 1960). Others have researched the internationality of groups by measuring their attitudes towards international issues, i.e., the role of the U.N., economic versus military aid, international alliances, etc. (Campbell, et al., 1954). And at least several attempts have been made to measure the world-mindedness of individuals by exploring the degree to which persons have an international frame of reference rather than specific knowledge or interest in global affairs (Sampson and Smith, 1957; Garrison, 1961; Paul, 1966).

Whatever the terminology, the definitions and metaphors allude to a person whose essential identity is inclusive of life patterns different from his own and who has psychologically and socially come to grips with a multiplicity of realities. We can call this new type of person multicultural because he embodies a core process of self verification that is grounded in both the universality of the human condition and in the diversity of man's cultural forms. We are speaking, then, of a social-psychological style of self process that differs from others. Multicultural man is the person who is intellectually and emotionally committed to the fundamental unity of all human beings while at the same time he recognizes, legitimizes, accepts, and appreciates the fundamental differences that lie between people of different cultures. This new kind of man cannot be defined by the languages he speaks, the countries he has visited, or the number of international contacts he has made. Nor is he defined by his profession, his place of residence, or his cognitive sophistication. Instead, multicultural man is recognized by the configuration of his outlooks and world view, by the way he incorporates the universe as a dynamically moving process, by the way he reflects the interconnectedness of life in his thoughts and his actions, and by the way he remains open to the imminence of experience.

Multicultural man is, at once, both old and new. He is very much the timeless "universal" person described again and again by philosophers through the ages. He approaches, in the attributions we make about him, the classical ideal of a person whose lifestyle is one of knowledge and wisdom, integrity and direction, principle and fulfillment, balance and proportion. "To be a universal man," writes John Walsh (1973), "means not how much a man knows but what intellectual depth and breadth he has and how he relates it to other central and universally important problems." What is universal about the multicultural person is his abiding commitment to essential similarities between people everywhere, while paradoxically maintaining an equally strong commitment to their differences. The universal person, suggests Walsh, "does not at all eliminate culture differences." Rather, he "seeks to preserve whatever is most valid, significant, and valuable in each culture as a way of enriching and helping to form the whole." In his embodiment of the universal and the particular, multicultural man is a descendent of the great philosophers in both the East and the West.

What is new about this type of person and unique to our time is a fundamental change in the structure and process of his identity. His identity, far from being frozen in a social character, is more fluid and mobile, more susceptible to change and open to variation. The identity of multicultural man is based, not on a "belongingness" which implies either owning or being owned by culture, but on a style of self consciousness that is capable of negotiating ever new formations of reality. In this sense multicultural man is a radical departure from the kinds of identities found in both traditional and mass societies. He is neither totally *a part* of nor totally *apart from* his culture; he lives, instead, on the boundary. To live on the edge of one's thinking, one's culture, or one's ego, suggests Paul

Tillich (1966), is to live with tension and movement. "It is in truth not standing still, but rather a crossing and return, a repetition of return and crossing, back-and-forth—the aim of which is to create a third area beyond the bounded territories, an area where one can stand for a time without being enclosed in something tightly bounded." Multicultural man, then, is an outgrowth of the complexities of the twentieth century. Yet unique as he may be, the style of identity embodied by multicultural man arises from the myriad of forms that are present in this day and age. An understanding of this new kind of person, then, must be predicated on a clear understanding of cultural identity.

The Concept of Cultural Identity: A Psychocultural Framework

The concept of cultural identity can be used in two different ways. First, it can be employed as a reference to the collective self awareness that a given group embodies and reflects. This is the most prevalent use of the term. "Generally," writes Stephen Bochner (1973), "the cultural identity of a society is defined by its majority group, and this group is usually quite distinguishable from the minority sub-groups with whom they share the physical environment and the territory that they inhabit." With the emphasis upon the group, the concept is akin to the idea of a national or social character which describes a set of traits that members of a given community share with one another above and beyond their individual differences. Such traits most always include a constellation of values and attitudes towards life, death, birth, family, children, god, and nature. Used in its collective sense, the concept of cultural identity includes typologies of cultural behavior, such behaviors being the appropriate and inappropriate ways of solving life's essential dilemmas and problems. Used in its collective sense, the concept of cultural identity incorporates the shared premises, values, definitions, and beliefs and the day-to-day, largely unconscious, patterning of activities.

A second, more specific use of the concept revolves around the identity of the individual in relation to his or her culture. Cultural identity, in the sense that it is a functioning aspect of individual personality, is a fundamental symbol of a person's existence. It is in reference to the individual that the concept is used in this paper. In psychoanalytic literature, most notably in the writings of Erik Erikson (1959), identity is an elemental form of psychic organization which develops in successive psycho-sexual phases throughout life. Erikson, who has focused the greater portion of his analytic studies on identity conflicts, has long recognized the anchoring of the ego in a larger cultural context. Identity, he suggests, takes a variety of forms in the individual. "At one time," he writes, "it will appear to refer to a conscious sense of *individual identity;* at another to an unconscious striving for a *continuity of personal character;* at a third, as a criterion for the silent doings of *ego synthesis;* and, finally, as a maintenance of an inner *solidarity* with a group's ideals and identity." The analytic perspective, as voiced by Erikson, is only one of a variety of definitions. Most always, however, the concept of identity is meant to imply a coherent sense of self that depends on a stability of values and a sense of wholeness and integration.

How, then, can we conceptualize the interplay of culture and personality? Culture and personality are inextricably woven together in the gestalt of each person's identity. Culture, the mass of life patterns that human beings in a given society learn from their elders and pass on to the younger generation, is imprinted in the individual as a pattern of perceptions that is accepted and expected by others in a society (Singer, 1971). Cultural identity is the symbol of one's essential experience of oneself as it incorporates the world view, value system, attitudes, and beliefs of a group with whom such elements are shared. In its most manifest form, cultural identity takes the shape of names which both locate and differentiate the person. When an individual calls himself an American, a Christian, a Democrat, a male, and John Jones, he is symbolizing parts of the complex of images he has of himself and that are likewise recognizable by others. The deeper structure of cultural identity is a fabric of such images and perceptions embedded in the psychological posture of the individual. At the center of this matrix of images is a psychocultural fusion of biological, social, and philosophical motivations; this fusion, a synthesis of culture and personality, is the operant person.

The center, or core, of cultural identity is an image of the self and the culture intertwined in the individual's total conception of reality. This image, a patchwork of internalized roles, rules, and norms, functions as the coordinating mechanism in personal and interpersonal situations. The "mazeway," as Anthony Wallace calls it, is made up of human, non-human, material and abstract elements of the culture. It is the "stuff" of both personality and culture. The mazeway, suggests Wallace (1956), is the patterned image of society and culture, personality and nature all of which is ingrained in the person's symbolization of himself. A system of culture, he writes, "depends relatively more on the ability of constituent units autonomously to perceive the system of which they are a part, to receive and transmit information, and to act in accordance with the necessities of the system. . . ." The image, or mazeway, of cultural identity is the gyroscope of the functioning individual. It mediates, arbitrates, and negotiates the life of the individual. It is within the context of this central, navigating image that the fusion of biological, social, and philosophical realities, then, form units of integration that are important to a comparative analysis of cultural identity. The way in which these units are knit together and contoured by the culture at large determine the parameters of the individual. This boundary of cultural identity plays a large part in determining the individual's ability to relate to other cultural systems.

All human beings share a similar biology, universally limited by the rhythms of life. All individuals in all races and cultures must move through life's phases on a similar schedule: birth, infancy, adolescence, middle age, old age, and death. Similarly, humans everywhere embody the same physiological functions of ingestion, irritability, metabolic equilibrium, sexuality, growth, and decay. Yet the ultimate interpretation of human biology is a cultural phenomenon; that is, the meanings of human biological patterns are culturally derived. Though all healthy human beings are born, reproduce, and die, it is culture which dictates the meanings of sexuality, the ceremonials of birth, the transitions of life, and the rituals of death. The capacity for language, for example, is universally accepted as a biological given. Any child, given unimpaired apparatus for hearing, vocalizing, and thinking, can learn to speak and understand any human language. Yet the language that is learned by a child depends solely upon the place and the manner of rearing. Kluckhohn and Leighton (1970), in outlining the grammatical and phonetic systems of the Navajo Indians, have argued that patterns of language affect the expression of ideas and very possibly more fundamental processes of thinking. As Benjamin Whorf has suggested (1957), language may not be merely an inventory of linguistic items but rather "itself the shaper of ideas, the program and guide for the individual's mental activity."*

The interaction of culture and biology provides one cornerstone for an understanding of cultural identity. How each individual's biological situation is given meaning becomes, then, a psychobiological unit of integration and analysis. Man's essential physiological needs, hunger, sex, activity, and avoidance of pain, are one part of the reality pattern of cultural identity; similarly with those drives that reach out to the social order. At this, the psychosocial level of integration, generic needs are channeled and organized by culture. Man's needs for affection, acceptance, recognition, affiliation, status, belonging, and interaction with other human beings are enlivened and given recognizable form by culture. We can, for example, see clearly the intersection of culture and the psychosocial level of integration in comparative status responses. In America economic status is demonstrated by the conspicuous consumption of products; among the Kwakiutl Indians, status is gained by giving all possessions away in the "potlatch"; and contempt or disrespect for the status of old people in many Asian societies represents a serious breach of conduct demanding face-saving measures.

It is the unwritten task of every culture to organize, integrate, and maintain the psychosocial patterns of the individual, especially in the formative years of childhood. Each culture instruments such patterns in ways that are unique, coherent, and logical to the premises and predispositions that underlie the culture. This imprinting of the forms of interconnection that are needed by the individual for psychosocial survival, acceptance, and enrichment is a significant part of the socialization and enculturation process. Yet of equal importance in the imprinting is the structuring of higher forms of individual consciousness. Culture gives meaning and form to those drives and motivations that extend towards an understanding of the cosmological ordering of the universe. All cultures, in one manner or another, invoke the great philosophical questions of life: the origin and destiny of existence, the nature of knowledge, the meaning of reality, the significance of the human experience. As Murdock (1955) has suggested in "Universals of Culture," some form of cosmology, ethics, mythology, supernatural propitiation, religious rituals, and soul concept appears in every culture known to history or ethnography. How an individual raises and searches for ultimate answers is a function of the psychophilosophical patterning of cul-

---

*A technical reference to the controversial literature examining the "Sapir-Whorf Hypothesis" can be found in "Psycholinguistics" by G. Miller and D. McNeill in Volume 3 of the *Handbook of Social Psychology,* edited by G. Lindzey and E. Aronson (Reading: Addison-Wesley Publishing Company, 1968).

tural identity. Ultimately it is the task of every individual to relate to his god, to deal with the supernatural, and to incorporate for himself the mystery of life itself. The ways in which individuals do this, the relationships and connections that are formed, are a function of the psychophilosophical component of cultural identity.

A conceptualization of cultural identity, then, must include three interrelated levels of integration and analysis. While the cultural identity of an individual is comprised of symbols and images that signify aspects of these levels, the psychobiological, psychosocial, and psychophilosophical realities of an individual are knit together by the culture which operates through sanctions and rewards, totems and taboos, prohibitions and myths. The unity and integration of society, nature, and the cosmos is reflected in the total image of the self and in the day-to-day awareness and consciousness of the individual. This synthesis is modulated by the larger dynamics of the culture itself. In the concept of cultural identity, then, we see a synthesis of the operant culture reflected by the deepest images held by the individual. These images, in turn, are based on universally human motivations.

Implicit in any analysis of cultural identity is a configuration of motivational needs. As the late Abraham Maslow (1962) suggested, human drives form a hierarchy in which the most prepotent motivations will monopolize consciousness and will tend, of themselves, to organize the various capacities and capabilities of the organism. In the sequence of development, the needs of infancy and childhood revolve primarily around physiological and biological necessities, i.e., nourishment by food, water, and warmth. Correspondingly, the psychosocial needs of the individual are most profound in adolescence and young adulthood when the individual is engaged in establishing himself through marriage, occupation, and social and economic status. Finally, psychophilosophical drives are most manifest in middle and old age when the individual can occupy himself with creativity, philosophic actualization, and with transcendental relationships. As Cofer and Appley (1964) rightly point out, Maslow's hierarchy of needs is not an explicit, empirical, verifiable theory of human motivation. It is useful, however, in postulating a universally recognized but differently named process of individual motivation that carries the individual through the stages of life. Each level of integration and analysis in cultural identity, then, can be viewed as both a part of the gridwork of the self image as well as a developmental roadmap imprinted by the culture.

The gyroscope of cultural identity functions to orchestrate the allegiances, loyalties, and commitments of the individual by giving them direction and meaning. Every human being, however, differentiates himself to some degree from his culture. Just as no one is totally free of cultural influence, no one is totally a reflection of his culture. The cultural identity of an individual, therefore, must be viewed as an integrated synthesis of identifications that are idiosyncratic within the parameters of culturally influenced biological, social, and philosophical motivations. Whether, in fact, such unity ever achieves sufficient integration to provide for consistency between individuals within a given culture is an empirical matter that deals with normalcy and modal personality. The concept of cultural identity, then, can at best be a schema for comparative research between (rather than within) cultures. This schema of cultural identity is illustrated in figure 1. Though

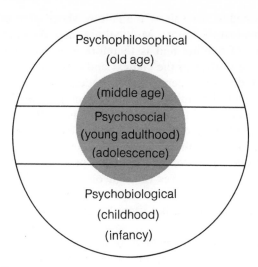

Figure 1

admittedly a fundamental rule of social science must be human variation and the unpredictability of models and theories, a schema of cultural identity and the interplay of psychological and cultural dynamics may lay a groundwork for future research and conceptualization. Particularly useful may be the "eiconic" approach proposed by Kenneth Boulding (1956). His typology of images which include the spatial, temporal, relational, personal, value, affectional, conscious-unconscious, certainty-uncertainty, reality-unreality, and public-private dimensions, may add important perspectives to the comparative study of cultural identity.

The Multicultural Identity

The rise of multicultural man is a significant phenomenon because it represents a new psychocultural style of self process. He arises amidst the metamorphosis of both traditional and mass societies, in a transitional time in which man is redefining himself politically, socially and economically. Multicultural man is a radically different sort of human being. Three characteristics distinguish his style of personality from the traditional structure of cultural identity. First, the multicultural person is psychoculturally adaptive; that is, he is situational in his relationships to others and his connections to culture. He maintains no clear boundaries between himself and the varieties of personal and cultural contexts he may find himself in. The multicultural identity is premised, not on the hierarchical structuring of a single mental image but rather on the intentional and accidental shifts that life's experiences involve. His values and attitudes, world view and beliefs, are always in reformation, dependent more on the necessities of experience than on the predispositions of a given culture. For multicultural man, attitudes, values, beliefs, and a world view are relevant only to a given context (as is usually learned as a result of the culture shock process) and cannot be translated from context to context. Multicultural man does not judge one situation by the terms of another and is therefore ever evolving new systems of evaluations that are relative to the context and situation.

Second, the multicultural person is ever undergoing personal transitions. He is always in a state of "becoming" or "un-becoming" something different than before while yet mindful of the grounding he has in his own cultural reality. Stated differently, multicultural man is propelled from identity to identity through a process of both cultural learning and cultural un-learning. Multicultural man, like Robert J. Lifton's concept of "protean man" (1961), is always recreating his identity. He moves through one experience of self to another, incorporating here, discarding there, responding dynamically and situationally. This style of self process, suggests Lifton, "is characterized by an interminable series of experiments and explorations, some shallow, some profound, each of which can readily be abandoned in favor of still new, psychological quests." The multicultural man is always in flux, the configuration of his loyalties and identifications changing, his overall image of himself perpetually being reformulated through experience and contact with the world. Stated differently, his life is an on-going process of psychic death and rebirth.

Third, multicultural man maintains indefinite boundaries of the self. The parameters of his identity are neither fixed nor predictable, being responsive, instead, to both temporary form and openness to change. Multicultural man is capable of major shifts in his frame of reference and embodies the ability to disavow a permanent character and change in his social-psychological style. The multicultural person, in the words of Peter Berger (1973) is a "homeless mind," a condition which, though allowing great flexibility, also allows for nothing permanent and unchanging to develop. This homelessness is at the heart of his motivational needs. He is, suggests Lifton, "starved for ideas and feelings that give coherence to his world . . .," that give structure and form to his search for the universal and absolute, that give definition to his perpetual quest. The multicultural man, like great philosophers in any age, can never accept totally the demands of any one culture nor is he free from the conditioning of his culture. His psychocultural style, then, must always be relational and in movement. He is able, however, to look at his own original culture from an outsider's perspective. This tension gives rise to a dynamic, passionate, and critical posture in the face of totalistic ideologies, systems, and movements.

Like culture-bound man, multicultural man bears within him a simultaneous image of societies, nature, personality, and culture. Yet in contrast to the structure of cultural identity, multicultural man is perpetually re-defining his mazeway. No culture is capable of imprinting or ingraining the identity of multicultural man indelibly; yet, likewise, multicultural man must rely heavily on cultures to maintain his own relativity. Like human beings in any period of time, multicultural man is driven by psychobiological, psychosocial, and psychophilosophical motivations that impel him through life. Yet the configuration of these drives is perpetually in flux and situational. The maturational hierarchy, implicit in the central image of cultural identity, is less structured and cohesive in the multicultural identity. For that reason, his needs and his drives, his motivations and expectations are constantly being aligned and realigned to fit the context he is in.

The flexibility of multicultural man allows great variation in adaptability and adjustment. Adjustment and adaptation, however, must always be dependent on some constant, on something stable and unchanging in the fabric of life. We can attribute to multicultural man three fundamental postulates that are incorporated and reflected in his thinking and behavior. Such postulates are fundamental to success in cross-cultural adaptation.

(1) Every culture or system has its own internal coherence, integrity, and logic. Every culture is an intertwined system of values and attitudes, beliefs and norms that give meaning and significance to both individual and collective identity.

(2) No one culture is inherently better or worse than another. All cultural systems are equally valid as variations on the human experience.

(3) All persons are, to some extent, culturally bound. Every culture provides the individual with some sense of identity, some regulation of behavior, and some sense of personal place in the scheme of things.

The multicultural person embodies these propositons in the living expressions of his life. They are fundamentally a part of his interior image of himself and the world and as much a part of his behavior.

What is uniquely new about this emerging human being is a psychocultural style of self process that transcends the structured image a given culture may impress upon the individual in his or her youth. The navigating image at the core of the multicultural image is premised on an assumption of many cultural realities. The multicultural person, therefore, is not simply the person who is sensitive to many different cultures. Rather, he is a person who is always in the process of becoming *a part of* and *apart from* a given cultural context. He is very much a formative being, resilient, changing, and evolutionary. He has no permanent cultural character but neither is he free from the influences of culture. In the shifts and movements of his identity process, multicultural man is continually recreating the symbol of himself. The concept of a multicultural identity is illustrated and differentiated from the schema of cultural identity in figure 2.

The indefinite boundaries and the constantly realigning relationships that are generated by the psychobiological, psychosocial, and psychophilosophical motivations make possible sophisticated and complex responses on the part of the individual to cultural and subcultural systems. Moreover, this psychocultural flexibility necessitates sequential changes in identity. Intentionally or accidentally, multicultural persons undergo shifts in their total psychocultural posture; their religion, personality, behavior, occupation, nationality, outlook, political persuasion, and values may, in part or completely, reformulate in the face of new experiences. "It is becoming increasingly possible," writes Michael Novak (1970), "for men to live through several profound conversions, calling forth in themselves significantly different personalities. . . ." The relationship of multicultural man to cultural systems is fragile and tenuous. "A man's cultural and social milieu," continues Novak, "conditions his personality, values, and actions; yet the same

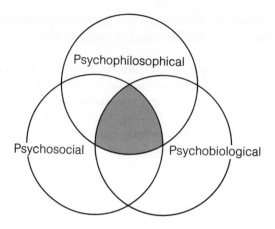

Figure 2

man is able, within limits, to choose the milieus whose conditioning will affect him."

Stresses and Tensions

The unprecedented dynamism of multicultural man makes it possible to live many different lives, in sequence or simultaneously. But such psychocultural pliability gives rise to tensions and stresses unique to the conditions which allow such dynamism in the first place. Multicultural man, by virtue of the fact that his boundaries are indefinite, his experience more intense, and his lifetime telescoped into modules of congruency, is subject to stresses and strains that are equally unique. At least five of these stresses bear mentioning.

First, multicultural man is vulnerable. In maintaining no clear boundary and form multicultural man is susceptible to confusing the profound and the insignificant, the important and the unimportant, the visionary and the reactionary. "Boundaries can be viewed," suggests Lifton (1967), "as neither permanent nor by definition false, but rather as essential. ... We require images of limit and restraint, if only to help us grasp what we are transcending. We need distinctions between our biology and our history, all the more so as we seek to bring these together in a sense of ourselves. . . ." Without some form of boundary, experience itself has no shape or contour, no meaning and importance; where the individual maintains no critical edge to his existence everything can become confusion. Experience, in order to be a particular experience, must take place amidst some essential polarity in which there is tension between two opposing forces. Where there is no sense of evil, there can be no sense of the good; where nothing is profane, nothing can be sacred. Boundaries, however indefinite, give shape and meaning to the experience of experience; they allow us to differentiate, define, and determine who we are in relation to someone or something else.

Second, multicultural man can easily become multiphrenic, that is, to use Erikson's terminology, a "diffused identity." Where the configuration of loyalties and identifications is constantly in flux and where boundaries are never secure, multicultural man lays himself open to any and all kind of stimuli. In the face of messages which are confusing, contradictory, or overwhelming, the individual is thrown back on himself and his own subjectivity, with which he must integrate and sort out what he allows himself to take in. Where the multicultural man is incapable of doing this he is pulled and pushed by the winds of communication, a victim of what everyone else claims he is or should be. It is the task of every social and cultural group to organize messages, images, and symbols into terms that the individual can translate into his own existence. But where the messages and stimuli of all groups are given equal importance and validity, the individual can easily be overwhelmed by the demands of everyone else.

Third, multicultural man can easily suffer from a loss of the sense of his own authenticity. That is, multicultural man, by virtue of the fact that he is psychoculturally adaptive, can potentially be reduced to a variety of roles that bear little or no relationship to one another. Multicultural man can lose the sense of congruence and integrity that is implicit in the definition of identity itself. Roles, suggest psychologists, are constellations of behaviors that are expected of an individual because of his place in particular social or cultural arrangements. Behind roles are the deeper threads of continuity, the processes of affect, perception, cognition, and value, that make a whole of the parts. Multicultural man can easily disintegrate into a fragmented splinter who is unable to experience life along any dimension other than institutionalized, routinized expectations placed on him by family, friends, and society.

Fourth, and related to this, is the risk of being a gadfly and a dilettante. Multicultural man can very easily move from identity experience to identity experience without committing himself or his values to real-life situations. The energy and enthusiasm he brings to bear on new situations can easily disintegrate into superficial fads and fancies in which the multicultural person simply avoids any deeper responsibilities and involvements. Flexibility can easily disguise a manner of self process in which real human problems are avoided or in which they are given only superficial importance. Especially in the Western societies, where youth is vulnerable to the fabricated fads of contemporary culture, the multicultural identity process can give way to a dilettantism in which the individual flows, unimpaired, uncommitted, and unaffected, through social, political, and economic manipulations of elites.

Fifth, and finally, the multicultural person may take ultimate psychological and philosophical refuge in an attitude of existential absurdity, mocking the patterns and lifestyles of others who are different from himself, reacting, at best in a detached and aloof way, and at worst as a nihilist who sees negation as a salvation for himself and others. Where the breakdown of boundaries creates a gulf that separates the individual from meaningful relationships with others, the individual may hide behind a screen of barbed cynicisms that harbours apathy and insecurity. In such a condition nothing within and nothing outside of the individual is of serious consequence; the individual, in such a position, must ultimately scorn that which he cannot understand and incorporate into his own existence.

These stresses and strains should not be confused with the tensions and anxieties that are encountered in the process of cross cultural adjustment. Culture shock is a more superficial constellation of problems that results from the misreading of commonly perceived and understood signs of social interaction. Nor is the delineation of these tensions meant to suggest that the multicultural person must necessarily harbor these various difficulties. The multicultural style of identity is premised on a fluid, dynamic movement of the self, an ability to move in and out of contexts, and an ability to maintain some inner coherence through varieties of situations. As a psychocultural style, multicultural man may just as easily be a great artist or neurotic; he is equally as susceptible, if not more so, to the fundamental forces of our time. Any list of multicultural individuals must automatically include individuals who have achieved a high degree of accomplishment, i.e., writers, musicians, diplomats, etc., as well as those whose lives have, for one reason or another, been fractured by the circumstances they failed to negotiate. The artist and the neurotic lay close together in each of us suggests Rollo May (1969). "The neurotic," he writes, "and the artist—since both live out the unconscious of the race—reveal to us what is going to emerge endemically in the society later on ... the neurotic is the 'artiste Manque,' the artist who cannot transmute his conflicts into art."

The identity process of multicultural man represents a new kind of person unfettered by the constricting limitations of culture as a "totalistic" entity. Yet, like men in any age, multicultural man must negotiate the difficulties of cross cultural contacts. The literature of cross cultural psychology is rich with examples of the kinds of problems encountered when people are intensely exposed to other cultures. Integration and assimilation, for example, represent two different responses to a dominant culture, integration suggesting the retention of subcultural differences and assimilation implying absorption into a larger cultural system. The relationship between assimilation, integration, and identification, writes Sommerlad and Berry (1973), "suggests that if an individual identifies with his own group, he will hold favourable attitudes towards integration; on the other hand, if he identifies with the host society, he should favour assimilation." Related to this are the various negative attitudes, psychosomatic stresses, and deviant behaviors that are expressed by individuals in psychologically marginal situations. "Contrary to predictions stemming from the theory of Marginal Man," writes J. W. Berry (1970), "it tends to be those persons more traditionally oriented who suffer the most psychological marginality, rather than those who wish to move on and cannot." Multicultural man is, in many ways, a stranger. The degree to which he can continually modify his frame of reference and become aware of the structures and functions of a group while at the same time maintain a clear understanding of his own personal, ethnic, and cultural identifications may very well be the degree to which the multicultural person can truly function successfully between cultures. Berry's ideas are developed further in his paper for this volume.

Although it is difficult to pinpoint the conditions under which cultural identities will evolve into multicultural identities, such changes in psychocultural style are most likely to occur where the foundations of collective cultural identity have been shaken. "Communities that have been exposed too long to exceptional stresses from ecological or economic hardships," writes J. W. Cawte (1973), "for from natural or man-made disasters are apt to have a high proportion of their members subject to mental disorders." Cawte's studies of the Aboriginal societies of Australia and Turnbull's studies of the Ik in Africa (1972) document how major threats to collective cultural identity produce social and psychological breakdown individuals. Yet, potentially, multicultural attitudes and values may develop where cultural interchange takes place between cultures that are not totally disparate or where the rate of change is evolutionary rather than immediate. The reorganization of a culture, suggests J. L. M. Dawson (1969), "results in the formation of in-between attitudes" which Dawson considers "to be more appropriate for the satisfactory adjustment of individuals in transitional situations." The multicultural style, then, may be born and initially expressed in any society or culture that is faced with new exposures to other ways of life.

Conceptualization of a multicultural identity style in terms of personality types, behavior patterns, traits, and cultural background is, at best impressionistic and anecdotal. Yet, the investigations of cross cultural psychologists and anthropologists give increasing credence to the idea of a multicultural man who is shaped and contoured by the stresses and strains which result from cultural interweaving at both the macro and microcultural levels. Seemingly, a multicultural style is able to evolve when the individual is capable of negotiating the conflicts and tensions inherent in cross cultural contacts. The multicultural person, then, may very well represent an affirmation of individual identity at a higher level of social, psychological, and cultural integration.

Just as the cultures of the world, if they are to merit survival amidst the onslaught of Western technologies, must be responsive to both tradition and change, so too must the individual identity be psychoculturally adaptive to the encounters of an imploding world. There is every reason to think that such human beings are emerging. Multicultural man, embodying, as he does, sequential identities, is open to the continuous cycle of birth and death as it takes place within the framework of his own psyche. The lifestyle of multicultural man is a continual process of dissolution and reformation of identity; yet implicit in such a process is a sequence of growth. Psychological movements into new dimensions of perception and experience tend very often to produce forms of personality disintegration. But disintegration, suggests Kazimierez Dabrowski (1964), "is the basis for developmental thrusts upward, the creation of new evolutionary dynamics, and the movement of personality to a higher level. . . ." The seeds of each new identity of multicultural man lie within the disintegration of previous identities. "When the human being, writes Erikson (1964), "because of accidental or developmental shifts, loses an essential wholeness, he restructures himself and the world by taking recourse to what we may call 'totalism.' " Such totalism, above and beyond being a mechanism of coping and adjustment, is a part of the growth of a new kind of wholeness at a higher level of integration.

Conclusions and Summary

This paper does not suggest that multicultural man is now the predominate character style of our time. Nor is it meant to suggest that multicultural persons, by virtue of their uninhibited way of relating to other cultures, are in any way "better" than those who are mono- or bi-cultural. Rather, this paper argues that multicultural persons are not simply individuals who are sensitive to other cultures or knowledgeable about international affairs, but instead can be defined by a psychocultural pattern of identity that differs radically from the relatively stable forms of self process found in the cultural identity pattern. This paper argues that both cultural and multicultural identity processes can be conceptualized by the constellation and configuration of biological, social, and philosophical motivations and by the relative degrees of rigidity maintained in personal boundaries and that such conceptualization lays the basis for comparative research.

Two final points might be noted about the multicultural man. First, the multicultural person embodies attributes and characteristics that prepare him to serve as a facilitator and catalyst for contacts between cultures. The variations and flexibility of his identity allows the multicultural person to relate to a variety of contexts and environments without being totally encapsulated or totally alienated from the particular situation. As Stephen Bochner (1973) suggests, a major problem of cultural preservation in Asia and the Pacific "is the lack of sufficient people who can act as links between diverse cultural systems." These "mediating" individuals incorporate the essential characteristics of multicultural man. "Genuine multicultural individuals are very rare," he writes," which is unfortunate because it is these people who are uniquely equipped to mediate the cultures of the world." The multicultural person, then, embodies a pattern of self process that potentially allows him to help others negotiate the cultural realities of a different system. With a self process that is adaptational, multicultural man is in a unique position to understand, facilitate, and research the psychocultural dynamics of other systems.

Second, multicultural man is himself a significant psychological and cultural phenomenon, enough so as to merit further conceptualization and research. It is neither easy nor necessarily useful to reconcile the approaches of psychology and anthropology; nor is there any guarantee that interdisciplinary approaches bring us closer to an intelligent understanding of the human being as he exists in relation to his culture. Yet, the multicultural man may prove to be a significant enough problem in culture learning (and culture unlearning) to force an integrated approach to studies of the individual and the group. "Psychologists," writes Richard Brislin, et al. (1973), "have the goal of incorporating the behavior of many cultures into one theory (etic approach), but they must also understand the behavior within each culture (emic approach)." Empirical research based on strategies that can accurately observe, measure, and test behavior, and that incorporate the "emic versus etic" distinction will be a natural next step. Such studies may very well be a springboard into the more fundamental dynamics of cross cultural relationships.

We live in a transitional period of history, a time that of necessity demands transitional forms of psychocultural self process. That a true international community of nations is coming into existence is still a debatable issue; but that individuals with a self consciousness that is larger than the mental territory of their culture are emerging is no longer arguable. The psychocultural pattern of identity that is called for to allow such self-consciousness, adaptability, and variation opens such individuals to both benefits and pathologies. The interlinking of cultures and persons in the twentieth century is not always a pleasant process; modernization and economic development have taken heavy psychological tolls in both developed and third world countries. The changes brought on in our time have invoked revitalistic needs for the preservation of collective, cultural identities. Yet, along with the disorientation and alienation which have characterized much of this century comes new possibility in the way human beings conceive of their individual identities and the identity of man as a species. No one has better stated this possibility than Harold Taylor (1969), himself an excellent example of multicultural man:

> There is a new kind of man in the world, and there are more of that kind than is commonly recognized. He is a national citizen with international intuitions, conscious of the age that is past and aware of the one now in being, aware of the radical difference between the two, willing to accept the lack of precedents, willing to work on the problems of the future as a labor of love, unrewarded by governments, academies, prizes, and position. He forms part of an invisible world community of poets, writers, dancers, scientists, teachers, lawyers, scholars, philosophers, students, citizens who see the world whole and feel at one with all its parts.

References

Berger, P. and Berger, B. *The Homeless Mind.* New York: Random House, 1973.

Berry, J. W. "Marginality, Stress and Ethnic Identification," *Journal of Cross Cultural Psychology,* 1970, 1, 239–252.

Bochner, S. "The Mediating Man and Cultural Diversity," *Topics in Culture Learning,* 1973, Vol. 1, 23–37.

Boulding, K. *The Image.* Ann Arbor: The University of Michigan Press, 1956.

Brislin, R., Lonner, W., and Thorndike, R. *Cross Cultural Research Methods.* New York: John Wiley & Sons, 1973.

Campbell, A., Gurin, G., and Miller, W. E. *The Voter Decides.* Evanston: Row, Peterson and Co., 1954.

Cawte, J. E. "A Sick Society," In Kerney, G. E., de Lacey, P. R., and Davidson, G. R. (Eds.), *The Psychology of Aboriginal Australians.* Sydney: John Wiley & Sons Australasia Pty Ltd., 1973, 365–379.

Cofer, C. and Appley, M. *Motivation: Theory and Research.* New York: John Wiley & Sons, Inc., 1964.

Dabrowski, K. *Positive Disintegration.* Boston: Little, Brown, & Co., 1964.

Dawson, J. L. M. "Attitude Change and Conflict," *Australian Journal of Psychology,* 1969, 21, 101–116.

Erikson, E. "The Problem of Ego Identity," *Psychological Issues,* 1959, Vol. 1, No. 1, 101–164.

Erikson, E. *Insight and Responsibility.* New York: W. W. Norton and Company, 1964.

Garrison, K. "Worldminded Attitudes of College Students in a Southern University," *Journal of Social Psychology,* 1961, 54, 147–153.

Kluckhohn, C. and Leighton, D. "The Language of the Navajo Indians." In P. Bock (Ed.), *Culture Shock.* New York: Alfred A. Knopf, 1970, 29–49.

Lasswell, H. *The Future of World Communication: Quality and Style of Life.* Honolulu: East-West Center Communication Institute, 1972.

Lifton, R. *History and Human Survival.* New York: Vintage Books, 1961.

Lifton, R. *Boundaries.* New York: Vintage Books, 1967.

Lutzker, D. "Internationalism as a Predictor of Cooperative Behavior," *Journal of Conflict Resolution,* 1960, *4* (4), 426–430.

Maslow, A. *Toward a Psychology of Being.* Princeton: D. Van Nostrand Company, Inc., 1962.

May, R. *Love and Will.* New York: Dell Publishing Co., Inc., 1969.

Murdock, G. "Universals of Culture," In J. Jennings and E. A. Hoebel (Eds.), *Readings in Anthropology.* New York: McGraw-Hill Book Company, 1955, 13–14.

Novak, M. *The Experience of Nothingness.* New York: Harper & Row, 1970.

Paul, S. "Worldminded Attitudes of Panjab University Students," *Journal of Social Psychology,* 1966, 69, 33–37.

Sampson, D. and Smith, H. "A Scale to Measure World-minded Attitudes," *Journal of Social Psychology,* 1957, 45, 99–106.

Singer, M. "Culture: A Perceptual Approach," In D. Hoopes (Ed.), *Readings in Intercultural Communication,* Pittsburgh: RCIE, 1971, 6–20.

Sommerlad, E. and Berry, J. W. "The Role of Ethnic Identification," In Kearney, G. E., de Lacey, P. R., and Davidson, G. R. (Eds.), *The Psychology of Aboriginal Australians.* Sydney: John Wiley & Sons Australasia Pty Ltd., 1973, 236–243.

Taylor, H. "Toward a World University," *Saturday Review,* 1969, 24, 52.

Tillich, P. *The Future of Religions.* New York: Harper & Row, 1966.

Turnbull, C. *The Mountain People.* New York: Simon and Schuster, 1972.

Wallace, A. "Revitalization Movements: Some Theoretical Considerations for their Comparative Study," *American Anthropologist,* 1956, 58, 264–281.

Walsh, J. *Intercultural Education in the Community of Man.* Honolulu: The University of Hawaii Press, 1973.

Whorf, B. In J. B. Carroll (Ed.), *Language, Thought, and Reality,* Selected Writings of Benjamin Lee Whorf, Massachusetts: Technology Press of MIT, 1957.

Suggested Readings

Brislin, R. W., W. J. Lonner, and R. M. Thorndike (eds.), *Cross-Cultural Research Methods* (New York: John Wiley & Sons, 1973). This collection presents, in a cohesive and well-organized form, various strategies, methodologies, and problems faced by the researcher interested in cross-cultural projects. The book is divided into ten chapters. Each chapter deals with concepts related to translation, survey methods, experimentation, and appropriate psychological tests.

Brislin, R. W., S. Bochner, and W. Lonner (eds.), *Cross-Cultural Perspectives on Learning* (New York: Halsted Press, 1975). This book contains a collection of essays that emanated from a conference on culture and learning sponsored by the Culture Learning Institute of the East-West Center in Honolulu, Hawaii. Included are essays that deal with the problems of learning another culture, studies of perception and cognition, and a variety of different perspectives for approaching intercultural communication.

Emmert, P., and W. Brooks (eds.), *Methods of Research in Communication* (Boston: Houghton Mifflin Co., 1970). This volume brings together a collection of essays that examine many aspects of behavior science methodology and apply that methodology to the special considerations of communication research. This collection is very important reading for the serious communication researcher.

Porter, R., and L. Samovar, "Intercultural Communication Research: Where Do We Go from Here?" in *Readings in Intercultural Communication,* vol. 3, edited by D. Hoopes (Pittsburgh: Regional Council for International Education, 1973). The authors explore specific needs in intercultural communication research and development during the next decade. Among the suggestions offered are the development of cultural data banks, the expansion of cultural training facilities, and the investigation of how communication variables operate in a variety of cultures.

Rogers, E. M., and F. F. Shoemaker, *Communication of Innovations: A Cross-Cultural Approach,* 2nd ed. (New York: Free Press, 1971). This book is concerned with the question of how innovations (defined as ideas, products, and practices perceived as new by an individual) diffuse to the members of a social system. The new ideas studied range from tractors in Turkey to family planning techniques among Hindu housewives.

Wedge, B., "Communication Analysis and Comprehensive Diplomacy," in *International Communication and the New Diplomacy,* edited by A. S. Hoffman (Bloomington: Indiana University Press, 1968), pp. 22–47. This essay stresses the theme that "misunderstandings of the most concrete and literal kind have played a large role in conflicts between nations." It is Wedge's contention that these conflicts are usually based on differing value systems and orientations. To stress this point, actual cases in international diplomacy are examined.

Additional Readings

Allen, F., *Socio-Cultural Dynamics* (New York: Macmillan, 1970).

Allport, G., *The Nature of Prejudice* (New York: Doubleday & Co., 1958).

Brueing, W., "Racism: A Philosophical Analysis of a Concept," *Journal of Black Studies,* 5 (September 1974), 3–17.

Cherry, C., *World Communication: Threat or Promise* (New York: John Wiley & Sons, 1971).

Glenn, E., R. Johnson, R. Kimmel, and B. Wedge, "A Cognitive Interaction Model to Analyze Culture Conflict in International Relations," *Journal of Conflict Resolution,* 14 (1970), 35–48.

Hayes, A., "A Tentative Schematization for Research in the Teaching of Cross-Cultural Communication," *American Journal of Linguistics,* 28 (1962), 155–167.

Jacobovits, L., "The Affect of Symbols: Towards the Development of a Cross-Cultural Graphic Differential," *International Journal of Symbology,* 1 (1969), 28–52.

Kelman, H., and R. Ezekiel, *Cross-National Encounters* (San Francisco: Jossey-Bass, Inc., 1970).

Kessler, E., *Anthropology: The Humanizing Process* (Boston: Allyn & Bacon, 1974).

Kraar, L., "The Japanese Are Coming—With Their Own Style of Management," *Fortune,* 91 (March 1975), 116–121, 160–161, 164.

Lerner, D., and W. Schramm (eds.), *Communication and Change in the Developing Countries* (Honolulu: East-West Center Press, 1967).

North, R., "International Conflict and Integration: Problems of Research" in *Intergroup Relations and Leadership,* edited by M. Sherif (New York: John Wiley & Sons, 1962).

Seelye, H., *Teaching Culture: Strategies for Foreign Language Educators* (Skokie, Illinois: National Textbook Company, 1974).

Robers, E., *Modernization Among Peasants: The Impact of Communication* (New York: Holt, Rinehart & Winston, 1969).

Singer, M., *Weak States in a World of Powers: The Dynamics of International Relations* (New York: Free Press, 1972).

Tanaka, Y., "Psychological Factors in International Persuasion," *The Annals of the American Academy of Political and Social Science,* 398 (November 1971), 50–60.

Triandis, H., V. Vassilious, G. Vassilious, Y. Tanaka, and A Shanmugam (eds.), *The Analysis of Subjective Culture* (New York: John Wiley & Sons, 1972).

Concepts and Questions

1. What do you see as most necessary to the improvement of intellectual communication during the next decade?

2. How can intercultural communication be improved domestically? Internationally? Is one more important than the other? Why?

3. Given all of the complexities associated with intercultural communication, is there really hope for the future?

4. How would the four implications discussed by Becker aid the researcher in intercultural communication?

5. What are some problems faced by researchers in the field of intercultural communication?

6. Becker concluded his article by raising three questions related to communication and research. Can you think of others?

7. What does Mead suggest when she states, "The American is used to experiencing the whole symbolic system of his society, in a series of fragmented and contradictory contexts"? How does this concept vary from culture to culture?

8. What are "monopolistic communication systems"? Why do totalitarian cultures employ this type of system?

9. How does Mead recommend that the United States maintain the honesty and integrity of its communication systems?

10. What does Adler mean by Multicultural Man? Is such a state ever possible?

11. Can you think of examples of people who might fit the description of multicultural man?

12. What are some of the difficulties in achieving multicultural man?

13. Are there advantages in being multicultural man? Are there disadvantages?

Index of Names

Index of Subjects